To Martin

Richd A Frosn
24th Jan
2008

Air Road to the Isles

Air Road to the Isles

The Memoirs of Captain E E Fresson OBE

Second Edition

kea publishing

First published in 1966 by David Rendal Ltd.

Second edition published in 2008 by
kea publishing
14 Flures Crescent
Erskine
Renfrewshire PA8 7DJ
Scotland

British Library Cataloguing in Publication Data

Fresson, Edmund Ernest, 1891-1963
    Air road to the isles : the memoirs of Captain E.E. Fresson, OBE. - 2nd ed.
    1. Fresson, Edmund Ernest, 1891-1963 2. Air pilots - Great Britain -
    Biography 3. Airlines - Scotland - History - 20th century
    I. Title II. Blake, John
    629.1'3'092

    ISBN-13: 9780951895894

Printed in Scotland by Cleland Crosbie Limited, Beechfield Road, Willowyard
Industrial Estate, Beith, Ayrshire KA15 1LN

Contents

Foreword to the First Edition

by Eric Linklater

In the *Shorter Oxford Dictionary* a pioneer is defined as 'one who goes before to prepare the way; one who begins some enterprise, course of action, etc; an original investigator, explorer, or worker.' These descriptions, excellent as far as they go, fail to indicate that the pioneer may also, like the artist, be a true creator. It is necessary to be aware of this before trying to form a balanced view of the initiatives undertaken and the results achieved by that remarkable man who, in the north of Scotland where he became famous, was generally known, not by some nickname or familiar Christian name, but as *Captain* Fresson.

This curious fact is some indication of the unusual respect that he enjoyed in those sparsely populated parts between Inverness and Shetland, between Inverness and the Western Isles. Fresson was a pioneer in that he explored the possibilities of establishing air services between the north of Scotland and its adjacent islands, and he was also the creator of new habits of life, a new comfort in life, because his aeroplanes brought to a people, who had previously travelled at the fastest by horse and gig, the thrills of hurtling through the air at a hundred miles an hour or more. And the natives of the outlying islands took to that brand-new form of transport with alacrity.

Fresson has served his apprenticeship to flying during the first Great War. Then in China, with overtones of considerable courage, he experienced and survived both commerce and service with some of the monstrously dictatorial Chinese war-lords of the 1920s. When he came home he was still a young man, and to the great benefit of all who were living in the far north of Britain, he saw that the aeroplane could usefully supplement the railway train and the steamer. He began his service with a minimum of capital but a maximum of vision, with a sufficiency of knowledge and an experience capable of growth. Initially, his resources were slender. I remember the earliest years of Highland Airways, and a day when, his only commercial machine having developed some engine fault, Fresson hired an even smaller aeroplane and a pilot who had never been north of Inverness before. In those days there were no modern aids to navigation, such as radio, and when we ran into fog we were soon lost. But suddenly we came down in a patch of fortuitous sunlight, and below us were the Highland Railway and the name – all too clearly legible – of a little wayside station. Hastily we turned and, a hundred feet above the bright steel lines, flew towards Inverness.

Fresson writes feelingly of the difficulties of flying without aids to navigation or foreknowledge of the weather. There was the particular summer hazard, north of Helmsdale, of dense cloud which sometimes lay only a couple of hundred feet above the sea, and it was necessary to fly between the wrinkled water and that low white ceiling. I have flown with him in such conditions, and I remember the confidence with which he navigated the narrow shelf of visibility above Sinclair Bay and the Pentland Firth. They looked as strange and unfamiliar as the coastal waters of New Zealand when Captain Cook first sailed them; but Fresson, like Cook, had a genius for finding his way about.

The aeroplanes that were the mainstay of Highland Airways were small biplanes of exceptional virtue called DH Rapides. Fresson and his regular pilots flew them daily through the violent, unpredictable weather of the northern and western isles. They were hardly ever storm-stayed, and they never had a serious accident. Their maintenance men were few in number, but expert and devoted to their task. Fresson flew mail and newspapers to the farthest isles with a punctuality and regularity that have never been surpassed, and not always equalled, by the great organisation that took over the service he had established. He and his pilots flew throughout the war, and soon after the return of peace Fresson was deprived of his livelihood. Over the routes that he had pioneered flew the larger machines of British European Airways, and in the earliest years of its existence the Scottish service of BEA was much less efficient than the service of the man it had ousted. Fresson got no reward for his good work, but was treated with conspicuous shabbiness.

In addition to his genius, he was a friendly, agreeable man with a great deal of interesting conversation. But the bureaucrats may have found him difficult to deal with, for he was proud and independent and had grown accustomed to having his own way. He was in all ways an admirable man, but he could sometimes be as unpredictable as the weather through which he flew. Once, I remember, I drove to Kirkwall in a great hurry, without having booked a passage, and pleaded with Fresson to take me to Inverness. He said, 'I am flying a full load of mail, but if you like to lie on top of the mail bags, you can come.' After we had crossed the Pentland Firth, he turned and shouted, 'I hope you won't mind if I go out of my way a bit. I've got very interested in fulmar gulls, and for the last week or two I've been counting their nests.' Then, to my horror, he drove his aeroplane along the top edge of the Caithness cliffs, weaving in and out, with his head over his right shoulder and his right hand scribbling notes and details of what he saw. But his DH Rapide behaved as if it were an extension of Fresson himself. He had a host of devoted friends, and machinery gave him perfect obedience.

It is a remarkable story which I have the honour to introduce. With the simple honesty of genius, Fresson tells precisely what he did, and how it was done, and it is my privilege to speak for the people of the Highlands and Islands of Scotland, and express the gratitude of all those whose lives he enlarged and whose comfort he increased. He was benefactor as well as pioneer, and he created, not only Highland Airways, but a legend that will endure.

3

Foreword to the Second Edition

by Magnus Linklater

I cannot have been much more than thirteen or fourteen, when I first met Captain Fresson. Or rather, when I first caught sight of his little Gipsy Moth biplane as it came in to land on what seemed an impossibly small field of rough grass near our house in Easter Ross. I remember two things about it. The great leap the plane made as it hit the ground, and the fact that its pilot did not even glance at us when he climbed out. Instead, the first thing he did was pace out the distance between the nose of his plane and the fence at the end of the field. Captain Fresson was a practical man. He needed to know whether or not he would be able to take off again.

By that stage he was a famous figure in our lives. We had been brought up on tales of his derring-do – my father, Eric Linklater, told us about the way he had pioneered air travel in the Highlands in the 1930s, about thrilling flights with him from Orkney to Inverness in his D H Rapide plane, dipping down to monitor the fulmar nests along the top edge of the Caithness cliffs, 'weaving in and out, with his head over his right shoulder and his right hand scribbling notes and details of what he saw.' We could almost recite, word for word, the account of the day, before modern aids to navigation such as radio had been introduced, when my father and Captain Fresson, flying down from Wick, ran into fog and got lost. Suddenly, there was a break in the cloud and they spotted the tracks of the Highland Railway below them, and a station coming up ahead. 'If I bring the plane down low enough, will you read the name of the station?' he is said to have asked my father. Straining to see through his binoculars, as Captain Fresson brought the plane down till it seemed to be skimming the rails themselves, my father called out triumphantly: 'Fearn Station!' 'Excellent,' said the Captain, 'we're making good progress.'

True? A touch exaggerated? Maybe. But anyone reading this under-stated but compelling account of the early days of air travel will rapidly discover that finding Fearn Station would rank as one of Fresson's milder stories compared to some of those that he recounts. Crash-landing on one wing, then rescuing his passenger as petrol sprayed out from a ruptured tank; almost colliding with a navy cruiser off the coast at Helmsdale in thick fog; losing a port engine in a blizzard off Tarbat Ness; delivering mail on the west coast in a 70 mph gale with the outer wing struts bent by the force of the wind; coming under fire from an Australian naval ship as he ferried the Prime Minister-to-be Clement Attlee on a flight to Orkney. These are just some of the tales he has to tell.

Throughout these hair-raising adventures, Captain Fresson remains imperturbable, matter-of-fact and down-to-earth. His punctuality and reliability, in fair weather or foul, won business as well as the confidence of his customers. The famously tight-fisted George Law, senior manager of *The Scotsman*, gave him the sole contract to fly his newspapers to Orkney, and even helped buy him a new plane. I would wager that the distribution of the newspaper I once had the honour of editing was more efficiently carried out by Captain Fresson in the 1930s than in my day when the paper was usually a day late getting to Orkney.

What emerges too from these memoirs is a steely will, and the sense that this man suffers no fools gladly. As my father wrote in his own foreword to these memoirs more than 40 years ago: 'The bureaucrats may have found him difficult to deal with, for he was proud and independent and had grown accustomed to having his own way. He was in all ways an admirable man, but he could sometimes be as unpredictable as the weather through which he flew.'

What this meant, I think, was that, in those pioneering days, he trusted his own instincts rather than the rules and regulations which were soon to govern commercial aviation, and which drained it, not just of its romance, but of its ambition. He showed, long before it had been dreamt possible, that isolated communities could be brought closer together by air travel, that the life of a sick child on Papa Westray could be saved, that a farmer's wife on North Ronaldsay could do her shopping in Kirkwall, and still get back in time for tea – which is precisely what she is still doing today.

Captain Fresson, however, did it first – and he did it 75 years ago. For anyone living in the Highlands or the Islands today, that spirit of enterprise still deserves our gratitude and our respect.

Preface

When I first discovered the Orkney Islands in Gipsy Moth, G-AAWO, on Sunday 19 April 1931, it was like flying into another land. The population appeared different in some intangible manner. My passenger, and owner of the Moth, Miss Helen Pauer, whose home was in Trentham, Staffordshire, was of the same mind., We spent half an hour talking with the crowd that surrounded our small plane, itching to touch and prod it as if it was made of solid wood.

My instant impression of the Orcadians was their desire to be of assistance and, on my second visit some months later, I found the same nice trait in the people with whom I came into contact. It was not really surprising, that feeling of strangeness which smote the visitor who descended from the sky that Sabbath afternoon because, we learned later, the population of Orkney and its neighbouring islands eighty-six miles to the north, Shetland, were of Norse descent. That first journey of exploration was to earn me many years of close contact with the Orcadians so that I had the opportunity of establishing a firm friendship with the people of Orkney. I found it more difficult to get close to the population of Shetland, whom I came in contact with a few years later. They appeared far more reserved in themselves and in their habits. For instance, it took very much longer to wean the population from surface transport to air, whereas the Orcadians took to flying as a duck did to water. However, once you made a friend in Shetland, he was your friend for life, and that was very noticeable to me when I recently made a return visit to the two groups of islands after an absence of fourteen years.

In writing an historical account of past events, it had been my endeavour to quote actual facts and, in some instances, express my reactions to certain happenings. It has also been my intention to avoid anything that might wander into the realm of fantasy or inaccuracies. So I hope, that in dealing with the activities of Aberdeen Airways which subsequently crystallised into Allied Airways of which my good friend Mr Gander Dower was the owner, that he will not hold it against me when I describe the events as they occurred in the internecine war which he and I fought over a period of thirteen years. There was little doubt that his operations along the routes I had established, and with which I was first in the field, caused Highland Airways Limited many heartaches as the population simply did not exist in the area to justify two companies in competition. We were at an added disadvantage as we did not possess the finance to fight a war of attrition. Accordingly, we were forced into tying up with big business which eventually superseded our local authority. However, those heartaches are of the past and were erased in my mind when it became my unhappy lot to take over Mr Gandar Dower's firm after the State had grabbed the fruits of our combined labours for which we had worked so hard over the years. I am happy to say that we are friends now in adversity and I often have the pleasure of calling at his attractive residence overlooking one of the parks in London, always receiving a real 'Scottish Welcome.'

With regard to my more drastic references to the State Corporation which grabbed our livelihood, I make no apology. Their actions were callous and quite un-British. However, it should be clearly understood that the British European Airways I chastise refers to the Corporation which existed in 1947-1948 when it was ruled by the personnel of the wartime Air Transport Auxiliary, who applied wartime 'know how' to commercial operations which were doomed to disaster from the beginning. When Mr Peter Masefield took over the management, BEA was reborn and became a business-like organisation. Before long, under his management and leadership, the huge losses of the previous years were turned into a profit. That high standard has been perpetuated and it is common knowledge that the present day BEA's Continental operations are a model to its competitors. The same goes for the London-Glasgow route which I frequently have the pleasure of travelling on. I bear no ill will to the BEA of today. They were not involved in the regrettable happenings of 1947-1948 that are recorded and described in the last chapters of my narrative.

E E Fresson
Inverness, 1963

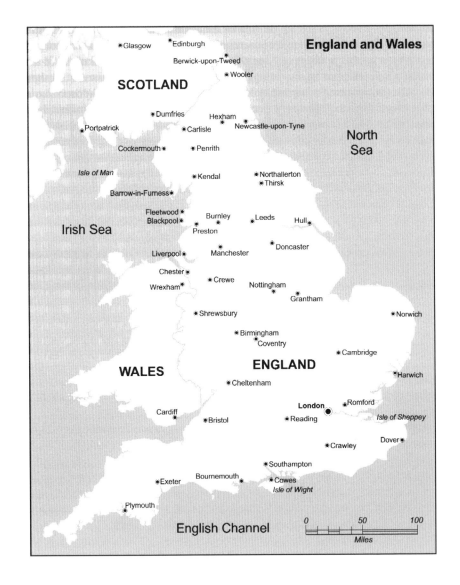

England and Wales

SCOTLAND

NORTH
Sea

Irish Sea

WALES

ENGLAND

London

English Channel

0   50   100

Miles

1

China and the Great War

I first became interested in aviation in 1907. At that time, Louis Blériot, Henri Farman, Gabriel Voison and others were conducting experiments with their home-built planes while the famous Wright brothers, Orville and Wilbur, were giving advanced exhibition flights in France with their biplane.

Early in the summer of 1909, I was spending my holidays at Minster on Sea on the Isle of Sheppey and, when cycling one day through the countryside on the east end of the island, I found myself at Leysdown marshes. Early air pioneer brothers, Eustace, Oswald and Horace Short, had built themselves an air-shed on the flat marshland and were constructing an aeroplane of their own design. There were also a group of enthusiasts trying to teach themselves to fly and I watched a few making quite long hops. I was greatly interested and cycled back day after day to watch the experiments. Among the more successful was Moore Brabazon, now Lord Brabazon of Tara, who later in the year won the *Daily Mail* prize of £1,000 for successfully making the first circular flight on an all-British aircraft, a Short biplane. Also there were Frank McLean, Hon Charles Stewart Rolls who was later killed when gliding in to land at the Bournemouth flying meeting, Maurice Egerton and John W Dunne. The latter designed and built the first tail-less biplane, which was inherently stable. A mechanic working with Dunne went on, many years later, to become a famous aircraft designer and constructor. His name was Richard Fairey.

In those days, I was also madly interested in the motor car, which was rapidly developing, but at the same time was a rarity on the roads. On one of my visits, to my delight, I met the would-be pilots packed into an early Panhard Levasseur open car chugging across the marshes, evidently on their way to the village pub for lunch. On 26 July 1909, a Monday, flying made its big impact on me.

Crossing Blackfriars Bridge that morning, I observed a *Daily Mail* poster carried by a 'sandwich-board' man. In large type it presented the startling news: 'Blériot flies the Channel.' Like many other people, I was thrilled over such an important event, which portended a considerable change in our insular position. There had been considerable excitement throughout July 1909 as Hubert Latham with his beautiful Antoinette monoplane had been waiting for favourable weather at Calais to make the first crossing by a heavier than air aircraft and so win the prize of £1,000 offered by the *Daily Mail* for the first heavier-than-air aircraft to fly across the English Channel. Latham made his first attempt on Monday 19 July, but was forced down on to the sea by motor failure. While the

Antoinette was being reconditioned for another attempt, Louis Blériot arrived at Calais determined to make a desperate bid to get across the Channel before his rival. He was suffering and in great pain from a badly burned foot and ankle, the result of a petrol explosion. He walked on crutches and had to be lifted into his plane. At 4.30 am on Sunday 25 July 1909, Blériot was called by his mechanic.

'It's a fine morning, Monsieur. The wind has abated. Shall I get the monoplane ready?'

Blériot gave the order and with difficulty dressed and made his way out to the flying field. His mechanic helped him into the small, single-seater monoplane Type XI. He was soon airborne and heading towards the English coast. His plane was fitted with a twenty-five horse power Anzani three cylinder motor that had to be run flat out to maintain the small monoplane in the air. Half way across the twenty miles of sea it was reported that the motor commenced to overheat and appeared likely to seize up, but luckily he was saved by a heavy rain storm that cooled the white-hot cylinder heads thus enabling him to reach the cliffs of Dover. Unfortunately, Blériot had to make an emergency landing owing to the overheated motor and was forced to land downhill damaging his history-making plane. A piece of the air screw blade is today hanging as a souvenir in the Royal Aero Club premises in London.

The flying bug had now bitten deeply into me and I commenced trying to teach myself the rudiments of flight by building numerous models. No one appeared to know much about centre of gravity in relation to centre of lift and thrust or inherent stability. I had to find out the hard way by trial and error and not having any clear idea what I was searching for. My parents were then living in the pretty little country village of Wickford, on the London to Southend railway. Opposite their house, *Whyteways*, was a large field that I used for flying tests. The kitchen table served as a bench and I worked into the small hours of the morning building my models. A few hours sleep and I would be up at six o'clock to carry out flight tests in the field with my latest model before catching the nine o'clock express train for London. In those days, I was employed by a London firm of Far Eastern merchants and training to take up a post in China. Their offices were situated in Mincing Lane House, Eastcheap. The firm were essentially tea merchants, but they also carried on an export engineering business for their branches in China. The Far East was developing rapidly in those days. Railways were being constructed and factories were being built, calling for heavy imports of machinery and equipment by their Hankow, Shanghai, Mukden and Foochow branches. I was attached to the Engineering Section, having been trained in the Western Electricity & Thames Iron Works near Greenwich.

Many models were made and written off and it was at least six months before I really got one to fly well. I was greatly excited over my first success and the whole family had to line up in the field to watch a demonstration. I felt they also deserved a share in my success for their sleep had been constantly disturbed by the noise I created with my midnight carpentry sessions.

The following year, 1910, there were a number of air displays held in Britain that were well attended by the French and British flying 'aces'. Blackpool, Lanark and Doncaster were a few of the most important meetings, which were crowded with spectators anxious to see an aeroplane in flight and who were charged an entrance fee.

It was at Hendon airfield, belonging to Mr Claude Grahame-White, one of Britain's first French taught pilots, that I saw my first aeroplane fly. It was designed by a Mr Barber, flew tail first, and was called a 'Canard.' Powered by a 35hp Green water-cooled four cylinder motor, Mr Barber would circle Hendon airfield time and time again, flying most gracefully at fifty feet or so. Another great attraction for me was Claude Grahame-White arriving at the airfield on a brand new 3½ hp Triumph motorbike, complete with cap on back to front and a pair of goggles raised over his eyebrows in truly sporting fashion. I greatly envied him that motorbike, which I would have given the earth to have possessed.

With the advent of the 50hp Gnome rotary motor in 1910, flying advanced very quickly and long cross-country flying became the order of the day in France. In England, long-distance flying was also beginning and, in April 1910, Claude Grahame-White entered for the London to Manchester flight for which the *Daily Mail* had offered a prize of £10,000. Grahame-White had learned to fly at the Louis Blériot and Henri Farman schools in France.

On the morning of Saturday 23 April 1910, Grahame-White took off from Wormwood Scrubs and reached Lichfield 117 miles away. While refuelling, the Henri Farman biplane was blown over by an unexpected squall of wind. Hurriedly, the plane was returned to London for repair so that an early restart could be made. In the meantime, Louis Paulhan, a young Frenchman, also had designs on the *Daily Mail* prize. As soon as he heard of Grahame-White's bad luck, he forthwith packed up his new, racing Farman and came to England. Paulhan's plane did not reach Hendon, his starting point, until Wednesday morning just as Grahame-White's damaged aeroplane was ready for flight. Grahame-White however had decided that, as the wind was gusty, he could safely wait until the calm hours of the morning before making a fresh start, and turned in to rest. Like Hubert Latham a year before, his sleep was disturbed by the unwelcome tidings that his rival had started. He immediately set off in pursuit, and actually caught Paulhan up and passed him when engine trouble forced him to land. That was Paulhan's opportunity. Before repairs were finished, the crushing tidings came that the Frenchman, starting at half past five in the morning, had reached his goal and won the coveted £10,000.

Four months later in the summer of that year, the famous Circuit de l'Est was flown. That brought at least a dozen aircraft across the Channel to the Hendon aerodrome for the English leg. I was out early in the morning, a beautiful sunny day, to watch the departure of those pilots for the Continent. I have a vivid recollection of the then-famous French pilot Jules Védrines taking off in a Morane monoplane. He was off the ground in sixty yards and went into a steep climbing turn to the right over the sheds. The performance of the Morane monoplane with the Gnome rotary motor was astounding. All the competitors left like clockwork and landed safely in France, and yet, only one year before, Latham and Blériot were struggling just to make the 20-mile Channel crossing.

The following summer, 1911, which incidentally was the last I was to spend in England for seven years, the Round Britain Race was flown. A large number of entries were received for the race and the competitors left Brooklands on the afternoon of 22 July for Hendon, the first sector. They would stay over until Monday 24 July before starting the race in earnest. Among the starters were the usual famous names of the day – André Beaumont in a Blériot monoplane, Védrines in a Morane monoplane, James Valentine in a Deperdussin monoplane, S F Cody in a Cody biplane which was known as the Flying Cathedral owing to its large dimensions, C Howard Pixton in a Bristol biplane, and a further twenty-six entrants, a number of whom did not start, or at any rate did not get further than the Hendon to Harrogate sector. The course was 1,010 miles and was won by André Beaumont in 22 hours 30 minutes flying time. He was closely followed by Jules Védrines over the whole course, with James Valentine some way behind. It was Wednesday when the winners arrived back at Brooklands on the third day after leaving Hendon having averaged 335 miles a day. This was a remarkable performance in those days.

At the time of that race I was staying with my cousin, Mrs Amy Troldahl, who lived at Hexham-on-Tyne. Her son, Bob, was some years younger than myself and equally interested in the air race so we decided to be at Gosforth Park, Newcastle on Tyne, on Monday morning in time to see the arrival of the leading competitors. They were scheduled to arrive at Gosforth, having landed at Harrogate en route, at nine in the morning. We were up before six, caught an early train from Hexham into Newcastle and then boarded a tram car for Gosforth Park. We sat on top and so had a clear view of the sky. It was a beautiful sunny morning, but very hazy.

Approaching Gosforth I suddenly spotted a Blériot monoplane high in the sky gliding down towards the Park. I shouted, 'Look Bobs, look up there,' pointing, 'can you see it? A Blériot monoplane. I'll bet that's Beaumont – dead on time.' It had only just passed nine o'clock. We jumped off the tram outside the park gates, paid our entrance money, and raced to find the landing spot. We got there out of breath to see Beaumont lying under the wing of his monoplane,

resting while mechanics were filling up with 'essence' (petrol) and oil. Another mechanic was checking the motor and aircraft. He had flown from London in the record time of four hours twenty minutes, half the time taken by an express train in those days. A few minutes later a shout went up 'There's another plane coming in.' On landing it turned out to be Védrines in his Morane monoplane. He had covered the distance in four hours eleven minutes, but had spent more time on the ground at Harrogate than Beaumont. They both got away for Edinburgh after a very short stop.

We waited for another hour before the third competitor, James Valentine, arrived in a Deperdussin monoplane. He filled up and was away within twenty minutes. By then, a choppy wind had got up and I remember seeing the Deperdussin rocking badly after taking off until altitude was reached. Heading north, he disappeared from sight in a few minutes. Bob and I waited around until lunch time and, as no further competitors arrived, we decided to make for town for a late lunch before returning to Hexham. We learned later that the other competitors were strewn all along the course, some with engine failure and many hopelessly lost. It had been reported that the visibility was not good by the time the first three arrived and, unless a pilot could fly a compass course with accurate map reading, it was hopeless. There were no specially designed aero compasses in those days and the marine compass used was exceedingly difficult to operate owing to vibration and difficulty in swinging. The French pilots were far ahead in that technique for they were constantly making long inter-city flights on the Continent whereas our pilots contented themselves by flying around aerodromes at flying meetings, no doubt influenced by the cash returns offered.

That race made a great impression on me and I was determined that one day

I would learn to fly. It was not until six years later that my chance came when I joined up with the Royal Flying Corps (RFC) in Canada.

On our return to Hexham, my cousin was interested by what we had to tell of our experience that day and asked many questions. She was amazed to hear that the journey from London to Newcastle had been flown in half the time of an express train.

I had brought with me one of my model airplanes which interested Cousin Bob. It was capable of flying over two hundred yards. We spent an hour or two the following day flying it backwards and forwards across a ravine near the house, operating an assimilated postal airmail service with pencilled messages to each other aboard.

A few days later my holiday came to an end, I returned to London by the coastal steamship service and was back at work within a few days. My parents were also very interested in the great Air Race and I had to recount again most of what Bob and I had seen at Gosforth Park.

At the end of August, Mr Simpson, our managing director at the office, told me I was to be transferred to the company's Shanghai branch the following November. I was given a list of the special kit required for very hot summers and extremely cold winters and told to make all special preparations to travel. During August, the Shanghai manager of the company's Engineering Department, James Stanley MacNider, visited England on leave. He hailed from the USA and was a real hustler. I would be placed under his care and tutelage when I arrived in China. He had recently arrived from America and was on his way back to the Far East by the Trans-Siberian Railway.

Three months later, I left Liverpool Street Station for Harwich early in November 1911. My parents, brother, uncles and aunts came to see me off and bid me godspeed on what was in those days considered an eventful journey for I also was about to take the Trans-Siberian route to the Far East. But first of all I was to visit some steel works in the Rhineland to pick up one or two agencies for the Shanghai branch of our company. I would then go on to Berlin to spend a week's holiday with some German business friends. They lived in the fashionable part of Berlin and they gave me a wonderful time. They took me to the top night clubs and I remember one in particular in which many young Germans had bright scars on their faces. I was told that they were very proud of such disfigurement as the wounds had been obtained duelling while serving their military training.

I left Berlin at ten o'clock at night a week later for Warsaw and Moscow. When I awoke next morning we were near the German border with Poland when we ran into snow-covered country. I had to change trains at Warsaw because the Russian-gauge rail lines were wider than the European, the reason being that European rolling stock could not be used on the Russian railroads in case of war.

14

I had half a day to spend in Warsaw and took the opportunity of visiting the cathedral to see the great composer Chopin's grave. After lunch, I was driven in a drosky through the Warsaw 'ghetto' to the Russian departure station some four miles distant. I was terrified. The ghetto occupants looked as if they would cut anyone's throat for a few pence and the drosky driver looked just as bad. There was nothing to stop him robbing me of my possessions, delivering me to the wolves, and then dispensing of me if they felt so inclined. In that case, I would never have been heard of again and not missed for weeks, or until the time I was due to arrive in Shanghai. I had with me a six-chamber .38 revolver with which I was determined to save my life. However, my fears were unfounded and the drosky driver delivered me safely to my train. I let out a terrific sigh of relief when the station came into view.

I spent three days in Moscow at the Metropole Hotel. The snow lay thickly on the streets and I was driven from the station in a drosky on sledge runners. The horse had a large hoop over its head with a small bell attached which jingled as we glided over the snow. What a magnificent hotel that was in the days of the Czars' reign. The splendour of the receptions and dinners held in the hotel and the glistening of the women's magnificent diamonds and jewellery had to be seen to be believed. I will never forget pre-Bolshevik Russia. Next day, the hotel porter found a guide to take me around the interesting places in Moscow. The Kremlin fascinated me as also did the Russian society mansions.

Two days later, in the evening, I boarded the train for Harbin. The journey was to take twelve days and we were to pass through Ekaterinburg where the Czar and his family were butchered to death some seven years later. From there the long rail haul took us through Omsk and Tomsk on to Irkutsk. I found the going very hard at first, as I could not sleep owing to the noise. It was three days and nights before I eventually got to sleep. From then on, I had no further trouble and slept soundly from sheer exhaustion. I was only twenty years old and my journey was looked upon in those days as a great adventure. It was certainly all very strange to me. The language problem was difficult if one did not speak French or Russian. Fortunately, I knew a little French, which got me by, plus a little German.

On the train, I became acquainted with an Englishman who had been in China for a number of years and was returning from leave in England. Having a human being to talk to broke the monotony. He also knew the ropes and shepherded me along the seven thousand miles of rail travel. He told me there was a plague epidemic in Manchuria and China and advised me of the precautions to take.

After leaving Irkutsk, the train had to wind its way around the southern shore of Lake Baikal. There must have been one hundred miles or more of tunnelling and sharp curves around that rocky shore. We were pitched from side to side constantly. The moon was shining and occasionally I would catch a glimpse of the lake which looked very beautiful in the moonlight. Later in the season, in the depths of winter when the lake was frozen to a depth of many feet, the railroad engineers would lay a track straight across the ice from shore to shore, thus saving many miles and hours of tortuous travel. When we awoke next morning, we were climbing up the Transbaikalia Plateau. We arrived in Chita before noon where we refuelled the locomotive with wood logs and replenished the dining car victuals. On the morrow, we entered Manchuria after crossing the great Khingan Mountains. It was not long before I began to realise what an eastern plague meant, for the train began to pass long mounds adjacent to the railroad track several hundred feet long, some eight to ten feet high and many feet wide, under which the plague victims were buried en masse. It frightened me and I remember wondering how long I might live under such conditions.

After being on the train for ten days, we ran into Harbin around eleven o'clock in the morning. The train was proceeding to Vladivostock and so I had to change over to the South Manchurian Railroad. There was no direct train to the seaport of Dairen so we were obliged to stay the night at the Railway Hotel in Mukden. It was all very strange to me and I felt a long way from home. Next morning, we embarked on the train to Dairen and, after rolling through undulating country all day, reached our destination around teatime. We were told we would have to stay a night at the Japanese-run Yamato Hotel as the Shanghai steamer, which plied across the Yellow Sea, would not depart until next morning. That night I went to a local Japanese cinema, very crude in those days and I got badly bitten by fleas, which forced a hasty retreat to the hotel long before the very inferior film came to an end.

We sailed next morning in brilliant sunshine. The steamer was fast, steaming at twenty knots, but rolled like a barrel. It was not long before the passengers were mostly down below, but I managed to weather it that trip, although on a subsequent one, some years later, I succumbed to my first attack of sea sickness. The Yellow Sea is comparatively shallow and the wind soon whips up a terrific swell. The name 'Yellow Sea' is very well termed as the water was a dirty muddy yellow.

On arrival in Shanghai, I ran slap into the 1911 revolution, which changed China from a Dynasty to a Republic. The killing and bloodshed that I witnessed for the first few months was a fearful introduction to a new country for a young man. I was taken under Stanley MacNider's wing, and I rapidly learnt the considerable difference of living in rural England to that of the Far East. He had a flat in the Kukiang Road and he entertained on a large scale. At such parties one met the business people who counted. During the day, I was tutored into the business routine at the office. As is said in the operetta, *Oklahoma*, and which could be applied to me in those days, 'I came to Oklahoma [Shanghai] on a

Friday and on Saturday I had learnt a thing or two,' for I learnt many things in a very short time in Shanghai. I stayed there until the end of January 1912 and, by that time, had obtained a good grounding in the company's procedures.

In February 1912, I was sent up to Hankow where the revolution was still raging. Junks used to come drifting down the river Yangtze, which was a mile wide at Hankow, full of dead refugees. They had been machine-gunned from the shore up river. If one tried to walk outside the Concessions, you had to step over the dead every few yards. It was a frightful state of carnage, which affected me considerably. By the summer, the situation became more normal and I fell into the way of life, boxed up in a few square miles, 600 miles from the coast. Our only connection with the outside world was the river steamer, which took three days to make the journey between Hankow and Shanghai.

I could write a separate story of my next five years in China. I was very interested in my work, which took me over many thousands of miles of the interior. There were no roads in China in those days and I was kept busy travelling the hard way, on foot mostly. It was nothing for me to walk twenty miles a day for several days on end. Then there were the rivers, the great Yangtze Jiang and its many tributaries. I had a sampan especially constructed by the Yangtze Engineering Works and installed with a 5 hp single cylinder De Russet motor, which would take me hundreds of miles inland serving the constructional units of the Canton Hankow Railroad sections.

The Great War came along in August 1914 and I signed on to join the first Volunteer Contingent, leaving Shanghai in October. In September, I contracted typhus fever and all but died of it. I was laid up in the Hankow Hospital until the middle of November and it took me several months longer to regain my strength. In the meantime, the first Contingent had sailed for Britain. Very few of those volunteers came out of the war alive, so perhaps the typhus fever saved me instead of claiming me.

When I was fit, our Consul put me on the indispensable list and I was not allowed to offer myself as a volunteer for other Contingents that sailed. It was not until the early part of 1917 that I managed to get the restriction lifted by writing to the British Embassy in Peking. I left for home on my own to join up, travelling via America and Canada. I sailed on the *Tenyo Maru* from Shanghai to Honolulu and San Francisco. We spent a few days in Honolulu, surf-riding and seeing the sights. It was a wonderful place in those early days and unspoilt by tourism. I spent a month in California, touring the country on a Red Indian motorcycle that I bought in San Francisco. I made it a good holiday as I thought it might be the last I would ever have. On arrival back in San Francisco, I joined up at a recruiting station for the Army, passed the medical board, and I was to go back next morning to be sworn in and receive the King's shilling. That night, some friends in Los Angeles phoned me. 'Come back right away,' they said, 'for there's an RFC Officer just arrived and he's recruiting for the Royal Flying Corps.' I had told them I was anxious to get into the RFC. I ignored my interview of that afternoon with the Army boys and left next morning at half past four on my Red Indian motorbike for Los Angeles, four hundred miles away. The roads in those days were mostly dirt surface and the trip over the mountains approaching Santa Barbara was tough going and slowed me down so much that I did not arrive there until six that night. I had to ride through three small rivers which were unbridged, and got thrown into the water at the middle stream as the front wheel hit a big stone. On reaching Santa Barbara I was thirsty, hungry and deadbeat. I went into a coffee bar and drank at least six big cups of coffee with my meal and then went along to the beach to have a sleep before tackling the remaining 100 miles. Unfortunately, the coffee worked against tiredness and I was unable to sleep. So at three in the morning I started off for Los Angeles, arriving there at around six thirty. I went to my friends' house. They were all asleep at that hour, but there was a hammock swung on the veranda, which I skipped into. And that was where they found me at eight o'clock in the morning, dead to the world.

My friends were English. One was a Dr Frances who had emigrated to USA some years back. He was married to an English lady and had a family. They owned a very pleasant home on the outskirts of Los Angeles. Dr Frances got in touch with the RFC officer, who was staying at one of the principle hotels, and made an appointment for me next day. I was duly ushered in and presented to a Captain Paul Arbon. I was put through a lot of questioning when he suddenly enquired where I was educated.

'Framlingham College,' I answered.

He looked up, surprised. 'What years were you there?' he shot at me.

I told him.

'What year were you in the Remove form,' he countered.

'Around 1903,' I replied.

'My God! I've placed you,' he said. 'I remember you now.'

And he mentioned the name of a cousin of mine, Rowland Fenn, who was also in the Remove. He went on talking about several anecdotes and my mind began to focus back fifteen years. Suddenly, I recalled him, a medium-height boy with black hair, very unassuming and who kept much to himself.

That was a moment of great celebration and what a million to one chance to celebrate on. There was no further questioning, I was signed in on the dot for the RFC in Canada, and given a steamer and rail ticket to Toronto where I was to report for a medical examination. I stayed in Los Angeles a week and we met frequently. Paul was very well-to-do, having invented certain improvements in oil drilling gear. I took him back to the Frances home and introduced him. They were amazed over such an extraordinary reunion and asked him to stay for dinner. It then transpired that a near relative of Mrs Frances had also been educated at Framlingham, 'another extraordinary coincidence.'

The time came to say goodbye again to Doctor Frances and his wife and Paul Arbon. He promised to look me up when he returned to Toronto in a month or so. A few days later I sailed from Los Angeles for Vancouver. I left my trusted *Indian* motorbike with the Frances family who promised to look after it for me until the war was over. If I survived, I planned to return to my job in China, which was open for me, via America, and I would call at Los Angeles to see the Frances family again and make arrangements to have my motorbike shipped to Shanghai. This is precisely what happened, for not only did I survive the war, but I did return to China via Los Angeles.

I travelled up to Vancouver by sea and spent a few days there before proceeding across the Canadian Pacific Rockies to Toronto by train, which carried an observation car. They were a stupendous sight, and I have never met their grandeur anywhere in my subsequent travels, which have been fairly extensive. I could write many chapters on that journey, but this is not a travel story.

I stayed over in Banff Springs Hotel for a couple of days before continuing on to Toronto. The swimming pool was filled with natural hot spring water. The hotel was set in a valley surrounded by fir and spruce trees and faced the Lower Bow Valley running through high mountains. Behind the hotel, the mountains reared up to over 10,000 feet. Lake Louise, another beauty spot with a magnificent hotel built alongside the lake, was not very far away from Banff Springs. Both hotels were operated by the Canadian Pacific Railway and were super-luxurious. On the following morning, after a swim in the hot springs bath, I went for a walk in the woods after breakfast. I had gone about half a mile down the track in the forest when, turning a corner, I ran straight into a huge black bear. As soon as it saw me, it reared upon his hind legs, at the same time letting out a roar. I turned and fled back to the hotel, expecting to hear the bear thundering after me. I don't think I have ever done a quarter of a mile in better time. When I mentioned the matter to the head porter, he laughed and said that the bears were often seen roaming the forest, but rarely attacked unless under provocation. However, I didn't feel like giving it a second chance and I kept clear of the forest for the rest of the day.

Getting near Toronto, we stopped at a wayside station named Borden, roughly seventy miles north of Toronto city. While exercising along the platform in the sunlight, a plane flew over. It was a Curtiss JN4 and a porter said it came from a nearby military airfield. I had cause to remember that statement later. On arrival in Toronto, I booked in at the King Edward Hotel and presented myself next day at Royal Flying Corps Headquarters, handing over Captain Arbon's confidential letter which he had given me for the authorities. After the usual form filling, they sent me along to the medical section for a report on my physical fitness to undertake flying training. I thought I was in first class condition, but the doctor examining me thought otherwise. He told me my blood pressure was phenomenally high and he was unable to pass me unless I could reduce it. I could not believe my ears. I had always been very fit, but then I thought of the typhus fever three years before. I told the medical officer (MO) about it and said, in despair, 'Just fancy coming all the way from China to join the RFC to be told I was medically unfit.'

The MO was a really decent sort and when he heard where I had come from, he asked me how long I had been in Toronto.

'I've just arrived. I left Los Angeles a week ago and have been travelling most of the time since.'

'Ah!' he ejaculated, 'that may be the cause of your trouble.'

'What! Travelling?' I said.

'Yes, railroad travel can be hard on the blood stream. Go back to your hotel, starve yourself and take Epsom Salts for a couple of days, three or four times a day, and keep quiet. Then come back and we'll have another go.'

I don't think I have ever spent such a harassing two days in my life. Magnesium sulphate is not exactly an exotic diet, but I kept strictly to orders and presented myself on the third day for another test. I asked for the same MO and he greeted me with a 'How did you get on?' Don't fret', he said, 'that will only make matters worse.' So again the arm band was pumped up, one – two – three times – the MO saying nothing. At the third go, I thought my doom was sealed, but almost simultaneously the doctor said, 'Fine, the salts have done the trick.'

'Thank you very much, doctor,' I said gratefully. Had I failed that medical board I was tempted to pack up and return to China.

A day or two later, I went before a board and was accepted as a Cadet and posted to the RFC Officer Corps at Toronto University for preliminary training. This consisted of route marches and living in uncomfortable conditions in a tent, sleeping on the hard ground on a ground sheet until my bones ached so much that I could hardly stand. On top of that, Army rations helped to make life more miserable. Reporting at the university that evening, I drew my kit. They told me to be down on the campus at nine o'clock sharp next morning for a parade. Unfortunately, my watch, unknown to me, was a few minutes slow, and I was three minutes late. There they were, at least fifty other cadets all lined up on parade with a bawling Irish sergeant addressing them. As soon as he saw me, he let out a howl, 'Are you Cadet Fresson?' he shrieked.

'I'm very sorry, Sergeant ....,' I commenced. I was not allowed to finish my explanation.

'Look at him,' the Sergeant bawled. 'Thinks himself a bleeding officer already. Fall in quick, and remember don't be late on parade again.'

The rest of the cadets enjoyed the scene at my expense immensely. Actually, at heart, Sergeant Higgins was not a bad sort. I sought him out after the parade and explained what had happened. He just laughed and told me I would soon get into the swing of things. By that remark, I assumed I was excused. We spend six weeks at the university, mostly on route marches and a discipline course. After two weeks of marching, one of my ankles became so sore that I developed a limp. Sergeant Higgins, coming up from behind, spotted me limping along. Each step was painful, but the only sympathy I got was a bellow, 'Hey you with the Oceanic Roll, pick 'em up!' There were titters from my fellow cadets. I still went on limping. I could do nothing else and every step for another two miles was agony. Eventually, Sergeant Higgins called me out of the squad.

'What's wrong with your foot?' he asked, a little more humanely.

I told him.

'Have you been to see the MO?' he asked.

'No, not yet.'

'Well the sooner you go, the better for you.'

So with that I duly reported at medical headquarters, had the sore dressed, and was excused route marching for a week until the wound had healed.

I got to like Sergeant Higgins. Under the rough exterior of a disciplinary instructor, he had a heart of gold. He was efficient at his job and just the man for breaking in raw recruits who had to be taught the difference between civilian life and hard military discipline.

Eventually the next move came and we were sent down to a place called Long Branch, on the edge of Lake Ontario, and some fifteen miles out of Toronto on the Hamilton Highway. There we also lived in tents, but with the comfort of camp beds, only two in a tent, and an excellent dining hall in an ex-corrugated iron barn. We attended lectures and radio instruction and, in between, a certain amount of drilling. The winter had now set in and it was bitterly cold. We took our baths by smashing the ice on Lake Ontario and washing ourselves down in the freezing water. The whole course was to make one tough. The part I hated most was 'sentry-go' at nights. Two of us were seconded for three nights at a time and we shared sentry go at the Main Gate on four hour shifts. Being on the main road, there were plenty of automobiles passing by at night. How I used to envy the occupants. Before passing out, back at the university we were given a month's intensive training on machine guns – interrupter gear, which enabled the bullets to pass between the blades of the air screw without touching them – aircraft rigging – engine maintenance – and artillery observation and bombing using a rotation map which passed under a tower on which we were ensconced.

It was now the beginning November and the snow was not far away. I was posted for flying training and, to my surprise, the name of the airfield was Camp Borden, situated nearby the station we had stopped on my journey over from the west. Arriving around one o'clock midday we were rushed to the camp for lunch.

Somehow or other, it had got around that I could play the piano and from that it was assumed the organ also. I was considerably surprised when an officer came up to me at lunch saying, 'I understand you play the organ, Cadet Fresson.'

I replied that I could indifferently.

'Never mind that', he said. 'You are detailed to play this afternoon at the funeral of 'Cadet X' who was killed yesterday in a crash.'

It was hardly a cheerful beginning to my flying instruction. Shortly after, it appeared they were killing one to two cadets a day in the rush for turning out pilots to be sent overseas to make up the heavy casualties on the Western Front.

I started my flying instruction next day, Thursday, in a Curtiss JN4 two-seater aircraft powered by a 60 hp O.X motor. The plane just flew at 40 mph and its all-out speed was about 55 mph so there wasn't much to play with. It also meant that the motor was running at 85 to 90 percent of its power output and so was very unreliable. In consequence, forced landings were the order of the day. Between Thursday and Saturday afternoon I received four and a half hours instruction. On the Saturday afternoon, and as dusk was falling, my instructor, Lieutenant Speakes got out of the front cockpit and said, 'I guess you're good enough to go solo. How do you feel?'

To the best of my recollection, I answered, 'I'm not so sure, but if you think I am competent, I'll have a go.'

'Just keep her straight on the take-off and you will be all right.' he replied. 'Good luck!'

It was 4.55 pm on 13 November 1917. I was frightened and I didn't mind admitting it. I thought, 'no wonder they are killing so many cadets, with so little instruction,' and then said to myself, 'you have just made a circuit, on your own with Lieutenant Speakes, so why not again? And isn't this the moment you have been waiting so long for?'

With that, I set my teeth, opened the throttle, zigzagged a little until the tail came up, and I was quickly off the ground and climbing. I remember making a left circuit at 500 feet and following a dried up stream back to the airfield, dropping off height for the turn in and making a first rate landing not so far from the perimeter of the airfield. Lieutenant Speakes came running up to me.

'Well done', he said, 'that was a very good first landing.'

I was very pleased with myself. I had at last attained my ambition of becoming a pilot.

Next day, our cadet course was ordered to Camp Everman, Texas, for further training. Snow was beginning to fall in Ontario province and, to avoid converting our aircraft to skis, the RFC authorities came to terms with the USA to lease us an airfield in Texas. We were packed up and ready to go in two day's time and we left by train on 15 November 1917. That was a long journey of over 1,000 miles. It took us three days to reach our destination. Excepting for a long stop at Little Rock, Arkansas, which enabled us to march around the small town for much needed exercise, we were cooped up in a crowded troop train.

We got quite a shock at Camp Everman, Fort Worth. The airfield was by no means completed, we had to live in tents, and the only meals one could obtain were from very badly organised camp catering. Along the road running past the airfield were a number of hastily erected shacks whose occupants turned out very good eggs and bacon at a reasonable charge and they were well patronised by the cadets including myself. Flying started soon after our arrival. I was given another half hour's dual by a Lieutenant Halliwell and I made my second solo in Texas on 21 November. Texas, around Fort Worth, was very flat country and the sun usually shone every day. The planes were not furnished with compasses and, as the countryside was featureless, it was very easy to get oneself hopelessly lost. It was therefore wise to fly by the sun's position and the layout of the railroad system which formed a square to the west of Camp Everman. I found this method accurate because I wandered quite a way from the airfield as time went on and always got back by hitting one of the railroads running into Fort Worth which, from the air, was within sight of Everman airfield. Some weeks before we moved from Camp Borden, an advance party of mechanics had been sent ahead to prepare for aircraft maintenance in order that flying instruction might commence with the least delay on the arrival of the cadets.

At weekends, we were allowed into Fort Worth town and, to be properly dressed, Cadets were required to wear white bands on their forage caps, which indicated they were 'ab-initio' air pilots under instruction. It soon became evident to us that we were being ostracised by the opposite sex and, however hard we tried, we could make no headway socially. To make matters more galling, the air mechanics were in great demand and would sail past us accompanied by the beauties of the town, with wide grins on their faces. This situation went on for a week or two before we got wise to what was happening. By then we had got to know some of the businessmen of the city and we discovered through them that, before we had arrived, the air mechanics had spread the story around that they were the flying pupils and that shortly a bunch of guys would arrive with a white band round their forage caps. This white 'band,' they said, served to indicate that the wearers were under 'medical treatment' and should be strictly avoided – anyway, they added as a 'coup de grace', they are only the mechanics. We had to give it to those boys, they had certainly put it across us, and we set to, to discuss ways and means of putting this smart trick straight. Almost at once, the answer was solved for us by a ruling of the camp commandant that, in future, on Sunday mornings the population of Fort Worth would be allowed, to watch the flying at Everman airfield. In those days, flying was a rarity and of great public interest, so the response was terrific. A large crowd turned up the first Sunday morning and the ladies to their amazement saw their so called 'Pilot Cavaliers' in grubby mechanics' overalls attending to the aeroplanes while the so-called tainted 'White Caps' were doing all the flying. From that moment on, the cadets had it all their own way and the trick the mechanics had played boomeranged severely upon them.

We had some new Instructors at Fort Worth, among them the celebrated dance instructor, Captain Vernon Castle. He was very interested in me when he learned I had come over from the Orient to join the RFC. He, naturally, being so famous, had many influential friends in Fort Worth and my entrée to social life was complete. My flying training at Camp Everman continued for five weeks, which brought us up to Christmas Eve. I went north to Buffalo and Niagara on the Lake, to stay with friends over Christmas and New Year, returning to Fort Worth and to a new airfield of Aerial Gunnery on 9 January 1918.

I had already visited my Buffalo friends at Niagara on the Lake when I was at Long Branch Camp on the opposite side of Lake Ontario in early October 1917. The house was only a few miles from the famous Niagara Falls and I had taken the opportunity then of venturing underneath the main fall. To do this, one had to don special waterproof garments and a guide took sightseers in a party under the falls. It was an awe inspiring sight. The force of the water flow in the Niagara River caused the water to shoot forward over the precipitous drop of some hundreds of feet and a passage was left hard up against the cliff face along which one was able to walk. The width would have been some six to seven feet, and the length probably a hundred and fifty feet or more. On reaching the middle, one stood and watched thousands of tons of green water crashing on to the rock. The noise was incredible and the viewer was soaked in spray. My mind went back to the indomitable Captain Webb who risked his life shooting the same falls in a barrel some years before.[1]

Having reached the opposite side, one made the return journey back to base, so to speak. Many of the people in the party were scared stiff and quite a few turned back at the start. I was with a friend I had met when travelling up from Los Angeles to Vancouver on the steamer, who had also been accepted in the RFC and was on the same course as I. Like myself, he was troubled with the slimy state of the rock we had to walk along under the falls, one good slip and that would have been the last slip one made.

At Hicks airfield, on the other side of Dallas, we received a concentrated course in camera work, firing at silhouette targets on the ground – towed target gunnery. The tests having been completed satisfactorily, we were shipped up to Toronto where we eventually joined the next overseas contingent and entrained for Halifax. That was a nightmare journey. It took three to four days, the ground was feet deep in snow and the temperature well below zero. We were placed two in a narrow train bunk which made it virtually impossible to sleep and, to make one's life more unbearable, the water system froze solid. That meant no washing and very little food. One afternoon, we stopped at a wayside station to let the Halifax-Montreal express through. I joined one of our instructors and another cadet for a walk along the platform to watch the express arrive. Our instructor, Captain Mackenzie, hailed from Scotland and wore the Service kilt. The express pulled in and the restaurant car stopped right alongside us. How our mouths watered to see the passengers enjoying their afternoon tea in luxurious comfort. There were two elderly ladies at one table and one was pointing at Captain Mackenzie. The kilt was evidently intriguing them. Mackenzie took great umbrage at being the object of their inquisitive study. Without warning, he turned, faced the two old ladies and pulled his kilt right above his head. He was one of the tough kilties who did not wear 'trews.' The two old ladies, held up their hands, gave one shriek and ducked. Captain Mackenzie walked on, murmuring, 'I hope that satisfied their curiosity.' The other Cadet Officer and myself were buckled up with laughter. We had never seen anything so funny as the look of outraged horror on the two old ladies' faces.

We arrived in Halifax, frozen, dirty, hungry and in low spirits after a four day nightmare journey. The town of Halifax was in a bad state. A month before, on 6 December 1917, an ammunition ship had blown up, flattening a great part of the town at a terrific cost in life. There was one hotel left which we repaired to and we were able to get superficially cleaned up and have a decent breakfast. We

---

[1] From the late nineteenth century, several people descended Niagara Falls in a barrel with a variety of outcomes. Captain Matthew Webb (1848-1883), swam the English Channel in 1875 and attempted to swim the Niagara River below Niagara Falls in 1883 – his body was recovered four days later.

were then escorted to the docks and boarded, if I remember correctly, the *SS Megantic* of the White Star Line. We were nonplussed with what we saw: a beautiful dining room laid out with spotless white linen and staterooms fit for the rich. What a contrast to our cadet camp life and uncomfortable long journey all the way up from Texas. At Toronto, we had been given our commissions as fully qualified pilots and so we were travelling first class, with the troops and non-commissioned officers below. We suffered no illusions as to what might befall us on the way over the Atlantic to Liverpool, our port of destination. The U-boat warfare was at its height and we were heavily escorted by destroyers. On two occasions, we could see the destroyers break formation and tear off to a certain section of the ocean, and the huge explosions which occurred from their depth charges which shot high columns of sea water into the air, indicated there were U-boats around. However, we were lucky for we did not suffer any casualty to our convoy, but it was a funny feeling waiting for what might happen, especially in the middle of the night. My friend Walter, whom I met on the trip up to Vancouver, was ahead of us with another contingent on the *SS Olympic*. They had great excitement as their ship rammed a U-boat, cutting it in half, the two ends of the submarine appearing on each side of the liner, so it was said. One or two ships were also lost in the convoy. Walter Pawson and I parted at Liverpool. He was posted to an airfield in Hampshire and I to one at Narborough in Norfolk. Shortly afterwards, I learned that Walter had killed himself trying to land in a field near some house in the country where he was keeping a date for afternoon tea. He apparently undershot the hedge, striking it, and the plane turned over, crushing him in the process.

After more instruction at Narborough, I was posted to a small airfield at Holt where we carried out coastal patrols for U-boats slinking down the North Sea. Our planes were fitted with wireless telegraphy, and we could only transmit but not receive. I was very excited one day when, picking up a ship convoy steaming south towards the Straits of Dover, I spotted a U-boat stalking the convoy. It was submerged and to the rear of the ships, which were steaming along quite unaware of the danger lurking beneath the waves. I at once tapped out a message on my Morse key to base reporting the situation and they in turn contacted the naval authorities who sent a destroyer to investigate. I heard later that the U-boat was located and destroyed by depth charges.

On 1 April 1918, a great change was effected in the set up of the Royal Flying Corps when it was merged with the Royal Naval Air Service and we became the Royal Air Force. At the time, it did not make much difference to us and life went on as usual. After some months on coastal patrol, I was transferred to Duxford airfield, some 10 miles south of Cambridge, as an instructor. We were the first squadron to take up duty on that airfield. I flew over from Thetford with my belongings in the back seat of an RE8 biplane and my bicycle strapped to the side of the fuselage with the wheels resting on the lower plane. The arrival caused great excitement amongst the mechanics when I taxied to a stop outside the hangars. They had never seen anything like it before and I don't suppose such a sight was ever repeated.

In the early part of the summer, the war nearly claimed me as a victim, not through any effort of the enemy, but by a large scale attack on me by the virulent Spanish flu which raged through Britain during 1918. To make matters worse, a repeat dose of malaria, which I had contracted two years before in Hankow, smote me. I was seriously ill in the RAF hospital in Hampstead for a number of weeks and, for two days, it was touch and go whether I would recover. It was not until the late summer that I was again fit for flying duties. There had been a suggestion that I was to be transferred to the Independent Air Force, which was operating from the Nancy district in France, but in view of the severe illness I had just recovered from, the authorities sent me back to continue instruction at Duxford.

A few months later, in November 1918, the enemy asked for an armistice, which produced hectic jubilations in London. Some of our chaps landed up in Vine Street police station that night.

I was demobbed in June 1919. In July, I was married to Dorothy Cumming whom I met at the home of friends in Hitchin the year before. The reception was given at my parents' home in Wickford and the ceremony was performed in the old village church in the parish of Runwell, next door to Wickford. We went to Devon and Cornwall on a three-week honeymoon in my little *Swift* cycle car powered by a two cylinder 7 hp water-cooled engine. On our return to Cambridge, we left by air for the seaside resort of Skegness. Prior to my marriage, I had contracted with the Cambridge School of Flying to carry out a two weeks' joy-riding tour from the beach of Skegness with an Avro 504K converted three seater. We flew up one evening, passing over my old airfield at Narborough in Norfolk and then Kings Lynn and out over the fifteen sea miles crossing of The Wash. Halfway across, the motor stopped dead on us. Although we were flying at 3,000 feet, we were too far from shore to reach dry land on the glide. It looked as if we were going to have a long swim or be drowned in the process when suddenly I noticed the petrol feed pressure gauge was reading zero. As I was flying from the front seat I was unable to reach the auxiliary hand pump situated in the rear cockpit. I let go the controls and leant over to the rear and shouted to my wife, Dorothy, to lean forward. She responded quickly and I pointed out the pump handle and told her to keep pumping until further notice. As I sat down in my own seat the engine came to life while we were in a pretty steep dive. We had lost a lot of height by the time I got the plane flying level again for the altimeter only read 700 feet. My wife had to keep pumping until we reached our destination half an hour later. From the awkward position in which she was sitting, it was very tiring work. She had, however, saved our lives.

By the time we arrived at Skegness, dusk was falling. I had no time to go looking for the field that the Cambridge people had hired for us as a parking place, so I put down in a favourable looking patch just outside the town. Unfortunately, there were one or two bulls grazing that green sward and, as soon as the plane came to a standstill, the bulls made ready to charge the intruder in their midst. I jumped out, tore off my leather flying coat and waved it at them. They hesitated a moment and beat a retreat. However, after a moment of furious tail wagging, they re-formed and charged again. This time my flying coat did not frighten them and I was obliged to jump back on the plane to avoid being tossed. It looked as if our Avro aeroplane was about to be completely destroyed by the angry beasts when, fortunately, the farmer and his cattleman arrived on the scene. They drove the bulls into another field and we descended and got acquainted with one another. In those days, an aeroplane was a rarity and so the farmer welcomed us both and apologised for the plight we found ourselves in. After picketing the Avro down for the night, I explained to him that we had rented a field on a certain farm, but owing to darkness setting in so quickly we had to make a quick landing. He said he knew the owner and would take us over next morning to show us the field and introduce me to him. The farmer drove us to Skegness in his car and we checked into our hotel for the night.

A day or two after we had become settled in our hired field, two ladies and a gentleman came along for a flight before we had moved over to the beach. They introduced themselves as the Misses Cash and I forget the Cavalier's name. After the flight, they invited Dorothy and myself to their summer residence in Skegness. They came from Farnsfield Hall, near Nottingham, and were members of the Cash family, famous for their 'woven name' tabs. One of the sisters was named Etta, but I forget the name of her sister. I was not to meet them again for fourteen years, and my wife not at all.

I was kept very busy for the next ten days, flying off the beach and taking several hundred passengers up for an aerial view of their town. It was a great novelty for almost no one in the civilian population had flown in those early days of flying, nor seen an aeroplane at close quarters on the ground.

Towards the end of the month, September 1919, the rail strike of that year descended upon us before we had completed our flying tour. The authorities would not allow us to draw any petrol and so I had to cease giving pleasure flights. To make matters worse, I could not even obtain sufficient petrol to take me back to Cambridge. After five days, matters were getting extremely awkward for us. I had to get the plane south by the end of September owing to our impending sailing for New York on our return to China.

At first the civil authorities would not yield to my pleas, but at last they gave way on one condition, that 'we would carry the several days' collection of mail to Cambridge' and deliver it to the postmaster there. It was not clear in my mind where I was going to stow the mail as I could not leave my wife behind and she occupied most of the stowage room in the rear cockpit. However, I compromised and said I would carry as much as there was stowage room for and, on that basis, petrol was made available for the return flight.

By the time we had finished loading the mail, my poor wife was surrounded by mail bags, but she stuck it out in great discomfort for the one hour and twenty minutes we were in the air. On that return flight we observed many convoys of lorries on the main north road carrying urgent supplies, which the railways would have normally carried. There was none of the softness shown to strikers who held up the national services in those days, as is the case today.

I still possess the receipt of the Cambridge Post Office for the mail sacks delivered to them on 30 September 1919, which was probably the first official air mail carried in Great Britain which was not an organised stunt.

In the middle of October, we sailed for New York from Liverpool on the White Star liner, *Baltic*. There were several celebrities on board, namely Mr George Grossmith, the actor, Mr Ian Hay, the author, and Jimmy Wilde, the lightweight boxer. The crossing was rough but very pleasant as we had several concerts and plenty of talent. We spent several days in New York staying at the Pennsylvania Hotel and we were taken around New York city by a Mr Hecht, the New York director of Harrison & Crossfields who were connected with the firm I was working for. We travelled west by the Santa Fe Railroad to Los Angeles and spent a few days with my friends, Dr Frances and his wife. I arranged with them to have my motorbike shipped to Shanghai and we left by the Shasta route train for Seattle, passing through San Francisco at night. At Seattle, we boarded the steamer for Yokohama and from there travelled by train to rejoin the steamer at Nagasaki. We visited Kobe and Kyoto on the way. The scenery of that route was wonderful and which words cannot adequately describe.

We spent Christmas Day 1919 in Nagasaki and had a big party on board. A year later to the day, my wife died in a Shanghai Hospital from typhoid fever, leaving me with a small daughter three months old.

While in America, I was given an introduction to a high ranking Japanese naval air officer in Yokohama. He invited me to visit the Yokosuka Naval Air Station, some thirty miles away. The station commandant was anxious for me to lecture the cadets on 'Air Fighting and Armament'. He said his cadets would be most interested to hear first hand knowledge from the Western Front. After giving an hour's talk, and receiving an appropriate vote of thanks, I was escorted over the naval air station. Not far away, I observed a low hill some two hundred feet high, which was swarming with Japanese men and women. On enquiring what was going on, I was informed they were removing the hill by hand shovels and picks, loading the earth and rock into small baskets and tossing them down a human chain which extended at least half a mile to the sea. They were dumping the contents into the water in order to extend the land aerodrome. It was the same principle they adopted in coaling ocean-going steamers. A barge draws alongside the ship and a human chain, usually women, extend from the barge hold to the steamer bunkers and the baskets full of coal are thrown from hand to hand at an extremely rapid rate and dumped into the bunker. Hundreds of tons of coal are dealt with in a remarkably short time. I learned later that the hill at Yokosuka had been flattened inside six months.

The Japanese naval authorities were using a locally designed float biplane built at the Yokosuka station. It flew very well, but I noticed a most curious feature with the wing bracing. Biplanes had the wing bracing wires, which carried the load when the aircraft was airborne, duplicated, and the wires which carried the weight of the wings when the aircraft was on the ground were single. It the case of the Yokosuka biplane, they had it in reverse, namely single flying wires and duplicated landing wires. That was a very dangerous design error. On enquiry, I learned several aircraft of that type had broken up in flight, which they could not account for. I mentioned the error in design, and the danger of flying aircraft with insufficient bracing of the wing structure while in flight, to the station commandant. He was amazed by my report and I received a letter from him later saying that the design had been corrected and thanking me for the valuable advice I had given them.

I did not get much flying in for the next few years. Occasionally, I visited a Chinese government airfield in Peking and at Pao-Ting-Fu and managed to get some flying practice as some return for technical advice given to the local school. After I had been back in Shanghai for a year, a Major Willie McBain, an ex RFC pilot, imported a 160 hp Armstrong Whitworth biplane and levelled out a small airfield at his farm on the Hunjac Road, some ten miles from the Shanghai Bund. I assisted in the erection of the aircraft and he made the first test flight. Major McBain flew the plane a few times, but tired of it quickly. I think he met with opposition from his wife. Anyway, he didn't like the small airfield, which was unsuited to a plane of that power. I, however, continued to fly his Armstrong Whitworth for hire and reward and business giving joy-rides over Shanghai was brisk. I flew up to the Heng-li Regatta, some fifty miles north west from Shanghai, and up the Soochow Creek with a photographer and he took the first aerial pictures of that annual event, which was an affair of some magnitude and run on the 'English Henley' lines. Eventually, just after taking off with an old friend of mine, Donald Leach, I had an engine failure. There was nowhere to make a forced landing and I had to crash-land the plane on rough ground covered with Chinese coffins and surrounded by split bamboo poles sticking into the air. Indeed, the machine was impaled on them and Donald and I narrowly missed becoming speared. Neither of us was injured, but the plane was a write-off.

I immediately set to work to reconstruct it in the bamboo hangar we had erected at the Hun-Jac farm. In less than six months, it was ready to fly again, but we had no spare air screw. The importation of aeroplanes and spares had recently been forbidden by the Peking Government and the two new air screws I had ordered from home were lying in bond at the Shanghai Customs. We were refused a permit to import, so some other method of obtaining those air screws had to be thought out. In the end, we shipped them to British Territory in Hong Kong and got a friend to wrap each air screw up in a bundle of sugar canes and sacking and re-ship them to Shanghai by one of the native crew on a local coastal steamer. When the ship arrived, we hired a sampan to go alongside the steamer, lying at the jetty, at night. The two bundles of supposed sugar cane were then lowered over the side to the sampan and brought ashore. Within a few days, the plane was tested and flew better than ever. I was frequently quizzed on how I came by those air screws. I evaded the question by saying we had made one ourselves. That explanation was accepted, but I don't think it was believed.

A year later, the local Shanghai 'War Lord' bought an Avro 504K fitted with a 90 hp Renault engine and, as he came under Peking jurisdiction, managed to obtain a permit from the Peking Government to import it. Having taken delivery of the crates, they were unable to erect and test the plane. I was approached as the Chinese knew I had erected Major McBain's aircraft. I agreed to do the work for an impressive fee, and eventually tested the plane on the Kiang Wan military parade ground, some 400 yards in length but with bad approaches. However, it was sufficient for that type of plane, and I completed the contract in quick time and pocketed my fee.

Shortly afterwards, my firm transferred me to Hankow so I had no further contact with aircraft until 1924. Towards the end of 1923, I was approached by the Chinese regarding the establishment of an aircraft factory at Tai-Yuan-Fu in the northern province of Shansi, very mountainous country and bordered on the north by the famous Gobi Desert. I was invited by Governor Yen Shih Shan to visit him in his capital, Tai-Yuan-Fu. That involved a rail journey of some 1,100 miles. To get there, I had first to travel by train via Nanking, cross the Yangstze River, which was over a mile wide, by launch to Pukow and then entrain for Peking. From Peking I had another train journey 140 miles south on the Hankow-Peking railway, to a little country station named Shih Chia T'swang, which was the junction for the railway running up to Tai-Yuan-Fu. There was a lot of inter-provincial fighting going on in that area. One of the local war lords was trying to take a neighbouring war lord's territory and it was advisable to keep clear when these outbursts of internecine fighting erupted. I felt I had to take a chance as it was important I should be in Tai-Yuan-Fu as quickly as possible. In any event, it would not be the first time I had become mixed up – and been shot at – in one of the many civil wars which went on in China in those days.

I left Peking one winter's night. There were no proper coaches and I had to travel in an open truck with the natives. It was freezing and bitterly cold although I was dressed in my flying kit, that is leather flying coat, flying helmet and fur-lined gloves and boots. The natives were swaddled in cotton wool lined garments, and seemed accustomed to travelling in open trucks under freezing conditions. The night dragged on and, in a few hours, we passed through Pao-Ting-Fu, some hundred odd miles down the line and which boasted a military airfield and training school. The train crawled along at around thirty miles an hour. It was a beautiful starlit night and the moon shone brilliantly, but I was far too cold and hungry to appreciate the heavenly beauty. We arrived in Shih Chia T'swang around one in the morning and I promptly made for the local Chinese hotel by the station to wait for the connection on to Tai-Yuan-Fu next morning. I got a room on the first floor and, after some hot tea well lined with whisky I had brought with me, I turned in to sleep. I was utterly exhausted and was asleep very quickly, but it was not for long. I was suddenly awakened by utter pandemonium. There was heavy machine gun firing and mortars cracked sharply above the noise; people were shouting and screaming with fear. As I got out of bed to see what was going on, the window glass was shattered by bullets which hit the wall just above my bed. I promptly ducked, grabbed my pillow and blankets and got underneath the bed. I could hear running and the crunch of heavy footsteps up the stairs, and cries of terror as Chinese guests were being dragged from their beds by the Chinese soldiers. Then executions commenced outside the hotel as political prisoners were put to death by beheading. My bedroom door was suddenly burst open and, from floor level, I could see heavy boots stump into my room.

The owner of those boots did not, fortunately for me, take the trouble to look under the bed although I could hear the wardrobe being flung open. As suddenly as the searcher arrived, he departed, and I spent the rest of the night huddled up on the floor. The firing went on all night and only died down at sunrise. I noticed many bullets had splattered the walls of my room when I eventually crawled out from beneath the bed next morning. By breakfast time, as all had been quiet for an hour or two, I ventured down the stairs. The sight outside the hotel was a horror. The dead were lying all over the place with several executed bodies, minus heads, lying around. Eventually, I found a Chinaman connected with the hotel, who told me that the town had been attacked by a rebel army who were looking for persons of rank in the army who were holding the area in that part of the country. Such raids in those days were so commonplace and an accepted fact that the train for Tai-Yuan-Fu was ready to depart at its scheduled time of 1.00 am. When I left, the hotel staff had recovered their equilibrium and were cleaning up and getting back to a normal day. The Chinese were very stoical to such raids. Needless to say, I was mighty glad to get away in one piece.

I hadn't had much sleep that night, so I made up for it on the six hour journey through the mountains to Tai-Yuan-Fu. I had a good view of the wonderful Chinese Wall built hundreds of years ago by the Manchus. I booked in at the principal Chinese hotel in Tai-Yuan-Fu and sent an emissary to let the governor know I had arrived. A reply came back asking me to visit him next morning.

That interview was a long one and I had many difficult questions to answer, technically and otherwise. Eventually, the governor said he was prepared to sign a contract for me to build three prototype aeroplanes. If they flew successfully, I was to obtain a contract for fifty more. That was something really worth going after for I reckoned to make a thousand pounds on each plane. With the signed contract in my pocket, I returned to Shanghai by the same route as I had come and was fortunate in making a connection with a northbound train from Hankow at the junction at Shih Chia T'swang for Peking, thus avoiding another night's stay there for which I was truly thankful.

As soon as the deposit was paid into my bank account in Shanghai, as called for by the contract, I resigned my position with the company for which I was working. Lists of equipment and materials were compiled and forwarded home to my suppliers, The Aircraft Disposal Company Limited in Kingsway, London. Major Jack Stuart was the manager and I dealt through him.

I knew of a German engineer in Shanghai who had some experience in aircraft construction. He was out of work so I managed to obtain his services. That was a bad day's work for me as will be seen later. I gave him the layout of the aircraft I had in mind and we got down to designing a plane based on the stressing of the Armstrong Whitworth biplane that Major McBain had imported. We used all the measurements and sections, but recalculated the centre of gravity which would place the two cockpits behind the main planes instead of the passenger sitting beneath the top wing, as was the case with the Armstrong Whitworth. We knew of a first class Chinese carpenter and woodworker and tied him up under contract. His name was Loh.

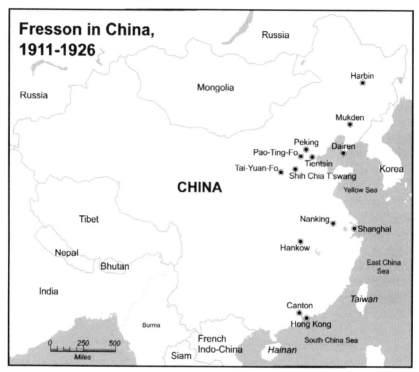

While the general arrangement drawings were being made in Shanghai, I returned to Tai-Yuan-Fu, to arrange for the construction of the workshops we would require and which would be sited within the Tai-Yuan-Fu arsenal. It was on that trip I met the arsenal mechanical adviser. He was an Englishman by the name of Wright and he was an expert mathematician. He gave great assistance in calculating the stresses for us. As soon as the workshops and equipment were nearing completion, and the engine test bench completed, I sent for the German engineer and carpenter Loh. In the meantime, the first order I had sent home for air motors, timber and steel sheeting had arrived at Shanghai. As I have said, the Peking Government had clamped down on all aircraft or spares being imported into the country unless required by the central government in Peking. Even Governor Yen, with the influence he held in Peking, could not get them to budge and give us a permit. So everything had to be made on the spot. We could not, however, make the aircraft wheels or instruments. We managed to import these accessories as motor car parts and they came through without any trouble. Welding equipment was bought in Shanghai and, by the late spring of 1924, we were ready to commence construction. The 160 hp motors were imported as motor boat engines and, on arrival in Tai-Yuan-Fu, were put on the engine test bench and given a run in, ready for installation. By the beginning of September, the first plane was nearing completion and ready for motor installation, when a disturbing report reached us. A French firm were endeavouring to sell Governor Yen some Breguet aeroplanes and one was on its way by rail with a French pilot for demonstration. It was essential that our plane flew first, otherwise the subsequent order for fifty machines might be in jeopardy. We eventually got our aircraft to the airfield that I had surveyed and had constructed some six miles to the north of Tai-Yuan-Fu. It had an eight hundred yard run which was a large airfield for those days, but as the altitude of the airfield was close on 4,000 feet above sea level, I expected the take-off would be quite a bit longer than at sea level. The body of the aeroplane was pushed along the dusty road on its wheels by coolies and the boxed wings, port and starboard, carried out separately to the bamboo hangar which had recently been erected. The final assembly of our aircraft was commenced as the French machine arrived on the aerodrome. That afternoon I had been engaged in welding a fitting without any eye shield. That night my eyes began suffering badly from burning. I was obliged to stay in bed in the dark. After I had been confined to bed for several days, news was brought to me that the Frenchman was nearly ready to demonstrate his plane. I cursed myself for my folly in omitting to use a shield and getting myself laid up at that crucial moment. I was a week in the dark before the doctor would let me out and, on that day, the Frenchman made his test flight at noon. A few more hours and I would have managed to get the first flight in, so I went into lunch heavy hearted, and feeling far from hungry because I was so upset. Within an hour, my German engineer brought me the news that, just after the Frenchman had taken off and risen to a hundred feet or so, his motor cut dead. He stalled his Breguet biplane and it fell to the ground, killing himself and completely wrecking his plane. That finished the Breguet affair, and a gala day was called a few days later for the testing of our home-made plane.

The governor and his ministers would appear on the airfield in the afternoon for the demonstration flight. There was great excitement in the town. There had been a lot of propaganda from the Chinese French camp that our plane would never fly, and the governor was anxious that these rumours should be given the lie. There were some ministers in his 'Ya-mun' that I suspected of being in the pay of our would-be competitors, and they were present in the Tuchun's (governor's) retinue hoping that we would be humiliated.

The motor started up first go and, after being warmed up on the chocks, I waved them away and commenced to taxi the eight hundred yards to the south end of the field as the wind was blowing from the north. The spectators did not appreciate what was happening. They had never seen an aeroplane before and, as my plane waddled down to the south end of the airfield, they started up a cry, 'The great bird cannot fly.' Roars of mirth followed and, by the time I had got to the end of the field and turned into wind, the poor governor was also convinced he had been sold a pup. I took my time, quite unconscious of what was going on, and tested both magnetos on the motor to be sure they were functioning correctly. I then opened the throttle wide. I was tense. 'Would the plane fly?' I asked myself. If so, I decided to fly low for a few hundred yards to test the controls, land and then start the run again for a higher flight. To my pleasant surprise, our locally made plane roared off the ground in a little more than a hundred yards run which, at that altitude, was incredible. I levelled out, and I did not need to wait to know that she was flying normally although she felt a bit tail heavy. As I came up alongside the grandstand, I pulled the stick back and the plane climbed at a sharp angle, passing the governor at not less than four hundred feet and still gaining height. I felt a great exultation. We had succeeded and the big order must surely follow, which would rope me in fifty thousand pounds. I learned afterwards that, when the crowd saw the plane suddenly in the air and starting to climb, they let off a big sigh of wonderment. Eyes were gaping and the governor's ministers who were on the French 'Band Wagon' looked completely mortified and angry. The governor was enraptured. I cruised around Tai-Yuan-Fu for ten minutes at 800 feet. The whole population turned out to see the 'Fey Johee' (Flying Engine). I could see their heads staring up. After several circuits, I returned to the airfield. I was anxious to see how the landing would work out. It would be heart-rending if anything went wrong and the plane got damaged just as success was ours. The approach was made on a very flat glide and the landing effected almost in front of the governor and his ministers. The plane was faultless in its handling and controls. When I reached our hangar, a message was waiting for me, that the governor wished to see me right away. He told me how pleased he was and that he wished me to call on him next day, at his Yamun (official residence). Naturally, our own camp was greatly excited at the success of our many months hard labour. We had a good look around the motor; there were no oil leaks and everything appeared in order, so I decided to make another flight with full tanks, which gave a range of six hours. I wanted to know the stalling speed and flat out speed of the machine, also the climbing characteristics with full fuel load. I took off again at forty minutes past four, this time with Loh, our carpenter, as passenger, and flew for two hours around the neighbourhood to give the motor and installation a good testing. During the flight, I came to the unpleasant conclusion that the plane with a passenger was very tail heavy. Even using full tail trim, I was unable to trim the plane for level flight. The motor was too far back and needed moving roughly eight inches forward and that meant redesigning the engine bay. This alteration could quite easily be incorporated in the remaining two aircraft, which we had not as yet commenced to assemble.

The *Peking & Tientsin Times* dated 29 September 1925 quotes the occasion as follows:

The first aeroplane flight in Shansi
Made in and flown over Tai-Yuan-Fu
An excited populace and Taipan

On 20th September, 1925 [my birthday] the first aeroplane flight was made in Tai-Yuan-Fu by Mr E E Fresson on a locally constructed machine. For several days it had been rumoured that the machine would be tested that morning, and quite early in the morning, people were streaming along the road North of the City to the Aerodrome to witness the unusual sight. Owing to the many adjustments that were necessary, the Plane did not get away until four in the afternoon. The weather was uncertain. The Aeroplane which is finished in aluminium, sparkled in the sunlight as it was taxied down the ground to get into position for the take off run.

After a very short run the machine was off the ground, and as it passed in front of the Spectators, the airman was given a vigorous cheer. After circling around the Town and aerodrome for ten minutes, a perfect landing was effected and the Pilot was warmly congratulated by the many People present. The health of Mr Fresson who is the Contractor and organiser of the Factory, was toasted in Champagne. The following day another demonstration was given for the Governor and Officials. [This was an inaccurate report as the Governor was present on the first flight.] As the proceedings had been published in the previous newspapers, a large crowd gathered. Shortly after Tuchun Yen Shan arrived, the plane was in the air and circled over the Airfield much to the interest of the Governor and his Officials, many of whom were witnessing a heavier than Air machine in flight for the first time. Upon descending, the Tuchun shook hands with Mr Fresson and congratulated him for being the first to fly in Shansi Province and on a plane made by Chinese labour in his Province.

On Tuesday the same pilot flew over the City at 2,500 feet for half an hour dropping pamphlets to the population. The Streets were crowded and the population cheered and clapped in their excitement at the unusual spectacle presented. It is hoped shortly to make a long distance flight with this machine in order to obtain fuller details of its air worthiness and staying capabilities.

Two days later, I made a flight 150 miles west to the Hwang Ho River (Yellow River) and returned non-stop. The flight took three and a half hours and was flown over mountainous country where a forced landing would probably have been fatal. The governor accepted the prototype after that flight and we began to make and plan arrangements for mass production and setting up a flying training school for army officers.

Before long, however, dark clouds began to appear on the horizon. A German representative of the Junker Aircraft Company in Germany suddenly appeared in Tai-Yuan-Fu. No doubt he had read the newspaper report of the successful flights of our locally made aircraft. Within two weeks or so I learned he was spending a lot of time at nights with my German engineer, and then my friend, General Li, the director of the arsenal, told me that the Junkers representative had asked for an appointment with Governor Yen Shih Shan. Through General Li, I was kept informed, and it soon appeared that my engineer had gone over to the Junker camp. To combat that bit of double crossing, I immediately made enquiries to obtain a British engineer to take on the mass production order I had been promised, and I have little doubt that the governor would have kept his promise had this arrangement been put into practice. There is an old saying, 'It never rains but it pours' and that was surely the simile in my case, for without warning, communist-organised student riots occurred in the Nanking Road, Shanghai, and the British Police were forced to open fire, killing a number of students. That sent a wave of anti-British feeling over China and was taken up by the students and agitators in Tai-Yuan-Fu. One afternoon, a day or two later, I was in my room in the Chinese hotel where I was staying, when my personal boy (servant) came running to me in an excited state:

'Master! Master!' he said in Chinese, 'There is a mob of loafers outside the hotel wanting to know where you are. They mean to kill you!'

He had scarcely finished speaking when I could hear the howls of the mob outside, demanding from the Chinese owner to be told of my whereabouts. My room was situated in the inner courtyard, which was connected by a narrow passage with the front of the hotel. There was no other exit but the front entrance, so I was cornered like a 'rat in a trap'.

'What is it that these people want with me?' I asked my boy.

'Master', he answered, 'they say you are an "Ing-Gwer-Ruen" [Englishman] and that your people have shot Chinese students in Shanghai. They mean to kill you', he repeated.

What was I to do? I had to think quickly. I could hear the shouting and fury of the mob, while they ransacked the front part of the hotel. There was no escape as the one entrance was besieged. I would have to try and bluff my way out. As I have said, the courtyards in Chinese buildings are interconnected by narrow passages. The passage connecting my courtyard was not more than two and a half feet wide. That meant only one Chinaman could get down at one time. I had two automatic pistols in my room, holding sixteen shots. Quickly, I grabbed a chair and placed it at the entrance of the passage, sat down and waited. Within a few minutes, the mob broke into No. 1 courtyard and started for my passage. I fired one shot over their heads. They came to an abrupt halt.

'Who's your leader?' I shouted in Chinese. 'I want to speak with him. Any of you entering my passage will be shot dead.'

A great murmur went up. They had received a shock, I sensed. The leader came forward.

'Stand in front of the passage,' I told him. He did so.

'Now', I asked, 'what do you want with me and why are you breaking the hotel up?'

'The English police have shot our students in Shanghai,' he answered, 'and we mean to take our revenge.'

'But I was not in Shanghai when the police shot your students,' I answered. 'What had it got to do with me? I am here as a guest of your Tuchun to build aeroplanes. Why insult your Tuchun's guest?'

He spoke rapidly to the mob.

Before he could speak to me again, I told the leader, 'Go home and leave me alone. If you try and force this passage, there will be another sixteen dead Chinese. Are you prepared to pay such a price just to kill me? And don't forget, the Tuchun will certainly behead you, should I be harmed.'

That created a problem for him. Chinese custom made a guest almost sacred. He turned round and harangued the mob. I could only catch bits of what he said. He spoke the local dialect which was very different to the Mandarin dialect which I knew. The leader said no more. Suddenly, they turned and left the hotel. By that time, the sweat was pouring down my face. How lucky, I thought, that I could speak Chinese and that the mob's leader understood Pekingese dialect. After they had gone, I went to look at the front of the hotel. It was smashed to pieces and would take a lot of repairing. I immediately got on the telephone to General Li at the arsenal and told him what had happened. He said he would come down to see me. He did, and went to see the Tuchun.

There was no further disorder as the military were out in force. Next morning, the Tuchun sent for me. He said how very sorry he was that I should have been insulted and in such danger in his province. The culprits would be punished. They were – several heads came off. After that there was no further trouble.

The next move in the German camp came shortly afterwards. One morning, I saw our plane in the sky over Tai-Yuan-Fu. I rushed out to the airfield and found the Junkers pilot was flying it. He had obtained permission from someone in the Yamun (Local Government Office). I was furious and went back to General Li. He was annoyed and very sorry for me. He then told me that my very 'loyal' German had come to an arrangement with the Junkers agent and that they had the governor's ear. The Junkers representative was able to promise the governor the whole support of the Junkers factory and he promised they would turn out the aeroplane cheaper than I had quoted. Even then, I don't believe Yen Shih Shan would have let me down. He was, however, greatly disturbed about the recent rioting, and felt he could not be responsible for my safety, more especially as the troubles in Shanghai had by no means died down. In the end, he gave me a considerable sum in compensation and asked to be freed from the mass production contract. I could see his mind was made up and it was no use arguing, so with a heavy heart I was obliged to accept his offer. I had spent almost two years under the greatest discomfort and poor food, cut off from my own kith and kin and working round the clock to get that contract for the fifty aircraft. Mechanical success had come my way and I had taken a big chance in flying an untried aeroplane of local design and had succeeded, now only to fail through circumstances beyond my control. That was early 1926. Twenty-two years later, history was to repeat itself as the continuing chapters will show.

I returned to Tientsin and stayed for a while with R H Rowlatt, my old boss during my early days in Hankow. He was very upset at the raw deal I had received and the grave disloyalty of the German I had befriended in Shanghai who, as I have said, was out of work at the time I employed him and on his beam ends. I returned to my house in Shanghai and had a holiday. I was very tired, but a month's relaxation in a civilised town soon put me right.

In the spring of 1926, I received particulars of the first de Havilland Gipsy Moth, which had recently made its maiden flight and was about to be mass produced for the flying clubs in Britain and the Colonies. In Mukden, General Chang Tso Lin was building up an air force. Most of his aeroplanes were of French design. I had a contact in Mukden, General Sutton, who had designed a new type of mortar, which the Mukden arsenal was producing in quantity under his supervision. I wrote to him and sent him the particulars of the Gipsy Moth, asking if he would make enquiries as to such an aircraft finding favour in the Mukden camp. He answered and advised me to come up to Mukden. He told me that General Chang Tso Lin's son was in charge of the aviation side and would be interested in discussing the question with me.

I had another friend in Mukden, Mr Butchart, who was Mukden manager for the Jardine Engineering Company in Shanghai. He also had contacts with the local government. For the first few nights, I stayed in the Mukden station hotel, which brought back memories of November 1911 when I first stayed the night there waiting for a train connection to Dairen. Chang Tso Lin's son, the 'Young General' as he was known, was impressed with the Gipsy Moth layout, the simplicity of the Cirrus 1 Motor, and also the price.[2]

---

[2] The son of Chang Tso Lin was Marshall Chang Hsueh Liang.

I suggested he should order half a dozen to try out in his training school. They were using the French Caudron Biplane, which was a very good little plane with the wartime 80 hp Renault V type engine. However, it cost more to buy and operate than the Moth and I hoped that might be a selling point. I stayed up there three weeks, but could make no progress in tying the Young General down to an order. I fell back on Sutton who made some enquiries behind the scenes. He learned that the Young General was committed with the French authorities whom, it was suggested, were making financial concessions and Chang's Financial Advisors were unwilling to risk any possibility of upsetting the French Legation. A year or so later, I learned that the Young General had got over his financial difficulties with the French authorities and had ordered six DH Moths. I never heard whether they arrived. But if they did, I had 'missed the bus' by a short hop for the second time. I returned to Shanghai and, in the autumn, left for California to see the Ryan Aircraft Company in San Diego which was in the process of making a monoplane for Charles Lindbergh for a proposed non-stop Atlantic flight from New York to Paris.

My daughter's godmother, a Mrs Newton, lived in Los Angeles. She also had a very nice summer house at Oceanside, a few miles north of San Diego. After spending a few weeks in Los Angeles, I went to stay with her. I had ideas of making a goodwill flight, which was the rage in those days, from Yokohama to Singapore, on a sales mission and I wished to tackle the Ryan Aircraft Company to see if they were interested and would provide the aeroplane. Mrs Newton had a friend who knew one of the Ryan brothers and he motored me in to San Diego one morning and introduced me. They were interested in my proposal, but were at the moment so wrapped up with the Lindbergh plane that they had no time to consider anything else until they had completed the *Spirit of St Louis*, which was the name Lindbergh had given his plane in honour of the city that helped to finance his famous flight and which was soon to thrill the whole world.

I was taken to their airfield and, after my log book was inspected, they invited me to fly one of their monoplanes powered by a 200 hp Wright 'Whirlwind' radial motor. I was very impressed with the high climb performance and its handling. The longitudinal trim was quite a different cup of tea to the Tai-Yuan-Fu plane.

A day or two later, I was in the Ryan factory picking up information when Charles Lindbergh arrived. We were standing by his plane at the time with Mr Ryan directing certain constructional details. He introduced me as an interested aviator from the Orient. We talked about Tai-Yuan-Fu and its outcome and his forthcoming Atlantic flight. He then asked to be excused as he had a lot of detailed work to discuss with the manufacturers regarding the plane they were building for him. At the time, I thought he was quite mad, contemplating a flight across the Atlantic in a small single-engine aircraft of only 200 hp. I felt sure it would be the last we would ever hear of him once he had left Newfoundland. And I was not the only one in San Diego who felt that way, because I sensed the Ryan brothers were also sceptical, but of course would not commit themselves. I was to meet Lindbergh again seven years later in Inverness when he flew in from the USA by the northern route with Mrs Lindbergh on a Lockheed float monoplane, as I will record later on in my story.

The outcome of my visit to the Ryan works was negative for the time being. As I have said, all their thoughts were concentrated on the Lindbergh plane and it would be some months before that aeroplane was completed. There was a General Strike on at home and I was not anxious to be caught up in that, so I returned to Los Angeles and met up with a man who had a Travel Air two-seater plane at Santa Monica airfield. I went on a number of cross country trips with him, which gave me an extremely interesting insight to Californian topography. By October, the strike at home was over and I left for Britain having decided to drop the 'Ryan Goodwill Flight' proposition. At home, I had a young daughter named Betty and some six years of age whom I had not seen since 1921. As already mentioned, she was sent home when she and I lost her mother to typhoid in Shanghai on Christmas Day 1920. I travelled via Salt Lake City and the Grand Canyon. First, I wished to see where the Mormons lived and then the wonderful spectacle of the Grand Canyon where the railroad winds its way through nothing less than a crack in the mountains, the perpendicular sides of the cliffs rearing up for many hundreds of feet. Viewing Grand Canyon from the railroad tourists' stop was just like looking at a slit in the sky. The train track was built out over the river in places and it stopped at the show place for the passengers to get out and view that wonder of nature.

From there I went to Chicago to see some old China friends and on up to Toronto for the purpose of inspecting some property my father owned, some seventy miles away. That job completed, New York City was the next stop and where I was to embark for Liverpool. I looked up my old friend James Stanley MacNider whom I have referred to earlier in this chapter. He had an office in one of the city skyscrapers and he was engaged in the broking business. I sat by his desk surrounded by constantly ringing telephones. I well remember my admiration over the manner in which he so expertly handled several calls coming in at the same time and settling bargains all in the same breath. I said a prayer of relief that I was not in the broking racket in New York City. The speed was far too hectic. He was so very glad to see me. We had a long talk in one of the hotels afterwards. That was the last time I ever saw him. He died a couple of years ago, around 1960. We were, however, always in contact by correspondence. He was a wonderful letter-writer. I had a very soft spot in my heart for 'Mac' as he was known to us, for he taught me most of what I knew about business and a very fine instructor he was.

A day or two later, I sailed for Britain and on board I met Sir Eric Geddes. He was interested in my travels in the Far East and we met on the boat deck many mornings for a 'get-together' chat. The boat train from Liverpool was met at Euston station by my mother and small daughter. She was so shy that she seemed to find the platform of particular interest. That was March 1927.

Two months later, in May, Lindbergh flew the Atlantic. I was laid up at my mother's house in Kenton, north of London, with flu, itching to get down to Croydon to see the 'Atlantic Hero' arrive after his Paris visit, but the doctor would not let me out of his sight. That frail plane I saw in San Diego six months before had actually stayed in the air for over thirty-three hours and Lindbergh, with inadequate instruments, had flown about half of that time in cloud. I think it still remains the epic flight of aviation history and one of the finest order of courage that has yet to be matched.

The political situation in China was going from bad to worse with the Japanese, so I decided I would not return there. Therefore, in 1928, I joined Berkshire Aviation Tours operated by F J V Holmes. He ran a joy-riding circus with headquarters at Shrewsbury in Shropshire. I remember seeing an advertisement in the *Flight* aviation magazine. It ran something like: 'Wanted, a Pilot for the season, with experience of Le Rhône and Clerget Motors.' As I had that experience from my war training and had joy ridden at Skegness at the end of the war with an Avro 504E fitted with a Clerget motor, I applied for the job and got it.

I motored up to Monkmoor airfield just outside Shrewsbury and signed on. I was then shown around and, as we came to the gates, which allowed the planes to be moved across the road to the flying field from the hangars, I was introduced to my prospective engineer, Bert Farminer. The poor chap was down a deep hole digging for the erection of new gate pillars. At the time, I thought that was a peculiar job for a licensed air engineer, but I soon got to know that in that organisation, or any joy riding organisation for that matter, one had to be a 'Jack of all trades.' I spent that summer joy riding in Shropshire and Lancashire, in Scotland at Dumfries, and then at Renfrew during that year's King's Cup race. That Saturday afternoon I made one hundred and fourteen landings and take-offs. The place was packed with would be customers wishing to fly. I was staying with a family near the airfield and I returned to the house for a late tea in my overalls soaked in castor oil from the Le Rhône rotary motor. As I was too tired to go into the dining room, I was sitting on the bed when they brought it into me. The next thing I knew, it was four in the morning, the tea untouched and cold, and, horror of horrors, the bed soaked in castor oil from my overalls. Next morning was an awkward one for I was not at all popular with my hostess. However, she behaved very nicely when I told her how much flying I had done the day before.

After that, we moved to the beach at Ayr where we flew for over a week. This involved tricky cross-wind take-offs and landings the whole time. I was then transferred south to work in Shropshire and Yorkshire. It was then, while flying at Leeds, that I met Lance Rimmer, Berkshire's chief pilot. We saw quite a lot of each other after flying duties and, before I left at the end of the season, we had agreed to form a joy riding company of our own for next year. I was to raise the finance and he would become joint director and bring the 'know how'.

That winter, we arranged to purchase two Avro 504K Le Rhône-engined planes from the old Beardmore Flying School at Renfrew which had closed down. We were to collect the Avros early in the year. My engineer, Bert Farminer, was willing to join us and, with the help of an old friend in Cambridge, Bertram Chater, who was an accountant, the North British Aviation Company Limited was floated in January 1929 with headquarters at Hooton Park airfield, an old time World War One air base. We rented part of a hangar there and, to my surprise and pleasure, found there was a small flying club with clubhouse which was glad to admit me as a member.

In January, I went up to the Blackburn Aviation Company at Brough to carry out my RAF Reserve Training on twin-engine Kangaroos. It was a curious machine, designed at the latter end of World War One for coastal patrol work and looked rather a weird object when standing on the ground. On the cross-country flight at the end of the course, I had to fly to Grantham. On my return, I landed at the RAF station at Digby for lunch as my youngest brother, Noel, was undergoing his training for a Commission. The Blackburn Kangaroo was an object of great interest. Apart from its peculiar look, twin-engine aircraft were an unusual sight in those days and the senior officers were anxious to find out all the details. After lunch, quite a large number of the RAF personnel gathered to witness the take-off. The two Rolls-Royce 'Falcon' 260 hp motors gave a healthy roar as I opened the throttle full out. After a very short run, the big plane was soon climbing and heading north for the Blackburn Training School at Brough on the River Humber.

In the first week of February 1929, Lance Rimmer my partner, our engineer Bert Farminer and myself motored up to Renfrew in Scotland to collect the two Avros we had purchased from the Beardmore Aviation Company, which had recently closed down its flying school at Renfrew airfield. After testing the planes in the air, it was found necessary to change one of the motors. It was a back-breaking performance as there was no lifting tackle available to raise the motor, which weighed some 330 lbs. The operation had to be done by the three of us manually. We struggled, cursed and sweated trying to lift that engine five feet into the air and into position while Bert bolted the motor to the face plate attached to the fuselage. After three attempts we finally succeeded.

The following day, 5 February, after further test flying, we departed for Hooton Park airfield 180 miles away. We flew in formation and Bert Farminer ferried the car back. I well remember the trip for it was great excitement possessing one's own aircraft and starting an air business. It was a perfect day and the flight was completed in two hours and forty-five minutes. The only section of the flight I disliked was the sea crossing from Barrow-in-Furness to Fleetwood. I was, by habit, distrustful of rotary motors. They had a nasty habit of packing up when least expected and twenty miles of water did not inspire confidence under such circumstances. However, we were flying at 3,000 feet with a slight following wind and were soon across and home.

Several weeks were spent in thoroughly overhauling the aeroplanes and their motors, which were in good condition and it appeared we had obtained a good bargain at £200 each. The North British Aviation Company Limited commenced operations at Huddersfield on 29 March 1929. After two weeks brisk business, we returned to St Helens, famous for the Pilkington Glass Works. We were visited by members of the Pilkington family who were extremely interested in viewing their home, Rainford Hall, from the air. They had many flights with me and during our visit I was invited to Rainford Hall for lunch. I kept the engagement by flying over in the Avro and landing alongside the kitchen garden. The incident caused much local interest. After that occasion, I made several visits while we were flying at St Helens and after I had returned to our Hooton base at the end of the season. To wind up our visit, the two Miss Pilkingtons flew with me to Kendal when we moved on two weeks later.

On the second Sunday, the last day at St Helens, the famous comedian Dave Morris arrived at the flying field and booked one of our planes to fly him to London that afternoon. He was required to attend a court case in London next morning and when that was finished we were to fly him up to Huddersfield in time for him to take part in the evening performance at the local theatre. It was decided I would take the flight and we set off at four o'clock in the afternoon in fine weather. There was a slight headwind that slowed us down and we were obliged to refuel at Coventry, which delayed us further. So, by the time Aylesbury was reached it was almost dark. I chose a field on the edge of the town as close to the railway station as possible and effected a good landing in the twilight. It was not long before help arrived from the owner of a house close by who, when the situation had been explained to him, kindly offered to run Dave to the station. I picketed my plane down quickly and went with Dave Morris to see him off and make arrangements for the next day. It was decided he would meet me at the de Havilland airfield at Stag Lane at two o'clock next day. Huddersfield was 155 air miles from London and, as the Avro cruising speed was only 60 mph in still air, we planned to arrive at not later than five o'clock. I would arrange for a taxi to meet the plane at our landing ground and Dave would arrive at the theatre with an hour to spare. But things did not work out that way. I was at Stag Lane airfield before lunch and one of the de Havilland engineers went over the Avro motor ready for the afternoon flight. While that was being done, I went into the clubroom for some lunch. Who should I run into but Cyril Murrell, one of Aerofilms Limited's camera operators. During the period we were forming the North British Aviation Company we had come to an arrangement with the Aerofilms company to charter our aircraft whenever we were flying in a district where they had air filming contracts. Over lunch, Cyril told me he had two or three days' work in Huddersfield and, when he learned I was flying up that afternoon, he suggested he should join the flight and I would stay in Huddersfield and carry out his air picture contracts with him. A further advantage, he would navigate me by map-reading from the front seat in the rear cockpit. To do that he tied a loop of rope like a rein to each of my arms, with himself retaining the loop end in his lap. All he had to do then was to pull on each rein as he would in the case of driving a pony and trap. It worked fine and I was relieved of map-reading and flying the plane at the same time, which was hard mental work.

Dave Morris arrived on time and we were airborne by two o'clock. He was delighted to have company and readily agreed to Cyril Murrell coming along. All went smoothly until half way to Nottingham when we ran into a strengthening gale, which slowed our ground speed down to 30 mph. At that rate, and especially should the wind get stronger, we would never reach Huddersfield in time before the theatre opened. I beckoned to Cyril to lean over to my cockpit so that I could converse with him. We agreed our friend Dave would stand a far better chance if we landed at Nottingham and engaged a high powered car to rush him the last sixty miles to Huddersfield. Cyril put the proposition to Dave Morris and he said, 'Yes.' A fast car was out at the airfield within a quarter of an hour. We bade Dave goodbye and good luck. When we met him next day, he told us that he arrived at the theatre a quarter of an hour before the show was due to commence.

On Tuesday, Cyril Murrell and I were presented with complimentary tickets for that night's performance at the theatre. Dave excelled himself and put over some very clever 'quips' about his flight from St Helens to London and up to Nottingham. We stayed on for four days so that Cyril Murrell could obtain his air pictures and on 3 May returned to St Helens via Manchester on charter to Aerofilms Limited. The following day I bade Cyril goodbye. 'I'll be rejoining you again shortly,' he commented. He was as good as his word for he turned up at many places we were flying at that year and several years after. His company paid us well and were of great assistance to us in our early days of consolidation.

I left St Helens to join Captain Rimmer at Kendal in Westmorland. As I have said, Miss Pilkington and her sister joined me on that flight. They sent their car up to take them home. They were delighted with the experience of their first cross country flight. We were kept very busy during our fortnight's stay at Kendal, for there were many people who were anxious to see Lake Windermere from the air. Our next port of call was Dumfries, across the border. The night before we were due to depart, my sister Christine arrived on the night train from London so that she might fly up with me the following day to visit friends who resided in Dumfries. It was her first long-distance flight. She was lucky, for the day was sunny and there was not a cloud to be seen in the sky. The view crossing over the Cumberland mountains and the Lake District was magnificent and the colouring had to be seen to be believed. We crossed the border after we had passed over Silloth and flew out over the Solway Firth to the Scottish coast. It was then not long before we were circling Dumfries preparatory to landing at Mr Wylie's farm at Tinwald Downs. Our plane was spotted by my sister's hostess and they were soon out at the airfield to greet us and take us back to town in their car.

The middle of June found us flying at Penrith and our next engagement was at Groomsport, Northern Ireland, situated on the coast at the top end of Belfast Lough. We had a job getting across the Irish Sea. We carried no compass in our aircraft so we had to see the coast on the other side before we lost sight of the Scottish coastline. We arrived at Portpatrick, south of Stranraer, which was our jumping off point on the Scottish coast and found the visibility down to five miles out to sea. We were obliged to return and landed in a field alongside the lighthouse. We pegged the planes down and got a lift into Stranraer where we spent the night at the Kings Arms Hotel. The following day, visibility was a little better, but we still could not see the coast of Northern Ireland. This was a dilemma as we were advertised to fly that afternoon. We waited till after lunch, but conditions remained the same. Rimmer and I just stood and glared vacantly at one another. Suddenly, I remembered the relay races we used to run at school.

Why not apply that system to our problem?

'Look, Rimmer,' I said, 'with the present visibility around eight miles, we ought to be able to get across if we both fly out together until we begin to lose sight of the Scottish coast. One of us then commences to circle keeping the coast in view. The other continues on his course by keeping the circling plane on his tail. If the Irish coast becomes visible before the rear plane is lost from sight then the first plane commences to circle. The rear plane will then follow on, join the first plane, and both fly on together. If the Irish coast is not picked up by the first plane, then he returns to the rear plane, and back we go to Portpatrick.'

'By Jove!' Rimmer said, 'That's a brainwave. Let's try it. I'll go on while you circle and you wait for me to signal.'

So that's how we did it. Rimmer commenced circling roughly five minutes after leaving me, which in terms of distance represented roughly six miles. I joined him as quickly as possible and all of a sudden the Irish coast could be discerned through the haze. Slowly, the outline of Belfast Lough came into view and we were over Groomsport within ten minutes to be greeted by a large crowd. It was an uncomfortable sensation crossing that twenty-five miles of sea. There was no shipping to be seen and I should say there was very little chance of rescue had either of us gone down.

We commenced flying as soon as we had unloaded the planes and were kept busy until nightfall. During our three weeks stay we took a lot of money at that town. I remained with Captain Rimmer for ten days, then I left him to carry on for the holiday period so that I could fly at Donaghadee, another seaside town a few miles down the coast. After three weeks, I returned to Scotland to give a flying display at Stranraer. That time, I had the sea crossing to do all alone except that I had my engineer in the back seat. We both had blown-up car inner tubes around us to act as lifebelts in case of trouble. We arrived on 24 August and, two days later, towards the end of the day, I had to misfortune to damage my plane when taking off over the main road telegraph wires. I had passed the point of no return when I got caught in a vicious downdraught. I could see I was not going to clear the wires so tried to duck underneath them. The undercarriage caught the top of the hedge and brought me down in the field on the other side of the road. The passengers and myself were unhurt, but the plane was badly damaged and had to be railed back to our headquarters at Hooton Park for repair. Curiously, on the trip before, I carried two passengers who were both unknown to me. But one of those passengers was named Willie White. I met him at a party a few months ago, thirty-three years later. I happened to be talking about the flights I made at Stranraer in 1929 and he asked me if it was I who had crashed into the hedge. It was when I answered in the affirmative, that he told me he took a flight with me on the trip before the accident. I have met him several times since as he is a friend of our solicitor, John Paterson, in Inverness, and they have business interests in common. That was a million to one chance.

After the damaged Avro had left Stranraer by rail, I went back to Hooton to collect one of the two Avros we had bought as spares. Its registration was G-EBGZ and that plane lasted me until the end of the 1932 season. It flew as far north as the Orkney Isles. I joined Captain Rimmer in the third week of September at Burnley and, after that, flew back to Hooton to finish the season at nearby villages. On the way, I landed at Rainford Hall to implement an invitation the Miss Pilkingtons gave me before they left Kendal earlier in the year. It was teatime, if I remember correctly, and I stayed on for a while telling them about my experiences since I had bade them goodbye. Just before leaving, I had the pleasure of being introduced to their brother, who was either managing director or chairman of the glass company. I visited them again several times at the end of our flying season and during the following year, landing in a field near the hall. I was sorry when I moved up to Scotland and the acquaintance which had sprung up between us terminated.

The following year, 1930, we changed our operational policy and split up into two 'schools' as I had now learnt the 'know how' of running the business. By that means we doubled the territory covered and, what was more important, our receipts. 1930 saw me up in Scotland on my own and, for my future career, that year proved a decisive one.

2

Barnstorming with Berkshire Aviation

I have frequently been asked, 'What made you think of starting an air service to Orkney?' The answer to that is, 'I didn't think about it.' The need suddenly presented itself to me later in the year whilst I was routing the extreme north of Scotland and Orkney during August and September 1931.

On 13 April of that year, Miss Pauer and myself left our headquarters, Hooton airfield, in Moth 'A-WO' on a site-hunting tour for the coming joy-riding season. The Moth I was using was the latest type powered by a Gipsy Mark 1 engine and made by the de Havilland Aircraft Company at Stag Lane, Edgware, London. It was owned by Miss H Pauer who lived at Trentham, Staffordshire.

I met this lady because she flew frequently with us when we were flying at Trentham the year before. She became a most enthusiastic aviatrix and commissioned me to find her a suitable aircraft on which she could learn to fly. The registration of the Gipsy Moth was G-AAWO. The last three letters, AWO, represented a Chinese name 'Ah-WO', so we christened the Moth by that name and had the name painted on the side in Chinese characters. I gave Miss Pauer instruction at our Hooton airfield base, situated in the Wirral peninsula, Cheshire, which was within easy reach of Trentham by car. Sometimes she would join us on tour and would fly from place to place when I ferried the Moth, which she had generously loaned me for performing the 'aerobatic' displays each week-end. In return, we housed the Moth in our hangar at Hooton during the winter months and serviced it for her. Without that aeroplane, I could not have made the survey of the northern air routes and, incidentally, created the public interest which resulted from my comings and goings by air in Inverness and Orkney.

Our first port of call was Walsall and from there we worked our way north arriving at Nairn on 18 April 1931. We had planned to work the extreme north of Scotland, including Kirkwall in Orkney, during the summer months as those places had never seen a joy-riding aeroplane before and breaking virgin territory was usually highly profitable. Taking off from Nairn the following day, we flew up to Wick, and after circling around the south of the town for a while, found a suitable field to land on at a farm named Barnyards adjacent to the main road running south to Helmsdale and Inverness. The farmer went out of his way to help us and we made arrangements with him to guard the Moth from the crowds that soon gathered to have a look at the unusual sight of an aeroplane. One of the spectators kindly offered to drive Miss Pauer and myself to the Station Hotel in Wick. After booking in, we went to our rooms to get washed and changed.

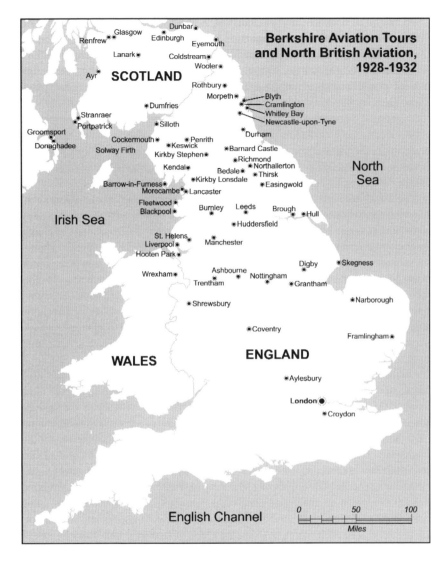

Berkshire Aviation Tours and North British Aviation, 1928-1932

I was feeling dry after the flight, which had opened up entirely new vistas. I rang the bell, and shortly the 'Boots' arrived.

'Will you bring me a double whisky?' I enquired.

'I'm sorry Sir', he replied, 'but this is a dry toon.'

My face must have denoted my feelings. When the Boots understood from my conversation that I was the pilot of the plane which had just landed on the hill at the south end of the town, he led me to the manager in his private room.

'This gentleman, Sir, is the pilot of the aeroplane which has just landed and needs a little medicine after a long trip.'

'Ah!' said the manager. He got up, locked the door, went to a cupboard and produced a bottle of whisky. White Horse, if I remember correctly. He poured me out a man's dose and said confidentially, 'Any time you are feeling faint, again, just come along!'

He turned out to be the owner of the hotel and, as time went on, we became good friends. After dinner, I commented to my passenger that, north of Helmsdale, the terrain had become wild and rugged, followed by miles of peat country with little or no habitation. It appeared to me as if I had flown into another country and my passenger fully agreed.

We left Wick for Kirkwall at lunchtime next morning, Sunday, and flew north over the famous motoring hotel at John O' Groats and out across the Pentland Firth. It was a fine day, slightly overcast and visibility as far as the eye could see. As we came up by the island of Swona, I became conscious of a large number of sunken vessels on the starboard side. I spoke with Miss Pauer over our intercom about the phenomena and neither of us could hazard a guess as to how those vessels came to be there. Later, we learned they had been deliberately sunk during World War One in order to block the channels into the Scapa Flow naval anchorage. On reaching Kirkwall a few minutes later, we circled around looking for a likely joy-riding field. I spotted one or two likely places on the north side of the town.

Kirkwall on a Sunday looked strangely deserted and we selected a field near the Balfour Hospital on the Scapa Pier road alongside the town boundary for a landing. After a dummy run in to test the approach and surface of the field, a smooth landing was effected. We had been battling a fairly strong northerly wind over the Pentland Firth and, as the wind had been backing most of the morning, I suspected bad weather was on its way in so I wanted to complete the business on which we were engaged as quickly as possible. In no time, the town of Kirkwall came to life and the field was crammed with interested sightseers. Within a matter of minutes, a cultured voice behind me enquired, 'Can I be of any use to you?' I turned and found a man of middle height and pleasant demeanour. He introduced himself as the surgeon for Orkney; his name was Ian McClure. I thanked him for his offer and explained my wish to locate a suitable flying field for operating a joy-riding air visit for the summer. He appeared deeply interested.

'I've my car here', he said. 'Come along and I will show you around. Have you any particular site in view?'

'Yes. I saw several during our search from the air', and I pointed the fields out to him on my map.

Leaving Miss Pauer in charge of the Moth, I set off with my newly found friend. Already, many boys were trying to clamber up on the lower wing to take a look at the inside of the cockpit. Fortunately several onlookers offered to help her, so I figured I could safely leave. On our way, Surgeon McClure told me he had been in the RFC during the war, so we had something in common. I told him I was in a hurry owing to possible deterioration in the weather and also that we had to return to Newcastle-upon-Tyne that evening. So he hurried me around, I pinpointed one or two fields that I thought were possibilities, and we quickly made our way back to the Moth.

Thanking Mr McClure for his kindness and saying I looked forward to seeing him again in August, with difficulty we herded the crowd to one side of the field and I took off into a good thirty miles per hour northerly wind towards the houses at the north end. I was a little nervous that we might not clear the obstacles as the run was not very long and slightly uphill, but I need not have worried for A-WO roared off the ground half way across the field. With the wind behind us, we reached Wick in a little over fifteen minutes and landed to fill up with petrol, which I had arranged with the local garage to deliver to the farm that morning.

I had spent the first part of the morning in going over the motor very thoroughly and so I decided, in order to save time, to make the sixty mile sea crossing to the Banffshire coast and carry on straight over the mountains to the Firth of Forth. With a strong wind on our tail, we reached Newcastle-upon-Tyne in two hours and forty minutes, touching down at Cramlington at six thirty in the evening. Dusk was beginning to fall as we reached Newcastle.

Next day we returned to our base by taking a direct course to Keswick in the Lake District then due south to Liverpool and to Hooton on the other side of the Mersey. In little over a week, we had covered 800 miles and settled most of the joy-riding sites for the season. It would have taken three weeks to have done the same work by surface transport, if not longer.

I commenced the season with a second visit to Kendal, Westmorland, on Sunday 26 April, then working my way via Cockermouth and Keswick to Hornsea, Yorkshire. While there, I took the opportunity of carrying out my annual RAF training on seaplanes at the Blackburn School at Brough on the River Humber, Hornsea being within a half hour's flight of that place. The course lasted ten days and I was able to carry out joy-riding at Hornsea over the week-end.

During the early part of my training, I was flying over the North Sea when engine failure forced me to land on the water, about five miles off the seaside resort of Cleethorpes. It was a hot sunny day and the time around eleven in the morning. I dropped anchor in some fifty feet of water and got back into the cockpit to await rescue. An hour went by and then another and still not a sign of any boat. The sun was extremely hot and I was getting thirsty. There was nothing I could do except pray that an off-shore wind did not get up and blow me further out to sea. The anchor was only a small one and I did not expect it would hold against a strong wind. By the time three hours, then four. had gone by, making the time three in the afternoon, I was really getting alarmed. I had no means of signalling and it was quite possible I would not be found. The motor was as dead as a crushed cockroach so I could not taxi towards the shore. To add to my discomfort, I was beginning to feel very hungry and my thirst was unbearable with the sun beating down on me pitilessly.

All of a sudden, a noise broke the lapping of the water against the plane's floats. I looked up and there was a motorboat coming towards me. 'Thank God,' I said to myself, 'help is at last at hand.' I scrambled down on to the floats to greet the motorboat skipper and to see he did not damage the plane with his boat. As he drew near, I could see it was full of females evidently on an excursion trip out from Cleethorpes. They were all waving to me and, to my dismay, the skipper started circling the Blackburn Dart seaplane several times and then sheered off and made for the shore. I yelled at the top of my voice for help, and beckoned him back, but he just kept on his return journey. I got back into the cockpit and tried to figure things out. It was four o'clock and it would be dark in a few hours. What was I to do? Things were really getting desperate. Anyhow, the boat skipper knew I was there so perhaps he would notify the Coastguard.

Shortly after that, another sightseeing motor boat faired up on me. Evidently, the first boatman had told his pals and they were running excursions at good profit for the holidaymakers to have a look at such an unusual spectacle. Again the boat started circling, although I shouted and waved for the skipper to come alongside. He also went round me two or three times and made off towards the shore, his female passengers waving like the other lot did. Surely, I thought, they are not going to let me perish; they must surely know something is wrong. The uncertainty was wearing me down, and oh, what would I give for a pint of beer. I had never been so thirsty in my life. I was completely helpless and could only return to the cockpit and wait. Five o'clock had passed with no sign of any further boats.

It looked as though I was going to spend the night at sea and, if my anchor parted company with the bottom and the plane started to drift, I was in for a sticky and painful end. I was sunk in apathy at the thought and did not hear the approach of another boat until it was right on me. I suddenly looked up and there was a powerful motor launch fairing up to the plane. This time there were no passengers, but two or three people amidships near the wheel. They hailed me to get down on the floats and catch a rope. Then I knew that it was a relief launch come to my rescue. The time was shortly after six pm. As the boat came alongside, I recognised my instructor from Brough Seaplane Base, Lieutenant Woodhead. What a relief. I had been on the water for seven hours. I was soon on board, the seaplane was roped on tow and we started back for Hull over twenty miles away.

Woodhead told me that the motorboat skipper on the first trip had reported my plane down on the water to the Coastguard and he had hurried down to Hull to pick up the launch and tow me in. The skipper of the pleasure cruise had said he was frightened to come too close to me in case he damaged the plane by collision. Woodhead asked me what had happened.

I said, 'Give me a drink first, and I will tell you. My tongue is sticking to the roof of my mouth and I am so thirsty.'

'Sorry old chap', he replied, 'there is nothing on board to drink. You'll have to wait until we reach Hull.'

That was two hours and it seemed twenty! At last we arrived and I said to Woodhead, 'Get me to the nearest hotel as soon as possible,' which he did. Never have I tasted such fine beer as I did that night. Over dinner, I told Woody, as he was known to us, about the forced landing. That I was cruising down the coast at three thousand feet when suddenly there was a terrific bang from the motor and it stopped dead on me. He told me I had done a very fine job landing that plane on the water with a dead motor. We had an excellent dinner at the hotel and then boarded a car to return to Brough. Next day I learned that the engine had partially seized up so no wonder it had stopped. I did not forget that experience for some time to come and never wandered so far out to sea on future flights. If there was to be another forced landing it would be near the shore!

From Hornsea we went on to Whitley Bay, Kirriemuir, Nairn and arrived at Grantown-on-Spey on 7 August 1931. On the Saturday night, a wager was made between a young man in the hotel where I was staying who fancied that he could win a race with my Avro plane from Grantown to Nairn with a fast sports car if I gave him half an hour's start. I worked the flying time out quickly in my head and took him on for the sum of £20. The only condition I made was that the wind remained appreciably the same as it was that day.

The contest commenced next day at eleven. It was a fine Sunday morning. We agreed the finishing point at Nairn would be the entrance to the field at which I had been flying the week before. One umpire remained at Grantown and the other had left for Nairn. Promptly at eleven, our motorist friend departed in his sports car with a roar. A few minutes before I was due to take off, my engineer swung my propeller and, by the time the half hour arrived, the motor was warmed up and I left the ground dead on time. At 2,000 feet I could see the coastline and was accordingly able to steer a straight course without a compass. I caught up with the sports car within three miles of Nairn and had been on the ground a few minutes when my sporting friend arrived. He graciously conceded me to be the winner and handed over his wager. The finish was a very close one and the race was therefore all the more interesting and most certainly a very novel one. We repaired to the Marine Hotel in Nairn for lunch and then set off back to Grantown-on-Spey to carry out a heavy Sunday afternoon's joy-riding.

On Tuesday 18 August we were due to depart for Wick, our next port of call. I detailed my groundsman to take the heavy luggage up to Wick in our service car. We took off at five in the afternoon in brilliant sunshine in Avro, G-EBGZ. The plane was heavily loaded. My ground engineer occupied the back seat and the rest of the luggage was stowed in front of him. In addition, there was a ladder some six feet long tied to the port wing inner inter-plane struts, that was used for assisting the passengers in and out of the rear cockpit.

Crossing over Nairn, we headed out to sea, picking up the Sutherland coast at Golspie and then we altered course to follow the coastline for Wick. As we neared the cliffs at Helmsdale, the weather began to change. Clouds began to form, forcing me down from 2,000 feet to 100 feet over the water. I was not aware of the weather phenomena, which at times embraces the Helmsdale area. Surrounded as it is by mountains to the landward side, cloud forms under certain atmospheric conditions and I was to become well acquainted with this later. It is very local and does not usually extend more than ten miles up the coastline. The cloud spills down the mountains and over the cliff tops, which are some 300 feet high, leaving a passage of around 100 feet clear over the sea.

As I was unaware of these conditions, caution was necessary. We did not carry radio or cloud flying instruments. In fact, they did not exist. We did not even have a compass aboard. I was unaware what lay ahead and was about to turn back into the sunshine when I spotted a field at the base of the cliffs, two miles north of Helmsdale, and I promptly sat the Avro down on it.

We were barely out of the plane when people came rushing towards us. Among them was the farmer upon whose ground we were trespassing. He shook me by the hand and welcomed us: 'You are the first airmen to land in these parts. Aeroplanes are quite unknown hereabouts.' I explained the cause of our impromptu landing and he asked us up to his farmhouse for tea. On the way, he explained that the low cloud which was bothering us often occurred, but added that it was very local and the weather would improve ten miles north where the mountains terminated. With that assurance, and after having enjoyed our tea and been introduced to Mrs 'Farmer', I decided to push on. We took off down the hill and downwind towards the sea with plenty of room to spare. I dropped down over the water to fifty feet or so and could see the mist halfway down the cliff for a mile ahead. We scuttled along, fearful that the fog would suddenly merge with the water. Without a compass and cloud flying instruments, envelopment in cloud would mean loss of control and direction, and could easily cost us our lives.

I prepared to turn back at the slightest worsening of visibility, but it did not occur. It appeared very weird with the oily sea beneath, the dim light caused by the cloud almost on top of us, and the jagged cliffs rising sheer into the mist on our left. After ten minutes or so of tenseness, the farmer's words came true for the fog commenced to rise and the visibility improved. In another five minutes we were clear and the sun could be seen shining on the sea ahead.

Soon we were dropping down to land on our pre-arranged field at Wick after one and a half hours flying time from Grantown-on-Spey. Our car, of course, had not arrived yet. After pegging the plane down for the night and clearing the usual crowd that had gathered on the field, an onlooker kindly took us down to the town in his car, dropping us at the Station Hotel. The proprietor remembered my visit earlier in the year so my wants were well attended to.

We commenced operations next day with a publicity flight over the town which incorporated a few aerobatics. At midday, my friend the 'Boots' and a pal turned up for a flight round the town. I gave them a free trip for his good services. On landing he told me that he came from Kirkwall and enquired what a return flight to Kirkwall would cost him. As I had to fly over there during my stay in Wick to select and license the field for my impending visit in a few weeks time, I quoted him a low price. He accepted on the spot and we took off at once.

As on my previous visit, I was intrigued in the host of sunken ships at the east end of Scapa Flow. They were all shapes and sizes and were blocking all the sea channels into the Scapa anchorage. It was a remarkable sight and my passengers were most interested. We landed some thirty-five minutes later in a field some three miles out from Kirkwall on the Deerness Road. The usual boat and road journey would have taken six hours at least via Thurso, so that was a saving of roughly five and a half hours for a thirty-five mile journey.

We had barely scrambled out of the plane when a man came running across the field from the road.

'Has anyone been hurt in the crash?' he enquired.

We looked at him in amazement. 'What crash?' we asked.

He looked blank and said, 'Haven't you crashed?'

'Not as far as we know', we answered. 'Take a look at the plane.'

'I'm so sorry,' he said, 'I've never seen a plane before. Can I be of help?'

'If you would take us into town, we'd be most grateful.'

'Jump in,' he said, and off we went.

On the way, we told him he had just witnessed an historical event. 'These two gentlemen are the first fare paying 'air passengers' to arrive in Orkney from Wick and they will make the return journey after lunch all within a little more than an hour of travelling time. Think what that means compared to the usual surface journey.'

He goggled a bit, but I think it sank in. The date was 22 August 1931. I wonder if that man is still alive. If so, no doubt he will remember the incident.

Our arrival in Kirkwall created quite a stir and the representative of the local newspaper, *The Orcadian*, lapped up all the news we could give him. This newspaper was owned by James Mackintosh who became dedicated to my later effort in establishing airline connections to the south. He was a tall man and somewhat portly and, when roused, he had a fiery temper but he was also blessed with a geniality and loyalty to myself in the super task which was to come. His columns were always at my disposal no matter how many I required. I remember an occasion later in 1934 when he got word that there were two passengers arriving at Wick by the train from the south and too late for the scheduled service. He told me I had to fetch them. As he was acting as our agent on a voluntary basis, I gracefully made a special flight over to Wick. I could not find the passengers anywhere and our Wick agent knew nothing about them. So, after hanging around the airfield for half an hour, I returned to Kirkwall empty.

Mr Mackintosh was awaiting the plane at the airfield. When he saw me step out, he went purple in the face.

'Why haven't you brought the two passengers?' he enquired indignantly.

'Because they were nowhere to be found,' I replied.

'Of course they weren't,' he bawled. 'The train didn't get in until five minutes after you left Wick.'

'Well,' I said, 'I've made one empty flight, I can't go across again.'

By this time, I thought he was going to have an apoplectic fit. He went purple in the face and shouted, 'If you don't get them, you can look for another Agent.'

With that he slammed in the clutch of his car and the car leapt forward, nearly knocking me into the ditch.

'By gum,' I thought, 'I can't afford to lose him and the publicity of *The Orcadian*.' So I climbed into the plane and returned to Wick for the elusive passengers. I duly found them waiting at the airfield and brought them back to Kirkwall. James Mackintosh was his usual self next day. But to get back to my story, I gave *The Orcadian* plenty to write about our forthcoming barnstorming visit and it was well advertised without cost, long before the happy day.

While at lunch in the Kirkwall Hotel, the first person who came to see me was no other than Surgeon Ian McClure who, it will be remembered, had helped me on my previous Moth visit with Miss Pauer, by motoring me around the countryside looking for a suitable landing field. After lunch, he again very kindly placed himself and his car at my disposal until a field was found about a mile out of town, on the Stromness Road. It belonged to Hatston Farm. I found the farmer and booked the field for August. His name was Ritchie and a very nice person he turned out to be.

Ten years later, Hatston Farm was incorporated in the Naval Air Station from which planes took off for the bombing of Norway and patrolling the North Sea for u-boats and enemy aircraft. On our return to town, I met the Provost and some town councillors who were more than ordinarily interested, judging by the number of questions they asked about the first mainland to Orkney flight with fare paying passengers whom I had flown over that day.

The return flight took thirty minutes and, on landing, I found a number of passengers waiting for flights. News of the return Orkney flight soon got around the town and my friend the 'Boots' and his pal were the subject of great interest. Certainly, I could not have wished for better advertising agents.

Sunday was always a busy day for us and Wick was no exception. The field was crowded and the flights went on incessantly until after dark. As usual, I was flying by the aid of car headlights for landing and take-off.

We drew our petrol supplies from a garage alongside the Station Hotel situated beside the river. It was owned by a Colonel Robertson. He was greatly interested in the passenger flight to Orkney and I subsequently got to know him very well. He went out of his way to assist us. He thrilled the locals by accompanying me on the exhibition flight I had been hired to carry out at the Wick annual gala. It was, I believe, his first flight and he was put through every aerobatic it was possible to do on an Avro 504K – and that was quite a lot. He got a great ovation on landing which was very well deserved for a first effort.

We made three more trans-Pentland return flights during our Wick visit. After ten days, we moved over to Thurso. Our flying field was a mile from Scrabster Pier from which the trans-Pentland steamer *St Ola* sailed daily to Stromness and Scapa under the command of Captain Swanson. During our visit, we often used to fly passengers out to sea, circle the *St Ola* and then return for another load. These flights caused great interest and excitement for already our passenger trans-Pentland flights from Wick to Orkney were being talked about in Thurso and the implications for the future were being mooted in bars and hotels and no doubt in private houses.

Our first Sunday was a fine day. We had a grand crowd waiting to fly and to see the exhibition flight later on in the afternoon. The crowds were swollen by people who had come in from the villages to the west as far away as Tongue. I was kept busy, going on until well after dark. Passengers appeared to like seeing a town lit up from the air and we never appeared to lack for night flyers. Our operations appeared to impress the Thurso inhabitants and there was little doubt there were many potential passengers for the coming week.

I was staying at the Royal Hotel and during the week the proprietor, Mr James Wilson, introduced me to a Mr Peter Angus who represented one of the large wholesale firms in Edinburgh. Apparently he has heard about the Wick Hotel 'Boots' flight and said he was anxious to be the first Thurso to Kirkwall return passenger, and the first commercial traveller to call on his customers in Kirkwall by air. We arranged, weather permitting, to leave at noon the following day, have lunch at the St Ola Hotel. He would make his business calls in the afternoon and fly back in time for tea at Thurso. It was a cute move on his part. The publicity was immense and he did big business in Kirkwall. We landed at the field at Hatston at 12.45 pm and on arrival at the hotel he introduced me to Mrs Stevens the proprietrix who became a helpful and trusted friend in days to come.

Mr Angus was very impressed with the trip across the Pentland Firth. I don't think I ever met anyone so alive to the potentiality of commercial flying in the north of Scotland. He literally became a travelling agency for me later on when my plans began to develop in terms of commercial air transport.

We left at four in the afternoon, landing at the Thurso field thirty minutes later. That night Peter was in great demand by his fellow business friends. They all wanted to know how he had got on. 'First rate,' said Peter. The publicity from being the first business man to 'make his calls by air' was great. The return fare of ten pounds had been more than worth it in orders, and extra ones at that, which he had received as a result of his 'air publicity.'

Towards the end of the first week in September we moved over to Kirkwall. The Air Ministry licence had come through for Hatston. As in the case of Wick and Thurso, there was no lack of customers and our visit laid the foundation for future events. Mr Angus had suggested to me that a trans-Pentland air service would be a great boon to the travelling public and I had also been thinking in and along the same lines. In fact, it became obvious. A modern plane could fly the cross-Pentland journey of thirty-five miles from Wick or Thurso to Kirkwall in twenty minutes. The steamer took four to five hours. The Pentland Firth could be very rough; the air could be much smoother. Providing the traffic density was sufficient, an air ferry just couldn't go wrong.

I hadn't been in Kirkwall a week when, on arriving back at the St Ola Hotel after flying had ceased, I was invited into the Private Room and introduced to the Deputy Town Clerk and several business friends. After a generous supply of liquid refreshment, they enquired if I was thinking of an air ferry service across the Firth. 'We've been impressed by the flights already made,' they said. They went out of their way to impress me about the stormy winter crossings in the *St Ola* steamer and how ill the passengers became in bad weather. I was interested. Other people were thinking along the same lines as Peter and myself. I said I would think it over and we might have another meeting before I left for the south.

During the many up and down flights made during the next few days, I constantly turned this matter over in my mind. The more I thought about it, the simple axiom dawned on me that 'where there were routes which involved sea crossings, air travel had great possibilities.' There were no internal airlines in those days to obtain any comparison from, but I felt sure that I had hit on something which had great possibilities.

With such thoughts in my mind, I met the boys again and told them I was prepared to explore the possibilities, but of course the over-riding consideration was the raising of finance to float an operating company. Up-to-date aircraft would be needed and airfields would have to be constructed. That would cost a lot.

'How many of you would subscribe to such a venture?' I asked.

They all had excuses as to why they couldn't subscribe. And then a voice chirped up, 'Why not make Inverness your base and fly up the mails which arrive by train from London and the south in the morning? After lunch you would fly the mails south to catch the London express and Glasgow and Edinburgh trains. That would speed up the mails some twenty-four hours.'

We were now getting into a much bigger issue. but with more attractive commercial possibilities. With a mail contract, I thought, a regular load would always be available and with the mail, why not the newspapers?

In my mind, the matter was clinched. I would go south, ask for an interview with the Director of Postal Services and contact one of the national daily newspapers. Should I be successful in obtaining such support, I would have a good lever to raise finance to float an air company. To accelerate this idea in my mind, there was little doubt that the days of barnstorming were coming to an end. Most of the towns in Britain had had their fill and in two or three years my livelihood would cease. And that is just what occurred to those left in that type of flying.

There were a number of further charter flights across the Pentland Firth to Thurso, which appeared to be the natural mainland terminal owing to the train and steamer service operating from that port. From an operational point of view, Wick would be the better port for an air service operating Inverness to Kirkwall as it lay directly on route and, in addition, it was the major town in Caithness.

Before returning south, I went over to Stromness for a few days by invitation. The manager of the distillery, a Mr Kelly, was anxious that the town folk should have the opportunity of seeing their homes from the air. I gave one aerobatic display at Stromness and our Mr Kelly paid a handsome fee to go up with me. He brought a camera to take pictures. By the time he had been looped and rolled many times and then ending up with a fifteen hundred feet spin, he was in no fit condition to take air photos. He, however, stood the strain very well, but was subjected to a lot of leg pulling and chaffing from his friends when he got out of the plane looking slightly anaemic. However, he received a great reception from the crowd. I thought he had good courage, like Colonel Robertson of Wick, to do all that on a first flight. Perhaps, however, it was a case of 'where ignorance was bliss.' I have met Mr Kelly many times in recent years and always get a bit of fun chaffing him about that afternoon with his camera.

One fine morning, I set off from Hatston with Mrs Stevens of the St Ola Hotel as passenger. It was her first flight. She also took to flying like a duck to water and was overjoyed with the view she obtained of the islands from 2,000 feet. She was full of enthusiasm for air travel and converted many a 'local' later on 'to go by air.'

We spent four days at Stromness and during that time there was a further demand for flights to Thurso and return. It was becoming quite a habit, but I called a halt at the last one which was the thirteenth. I am not naturally superstitious, but I jibbed at that one. The Avro 504K was not suitable, nor really safe, for so many sea crossings. The motor had been worked hard all the season and if that one engine failed in the middle of the Pentland Firth, it would have been certain death for my passengers and self in the usually rough sea and dangerous currents. Even with life-saving equipment, it was most unlikely we would be picked up in time as shipping was not that numerous. I believe the passengers understood when I explained the danger to them of tempting providence too far. I had acquired what I wanted in the dozen flights I had made, namely, intense interest in air travel between the mainland and the islands. A serious mishap at that stage would undo all that had been gained.

Curiously enough, next day and on the thirteenth Pentland crossing, engine trouble occurred on my way to Thurso and Dalkeith where I was next booked. The engine spluttered and lost power, and the plane began to lose height. I was fortunately flying high and just managed to scramble into the field at Scrabster. I have often thought I must have received psychic warning the day before because I could never have reached the shore with a full load of passengers.

I spent twelve days flying in Kirkwall and Stromness, and one month with the inclusion of Wick and Thurso. During that period we made five hundred and fifty-five take-offs and landings and carried 1,110 passengers in an open two-seater aircraft.

What more ample proof was necessary that the people of the north of Scotland were 'air-minded?' It was an excellent omen for an air service, more especially if the people of Inverness and district, and of Glasgow and Edinburgh, took to flying as easily.

My flight engineer was with me and we soon carried out repairs to the valve-operating gear which had come adrift on one cylinder. Within an hour we took off for Dalkeith but had to land at Huntly for petrol. My log book shows that we flew at 4,000 feet straight across the desolate moors to the coast. Approaching the mountains behind Helmsdale, we experienced terrific upward air currents, which pushed us up to 6,000 feet within minutes. The plane was going up so quickly that I shut the motor off to check the ascent, but height was still maintained and so the plane was actually soaring.

Over Helmsdale, I decided to again risk the sea crossing of forty miles across the Moray Firth to Fochabers to save time. The day was sunny and visibility was unlimited. We were flying at 6,000 feet and as we had just checked over the motor, I thought the chance a reasonable one. To make sure, I eased the load on the motor by throttling it down half way over and making the shore on a long glide. We landed at Huntly on my joy-riding field of the previous year a little after noon. After lunch at the farmhouse, the aircraft was filled up with petrol, which was ordered over the phone, and we departed on the second leg of our journey around three in the afternoon. Eventually picking up the Firth of Forth, we landed at Dalkeith after two hours and fifty minutes flying time from Thurso.

There was a large crowd awaiting us and the following day, Sunday, carried 110 passengers, two at a time. We stayed a week and the owner of the farm we were flying from, Archie Dodds, made life very pleasant for us. His house was just up the hill and a five minute walk from the flying field. We spend much of our off-duty time there with Archie's charming mother and sister seeing to our wants. The time passed all too quickly. We moved on to Haddington where we were booked to fly in the early part of October. Archie became a friend whom I used to see a lot of up to the outbreak of World War Two. His mother subsequently bought a house at Longniddry on the Firth of Forth. We used to call in when passing on our way south by car and always received a welcome to lunch or tea.

Our season was drawing to a close. We worked our way back to our Hooton headquarters via Denny, Alloa and Kirkintilloch which terminated the 1931 tour. The Kirkintilloch field was flooded by heavy and continuous rain and operations on the Sunday afternoon resembled a seaplane taking off and landing. The middle of the field was quite deep in flood water, and landing and take-offs had to be made in a semi-circle so as to keep clear of the water. After carrying seventy-five passengers under such difficult conditions, I called it a day and made off next day for Hooton Park via Carlisle, Shap, Kendal and Preston, skirting Liverpool to the east and across the Mersey into Hooton on the south bank.

I had clocked 280 hours flying for the season and most of that in up-and-down flights lasting three minutes. That represented approximately four thousand take-offs and landings, which was very strenuous work. In addition to that, I had flown to the top end of the British Isles and back and put in quite a lot of night flying without proper lighting equipment at flying fields and no cockpit lights. Quite a bit of open sea had been flown over. Motor failure during such periods would have been disastrous and always represented an extra strain. One might therefore say in Gilbertian paraphrasing, 'A Barnstorming pilot's life was not an easy one.'

After a few days of rest at Hooton at my hotel quarters adjacent to the Eastham ferry, I began to plan the ideas I had formulated during my Orkney tour. I felt certain I had something of great promise, but to organise such a project appeared insuperable. It was going to cost a lot of money and capital was not easy to raise in those days. I repeatedly asked myself, 'How was I to begin?' I discussed the matter with my partner Lance Rimmer, but he did not appear very interested, but he changed his ideas later, when success was within my grasp.

I went to bed and slept on it. I decided next morning that I would pay a visit to London as soon as our winter overhaul programme was underway. That was a major operation as aircraft and engines had to be completely stripped, and an inspection made by the Aircraft Inspection Department of the Air Ministry. On completion, the planes had to be flight-tested and only then would they be ready for the next season's tour.

In the first week of November 1931, I flew Moth A-WO to Cramlington, Northumberland, for the Annual Renewal of Certificate of Airworthiness. Cramlington was an old World War One airship base which boasted a huge hangar which used to house the blimps used in those days for coastal patrol. The Certificate of Airworthiness overhaul was to be carried out by the Cramlington Aircraft Company, managed by Miss Connie Leathart, a well known lady aviatrix. I stayed for a day while the survey was made to find out how much work was required. I was then told I could collect the Moth the day before Christmas, 24 December 1931.

On 22 December, I went north by car to collect the Gipsy Moth from Cramlington. The same lady, Mrs Gwen Simons who drove my car up to take me back to Hooton when I put the Moth in for overhaul at the beginning of the month accompanied me so that she might fly back in the Moth, and one of my engineers came with us to drive the car back. Little did I know it at the time, but some three years later that lady was to become my second wife.

The Moth was almost ready and looked very smart. I flight-tested it on 24 December and at ten o'clock that morning, Christmas Eve, we took off from Cramlington and steered a direct course for Hooton across the Pennines, one hundred and fifty miles away. After passing Consett in Durham, we were forced to climb above a layer of thick cloud as the ground was rising and the ceiling was only some fifteen hundred feet. For half an hour or more we flew on without seeing any break in the cloud and the opaque mass beneath us was getting higher the further south we flew. As I had no means or aids to check my course and whether I could safely descend below the cloud when the estimated time of one hour and three quarters had been completed, I reluctantly turned back and retraced my steps. When we eventually got back to the edge of the clouds, I ducked down beneath them and steered south-east for Harrogate, intending to make for the Penistone Pass and over the mountains by Holmfirth. The cloud base got lower and lower and I nearly knocked the steeple off Ripon Cathedral. I was relieved to pick up Harrogate and land on the Stray, a large area of grassland south of the 'old town'. I phoned through to Hooton to be told the weather was not too bad there. After an hour or so the cloud base improved and we set off for Penistone Pass. As we got near the top, the cloud began to merge with the ground again and, as it was getting late, I deemed it wise to land in a field at Holmfirth where we spent the night. My passenger was worried that her sister would be anxious at our non-arrival, so we phoned through to explain the position. I said we would start first thing next morning, Christmas Day, weather permitting.

Next morning the weather had improved so I did not bother getting a weather report from Hooton. Therein lay the biggest mistake I had ever made in my flying career. Unknown to me, a bad weather front was rapidly descending on us, which meant low cloud and poor visibility with rain, and it nearly resulted in the death of my lady passenger and myself.

It was a difficult uphill take-off with two people in the Moth, but the wind was strong which helped a lot, and we cleared the four foot stone dyke with a good twenty feet to spare. I headed south for the main road and, after picking it up, set a compass course for Hooton Park in case I had to go up into the clouds. I followed the road for a few miles as it wound its way up the Penistone Pass and, as I neared the top, I was only a few feet above the road. Then the clouds merged with the ground and I had to pull up into them. My last impression was a man on a motorbike looking up in astonishment as we roared over his head and disappeared in the overcast above. We came out on top at 3,000 feet, which meant I had climbed through nearly 2,000 feet of cloud, and there the weather was not too bad with distant visibility. I settled down on to a compass course, wondering what the cloud base would be at Hooton airfield.

The distance to Hooton was only fifty miles and, at eighty-five mph and without any head wind, I estimated that we should reach there in thirty-five minutes. But I did not know what the wind was doing at that altitude. It was evident to me, as the cloud height was increasing, that the weather front was upon us and, whereas the wind was strong south-west when I took off, it could be quite different at 4,000 feet, the altitude at which I was flying. I decided to hold the course and allow for a wind from the south-west. After ten minutes or so, I saw the top of a mountain sticking through a hole some way down, which meant I was still over the Pennines. Then to the south, I thought I saw the canal running from Chester to Nantwich – and I then made grave error number two. I turned off course and made for the canal only to find, after flying for some fifteen minutes, that it was not there and that I was still above complete cloud coverage. I studied my map and came to the conclusion that I should be over Crewe, so I decided to go down through the clouds. Down I dropped and at 2,000 feet on the altimeter I suddenly saw, only some 50 feet below me, the corner of a stone dyke with several sheep in the corner. Evidently I was still over the mountains and a long way off my estimated position. I immediately started to climb at full throttle, waiting every moment for a shattering bang as we hit a mountain. Luck, however, was with us and I got on top again. I was severely shaken, more especially as the Moth did not carry cloud flying instruments. I had to rely on my compass for direction, which was not very accurate owing to a certain amount of lag which compasses experience in northern latitudes; a horizontal spirit level for lateral control, and the air speed indicator for fore and aft position. I had been in cloud for nearly quarter of an hour and was a bit fuzzy. 'What's to be done?' I asked myself. I turned the facts over in my mind and decided to fly west for ten minutes. By this time the cloud top was 5,000 feet and I was then certain I was caught up in dangerous weather underneath with probably little cloud base over flat ground and poor visibility. I looked to see how my passenger was faring. The only thing I could see was just the top of her flying helmet. Later I learned she was thoroughly frightened, and no wonder. I was feeling near that way myself. There was nothing for it but to go down again, but I hesitated. I remembered a well-known book I had read on weather written by an American expert. It was called *Through the Overcast* and mention was made of the happy-go-lucky pilot who said, 'Let's go down and have a look.' Then it read on, 'That's the last time he ever took a look.'[1]

So I flew on a bit longer. Had I known it, I was then flying into the teeth of a westerly gale blowing at fifty to sixty mph, so that meant I was only doing about twenty-five mph over the ground.

Down I started to go. At 2,000 feet, I could see nothing. At 1,000 feet, I could see nothing. And I was being bumped all over the sky which made cloud flying

---

[1] Assen Jordanoff, *Through the Overcast: The Weather and the Art of Instrument Flying*, first published in 1938.

almost impossible without proper instruments. I had to concentrate on keeping the plane level and on a correct descent angle. Suddenly, I caught a glimpse of a field at 800 feet. At 700 feet I could see fields slipping directly by underneath and I passed over a field bordered by high trees. I had to make instant decision. I did not think I could successfully keep control of the plane if I tried to go up again as my senses had suffered savagely on that last bumpy descent. I instantly made up my mind to take a most drastic step. If I tried a blind landing in a field I would almost certainly run into something at forty-five mph and that would most certainly be fatal for my passenger, even though I, in the back seat, may have got away with it. So after the next hedge which I passed over, I shut the motor off, pulled the nose up, and side slipped the plane down on to one wing. There was a crunching roar, the poor Moth folded up and we were on the ground. I was alright except for a cut over my right eye. I jumped out of the wreckage and looked for my passenger. Poor soul, she was not to be seen except for a part of her fur coat which was sticking out from under the top wing petrol tank, which had collapsed and was spurting petrol all over her. What a lucky thing the engine was off. Even so, the hot exhaust pipe might have ignited the cloud of petrol vapour that was pouring out. I tugged at the wreckage but could not lift it by myself. I was in despair when suddenly I noticed two farm hands gawping at me.

I shrieked at them, 'Don't stand there like two idiots. Come and give me a hand. There is a lady underneath that tank.'

They hadn't realised it apparently as she was not to be seen. The reaction was swift.

I said, 'Lift this edge, you,' and to the other, 'That edge, you.'

I took another corner and, between us, we managed to lift the wreckage and clear Mrs Simons who was lying ominously still and soaked with petrol. With the assistance of the farm hands, we got her out and laid her on the ground. She was breathing, thank goodness. I tore her fur coat off and gave her my leather flying jacket, or rather put it over her. After a while she began to come round. In five minutes she was sitting up, but evidently badly concussed as she was mumbling senselessly. By that time the farmer had arrived and I asked him where we were.

'You are seven miles away from Leek and to the east', he replied.

'Have you got a car?' I asked.

He said, 'Yes. I will phone for an ambulance from Leek Hospital. She looks badly hurt'.

He acted quickly, away he went and in no time an ambulance appeared. I accompanied my passenger into Leek, leaving the two farm hands to guard the wreckage until I could get back.

The clouds were on the ground at 700 feet and, as we drove downhill into Leek losing height, the going became clear at about 500 feet. This meant that,

had I flown west for another five minutes, I would have found clear ground and could have made a normal landing. Shocking bad luck, I thought. I got Mrs Simons into the hospital which was all agog. They had never had an air casualty before. The doctor, after a somewhat lengthy examination, came and told me that she had no broken limbs or other injury as far as he could ascertain, but was, as I had surmised, suffering from concussion. She was put to bed and spent Christmas Day and a few days after that in the hospital before being allowed to return by road to Hooton. In the meantime, I phoned Mrs Simons' sister, Mrs Elaine Pobjoy, explaining what had happened. When she understood that her sister was not seriously injured, she said she and her husband would be over next day to see her.

I made my way back to the crashed plane and, to prevent pilfering, I arranged for a guard. The farmer was very helpful and interested to know the details of the flight which led to the crash, and he undertook to see that the Moth wreckage came to no harm. On arrival back at the hospital, the doctor stitched my cut eyebrow which was bleeding profusely. I booked myself in at the local hotel and returned to the hospital to spend Christmas afternoon with my victim. To my surprise, I found her sitting up in bed in the midst of a Christmas party. She was surrounded by many of the visitors, who were obviously intrigued with a patient who had arrived by air in such an unorthodox manner. That night, before going to sleep, I went over the happenings of the day. Two incidents stood out glaringly. Firstly, I should not have taken off from Holmfirth without a weather report. Secondly, having obtained it and ascertained that the cloud height at Hooton was reasonable, I should have kept to my compass course above the clouds and not gone off course looking for canals or cloud breaks, which had turned out to be nothing more than a mirage, and a very realistic one at that. Thirdly, I thought how lucky we were to have got away with our lives. It was really a miracle that we were not killed. There would be a heavy bill in rail charges and rebuilding of the Moth. Actually it came to close on £100. A costly error, but one that taught me a salutary lesson in subsequent years when flying over the north of Scotland air routes in all weather.

Next day Mr & Mrs Pobjoy arrived by car from Hooton and spent the afternoon with the patient. She was much better, but could not remember anything prior to or about the crash and kept on asking why she was in hospital. The matron had warned us not to mention the crash so we sidetracked the conversation when it veered that way. The doctor agreed it would be alright to leave Mrs Simons as she was in no danger, so after promising to return next day, I departed for Hooton airfield with the Pobjoys to set the wheels in motion for shipping the Moth for repair and arranging with the insurance company regarding a claim. I was uncertain if they would accept responsibility owing to my faulty navigation, but they came up trumps and settled on the basis that I paid the first forty pounds. They instructed me to return the wreckage to the Brooklands Aviation Company in Surrey for rebuilding.

I returned to Leek next day and found my passenger much better. However, as she had received a severe blow in the crash, it was deemed advisable to keep her in hospital for a little longer so as to be sure that no complications arose. The station master at the country station near the scene of the crash was most cooperative and, with the aid of the engineer I brought over with me, we soon had the wreckage loaded on a truck and railed south three days after the accident. It arrived at Brooklands towards the end of December 1931.

That done, I motored Mrs Simons back to Hooton, firstly taking our farewell of the matron, doctor and hospital staff. They had been most kind and attentive. When I thanked them, they said, 'We do not have air patients every day, so we had to make a good job of our first case.' We saw the New Year in a day or so later at a hectic party at Hooton airfield. By that time, my passenger was safely tucked away in her sister's house which was situated at the east end of the airfield. During World War One, it had served as the airfield hospital for the Royal Flying Corps. There was a small mortuary behind it which had been converted into a coal shed! Mrs Simon's brother-in-law, Douglas R Pobjoy, had founded an aircraft engine factory on the airfield the previous year, trading under the name of Pobjoy Airmotors Limited. I was to become closely associated with that firm in the days to come.

3

Financing an Airline

I collected the Moth from Brooklands in early part of February 1932 and flew north, with Miss Pauer as passenger to Kirkwall, in order to raise support. Like the first trip ten months before, we ran into a strong northerly wind in the Orkneys. We landed after a rough and tiring trip around five in the afternoon, in a field adjacent to the Peerie Sea on the outskirts of the town. The wind gusts were so strong that I decided I had to find shelter for the Moth somehow or other. To have left it pegged down in the field overnight would most likely have resulted in finding the machine on its back the next morning. So, leaving Miss Pauer to hold the Moth down with the help of some sturdy looking men who had arrived to look at the plane, I walked the half mile into town to look for a possible hangar.

I found it with the leading firm of coal merchants in Kirkwall, J G Shearer in Albert Street. It was a corrugated shed with just sufficient span to allow the Moth to enter with the wings folded. Mr Shearer found a boatman who had a small trolley which would be necessary to place under the tail skid so that the plane could be wheeled along the road. In addition, he found a couple of stonemasons who would pull down the stone dyke that separated the field from the road to allow the Moth to pass through. They would likewise rebuild it after we had left. Then there was the farmer to visit to obtain his permission about the onslaught on his dyke. Within an hour we had the Moth trundling along the road into Kirkwall and pushed into the coal merchant's shed.

That night, my weather forecast came true for a gale of over sixty mph sprang up, with heavy gusting. Listening to it in bed, I was thankful that our trusty steed was safely tucked away in that shed. We stayed two days and I quickly got down to business for that night I met my friends again and we discussed the best method of raising finance. They suggested I should start on one of the two directors of the local distillery. So an appointment was made and an introduction effected to Charles Hayden of Highland Park Distillery. I told my story, stressing the advantages of a mail service, the delivery of newspapers at lunchtime, and the advantages to the business population for fast transport south. Mr Hayden looked at me as if I was a creature from another world which had descended upon him. He told me that aeroplanes that flew in Orkney during the last war [World War One] were seldom able to get into the air owing to the violent air currents and the pilots found great difficulty in keeping their aircraft on an even keel. 'But that was over 10 years ago', I said to him. The design of aircraft has moved ahead since then. I also reminded him of the recent flying we had carried out in the late summer at Kirkwall and

Stromness. It was this type of trivial objection and excuse that I encountered throughout Orkney, and was due to a cause which I did not know of, or appreciate, at the time. 'Have a dram', said my host, and we had one and several to follow.

After a while he became friendlier and he asked me how much I wanted. I told him the capital I should require and I was pleased to accept any sum to make up that figure. 'Of course,' I said, 'a limited liability company will be formed, and there will be capable directors.' He thought a while, then said, 'Go and see my partner, Walter Grant. Tell him what you have told me, and I will come in with you if he will do the same.' Mr Hayden directed me to Walter Grant's house which was situated on top of the cliffs overlooking Scapa Flow.

I found Mr Grant at home. He was a very well known personality in Orkney and became a very good friend of mine at a later date. I told him what his partner had said. He didn't ask so many questions, but was keen on getting me to drink some of his distillery's 'extra special.'

At last he said, 'How much?'

'Same as up the hill', I said.

'What's that?' he asked.

'Five hundred pounds,' I answered off hand.

'Right, bring Hayden's cheque for me to see and you shall have the same amount.'

As neither would part with their investment without seeing the other's cheque, I had eventually to admit defeat. Three years later, when we sold the company to merge with a bigger concern in the south and made a good profit, Walter Grant actually chided and blamed me because he had not got any shares. So that was the way of it.

My mental spirits were low when I returned to the St Ola Hotel and told my well-wishers. One of them, John Shearer, said, 'I should not despair.' He was sure the owner of the Kirkwall Hotel, Mr MacKay, would be interested.

'Look at the extra visitors you would bring him,' he said.

I called next morning, but Mr MacKay looked a sick man. I took to him right away, but he was on the defensive.

I explained my plans to him for an air service and the benefits described to Messrs Hayden and Grant. I added the extra number of visitors I hoped to bring to the islands, told him I was looking for capital, and asked if he would take up a batch of shares.

'Captain Fresson,' he answered, 'would you be prepared to put up money to have all your business taken away from you?'

'I don't quite understand you Mr MacKay. Who is going to take your business away?'

I was secretly wondering what evil 'gremlins' existed in Kirkwall.

To my astonishment, he answered, 'You. With such quick travel, the visitors won't want to stay more than a night or so, whereas at present, they stay weeks.'

'Come, Mr MacKay', I answered, 'You've got it in reverse. Quick air travel will bring so many passengers to Orkney when the travelling public realise they do not have to face the dreaded Pentland Firth sea crossing, that you won't be able to take them all in.'

We talked on, but I could not persuade him to my point of view. Again I had to admit defeat. Mr MacKay and his wife ultimately became two of my best customers, flying frequently south and returning in due course. On one of those trips, two years later after I had been operating a year or so, he called me aside at Inverness when I was preparing for the morning flight north.

'Captain Fresson,' he said, 'I have felt for some time that I owe you an apology. You will remember the thoughts I expressed when you came to enquire whether I would take up shares in your company a year to two ago.'

'I remember very well,' I replied.

'Well, you have proved me to be so very wrong. I am amazed at the extra business your air service has brought me and the Kirkwall Hotel and regret that I do not possess any Highland Airways shares today.'

I told him that I appreciated his frankness, but he was not the only one in Orkney who thought as he did at that time. A year later he died. It turned out that all the trips he had been making by air on his way to Edinburgh were for medical and surgical treatment for a serious internal complaint of which I was unaware, and I was very sorry to see him no more. His wife, however, carried on the Kirkwall Hotel for many years and she continued to travel with us on many occasions.

In desperation, having drawn a complete blank in Kirkwall, I went back to Mr Walter Grant. He then made it clear that he thought the project too much of a gamble, but he relented a bit and gave me indirect assistance. 'I tell you what I will do,' he said. 'You said you were interested in the carriage of newspapers. I will give you an introduction to the senior partner in *The Scotsman*, Edinburgh,

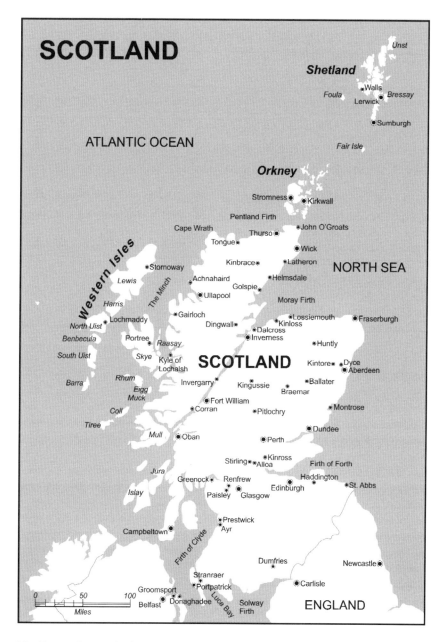

Mr George Law, who is a very good friend of mine. He could be of great help.'
Thereupon, he sat down and wrote a letter to Mr Law telling him of my plans for
an air service and asking him to give me what help he could.

'You know,' said Mr Grant, 'George Law is very keen on the pipes and it is more than likely you will be taken to a practice centre, so try and take an interest and you will make a friend for life.'

Although I am musical, at that time I had not mastered the exceptional harmonical progressions which the pipes called for.

I went back to my hotel, the St Ola, and the small band of enthusiasts again assembled that night to toast success to the venture and I told them of my almost fruitless search for financial backing in Orkney. I did not tell them about Walter Grant's letter. One of them, John Shearer, said they were sorry they could not raise enough to make a worthwhile contribution, but wished me better luck when I got south.

We left Orkney early on 11 February 1932 and flew over to Thurso for a meeting with Mr Wilson, the owner of the Royal Hotel. We then went on to Wick for a discussion with Colonel Robertson whom it will be remembered was my passenger on the exhibition flight given at the Wick gala the previous summer. Both Mr Wilson and Colonel Robertson were of the opinion that my plans were sound, and Colonel Robertson proved of great assistance in raising finance at a later date. Mr Wilson, who had far more to gain from an air service as it would bring visitors from the south to his hotel, raised nothing but lip service. We departed for Inverness after lunch with a strong tail wind to assist us and arrived in Inverness in forty-five minutes as against the usual hour.

The first chore was to write to Mr Law, enclosing Walter Grant's letter of introduction and saying I would by flying down within a day or so. I asked if he would he kindly let me know if he would see me and, if so, the day and time. That done, I called on Mr Donald, managing director of the well-known Inverness motor engineers, Macrae & Dick Limited. I had first met him when I was joy-riding at Nairn the year before and I had been up to his house on several occasions. During our conversation I had learned he had been stationed during World War One at one of the large aviation repair bases in France and I gained the impression that he was interested in aviation. I found him at home and confided my hopes and plans for an Inverness-Orkney air service and told him of the blank I had drawn in obtaining financial backing in Orkney. I mentioned the introduction I had obtained to Mr George Law and the plans I had in mind for the carriage of mails to Orkney by air. At the mention of an Air Mail contract, I noted a stir of business-like interest.

'Why not?' he said. 'It would save a lot of time.'

He questioned me for a while and I suppose my answers must have been fairly satisfactory for he gave the provost a ring on the phone and said he was sending me over to him. The provost, Sir Alexander McEwan, listened to my proposals which were, I would say, word perfect by then as I had repeated them so many times.

'How much capital do you want?' he enquired.

'To commence with, £3,000, and probably another £7,000 should the first year turn out successfully with a mail and newspaper contract secured.'

My hopes rose as he sat thinking.

Then he said to me, 'Go and see Mr Hugh MacKenzie at the Waverley Hotel. If he says the proposal is worth backing, you will obtain the capital you require.'

The Waverley Hotel was only a few minutes walk from Sir Alexander's office. The Boots took my message to Mr MacKenzie and within a few minutes I was ushered into his office. I repeated what I had told Sir Alexander McEwan who had evidently phoned him while I was on my way. Mr MacKenzie told me he was connected with the Highland Transport Company who operated an extensive motorbus service in the north of Scotland. He was accordingly interested in transport and listened intently to what I had to say.

After asking me a number of questions, he went on, 'Sir Alexander tells me you require £3,000 to commence with and a possible £7,000 extra for development if the service is successful.'

'That's correct,' I agreed.

He thought a while and questioned me about the possible newspaper and mail contract. Then, without any more to do, he said, 'That's a small sum. You can have the money on one condition.'

My heart gave a beat of exultation.

'What's that?' I enquired.

'That I become managing director,' he replied.

I was taken aback. How could he fulfil that office without any knowledge of the complexities of air transport? It could not be run like a motorbus company. I thought quickly.

'I feel I would have to hold that position as I would have to make all the decisions technically and operationally,' but if you would accept the chairmanship of the air company, I would be pleased to take that offer up.

'No,' he said without any hesitation, 'managing director or nothing.'

I tried to reason with him explaining some of the problems which he would know nothing about and, as managing director, would have to make decisions on. But he remained adamant.

'Well Mr MacKenzie,' I said with my heart in my boots, 'I am afraid I must bid you good afternoon. I could not consider giving up the right to the authority I would require to successfully tackle the immense problems which lay ahead.'

With that, I returned to Mr Donald. 'How did you get on?' he enquired. I told him how near I had been to raising the capital, but when he heard the terms, he said I had been quite right in not giving way.

'When are you going south to see Mr Law?' he asked.

'As soon as I hear from him.'

'Alright, look in and see me before you leave.'

I went back to the Queensgate Hotel where I was staying and spent a dejected night. I had got so near to my journey's end only to be robbed by one man's obstinacy for power. If Mr MacKenzie, I thought, could tackle successfully the specialised problems which lay ahead, I might have given in. I knew I could not have done so. It would never have worked. So I went to sleep hoping for better fortune next day with Mr Law. Once I had the newspaper subsidy which I was after, I felt sure I would find the capital somehow.

The morning after, I packed my bag and called in at Mr Donald's office on my way to Dalneigh Farm, where we had landed.

'Hullo, Captain Fresson', he said, 'did you have a good night? At least the weather is good to you today.'

He was right, the sun was shining and with the sun, my spirits rose, and they rose still more after my talk.

'You know,' he said, 'I have been thinking a lot about what you have told me of your plans. If you have a successful talk with Mr Law and are sure you can operate a service to Kirkwall with sufficient regularity so as to stand a good chance of obtaining a Post Office contract, my firm will interest themselves in the project and we will bring in others to support us. And you will, of course, be managing director. We will have the right to appoint the chairman.'

'That's splendid,' I replied and thanked him. 'I will get that contract off Mr Law somehow or other.'

He agreed to phone Mr Law to tell him I was on my way and that I would call him at his office after landing. 'Let me know the results of your meeting as soon as possible. You should have a pleasant flight over the Cairngorms today. How long do you expect to make Edinburgh in?' 'Direct across the Grampians? In one hour and a quarter.' With that I left him and, soon after, was airborne on my way to the Scottish capital.

I climbed above a cloud layer to seven thousand feet and crossed the Grampians in sunshine and blue sky. The clouds broke up on the other side of the mountains and I dropped below them as I drew near the Forth Bridge. Shortly afterwards, I found a field at Murrayfield on the south side of the main Edinburgh-Glasgow road and not far away from Mr Law's house. The surface of the field was good and I made an easy landing. After picketing the Moth down in the field and covering the cockpits with their canvas covers, I got my bag out of the back luggage locker and hied into town, booking myself in at the George Hotel.

I phoned Mr Law and he asked me if I liked bagpipes. 'God Lord,' I thought. 'It has come already.' I controlled myself, remembering Mr Grant's advice and said I loved them and was most interested.

'Good,' said Mr Law, 'meet me at the Highland Rooms at seven o'clock.'

I had an early meal and got to the rooms on time. I was taken to Mr Law who was sitting in the main room with other onlookers surrounding the pipers. And then the fun started. I had to sit through the pipers' practice for two hours. In between times, Mr Law asked me about my plans. I found it very difficult to put on good sales talk in such a discordant and interrupted atmosphere, or so it appeared to my untrained ear. Between the skirls of the pipes I unfolded my proposition. Mr Law didn't seem very impressed. He appeared more interested in Walter Grant and asked me if I knew him very well.

'No, I only met him for the first time during my recent visit to Kirkwall.'

'How much did you get from him?'

'Only a letter to you, Mr Law,' I replied.

He appeared surprised, but thought that was extremely amusing and he suddenly went off into raptures over a lament on the pipes played by some special exponent of the art. By that time my head was in a whirl when, to my relief, Mr Law said, 'Time we were going. Come to my house and have some supper.' He bade his farewells to his piping friends and took me to his car.

On arrival at some massive gates, which automatically opened as he rang the bell, I was led into a very fine house. Before we sat down to supper, Mr Law took me into his study and, when we were seated, said to me:

'I'm interested in the proposal you have made. If you like to give me the sole rights for *The Scotsman* to be carried on your air service for a period of one year, I will back you. How much do you want?'

I said, '£500 plus 3d a pound for the carriage of *The Scotsman*.'

'How much can your plane carry?'

I was determined to carry all the *Scotsman* newspapers Mr Law might ask me to, even if I had to make two trips a day.

So I countered, 'What load do you want?'

'I'll let you know in the morning.'

Before I left Edinburgh for Inverness to report to Mr Donald, I called at Mr Law's office at North Bridge and was introduced to the circulation manager, Mr Chisholm.

'Now, Mr Chisholm, Captain Fresson is organising a daily air service from Inverness to the Orkneys and will carry *The Scotsman* by air to Kirkwall as soon as he can get his air service launched. How much weight will you be wishing to despatch?'

Mr Chisholm's eyebrows went up and he went off to make enquiries.

On his return he said, '60 lbs to commence with.'

'Good God,' I thought, 'Is that all?'

Aloud, I said I was sure we could manage that.

'Well done,' said Mr Law, 'we will pay your company 3d per lb freightage and a subsidy of £500 for the first year's sole rights for the carriage of *The Scotsman* by air to Kirkwall. When you get back, write and let me know when you hope to form your company and also let me have the date you expect to commence operations.'

I was overjoyed at the generous terms offered. I promised to do that and I assured him that, if we could obtain delivery of the Monospar in time, I would make every effort to start the following September 1932.

'Anyhow, I will keep you constantly informed.'

It was not until later that I was to realise what a good friend I had made and the immense support that he would give when I got under way.

I was back in Inverness by lunchtime. 'A-WO' had not been pulled to pieces by the crowd that was gathered around when I got back to the field preparatory to take-off thanks to a policeman who was standing by. He asked me for my licence and aircraft registration, which I produced, and I was then free to take-off.

Mr Donald was very pleased at my good news and we confirmed what I had arranged by letter to Mr Law. Mr Donald told me I had better place a firm order for the Monospar monoplane as quickly as possible and, when we knew the date for collection, I was to come north again and make the final arrangements for licensing the fields. Steps would then be taken to float the company, which was to be known as Highland Airways Limited.

That afternoon, I visited the Town Clerk at Inverness, Mr Smith-Laing. He was most surprised, but charming and so very helpful, when I asked him if his Council would consider turning the Longman fields into a municipal airport. I explained to him about the proposed air service and the progress we had made. He told me he would take the matter up with his Council as quickly as possible and he felt sure they would be highly interested. He sent for the burgh surveyor, Mr Mackenzie; maps were speedily produced and I marked off the area I would require. Then there was the question of a long line of telephone wires which would have to be removed and re-sited.

'Right,' said Mr Smith-Laing, 'we will contact the Post Office and ask them if they can get them moved.'

I had a long talk with the burgh surveyor, Mr Mackenzie, and gave him the details of Air Ministry requirements for surfaces and length of runway at four points of the compass. He thought there might be some difficulty about the south-west corner as the ground in that quarter was incorporated within a farm which was let. I left it to him to use the necessary persuasion, which he successfully did.

I then flew south to our base at Hooton Park and spent a week there putting the final touch to our joy-riding tour for the first half of 1932. Within the week I was ready to leave for London. I phoned my parents at Northwood to tell them to expect me and set off in the Gipsy Moth after breakfast. I had a lady passenger with me, the wife of Mr Pobjoy, the designer of the air motors bearing his name. I was to land her at Aylesbury in a field near her mother's house. She sat in front of me and, from the first, the going was rough and bumpy and thoroughly unpleasant. As we passed over the lower Pennines it got worse, and my passenger's head disappeared inside the cockpit. A short while afterwards a handkerchief went overboard, a few minutes later a scarf – and then my passenger's felt hat disappeared.

The journey got rougher and the Moth was bucking like a steer when the climax of the jettisoning ended with a salmon-coloured piece of apparel fluttering past me, which looked uncommonly like an undergarment. I wondered what was happening and it was not until we landed at Aylesbury forty minutes later that I discovered my poor passenger had been frightfully airsick and sooner than be sick on the floor of the aeroplane, had nobly discarded various garments, at some cost to her husband, as a means of overcoming her dilemma. Poor woman, she looked very pale and pleased to get on terra firma again.

It was a pleasant and sunny day with little wind on the last stage of the flight. My mother and father were delighted to see me and there was plenty to talk about that night. I told them all about my plans for starting the first internal British airline between Inverness and Orkney. 'That seems a big undertaking,' they said. I explained to them that speedy air communication in the north could but succeed as rail and steamer services took days to carry out what an aeroplane could do in hours. Father seemed impressed and we talked about the details well into the night. Next day, I flew over to Croydon to see the General Aircraft Company which was producing a twin-engined monoplane which had very interesting possibilities.

I had a friend at Court there who used to be with the Aircraft Disposal Company Limited from whom North British Aviation bought their Le Rhône engine spares. They had their hangars at Croydon Airport. My friend introduced me to Captain Schofield, manager and test pilot for the company, who took us to the hangar to inspect the prototype aeroplane. It was a monoplane and looked a trim little aircraft, carrying five passengers, excluding the pilot, with a specially-designed locker which could be attached under the fuselage and capable of carrying at least 60 lbs of mail and newspapers. In addition there was a locker at the back of the cabin which took a limited amount of passenger luggage.

The production model was to be powered with two Pobjoy 80 hp 'R' type radial motors, thus giving 160 hp for take-off. The price of the plane was attractive at £1,500 for an all-metal aircraft. Captain Schofield said he was flying down to Cowes that morning in the prototype and enquired whether I would like to accompany him. 'I'd be delighted,' I answered. We landed at Saunders Roe's private airfield up on the hill behind Cowes. On the return flight, I piloted the plane and was impressed with the performance although it was only powered by two 50 hp Salmson radial engines. I was impressed by its all-round performance. There and then I asked him to put my name down for one of the first machines off the production line, which they hoped would be ready during the middle of 1932.

The prototype monoplane was made of three-ply and spruce, but the production model was to be made in Duralumin alloy and would be called the General Aircraft ST4 Monospar. The main wings only had one main spar which were specially stressed with kingposts and swage rods. This system also applied to the fuselage, the idea being to save weight which gave the plane a better payload. This was of major importance to my project. As I have said, the air motors were manufactured at our headquarters at Hooton Park airfield by Pobjoy Air Motors Company Limited and already they had proved to be reliable engines. They were exceedingly light for the power they produced, which helped to increase payload.

Around that time, an Australian named Cecil Arthur Butler flew a Comper Swift monoplane fitted with a Pobjoy 'R' type motor to Australia in record time, and another pilot, Charles Taylor, crossed the Andes at high altitude in a similar plane. These engines had not, however, been given the gruelling test of commercial airline work and Highland Airways subsequently proved to be a hard testing ground, which helped the makers to iron out any inherent weak spots that developed as will be recorded later.

Now that I had a plane available, my next move was to contact the Post Master General's Department, but I waited for a few days to get the proposition properly presented. That accomplished, I wrote and asked for an appointment and briefly explained my business. A reply came back very quickly saying Sir Frederick Williamson would be pleased to see me if I called at a stated time. I was feeling a bit apprehensive, but Sir Frederick immediately put me at my ease and introduced me to another official sitting by him. I do not remember his name, but he was from the Air Ministry.

'Now what is your proposal, Captain Fresson?' Sir Frederick asked.

I described my recent visit to Orkney and the time which could be saved if the mails could be flown from Inverness to Orkney, and later joining up with Wick, thus serving the extreme north of Scotland.

Sir Frederick asked, 'Have you an established company to operate this service?'

'Not yet', I said. 'This meeting you have kindly arranged is for exploratory purposes and to find out whether the Post Office would approve in principle, the carriage of air mail between Inverness and Orkney, should an air service be available. Naturally it would make matters very much easier for me to establish an operating company if I could say that the Post Office would be interested in such a project. Besides offering a regular daily load, it would attract passengers and newspaper freightage.'

Sir Frederick looked at me seriously for a moment before replying.

'We have had many propositions like this put to us before, but they have all turned out to be without substance. What assurance can you give us that you are capable of maintaining a safe and regular air service that would justify us entrusting His Majesty's mail in your care?'

'I am willing to run a service for a trial period, to be specified by you, which will enable you to judge for yourself, and as long as I know the Post Office is behind me in the event of the desired regularity being achieved, I would be in the position to raise the capital to form an operating company'.

Sir Frederick appeared satisfied with my answer and then referred to the Air Ministry official sitting by his side. He only asked me one question.

'You are aware, Captain Fresson, that the route you are talking about is a very stormy one and subject to rapid weather changes. As there are no weather stations along that route, how do you propose providing yourself with the meteorological conditions each day before commencing the flight?'

Sir Frederick was looking at me quizzically.

'That's easy,' I countered without hesitation, 'I will obtain telephone reports from my own observers, whom we shall train for the job. All we shall need is cloud height, visibility and approximate strength of the wind.'

The Air Ministry man appeared non-plussed over such unorthodox methods, but Sir Frederick smiled, and I felt I had gained a point with him.

The outcome of the meeting left it open for me to approach the Post Office again at a later date when I was further on with my plans. Sir Frederick Williamson's last words to me were:

'Send us regularity figures for a year's operations and *we will consider a contract* if they are good enough.'

With that, I considered we had enough ammunition to complete the financial arrangements. I had a plane available, a possible newspaper contract plus the mail at a later date, and an air minded public. That seemed to me a good foundation with which to commence trying to float the air company. I returned to my parents' home that night and they were deeply interested in what I had to tell them. We talked on and on, my father asking me a lot of questions and the night was well on before we turned in to sleep.

Next morning, after breakfast and having bid my parents goodbye, I flew Moth 'A-WO' back to Hooton airfield. My first job was to write a letter to the General Aircraft Company confirming my order for the ST4 Monospar plus the newspaper tray to be fitted underneath the fuselage. I requested delivery for June 1932.

I found my engineer, Bert Farminer, had the winter overhaul mostly complete and the motor of my plane had received a complete overhaul. The North British Aviation Company was ready to go into action early in the spring. I was expecting the next six months would put 'finis' to my joy-riding days. I had completed four strenuous years at the game and so looked forward operating a regular air route. I'm afraid I did not realise it at the time, but my new occupation would call for far higher endeavour and effort than that required for 'barnstorming around the countryside.' If the weather was bad, no one wanted to fly. So, we just sat on the ground and amused ourselves. That was not to be the case with an airline and it was the bad weather days that took a heavy toll on me.

4

The beginning of Highland Airways

By the time April 1932 arrived, negotiations for an airfield at Hatston Farm were dragging on and so I returned to Orkney for a final all out effort to get this thorny question disposed of. First I contacted Mr Ritchie who farmed the Hatston land that I had used the previous summer for our joy-riding visit. He was most willing to help me, for he was one of the few to perceive the advantages of air transport to isolated Orkney. He was however controlled by the agents of the owner of the Hatston Estate, a Mr Bell, who lived at St Abbs Head in Berwickshire.

'Why don't you go along and see Mr Robertson?' Mr Ritchie said, 'You can tell him I am agreeable to you having the fields as long as my evening grazing rights are protected, and see if you can come to a final arrangement.' Mr Robertson was one of the leading solicitors in Kirkwall and I made an appointment for the following day. We had not been talking long when I perceived my proposition was not well received. Negotiations were long and protracted. Every time an obstacle was overcome, another cropped up, and it became evident I was up against evasion and stonewalling.

In desperation, that night I phoned the owner, Mr Bell, at St Abbs and asked if he would see me if I called on him next day. Mr Bell evidently knew about me for he said he would be delighted to meet me. Come to lunch he said and he described the position of his house in relation to St Abbs Head. I set off next morning and was over St Abbs Head just after noon. I espied a house which I thought might be the correct one and landed in a field nearby. As usual, the locals soon put in an appearance and one of them told me that the house I was looking for was a couple of miles to the north. In fact one could just see it on top of the hill. Taking off, I was soon down near the right mansion and Mr Bell was out to take me up to his home.

We spent a lot of time discussing my plans. Mr Bell was extremely interested and wanted me to have Hatston.

'I can't think,' he said, 'why Mr Robertson is so much against it if Ritchie is agreeable. After all he is the one who has to farm the land. I will write to Mr Robertson asking him to give you the facilities you want unless he has any serious objections which I do not know about.'

I took off on the return journey at half past three in the afternoon after thanking Mr Bell for an excellent lunch and such a good welcome.

'I hope to be flying up to Kirkwall with you before long,' he shouted as I revved up the motor to take off.

On the way north I felt pleased with myself for having overcome the stonewalling, but I did not know my Mr Robertson. He was resentful that I had gone over his head and he firmly dug his feet in and refused to listen to his client pleading on my behalf. It was a day or two later that I realised I would have to find another site, as Hatston was definitely denied me.

So, after breakfast, I set off by car. I went to the old war-time airfield at Houton, about nine miles out in Orphir. It was far too small for the modern requirements of the day. I swept the country side, but it was impossible to find a site that had the necessary 500 yards length of runway in all direction. At last I found one site at Braebuster, in Deerness, but the ground was almost totally waterlogged in winter and it was ten miles away from Kirkwall, so that was out. I returned to my hotel tired and dispirited. I met the boys in the St Ola lounge that night and discussed the problem with them and I began to understand the resistance I was meeting on the Hatston proposal. They said that quite a number of people in the town held shares in the shipping company and, like my friend Mr MacKay of the Kirkwall Hotel, they thought an air service would be injurious to the shipping interests and so they were out to do anything which would block air facilities in Orkney.

'Oh, that's it!' I exclaimed. 'And I have a sort of feeling they are right in what they say, for a successful air service, crossing the firth from Thurso to Kirkwall in twenty minutes and in comparative smoothness, would most assuredly make a big hole in the steamer passenger bookings.'

I later gleaned that Mr Robertson was thinking along the same lines, so somehow I had to find another site over which he had no control.

Next day I went out again. This time I flew the Moth around and found one or two likely places, but always there was something wanting. When I got back that night, there was an invitation to tea next day from Mr Hayden whose house was near that of Mr Grant. He had two good-looking daughters who had flown with me when I was giving flights last summer. I rang up to say I would be pleased to accept and, next afternoon, after another day's fruitless search, I presented myself.

In answer to their enquiries, I told them that, short of obtaining Hatston, which looked impossible, I was beaten in finding a suitable site within reasonable distance of Kirkwall and which could be made into an airfield at reasonable cost. The girls were very keen on getting an air service as they frequently went south and were not good sailors.

The eldest sister, Patty, said to me, 'Have you looked over the top at Wideford Hill?'

This was just behind them to the east. I said I had covered most of the ground without success.

'Well,' said Patty, 'let's take a walk up to the top after tea and have a look at Wideford Farm.'

It was a steep climb and there were many stone dykes to be scaled, but Patty and her sister, Jean, romped over them like goats and I did my best to keep up.

On arrival at the top, the girls said, 'That's Wideford Farm,' pointing down in front of a slight slope.

I gave a casual look and then stiffened. I could not believe my eyes. There in front of me was a site even better than Hatston. It gave me a south-east run, whereas Hatston did not unless the main road was diverted.

'My God', I said, 'you have surely saved the situation. This is the place without any doubt. Let's get down and pace the field out.'

Sure enough, I obtained two runs of five hundred yards and two of around four hundred and fifty. If the wind was strong enough to warrant using the two shorter directions, then the length was sufficient. The surface was mostly good and could be put in order at low cost. There were no obstructions on the perimeter and, best of all, the NW-SE runway was downhill for 100 yards, which on calm days and when the field was soggy in the winter, offered a catapulting effect to the take-off with a full load. The really big job that required attention was the bridging of the four feet wide ditch which ran through the middle, north-west to south-east. The field turned out to be only one and a half miles from the town.

'Where does the farmer live, Patty?' I asked.

'Over there in the house by the road.'

'What's his name?'

'Mr Anderson,' they both replied.

'Do you know who owns the ground?'

Patty answered, 'He does, I think.'

'Will you introduce me please?'

We went up to the front door and rang the bell. Mr Anderson himself answered it.

'Oh good afternoon, Miss Patty and Miss Jean', he said.

'May we introduce Captain Fresson to you?' they replied, 'He is looking for somewhere to land his planes and he would like to talk with you.'

I greeted Mr Anderson: 'I understand you own this farm?'

'I do,' he replied.

'Well, I am urgently in need of your assistance. I am in an awful fix.'

I then explained to him that we were ready to form a company to operate an air service to Orkney from Inverness and serving Wick and Thurso, but I could not find any suitable place to make an airfield in or around Kirkwall.

'Hatston is barred to us as there appears to be clash of interests in the town and the only other suitable place I can find after days of hunting are these fields of yours. Can we do a deal?'

He asked me many questions as to how much ground I wanted and how many services we would run daily. Also, what would be the time of the last service because he would require the ground for sheep grazing after five in the afternoon. I realised from his conditions that he was willing to help if we could work our respective interests in a tied pattern. I explained to him the work required to make the ground suitable, and that I might even have to lay drainage if the ground became soggy in winter. He agreed to the ditch being bridged and said I could have the ground on a five-year lease at a very reasonable annual rental. I felt faint with relief. The last obstacle had been overcome and the 'Hatstonites' could go to the nethermost regions. I was all set now to return to Inverness and to form the company as soon as I knew when we could obtain delivery of our monoplane.

I went back to the hotel that night and, as usual, the old friends were collected in the private room. They were delighted at my news and the makings of a big night to celebrate the important event developed. One of them, a building contractor named Baikie, known to his friends as the 'Baron', and a big built very friendly man, said he would get the ditch covered at cost price and another said he could arrange for the ground to be levelled off. 'The Baron' also said he would build us a reception hut at low cost and I then knew I had valuable aid behind me which subsequently proved well founded.

We broke up around midnight and, with John Shearer and the Deputy Town Clerk, we were invited round to Mr Baikie's building yard. He took us into the office and produced a bottle of good Scotch. By that time I was wondering how I was going to fly south next day, so I hurriedly excused myself. Having bid my friends 'au revoir', I eventually got back in the early hours to the hotel and slept soundly until I was called next morning. I had told Mr Anderson at Wideford that our Inverness solicitors would draw up an agreement and a rough copy would be sent to him for his approval. What a kindly man and valuable ally he turned out to be in our early struggle.

I arrived back in Inverness in time for lunch and at once went to see Mr Donald. He was delighted with my news and agreed that, as soon as we could ascertain the delivery date of the aircraft which would enable us to commence operations in 1932, immediate steps would be taken to form the company. He took me along to see his solicitor, Mr Robert Wotherspoon, who was also interested in the project and who would later join the board as a director. Mr Wotherspoon was to act as the company's legal advisor and Mr Donald's firm, Macrae & Dick Limited, would provide office space while their Secretary, Mr William Hamilton, known to his friends as 'Willie', would be responsible for the books and statistics. Both of these gentlemen would also join the board with myself as managing director and chief pilot.

There now only remained the confirmation regarding the Inverness airfield at Longman to complete the preliminaries, so I called on the Town Clerk, Mr Smith-Laing, before setting off in the Moth for Hooton Park. 'Hello, Captain Fresson', he said, 'how did you get on in Orkney?' I told him I had at last found and obtained the use of a good airfield and now I only wanted to be assured about the Inverness landing ground at Longman. I would attend to Thurso later. Mr Laing told me that it was agreed in principle that the Town Council would grant facilities and, if I would acquaint him with the date we proposed to commence the air service as quickly as possible, the ground would be prepared in time by the Council. At last, the operating requirements were completed, so I now only needed the aeroplane – and an engineer to maintain it.

The day after my arrival at Hooton, I flew to Croydon to see General Aircraft Company and urged them to hurry up the delivery of my plane. I also asked if they would look around and find me a competent engineer to maintain the Monospar and its two Pobjoy engines. If they could do that, I would arrange for the engineer to take an immediate course on the engines at the Pobjoy factory at Hooton.

I still had a lot to do if we were to commence operations that year. There was the administration to look to – advertising, road transport at terminals, ground staff and office staff, and a host of smaller matters.

I was speaking with the General Aircraft Company's general manager and chief test pilot, Captain Schofield. The production and works manager was also present. He told me that the production line was obscure at that moment as they were in the midst of carrying out certain tests with the prototype and until those tests were completed, they were unable to make any promises. However, the works manager said he hoped to have news for me within a few weeks. Captain Schofield then sent for the engineer he had recommended me. His name was Cyril Pugh and he appeared keen at the idea of joining me in Inverness. We discussed terms and I promised to send him a contract to sign when I arrived back in Hooton. I mentioned the Pobjoy motor training at the works at Hooton and he said he had been working on the Pobjoy engines for a month or so and had a fair knowledge of the engine. At the same time he was anxious to make use of a course at the Pobjoy factory. I was very pleased with this turn of events, more especially as he had the Gipsy 1 motor on his licence and so could service the Gipsy Moth.

I went to my parents' home in Northwood for a couple of days. They were anxious to know how my plans were maturing for the Orkney air service. I made the most of those couple of days as I felt that, once the air service was operating, I would not be seeing much of them and for them 'time was marching on.' Two days later, I took off from Brooklands airfield, with Miss Pauer as a passenger, to fly up to my old school at Framlingham in Suffolk. It was a misty day with limited visibility. The country was featureless and a fair crosswind was blowing. My estimation of the drift must have been fairly accurate as we hit Framlingham Castle dead-on after one hour and thirty-five minutes on a strict compass course. The school pupils were out in force playing football. I gave them an aerobatic display over the playing fields with the result that the match appeared to come to a halt after the first couple of loops and rolls. I landed in a field by the old castle, which I used to play around as a boy, and got myself fixed up in the Crown Hotel for the night.

I then went up to the College and called on the headmaster and made myself known.

'You are just in time for tea,' said the Head's wife. 'This is quite an event.'

I gladly accepted and, as the talk progressed, I reminded them that this was the second time I had paid them a visit by air. They seemed surprised.

'When was that Mr Fresson?' the headmaster asked.

'In April 1918, during the War, I flew down from Narborough in Norfolk, landed at an RFC landing ground some seven miles away, borrowed a bike off a farmer's lad, and cycled in to see Dr Stokes who was Head then. Mrs Stokes was giving a party and asked me to tea, so this is the second time I have had the pleasure of saying 'yes' to a good tea offer in your house'.

I met my old music master, Mr Barnicott, and the Head of the Senior School, Mr Towel. These two masters later accompanied me back to the Crown Hotel and we sat in the bar well into the night talking about 1900-1904 days when they had the pleasure, or displeasure, of teaching me. They remembered my earlier flying visit at the end of World War One quite well.

We left next morning, a Sunday, my passenger and I taking off for Ratcliffe Hall in Leicestershire which was the home of Sir Lindsay Everard. He kept a private airfield and Miss Winifred Spooner, who was one of the early women flying aces, acted as his private pilot. She had invited me to drop in if I was ever passing, so here was a good opportunity. We were made very welcome and Sir Everard came down and had a chat with me in the charming cottage which he put at Miss Spooner's disposal. Sir Everard was chairman of the Royal Aero Club and he was genuinely pleased to see me.

'I have read about your air service plans to the Orkney Islands,' he said. 'I'm most interested and admire your pioneering spirit. You will be the only operator outside the Imperial Airways group, you know. When do you expect to commence operations?'

'That is difficult to answer,' I replied. 'It all depends when the General Aircraft Company can deliver the monoplane I have on order. However, I am hoping to get under way by the beginning of September.'

He went on chatting and asked many questions about the meteorological conditions in the north.

'I have always heard' he said, 'that it's pretty stormy.'

'You are not far wrong,' I replied. 'However, I feel confident we shall be able to overcome the hazards which may exist.'

'Let me fill your glass', he said, 'then I must be getting along. Miss Spooner tells me she has invited you to lunch and I'm sure you will be well looked after.'

He got up, and bade us goodbye.

'Call in again whenever you are passing. I shall watch your progress with great interest.'

Unfortunately, I never saw him again for Scotland kept me tied to the northern latitudes and they were off the beaten track for the flight down the east coast to London. We sat down to an excellent lunch.

'You have a delightful place here,' I remarked over the soup course. 'Do you get much flying for Sir Everard?' I enquired.

'Oh yes,' Miss Spooner answered, 'Sir Everard gets around quite a lot. Backwards and forwards to London and quite a few trips to the Continent. We also visit a number of air rallies so I am kept pretty busy from the flying point of view.'

I asked her many questions about her long distance flights of the previous year and the conversation never flagged.

After lunch and when we had finished coffee, Miss Spooner said she had several jobs to do.

'Just make yourselves at home and I'll be back as quickly as possible.'

I thanked her, but as we wished to get back to Hooton before dark and there was a fairly strong head wind blowing, I said we had better be getting along. She came to see us off.

'I'll swing your 'prop',' she said.

Noting my surprise, she commented, 'I have to do it for our Moth so why not yours?'

We bade her farewell and after thanking her for her kind hospitality, we clambered aboard, fixed our harnesses, and in no time Miss Spooner had the motor going. As she stood alongside me while I warmed up the motor, I asked her to visit us in Inverness with Sir Everard. She seemed dubious about getting Sir Everard so far north.

'However,' I said, 'I hope we may meet again.'

I taxied out and we were soon airborne and on our way to Hooton.

In those days there was much chivalry between private flyers, which completely disappeared after World War Two. There were numerous flying clubs and the spirit of competition and camaraderie of the air were strong. One was always made welcome if you flew in to a club, even though you had not been there before, and one never lacked plenty of people to talk to at the club bar. They were interested in your flying experiences as much as you were with theirs. Brooklands Air Club was one of the most enterprising clubs, founded and operated by Captain Duncan Davis. He organised the famous 'Dawn Patrol', which operated in the summer months. It was based on the early morning air patrols adopted by the Allies in World War One. Brooklands would have its squadron of Gipsy Moths and other light aircraft and other aero clubs on the South coast would assemble a similar force. They would start the patrol from each base, Brooklands being the Home Squadron and the outside air clubs would represent the enemy. As soon as one side picked up the other, a mock air battle would ensue. I am uncertain as to the methods used to score points which would enable the victor of each engagement to be decided, but to suffice, a score was kept throughout the season and the victorious club would be the one which had won the most battles and the handsome prize. There was great enthusiasm displayed in the 'Dawn Patrol' which resulted in much inter-club camaraderie.

Back at Hooton, I got dug into the North British Aviation programme for the coming season. If I could not take part, then my partner Lance Rimmer would work on his own. Alternatively, if the aircraft for the air service would not be available in time, I would take my share in the operations.

A week or so later, a letter arrived from the General Aircraft Company which caused us much concern. It informed me with regret that their experimental aircraft had been severely damaged after a test flight. That meant at least a year's delay in commencing production. It finished by expressing their great regrets and assuring me that every effort would be made to deliver my aircraft early April 1933.

At once, I advised the three municipal councils in Kirkwall, Wick and Inverness the contents of this letter and said this delay would mean putting back the air service opening date until Spring 1933. I also wrote a letter to the newspapers in each town explaining the situation and asking them to make an announcement in their next issue. Inverness and Wick accepted these events for which we could not be held responsible, but in Kirkwall, the hard core, to which I have referred previously, immediately rubbed their hands and were vociferous in their 'I told you so' attitude that no aeroplane could operate across the stormy Pentland Firth. They failed to say that their steamer also had the greatest difficulty at times.

The press received the General Aircraft Company announcement sympathetically. One report later read:

In all, eight trips were made by Captain Fresson from the south, spread over two years, before all obstacles were overcome, and during this time much valuable data was obtained respecting meteorological conditions that are encountered in these climes at various times of the year. When success was within his grasp and it was hoped to commence the service, the "monoplane" that was intended for the run, which was of an entirely new type, was damaged during trials at the manufacturers aerodrome and this put the makers so far back in their programme that it was found impossible to find a plane in time for the service to be commenced that season. The service, accordingly had to be abandoned for that year and the pessimistic shouted aloud 'That's that', but news now comes through that perseverance has won and that final arrangements have been completed for the opening of the Inverness-Orkney air route – which will coincide with the opening of the Inverness Municipal Airfield on 5th and 6th May, 1933.

Now that the position was known, it was clear I had to finalise preparations for a joy-riding tour for the 1932 season. So firstly I tackled my engineer, Bert Farminer, regarding the overhaul of my Avro aeroplane, which had been left unattended pending the decision to commence the air service. The motor had done really hard work during the past season and required a complete overhaul. That meant taking the motor out of the aircraft. As has been said, Bert was an old hand from the pre-war days of flying. He had joined the Sopwith Company as a boy apprentice and so grew up with rotary engines and, with the experience he had gained with years of joy-riding behind him, what he didn't know about the 110 hp Le Rhône rotary motor could be written on an old time three-penny bit.

I got busy planning the tour. Some towns were already signed up to the end of May, so that left the summer and autumn to button up. Before I had the Moth I used to do this job by car and it took a long time. With the Moth, it was a far quicker process.

Firstly, having decided on the town, one could spot likely fields from the air more quickly and easily, come down low, test them for approach, and if the surface looked good, effect a landing, walk the field over and measure the runs by pacing, as this information would be required when applying to Air Ministry for a licence to operate a temporary aerodrome. Lastly, if the conditions appeared in good order, I would search out the farmer and endeavour to sign him up for as reasonable a fee as possible.

One has no conception of the host of objections we had, in many instances, to overcome with farmers, especially when one particular field in the neighbourhood was the only suitable place for flying. However, on the whole, we found the farmers very helpful and co-operative, and in many instances they became our very good friends.

Within a month, I had completed arrangements for the second tour which was to take me to Ashbourne in Derbyshire, Wrexham, Kirkby Stephen, Keswick, Penrith, Kirkby Lonsdale, Bedale in Yorkshire, Richmond, Barnard Castle, Durham, Easingwold, Northallerton, Thirsk, Morpeth, Whitley Bay, Dunbar, Cramlington, Blyth, Wooler, Rothbury, Coldstream, Musselburgh, Portobello, Pitlochry, Banchory, Aboyne, Ballater, Eyemouth, and North Shields to finished in first week of November 1932 at Durham.

I have gone to some length in quoting the towns visited in a season to show the area covered in a normal barnstorming tour. As may be imagined, it was hard work as literally thousands of take-offs and landings were accomplished in a season. Of course, each week-end there was also an aerobatic display to be given to the crowd who had paid gate money for admittance to the heavily screened flying field. Not only did we charge for the flying, but there was a gate admittance of sixpence. Many people in those days had not seen an aeroplane at close quarters and, providing they could not watch free of charge from the roadside, they would come in and pay their 'tanner' and it was not uncommon for a one man show to take fifty to sixty pounds gate money on a Sunday afternoon. That meant an attendance of 2,000 people or more. To ensure privacy of operations when there was no high hedge to shield us from the outside onlooker, we carried several hundred yards of sackcloth with poles, ropes and pegs and a screen would rapidly be thrown up.

There were several incidents on this, my last tour of joy-riding, which are perhaps worth describing. The first was Keswick in the Lake District. Many, many, joy-riding firms had tried to find a field to operate from there as it was correctly assumed to be a lucrative place containing many people on holiday and a number of fair-size neighbouring villages with frequent transport services to draw from. I told my partner, Lance Rimmer, that I was planning to obtain a field there. He laughed at me and told me about the past efforts made by himself and others in that direction.

In spite of what he said, and not feeling hopeful, I decided to visit Keswick. Accordingly, I went up by car as there would not likely be any suitable place for a chance landing in the Moth. I also had to find a field at Cockermouth. I decided to stay the night at Keswick and make an all-day search. I tried every road out of the town for three miles and, at last, two miles up the hill on the left of the main south road to Ambleside, I spotted a fairly large area of ground. It was well shielded from the road by trees and a big hay barn. I jumped over the gate and saw a field of some three hundred yards in most directions with the east side sloping uphill. Most of the surface was in good condition although a bit rough in places, but there was a snag, which was no doubt the cause of other site hunters having walked off in disgust. Scattered in at least a dozen places were outcrops of rock about one to three feet high, which interfered with the runways. I cursed my luck as this site was the last and only possibility and was about to give up. As I was entering my car, an idea struck me. 'Why not blow those rocks up by blasting?' I thought. 'Even if it costs fifty pounds it would be worth it.'

Back in town, I sought out a contractor and told him what I wanted.

'Yes, Captain Fresson, I think I can help you. Come along and I will introduce you to a friend of mine who specialises in blasting for road material.'

This friend accompanied me up the hill, took a careful look and, to my relief, said, 'The job could be done, but it will be expensive.'

'How much?' I asked.

'Twenty pounds,' he said.

With a pained look on my face, but inwardly rejoicing, I said, 'Couldn't you do it for £15 and we will give you and your family a free flight?'

He thought a moment and had another look and counted the rocks again.

'Well,' he said, 'I wouldn't make much out of it for that, but I will take it on.'

In the first season, I took £600 in ten days with the help of another aircraft which came up from Hooton to join me on the two Sundays. So I gave the contractor his £20 plus the free flights. He made a good job of the blasting and in levelling out several other rough places and so the seeming impossible had been achieved.

My partner Lance Rimmer would not believe me when I got back and told him I had found a site. He was amazed and well pleased when he saw the flying ground later on. The second season, I took another £400 from the same site so a total of £1,000 for twenty days flying was a good return for twenty pounds.

Later, at Barnard Castle, while taking off in the Moth one morning, I hit the top of a tree with the port wing. The plane sagged and nearly nosedived into the ground. Quick action got me down in the next field without accident. Examination disclosed that the port wing was fractured and it would be a workshop job to repair it. The nearest place was Cramlington, north of Newcastle-on-Tyne. I had no engineer capable of dismantling and re-rigging the wing so had to do the job myself. I soon got it off and with the help of a friend, the Hon. Joey Pease, who loaned me a large car, we got the wing tied on to the roof and took it up to Cramlington by road. In two weeks it was ready. We carted it back by the same means, I re-erected the wing in a couple of hours and the wee Moth was flying again in good trim.

Another incident occurred when I was operating at Cockermouth. Miss Pauer, the owner of the Moth, was accompanying us while we were on tour so that she might receive flying instruction. The flying field at Cockermouth had a very rough surface. The pupil sat in the back seat and the instructor in the front, while the control stick in that cockpit was detachable, being locked in place by a pin and spring clip. One day we were taking off and had nearly reached flying speed when the bouncing over the rough ground jolted the control in my hand free from its housing. There I was with the loose stick in my hand and completely without control of the aircraft.

The hedge was rushing towards us and certainly not more than 100 yards away. A crash appeared imminent. Our only hope of avoiding a bad accident lay in my pupil's hands. So as not to fluster her, I calmly directed her to ease the control stick back a little and fortunately my pupil responded quickly. The aircraft rose from the ground as the hedge was upon us and we cleared it by a few feet. I continued to give directions until we had climbed to 1,000 feet and then I told her to level off and fly straight. I then had an opportunity to mop my brow. It was indeed fortunate for us that Miss Pauer had reacted so well. Now that we were flying straight and had plenty of altitude, I managed to replace the control stick into its socket, but I was unable to lock it. However, with care, it would function sufficiently for me to take over the landing. After landing, I told my pupil how she had saved us from a nasty crash and the destruction of the plane by so quickly obeying my instructions. She was overcome with amazement and pride for she had no idea she had complete control of the take-off. Had she been aware of this, perhaps we would not have got away with it so well.

Later in the season we were engaged to give a stunt exhibition at a flying display held at Cramlington airfield. My advertising manager, J C Dixon of Whitley Bay, was the wing walking expert and he gave a thrilling demonstration of riding the top wing standing up. Indeed the plane took off with him in that position and we landed with him still on top. In addition, he gave a demonstration of walking out to the extreme tip of the wings. On landing, he received a great ovation from the crowd of spectators. That display earned us a good fee and the thanks of the management committee. That stunt resulted from an experience I had when flying half way between Morecambe and Lancaster some four years previously. I was then flying for Berkshire Aviation Tours Limited and there was a long queue of people waiting to fly.

We had three aircraft going 'hammer and tongs'. There was a strong and gusty wind which made the circuits at low altitude very uncomfortable for the pilot. I had made perhaps a couple of dozen trips with everything going normally when, on the next trip with two passengers, the plane suddenly went funny. We were flying at around three hundred feet and I could not make out what was wrong with the controls. The aircraft was very difficult to keep on an even keel and the fore and aft control was soggy. 'Whatever can be the matter,' I asked myself. The idea of structural failure flashed through my mind. I went hot and cold at the thought. 'Must get down as soon as possible' I said to myself when suddenly we were hit by a terrific gust. The left wing dropped badly and I could not right the airplane. After what seemed an eternity, but which probably was not more than a quarter of a minute, the plane gradually came up with full lateral control on, or as much as I could give it as it was incredibly stiff to operate. I hurried in to land and, having rolled to a stop, my engineer, Bert Farminer, ran up to find out what was the matter.

I shouted over the noise of the motor, 'There is something wrong with the plane. I'm switching off for an inspection.'

By this time the engine had stopped and Bert said in a more normal tone, 'What do you expect? You have a ruddy passenger standing on top of the plane and he has been hanging on to the lateral control wire'

This worked the ailerons and in turn controlled the lateral balance of the plane. No wonder the lateral control was stiff and heavy. I looked back into the passenger cockpit and sure enough there was only one passenger sitting in it. And then I saw a leg coming down from the top wing and the second passenger appeared looking very wind-swept and red in the face.

'What in the hell do you think you have been doing,' I shouted at him. 'You nearly killed the lot of us.'

'Sorry, Mister' he replied. 'I thought I would give my pals and the crowd a thrill. They bet me a quid I wouldn't do it.'

At that moment, the tour manager arrived with a policeman who arrested him.

After giving the 'sailor', which my passenger turned out to be, a severe reprimand, the police let him go. They said he was used to heights climbing masts, but that was not much comfort to me. That episode gave me the idea. It had gone down well with the crowd of spectators one hundred per cent and must have looked very thrilling from the ground. I had a talk with Bert Farminer and during the last winter season we designed some foot loops of steel cable and bolted them to the top wings at the centre section. We also fitted a steel wire rein which was attached to the same bolts for the wing rider to hold on to. After practising the stunt, we had then been giving the crowd a thrill at all our weekend shows that year. It had earned us a lot of money because the display drew large crowds of spectators, thus increasing our gate receipts.

The last episode that year occurred at Pitlochry, north of Perth. We had advertised: 'Come and see a local lady, who has never been in an aeroplane before, try to fly one of our planes.' Crowds turned up and awaited the hair-raising event. We had hired a cottage on the other side of the road from the flying field where we kept our portable belongings. The idea of this stunt consisted of myself dressing up as a woman with a red wig and old fashioned ladies' split knickers with a pocket for a powder puff sewn on to the leg. I would then mingle with the crowd of onlookers. Our publicity manager was standing in front of the plane talking nonchalantly with our engineer when suddenly he would announce in a loud voice, 'We offer five pounds for any lady in the crowd who will come along and fly this plane.'

No one stirred. Again he would shout, 'Surely there is one of you nice looking girls who would like to make a fiver. It's quite easy! We will show you what to do!'

I then raised my voice and said, 'I'll try it if you think it would be safe, Mister.'

'Of course it will be safe,' replied our publicity man.

At that I marched forward. There would be a great stir in the crowd, and with some of the women gawping.

'Well,' says the engineer, in a loud voice for all to hear, 'let me show you the works,' leading me to the propeller and explaining: 'That sets the plane going.'

At that moment he turned the propeller over and the engine made a noise. I reacted with a jump as if trying to get away. The crowd laughed at the discomfiture of the red headed lady.

'Now come round to the cockpit and if you will get in we will show you how to work the controls.'

All these instructions were given in a loud voice so that the spectators could hear.

'How do I get in?' I querulously asked.

'Like this,' says the engineer and at that, he gives me a good heave and I fall head first into the cockpit with my skirt falling over my head thus exposing the old fashioned pantaloons and I let out a shriek. The crowd let out a mighty roar and by this time were getting really worked up. I then jumped out of the cockpit and tried to run off. The engineer chased me and cajoled me back into the plane, dangling a five pound note in my face. At last, I got in, the motor was started and I proceeded to make a zigzag course taxying to the end of the field. I turned around and, opening the engine full out, I swerved in alarming fashion from side to side on the take-off run. Alongside the spectators, I pulled the plane into the air, standing up in the cockpit, yelling and waving my arm around and then I started climbing, doing the craziest flying it is possible to do.

The crowd, by this time, have completely bought the stunt as a genuine performance. I made a circle in erratic fashion and came in for a landing. I flattened out ten to twenty feet above the ground in front of the spectators and quickly threw up both arms in the air, holding the control column between my legs and yelling, 'Help, help, help, I can't get down.'

The spectators went mad with excitement but there was a policeman in the crowd who took a different view. Eventually, I made a zigzag approach bumping over the ground and, before the plane had time to come to a standstill, I jumped out, rolled over on the ground and, picking myself up, started to run for my life. Like a shot from a gun, the policeman left the crowd and chased after me. I saw him coming and ran slower so as to let him catch me.

'Hey, you,' he said, taking me by the arm, 'Where is your flying licence? You're drunk. I'm taking you in.'

At that point, the crowd were nearly off their heads with hilarious excitement. My assistants told me later that they were speculating who the tough looking 'bitch' was as no one seemed to know her. I let the policeman lead me away to the road and cottage, where I had told him my licence was, and my publicity manager came running up behind.

Out of earshot from the crowd, and with my manager alongside, I turned to the policeman and said, 'Thank you Copper for putting on such a good show. The crowd appear to have appreciated it no end.'

'What do you mean,' he said, red in the face and angry. 'You're drunk and coming with me. I have never seen such a dangerous display in all my life.'

About time to end the farce, I thought.

'Let me get my licence first,' I said.

He let me into the cottage with my manager standing by him. In a few minutes I reappeared in my proper flying kit and with my licence.

My friend, the policeman, said, 'Where's that drunken bitch?'

'Here', I naively replied.

He stared at me and didn't believe me, but my manager told him it was correct and that I was the pilot of the plane, and furthermore I was far from being drunk.

'You have been badly had, and I consider it a compliment,' I said.

He was still not thoroughly convinced until I took him into the cottage and showed him the female garb I had been using for impersonation. At that, he was convinced, and he said he would never have believed it possible.

'We do this stunt all round the country', I told him, 'but you are the first copper who ever tried to arrest me.'

He retired crestfallen. I saw him several times before we moved on. He took the joke in good part. We never disclosed the trick which had deceived 'their policeman' to anyone. Otherwise his life wouldn't have been worth living!

We moved on to Aboyne where my Sunday flying was ruined by a very tricky forced landing which occurred just after taking off on the second flight of the day. The plane had reached about fifty feet and was over a small wood when the engine spluttered and cut. On the far side of the wood there was a field about 200 yards long, much too short as the height of the trees along the edge made a low approach impossible. I managed to drop the plane and my two passengers into the field in a semi-stall. In so doing, the under-carriage suffered some damage which took all the afternoon to put right. The cause of engine failure turned out to be a broken connecting rod inside the motor. Considering the right fix I was now in, we all agreed we had come out of it very cheaply as the whole plane could easily have been severely damaged, thus necessitating dismantling and return by rail to Hooton Park for rebuild. It was bad enough, however, to lose a whole Sunday's revenue of around £100.

We worked our way up the valley to Ballater and had a grand view of Balmoral Castle on the way. From Ballater, we flew south to Eyemouth, Berwickshire. It was the middle of October and we found our licensed stubble field waterlogged, although it had been dry and hard surfaced when I inspected if for licensing earlier in the year. There was a grass field alongside which was quite dry and the same size. Accordingly, we shifted into that. After Sunday operations, a policeman came to the house where I was staying. He informed me that the field we were using was unlicensed and that the licensed field was the waterlogged one next door. I explained our difficulty and pointed out that the licensed field was unsafe to operate from, on account of the soft state of the waterlogged ground, so common sense directed us to use the safe field. 'Sorry, Sir', he said, 'we shall have to report you.'

Such is the red tape of the law on occasions. Here was a situation where we were legally licensed to carry out dangerous flying, but because we chose a safe hard surfaced alternative, of the same dimensions, immediately alongside our licensed field, we were to be summonsed for using our common sense and good judgement. It summed up the fact that the law is 'sometimes an ass'. The need of ground licences was in force to protect the public against dangerous fields being used. The authorities waited until I had returned to Hooton, Cheshire, a month later, before they summonsed me to appear at the court in Duns, Berwickshire, which involved an expensive journey, four times greater than the two pounds they fined me. I pleaded a technical breach of the law for public safety and asked for a nominal fine of 1/0d, without success.

We landed up in Durham in the first week of November 1932 for the last Sunday of flying. It was a filthy day, raining and misty and a dead loss. As soon as the weather cleared, we flew back to Hooton.

That ended my last season of joy-riding for next year was to be the year I had been planning to leave Hooton Park and settle down to live in Inverness. In early December, I received a letter from the General Aircraft Company saying they could guarantee delivery of my monoplane in the early part of April 1933, so I severed my working connection with the North British Aviation Company Limited and flew back to Inverness where I intended to stay until the three airfields were well on their way to completion and to my satisfaction.

I returned from the north of Scotland in the third week of December and left the Moth at Cramlington for its annual overhaul and renewal of its Certificate of Airworthiness. I had found airfield sites at Thurso and at Wick, and had arranged booking agents in Wick at Robertson's Garage on High Street next door to the Station Hotel, which would act as a 'Waiting Room'. At Inverness, Macrae & Dick Limited were attending to the registration of the operating company which was to be known as 'Highland Airways Limited'. Work was proceeding well in preparing the Kirkwall airfield and the ditch was well on the way to being covered over.

The home-bound trip was difficult. At Keith, I ran into fog and landed in a tight field and stayed the night. The sun shone next morning when I took off for the south with my passenger, Miss Pauer, only just scraping over the fence. Approaching the coast south of Aberdeen, we again ran into fog, but we managed to duck underneath it, and fly down the Dee Valley to the coast. We then followed the coastline at a few feet above the sea and with very limited visibility. I was afraid of becoming completely enveloped, and if that had happened I had planned to turn out to sea, climb high and fly inland to the west which was in the clear. At Montrose, the ceiling improved, but on reaching Leuchars there was more fog stretching south so we landed at the RAF airfield and decided to stay the night. Cramlington was reached next day in good weather, the fog having dispersed overnight with a change of wind.

The middle of January 1933 saw me at Croydon inspecting my General Aircraft Company ST4 aircraft which was beginning to take shape. Captain Schofield, the test pilot, was flying down to Cowes again, this time in the company's production metal monoplane, and for the second time I accompanied him and got some dual flying practice in. The plane handled very nicely. The Saunders Roe company officials asked us to lunch and were very interested when they were told of my plans to commence an air service to the north of Scotland. We flew back to Croydon in the afternoon.

Next day I returned by road to Cramlington airfield to collect the Moth after its overhaul. The test flight proved that everything was in good order and I took off for Inverness, via Edinburgh. Heavy snowstorms were encountered and I had to fly around in circles for half an hour waiting for a particularly black storm to pass over the Cheviot Hills. The weather report was not good: heavy continuous snow. So I bedded down in Edinburgh until next day when I managed to get through to Inverness above the clouds in blue sky and sunshine. My presence was needed to take part in the final arrangements for floating the air company.

With that essential business completed, I inspected the work of constructing the airfield which was in progress, and then called on Mr Smith Laing, the Inverness Town Clerk, to congratulate him on the speed at which the airfield was being built. I told him we were planning to commence the Orkney service on 8 May 1933. That afternoon, I left for Hooton Park to finally settle my affairs with the North British Aviation Company Limited.

The beginning of March found me back in Inverness with Miss Pauer as my passenger. I gave a number of short flights in the Moth at Inverness and nearby towns to advertise the coming air service. The Inverness airfield was almost finished and it only remained to drop the telephone wires. I found it a very nice airfield to operate out of and Mr Mackenzie, the burgh surveyor, had made a good job of it. The terms of use were discussed and the Inverness Council were very generous in granting us free use of the airfield for the first year, a low rent for the second year, and a final and very nominal rent thereafter. Wick also did the same for us, but in Kirkwall the same stonewalling influences were at work and we got no financial help from Orkney Council. However, farmer Anderson, the owner of the airfield, was extremely generous to us and made up for the council's omissions.

I have often thought about the official Orkney attitude at that crucial time in as much that Orkney had so much to gain from an air service. After all, only a limited number of the population could have shares in the steamer company whose interest they were evidently trying to protect and which held public power. They little suspected at that time that the North of Scotland Steam Navigation Company Limited, which operated the steamer service, would very soon join the board of Highland Airways Limited. Their managing director, Mr McCallum, became a great supporter of Highland Airways and subsequently gave valuable assistance to the development of the air service.

I returned south at the end of March. Information was awaiting me that our monoplane would be ready at the beginning of April, right on time. I spent three days at Croydon observing the finishing touches being put to the aircraft, registration G-ACEW, and which was subsequently christened *Inverness*. On 7 April 1933, I flew on the test flight with Captain Schofield. After half a dozen take-offs and landings with him, he got out and I made another three landings on my own. Next day, I took off for Hooton Park with Mrs Simons who had come down specially for the flight.

It was a lovely day and we crossed over to the west side of London to Heston airport and from there headed for Stoke-on-Trent airfield, situated seven miles to the east at Meir. There was a pilot there whom I wished to interview in case, within a few months, I might want flying assistance. After the interview, which was purely exploratory and with interest shown, we left for Hooton arriving there in time for tea. We were greeted by the Pobjoy family and Mr Pobjoy was interested as to how the motors had performed on the two hours and twenty minutes flight from Croydon.

Next day, Sunday, Mr Pobjoy, who was known to his friends as 'Pobby', his wife and Mrs Simons, flew over with me to tea at Woodford airfield where the arrival of the Monospar created much interest. Woodford was the home of the Lancashire Flying Club and situated some ten miles south of Manchester. Being a Sunday afternoon, there was a good attendance of club members and we were given a VIP welcome. It was not every day, as one member said, they were honoured with the visit of a twin-engined five-seater aircraft!

On Wednesday 12 April, Engineer Pugh, who was seconded to me by General Aircraft Limited, arrived from Croydon and we left immediately after lunch for Inverness. The first stop was Cramlington, Newcastle, and then on to Edinburgh where we stayed the night, for by now, there was a strong head wind of some forty miles per hour blowing, and it appeared we would not make Inverness before dark. Next afternoon, with a bad weather report, we set off. On reaching Blair Atholl, there was a black snow storm ahead and it appeared as far as the eye could see east and west. Consequently, I altered course and flew east alongside the blizzard and worked my way up to the Dee Valley only to find the black wall of snow still blocking our way to Inverness.

I said to Pugh: 'It doesn't look as if we can get through to Inverness unless we take the long route round the coast. I think we will land in the field I used last year for joy-riding at Banchory and stay the night.'

'Good idea, Captain Fresson,' he said.

So I altered course to the west and came to our field which was well in the fringe of the blizzard.

It was snowing hard, making visibility difficult. I was not sure whether the field was long enough for a plane which stalled at fifty-five miles an hour, so had to make a dummy run. The snow beat on the windscreen and the turbulence was terrific. It was with great difficulty that I managed to turn in the valley in order to get into the wind for landing. The strong wind helped a lot and we settled down in a matter of two hundred yards leaving as much again to spare. We picketed the plane down and hailed a passing motorist who took us into town to the local hotel where mine host of the year before gave us a warm welcome. He produced some extra special Scotch to thaw us out. We were certainly very cold.

Next morning was lovely sunshine. 'Come on Pugh,' I said when we met downstairs. 'Let's get through breakfast quickly and get going before the weather-god changes its mind. It seems in these parts you can't tell from one moment to another what the weather is likely to be.'

We phoned Inverness and were given a good weather report. 'We shall arrive at the Longman airfield at eleven o'clock that morning. Will you send a car to meet us?' I explained about the hold up the night before. Mr Donald said he was worried about our non-arrival, but guessed the weather was the cause. On arrival at the Banchory field, we found the monoplane was surrounded by a number of locals. The wind had died down and, in place of the strong westerly blow of the night before, it now blew gently from the east. 'Would the Monospar clear the four foot stone dyke at the end of the available run in time?' I worried. I had not as yet determined exact unstick performances in the short time I had been flying the plane as all my landings and take-offs had been at proper airfields with plenty of room to spare.

I first paced the field out. It was just four hundred yards. The petrol tanks were not full and there was only one passenger. I thought about my previous take-offs at Croydon, Hooton and Meir and guessed the plane was taking about 350 yards to get unstuck.

'Come on Pugh,' I said, 'I think she will just do it.'

We got the tail right up against the west dyke, opened the engines up after a good warming with the brake full on, and then I let go. The tail came up quickly and we were off the ground a little over half way down the field. I climbed the plane hard to 5,000 feet and made off on a direct course for Inverness. Passing over some high mountains, we picked up the Spey Valley by Grantown-on-Spey and within forty minutes of leaving Banchory we were circling Inverness in brilliant sunshine at twenty minutes to eleven, ahead of our schedule.

I hung around over Macrae & Dick's garage for a while to let them know we had arrived, and then passed over the airfield preparatory to effecting a landing, when I espied a car and two or three people standing on the edge of the airfield. On landing, Robert Donald and Willie Hamilton came forward to welcome us and they looked pleased with the trim monoplane I had brought up. 'So you ran into bad weather,' Donald said to me. 'It was not looking at all good here yesterday afternoon and there was a big storm raging just over the hills. I think you did the wise thing putting down at Banchory.' That morning the day was perfect and Inverness looked like a fairy town from the air, glittering in the sun, with the Moray Firth blue as blue could be, lapping almost up to its back door and along the edge of the Longman airfield. 'Let's get the plane into the shed, Pugh,' I said. To do this we had to fold the wings. To save initial cost, I had the smallest hangar possible made to house our first aircraft. The wings folded very easily and quickly, and in no time we had the plane inside. It was arranged that I would give Donald a flight that afternoon.

Next day we had our first board meeting. The Company was registered and the directors were Dr Alexander of Elgin, Chairman; myself as Managing Director; Mr R Donald, Director; Mr R Wotherspoon, Director and Legal Advisor; and Mr W Hamilton, Secretary. Offices were provided at Macrae & Dick's garage, Academy Street. It was agreed that we should commence the first service on Monday 8th May 1933, a little over three weeks ahead. In the meantime, I was to give local flights to show and advertise the aircraft, and get the people of Inverness interested in flying. The local newspapers co-operated loyally and their reports were quoted in the national papers, which generated the publicity that we required.

On 22 April, a Saturday afternoon, I visited Tain and initiated 161 passengers to become potential air travellers. During the ten days of operations at Inverness airport, we carried three hundred and fifty-eight passengers on ninety-four flights.

We next visited Elgin for two days and one hundred and fifty one of its inhabitants took to the air. Kirkwall became the next port of call for one afternoon when only forty passengers booked flights. The following day, we flew to Golspie via Thurso and Wick. On that trip I had my first real taste of coastal fog and was obliged to fly above it at 2,000 feet. Fortunately it cleared south of Helmsdale and the weather was clear for the Golspie operations. There was great interest and keenness for such a small place. I was kept going hard for the whole afternoon, carrying no less that one hundred and sixty-one passengers in three and a quarter hours of continuous flying.

Comparing the forty passengers at Kirkwall with the other towns visited, it was easy to see how little interest Kirkwall took in this tour. And yet, when I had given short flights there last year, the support was excellent. It seemed only too apparent, the same influential interest was still acting against the proposed air service. However, after we had been operating a short while and the mail contract was granted, Kirkwall redeemed itself, and they took to the air like ducks to water. Also, they turned out to be very loyal to Highland Airways in the competition we had to combat later on.

These happenings I have recorded were the last of the lengthy preparations for, two days later on 8 May 1933, the air service became an established fact.

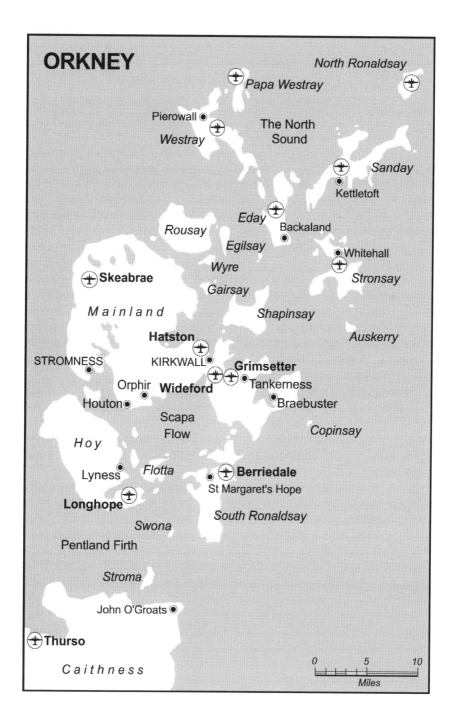

ORKNEY

North Ronaldsay

Papa Westray

Pierowall

Westray

The North
Sound

Sanday

Kettletoft

Eday

Rousay

Backaland

Egilsay

Whitehall

Wyre

Stronsay

Skeabrae

Gairsay

Mainland

Shapinsay

Auskerry

Hatston

STROMNESS

KIRKWALL

Grimsetter

Orphir

Wideford

Tankerness

Houton

Braebuster

Scapa
Flow

Copinsay

Hoy

Lyness

Flotta

Berriedale

St Margaret's Hope

Longhope

South Ronaldsay

Swona

Pentland Firth

Stroma

John O'Groats

Thurso

Caithness

0   5   10

Miles

5

Launch of Highland Airways

The day dawned fine and sunny. My thoughts on that morning, as I was dressing in the Queensgate Hotel, were apprehensive to say the least. My journeying backwards and forwards in the Moth left me in little doubt that I was up against a really tough proposition and some of the worst weather to be found in the British Isles, which I would have to combat on my own. When the visibility was down to almost zero, I had no radio facilities to assist me, which would have enabled me to climb into or above the clouds to a safe altitude and 'home' on the station for which I was heading I was. Neither did I possess the Sperry artificial horizon and directional gyro, which are installed in all modern aircraft and are essential for accurate control of the aircraft in cloud. Under such circumstances, one was confined to crawling along, low down under the overcast and on misty or foggy days, when visibility was down to a few hundred yards, piloting became very difficult and was a severe strain on me.

I was to have more than my share of that type of flying in order to maintain a high enough degree of regularity which would enable me to claim the coveted mail contract at the end of the first year's operations.

My thoughts wandered on. 'This won't do,' I said to myself. 'Don't shy at your hurdles until you reach them,' To raise my morale to a higher level, I wound up my portable gramophone and put on the first movement of Dohnányi's Piano Concerto 'Variations on a Nursery Theme', the theme of which, of course, is based on the nursery tune of 'Ba Ba Black Sheep'. The calm this music created within me soon restored my confidence and I was quickly dressed and ready for breakfast.

By the time we got down to the Longman airfield, there was a sizeable crowd gathered to witness the opening ceremony.

The most urgent matter I had to attend to was the loading of the *Scotsman* newspapers. We had a load of some 70 lbs, specially done up in bundles not exceeding six inches thick. This was essential because we had to load the bundles into the special tray which was designed and attached underneath the seating compartment of the aircraft and only some eight inches deep so that it would not interrupt the airflow of the fuselage. This special tray was necessary as there was no room inside the plane when carrying a full load of four passengers and their luggage. Mr Chisholm, the *Scotsman* despatch manager, was present to see that his company's interests were properly looked after. Mr George Law had seen to that. He also brought a letter from Mr Law wishing me the best of good luck on this first trip and for the future.

Provost Macdonald and his wife officiated at the proceedings on behalf of the town council and Mrs Macdonald christened the monoplane *Inverness*. The official opening of the airport was left over to the middle of June.

I quote the press report of the proceedings on that auspicious morning:

To the North by Air
Epoch Making Plane Service
Inverness Linked with Orkney

9th May 1933. History was made yesterday by the opening of the air service between Inverness and Orkney, the double journey occupying somewhat under two and a half hours.

In a perfect May morning, the beautiful twin-engined monoplane *Inverness* of Highland Airways Limited, took the air from the Longman Municipal Aerodrome. Appropriately christened with 'Highland Dew' by Mrs Macdonald, wife of Provost Macdonald, the plane set off promptly at ten o'clock with three passengers and the pilot, Captain E E Fresson, on board. The passengers were Sir Edmund Findlay, Bt., of the *Scotsman*, Mr Douglas S Gabriel of the Anglo American Oil Company and Mr D Smith of the White Horse Whisky Company. A large and representative gathering was present at the christening ceremony and the Town Council was represented by Bailie A A Noble, Dean of Guild John Mackenzie; Councillors H A Braine, H Munro and N D Mackintosh; Mr G Smith-Laing, Town Clerk; Mr James Maxwell, Town Chamberlain; Mr D Mackenzie Reid, Town Clerk Deputy; Deputy Chief Constable Wm Dalgleish, and Mr Wm Emm, County Assessor; Dr Alexander, Elgin, Chairman of Highland Airways Limited; Mr R Donald, director and Mr Robert Wotherspoon, director and legal advisor to the company and Mr Wm Hamilton, secretary, were also present.

Bailie Noble remarked that the delightful morning was a happy augury for the success of the venture. 'Captain Fresson,' he said, 'was regarded as the pioneer of air service in the North of Scotland.' He deserved their congratulations for the enthusiasm and the initiative he had shown in promoting the air service from Inverness to the far north. The air service was deserving of every success. Not only was it of incalculable value to businessmen but also to the ordinary person who wished to see the far places of his own country. 'It takes a long time by ordinary mode of travel to reach the Orkney Islands,' said Bailie Noble, 'but by the air service it is only a matter of an hour or so. I was only once in the Orkneys and at that time there was such a storm that I had to stay longer than I anticipated. However, I would welcome the opportunity of exploring the delightful islands and this makes such a journey possible. I hope and trust that this service will be so successful that the promoters will extend it so that it will include the Western Isles. I would like to see His Majesty's Mail being loaded on the plane this morning, but as an old Post Office official myself, I know that their motto is 'Wait and See' (laughter). Well, I am sure they will not have long to wait to see how successful the service is (applause).'

With a bottle of whisky in place of the traditional champagne, Mrs Macdonald christened the plane *Inverness*. 'This is a unique occasion in the history of transport in the Highlands. It will bring the remotest part of Scotland to our front door. I wish the service every success.' The bottle crashed on the propeller of one of the motors and liberally besprinkled it with the 'Dew of the Highlands'.

Dr Alexander, who returned thanks to the Council for the great interest they had shown in the venture and the facilities they provided, foreshadowed an extension of the service to the Western Isles. Captain Fresson also spoke warmly, thanking Mrs Macdonald and Sir Edmund Findlay for their interest. Captain Fresson's time from Inverness to Wick was 50 minutes. A stop of fifteen minutes was made at Wick and the completed flying time to Orkney was one hour and fifteen minutes. Weather conditions were not good between Helmsdale and Latheron but cleared up by the time Wick was reached. The plane flew at 200 feet above the sea for fifteen miles to keep under the overcast. On the return journey the weather south of Wick had improved, and the elapsed time for the Kirkwall-Inverness journey was one hour twelve minutes. The plane landed at Inverness at twenty minutes past five in the afternoon. This was not the regular time of returning, but was made so as to suit the convenience of the passengers. Both Mr Gabriel and Mr Smith conducted business in the town of Kirkwall before flying back to Inverness. The Inverness landed at Hillhead, Wick. The passengers were delighted with the trip and praised the scenery between Inverness and Wick which they described as unexpectedly beautiful.

Fine weather prevailed at Kirkwall when Mr J Storer Clouston of Orphir, the novelist and Convenor of the County, with Provost John M Slater of Kirkwall, extended a welcome at Wideford Airport to the passengers of the plane and the pilot.

Such was the version of the press and it depicts an accurate account of the first trip with the exception of the last reference. Provost Slater cut me dead on arrival and I do not think Mr Storer Clouston noticed me, he was so taken up with Sir Edmund Findlay. It was in line at that time with the hard core against air transport, already described during the early days. I suspect the Provost was interested in other means of transport. Whatever it was, I got no support from him for some time to come.

The deterioration of weather mentioned between Helmsdale and Latheron was similar to that experienced on my first trip up north in the Avro 504K described in Chapter Two and I had noticed it on several occasions during my journeys in the DH Moth. I knew by then what I had to cope with and acted accordingly.

For the remaining twenty-three days of May, I had my fair share of bad weather. No less than ten days were either foggy or I encountered extremely heavy rain storms along the route. On several occasions I climbed above the fog hoping for a hole to fly down through on reaching Kirkwall. The foggy weather usually started at Helmsdale so on those occasions it was worth trying to fly above the murk as the weather to the south was clear and one could always return safely. On the really bad days, when we had fog from Inverness all the way up the coast, I would take a run up in my car to Culloden Moor to see if the weather was free of fog. I had a landing field located there alongside the famous battlefield so, when Inverness was fogbound and Culloden Moor in the clear, I would take off and climb through the fog which was seldom more than three hundred feet high. On returning I would land in the field at Culloden Moor. A car would meet us and the journey to Inverness would be completed by road.

On 24 May, I had my first miss and the Kirkwall trip was not completed, the weather being clamped down at Kirkwall. After service hours during the early days, we organised short flights around the countryside in our continued effort to make the people air-travel conscious. That particular afternoon we were booked to fly at Kingussie. It was raining hard with low cloud over the mountains, but nevertheless I managed to reach that place. In spite of the rain, the locals turned up in their hundreds. With the windscreen of the plane blurred with water, which made taking off and landing very difficult, 112 passengers were carried in three hours flying. We returned to Inverness at dusk and had difficulty in scraping over the Slochd pass through the rain-swept clouds enveloping the hills.

By the end of May, we had carried one hundred and forty three passengers on the daily service and through a particularly bad spell of weather. I had thus proved that it was possible to maintain a regular service by flying in contact with the ground and sea during bad visibility. But, as I have said, it was a nerve-wearing form of flying that I disliked intensely.

The first half of June produced an improvement in the weather and on 17 June 1933, the Duke and Duchess of Sutherland officially opened the Inverness Longman airfield. After flying hours for the past month, I had worked long into the night with the help of a secretary organising that event. A big air display was planned and it was advertised from Cape Wrath to Wick in the north and a line drawn across the map from Dundee to Fort William in the south. My good friend Mr Donald was getting a bit anxious over the money I was spending on advertising and one day he asked me how many people I expected to draw at the gate for which a charge of admission was levied. My answer of 20,000 amazed him. I can see his look of incredulity as he shot back at me, 'If you get 2,000 in these parts you'll be lucky.' 'Inverness is not like the south, you know,' he warned me. It was left at that and I went ahead.

An air pageant ball was given at the Station Hotel the Friday night before the event. At 8/- per head, it was crowded, which I thought a good omen for the next day's air display. I had arranged for many well-known fliers to come up from England as our guests and John Tranum, the well known parachutist, arrived to do a drop. Next day, Saturday, a luncheon party was given by the town council to the Duke and Duchess and local celebrities. Mr Donald, Mr Hamilton and myself were invited, although I felt I should have been at the airport to keep an eye on catering for the crowds I expected to attend. I left early for the Longman airfield only to find that a crowd of thousands of people had crashed through the gate and were enjoying a free view of the proceedings to come. They were also along the road adjoining the airfield, which had been closed by the authorities for the day. I quickly gathered all the police I could and marched them across the aerodrome to the end of the road situated alongside the airport. We closed arms and marched forward, holding the barbed wire barrier in front of us, the police at the same time shouting to the crowd to get back. Gradually, they retreated and at last we got them behind the houses on the Longman Road. We then admitted them after payment of the admission fee. My early departure from an uneasy lunch had saved a substantial part of the gate money. It was later estimated from the air, that there were at least 20,000 spectators present.

On the programme which followed, I cannot do better than quote Mr C G Grey, then editor of the magazine, *The Aeroplane*, in the issue dated 21st June, 1933:

On 17 June, the municipal airport of Inverness was opened officially by His Grace the Duke of Sutherland, who was accompanied by the Duchess, and thus a fresh step forward was marked in the history of British Civil Aviation. Actually the meeting began on Friday 16th, when certain brave visitors found their way to Inverness by air in spite of the weather. The first arrival was on Thursday, when Mrs Fairlie landed her Klemm. She came from Heston, West London, and brought Miss Stephenson of the Newcastle Club with her. Surely a good omen for the future of the Airport. Early on Friday, Mr Ivor McClure of the AA and Mr Elwell of National Benzole got through, followed by Mr Dick Bentley of the Shell Organisation, and Mr Cree of the Scottish Flying Club. Four Wapitis of No. 603 City of Edinburgh Bomber Squadron, Auxiliary Air Force also got through.

That night the Directors of Highland Airways gave a Grand Ball at the Station Hotel. It was a very cheery affair and kept going until 03.00 hours. There is no real darkness in those latitudes at this time of year, so all went to bed in broad daylight.

On Saturday, Captain Fresson was stage manager, box office manager, property man, call boy, leading comedian and everything else for the display. Dick Bentley took the *Scotsman* newspapers to the Orkneys in Highland Airways' Moth. Lots of people arrived by air – considering that there were three or four important meetings in England to keep the Sassenachs at home or to tempt the Scotsmen to go south. Long before the opening hour, hordes of people arrived by car and on foot, to the embarrassment of the inexperienced gatekeepers and ineffective policemen. Judging by their handling of the crowd on the aerodrome, I should think they are ex shepherds. Happily Macrae & Dick's huge garage affords a haven of refuge from them. It is a splendidly run affair and Mr R Donald, who is in charge, was an officer of the RFC and RAF at the great engine depot at Pont de L'Arche during the 1914/18 war, so aviators are always welcome there, apart from Mr Donald's connection with Highland Airways Limited.

The first event was an excellent display of flight formation of 603 Bomber Squadron given by Flt Lt T M McNeil, Fg. Offs G A Reid and Allen Wallace. In spite of a gusty wind, their flight formations line astern – echelon right and left – and in line abreast were close and neat. Flt Lt McNeil's leading was excellent. He took the formation round so that it could be seen to the best advantage by everyone, and when the flight broke up to land, by diving in turn out of a right echelon, it was done most effectively in front of the enclosure. Thereafter Captain Fresson, heavily disguised and in a Moth, showed how a local lady and without knowledge of flying should not make her first solo flight. It was very funny and the crowds were in fits of laughter, including the Duke and Duchess. Then Mr Bentley did some very pretty flying in a Comper Swift (Pobjoy motor) which must have educated the crowd. After which he went off over the surrounding scenery, partly, he said, to prevent the crowd stamping on his machine.

After that, an 'Old Soldier' deputised for another aviator who had not arrived and gave in the Highland 'Moth' one of the best exhibitions of crazy flying I have ever seen.

After several other displays of trick flying, came Mr Tranum's parachute drop from a 'Spartan' aircraft piloted by Captain Fresson. He had travelled all night and most of the day, having done a jump at Eastbourne the previous day. As usual his judgement of speed and distance was excellent, even though he landed in a cabbage patch on the edge of the aerodrome.

After that Captain Fresson started joy-riding in the Monospar. Midland & Scottish Air Ferries Limited (Mr Sword's excellently run show) carried lots of passengers in an Air Speed Ferry, a DH Fox Moth and a Spartan, and the Scottish Motor Traction Company's three seater Avro Cadet and Fox Moth carried some few less.

On Saturday evening Highland Airways Limited gave a dinner to the visiting pilots. The versatile Captain Fresson took the chair. He thanked the visitors for helping him to make the show such a success and his friends in Inverness who had acted as stewards and had helped generally with the ground work. Mr Ivor McClure expressed the pleasure that all the visitors felt at being present at the opening of the first airport in the Highlands, and he congratulated Captain Fresson on organising and running such a successful affair single handed. And so said all of us. CGG (Editor)

That all happened on the Saturday. By Monday the visitors had returned south and we got back to normal.

June was a mixed month for weather, but there were no missed flights. Passengers increased to 206 for the month and then 3rd July brought disaster which rudely shook the confidence I was beginning to feel. On that day, I left Inverness for Kirkwall in fine weather with three passengers, *Scotsman* newspapers and luggage, which constituted a full load. The telephone report from Kirkwall gave fog at our Wideford airfield, but about 70 feet ceiling at Kirkwall at sea level. We ran into the fog at Wick and scuttled across the Pentland Firth under it, reaching Scapa pier and then Kirkwall town. Instead of putting down in the field at Hatston which was at sea level, as I should have done, I chose to follow the road up the hill to Wideford. Soon the plane was completely enveloped in swirling mist and I turned at right angles to the north to slip down the hill towards the sea. We got under it again and had another try to reach Wideford. As I almost reached our airfield, I started to run into swirling mist again and, as there was a nice flat field in front of me and uphill, I put the plane down just over the stone dyke. There was a terrific bump and the plane came to rest. What a sight presented itself when we got out of the aircraft. The two motors were hanging down as if they were falling out of the wings and the undercarriage was twisted and bent. We went back along the line of landing to find out what had happened and discovered there was a shallow pit which was completely overgrown with high grass. The landing wheels had struck about six inches below the sharp edge and the force of impact must have been terrific at the speed we were travelling. No wonder the plane was bent, and what frightful luck, for there was not another rough place in the whole field. Had I been five yards right or left or three feet higher, the plane would have missed that lone hole.

As I stood feeling completely overcome with despair, and with the condolences of my passengers ringing in my ears, figures came running towards us from the road. They turned out to be my car driver and a couple of people who were sightseers on the aerodrome. I told Norn, my driver, that the plane was damaged and to get me into town as quickly as possible. The passengers scrambled in behind and we were soon at our booking office in *The Orcadian* newspaper premises. Mr Mackintosh, the owner, was very kindly acting as our booking agent and he did this work free for a number of years until we had established ourselves sufficiently to open our own office. I told him what had happened and he was terribly upset as it meant the service might not be able to operate for weeks. The plane would have to be shipped south to Croydon for repairs, and that would give the Jonahs full rein to vent their spite. He was also angry with me, but later when he saw the field and the trap it harboured he graciously withdrew what he had said earlier.

I at once phoned Mr Donald at Macrae & Dick Limited, Inverness, and he suggested that we should endeavour to hire a plane to keep a skeleton service going while our plane was being repaired. 'Why not try Mr John Sword at Renfrew?' he said. Mr Sword, it will be remembered, had been at the opening of Inverness Airport and had a fleet of aircraft including some DH Dragon twin-engined eight-seaters. So I rang John Sword and told him what had happened. 'Can you hire us one of your Dragon aircraft with a pilot?' I enquired.

John Sword was sympathetic. 'Well, Captain Fresson,' he said, 'I'll see what I can do. Hang on while I have a talk with my chief engineer and see what planes we have available. By the way, how long would you want a plane for?'

'The monoplane will have to go back to Croydon for repairs so I should say a month at least.'

'Hold on,' he said, 'I'll only be a minute.' John Sword was back a few minutes later. 'I'm very sorry, but all our Dragon aircraft are in use. We are short of that type of plane as there are two undergoing annual overhaul. I can let you have a four-seater Fox Moth which, incidentally, carries the same load as your monoplane – along with Captain Coleman as pilot – during your absence in the south.'

'Let me think that one out for a minute,' I answered. I thought hurriedly. The Fox Moth certainly carried four passengers as was the case with our damaged plane, but it had no extra accommodation for newspapers, in the form of a newspaper tray, as did our aircraft. That meant we would have to forego one seat on the northbound journey, which would be used for loading *The Scotsman*. There was nowhere else where I could obtain a relief plane at a moment's notice so the Fox Moth had to do. Anything, I reasoned, would be better than closing the air service down so soon after commencing while repairs were carried out to our damaged monoplane. So, I picked up the phone, 'Are you there Mr Sword?'

'Yes,' he replied.

'We'll gratefully accept your offer. When can you send the Fox Moth up?'

'Right away,' came the reply.

'And how much will you charge?' I enquired.

'Don't bother about that,' he said. 'Wait and see how many hours the Fox Moth flies while in your service. You can trust me not to charge you too much'. With that, we hung up.

'Have you got a plane?' Mr Mackintosh enquired.

'Yes,' I answered, 'but we will only have three available seats for the northern run because of *The Scotsman* load.'

'That doesn't matter,' he replied, 'as long as the newspaper gets through. The people here look upon their early delivery of *The Scotsman* with great expectation.'

I felt as if my world had collapsed around me when I again took a look at our wrecked plane. I did not think Cyril Coleman could ever tackle the Orkney weather in a Fox Moth. And then there was the expense of sending our plane back to the makers in London and the cost of repairs. We had very little money in the kitty for such contingencies if the insurance company refused to pay up. They might say, I reasoned, that I should not have been flying in such weather. My ruminations were suddenly interrupted by a slap on the back and a 'Hullo, old chap'. I turned quickly and observed my previous benefactor, 'Surgeon McClure'.

'Cheer up,' he said, evidently seeing the look of despair in my face. 'You'll get over the difficulty somehow. Come up to the house and have lunch with us. A good dram will do you the world of good.'

'That's a good offer,' I replied, glad of the interruption to my thoughts, 'so let's get along to the car.' Within five minutes we reached his home, *Innistore*, on the edge of Kirkwall and I was warmly welcomed by Mrs McClure who introduced me to another visitor, Mr Thomas MacKenzie, chief of Metal Industries at Scapa Flow. It appeared that he was engaged in raising the sunken German warships from the bottom of the Flow where they were scuttled by the German Fleet after World War One. The lunch was a pleasant one and my spirits revived with so much hospitality. Meanwhile, a phone call had come in to say Captain Coleman was on the way, so I hurried up to the airfield to meet him and Engineer Pugh. On their arrival we all went along to see the monoplane *Inverness* lying in the next field over the road, so near and yet so far from safety.

'I'm afraid, Captain Fresson', Coleman said, 'you're not going to have the use of that aircraft again for some time.'

I agreed with him. 'What bad luck.'

Returning to the airfield, we saw him off with the southbound passengers and returned to the crashed plane. A thorough examination showed damage to the engine bearers and undercarriage struts, but we could not be sure about the main stub wing spars which the engine bearers were attached to. I left Pugh to get all the nuts and bolts freed and ready to take the wings off, then went down to town to obtain transport and some men to help lift the wings from the plane. I was back in an hour with a lorry and the men. Pugh had worked fast. Everything was ready for dismantling and we lifted the wings clear of the body and put them on the truck. We thought the undercarriage would stand up in its damaged condition and allow us to tow the fuselage behind the truck, so we pushed it through the gate and got the tail end roped on to the rear of the truck where Pugh sat. I sat behind the cab ready to signal the driver if anything went wrong and we wished to stop quickly. All went well, however, until we came to the edge of the town when another vehicle appeared coming towards us. There was not enough room for him to get by as the stub wings stretched right across the road. So, I had to jump off and get the driver of the oncoming car to back on to the main road, a short way off, which allowed us to pass. Then we were all set for a straight run to the edge of the town. I went ahead to keep the narrow streets of Kirkwall clear to the wharf and quay.

We put the plane on the quay with the wings standing on their leading edges each side, and covered it with tarpaulins. The North of Scotland Shipping Company, who were our competitors and who would have to carry the damaged monoplane to Aberdeen, were extremely nice to me. Far from being in a gloating mood over my misadventure, they did all they could to help and made special arrangements for the plane to be loaded on to the *SS St Magnus* which was arriving from Shetland next day. They were wondering about the length of the fuselage and where to stow it, but when the captain arrived he soon figured that difficulty out.

We set off by sea to Aberdeen next day along with the damaged plane. I appeared to be an object of interest to the passengers, but I have always wondered what they really thought. 'So much damage in such a short while.' Well, the next time was a very, very long while, because in the following fifteen years I did no further damage to my aircraft and I flew in far worse weather than that which was the cause of my present predicament.

On arrival in Aberdeen, Pugh and I supervised the transfer of the damaged plane from *SS St Magnus* to the London steamer and, when that was completed, we returned to Inverness by road. Arrangements were made over the phone and by letter with the General Aircraft Company Limited to effect repairs as quickly as possible and there is little doubt they must have dropped everything and given us first priority for the repairs were finished early August.

Captain Coleman reported to me on my return to Inverness and he had managed so far to keep an unbroken schedule, although he had been bothered a lot by fog. In fact he had put up a splendid show on the single-engined Fox Moth. I hated to think what would have happened if motor trouble had been experienced in that kind of weather.

A search then commenced for another plane to take the place of the monoplane, *Inverness*. Through the firm of Brian Lewis & C D Barnard Limited at Heston airfield, we located another Monospar, G-ABVH, and as we were negotiating to buy a DH Dragon eight-seater plane from that firm they hired it to us for a very nominal sum. So, on 15 July, twelve days after my misfortune in Orkney, I left Heston airport in the replacement Monospar and flew it to the de Havilland factory at Stag Lane airfield, near Hendon. After inspecting our new airplane on the stocks, I went home to my parents at Northwood for the night. They were having tea when I arrived. As my mother went out to get me a cup, Pater said, 'My son, you look well. What brings you south? Why didn't you let us know you were coming?'

'I couldn't', I said, 'as I was not sure I would be able to get out and see you until the last minute, you see. I have come to collect another airplane.' And then I told him of the accident I had had at the beginning of last month. They were worried.

'You're taking awful risks,' the old man said. 'Those islands have always had a bad name for stormy weather.'

'I know. But now I am getting to know what I am up against, I can guard against those risks. I have organised forced-landing grounds all along the route and, if I get caught out by weather again, I shall always have somewhere to put down and wait until the weather improves.'

'It sounds bad sort of country up there.'

'Oh, I don't know. Once you get to know it and its ways, it's not too bad, except, of course, on the odd occasion, but when the time comes and we can obtain wireless facilities, it will be a cinch.' My parents seemed a bit reassured at that remark.

Mother said, 'you're getting wireless?'

'Well, not just yet, but once we get that mail contract, we shall have a very good case with which to press the Air Ministry to obtain it.'

At that moment, my young daughter Betty came running in. She too was surprised to see me and greeted me shyly. Betty had lost her mother in 1920 in Shanghai when she was only three months old and I had sent her home with friends to my parents who had looked after her for me since then.

'Hello, Daddy,' she said, 'what a surprise seeing you, I've only just got back from school.' 'How long are you staying?' she enquired.

'I'm afraid, Betty dear, only tonight. I have to leave for Inverness early tomorrow morning. I am delivering a new airplane from Stag Lane.' And then I had to tell her all about the accident to the monoplane, *Inverness*.

She said, 'Can I fly up with you tomorrow, Daddy?'

I shook my head, 'No, I'm afraid you can't leave your lessons in the middle of term, but you can come up later on with your granny for the summer holidays'. That pleased her, for she ran up and hugged me.

I bid them farewell in the morning and hurried out to Stag Lane airfield. The de Havilland factory told me they hoped to finish our new DH84 plane by the end of the month, and it was arranged that one of the Brian Lewis pilots should fly it up to Turnhouse, Edinburgh, and I would collect and fly it up to Inverness. This was quite a different plane to the Monospar monoplane *Inverness*. It was a biplane and had a large fuselage with eight comfortable seats and room for mail and luggage behind. It was powered by two 130 hp Gipsy Major de Havilland engines and would cruise at 100 mph. It also enjoyed a good range of four hundred miles and was fitted with Sperry cloud flying instruments, ready for the day when we obtained radio facilities. The advent of this airplane with its comfortable seating and plenty of legroom immediately boosted our traffic and reduced our operating costs and it was not long before we were obliged to add another to our fleet.

I set off from Stag Lane airfield in the ST4 monoplane around eleven, arriving at Cramlington in time for a late lunch. I met Connie Lethart of the Cramlington Aircraft Company whose company, it will be remembered, used to carry out the Certificate of Airworthiness for Moth G-AAWO. She was most interested in our air service to the Orkneys and kept me chatting quite a while.

The weather north was reasonably good so I set off for Inverness, taking a direct course across the mountains. On arrival, I was pleasantly surprised to see Brian Lewis & C D Barnard's Dragon G-ACCE, and their sales representative, Bill Gairdner, who was piloting the airplane. He had apparently arrived several days before to see me, but as I was away, he stayed on and gave a helping hand to Captain Coleman in the Fox Moth as the traffic had completely swamped the carrying capacity of his small machine. Bill Gairdner remained for a few days extra, and that gave me an opportunity to fly the Dragon over the air route and put in some practice handling the plane, ready for the delivery of our own Dragon.

Captain Coleman bid us goodbye next morning and returned to Renfrew. He had done exceedingly well and I shall never forget his great service, while I was south, in maintaining an unbroken schedule during two weeks of continuous fog in that little single-engined plane. His personal skill in maintaining the Orkney run undoubtedly saved Highland Airways, for public confidence was maintained. It would have been shattered for some considerable time had we broken the continuity owing to that unfortunate mishap in the fog with our monoplane. The maintenance of continuity had also impressed the postal officials whom we were told were watching our operations very closely.

After several days operating the Dragon to Kirkwall, it was obvious that it was an ideal plane for the job. It was an easy and delightful plane to fly and had a remarkable take-off with full load which fitted in very well with our small airfields. Even in the few days the Brian Lewis plane had been on the run, there was a noticeable increase in our bookings and so I looked forward to the delivery of our new Dragon, G-ACIT, at the end of the month.

With the advent of that aircraft we would require another pilot, so I sent for the one I had interviewed at Meir, Stoke-on-Trent. He arrived on the morning train and I met him and took him to the hotel where I had booked him in. We got talking about the route and I suggested that, as I had a spare seat on the service at ten o'clock next day, he might like to come along, I could give him some dual instruction on the Monospar and he could also take a look at the route. I did the flying on the north trip. It was a good day and we had no trouble in reaching Kirkwall. I was informed we had a full load for the return trip so the new pilot had to stay behind, but he didn't appear to mind. I learned afterwards, he made straight for the Kirkwall Hotel bar. When I returned later in the afternoon to fetch him, our car driver told me he had difficulty in getting him away to take him up to the airfield so I had to wait a while for the car bringing pilot 'A' from the town. I thought he looked a bit queer, but after we had settled down on the return trip I handed the controls over to him. We seemed to steer a very zigzag course and he did not appear able to keep the plane in a horizontal position. First one wing would drop and then the other. I kept on telling him, but it did not appear to make much difference. The limit came when we reached Inverness and he tried to land in a large field some three miles to the west of Inverness Longman airport. He kept on insisting that this field was the airport and became angry when I took control and landed at our base. Out of the plane, he complained of not feeling well. I was suspicious, and took him round to our doctor for attention. I left him there and Dr Mitchell said he would see him back to his hotel. Next day, I met Dr Mitchell and asked him what was wrong with my new pilot. 'Drunk', he said, 'drunk as a tick.' That explanation confirmed my suspicions and so our friend was hustled south on the afternoon express. He must have had a real innings at the Kirkwall Hotel while waiting for my return.

I had to look quickly for another pilot, but where? They did not grow on trees. Luck, however, favoured me. I was in Aberdeen a day or two later and, on the outskirts of the town, I observed a three-seater airplane giving joy-rides off Anderson Drive. So I looked in to see who was operating it. I recognised the joy-ride firm's name but did not recognise the pilot. I watched him for a time and I thought to myself, that chap is no novice at the game, let's go and have a chat with him. Without disclosing who I was, in between passenger loads we got into conversation. His engineer called him Captain Holmes, but I could not recall having met him before. 'You appear to be busy, Captain Holmes.'

'Yes, we are not doing too badly', he replied, 'would you like a trip?'

I excused myself and got him talking. He told me he was flying for Scottish Motor Traction at Edinburgh and had several thousand hours flying to his credit, most of which I gathered had been gained with the RAF. What interested me mostly was the fact that, in his log book, he had quite a few hours flying DH84 aircraft (Dragons). I just had to have a pilot quickly, so I took the plunge.

'Would you like a job on the Inverness-Orkney Service?' I asked him. The question appeared to shake him, but I could see he was interested. He thought for a moment.

'Why? Have you anything to do with Highland Airways?' he asked me. I then told him who I was.

'Glad to meet you, Captain Fresson', he said, shaking me by the hand, 'I have read and heard a lot about you and have been hoping to meet you. Yes, your offer interests me. No future in what I'm doing at present. When would you want me?' I explained we had a new Dragon arriving at the end of the month and I should require his services immediately.

'Well, I don't know about that. You see, I have undertaken to carry out this job for another month. What would the salary be?' I told him a figure and made it clear we did not give flying pay as was the case with the joy riding companies.

I liked him for his frankness and loyalty to the job he had undertaken, so I said to him, 'I suggest you get in touch with your employers, be frank with them and ask how quickly they can release you and then let me know. Here is my phone number.'

'Right', he said, 'I will do that.' Within a week of my return to Inverness, Captain Holmes phoned me to say he had obtained his release from his employers and he would report to Inverness at beginning of the week.

At the end of the month, I went by car to Turnhouse airfield with six friends to collect our Dragon and, as we arrived, it came in from the south piloted by Bill Gairdner. I first met him at Hooton Park when he was Brian Lewis & C D Barnard's local manager. Bill told me I had got a first class plane in G-ACIT and the engines were particularly sweet, he said. Some years later, when the rail and air interests merged with Highland Airways he joined the new company, Scottish Airways of which Highland Airways became a member. After a chat and having handed over the documents of the aircraft, he left me. He planned to catch a train back to London that evening. Having got my friends on board, we took off and flew up to Edzell in Angus where we landed for tea, arriving in Inverness in time for dinner. My passengers were delighted with the trip and they commented on the comfort of the Dragon airplane.

Three days later, G-ACIT went into service on the Orkney run flown by Captain Holmes. I continued for a while to fly the monoplane as an 'extra'. The question now arose as to the best means of financing the DH84 Dragon. £3,000 had to be found. Inverness interests would go half of the way, so I suggested to Mr Donald that, on Sunday, we should fly over in the Moth and land at Mr Law's shooting lodge at Achintoul, in the hinterland of Sutherlandshire. I had already made one visit in the Monospar and had managed to get down and off, light-loaded on the heather moorland which was pretty rough. I phoned Mr Law to say we were proposing to pay him a visit.

'Splendid,' he said, 'I have some guests here for the week-end. Come and have lunch.'

We duly arrived over the lodge in DH Moth, G-AAWO, just after midday, Sunday, and landed up the hill on the moorland field by the side of the lodge. There were quite a few guests and the party developed into a good one, so much so, that Mr Donald did not espy me sneak off into another room after lunch with Mr Law for a talk.

When we were seated, Mr Law said, 'What is the trouble, Captain Fresson?'

I told him about the new airliner we had acquired.

'It carries eight passengers in armchair comfort,' I said 'and could carry more *Scotsman* newspapers.'

I explained that it would be ideal for carrying the mail contract which we expected to obtain next spring. However, we had to raise our capital to pay for this new and better airplane and I had flown over to ask him if he would take up some shares in Highland Airways Limited. I also told him we had been operating a DH84 Dragon for the past two weeks on loan to us from Brian Lewis and our passenger traffic had increased almost overnight as a result of this larger and more comfortable plane. George Law listened intently and asked me a few questions about our operations. Suddenly, he turned from looking out of the window and said to me:

'Captain Fresson, Mr Chisholm, our circulation manager tells me you have carried *The Scotsman* regularly since the service started two months ago and I hear the people in Orkney are delighted. So much so, that the demand for our paper has increased. I am very pleased with you. I think you are right about the larger aircraft. How much do you want?'

'One thousand pounds', I said quickly, holding my breath.

'You can have it', and on the spot he wrote me a cheque. 'You can tell your secretary, Mr Hamilton, to send the share certificates to me at Edinburgh.'

I was well pleased with the outcome of the visit and exceedingly relieved.

'Thank you.' I said, 'I am sure you will not regret your kind support. If you wish to increase the *Scotsman* load, we will of course see that it is carried even though it may mean off-loading a passenger.'

'I will speak to our circulation manager, Mr Chisholm,' he replied. 'I'm sure he will wish to take advantage of your offer. I think it is now time we joined the others or they will begin to think we have deserted them.'

Two years later, when Highland Airways amalgamated with United Airways, Mr Law received fifteen hundred pounds back, for his one thousand pound investment. I was proud to have repaid his faith in me so well. We stayed over until afternoon tea then Mr Donald said he thought we should be getting back to Inverness.

Having said goodbye to the guests and Mr Law, we all walked out to the Moth. The motor started at first swing and, after strapping ourselves in, we taxied the plane up the rough ground to the top of the hill and made ready for take off. There was about three hundred yards of rough heather ground to get off in. With the extra weight of a fairly heavy passenger, and the rough going, I felt anxious as I opened the throttle. Would the Moth make it? There would be no second chance once we were well underway. The plane gathered speed slowly, half way down the slope it had only attained thirty miles an hour and forty-five mph was needed for the Moth to become airborne. The fence rushed up to meet us and still the plane was glued to the ground. I took a quick glance at the airspeed indicator. It showed just over forty mph. It was now or never – 'one good pull on the stick.' At that moment we hit a bad hump, the plane catapulted into the air and then began to sag. Fortunately the ground sloped down over the road to Loch an Ruathair. Easing the control forward, flying speed was attained with the wheels brushing the top of the heather and we began to climb. 'Phew, that was a close shave', I said to myself. From what he said to me on the completion of the flight at Inverness, my passenger thought likewise.

It was a pleasant trip home over the mountains in brilliant sunshine. Picking up the coast at Golspie, we headed over the sea to Cromarty and down the coast to Inverness. Donald, of course, had no knowledge of the successful outcome of our visit, and on our walk up to town from the Longman airport he remarked rather dejectedly: 'That was a very nice lunch and flight, but we haven't got what we went for!'

'Oh, I don't know' I said laconically, 'I don't think we did too badly. This will do to go on with,' I said, handing the folded cheque over.

'What's this?' he said, unfolding it slowly. He stared at the cheque for a moment and did not seem to take it in.

Suddenly the penny dropped, 'By Jove, when did you get this?'

'While you were all taking after lunch.'

'Well, you are a fast worker. Well done,' he said. 'The cost of the Dragon aircraft is now assured.'

'By the way,' I said, 'Mr Law told me he is very pleased with the way the air service is going, especially as far as *The Scotsman* is concerned. He indicated they would be increasing their load immediately. There is little doubt we have a loyal and good friend there!'

On the Tuesday Captain Holmes took over the regular Orkney run, piloting our new Dragon DH 84 aircraft to Kirkwall on its maiden flight. The Dragon airplane was very well received in Orkney and the press had this to say:

Glittering silver and green – the new eight seater cabin plane which Highland Airways have added to the Pentland Firth service, arrived at Kirkwall Airport on Tuesday, 2nd August 1933, from Inverness. The machine made flights to Thurso and Wick with passengers, before returning to Inverness with other passengers for the 3.45 pm and 4.00 pm trains for the south. The pilot was Capt. G B Holmes who recently joined Highland Airways Ltd from the SMT Airplane Service department, Edinburgh. Capt. Fresson the Managing Director, piloted the four seater monoplane which accompanied the new airliner. The monoplane returned immediately to Inverness with passengers who wished to catch an earlier train!! The North Ronaldsay postman who was transferred by air from the Balfour Hospital to the Royal Infirmary, Inverness last week is making satisfactory progress. The following letter sent by Mr Ian H McClure has been received by Highland Airways. 'Thanks very much for taking my patient to Inverness Infirmary today. It will interest you to know that without very rapid facilities for taking him to the appropriate specialist, he would have had to undergo a serious operation entailing about two month's invalidism. I hear the job was done this evening and that he will be home perhaps the end of the week'.

During the middle of August, I returned the borrowed monoplane to Heston as repairs to our plane had been completed and it was awaiting collection at Croydon. It was a dirty trip the whole way with usual low cloud and heavy rain.

The General Aircraft Company had made a good job of G-ACEW and Captain Schofield laughingly said, 'Don't give it any more bumps like the last one. You may not be so lucky next time!!' After a test flight of our repaired aircraft, I bid them adieu and, with Mr Donald as passenger, we commenced the return journey. We had lunch in Edinburgh and then set off from Turnhouse airfield on the last leg. Approaching Perth, the starboard engine packed up. We were flying at around 2,000 feet over the centre of the city.

'We've got to find a field,' I shouted to Donald. 'She won't cross the Grampians on one motor.'

Circling the town, a possible field was spotted on top of the hill to the south and adjacent to the main road leading to the Forth Bridge. As we dropped off height, and approaching the hedge, my passenger shouted, 'Look out! The field is full of cattle!!'

We were too low to start climbing again on the remaining motor, so I shouted back, 'Never mind the cows. I've got to land.'

I caught a glimpse of him out of the corner of my eye and he looked a bit strained. I chose a run between the middle of the pack, hoping they would break, which is precisely what they did.

'There you are,' I said. 'What obliging creatures,' to which Donald heartily agreed.

In no time the usual crowd appeared. Airplanes were still a novelty on the ground in 1933. Having press-ganged two sturdy looking youths to guard the plane, we cadged a lift into town and telephoned Inverness. Engineer Pugh was soon on his way by road with a spare engine and arrived before dark. The job of changing the motor was completed next morning. Taking Pugh with us, we were soon back in Inverness.

In September, I again met my old friend, Peter Angus, who had hired the Avro 504K in 1931 to take him from Thurso to Kirkwall and back for a business call. He wanted to know if I could fly him to Brora for another commercial appointment. I didn't know of any landing place at Brora, but I knew from passing over Brora on my trips to Kirkwall that the fields there were exceedingly small and undulating. Nevertheless, we set off in the Moth and, a mile out on the Helmsdale road, found a somewhat tight field to land on. I went into the village with my passenger and waited at the Grand Hotel. Within an hour he was back, having made good use of his time and no doubt helped by the usual publicity the flight had brought him. Encouraged by this and the Thurso business air trip, Peter again pressed me in to service on 3 October to fly him to Shetland. I had not been to Shetland before, but knew it was possible to land on the links at Sumburgh, some 25 miles south of Lerwick. Peter Angus first wished to visit Kirkwall en route for business calls. We stayed the night in Kirkwall and left for Lerwick the following morning. Half way across the sea to Fair Isle, we ran into

low rain cloud and, without radio assistance, it was too chancy looking for the narrow landfall of Shetland under such conditions. From my early days in aviation, I always remembered an advertisement in one of the aviation magazines on behalf of one of the insurance companies which announced: 'The wise pilot is always he who knows when to turn back.' I took the hint on that occasion and we returned and landed on the island of Sanday, staying at the Kettletoft Hotel for the night. The field we landed in was most conveniently adjacent to the hotel's front door. Ultimately, that field became our landing ground for the island service.

Next day, the weather improved and we again set off and found good weather over the fifty-eight miles of open sea. Fair Isle soon came into sight and, through the haze to the north, I could discern Fitful Head, the southernmost point of Shetland. As we approached Sumburgh Head, where the landing field was situated, Peter said, 'Let's go up to the island of Bressay, just across the sound from Lerwick, and see if you can land there. I know of a number of flat fields.' Sure enough, there was one that was possible, but it was bounded on the south side by a telephone wire some fifteen feet high. However, I thought I could make it. After flying around Lerwick for ten minutes or so to let the inhabitants know of our arrival, we landed. The SS *St Magnus* was tied up at the wharf. This steamer belonged to the North of Scotland Shipping Company and was the very one that had carried the damaged monoplane to Aberdeen in July. The Captain had evidently become conscious of the competition from the air for, the story goes, on being told by the Mate that the plane he had watched flying over his ship a quarter of an hour earlier had landed on the island of Bressay, was quoted as having put his hand to his brow and commented in a hoarse voice: 'A plane landed on Bressay? Jesus Christ – a bad omen man, a bad omen.' The poor captain, however, had some respite, for it was not until three years later that we were able to extend our air service to compete with him on the Shetland run. And even then it took a long, long time to woo the Shetlanders away from sea travel. That was quite the opposite to the Orcadians who, after a matter of only several months, used air travel in preference to surface transport.

We spent three days in Lerwick, staying with Peter Angus's firm's agent, Mr Mowatt. During that time, I took Mr Mowatt and his family over to Bressay to look at the plane and, having previously arranged with the Post Office for them to 'drop the telephone wire', I gave three joy rides to our good friends. Again, my friend Peter did exceptionally well with his business. He told me he had obtained orders that had never come his way before. Everyone wanted to talk to him about his flight to Shetland. In those days this was big news.

We left on 7 October for the return journey, arriving in Kirkwall in time for lunch. Peter decided that further business calls in Orkney should be made and, flying through low cloud and heavy rain, we arrived back in Inverness late in the afternoon. It was the exact opposite to the sunshine of the day before, which shows how unpredictable the weather is in latitudes 58/60.

News of the business value of this trip rapidly spread, for a week later we received an urgent call from a businessman in Aberdeen who, with two business friends, wanted to charter G-ACEW for a similar flight direct from Aberdeen to Shetland. The problem in this case was that we knew of no suitable field for landing and taking off at Aberdeen. Mr J L Swanney, who was apparently the leader of the expedition, suggested Dyce. He said there was talk of an airfield being built there. I went over by car to look at the ground and found a number of small fields bordered by heavy stone dykes. I chose two of the largest and, after obtaining the farmer's permission, arranged for the middle dyke to be taken down leaving a gap of around one hundred feet. There was also a very large rock sticking out in the middle of the run. The contractor, Reggie Bissett, who subsequently became a very close friend of mine, soon blew that rock up and we then had a strip 400 yards long. Within two years, Dyce airfield was constructed around that site and so we were the first to use what was to become Dyce airport.

Departure for Shetland was arranged for Monday 16 October and I picked my three passengers up at two thirty in the afternoon at the prepared airstrip. It was a blustery day and was rapidly getting worse. I had a very rough trip over from Inverness so I warned my passengers, J L Swanney, E G Macrae and a Mr Williamson that we would have a strong headwind which would slow us down considerably and that the journey would likely be very rough. Mr Swanney sat in the front beside me and the other two sat behind with the luggage.

We left the Buchan coast at Macduff with sixty miles of foam-tossed sea ahead, between us and Wick. Our progress was very slow against a fifty mile an hour headwind, so I flew fairly low at 1,600 feet across the sea to avoid the stronger winds higher up. We were taking a good tossing and, around the middle of the journey, one of the passengers behind pulled my arm. I looked round and saw his friend holding a paper bag towards me. Thinking he was offering me a candy, I put my hand in the bag to take one. I pulled it away quickly, dripping with some warm substance, wondering what on earth was in the bag. It turned out, the poor chap had been violently sick and was handing me the bag to throw out of the front window. The other two were in fits of laughter and evidently in good form over my discomfiture.

We arrived in Kirkwall at five in the afternoon, having taken two and a half hours for a normal one hour and a quarter's flight. It would have taken close on two hours to reach Sumburgh in that gale so the passengers decided they had had enough and asked me to stay over in Kirkwall for the night. I was glad as we would have been hard put to reach Shetland before dark. We spent a comfortable night in the Kirkwall Hotel with plenty of 'good cheer flowing' and early next morning we departed for Shetland.

Like the last trip two weeks earlier, we diverted off course a bit to have a good look at Fair Isle. I spotted a possible landing ground on the south side of the island near the lighthouse, and dropped down low to make a dummy run in. It looked a bit rough perhaps and I decided to return one day by steamer and inspect it. We flew over Sumburgh and landed, for the second time, on the field at Bressay and again the phone wires had to come down. They had only been put back by the Post Office the day before. However, the Post Office engineers took it in good part and promptly sent their engineers to lower the wires.

My passengers decided to stay two days and, by the time they were ready to go back, they were also apparently very pleased with the results of their air visit. The third member of the party, who had been ill in the paper bag, decided to remain another day and would return by ship. Mr & Mrs Mowatt again made us very welcome and I was introduced to Mr R G Ganson who operated a garage and bus service. I had no illusions about Shetland – an air service to Aberdeen was a must at some time in the not too distant future, but radio directional service was absolutely essential for safety. I opened my mind to Mr Ganson and he undertook to be my agent in Shetland and to put on a bus service to Sumburgh to meet the plane when the service arrived. He took me by car to Hillswick on the west coast and showed me the centre of the island very thoroughly. After a long search, I could not find another flat place anywhere near Lerwick that could have been made into an airfield. The country was nothing but mountains and valleys.

The weather was not very good when we took off for Kirkwall and, having left Sumburgh behind, the visibility dropped down to a couple of miles or so. There was a fair crosswind blowing and it was essential for me to pick up Fair Isle to check my drift before turning off for Orkney. I had in mind two American flyers who, a year or so before, had left Shetland in a seaplane and had never been heard of again. So I decided to play safe. Swanney and his friend were relieved to see me turn back – I told them I was going to wait at Sumburgh for the visibility to improve. We waited till next morning, and even then it was not as good as I would have liked. However, I decided to have a go at it and we departed with our third passenger on board. He had arrived by car the previous night, having heard that we had not as yet left the island.

After fifteen minutes, I looked for Fair Isle but there was no sign of it on the port side. We flew on. I would give it another five minutes. Swanney, who was sitting behind me, casually remarked, 'That must be Fair Isle over there.' I looked up and there it was, at least four miles away on my starboard side. The drift was considerably more than I had expected for we were on the wrong side of the island and that just showed the wisdom of not taking chances over that sea in bad visibility without radio control. We pulled up to the south end of the island, I reset course and then steered a deliberate five degree error to the south to make sure we did not pass to the north of North Ronaldsay and thus get ourselves hopelessly lost out at sea. In any event, I was getting a bit short on petrol and had not enough to go looking for land for too long. We should have seen North Ronaldsay in twenty-five minutes, but it did not appear on the horizon. There was just a persistent yellow circle of mist about three miles radius around us. Thirty minutes went by, then thirty-five. We were well over the time now and I was beginning to get worried when a mournful voice from behind bleated, 'Say you chaps, do you remember those Yankees who left Shetland not so long ago and were never seen again.'

'Shut up,' said Swanney, who was versed in sea navigation and was beginning to wonder just where we were.

He knew we should have seen land before now and conveyed his thoughts to me.

I explained to him that I was steering an error course to the left so as to be sure we would not pass to the north of North Ronaldsay. 'If we don't see land in forty minutes, I will turn west'. There was no land to be seen at forty minutes and we altered course to the west. Shortly, a coastline showed up and soon we were over an island which I recognised as Stronsay. We had flown well south of our course and were that much nearer Kirkwall. After a short while, we suddenly

ran out of the mist into bright sunshine and the rest of the trip was easy. *The Times* of 7 October 1933, reporting on this charter flight, said:

> Highland Airways Limited, who link the Orkney Isles with the Scottish mainland, have sent a machine from Aberdeen to the Orkney Islands and Shetland, with three commercial travellers, who are the first persons to make a commercial flight to the islands from Aberdeen. They landed at Kirkwall Airport last night at dusk, having flown the 120 miles from Aberdeen in two hours in a 55 mph gale. They spent the night at Kirkwall and left today at eleven on the journey of ninety air miles between Orkney and Shetland. The plane will wait two days at Lerwick the capital of the Shetlands. The commercial passengers will, therefore, cover business in four days, which by train and boat would occupy fourteen days. The pilot, Captain Fresson stated at Kirkwall, that the trip from Aberdeen was one of the worst he had experienced in the north.

As my passengers had completed their business in Kirkwall on the trip north, we only stayed for lunch and flew back to Inverness where a car was waiting to take them back to Aberdeen.

At the end of October, we shut down the Inverness-Wick portion of the service and stationed the monoplane at Kirkwall to operate a trans-Pentland service to Wick and Thurso. The following news report later appeared in the Scottish national press of 3 November.

Air Ferry's gale feat
60 mph wind holds up Mail Steamer
Plane succeeds in making double crossing

The Orkneys would have been isolated yesterday, owing to the terrific gale which swept the east coast of Scotland, had it not been for the existence of the air service. In the teeth of the tempest, which at times reached a velocity of 60 mph, the Pentland Firth mail steamer, *St Ola*, was unable to reach Thurso from Orkney, but the monoplane 'Inverness' piloted by Captain E E Fresson, Managing Director of Highland Airways Limited, made the double crossing from Kirkwall and back. Captain Fresson told our Kirkwall correspondent, on his return, that the round trip had been a very steady one notwithstanding the gale. He emphasises that his crossing must not be regarded as running 'at any risk' in competition with the mail steamer, whose Master had found it impracticable to make the daily crossing. Captain Fresson said that wind was not so troublesome to an aeroplane as a steamboat which had the waves and currents to contend with. He added that with an air crossing of the Pentland Firth of only fifteen to twenty minutes, he could 'pop across' during lulls in the storm, whereas the Master of the steamer, who required three hours or more each way, had not that fortunate option.

That was our first tussle with the famous Orkney gales and I was relieved to know that we need not fear them as much as we thought we should do. The main difficulty was to avoid being blown over on the ground after landing. To overcome this we organised landing parties who would grab the plane as the tail dropped and we would then tie it down to a car, or sometimes a lorry if available. I shall have more to say about gale flying much later on in my story, for during the Second World War, I subsequently flew to Sumburgh and landed in a gale blowing at 80-90 mph.

On 1 November 1933 we commenced our trans-Pentland operations from Kirkwall. A hangar had been built at Wideford and Engineer Pugh moved north to maintain the aircraft. Captain Holmes and myself shared the flying on alternate weeks and we ran a once weekly return trip to Inverness so that we could switch pilots. There was not so much flying to be done on this restricted service, although sometimes we flew the Pentland Firth several times a day.

On 3rd November I undertook a charter to fetch two passengers from the island of Westray and take them to Wick. I found a field from the air and then flew over the local hotel to let the passengers know I had arrived. They were to observe the direction in which I landed and follow out by car. They duly turned up and to my surprise they had two dogs and guns with them. That was a bit of a jam for the monoplane which we were using for winter operations, but somehow or other, they managed to crowd in and we got to Wick without incident. At the end of the month, I had a charter to the island of Rousay for Mr & Mrs Walter Grant, the distillery director I had tried to interest in the Company in 1931. He had a large house, named *Trumland*, situated at the south end of the island.

Now that we had known fields on which it was possible to land in the North Isles group, we were soon called in by the County Council to attend to ambulance flights for the Balfour Hospital, Kirkwall. My friend Surgeon McClure was the prime mover and charter flights grew apace.

December soon came and passed, and we saw the New Year in with important developments pending for an airmail contract was to be entrusted to us and Aberdeen was connected by air to the Orkneys direct via Wick. The accomplishments gained during the year 1933 had firmly established Highland Airways and we made ourselves ready for greater conquests to come.

In closing this chapter, I think it appropriate to quote a poem, which was sent to us by a young lady who that winter flew on the Thurso service from Kirkwall.

G-ACEW

On June fifteen, one nine three three
Four fairies flew o'er the sea.
The way was long, the way was rough
The bumps off Dunnett Head were tough.
The pilot cried, 'quick, clutch your seat'
And up they shot three hundred feet.
T'was but a twice before they fell,
The fairies murmured, 'This is hell'.
It turned their tummies round about,
The paper bags were then brought out.
The shrieks and groans did soon subside,
As they beneath them land espied.
'Can this be Thurso?' Jean Hunt said,
Raising from Patty's knee, her head.
'Why, yes', said Fresson 'Here we are',
'I'll try and land the "Monospar".'
So having crossed the Pentland Firth,
They found themselves on Mother Earth.
There is a moral in this tale,
'Highland Airways' cannot fail.
(Alternative line: The pilot flies on 'Younger's Ale'.)

6

Expansion to Aberdeen

The New Year, 1934, brought with it a new Chairman. After a hectic board meeting in which I was involved as managing director, Dr Alexander departed on matters of disagreement in policy, and my good friend Mr Donald took his place. As a result, my work became easier and more agreeable. Under the new chairman, it was agreed that no time should be lost in establishing an Aberdeen-Orkney air connection in view of possible competition in the offing. We planned to commence the service on the anniversary of the opening of the Inverness-Orkney airline, namely Monday 7 May 1934.

In order to carry out these plans, we needed substantially more capital and I spent many searching hours as to where I could most likely raise it for, in spite of our success with the Orkney air connections, the public were still shy of venturing into aviation as a means of investment. One day, it occurred to me that operating out of Aberdeen would involve hotting up competition with the North of Scotland Shipping Company. We must have already bitten into their profits, and operations out of Aberdeen would substantially increase the drain. I wondered how they would take it and what steps they might adopt to counter our competition. Suddenly the answer clicked in my brain. Why not approach them to take a holding in Highland Airways? It would be mutually advantageous and would prevent them working against us for they were a powerful concern to fall out with. I had a talk with Mr Donald and we called a special board meeting of our directors and laid the proposition before them. The result was that Mr Donald and I were charged with the task of making contact.

A few days later found us calling, by appointment, on Mr MacCallum, the Managing Director of the North of Scotland Steam Navigation Company Limited in Aberdeen, where we laid our proposals before him. He was a short man and fairly well set with rather a square head. After a few minutes conversation it appeared to me that he was a hard-headed businessman and that he had been watching our operations very carefully. It was evident from what he said to us that the early days of their disbelief in air transport in the north of Scotland had now changed to the acceptance that air transport had come to stay and, what was more important to them, it was making a hole in their receipts. Furthermore, my two air trips and landings in Shetland had not gone unnoticed and they realised that it was only a matter of time before our services would be extended to 'Ultima Thule'. When we announced to him that we intended opening the Aberdeen-Orkney Service on 7th May, only a few weeks hence, he stiffened visibly in his chair, especially when I told him our airfield was on the bus route some three miles from the centre of the town.

We were accordingly well received, and after inspecting our traffic returns and accounts for the first years operations, which were substantially good, Mr MacCallum said he would place our proposal before his board of directors.

We returned to Inverness thinking we had got them interested and so it was within a few days we received a letter from Mr MacCallum saying that our proposals were accepted in principal and asking for a further meeting when terms and conditions could be discussed whereby the shipping company would take up a substantial holding in Highland Airways Limited.

Well before the opening date of the Aberdeen-Orkney run, they became shareholders in our company, Mr MacCallum being nominated to our board. Mr Adams, another director of the shipping company was intensely interested in the link up and I found him immensely helpful in guiding his fellow directors to see eye to eye with us until they accustomed themselves to the difference which existed between air and sea operations. As a result of this marriage, our position was considerably strengthened. It was a major triumph and we were now in a financial position to put into operation our plans for the commencement of the Aberdeen-Orkney service and a further Dragon DH84 aircraft was ordered. I collected this airplane from de Havilland at Stag Lane and flew it north on 25th April.

About that time we learned through the press that a Mr Eric Gandar Dower had purchased the property at Dyce, Aberdeen, where I had taken off for Shetland the previous autumn, and intended constructing a full-sized airfield. His plans were to commence a flying club and, in addition, rumour had it that competition might be in the offing between Aberdeen and Orkney, and later on to the Shetland Isles which we were now committed to. This was disturbing news as it was clear to us there was no room for competition on those routes. The density of traffic simply didn't exist for two companies. Accordingly, I slipped over by road to Aberdeen one Sunday morning having heard Mr Gandar Dower was visiting and staying at the Caledonian Hotel.

Arriving early to be sure of catching him, my name was sent up to his apartment. A female secretary appeared in order to enquire my business. I explained who I was and told her I would like to see Mr Gandar Dower in connection with aviation interests in the north of Scotland. I gave the secretary my card and she departed upstairs in the elevator. When she returned, she said apologetically, that Mr Gandar Dower was unable to see me. I was nonplussed and explained to her that I had come from Inverness that morning especially to see him. She returned upstairs for the second time and came back with a message that he would see me at 4.30 that afternoon. 'But that's five hours away and I've got to get back to Inverness', I exclaimed. The secretary looked embarrassed as she appeared to be a very nice person, and I learned later her name was Miss Hopkins. I got the impression she was a bit subjugated under the influence of a strong personality. However, very reluctantly she went upstairs again and succeeded in getting the time changed to 12.30 midday. I blessed her for her perseverance on my behalf. At 12.45 pm or thereabouts, my 'quarry' turned up a quarter of an hour late.

The secretary introduced us. I did not beat about the bush and after a few preliminaries came straight to the point.

'I hear you intend constructing an aerodrome at Dyce and intend commencing air operations to Orkney and Edinburgh.'

'That's materially correct, Captain Fresson,' he answered.

'Do you think there is room for two services in competition on the Orkney route?' I enquired. 'Those islands are very sparsely populated and there just isn't the business for two companies. We would both lose money and, in any event, Highland Airways are first in the field. You are aware, of course, that the North of Scotland Shipping Company are now interested in Highland Airways which means we have strong backing.'

He looked surprised.

'I have not heard that', he said. Coming directly to the point, he enquired, 'What's your proposition, Captain Fresson?'

'It's this.' I answered. 'We also are planning to run a service south from Aberdeen to Dundee, Perth, Edinburgh and Glasgow. That should be a very remunerative route, serving such large cities. I will recommend to my board to let that one go, if you will reciprocate by keeping off the northern routes, which we have pioneered and are at present operating from Inverness. It may also interest you to know that we are commencing an air service from Aberdeen to Orkney next month.'

He appeared a bit taken aback. 'Where will you operate from in Aberdeen?' he enquired.

'From Seaton, alongside the promenade. We have a lease on the ground and it is licensed and levelled.'

He gave me a penetrating look. 'You move quickly, Captain Fresson', he said. 'I am inclined to accept your proposition. Send me your proposals in writing regarding the Aberdeen, Edinburgh and Glasgow routes and your willingness to abstain from operating south and I will consider your proposition regarding the northern routes.'

My board duly approved the proposed letter which was despatched, but I do not recollect receiving any acceptance.

In a little over a year, Aberdeen Airways had been promoted by Mr Gandar Dower and, contrary to what had been discussed, commenced competition along our routes. From that date, a war of attrition began and was to last until 1939 when a licensing court, which sat under the Maybury Report recommendations and under the chairmanship of Mr Trustram Eve, robbed us of our Aberdeen services and gave all operations out of Aberdeen to the 'cuckoo in the nest'. It will be explained later how it all worked out.

Next day, Monday, fog blotted out everything along the Wick-Orkney route. The ten o'clock service had to be delayed until the weather improved. We still had no ground radio direction stations. There was only one passenger booked so I was using the monoplane *Inverness,* the load being light for that day. The passenger was a young businessman travelling to Wick. After an hour's delay, he began to get impatient. I learned he was the son of Mr D W Georgeson, a solicitor in Wick who, along with Colonel Robertson, were shareholders in Highland Airways. I thereupon gave him VIP treatment

'When do you think you will start, Captain Fresson?' he enquired.

'Just as soon as the fog lifts a hundred feet or so. It usually occurs around lunch time.'

He must have been down to the Longman Airport four times before lunch, urging me to leave. At two o'clock, the fog began to lift slightly. I was looking over at the Black Isle trying to gauge the height of the fog against the cliffs, when suddenly a voice behind me said, 'Captain, it looks fine now. Are we going?' I turned and there was my passenger again.

'I think we should wait a little longer,' I replied.

'I don't know what you're bothering about Captain,' he said. 'It's quite easy. All you have to do is to climb above the fog until you get to Wick, come down through it and we're there.'

'Really', I said. 'It sounds most simple and interesting, but I'm afraid it is not so easy as all that. How do you propose I should find my way above fog and drop down over Wick airfield without radio assistance?'

'Navigation, my dear Sir. Simple navigation.'

'And how do we navigate?' I enquired.

'Easy,' he said, 'If you can't do it, I will be your navigator.'

'Good God,' I thought, 'what an optimist. How can anyone navigate accurately without seeing the ground unless there is a radio station to work on?'

Trying to be as polite as possible, I ventured to say, 'That method might be a bit risky and we should end up by getting our necks broken.'

'Ha! Ha! Ha!' he laughed. 'Don't worry about that Captain, I'd just as soon die with you as with any other man.'

I gave up. If he was so keen on getting killed, he could do it without me. Half an hour later, the fog rose to about sixty feet and, much against my better judgement, but under intense pressure, I decided to have a go at it. We took off, crawling along the edge of the Black Isles cliffs to the Cromarty opening. Never seeing much more than half a mile ahead, we picked up one of the Cromarty

World War One 'look out' pill boxes perched half way up the cliffs and followed them round to Cromarty village. We then cut across the low ground on a compass course to Dornoch, skimming over trees and a small loch which I recognised.

The fog cleared a little but clamped down again as soon as we picked up Dornoch and the sea. Crawling up the coast at fifty feet or so, perspiration dripping off my brow, we passed Brora which was barely visible. Soon we were approaching the high cliffs of Helmsdale. Visibility ahead was then almost nil. I could just pick out the cliffs about 100 feet on my left. I was scared of running into them if they jutted out ever so little. All of a sudden, something black loomed ahead. I hadn't time to think. Automatically, I slammed on full power and pulled the stick back and put on rudder out to sea. The next moment, we were roaring over a large vessel moored close into the cliffs. My passenger said it was a naval cruiser. Apparently, they frequently exercised close inshore. In a moment, we were swallowed up in thick fog and I was committed to a most dangerous form of flying that I had been waiting all morning to dodge.

I hoped that the west coast would more than likely be clear, so I decided to turn west immediately we had reached 2,000 feet altitude and seek refuge on Achnahaird beach, west of Ullapool. At one thousand feet, the fog began to get lighter and at 1,200 feet we climbed into bright sunshine. That was a relief. I turned west and, to my astonishment, a couple of miles inland the land was in the clear. Turning on course, and following the edge of the fog on the landward side, we reached the main Thurso-Wick highway when all I had to do was to follow it low down to our landing field at Hillhead. The fog thickened as we approached the outskirts of the town, but the field was safely reached and, cutting both motors, we slid in over the fence and landed in one piece.

'Jolly good,' said my passenger, 'Jolly good old chap – I knew we could do it. Whatever did you wait so long for?'

By that time, I felt quite limp. We had escaped with our lives by a miracle. We hadn't cleared that cruiser's masts by more than a few feet and here was I being chided for not leaving earlier.

North of Wick, the fog was better and a phone call from Kirkwall reported there were many clear patches in the overcast. Thereupon I phoned Inverness to ascertain whether the emergency field at Culloden Moor was clear and, if in the affirmative, to phone the information through to Kirkwall.

That done, we loaded four passengers aboard and took off for Kirkwall, which was reached flying in sunshine above the fog. Slipping down through one of the holes in the fog, the landing was made at Wideford airfield without difficulty. As the aircraft was being unloaded, a message was handed to me by our traffic manager saying that Inverness reported that Culloden Moor was clear.

I took aboard the passengers for Inverness and overflew Wick. A car was out to meet us at Culloden Moor and, after picketing the plane down, we were soon in Inverness. Compared with that nightmare journey north, how easy the journey back, in sunshine with the white floor beneath us, had been.

I prayed that night that we did not have any more passengers like the one I had on the northern trip that day. It was not until sometime later that I learned that Harold Georgeson was an expert 'leg puller' and I had fallen for it that day, hook, line and sinker. Ultimately, we became great friends and we often used to laugh at that incident. I am now under the impression he was well aware how close we had come to disaster with the cruiser that afternoon when he observed its masts almost sticking through his seat.

With the opening of the Aberdeen-Orkney service approaching, another pilot, by the name of Greenshields, was taken on to operate it. He arrived during April which gave me time to put him through route familiarisation training on the Inverness-Orkney run. He was an ex-RAF Officer and so had some years flying experience at home and abroad. He turned out to be an excellent pilot and was able to fly through any weather without turning a hair.

On 5 April 1934, I was married to my unfortunate passenger, Mrs Simons, who crashed with me in the Moth at Leek in 1931. After the ceremony, I took the air service to Orkney and she accompanied me as I was to relieve the pilot on the Pentland crossing for a few days. We were pelted with confetti and some must have stuck to our clothes as one of the passengers remarked to me on arrival at Kirkwall, 'Has there been a wedding, Captain Fresson?'

'Why do you ask?'

'Oh, there is confetti all over the floor of the plane.'

I knew the passenger by sight. He was a businessman who travelled frequently with us. 'Do you know who it was?' he enquired.

'One of the members of our staff', I answered.

He got out of the plane and we left it at that. Some weeks later, he caught up with me.

'I've a bone to pick with you, Captain. Just to think I flew with you and your wife on the day you were married and you did not tell me. I would like to have wished you both all good happiness and good health over a dram, and you denied me that pleasure.'

To cool him off, we made up for it that evening at the Kirkwall Hotel.

During my stay in Kirkwall, I decided a landing ground at Halkirk by Georgemas Junction would be ideal for passengers catching the southbound train. It saved quite a lot of time compared to joining the train at Thurso and I thought the southbound passengers would jump at it. We tried it for a time, but it was not popular so after six months we gave it up. It appeared that most of the trans-Pentland passengers wanted to stay over in Thurso for business reasons.

Stornoway was, at that time, in my mind a lot. That was the next town I wished to connect by air with Inverness. The owner of the Caledonian Hotel in Stornoway, Kenny Ross, had been in to see me at my office many times. He was extremely keen to get an air service and offered to mark off a strip with sheets on the golf course at Melbost as soon as I could get over to survey a landing ground. I told him I would let him know as soon as the Aberdeen-Kirkwall service had established itself. He left my office saying, 'Now don't forget Captain, we will give you a right good welcome,' and he wasn't exaggerating when he said that as I found later on.

The 7th of May 1934 was close on us and the service was due to commence from Aberdeen to Orkney. We left Inverness on a Sunday afternoon to ferry the aircraft, which was to operate the new schedule which was to operate the new schedule, over to Aberdeen. On board were my wife, Mr Donald, Pugh our engineer, and Greenshields our new pilot. I was piloting the DH84 Dragon, G-ACIT. It was a nice sunny afternoon with scarcely any wind when we left the Longman airport. After passing Elgin, the weather began to change and a strong wind developed from the south-east which was roughly the course we were steering. By the time we had reached Huntly, the plane did not appear to be making any headway over the ground and the bumps were colossal. One of the passengers was laid out on the floor violently sick, and Greenshields, who was sitting immediately behind me, said my wife wanted me to return as she was very frightened. I wanted to reach my target that afternoon if at all possible and stayed on course for another ten minutes in which time we had only covered five miles over the ground. That represented a gale of 70 mph and a ground speed of only thirty miles an hour. As we had nearly forty miles to go, that was over an hour's flying. By now the passengers were in a bad way and I didn't think they could very well stand such a hammering for that length of time so, reluctantly, I turned about and made for Lossiemouth field where the Prime Minister, Mr Ramsay MacDonald, used to land in an RAF plane when he flew home from London. We arrived there in a few minutes with a ground speed of around 170 mph. The wind was not blowing so hard at Lossie, but I figured from the chimney smoke that it was at least fifty miles per hour.

So, before landing, I asked Pugh and Greenshields to get ready by the door. I was frightened that, without a landing party to hold it down, the plane might be blown over after it had landed. Immediately the plane came to a halt with the tail high in the air, those two were to jump out, dodge under the wing each side and grab hold of the outer wing struts while I let the tail drop. That worked fine. I then hurried out and screwed pickets into the ground and roped the aircraft down. We also lashed the tail and the plane rode the storm out safely through the night. Very soon, the usual crowd of sightseers gathered and there was no trouble getting a lift into Lossie where we put up at the Marine Hotel. Our first call was for sustenance to calm the passengers and, lastly, the crew.

Next morning dawned sunny and the wind had abated. We left early for Aberdeen, arriving at half past eight, an hour and a half before the service was due to commence. There was a large crowd awaiting our arrival on the airfield. The christening ceremony took place at half past nine and is best described by the *Press and Journal* report:

Aberdeen put on Air Map
Service to Orkneys

An important development in the history of transport in the Highlands, which places Aberdeen on the air map, was recorded today, when the regular daily air service between Aberdeen and Orkney was inaugurated. The seven seater plane which will maintain the service daily, was named *Aberdeen* by Lady Provost Alexander at the Aberdeen inauguration ceremony this forenoon on the flying ground at Seaton. The service will represent a great asset to the business and commercial interests, not only of Aberdeen and the north, but to the whole country in general.

Present at the ceremony were the Lord and Lady Provost, Directors of Highland Airways Limited including Captain Fresson, Managing Director; Mr R Donald, Chairman; Mr James McCallum, Manager and Secretary of the North of Scotland Orkney and Shetland Steam Navigation Company and Mr J W McKillop; and amongst the leading public men were Professor Hendrick, President of Aberdeen Business &

Professional Club; Mr A B Hutchinson, Past President; Mr Geo Slater, Mr Wm Veitch, Editor, *Press & Journal*, as well as a good representation of the general public.

Mr McCallum presided at the inauguration ceremony and commented on the importance of the occasion and expressed the Directors' indebtedness to the Lord and Lady Provost. The Lord Provost Alexander said it was a notable and interesting occasion, for they were about to inaugurate the first regular air service from the City of Aberdeen. There had been frequent casual visits of aeroplanes to Aberdeen, but today's event

marked the initiation of a regular service between Aberdeen and the North Islands. It was an event of unique commercial promise. There would always be a place for sea transport, just as there would be a place for rail and road transport, but all recognised that air transport had now arrived and would prove an admirable and useful addition to the excellent shipping facilities. The Lord Provost recalled a prophecy made by the late Mr Wm Slater in 1906, a year or so after the first aeroplane had made its first flight [the Wright Brothers, at Kitty Hawk, North Carolina, USA 1903]. He remarked to his brother that before long he would be flying in his own plane to the Orkneys and Wick, visiting his stations there, and be back in time for tea. His brother, who is still alive, was present. Today they saw that prophecy realised. They were indebted to the Directors of

Highland Airways and in particular to the energy and enterprise of Captain Fresson, Mr Donald and Mr McCallum and they wished the service all the prosperity it deserved, which in turn, would reflect on the happiness and prosperity of the north of Scotland (applause).

At the naming ceremony, a humorous little incident occurred. A bottle of champagne decorated with golden tartan was attached to the nose of the plane, but when the Lady Provost endeavoured to smash the bottle against the plane, the string snapped. Laughing heartily at the mishap, she lifted the bottle, wrapped a towel around its neck, and broke it saying, 'I have the honour to christen the aeroplane with the name of the *City of Aberdeen*'. The Lady Provost presented to Captain Fresson a mascot for the airplane, a full-sized Aberdeen terrier, decorated with ribbon. Captain Fresson accepted the mascot and placed it in the pilot's cockpit. Returning thanks, Captain Fresson pointed out that the inauguration was the anniversary to the day of the Inverness-Orkney service – the predecessor of the new service. The difficulties of running a service from Aberdeen had been considerable, owing to the problem of finding a suitable landing ground within easy reach of the city. The saving of time and, therefore of money, would enable people to make it worth their while to utilise the air services. Captain Fresson took a party consisting of the Lord and Lady Provost, Mr McCallum, Mr Slater, Mr Rogers and Miss Meston for a trial flight over the city. A second flight including Mr A B Hutchinson, Mr Wm Veitch, Editor of the *Press and Journal*, reporters and photographers was made over the city.

The plane then left for Wick and Kirkwall with a full load of return passengers. On their return they told the *Press and Journal* representative, they had all enjoyed the flight immensely. They obtained lovely views of the firth and mountains on the journey to Kirkwall which occupied one and three quarter hours. Great interest was shown in Kirkwall by the crowd at the airport in the Aberdeen terrier mascot presented to Captain Fresson by Aberdeen's Lady Provost. The return trip was completed in one hour and five minutes with the help of a strong tail wind.

This time, on arrival at Kirkwall, I received a hearty welcome and handshake from Provost Slater and from that day on, he did all in his power to help me. I suspect the North of Scotland Shipping Company's interest in our company at that date had a lot to do with the transformation.

Next day, pilot Greenshields took over the service. He was a remarkable pilot. I used to watch him arrive at Kirkwall airfield quite unruffled, having flown across sixty miles of open storm-ridden sea in atrocious weather without any navigational aids and he kept one hundred percent regularity. Even the steamer skippers complimented him and said they would not have believed it possible.

With the Aberdeen service underway, back in Inverness, my next attention was to survey the Stornoway route. I was anxious to get the whole of the north of Scotland tied up before outsiders started to poke their noses in. Already I had heard rumours of a southern aviation company having designing eyes on Stornoway, and I wanted to be in first. A long conversation on the phone with my friend Kenny Ross at the Caledonian Hotel, Stornoway ensued. He would mark off a 300 yard strip for me on the Melbost golf links in the direction of the prevailing wind. He said there would be two bunkers in the middle with only a thirty foot gap between – would that be alright?

'A bit close,' I said. 'The Dragon's wheels are around thirteen feet apart. That doesn't leave much room does it, Kenny?'

'Well, Captain, I don't see what we can do as there isn't another strip that long with a suitable surface.'

'Alright, Kenny,' I said. 'We'll have to make it do. Can you mark the top inside edge of the bunkers with a linen sheet and place one in between – in the middle of the run?'

'Certainly, Captain. We have plenty of old sheets in the hotel. I'll get that done.'

'Also,' I said, 'light a smoke fire as soon as I circle the golf links.'

'Yes, we'll do just that'.

A few days later, on a brilliant Thursday morning, we took off from Inverness in Dragon G-ACIT with Willie Hamilton, our secretary, Engineer Pugh and two other passengers, arriving over the Stornoway golf course at midday. The markings were clear as I dropped off height and took a dummy approach and low run over the strip. The smoke wind direction indicator was going strong and the bunker gap, although very narrow, was well marked and looked possible. There were quite a number of onlookers to witness the first landing on Melbost Golf Course, Lewis.

After another, circuit we dropped down low over the golf course, motoring in at minimum speed, and touched down almost on top of the first marker. By keeping the tail up I had no difficulty in steering for the middle bunker marker and we ran through the 'bunker straits' without any difficulty, pulling up with fifty yards to spare. Before going into town, we had a good look round the golf course and I found it had great possibilities for an airfield. I estimated it would cost a few thousand to remove bunkers, and to level and grade four strips of six hundred yards each.

I decided to make a report on the Melbost Golf Course survey and submit it to our next board meeting. Obviously we would need help from the town council to build an airfield in Stornoway in view of the magnitude of the work required.

And then there would need to be a good measure of public pressure to obtain the use of the golf course for our purpose. It would mean extensive alterations to the golf course layout, but I figured we could still retain the eighteen holes. After strolling over the links for an hour, we went into town to the Caledonian Hotel for lunch. Mine host, Kenny Ross, did us proud. By the time we had finished, it was three o'clock and we were all ready to brave anything which came our way on the flight back.

I changed course for our return trip and made a landfall at Kinlochewe. Dropping down to fifty feet above the water, we flew right down to the east end of Loch Maree, obtaining a magnificent view, and then pulling up the Glen Docharty pass and down the valley over Achnasheen, Garve, passing Strathpeffer on the left and up the Beauly Firth to Inverness. We landed exactly one hour after take-off from Stornoway.

The directors of Highland Airways accepted my report and agreed we should make an official approach to the Stornoway Town Council. We would also ask the Air Ministry to survey the site first in order to make sure that the golf course would be acceptable for licensing. Some months later, Major Mealing of the Civil Directorate duly arrived from London and flew over with me. He was very pleased with the site and gave it a clean bill. Thereafter the fun started. The golf club did not want to give up the ground or have it altered. The council were not prepared to make any contribution for the construction of the runways. Then, when we were beginning to make some sign of progress, a pilot from Renfrew flew up and said he would give Stornoway an air service by using float seaplanes. We considered the water was usually too rough for float planes and proved this by later sending the *Cloud of Iona* flying boat over to make tests. The report of the expert seaplane pilot, Captain Scott of Saunders Roe Limited, Cowes, Isle of Wight, confirmed our views. He also pointed out the hazard of flotsam and jetsam in the sea and, even although the rough water was ruled out, it would still cost a lot of money to operate motor launches to patrol the landing area for each landing.

The West Coast authorities would not believe this assessment and went on dealing with the Renfrew pilot whose name, I believe, was Glyn Roberts,[1] known to his friends as 'Rocky', and that well described him. To cut a long story short, bickering over that aerodrome dragged on until four years later, early 1939, before we got the site approved by the owners and golf community. We could get no local financial support and so Scottish Airways[2] had to finance the construction. It cost us around eight thousand pounds to produce those four

---

[1] Captain Glyn Roberts of West of Scotland Air Services Ltd.

[2] Scottish Airways was to be brought about by the amalgamation of Highland Airways and Northern & Scottish Airways of Renfrew from 31 May 1935.

runways. They were not finished until the end of August 1939. The Second World War came on 3rd September and we never used that aerodrome. Our eight thousand pound airfield, unused, was torn up and a large modern airfield was built by the government for the use of Coastal Command. I believe we obtained compensation from the government for the money we spent to no purpose.

It was not until 24 May 1944, towards the end of the War, that the Air Ministry allowed us to operate the first Inverness-Stornoway service. Out of all the governing local bodies I had to deal with, the West Coasters were the most difficult. Time meant nothing to them and they were not prepared to spend a 'bawbee'.

At the end of April 1934, Captain G Holmes decided to leave us as he had a job offered to him by Imperial Airways. We were most sorry to lose him as he had the confidence of the public and had kept an excellent schedule between Inverness and Kirkwall for our first ten months of operations. We, however, did not wish to stand in his way for advancement and so very reluctantly we released him with our best wishes. He was replaced by a pilot, who shall remain nameless, and who had recently returned from a short RAF service commission. He was a good pilot during his not very long stay with the company and managed to earn us wide publicity by dumping a honeymoon couple in the Moray Firth, alongside the Inverness airfield, just after take-off. It was not until after the immersion, when the good lady lost her false teeth in the icy cold ducking in freezing weather, that the very new husband found out that her teeth were not her own. There was the devil to pay and we faced a serious claim for hurt feelings and 'damaged baggage'. The reason for the forced descent was never really cleared up. The pilot claimed that ice on the main planes had contributed to the plane failing to remain airborne after taking off, but I doubt that explanation as the aircraft was only lightly loaded. At the end of the War, a similar accident happened to a Dakota taking off at Northolt (London) which finished up on the top of a bungalow on the edge of the airfield. That accident was attributed, by the expert team directed to enquire into the cause of the accident, to ice formation on the aircraft's wings.[3]

Our nameless pilot had more trouble ahead of him for, a year or so later, taking off at Wideford in Kirkwall, he failed to clear the dyke and dumped six passengers into a wide pit on the other side of the airfield. Two were injured, but fortunately not seriously, and the other four were badly shaken. Those two crashes lost him the confidence of the travelling public and he left to join Imperial Airways at Croydon. An amusing rumour filtered through later on that he had been given a nickname. They had christened him 'Saint George'. Upon

---

[3] This occurred on 19 December 1946 when Railway Air Services Douglas C47A, G-AGZA, came to rest on the roof of a private home at 46 Angus Drive, Ruislip.

enquiry why, we were told, 'Because he slew two "Dragons"' (a reference to the DH84 aircraft). I believe he did well with Imperial Airways. The next time I saw him was in Nairobi, some fifteen years later, around 1949. He had come over from West Africa to take part in the Air Ministry conference for African air administration. He was, I believe, Director of Civil Aviation on the Gold Coast.

May 29th 1934 was drawing near. On that date we were to be invested by the Director of Postal Services with an Air Mail Contract and Air Mail Pennant, and on that day I was to fly the first regular internal air mail service in Britain at ordinary letter rates. It was a red letter day for me as it meant I had conquered all that I had set out to do in those early days when I was hunting around Kirkwall for capital to finance the company.

We had now obtained the four essentials I had been looking for: finance, passengers, mails and newspapers. There had been a lot of bad weather during the past twelve months and George Holmes and myself had battled unaided through fog, gales and torrential rain to achieve our goal. We had no real airfields with hard airstrips like there are today. Our aerodromes were grass fields, mostly rough surface and often bogged with mud after heavy rain during the winter months. And on top of that, only short take-off and landing runs were available. The pilot had to accurately gauge the length of run required for the aircraft to take off with the load on board. Under bad conditions, the aircraft usually took the whole of the run available and so the pilot had to be certain that he would obtain sufficient flying speed in time to clear the stone dyke on the far end of the field. Failure to judge accurately meant a certain crash and risk to life and limb. It took long practice to become proficient in the art of judging these take-offs and so a trained pilot to us was invaluable. It was hard on the nerves when the ground was wet and soggy. I always heaved a sigh of relief when the plane became airborne.

Many of those winter runs were nightmare experiences because, in addition to restricted airfields, crawling along underneath low cloud or fog in high winds, which buffeted the plane severely, was frightening and prolonged. Today, the pilot flies high in the sky from 'A' to 'B' and has radar to bring the plane down to within a few hundred feet in line with the airstrip, just ahead. Ask a modern pilot to do the kind of flying we did and I doubt whether he would be willing to try.

George Holmes supported me in the flying on an equal basis. He knew that we would not get the mail contract unless we maintained a near one hundred percent service, so I was extremely sorry he had to leave us just about the time we obtained our reward for such hard joint efforts. Poor fellow, he was killed about a year later on the London-Cologne run. He was homing by radio bearings on the Cologne airfield radio station and the operator allowed him to pass over the station without changing his bearings to a reciprocal course. In consequence, he continued flying east, towards rising ground and descending in cloud.

Eventually the plane crashed on a cloud-covered mountain killing all passengers and poor old Holmes. After the enquiry into the accident by the German authorities, it was said that the faulty ground station operator, for the magnitude of his error, was shot on the orders of Hitler.

Towards the end of the War, I had a similar experience when homing on Kirkwall above cloud. The aircraft was within ten minutes of Kirkwall by dead reckoning when I commenced the series of bearings to bring me in over Wideford airfield. After the estimated ten minutes had elapsed, I was still obtaining a string of northerly bearings and I queried their accuracy with Kirkwall radio station. Confirmation came back that the bearings were correct. I went on flying northwards thinking I must have struck a very strong head wind. When ten minutes past my estimated time of arrival over Kirkwall airfield had elapsed, I sent another message to the radio station saying that I estimated that I was well on the way to Sumburgh and to check the bearings again. There was some delay and then a terse bearing giving me a course southwards which was, of course, in the reverse direction to that which I was flying. It took exactly ten minutes to reach Kirkwall station, which was the time I had estimated I had over flown Wideford airfield. After landing, I went along to see the radio operator and asked him what had gone wrong.

'It's a shocking error,' I said, 'especially after I had queried the accuracy of the bearings you were sending.'

'I'm very sorry. I don't know how I got so mixed up.'

'You need to find out,' I answered. 'Otherwise you will have a serious accident on your hands.'

I then recalled to him the recent Cologne accident in which Captain Holmes was involved. 'Do you remember what happened?' I enquired. His answer was negative.

'He hit a mountain descending through cloud owing to the German operator making the same error as you have committed and there was not a single soul left to tell the tale. It may interest you to know that Hitler had that operator shot, so you can thank your lucky stars you are not in Germany.'

Not so long after that episode, I had a similar experience approaching Shetland where the consequences might have been more serious owing to the mountainous nature of the terrain, but that operator woke up immediately when I queried his bearings.

The 29th of May 1934 dawned and Sir Frederick Williamson and his party were arriving on the night express from London to preside at the Air Mail ceremony for, after one year of operating at near 100% regularity, the Post Office had decided to entrust us with the Orkney Air Mail contract. Our postmaster, Mr Campbell, and Mr Measham, the Post Office surveyor of the Eastern District of Scotland were also present. While they retired to the Post Office, Mr Donald and myself, together with Willie Hamilton, hurried down to the airfield to ensure all was ready for the ceremony which was about to take place.

Our chief engineer, George Griffiths, had our fleet of aircraft lined up in echelon in front of the hangars and a small dais was erected in between the planes and the sheds from which the speech making would take place. The flagstaff was checked to ensure the Air Mail pennant would float aloft at the appointed moment. A large crowd began to appear at the advertised time. The postal officials were greeted by my directors and myself. The press report, taken from *The Scotsman* of Wednesday 30th May 1934 adequately describes that historical event:

Britain's First Airmail
Opening of Inverness to Orkney Service
Epoch Making Event

A new epoch in British postal history began in Inverness today, when General Sir Frederick Williamson KCB, Director of Postal Services, inaugurated the first inland airmail services in Britain, which will operate between Inverness and Kirkwall. Over 2,000 letters were despatched by the plane today, as well as the supplies of *The Scotsman*, which has been conveyed by the air service since its inception of over a year ago.

The occasion was marked by a simple ceremony, and the unfurling at the Municipal Aerodrome by Sir Frederick of a Royal Air Mail Pennant, the first pennant authorised by an inland service. Sir Frederick was accompanied by Mr F G Milne, Secretary of the Post Office in Scotland, and Mr R J R Measham, Post Office Surveyor of the Eastern District of Scotland. The weather was fine, and the aerodrome on the shores of Inverness Firth looked a very comfortable place for a starting point. A representative gathering present included, Provost John MacKenzie and the magistrates and members of the Town Council, Sir Alex McEwan and Miss McEwan; Mr A J Campbell, Head Postmaster of Inverness; Mr R Donald of Highland Airways; Mr Robert Wotherspoon, legal adviser, and Mr W Hamilton, General Secretary. Ex-treasurer John Young and Mrs Young; Mr J W McKillop, County Clerk, and Mr George Smith-Laing, Town Clerk, Inverness.

Provost MacKenzie said it was his privilege to introduce Sir Frederick Williamson who had come to the capital of the Highlands to inaugurate that mail service, which was an epoch making event in the whole of Great Britain. The service would have the effect of bringing into closer contact with the commercial community of those important districts which at the moment were rather remote from the other places of the world. For that purpose, the service was very acceptable to everyone engaged in industry of every kind. On behalf of the Corporation and his fellow citizens of

Inverness, he wished the new airmail service every success. (Loud applause).

Sir Frederick Williamson said it was with pleasure that he came to Inverness to inaugurate the airmail service between Inverness and Kirkwall. As the Provost truly remarked, it was the inauguration of an epoch in aerial service, for it was the first occasion they had established regular air mail services in Great Britain. Overseas air mail services were what he might term, commonplace, but up to the present, nothing permanent had been done to have a regularly established service of the kind in this country.

Owing to the energy and enterprise of Highland Airways, the Postmaster General was satisfied that the air service between Inverness and Orkney was sufficiently reliable to enable him to set up a mail service by it. Sir Frederick said he proposed to inaugurate the service by asking Highland Airways to accept from the Postmaster General an airmail pennant, which had just been introduced. The one he was now handing over to Highland Airways was the first authorised for an inland air service in Britain. Amid applause, Sir Frederick presented the pennant to Mr Donald, and a miniature pennant to be attached to the aircraft itself.

The pennant was attached to the flagstaff at the aerodrome and hoisted by Sir Frederick to the accompaniment of cheers. A letter from Provost MacKenzie to Provost Slater, Kirkwall, was handed to Mr Measham for delivery. The thanks of the Directors of Highland Airways was voiced by Mr Donald. No effort would be spared to justify the confidence shown by Sir Frederick in granting that airmail contract. They had just completed one year's operation between Inverness and Orkney and regularity of ninety-eight percent had been maintained.

Concluding, Mr Donald paid a high tribute to Captain Fresson, Managing Director and Chief Pilot, who would pilot the first 'air mail' from Inverness to Kirkwall. It was due to the foresight and sound judgement of Captain Fresson, who surveyed the route at his own risk and expense, that the Inverness-Orkney air route had become established.

Orkney's Welcome. A crowd of over a thousand awaited the arrival of the plane at Kirkwall Airport. Among those present were Provost John M Slater, Kirkwall; Mr J Storer Clouston, of Orphir, Convener of the Orkney County Council; Mr Alfred Baikie of Tankerness; The Lord Lieutenant of Orkney and Shetland; Provost J G Marwick, Provost of Stromness; Sheriff Brown, Kirkwall; Mr J J Tait, Postmaster, Kirkwall; Mr Wm J Heddle, Town Clerk, Kirkwall; Mr J E P Robertson, Town Clerk, Stromness, and members of Kirkwall Town Council.

Provost Slater said Kirkwall was deeply indebted to the Postmaster

General for selecting it for the first air mail service in the United Kingdom. The new service was a boon to all in the Orkney Islands. The Provost said he specially desired to pay tribute to Captain E E Fresson, the pioneer of air service to Orkney. With bulldog tenacity, Captain Fresson had overcome all difficulties. Sir Frederick Williamson, briefly replying, told the crowd they were witnessing an epoch in the history of British aviation. He paid tribute to the initiative of Highland Airways. The air mail involved no surcharge, the letters being carried at ordinary rates.

Twelve thousand letters were sent from Kirkwall to Inverness by the plane on its return journey, Mr J J Tait, Postmaster at Kirkwall stated.

The Provost, Magistrates and Councillors of the Royal Burgh of Kirkwall gave a luncheon in the Kirkwall Hotel to Sir Frederick Williamson and his colleagues, including our party, at which all the dignitaries of Orkney attended. It was a very large luncheon and went on to nigh on three o'clock in the afternoon. The menu and liquid embellishments were all to be desired, the most popular dish apparently being a sweet named 'Eve's Pudding' or 'the Pilot's Favourite', which caused much amusement and chaffing. I was not aware that I had given the locals, during my many visits to their city, any inclination of my sentiments of the opposite sex. But there it was stark and bold, in print.

During the first half of July, I spent my time touring the Orkney Isles and giving joy rides to test the attitude of the islanders to air travel, preparatory to opening a 'round the isles' service, with the monoplane *Inverness*. These Islands are so cut off, and the small steamer which plies between them so slow, that a plane can do in a few minutes what takes hours by sea. The islands visited were Rousay, Sanday, Westray, Stronsay and North Ronaldsay.

We made our headquarters on the island of Rousay and were the guests of Mr Walter Grant, my distillery friend whom three years before I had in vain tried to interest in the formation of Highland Airways. He had a beautiful mansion named *Trumland* on that small island and I used to fly back every evening, land near the mansion and picket my plane down for the night. Engineer Pugh was with me to maintain the aircraft and motors, which were being worked very hard. My wife accompanied me, and Mrs Grant was the fourth member of our party.

Rousay is one of the smaller islands of the Orkney northern group. It is mountainous and is fringed around the perimeter by gently sloping ground, which is farmed. *Trumland* is situated around 200 feet up the hill and facing south towards Kirkwall. It commands a beautiful view and, on a fine and sunny day, the island of Gairsay and the north coast of the Orkney mainland are clearly visible. In fact, it is only separated from the mainland shore by a strait some two miles wide. The island takes about two hours to reach by the island steamer and is within ten minutes by plane to Wideford airfield.

It is an historic island because, a few years ago, a broch, built by stone-age people 2,000 years ago, was found there. The broch is circular and the stone compartments can be seen clearly. The stones in what appeared to be a kitchen clearly showed signs of being burnt. During our stay, we were taken to see this interesting monument of ancient days. Its construction was of solid rock. The mortar used, we were told, was made of sea birds eggs and sand with egg shell mixed in to give the lime content. The mortar appeared still to be in good condition, probably better than modern cement mortar. Thousands of sea birds haunt the cliffs in Orkney so the ancients hadn't far to seek a plentiful supply of eggs.

We were talking after dinner on the night before our return to Inverness and Walter Grant asked me how I had got on at the various islands, and whether I had arrived at any conclusion in providing air connection with Kirkwall. I told him the islanders had given me, without exception, a great welcome and my impression from the numbers who flew with me in the past three days, when three hundred and seventy passengers queued up for and received flights, indicated that an isles air service would be well supported.

Undoubtedly the outstanding air conscious island was North Ronaldsay, the most northerly and isolated island of the North Isles group. Mr Swanney, their postmaster and spokesman, asked me to give them an early air service.

'We can't give you an air connection without an airfield to operate from,' I replied. 'There is no field large enough here which could be used as a landing place. It would require two fields converted into one.'

'Which two would you like?' he shot back at me quickly.

Thereupon, I spent an hour or so, looking around from the air and on the ground, and chose an excellent site alongside the post office which would provide the largest airfield of the North Isles group. I explained to Mr Swanney, that there was a lot of work to be done before we could use it. A three hundred yards stone dyke at least four feet high had to be removed, parts of the ground required levelling and thousands of fair-sized surface stones required gathering up before it would be suitable for an airfield.

'I'm afraid it would cost us too much to prepare for the amount of traffic we would obtain from the island,' I commented.

'Leave that to me,' said Mr Swanney.

He thereupon sent runners to all the houses on the island and asked them to report at the post office within half an hour. Meanwhile, I was asked into the house for tea and a very good one it was. I had barely finished when I was told the islanders had arrived. Indeed they had, almost every one of them, including the children.

The postmaster stood up on a box and proceeded to say:

'I have called you all here because I have an important announcement to make. Captain Fresson has assured me that Highland Airways will give this island an air service to Kirkwall providing there is a suitable landing field. He has this afternoon made a survey and has chosen two fields alongside the post office. These two fields belong to Farmer Rendall. Is he here?'

'Aye,' shouted a voice.

Said Mr Swanney, 'Are you prepared to allow your two fields to be used, and if so, will you allow the separating stone dyke to be pulled down, the ground levelled in places and stones cleaned up on the surface? If so, will you grant the use of the land for an air service free of charge?'

'Certainly', said Farmer Rendall of Holland Farm.

'Now,' said Mr Swanney, 'who is going to help in removing the dyke and preparing the surface? Hands up.'

Up shot a forest of hands, including the small boys!

'When will you begin?' enquired Mr Swanney.

'Tomorrow', was the unanimous reply.

The next day was fine. At ten o'clock, sixty men and twenty carts were on the fields. Just before dusk next day the job was completed. Schoolboys had joined in the work, mostly in the picking up of the loose stones scattered all over the surface. Yesterday there were two fields uneven of surface. By the evening of the day after, they were converted into a twenty-eight acre airfield, flat, free from obstacles, the finest in all the North Isles, 'made in a day'. What enthusiasm. I saw to it that the people of North Ronaldsay never had reason to regret the spontaneous effort of its populace, and many a time in later years, when they were cut off by storm with no outside contact with the world, Highland Airways and their successor's Scottish Airways planes, were always ready to go to the rescue.

I trained a team to catch our planes in, to prevent them being blown over, when there were high gales blowing and mountainous seas were pounding the coastline. We would fly food and mails in to them even when the winds were topping seventy miles an hour. No steamer service could operate under such stormy conditions. Anyone wanting to get back to Kirkwall would be taken on the return journey. When we eventually opened the air service early in August, full loads of passengers were available, taking their produce, such as chickens, ducks, eggs, etc., in to the market in Kirkwall and returning on the afternoon service. We ran two services a day, three times weekly, to give the return daily service. Visitors and business people would go out on the morning service, stay the day and return on the afternoon plane, which had brought the islanders back. It paid our company, and the islanders were more than satisfied with what their endeavour had brought them for they were no longer isolated. Later the post office gave them a postal service. The air trip took a little over a quarter of an hour compared to most of the day by the old steamer service.

148

The other islands, Westray, Sanday and Stronsay, were also helpful, but except for Sanday, we were able to find single fields on those islands large enough for full-load operations and which only required a little levelling. All the farmers gave us free landing facilities after the magnificent example set by North Ronaldsay.

The final and probably most important boon that the North Isles air service brought the inhabitants came about when the Orkney County Council, early in October, two months after the air service commenced, contracted with Highland Airways Limited to operate an air ambulance service. A great number of urgent cases were flown to the Balfour Hospital in Kirkwall and a number of lives were saved.

A view to educating the Aberdeenshire people to air travel found us, at the end of July, giving short 'air travel' demonstration flights at a country village named Inches and other towns in the district. While at Inches, I received an invitation to the opening of Dyce Airport constructed by Mr Eric Gandar Dower. Lord Arbuthnott, Lord Lieutenant of Kincardineshire, was to preside and present the prizes offered. The first one, which interested me, was the landing competition. A landing time was written on a card and placed in a sealed envelope in charge of the stewards. The pilot who landed his aircraft at the nearest time to that stated in the envelope would be the winner of a silver cup along with £30. During the previous afternoon's flying, I gave this matter some thought and decided to make a bid for it. There was a long afternoon's programme, commencing around 1400 hours, and so it appeared to me that the visiting aircraft would have to be on the Dyce airfield in good time and before 1400 hours. Many would be arriving from the south, so probably twelve noon would be about the time of the earliest southern visitors. Therefore, I could safely say the time on the card would be confined to between twelve midday and, say, 1345 hours. In between landings and take offs at Inches the previous afternoon I tried to make my choice from the 105 minutes thus presented. I was baffled, but thought just before lunch might be as good as any. They say that dreams are sometimes induced from prior concentrated thinking and, be that as it may, that night I had a most realistic dream that the time on the card was 1300 hours. In fact, I actually dreamt I had looked at the card. I do not usually remember dreams in detail the next morning, but this one was so clear in my mind that I decided to back its guidance. I calculated the time the flight would take from Inches to Dyce and left a bit earlier in Monospar G-ACEW with my wife so that I would be sure of arriving well on time. I would then slip off any surplus time by circling the airfield before landing.

The judge marked the touch down of G-ACEW off as 1301 hours. I joined the party fun and went into lunch and thought no more about the matter. There were several local air races which I joined. One I remember well. I had just taken off and was climbing when a DH Puss Moth cut right across me. I had to push the nose of my aeroplane down sharply to avoid it. I cursed the pilot for flying so dangerously and, when I landed, I made enquiries only to find that the pilot was no other than our host himself, Mr Eric Gandar Dower. I wondered whether the motive could have been to slow me down. I lost a minute or two regaining position, but I decided under the circumstances, to lodge no protest. Needless to say, I lost the race. When the races were completed, we sat around waiting for the winners' names to be announced. The landing competition was the first to be announced. The announcer's voice started up:

'The winning time on the sealed card for the landing competition is 1303 hours. The winning aircraft, G-ACEW, touched down at 1301 hours piloted by Captain E E Fresson, and so to him goes the prize of a silver cup and £30.'

I could not believe my ears – so my dream had come out trumps after all.

When I was about to mount the dais to receive my prize from Lord Arbuthnott, I felt a tug on my arm. Glancing down, there was mine host. 'I hope the thirty pounds, Captain Fresson', he murmured, 'makes up for the loss of an afternoon's joy riding.' I assured him that the honour of taking it off him more than compensated me. I then remembered that I had told him on my arrival, that I had given up an afternoon's flying revenue at Inches to attend the opening of his airfield. So, perhaps I was too hard on him.

I duly took the prize back to Inverness and reported my success at the board meeting which was held a few days after. One director, who shall be nameless, said I ought to hand the cup and thirty pounds over to the company. I remonstrated and said that it was usual in the flying world for the pilot to keep a prize of that nature. Mr McCallum of the North of Scotland Shipping Company immediately came to my support, and Mr Wotherspoon and Colonel Robertson of Wick also agreed, so I kept the swag. After all, it was *my* dream.

The opening of Dyce airport immediately began to create a problem. It appeared evident that the previous Caledonian Hotel arrangements, by which Highland Airways flew the northern routes and Mr Dower would fly the southern, were not going to be implemented, for we had news that Mr Dower was planning a competitive air service from Aberdeen to Kirkwall. To make matters worse, we were suddenly confronted with the stark fact that our airfield at Seaton was to be used for the Highland Show next year and we would have to seek another airfield to operate from. Mr Gandar Dower was sounded out about the use of Dyce, but we were met with a blunt refusal. Clearly, it appeared to us, he was out to freeze us off the Aberdeen-Kirkwall run for he knew as well as we did that, owing to the lie of the land around Aberdeen, our chances of obtaining an alternative field to Seaton were most remote. I certainly knew it as I had searched the countryside at all points of the compass without success before I found Seaton. It was a bitter blow. The Aberdeen-Kirkwall run, which we had so successfully operated and had educated the public to use, was now to be taken from us by the freezing process for the want of an airfield. And what bad luck about Seaton, for the Highland Show only visited Aberdeen once every five years and 1935 had to be the one year in five. Another site just had to be found, even if I had to look much further afield.

I decided to make a square search in our Moth, which we had recently purchased from Miss Pauer, its former owner. I landed in many fields and ended up at Kintore. There was a long field alongside the stream running adjacent to the railway to Inverurie, so I landed on it. It was a sunny Sabbath morning. I found the owner, but he said he could not spare the grazing. I explained our difficulty and asked him to help us.

'Why not go up and see Mr Barrack about quarter of a mile up the road past the cemetery on the left which leads to Inverurie,' he said. 'There are two good fields there.'

A good omen, I thought. At least we would not require to look far in case of an accident. I went up, walked over the fields and decided that, with several fences removed and a lot of levelling, we could make a satisfactory aerodrome. The cemetery did not bother us as an obstacle, but the main road telegraph wires would. The poles were a good twenty-five feet high and at least four feet deep with wires. They would have to come down. So, along I went to the farmhouse and asked for Mr Barrack.

'I have been sent up to see you by the farmer next door alongside the village. I was looking for an airfield as I have got to get out of Seaton owing to the Highland Show next year. This is the only place I can find. Will you help me?'

While I was speaking, Mr Hunter, his brother-in-law, joined us at the back door.

'Ah, Captain Fresson, we have read a lot about you. Won't you come in?'

I was ushered into their sitting room and a bottle of whisky was produced. Mr Barrack poured out liberal doses in each glass and by the time they were disposed of, we had got along famously.

They were prepared to help me when they got to know what a fix Highland Airways were in. We then walked out over the fields and I explained exactly what was required. Remembering the shot which so successfully registered at Wideford, Kirkwall, I said, 'Of course, gentlemen, we shall only require to use the field for an hour or so each day, so the grazing for the rest of the day would be yours.'

I could see I had again registered a 'bull's eye' and that settled it. They asked me the terms. I told them what I was paying for Seaton and they accepted the same figure. They were prepared to give me a long lease, I could build a hangar alongside the main road and to accentuate their extreme goodwill, they would attend to the removal of fences and levelling without charge. Back we went into the house and clinched the deal over another strong dram. They were incensed over the attempt to freeze us out of the Aberdeen-Orkney air route which we had established with the backing of the Aberdeen Civic Authorities.

'Gentlemen,' I said, as I was about to take my departure, 'you have been very good to us and saved the situation for my company. I will not forget. We will have an agreement drawn up and I will bring it over early in the week for signature'.

This agreement was duly signed, I managed to get the Post Office to drop the phone wires for a hundred yards and bury them underground, and in a few weeks, the airfield was ready for use. (That gap in the telephone wires on the main road can be seen today, just opposite the Kintore Cemetery. Our hangar can also be seen from the road). From that moment, a lasting friendship sprang up between Mr Barrack, who was the actual owner of the land, and myself. I saw him about a year ago, and I am always welcome at the farm whenever I am passing that way.

That winter, I got Mr Reggie Bissett, who had the year before cleared the runway for me at Dyce for my commercial charter to Lerwick, to erect a fifty-foot-span hangar capable of housing two DH89 Rapides. We moved over from Seaton early the following year. Our Kintore airfield was a better one than Seaton, operationally but, unfortunately, it was ten miles further from the centre of Aberdeen and we had to operate a car service to carry our passengers in and out, which added to our operation costs. We also would suffer from the advertising value of Dyce, but the name of Highland Airways was, by now, well known and that helped considerably to counteract that disadvantage.

During those early years, it seemed to me that I was always coming up against high walls that stood in my way to progress, but we survived all the problems imposed on us until January 1939.

By now, our passenger traffic, along with the mail, *Scotsman* newspapers and freight, was increasing rapidly. Accordingly, we considered testing out one of the new de Havilland DH89 Rapides. They were faster than the Dragon and had a better reserve of engine power thus giving improved one-motor performance, which would be a great asset on the Shetland run over so much open sea, and they carried a better load which was our immediate problem. We arranged that de Havilland would send up one of these aircraft and G-ACPO arrived at Inverness in the third week of October 1934. I spent several hours testing this aircraft giving particular attention to the distance this plane required for taking off with a full load and the run required on landing. Our fields would accommodate the take-off run, but as this plane was faster and carried a higher wing loading than the Dragon, it required great skill in landing and pulling up in still air on the existing small airfields. The answer was either to lengthen our airfields, which would be extremely difficult and very costly, or to persuade de Havilland to fit landing flaps which would permit a slower touchdown and slower stalling speed. The proposition was submitted to the de Havilland company and within six months they had a flapped demonstration Rapide ready for test. We tried it out and there was no question, our problem was solved. The flaps reduced our landing run considerably and we could operate this aircraft safely from our small aerodromes. I kept our board conversant with what I was doing and, when they received my report, we immediately placed our first order with de Havilland and our first Rapide aircraft was delivered to us the following spring.

The aircraft was most successful and helped us to more than hold our own on the Aberdeen run. We then decided to replace the slower DH84 Dragon planes with the Rapide. We also had Standard Radio installed and commenced pressing the Air Ministry for Direction Finding Stations at Inverness, Kirkwall and Sumburgh, Shetland. In the meantime, the Air Ministry arranged with the Post Office to allow us to experiment with their Shipping Radio Station at Wick. This station operated on quite a different frequency for shipping, but they agreed to alter their frequency setting for half an hour on certain days when we could experiment on homing. We experienced some trouble at first, but eventually we made contact and the tests were most satisfactory. Arising out of this test, the Air Ministry informed us they would install radio stations for aircraft under certain conditions. The main condition was that we would have to throw our airfields open to the public and that meant letting Mr Dower's company, Aberdeen Airways, into our Shetland airfield and, if necessary, Kirkwall. We considered this point at great length. Firstly, we were anxious to open the Shetland routes and, having regard to our airmail contract, we naturally expected the Postmaster General to extend the contract to Shetland. But without radio navigational assistance, we were under no misapprehension regarding our inability to maintain the required regularity without this aid. However, we were very conscious that our company had been refused the use of Dyce airport. It was, therefore, with great reluctance, that we opened Sumburgh airport to public use. Had we known how we were later to be betrayed by the Postmaster General after two years of nigh on one hundred percent service, we should have most certainly kept Sumburgh airfield private and let the Shetland airmail service slide.

From our experience of the winter months last year, we decided to carry on a daily Inverness-Kirkwall winter service. Our mail contract was only valid until the end of October and, without a connection in the winter, we would have to break the continuity and there was no telling what would then happen with threatening competition from Aberdeen. That was a wise decision as we were later given a permanent mail contract as far as Inverness-Orkney was concerned, and it was rumoured that at the beginning of December we were to be given the Inverness-Wick mails, which would be a substantial gain in prestige and load factor.

During the winter, we had a different type of weather to contend with than during spring and summer. In place of continuous spells of fog, we experienced gales up to 80 mph. Sometimes there was heavy rain and low stratus cloud which had the same bad effect on us as fog, but fortunately that type of weather was not so frequent as the fog. One other difference was that whereas one could usually climb above fog at 2,000 feet and fly in the clear, there was sometimes no getting above low stratus. As a rule, it was usually joined to higher stratus cloud. That meant instrument flying and its attending difficulties at that stage in our operations. We managed the high winds without much trouble. The Monospar monoplane was usually used under gale conditions as it had little or no tendency to blow over on the ground, whereas the DH84 Dragons could quite easily be blown over on their backs. When we were obliged to use the Dragon aircraft under gale conditions, owing to heavy loads which were beyond the capacity of the Monospar, we made provision for a landing party at Wick and Kirkwall. In the latter case, the aircraft had to wait over for two hours before the return journey and a lorry had to be on the landing ground so that we could tie the aircraft down to it during the wait. The usual picketing was not strong enough in high winds. This system worked well and we never, to my knowledge, suffered any damage through aircraft being blown over.

The pilots had to be trained in a special landing technique. The principal point was not to allow the tail of the aircraft to drop after landing until the landing crew had got a good grip on the plane. Approaching the airfield at, say, fifty feet, halfway down the strip the motors had to be shut down. By judicious use of the throttle and keeping the nose of the aircraft very slightly down, we were able in winds of sixty mph and over to drop down almost perpendicularly, like a modern day helicopter. It took a deal of practice, but all our flying staff had to learn the drill before being let loose in gales.

Towards the end of the year, the *Daily Express* reported:

North Air Mail Extension – and plans for two Counties
Post Office officials inspect Inverness Aerodrome

An air extension of the Inverness to Orkney Air Mail service, the first inland air mail in Great Britain to the counties of Caithness and Sutherland, may result from a visit paid this week to Inverness by Colonel Banks, Director General of the Post Office and Group Captain W H Primrose who is Air Mail Adviser to the Post Office. Captain E E Fresson, Managing Director of Highland Airways, who operate the present service, said to a *Daily Express* representative yesterday, 'Col Banks and Group Captain Primrose congratulated us on the extraordinary regularity of our air mail service between Inverness and Orkney since its inception in May last. During that time, I may add, we have missed only two journeys. The possibility of operating an air mail service for the counties of Caithness and Sutherland was under review.'

A month later, we were entrusted with the air mail for those two counties. The service commenced on 1 December 1934. We produced a special air mail cover for this occasion. On top of this development came the Orkney County Council air ambulance award to Highland Airways Limited for the transport to hospital by plane of all urgent cases occurring in the Orkney Islands and this became operative in November 1934. Later, this service was expanded to carry urgent Orkney cases to Aberdeen for specialised treatment.

As will be seen, 1934 proved a year of considerable progress. Highland Airways had now passed the fledgling stage and had become a factor that was creating considerable influence in the lives of the inhabitants of the north of Scotland. Southern national newspapers, which had looked at me with pity and which contemptuously turned me down when I called on them for their support in the days I was hunting for capital and support to launch Highland Airways, now became vociferous in their demands to have their newspapers carried by air to Wick and Kirkwall. They were, no doubt, well informed of the great increase in load of *The Scotsman*, which had occurred over the past eighteen months to their detriment. Those sole rights had been extended by our company for a further year with the understanding that Mr George Law of *The Scotsman* would consent to opening the door for outside interests at the end of the second year, namely 31st May 1935. We had been threatened by several newspaper barons with court proceedings to force us, as 'Public Carriers' to carry their newspapers north. We informed them we were not a public carrier and that they had their chance before I approached Mr Law of *The Scotsman* and turned it down. We could not do anything for them until *The Scotsman* contract expired. They then threatened they would operate their own planes in which case, we had to tell them, they would not be allowed the use of our airfields. We suggested they should have patience and await the completion of our *Scotsman* contract and we would be pleased to carry their freight from 1st June the following year. I never thought that the day would come when a small limited company would be in the position of saying 'no' to the national press, and I don't think they thought it either when they so magnanimously turned down my approach to them in 1932 before Mr Grant gave me that introduction to Mr Law in Edinburgh.

The Aberdeen service was making good headway, but as most Aberdeen passengers wanted to stay over in Orkney and the Orcadians were the other way inclined, wishing a few hours in the Granite City and return home for the night, we decided, as from 1st October, to alter our schedule and base the aircraft in Kirkwall, running an early service to Aberdeen and making our return departure from Aberdeen after lunch. This timing connected with the arrival of the southern train from Edinburgh and Glasgow and enabled passengers to reach Orkney the same night. This arrangement proved very successful and our passenger load increased appreciably.

The end of the second year was upon us and, when the festivities were over, we addressed ourselves to the new problems ahead. Shetland with the attending mail contract was our objective. Stornoway was very much in my mind, but most elusive. We had made no progress in spite of many visits to acquire an aerodrome in conjunction with the local authorities. However, we were constantly making a number of charter flights for which we had prepared an emergency strip in the tidal basin. They seemed to be satisfied with that, probably because they were not asked to put their hands in their pockets.

Night ambulance flights in those days called for a high degree of skill on behalf of the pilot and were not entirely without risk. The landing grounds were small, which meant the aircraft had to touch down immediately on the approach edge, and with indifferent ground lighting, which consisted of two cars shining their headlights in the form of an 'L' representing the boundary of the field and the vertical line of the 'L' the direction of the runway into wind, required very accurate flying and a considerable amount of practice. It was not possible, owing to the expense, to arrange a proper flare path system on the islands which, of course, would have made night landings much easier. I had foreseen this problem and had previously arranged that our pilots and myself went through training in this sort of night flying at Inverness airport when it was known that the ambulance contract was to be given to Highland Airways. We made a number of emergency night flights using this technique and no damage was done to any of our aircraft. Such methods caused consternation to the pundits who were accustomed to operating under the modern and slap-up conditions in the south. Pilot Hankins did most of the island night ambulance work and he was a pilot of outstanding ability. He was more deserving of a decoration, which he never received, than many civil servants who obtained CBEs for sitting at a desk.

Before seeing the old year out, it is interesting to mention the development of a plan in connection with the arrival in Orkney of Father Christmas by air for the benefit of the Kirkwall and Stromness children. Some weeks before Christmas day, Mr Jim Christie of Garden Brothers, Kirkwall, distributors for the well-known Leith firm of wholesale provision merchants A & J Todd Limited, approached me one evening when I was staying in Kirkwall at the St Ola Hotel.

'We want your assistance, Captain Fresson, to stage an "air arrival show" of Father Christmas at the airport on Christmas Day after lunch.'

I looked at him, wondering what kind of leg-pull he was trying on me.

'It's like this Captain. Our firm, as you may know, gives a big Xmas party every year for the children of Kirkwall and Stromness, and a Christmas tea at which Father Christmas appears in order to hand out the presents. Now our idea is this. We hire your monoplane *Inverness* with you as pilot, and you remove it to the field at Hatston before lunch. We will advertise that, before our tea party is due to begin, the children will be taken to Wideford airfield by lorries to witness the arrival of Father Christmas from the frozen north by aeroplane with Captain Fresson piloting. Our man, dressed up as Father Christmas, will meet you at Hatston and you will take off with him and fly in from the north, circle the field low down so the children can see Father Christmas in the plane, and then land and taxi up to the waiting children.'

He was prepared to pay us well for our part in the hoax. I told him I would co-operate.

My name, by then, was well-known to all the children in Orkney and it appeared that my connection with the scheme sold it as a real and genuine occasion. At the appointed time, the chap who was to impersonate Father Christmas arrived at Hatston. He looked wonderful in his make up. I got him into the monoplane in the front seat alongside me and at half past two we took off and headed north to get on the Shetland-Kirkwall track, and then turned on course for Wideford airfield.

I was amazed at the crowd of children that had turned up. So was my friend sitting beside me.

'This looks like being a real big do,' he said.

'Looks like it,' I replied, and it certainly was.

There was a fifty-five mile an hour gale blowing and the plane was moving at great speed on the downward course preparatory to landing. When we taxied up to the crowd of children and Father Christmas stepped out on to the wing, the look of amazement and complete astonishment on those children's faces had to be seen to be believed. They stared at me and they stared at my august passenger, and swallowed the situation 'hook, line and sinker'. When my erstwhile passenger began to move towards the children, the little ones appeared a bit awed and frightened, but my good friend Mr Christie soon got them on amicable terms and they departed in the lorries, with Father Christmas in the leading vehicle, for the scene of the party. It went with a bang, The organisers were more than delighted with the exercise and said there and then that they would make the 'air arrival' an annual event, which they did up to the outbreak of war, five years later. I appeared to share some of the glory, because I noticed after the party that the children used to look at me with great respect when I passed them in the street.

As a result of our newly found ambulance work, the following poem was written and composed by an inhabitant of North Ronaldsay. It was in honour of a difficult autumn flight in the dark to Kirkwall for an air ambulance case.

On one of the dark November days
A wire was sent to the airways base,
For Captain Fresson to start a flight
To the Orkney's Northern-most Isle that night.
The Captain entered his beautiful plane
In the darkening dusk and drizzling rain,
Tho' the wind was high and the seas did roar
He proceeded at once to the Sanday shore.
He picked up a man who was storm-stayed there
Then away again through the wintry air,
And quickly he flew to our Island home
And landed him safely on our aerodrome.
The whirring from earth with a run and a spring
And soaring aloft like a bird on the wing,
Mid the gathering gloom that November night,
In one short hour he had finished the flight.
He appeared again in the still Sabbath air
As the folks were assembling for praise and prayer,
But ere our Kirk service had even begun
He was speeding again on his homeward run.
Flying so swiftly for Kirkwall's fair town
Carrying his name on the role of renown,
With engines running so smoothly in space,
In twenty minutes completed the race.
Once more he came in the season of Yule,
Steering his course for Ultima Thule,
Scorning the seas and their treacherous tides
Down on our aerodrome gracefully glides.
Long life to the Captain and safe may he glide
To carry his freights over the great rolling tide,
May his eye be keen and his nerve well braced
And his perilous journeys be safely faced.

7

Hebridean incursions

During the previous summer of 1934, a very bad accident occurred with a DH Rapide aircraft belonging to Hillman's Airways Limited whose headquarters were at Romford, Essex. The aircraft was on a scheduled run to Paris. About noon, holidaymakers on the seafront somewhere near St Leonards heard the roar of an aeroplane just above them, but invisible in the heavy mist enveloping the town. Shortly after, a loud report was heard out at sea. Boats sent out to investigate came across the wreckage of a DH89 Rapide aircraft. The seven occupants and the pilot were dead. An Air Ministry investigation subsequently took place and the cause of the accident was attributed to the pilot having lost control of the aircraft in cloud.

Arising out of that incident, shortly afterwards a 'Notice to Airmen' was issued by the civil aviation authorities that no pilot's transport air licence would be renewed unless the applicant went through a satisfactory instrument flying test at the RAF station at Hendon. My own licence, one of the early ones, No. 310, (today there are now over 40,000) became due for renewal in May, so I had time to prepare myself for the conditions to be fulfilled. It was arranged for the two front seats in the Monospar cabin to be partitioned by a curtain, thus segregating the pilot from the passenger on his right. In addition, the pilot's cockpit windows would be blanked out with three-ply sheets cut to size. When that was completed, it produced the same effect as being caught up in dense cloud, as visibility was nil. On the other side of the curtain, on the right-hand side of the cockpit, another pilot sat as an observer with duplicated controls and full vision in case the pilot under test got into trouble, in which case he would act should an emergency arise. The test comprised the following requirements:

(a) Take the aircraft off the ground on instruments
(b) Climb to a prearranged altitude
(c) Complete three left and right hand turns and continue on the same course
(d) Complete three half turns and proceed on a reciprocal course
(e) To fly a triangular course of over half an hour and return on dead reckoning to as near to the starting point as possible.

I had been doing a considerable amount of instrument flying on the route, principally when it was foggy, so that I could get above the fog while the weather was clear each end of the route. The test showed up certain faults and I practised for ten hours. At the end of that time, I flew a plotted course blind from Inverness to Nairn, across to Cromarty and back to Inverness, landing about a mile off the airfield at Longman. There was not much wind and the courses were previously computed for each of the three legs. That, I thought, was good enough and, with interest, I awaited my test at Hendon the following May.

In the meantime, my other pilots were put through the same instruction and it was found to pay handsome dividends as it gave them so much extra confidence when they encountered bad visibility. They always knew that, in the case of emergency, they could climb up into the overcast and return to base and clear weather.

Also about that time we were informed that radio stations were shortly to be erected at Longman airport, Inverness, and Wideford, Kirkwall. We heard later on that the Sumburgh station could not be supplied until the following year. Radio station control meant we would be in a position to fly the whole Inverness-Orkney sector at altitude in cloud if need be, the radio station bringing us in overhead. We would let down through the overcast on a time and course procedure, known in those days as the 'Z' approach. To fly as accurately as this required modern cloud-flying instruments. We had taken the precaution to install our new Dragon aircraft with the Sperry artificial horizon which controlled the lateral and perpendicular position of the aircraft, and the Sperry directional gyro which indicated the number of degrees turns to right or left. While this instrument was unaffected by magnetic variation, it was subject to precession which necessitated a check and correction with the compass every fifteen minutes. Unfortunately, the aircraft manufacturers did not provide for these instruments to be driven by an engine-operated vacuum pump. They crudely chose to drive the instruments by two Venturi tubes attached to the side of the aircraft. Under icing conditions, these tubes would become frozen and the cloud flying instruments would cease to function. When that happened, we only had the Reid & Sigrist turn and bank indicator to fall back on. As it was difficult to maintain an accurate course in cloud on this instrument for long periods, if we were over high ground we usually made for the open sea and let down under the overcast with the help of bearings from the nearest radio station. Subsequently we found a fairly good method of overcoming the freezing of the Venturi tubes by remounting them alongside and to the rear of the hot exhaust pipe.

I have mentioned these problems difficulties and explained them at some length so that the reader may be able to appreciate the difficulties which beset us in the early days of instrument flying. Of course, we had no radio landing and approach system as is the case today. The radio station simply brought the aircraft overhead by a series of Wire Telegraphy bearings (using Morse code), or Radio Telephony if no radio officer was aboard. After that, the pilot had to find his own way down and on to the airfield. It is too complicated to explain the 'Z' approach method we used, but with practise we got extremely accurate with the let-down and could get into our airfield with cloud a few feet off the deck and with visibility a hundred yards or so. That is as good as, and sometimes considerably better than, can be done today with larger aircraft and their modern automatic approach radar equipment. In addition, we had now reached the stage when our aircraft engines required a special maintenance organisation operated by an engineer with specialist qualifications. Up until then, I had been responsible for the work in conjunction with Engineer Pugh, who came up with me from Croydon in April 1933. He was a first rate chap at field maintenance, but was not sufficiently qualified or experienced to organise and operate an up-to-date maintenance shop which would cover the complete overhaul of motors and carry out the annual Certificate of Airworthiness overhaul required by the Air Ministry. Hitherto, we had been obliged to ferry our aircraft south to the makers for this annual overhaul, which was very costly. Accordingly, we decided to engage a fully licensed engineer to carry out this work and I was fortunate in locating George Griffiths who, at that time, was employed by the SMT Aviation Department, Edinburgh, and who was looking for a change. He joined us around the middle of 1934. I have always looked upon that appointment as the luckiest shot of my life in business. Griffiths turned out to be a superlative craftsman. There was nothing he could not do. If he didn't know the answer to a problem, he found it within a matter of hours. When we commenced using radio, we found ourselves in difficulty because we had no radio maintenance. Every time a set went out of action, we had to get the manufacturers to send a mechanic to put it right. After several of these visits, which were costly, Griffiths commenced correcting faults himself. He had watched and questioned the factory mechanics and had already grasped the fundamentals of our radio sets.

Accordingly, I asked Griffiths if he would undertake a month's course at the Standard Radio Corporation's workshops if it could be arranged. He agreed and he took the maintenance course in London. On his return, he set up his own radio shop and carried out an efficient maintenance service until Theo Goulden joined us a year or so later. Goulden also knew radio backwards and was a great asset to our company.

Griffiths had learned in a month what would have taken an ordinary person twelve months to acquire. He stayed with me until we were nationalised after World War Two and then, within a few months under very difficult conditions, left the nationalised corporation and joined Rolls-Royce Aviation Department at Hillington, near Renfrew. Twelve years later, he still holds a responsible appointment with the Rolls Royce Company.

Under the new maintenance arrangement, it was not long before it became apparent that Pugh and George Griffiths wee out of tune with each other. It was accordingly, with great reluctance on my part, that Pugh should be asked to find another job. In view of the loyal service he had given me to date, I had insisted that he would be kept on with Highland Airways until he could find an alternative and satisfactory appointment. He had done a good job for me and we parted good friends. I was sorry to see him go.

The year 1935 was not very old when it became apparent that we were very soon to be faced with competition on the Aberdeen-Orkney route. An announcement in the Aberdeen press informed the public that Mr Gandar Dower at Dyce Airport had floated an air operating company known as Aberdeen Airways Limited.[1]

It appeared that the so called 'Gentlemen's Agreement' which I had previously discussed the year before in the Caledonian Hotel, was not going to be kept. The press announcements indicated that his concern intended operating alongside us on the Aberdeen-Kirkwall run and ultimately on the Shetland service. Our agents in Shetland informed us that Aberdeen Airways representatives had been making enquiries in Shetland, and in fact, had been trying to wrest the Sumburgh landing ground from us by approaching the Sumburgh Estate manager, Mr W Laidlaw MacDougall. They met with a rebuff as Mr MacDougall remained loyal to Highland Airways. A press report of the day summed up the position as follows:

Highland Airways Limited in a letter to the Zetland County Council announced that it is prepared to commence an air service to Shetland in May, which will be run just as long as there are passengers to support it. If the traffic warrants, states the letter, the services will be daily, Sunday's excepted, and in winter it may be possible to maintain either a once or twice weekly service. Highland Airways added, that the Air Ministry had definitely promised a 'radio beacon' for Shetland, and asked for an immediate reply from the council whether they would contribute £100 towards the annual maintenance of this beacon, which would cost the Ministry £1,000 per annum.

Captain Halcrow and other Councillors contended that Inverness was not anything like such a good jumping off or landing place for Shetland passengers as Aberdeen. The captain added that two representatives of the Aberdeen air firm were in Shetland last week and were quite willing to co-operate with the County Council. Mr Laidlaw MacDougall retorted that Highland Airways ran a service from Aberdeen to Kirkwall just now. The Aberdeen firm, he added, had entered the field rather late and seemed anxious to benefit from the pioneer work carried out by Highland Airways. The latter company had been exceptionally successful with their service to Orkney, and if they began a service to Shetland, he had no

---

[1] Aberdeen Airways launched scheduled services in 1934, initially between Aberdeen and Renfrew.

doubt, they would get the mails also. It was eventually agreed to pay £100 towards maintaining a radio beacon and to inform Highland Airways and the Air Ministry accordingly.

That was in the spring of 1935. We did not get the radio station at Sumburgh until a year later.

Up to the middle of March, I spent a lot of my time at Kintore overlooking the building of Kintore airfield and the hangar which was to house our first DH89 Rapide that was on order for the Aberdeen-Kirkwall-Shetland run. During the middle of that month, Provost Smith of Stornoway, along with Councillor Alistair MacKenzie who subsequently became Provost, and a Miss Margaret McIvor, arrived in Inverness from the south and booked a charter flight over to Stornoway. I flew them over in the Monospar, landing on the tidal basin alongside the golf course at low tide. Work had previously been carried out to enable the aircraft to be taxied up to the golf club above high tide. Having picketed the aircraft down, I accompanied the passengers into town and spent four days with the council, trying with the aid of Provost Smith and Bailie MacKenzie to get them to start construction of an airfield on the golf course. They had control over the golf club and the Stornoway Trust owned the ground. The council seemed either shy or afraid to use their authority. At the end of four days, I had got no further and, as I had passengers for the return journey, took off for Inverness with a Mr Hooper, a chartered accountant, and his friends who were resident in Inverness. Incidentally, Mr Hooper had been the first businessman to fly from Inverness to Stornoway some months before when he chartered the monoplane *Inverness* for the journey. It appeared he had regular audits to do in Stornoway and, as it only took him fifty minutes by air compared to all day and night by train and steamer, he found it a business proposition to charter a plane. We made many trips together.

I returned to Stornoway in April, having previously advertised a five-day visit for the purpose of giving short flights to cultivate air mindedness amongst the population of Lewis. I used the hard beach for this exercise and operated between tides. I took my chief engineer, George Griffiths, over with me and we had a very successful tour carrying two hundred and fifty passengers in three days of operation.

During the middle of our visit, Bailie Tolmie and Kenny MacKenzie, director of the local tweed mills, asked me to fly them across to Inverness in the morning and return at night. As the time of the tide was not very suitable for short flights that day, I accommodated them. The weather was not very good, low cloud covering the Minch, but Inverness was clear with high cloud. We climbed above the cloud after take-off and ran into good weather on the other side of the Minch. This phenomena with the weather often occurred on this route, as we came to know later. The weather would commence building up over the Summer Isles and persist right across the Minch. Also, it could be the other way round, which indicated different weather systems existed east and west of the mountains of Wester Ross.

We left Inverness late in the evening for the return trip and again ran into fog over the Minch. It was very thick and low, but patchy. Half way over, I talked the position over with my passengers and we decided it would be better to return to Enard Bay on the west coast and land on the Achnahaird sands. There was a good hotel a few miles away on the shores of upper Loch Broom opposite the Summer Isles, and we had it organised with the owners of the hotel, that if we dived on them three times, they were to send a car to Achnahaird beach. We spent and hour at the hotel during which time our host produced some very excellent whisky, and we took off again and set off for Stornoway. We had ascertained on the phone that Stornoway harbour was clear of fog. We ran in and out of fog for the next fifteen minutes and then flew into the clear. Ahead was a large bank of fog which appeared to cover the Chicken Head promontory. The tidal basin where we had to land was most likely in that mass of mist. It was tending to get dark and I had not much time to go looking for 300 yards of sand and, if I failed to find it, return before darkness set in to Achnahaird beach, thirty miles across the water. I decided it was too risky, so after a wide sweep out at sea, changed course on the return Minch crossing. The fog was thicker and I was thinking I would soon have to decide whether I would gain altitude for the return flight over the mountains to Inverness, when suddenly we burst into the clear and there was the rocky coastline of Rubha Mòr, some three miles west of Achnahaird beach. David Tolmie was sitting by my side when he saw Rubha Mòr hills ahead.

'Ah, Kenny,' he exclaimed, 'there's the Chicken Head.'

Kenny who was sitting behind, leaned forward from the rear seat and said, 'We shan't be long now.'

They had both mistaken the rocky west coast for Chicken Head, Lewis and failed to notice the half turn I had made in the bad visibility, some twenty minutes before. I said nothing thinking I would pull their legs. It was nearly dark and I had no time to give the diving signal to the hotel, so we swung round to the north and landed back on the Achnahaird beach. We all got out of the plane. My passengers looked around, a bit bewildered.

'Hey, Kenny,' said David Tolmie, 'where are we? This doesn't look much Stornoway.'

Kenny raised his head and looked around, 'It certainly doesn't, David. Where are we Captain? The other side of Lewis?' no doubt meaning Cross sands on the western side, off the north tip of Lewis.

'No,' I answered laughing, 'unfortunately, you are back where we started from – Achnahaird bay.'

They both looked amazed. It took a moment or two for it to sink in, which demonstrated how easy it is to completely lose one's sense of direction when careering around under foggy conditions. That made a good story on the island for many a long day.

A boy turned up on a bicycle. 'Hey, sonny,' I said, 'there's a shilling. Go and ask the hotel to send a car for us, will you?'

'Right-o, Sir,' and off he pedalled for dear life.

In the meanwhile, some other bodies turned up from a nearby croft and helped us get the monoplane to a sheltered spot behind a sand dune. I screwed the pickets into firm sand and tied the aircraft up before walking over to the road about three quarters of a mile away to await the car. By then it was pretty dark and we had only just made it.

The Achiltibuie Hotel was a very comfortable place in those days and the owner made us very welcome. He said we were the first air guests to have come his way and that called for 'several on the house.' That in turn called for a few more and it was well on into the night before we got to bed.

The following morning dawned fine and sunny. We made an early start, crossing to Stornoway in twenty-five minutes and were back at base ready for another busy day. Later in the year, I was to have another emergency landing at Achnahaird which I shall refer to later. I had only discovered that beach not so very long before and had made a survey on foot. On the east side ran a small stream and on the west side the beach rose up towards the eroded sand dunes. From the middle of the beach to the stream, the sand was exceedingly soft and an aeroplane would have turned over landing on such soft sand. From the middle towards the sand dunes, it became very hard and so the available safe run was as near to the sand dunes as possible. I had arranged with the crofter to build stone cairns along the division between the hard and soft sand and these acted as a safe guide for any pilot who was properly briefed. Seven years later, during the war, an RAF plane force-landed on those sands and he, of course, did not know what the stone cairns were for, even if he had seen them, which I very much doubt. However, he landed on the east side of the cairns. The aircraft sank into the soft sand and somersaulted on to its back. I think the pilot was badly hurt and I believe he was alone, but I am not sure on that point.

The result of operations to Stornoway over the past months, and the frequent use being made of that very small runway on the tidal basin for charter flights, confirmed without doubt that an Inverness-Stornoway air connection would be a success. I still had not solved the problem of getting all the interested parties involved with the golf course to come to some common agreement over the alterations to the fairways and the payment for carrying out the levelling and draining work required.

By the end of April, our airfield at Kintore was ready for operations. We shifted over from the old field at Seaton and commenced our summer service to Kirkwall some three weeks later.

We were worried about the competition which would commence almost immediately as at that time there was not sufficient traffic available for one airline, let alone two. The public had to be educated to this new form of travel and they still clung to slower sea transport. What were we to do? It was disgusting luck that we had spent so much time and money pioneering this route only to have a second party 'horn in' on us, thus depriving us of the chance of running this service, if not at a profit, at least not at a loss. I knew we were well backed by the North of Scotland Shipping Company Limited, but there was no knowing how long they would be prepared to help subsidise a service which was losing money. On the other hand, the shipping company knew that if we withdrew and left the Aberdeen-Kirkwall run to the Dyce operators, they would gradually strip the sea route of their passenger traffic, so the result would be as broad as it was long for them.

In early April, we received an enquiry from United Airways Limited whose headquarters were at Blackpool and London. They were backed by the wealthy Whitehall Securities Corporation and wished to know whether we would be interested in joining their organisation, but still retaining our identity.

We were interested in the enquiry and the matter was discussed at length by our directors. We came to the conclusion that a merger with such an influential concern might be the answer to our problem vis-à-vis the threat of competition from Aberdeen Airways Limited. I was authorised to write and ask for an appointment, suggesting Glasgow as the meeting place.

A date was ultimately arranged and Mr R Donald, our chairman, and myself as managing director, flew down in the monoplane *Inverness* to Glasgow on 1st May 1935 for a meeting in the Central Hotel with two directors of United Airways Limited. We booked in for the night and awaited the arrival of the United Airways representatives. They flew up from Blackpool, arriving at Renfrew late in the afternoon. Mr W D Roberts led the deputation, supported by Mr A R Ballardie, the secretary to Whitehall Securities. The discussion commenced before dinner and carried on right through the meal and for quite a while after. Mr Roberts opened up with a general survey of the internal airways situation and described the picture they had in mind for future operations. We in turn presented our views and spoke from strength as far as the extreme north of Scotland was concerned. We possessed the airfields, mail and newspaper contracts and, at that moment, all the passengers and their goodwill. United Airways appreciated our desire to retain our identity and both Mr Roberts and Mr Ballardie thought that a good thing as the name of Highland Airways now meant something to the travelling public, having created and established a feeling of goodwill. At that juncture, we hied ourselves down to a magnificent dinner in the Malmaison restaurant as the guests of our visitors. On top of the whisky, the wine flowed in abundance, and both Donald and myself felt there was little doubt we were up against two men who could easily see us 'under the table'. It was imperative to keep fit for the final discussion after dinner so we resisted the wine. After dinner, we went upstairs to the lounge and, over coffee, got down to final business.

Mr Roberts did most of the talking while his friend gave advice when needed. I instinctively liked Roberts and Ballardie, and I could see they were interested in our proposition. They definitely wanted us in their orbit – I could feel that – and for that matter, we wanted them to help combat the war that was building up in the north.

'Well, Mr Donald,' Roberts said when our talks drew to a close, 'how much do you want for a majority share holding in Highland Airways?'

Without hesitation he named a figure which would give our shareholders a fifty percent profit.

'We weren't thinking as high as that,' said Roberts. 'Won't you come down a bit?'

'No,' said Donald firmly. 'We don't have to sell, but we would like to have you with us providing you are willing to offer a worthwhile figure. We hold all the airfields. I think our offer very reasonable.'

There was a long pause. Roberts looked up at his friend Ballardie, 'I'm afraid, Ballardie, we've wasted a good dinner,' he said.

'Looks like it,' said Ballardie gloomily.

We talked on for a bit longer and, having thanked them for a very nice dinner, suggested we would be off to bed as we had to make an early start for Aberdeen in the morning. Mr Roberts then suggested we put our offer to them in writing, along with an undertaking that we were willing to sell on the understanding that we would continue to operate the north of Scotland routes under our own management.

'If you will do that, we will then put the proposal to our principals, Whitehall Securities, and will let you have our final answer at an early date. We retired to bed jubilant. There was little doubt the offer would be confirmed and new vistas would be open to us. We would be able to join up with the southern end of the group by operating a service to Glasgow, which would, in turn, join up with a network throughout England, the Channel Isles and the Continent. And most important, we should be in a very strong position to combat the Dyce competition.

Our board approved our negotiations and our offer was duly sent. We received a reply by the third week in May accepting. The press quoted the merger in the following terms:

Civil Aviation Merger
Highland Airways in National Combine
To Link Shetland and Channel Islands

The announcement was made in Inverness yesterday of the merger of Highland Airways Limited, the pioneer civil aviation company in Scotland now in its third year of operation, with United Airways Limited, London, the central company of a great national air combine. Highland Airways will retain its name with Captain E E Fresson as its managing director and also most of the local directorate. The merger had been anticipated for some time and it was understood that the agreement would come into operation on 31st May.

Behind the merger is Whitehall Securities Corporation Limited who, it is understood, have connections with United Airways Limited (London-Blackpool-Isle of Man-Carlisle-Glasgow), Jersey Airways Limited (London-Jersey) and Northern & Scottish Airways Limited (Glasgow-Islay-Campbeltown-Isle of Man). The London terminus of the combined companies in Heston Airport, Middlesex, and, in association, they will now operate air transport services from the Shetlands to the Channel Islands.

Developments foreshadowed

Highland Airways has developed a summer service between Orkney and Aberdeen and hopes soon to extend that route to the Shetlands. Its present aircraft includes two fast, modern twin-engined eight-seater biplanes and a five-seater monoplane. Early developments foreshadowed are services linking Inverness with Stornoway, Inverness-Aberdeen and Inverness-Dundee.

In two years of its active operation, Highland Airways have carried thousands of passengers and many tons of parcels and mails with creditable regularity in all kinds of weather and with complete absence of serious accident. In the merger, Highland Airways will retain its name. Captain Fresson will continue as Managing Director and Chief Pilot. He is a native of London and his aviation experience dates from 1916 when he joined the Royal Flying Corps, which later became the Royal Air Force. After the war, he did considerable air work in the Far East, being for a time Flying Instructor to the Chinese Military Authorities. He organised the first aircraft factory in China at Tai-Yuan-Fu.

We now felt more than ready to go into action and the whole of our attention was turned to making our Company the predominating air carrier between Glasgow and Shetland. Our first move was to build up-to-date maintenance workshops at Inverness and to substitute our DH84 Dragon aircraft with DH89

Rapides. To do this we would also require new hangarage at Inverness as the latter type of aircraft did not have folding wings like the DH84, and so our existing sheds were not of sufficient span. However, the old sheds converted nicely into workshops and so were not wasted. In those sheds we soon built up a first class organisation under George Griffiths' direction and our spares stores were the best that could be obtained. We wanted for nothing, down to the last bolt. Also, we added an engine test bench with instruments that enabled us to carry out our complete engine overhauls and we could rebuild any damage that our aircraft might sustain. Up to now, all this work had to be sent south and not only was the transport expensive, but a lot of valuable time was wasted.

We took on further engineers to cope with the extra work, two of whom were outstanding. A MacLennan, who came from around Fochabers, was an expert wood worker and he became the foreman of aircraft repairs. The other, Bert Farminer, had been brought up in aviation. In 1912, when a boy of fourteen, he had joined the Tom Sopwith sheds at Brooklands. What he did not know about rotary engines was not worth knowing. As mentioned in Chapter 1, I first met him at Monkmoor airfield at Shrewsbury in 1928, just after my return from China. I had taken on a job with Berkshire Aviation Tours Limited, managed by another old timer, Fred Holmes, and Bert was seconded to me as my engineer in the field. Subsequently, when Lance Rimmer and I set up the North British Aviation Company, Bert Farminer came over to us. So what was more natural than for me to ask Bert Farminer to join Highland Airways now that I could offer him secure employment. Certainly there would be no rotary Le Rhône engines for him to look after, but as he had always serviced the DH Gipsy motor in my Moth, he soon got into the way of caring for the larger Gipsy VI 200 hp motors. He was a born comic and always kept the team in good humour and, best of all, he got on excellently with George Griffiths who was now our chief engineer.

On the 31st May 1935, I duly reported to Hendon for the Instrument Flying Test. The aircraft, on which the test was to be carried out, was a Lynx-Avro with a hood over the front seat which I occupied. In the rear seat was an RAF Instructor who put me through the mill. On landing, he pronounced me as 'competent' and said the Air Ministry would be notified about the endorsement of my Transport Licence.

On 16 June I was back at Kintore. Aberdeen had been well advertised for an 'Air Demonstration Day' and short flights were given in one of our eight-seater aeroplanes that we used on the Aberdeen-Orkney route. It was very successful, 200 passengers having been flown during the afternoon despite heavy rainstorms. Great interest was displayed by the crowd which had turned up at Kintore in time for the arrival of the Orkney passenger plane, which, fortunately, was full with passengers. That gave a good impression.

In the third week in July, we undertook to fly the *Daily Mail* to Dornoch, off the morning train. We ran two services a day from Inverness. Along with the newspapers on the morning flight out, we carried passengers for a day on the sands at Dornoch. On the return journey, the local inhabitants flew in to Inverness for a shopping day. On the flight in the evening, the Dornoch shopping passengers were flown back, and we collected the beach party for their return to Inverness. This service did not prove very successful, and the flight was discontinued as the *Daily Mail* did not renew the contract for the next year.

Towards the end of July, we received notification from the Air Ministry that Major Mealing and a Mr Duncan from the Signals Department in London were visiting us with a view to locating the radio stations along the air route. I met them in Aberdeen and flew them up to Shetland and Kirkwall. Major Mealing approved the Sumburgh landing field and Mr Duncan, in striped trousers, bowler hat and umbrella, to the great amusement of the locals, wandered around the bleak Shetland countryside looking for a position to site the radio station. Major Mealing said he always did that and was quite impervious to the amusement which he caused the locals. The radio site decided upon did not turn out to be very practical because it was washed away by torrential rain during the first season and had to be moved to higher ground. On the way back to Kirkwall, the weather was far from good and we had to negotiate a big fog bank off Fair Isle. Major Mealing said he could quite understand why we were so insistent in having radio service on this inhospitable portion of the North Sea. I could guess how he was feeling as, of course, we were flying on dead reckoning and, if the fog got worse over Orkney, it would not be easy to locate Kirkwall.

'Do you think you'll make it?' he asked.

'I think so,' I said. 'You see, Major, this fog has a habit of tailing off just north of Kirkwall. We'll go on until North Ronaldsay island should appear and, if we don't spot it and the fog is worse, we will climb above the layer and return to Shetland.'

We arrived alright in Kirkwall with the conviction of our Air Ministry officials fully behind us on the need for radio communication. On their return to London, they used their influence to speed matters up.

We stayed the night in Kirkwall and flew on to Thurso next morning as Major Mealing wished to look at a site that Aberdeen Airways had chosen to use as a landing field and desired to obtain a licence for. We had 'flight tested' that field a year before, but turned it down as being unsafe. He was not very impressed, but a low grade licence was ultimately granted. The run was very short and there was only one runway at that, from east to west. A year or so afterwards, there were some nasty incidents on that airstrip involving a complete write-off of one aeroplane. It was raining heavily at this field, which was about three miles from Thurso on the main road to Castletown. We had given up using Thurso as we could not find a safe airfield to operate from.

After Major Mealing had completed his work, we went into Thurso to see James Wilson who owned the Royal Hotel.

'Hello, Captain Fresson,' he said when he saw me, 'Glad to see you. What brings you here?'

I introduced my companions and, when he heard that their visit was in connection with providing Thurso with a landing strip, he was elated.

'Come in, Gentlemen,' and he took us into the lounge and said, 'You must be a bit dry after a hard morning's work. Waiter, bring three large whiskies and soda.'

Major Mealing's face took on a sudden warmth. We chatted a while and went in to lunch. Mr Wilson had started life selling ginger beer and aerated water from a barrow and he now owned the Royal Hotel, which he had recently extended and almost completely rebuilt with accommodation for over one hundred guests. It possessed a very modern dining room and the menu was all that could be desired. My Air Ministry friends were most impressed, but could not understand how such a hotel could pay in such a small out of the way place as Thurso. I explained to him that the coach touring business was developing in the south and the idea was that the Royal Hotel would be the agent for the extreme north of Scotland.

As the years went by, the coaches came north every summer in ever-increasing numbers and Mr Wilson was rapidly becoming a very wealthy man. He was naturally also keen to build up an air passenger clientele and he was looking to Aberdeen Airways to provide these passengers. I had told Mr Wilson repeatedly that Highland Airways would provide all the air communication he required, provided the Council would construct a reasonable airfield which we would hire from them. This never came about although there was an effort made around 1938, which fell through. We had searched the Thurso area very thoroughly, but had been unable to find a large enough field which would give the safety margin we required. That afternoon, we flew back to Inverness in time for my friends to catch the half past four train to London.

Mr Duncan was looking out of the carriage window while waiting for the train to start.

'I'll do all I can, Fresson, to get the Inverness-Kirkwall and Shetland radio stations underway. You certainly need them on that route. It's a wonder how you have flown so regularly and without accident for so long without such aids.'

'I must admit, it has been pretty soul destroying at times,' I said.

Major Mealing then said that he and Duncan would be up again later on. 'I want to go over that Stornoway site with you, so we'll meet again soon.'

The train started to pull out and, as I stood waving farewell, I thought, 'What human and helpful individuals those two are compared to the usual run of civil servants one meets from government departments.' I heard later that the Thurso site had been granted a Grade 2 licence. I also learnt that accidents were beginning to occur which were upsetting the morale of the air travelling public.

Around the middle of August, a party from the D'Oyly Carte Opera Company from the Savoy arrived too late for the train which connected with the Stornoway steamer at Kyle of Lochalsh. We were asked to fly them over and the party of eight squeezed into one of our Dragon DH84s. Phone reports indicated that the weather was far from good over Stornoway although it was fine in Inverness. I told their manager about this and warned him it might not be possible to land. If he would like to take the risk, I would try and get them there. He agreed. Like the previous trip with the Stornoway councillors, we reached Chicken Head only to find it completely covered with low cloud and the cloud extended heavenwards for many thousand feet. I tried to dodge under it at sea level, but when it came to turning inland to the north to find the landing strip, it was like a blind in front of one and was hopeless. I was obliged to turn out to sea and return to Achnahaird beach. We had a consultation and I suggested they wait an hour or so and we would have another try. The party agreed. It was a fine afternoon that side of the Minch so my passengers went for a walk along the extensive beach while I sent the boy with a bike who had befriended us before for a car. We tried again two hours later, but this time found the low cloud had reached three quarters of the way across the Minch. That meant only one thing, a weather front was advancing from the west. So we turned tail and headed back to Inverness. I was as disappointed the way the flight had turned out as was the manager of the D'Oyly Carte Opera Company. It would have been first class publicity for us to have got them over to Stornoway in time to stage their show. I have forgotten the manager's name, but he heartily agreed with me that eight whole necks and a broken appointment was a much better proposition than eight broken ones with the same results.

172

Five days later, another charter cropped up, this time from Aberdeen to Stornoway, with six professors who were attending an important meeting. The weather included heavy rainstorms over the Minch, but the trip was successfully completed. I stress all these Stornoway charters to support my contention that an air service was urgently needed for Stornoway, and one would have thought the local authorities would have recognised this proof by now and got on with providing an aerodrome.

With this build up of evidence, I was hoping that Major Mealing would be able to make some impression on the councillors and loosen up their pockets when he returned. But, as will be seen, I hoped in vain. It appeared that the local rulers were still sold on the uneconomical flying boat service, which they hoped to obtain without any cash outlay. They were hoping some other company would come along and solve this situation. But they waited in vain. Our services were running to good capacity from Aberdeen. The distance from the town to Kintore did not seem to put passengers off. Also the Inverness planes were invariably filled to full capacity, what with rapidly increasing mail and newspaper supplies. We were now able to carry outside newspapers, the end of the second year's *Scotsman* contract having now terminated.

The merger with United Airways Limited brought us into working agreement with Northern & Scottish Airways Limited, Renfrew, which succeeded Mr John Sword's company, Midland & Scottish Air Ferries at the beginning of 1934. George Nicholson was the managing director and William Cumming was their very able secretary. Already, I knew them well. They operated the air services from Renfrew to Campbeltown and Islay and were beginning to extend north to the Outer Hebrides: Barra, South and North Uist, and hoping, like ourselves, to finally link up with Stornoway. So they were also an interested party in the establishment of an airfield there. We had both discussed the question of a seaplane service with Mr Roberts of United Airways. He thought we should survey the route in a flying boat and, as the company was connected with Saunders Roe of Cowes, Isle of Wight, who built small flying boats, it was agreed that an amphibian would be made available and sent up to Renfrew as the kicking off point.

One morning my phone rang. 'Hello, Fresson, is that you? This is George Nicholson, Renfrew,' a voice said.

'Yes, George,' I answered.

'We've just got word that Saunders Roe are sending up the *Cloud of Iona* with Captain Scott in charge and Captain MacIntosh (ex Imperial Airways) as second in command.'

'That's fine,' I said, 'when do they arrive?'

'Over the weekend and we intend setting off for the west coast on Monday after lunch. Can you come along?'

'Certainly, I can and will,' I answered. 'I'll meet you at the airport club in time for lunch. Is that alright?'

'Certainly,' answered George, 'we'll be glad to see you.'

I arrived by air at half past twelve and the *Cloud of Iona* was sitting on its two wheels on the tarmac ready for us. I made for George Nicholson's office and instantly recognised Captain Scott.

'We met at Cowes,' I said, 'over a year ago.' He looked a bit blank. 'I flew down with Captain Schofield in their demonstration Monospar.'

'Ah, yes,' he said, 'I remember. Are you coming with us on the West Coast survey?'

'That's the idea,' I said, 'hasn't George told you?'

George answered: 'They haven't arrived long and I hadn't got around to that. Have you met Captain MacIntosh?'

'No, but I know him by name very well. He was one of the 1920s pilots who had designs of flying the Atlantic east to west.'

We repaired to the club and, after an appetiser in the very nice lounge overlooking the airfield, we sat down to lunch. It was remarkable in those days, when one started chatting to anyone in the flying world, how familiar names kept cropping up and that time was no exception.

We took off after lunch, Captains Scott and MacIntosh in the front cockpit and George and myself in the cabin which seated six persons. It was a cloud-free afternoon and we climbed high to cross over the lower Argyll mountains to reach the coast at the north end of the island of Islay. I was invited up to the cockpit after a while and Captain MacIntosh went back and sat with George Nicholson. What a wonderful sight it was. I had never seen that part of the coast before. The broken coastline and innumerable inlets and small lochs, the blue sea in the distance and the heather-coloured mountains underneath looked superb. On reaching the sea, we turned northwards. Soon the familiar Cuillin mountains came into sight in the far distance and we dropped off height and slipped by the Sound of Mull with the islands of Muck and Eigg coming up on our port side. We flew up to Mallaig where we alighted on the water, the land wheels having been wound up. We looked for a sheltered bay, but there was nothing within ten miles of the next opening to the north. I jotted down Captain Scott's report on the Mallaig landing and we took off again, this time headed for Kyle of Lochalsh. Soon we ran into the Sound of Sleat with Loch Hourn on our right. In front of us, the mountains, some two thousand feet high on each side of the sound, seemed to converge into a tiny gap like the eye of a needle as we approached. On we flew, and the mountains appeared to be touching each wing. Suddenly, we were over the Kylerhea ferry, the horizon opened up and, turning to the left, there was Kyle of Lochalsh village directly ahead. What a breath-taking trip that had been, with the clear sky and sun shining on the mountains in the south west.

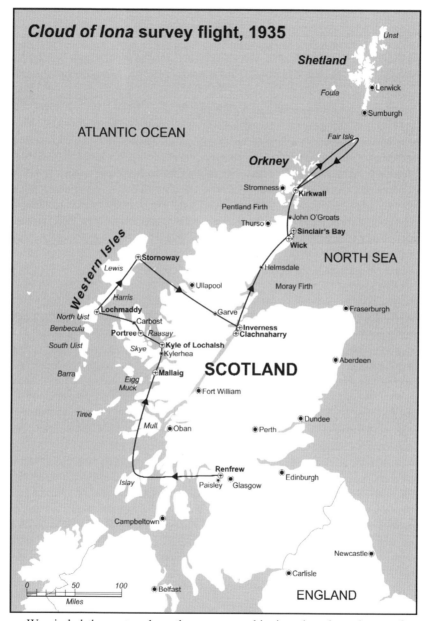

Cloud of Iona survey flight, 1935

Unst

Shetland

Foula • Lerwick

• Sumburgh

ATLANTIC OCEAN

Fair Isle

Orkney

Stromness ● ● **Kirkwall**

Pentland Firth

Thurso ● ● John O'Groats

● **Sinclair's Bay**

Wick

Western Isles

● **Stornoway**

Lewis

● Ullapool

NORTH SEA

● Helmsdale

Moray Firth

Harris

● **Lochmaddy**

North Uist

● Carbost

Benbecula

● Garve

● **Inverness**
Clachnaharry

Portree *Raasay*

South Uist

● **Kyle of Lochalsh**
● Kylerhea

Skye

● Fraserburgh

Barra

Eigg
Muck

● **Mallaig**

SCOTLAND

● Aberdeen

● Fort William

Tiree

Mull ● Oban

● Dundee

● Perth

Islay

Renfrew

Paisley ● ● Glasgow

● Edinburgh

Campbeltown ●

Newcastle ●

0   50   100
Miles

● Belfast

● Carlisle

ENGLAND

We circled the port and, as there was no shipping abroad, made a perfect landing opposite the hotel. Tying the boat up to one of the wharves, we scrambled ashore. We checked with the port authorities that the flying boat would be safe for the night where we had moored her and, with our suitcases in our hands, made for the hotel and booked in for the night.

'Kyle of Lochalsh,' said Captain Scott, 'would be very suitable for flying boat operations, but there was a big hazard caused by the flotsam and jetsam floating in the water. It would need a motor launch to patrol a sea lane for each landing.'

A very expensive proposition, I thought.

We found the hotel to be very well furbished and the flight had given us a thirst so we retired to the bar and planned our operations for the morrow. We decided to fly up to Portree, make a landing in the harbour if possible, and then cut across the centre of Skye and over to Dunvegan Head and across to Loch Maddy. From there, we decided, we would make for Stornoway that night. Such were our plans, but it did not work out that way. We retired to bed early after a very good dinner and agreed to meet for an eight thirty breakfast. To my surprise, the first person I was to meet when I got down to the dining room was George Nicholson.

'Hello, George,' I said, you've excelled yourself this morning.'

'You haven't done too badly yourself,' he said.

'The weather doesn't look very bright today does it George?'

'No,' he said, 'but it should be alright, providing the weather doesn't get any worse.'

When I observed the type of clouds hanging around, I had a nasty feeling that there was a depression advancing on us. At that moment, Captains Scott and MacIntosh arrived and they were of the same opinion as myself regarding the weather. We hurried our breakfast and decided to get on the move as soon as possible. We took off at around half past nine and headed up the sound and across the lower end of Raasay island into Raasay Sound. The overcast was undoubtedly getting lower the further north we went. We pulled into the Portree harbour, flew around a bit looking for suitable sea lanes, then dropped down in the harbour and went ashore. The *Cloud of Iona* was no stranger here as the Duke of Hamilton had given joy rides in her at Portree the year before and had taken up a large number of passengers.

We got on the phone to Lochmaddy for an actual weather report and it was bad. Cloud estimated at 400 feet, a mile visibility, heavy rain and a south westerly wind blowing at least forty mph. Captain Scott asked me if I knew the coastline over the other side.

'A bit,' I said, 'I have landed at North Uist once.'

'What do you think of making an effort?'

'If you can get clear of Skye without having to go into cloud,' I said, 'I think we can make it, but it is going to be hellish bumpy.'

'Righto,' said Scotty, as he was known to his friends, 'let's get going.'

By the time we were airborne the wind had freshened a lot and we headed up the valley to Carbost and then up Loch Snizort, hoping to cut across Vaternish peninsula at Loch Losait. The air was getting very rough and we were just skimming the base of the clouds at 400 feet. We scraped through to Ardmore Point with the hull of the boat just about kissing the peat. And on those five miles, Captain MacIntosh had to help at the dual control to keep the 'boat' the right way up, the turbulence was so great. George and I were strapped in our seats. I gave Captain Scott a course for Weaver's Point Lighthouse at the entrance to Loch Maddy sixteen miles away. The wind was now at gale force from the west and the sea was running high. As we only cruised at around 90 mph, I estimated we were not doing more than forty-five miles an hour against the gale over the sea. I calculated we would pick up the coast in about twenty-four minutes. The visibility had now dropped to not more than half a mile and we flew on into the storm, being thrown all over the sky. I didn't like it so low down as we appeared to be only 100 feet above the raging waves. Almost to the minute, we picked up the coast of Uist, and a few minutes later the lighthouse hove in sight and we turned into Loch Maddy. There the sea was protected by the land and was calmer. We landed in front of the pier. Although the water was sheltered here, the flying boat was nevertheless being rocked quite a bit. We made signs to some fishermen who were standing on the wharf. Shortly, a motor boat put out, towed us to a safe mooring and then took us ashore. It had taken us a little over the forty minutes to fly the forty miles from Portree. It had seemed like two hours and I was glad to be down.

The storm grew fiercer and, by the afternoon, there was a gale of around sixty mph blowing and the rain was coming down in sheets. There was nothing we could do so we sat down in the hotel lounge and played poker. As I have said, there is no accounting for the weather on the west coast, it can change so quickly. And so, next morning, Captain Scott was surprised to see the sun shining again and the wind down to a respectable 20 knots from the north-west. We got going soon after breakfast and made several landings off Lochmaddy wharf. It was quite good for seaplanes, but here again there was flotsam, consisting of cans and shore debris. We concluded the landings would have to be effected some miles away from the village where the water was cleaner. The flying boat would then have to taxi to the pier to discharge and pick up passengers.

We left for Stornoway around eleven in the morning and covered the fifty-eight miles in just under the hour. There was a fair headwind to contend with. However, the turbulence had subsided and we had a pleasant flight. We landed in the bay at Stornoway and were soon ashore. I took my friends along to see Kenny Ross at the Caledonian Hotel and introduced them. George Nicholson had not met him as he hadn't as yet, apparently, got so far north with his plans.

'Well, Captain Fresson,' said Kenny, 'it's a surprise seeing you land here in a flying boat.'

'Yes, Kenny, it sure must be, but we are trying the route out from the seaplane angle, as we cannot make any headway with an airfield.'

'Come along in, Gentlemen,' said Kenny Ross, 'no one comes to Stornoway without a good welcome.'

We were soon sitting down to a series of rounds, waiting for lunch to be served.

After we had eaten, I took Scott and MacIntosh along with George to see the golf links where I usually landed. We walked the whole area over and there was no doubt whatsoever in the minds of our friends that here was the answer to the problem. It was definitely a land plane route.

'Stornoway harbour is too unprotected for high winds and seaplane work, anyway,' Captain Scott told me.

I went along and saw one or two of my councillor friends and told them we had tried out the seaplane possibility, but we wouldn't take it on. So the sooner they got busy building their airfield the sooner they would get an air service, which, by now, everyone knew had to come.

We left around four in the afternoon, headed over the Minch to Ullapool and, amidst the great excitement of the villagers, landed off the pier in calm water. The whole village turned out. It was the first time they had seen a flying boat. The tide was low and we had a difficult scramble to the top of the pier before we hied ourselves over to the Royal Hotel for tea. Captain Scott thought the facilities at Ullapool good for a seaplane, but I doubted it in high winds as I knew to my cost how fierce the gusts were at the bottom of those hills opposite.

After tea, we took off from Loch Broom after quite a long run as the water was fairly smooth, climbing up to the Braemore pass and then down the valley to Garve. I shivered to think what would happen if one engine failed over that rough and rocky terrain because that 'boat' would not hold height on one motor.

We flew around Inverness and decided to land on Longman airfield instead of the Moray Firth as there were no boats available or suitable moorings. So down went the wheels and we made a smooth touchdown on our home airfield. George Nicholson decided to return to Glasgow by the night train as he had no interest in the northern operations and next day my wife took his place.

After lunch, we left for Kirkwall. Captain Scott was not too certain of getting the *Cloud of Iona* off the Longman airfield with us on board, so he took off alone and landed in the Beauly Firth. He taxied up to a broken-down pier at Clachnaharry and we crept over the rickety structure and somehow or other got aboard. Again the weather was good with little wind, but there was a slight swell on the sea and that helped a quick take off. We headed north and, flying at a high altitude, we passed Helmsdale. Captain Scott was behind in the cabin with my wife and myself and Captain MacIntosh was piloting. My wife commented that this was the way to fly.

'A landing ground as far as you can see,' she murmured.

She had barely got the words out of her mouth, when a terrific report occurred and the plane started to vibrate dangerously. Captain Scott, who was sitting alongside me on the port side with his feet up on the front seat, leapt out as if shot from a gun, disappeared through the narrow entrance to the cockpit and was in his seat in a matter of seconds. In the meantime, MacIntosh had shut off both motors and was diving towards the sea. We had just passed Wick and had lost a lot of altitude when Scott opened up the port motor full bore and eased the nose of the plane up to the horizontal. MacIntosh shouted to me to come forward.

'Is there a sheltered bay near here?' he asked.

'Yes,' I answered, 'Sinclair's Bay, about three miles ahead.'

He passed the information on to Scott. We were losing height slowly and it was anybody's guess whether we would reach the bay. We shot by Noss Head Lighthouse and landed about a mile off the sandy shore to the west. I was then told that the airscrew on the starboard motor had parted with the top of a blade, which completely upset the balance of the motor. In cases like that, it has been known for the motor to be torn from its mounting by the damaged airscrew. As we could not taxi towards the shore on one motor, we only went round in circles.

'What's to be done?' said Scott,' can you see a boat around?'

We searched the horizon without any success.

'Have you got a hack saw in the tool kit?' I enquired.

'I don't know,' he said, 'have a look, Mac, will you?'

A search fortunately produced one.

'What are you going to do with that?' queried Scott.

'Saw the unbroken propeller blade down to the same length as the damaged blade,' I said. 'That will reduce the vibration and you might then get enough power from the starboard engine to enable you to taxi ashore.'

Mac and I clambered on to the starboard wing where the engine was mounted and got down to sawing about a foot off the sound propeller blade. That done, we scrambled back and Scott started up the motor. By running the starboard motor twice as fast as the port engine, the boat got under way and we steered for the shore. There was some vibration, but not enough to worry about. We cast anchor some fifty feet from shore, in about two and a half feet of water. The beach was desolate and a long way from help. We held a council of war.

I said, 'I'll take my trousers and shoes off and wade ashore and see if I can find a cottager who might be able to help us.'

I found one about half a mile inland and the owner came back to the shore with me. Captain Scott asked him if he could get some men to help pull the *Cloud of Iona* up above the tide if he let the wheels down. The man said he thought he could find half a dozen bodies and went off. In the meantime a crowd seemed to appear from nowhere and predominantly the feminine sex. Scott asked me to take the ship's papers and our baggage ashore. I only had short aertex pants on, and in this garb started a number of trips to the beach. I took my wife ashore on my back on the first trip and then went backward and forwards for the rest of the gear. After a while, I noticed the crowd began to shriek with laughter as I turned to make for shore. This went on for a few trips when Captain Scott told me what was wrong. Unbeknown to me, my pants had slipped quite a bit and I had been creating quite a diversion with the women onlookers. My last trip out was to collect my trousers, shoes, socks and jacket. As I turned towards the seaplane, I noticed it turning around and, before I could reach it, it was moving out to sea with my clothes aboard. A small fishing boat had come up behind while I was ashore and, I learned afterwards, Scott had arranged for them to tow the seaplane back to Wick harbour.

Here was a fine predicament. I was practically naked and stranded on the beach. There was no transport and the Wick to John O' Groats road was a mile away across the marshes. My wife took off a woolly jumper she had on and I covered my shoulders. It was beginning to get chilly. I couldn't stay on the beach all night, so decided we would have to make for the road and one of the crofters said he would raise a car to take us into the Station Hotel at Wick some six miles away. It was rough going for my bare feet and I was grateful when the road was reached. Within a matter of minutes, the car arrived and we set off. On arrival at the Station Hotel entrance, there were three elderly ladies sitting in the sun porch. There was nothing to do, but to make a dash for it. I told my wife to go in and arrange for a room for the night and I followed her in my semi-nudity. When the three ladies saw me, they let out a trinity of squeals and held their hands high in the air in seeming horror. Could it be that they had never seen such a scantily clothed male before? I was past them in a flash, leaving them in a state of complete hysterics, genuine or otherwise I never found out. That was a good story for Wick and I heard about it for a long time afterwards.

The result of that experience ended up by my catching a severe chill and I was confined to bed for a couple of days. On the morning of my recovery, an engineer from the south arrived by air from Renfrew with a spare airscrew. He proceeded to the harbour where the *Cloud of Iona* had been towed and set about changing the damaged propeller. It was ready by a little after noon. Now came the problem of getting the plane off the water. It was too rough outside the harbour, and the length of run inside to the narrow opening in the harbour groyne was not much more than 300 yards. With the aid of a slight wind from the east, and with a small petrol load, Captain Scott thought he could make it alone. So we had to hunt around for cans to drain petrol off. This accomplished, the motors were started and well warmed up. The seaplane was then pulled right up to the jetty. We held our breath as the motors were opened up and the seaplane started to gather way. If Captain Scott failed to clear the concrete groyne on the far side of the harbour, he faced certain death in a terrific crash. He headed for the centre of the entrance through the groyne but, as there were not more than a few feet clearance each side of the wings, it was unlikely he could pass through the eye of such a small needle. He had to be off before he got there. Nearer and nearer he got. We all held our breaths.

Gwen said, 'He's going to crash.'

I thought so too, but he just made it. The boat came off about forty yards before the groyne and cleared it with a good ten feet to spare. We all felt limp as we walked back to the hotel. I phoned Kirkwall and told the traffic officer to send the de Havilland Dragon we had stationed there, over to Wick to take us to Kirkwall that afternoon. With that done, MacIntosh thought we were due a little 'pick me up' and Gwen and I agreed. Also, I thought it would help the chill that I was throwing off.

After lunch, we went up to Hillhead field and waited for Captain Rae, who was resident pilot at Kirkwall, to arrive. We had not long to wait and we were in Kirkwall within the hour. We found Scott and the *Cloud of Iona* waiting for us on the Wideford airfield.

'That was a narrow shave,' I said to Scotty, 'I didn't think you were going to make it.'

'I felt,' he said, 'after I had covered half the run, she would just make it. Otherwise, I should have shut off and postponed the take off until the sea outside had calmed down sufficiently.'

'Yes,' I said, 'an experienced pilot can usually tell if his aircraft is going to get out of a tight place. We often have the same problem here at Wideford when the ground is soft and muddy in the winter.'

We planned next day, Sunday, to fly up to Fair Isle and Shetland to have a look round. That night I was not feeling so well again, the temperature came back and, to my great annoyance, I was laid up next morning. I really wanted to have a go at landing on Fair Isle, or at least on the sea adjacent to it. Scotty said he had to return south next day and so it was that day or never, so he and MacIntosh set off on their own. They were back at lunch time. The weather was not good, a heavy sea was running off Fair Isle which made landing impossible, and the wind was rapidly gaining strength so they decided to call the Shetland section off. They left next morning for the south. So we bid each other goodbye. They were a couple of really nice guys. Scottie and MacIntosh both insisted we should look them up when we next ventured down to London, 'Don't forget,' were their parting words. We promised we would, but we never saw them again.

A couple of days later, we returned home on the afternoon service and my first job back in Inverness was to communicate with the Stornoway Town Clerk in writing requesting him to advise his Council that they could wash out any idea of a seaplane service as far as we were concerned, and to ask him to try again and get some solution to constructing the golf course airfield. It didn't do any good. They just withdrew into their shells and still did nothing. There was no escaping the fact that the onus would be on us if we were to establish an air connection to Stornoway, so we also decided to sit on the fence and make do with the charters that came along from time to time. There were quite a few and they were profitable for we were paid for a full load each trip. The Monospar *Inverness* was kept busy on that run as its seating capacity of four was more in keeping with the number of passengers travelling on charter work. Mostly they were couples.

I lost no time in writing my report on the technical side of the seaplane survey. I was also a qualified seaplane pilot having passed out at the Blackburn seaplane base at Brough, Yorkshire in 1929. So, on receipt of my report to Renfrew, Mr Nicholson asked me to attend a meeting that they were calling vis-à-vis the question of the use of seaplanes to the Western Isles. Landing grounds for aeroplanes were harder to come by in the Hebrides than in the north of Scotland, Orkney and Shetland. During the meeting, we all came to the decision that the cost was all against us and there would, without doubt, be considerable difficulty in finding sheltered water in many areas. So the use of seaplanes was abandoned.

During the middle of September, we received the first visit from United Airways management. A Captain Lynch Blosse and another official of the company, whose name I have forgotten, called on us with a letter from Mr Roberts saying that Captain Blosse had been sent up to make enquiries into our operational set up and asking me to show them around. His principal pre-occupation appeared to fall on the types of form we were using in the various stages of our work. He said, after he was seated in my office, 'I would like to look at the forms you use for traffic booking, daily inspection of aircraft, load sheets, and pilot's daily report on aircraft and engines.'

'Certainly,' I said, 'I will obtain them for you if you will excuse me while I phone the various departments who handle these documents.'

They were duly brought along and I handed them over. He looked through them and asked me if I thought we could standardise on the forms they were using at Blackpool and London, at the same time pulling a bunch of forms from his pocket. We studied them together, and they were well set out, but I did not think they were any better than ours and I told him so.

'You know, we have been using our system for some time now. They do the job and all the staff are familiar with them. We are very busy at this time of the year and our staff is a small one, one person doing several jobs. I do not think it would be wise to alter the system at the moment. Should United Airways wish to standardise the paperwork, couldn't we leave it until the winter when we will have more time? And as for the maintenance side, I am sure our chief engineer will not want to be involved at the moment.'

'All right,' he said, 'I will leave these copies with you and you can look into them and let me know later on.'

I took them and let them die a natural death. The matter was not brought up again to my relief. Lynch Blosse turned out a very nice chap. He was an Australian and a first rate pilot. I asked him up to our house to stay and we arranged a picnic over at Achnahaird beach on the Sunday. David Tolmie of Stornoway was also staying with us and we had a pilot, Johnnie Fielden, on loan from United Airways, who knew Lynch Blosse well, so we asked them along also. My wife, Lynch Blosse and David Tolmie flew over with me in the Monospar and Johnnie Fielden took our car with the picnic equipment and the official who was with Lynch Blosse accompanied him. I well remember that it was a beautiful sunny September day and we had a lovely flight. The car started before us and we caught it up at Braemar at the head of Loch Broom. Lynch Blosse and my wife were looking out for it. She was the first to spot it. They still had an hour and a quarter to go so we arrived well ahead of them. We had our bathing gear in the plane. The water at Enard Bay, which lapped the beach of the Achnahaird sands, looked a lovely emerald green and there was little wind. We circled around the beach and then flew over to Loch Broom so that Lynch Blosse could have a look at the hotel. It looked very quiet on the Sabbath morning. They were probably all at the kirk.

We then flew out over the Summer Isles, also bathed in sunshine, and surrounded by blue sea which hardly had a ripple on it. It was a beautiful sight and Lynch Blosse said he had never seen such scenery in Britain before. We flew up to Red Point, overlooking the Minch, and made a wide sweep dropping off height down the slope of a hill some 800 feet high and turned in to the approach over Loch Raa. Lynch Blosse saw the stone cairns on the beach ahead and asked me what they were for. I explained and we touched down on the firm sand to the left without him knowing we were on the ground. We taxied over to some dunes, which looked a good place for spreading our picnic when the car arrived. We then got into our swimsuits and had a bathe. It was so quiet and peaceful and hot. The sun blazed down on us. The water was clear translucent and ever so warm, and the oyster-coloured sand added a beautiful setting to a heavenly scene. I don't think one could have found a more peaceful spot and my wife, David Tolmie and Lynch Blosse, were of the same mind. Moreover, we had the whole place to ourselves. We got dressed and, at about twelve thirty, my wife said she would get going with the lunch and we stayed to give her a hand.

Johnnie Fielden, with Lynch Blosse's friend, arrived at that moment. They decided to go for a swim before lunch. Johnnie was a corpulent figure around his middle and had no swim suit. They set off in their shirts and underpants intending to swim in the nude. Some twenty minutes later, we heard feminine chuckles on top of a sand dune near us. We looked up to find we had company consisting of three young females sharing a pair of binoculars which they were pointing towards the far end of the stream running along the east end of the beach. To our astonishment, with his companion there was Johnnie Fielden complete in his birthday suit, with his clothes held above his head, wading across the stream and coming towards us. He looked the funniest sight with his huge girth wobbling from side to side, and his companion following behind him was missing the fun. We were all amused at the excitement and shrieks of laughter coming from the top of the sand dune on our left. One girl who was looking through the binoculars said, 'Oh, isn't he fat?'

'Let's have a look,' said both her companions, and one grabbed the glasses.

'Ha, ha, ha, just look at him, not a stitch on,' she said.

'Oh, Morag,' said the third girl, 'it's my turn to have look' and she caught hold of the binoculars. 'Oh! Ho, ho, ho,' she squealed in raptures, 'what a sight.'

Just then, Johnnie, who had been serenely ignorant of the appreciative audience, suddenly spotted the females. Quite unabashed, he gave them a wave and a broad grin, sat down on the sand and commenced to dry himself and dress. By that time we were weak with laughter and were brought back to more mundane matters when Gwen said she was going to spread the picnic lunch. We all had another swim in the afternoon, and then we got the tea basket out. My wife and David Tolmie left first on the return journey, which was around a three-hour run, and Lynch Blosse, Johnnie Fielden and the other chap returned later with me in the monoplane *Inverness*.

Returning through the hills during the early evening, it was a contrasting sight. All the colours were changed and we might as well have been in another world. We landed at Longman forty minutes later, put the aircraft away in its shed, and strolled up to Macrae & Dick's garage to see if there was a taxi available. Johnnie then said, 'It's not far to your house, Fressy. Let's walk.'

'Righto. How about the others?' They agreed and we walked into town to our house in Fairfield Road.

Lynch Blosse said, 'Thank you for a most wonderful day. It was well worth the journey up. You certainly have the scenery in Scotland.'

'Yes, on a fine day,' I replied. 'You should now see it on a day when the wind nearly blows you to pieces and the rain is pouring down. You wouldn't know it for the same place. We've been lucky today so let's have a drink on it.'

They returned to Blackpool next day. I accompanied them in the Spartan Cruiser monoplane in which they had arrived. There was no difficulty in persuading Lynch Blosse to pay us another visit. But good intentions sometimes go astray for he never visited us again. Gwen and I went to see him and his wife at Redhill next spring. I heard from him later on in the War, saying he had been posted to a Stirling bomber squadron. He had done several missions and had been shot up badly. He did not like the aircraft, he said. They were underpowered and very slow and cumbersome and badly defended. He wanted to transfer to another squadron, but before he could do so he was shot down over Germany. We were very grieved, my wife and I, to hear that bad news. He was a charming chap and his wife was equally nice. He had said in his letter that, if he didn't get away from that Stirling squadron, he would not have long in this world and his prediction unhappily turned out only too correct. The Stirlings were scrapped not so long after; the casualty rate was too high.

After my return from the south, David Tolmie chartered me to fly him back to Stornoway. My wife came along for the trip as we were to stay the night. As usual, we put up at the Caledonian Hotel with mine host, Kenny Ross. He was a wonderful host. He had been badly wounded in World War One and was literally sewn up with silver wire. It was also said that he suffered a lot of pain, but he never showed it. He was a great storyteller and he could mimic anyone. Kenny could imitate the locals so well that it was impossible to tell the difference when he was speaking out of sight. We were kept in fits of laughter all night over his well-told stories about the locals in the north of Scotland and we retired well into the early hours.

We departed for Inverness next morning with our Sealyham puppy. He curled up, as usual, in the back seat. I climbed to 2,000 feet for the Minch crossing. The sky was blue and, about half way over, I remarked to my wife how sweetly the two motors appeared to be running. Almost immediately after that remark, a strange thing happened. The Sealyham pup suddenly scuttled off the seat behind and wedged himself under my seat. He wouldn't move although my wife did her best to persuade him. A minute or so after, during which time the Sealyham seemed very agitated as he kept changing his position, there was a crack from the port motor and it immediately lost power and commenced to vibrate badly. We were at least eighteen miles offshore and I changed course for Achnahaird beach, throttling back the port motor and opening up the starboard for more power. Our airspeed dropped to seventy-five miles per hour and that meant at least an extra fifteen minutes to reach the beach. I was afraid to open the starboard engine too much in case it should overheat and also pack up. My wife was badly shaken and the pup, which had now left the precincts of his retreat, was trembling like a leaf.

I remember saying to my wife: 'Don't be afraid. We will reach the beach somehow or other.'

But I was not too sure for we were gradually losing height. The drag of the port engine's four-bladed airscrew was like a brake on our forward speed. Somehow, I had to reduce it or we would be in the drink, our altitude having dropped to 1,000 feet and with at least eight miles to go. I did not know what had happened to the port engine. If it was a broken connecting rod, the engine might break up if I opened the throttle, but if I did not obtain some power from that damaged engine, we would be down in the sea, probably upside down, and either way we would drown. So I was left with no alternative. Gingerly, I opened up the faulty motor to half speed and, although it ran roughly, the vibration did not increase and our speed pulled up to eighty-five mph. With the airscrew drag gone, the plane had no difficulty in maintaining height and we even climbed a little. I assured my wife that everything was alright now and we would be down in another ten minutes, but she didn't look very convinced and was trembling almost as much as the pup. Nearer and nearer we got to the beach of so many previous landings, and I commenced descent towards Loch Raa. As the beach came into view, I was staggered, even shocked, to observe that it was completely covered by sea water. Over the ten months that I had known of those sands, I had never seen it in that condition before. What to be done now? I could not risk the water crossing back to Stornoway and I could not climb high enough to cross the Wester Ross mountains to reach the flat fields on the Inverness side. I had no alternative but to land. I opened up the motors and flew around at 500 feet, trying to think this one out. As I got calmer, I remembered that the slope from the west side of the beach to the stream on the east side was very slight, so it followed that the water could not be very deep near the edge of the dunes. By now, my wife was in an extremely agitated state.

'Be calm,' I said. 'We'll get down alright. I'm going to land in the water as near to the edge as possible.'

I strapped her in and did up my own belt. Down we slipped and we passed the first cairn marker on our right. I held the aircraft a few inches from the surface and with the tail right down as we struck the water. The sea flew up over the wings and canopy and the tail came up a bit, but we were on firm sand and we quickly pulled up in one piece with nothing broken. I managed to find a level piece of the unsubmerged rough ground and taxied on to it. We got out and examined the faulty engine. I found a valve rocker had sheared on number five cylinder port motor. We walked up to the crofter's cottage half a mile back on the road leading to Achiltibuie. The family sent word to the hotel for a car and, on arrival, I managed to phone George Griffiths at the Longman airfield and told him what had happened.

'Have you got a pilot available?' I asked.

He said he would enquire and phone me back.

While we were waiting I was telling the hotel owner about the flooded beach and he said that happened once a month on the turn of the moon and it would be dry in a couple of hours.

'That's fine,' I said.

At that moment, the phone rang and George Griffiths told me he had found a pilot, 'But I don't know about him landing a Dragon on that beach.'

'Never mind the Dragon,' I said, 'Get the Moth out and get that pilot to fly you over with a spare cylinder.' George didn't seem too keen, but said he would do it.

'Now listen,' I explained, 'I will lay a white cloth down on the beach. Tell pilot 'H' to drop down just over the sheet and keep the plane straight until it pulls up, and if he looks like missing it, he should head off to go round again. The sand is very soft to the east and if he goes into that you will be on your back.'

'OK,' he said, 'I will see to it you can be sure.' This particular pilot was not very brilliant and was about to be replaced.

An hour later, we heard a drone from the east and shortly we discerned my Moth gliding down towards us. Pilot 'H' flew over the beach and came in quite accurately over the spread sheet. The beach had become almost dry by now. The landing was a bit bouncy, but they had arrived safely. Griffiths soon got dug into that motor and, in a little over the hour, had the new cylinder on and we were ready to get on our way. However, it was lunchtime so we repaired to the Achiltibuie Hotel for a meal before starting off home. Griffiths insisted on flying back with my wife and I so the Moth went back without its passenger. We were not, however, out of the wood yet. We had to cross over a ridge about 1,000 feet high just before reaching Garve and it was covered in cloud. I pulled up into the mist climbing to 2,000 feet. We had barely reached that altitude when the right motor spluttered. I tested the two magnetos by switching off one and then the other. The right hand magneto was not functioning at all and the left one was not too good. We continued on course in cloud and then the port motor started the same tricks and another magneto was found to be functioning badly. There was nothing I could do about it. Both my wife and George Griffiths were looking very unhappy and I too was sweating. If both motors stopped with the aircraft in cloud and before we had reached lower ground, we stood a jolly good chance of breaking our necks.

I remember saying to Griffiths while in cloud, 'It's a pity you didn't stay with the Moth, you would been safer after all.'

'What's wrong with those mags,' he said.

'I wish I knew,' I answered.

We had a very uncomfortable eight minutes in cloud until we flew out into the clear beyond Garve and over open country. Saying our prayers, we staggered back to Inverness and landed safely.

In several hundred hours flying in that monoplane I had never experienced such a chapter of mishaps. The cause of the magneto trouble appeared to lie in the rubber drive connections having partially sheared, thus upsetting the magneto timing. That was a new one on us and it was carefully noted for future inspection records. It never happened again. George Griffiths saw to that.

The Moth came in just after us. Its pilot had ducked down a narrow valley along the road and had thus avoided going into cloud. I would have done the same if I had known what was about to befall us. However, all was well that ended well, except a few shattered nerves. The Sealyham pup soon bucked up after he was on terra firma. I have always thought it was a very curious way that the puppy behaved some minutes before the motor failure. We know that a dog is able to hear higher vibrations than a human being, so it would appear that there must have been some ultra high vibration set up in the motor as the rocker arm began to fracture and shear. But then one might ask, why should a dog become alarmed at a change in the engine beat? We have never found the answer to that strange phenomenon.

8

Radio and Rivalry

I have already mentioned in the last chapter about the installation of 'Standard' radio transmitters and receivers in our aircraft, ready for the day when the promised ground stations arrived. Towards the end of 1934, we equipped our airfields with ordinary household radio receivers capable of receiving on 900 meters band and which could tune in to our aircraft. Our pilots were, therefore, able to keep in touch with our traffic staff at the stations they were heading for, giving the number of passengers, estimated time of arrival, position and any other useful information the captain thought would facilitate traffic operation. With the aid of this system, we began to keep track of our Aberdeen competitors who had taken a leaf out of our book and installed radio in their aircraft. In fact, it appeared every move we made was copied, even down to postage envelope advertising stickers. It was the case of 'everywhere Mary went, the lamb was sure to follow.' It has been said that imitation is the sincerest form of flattery, but it was not appreciated one little bit at the time.

I well remember that the first voice we picked up at our Inverness hangar belonged to Eric Starling, chief pilot for Aberdeen Airways Limited, who appeared to be wallowing around in cloud trying to reach Sumburgh, Shetland, on a charter flight. His voice laconically came over the radio calling his Stromness airfield in Orkney, 'Flying in cloud at fifteen hundred feet, estimated position Fair Isle.' Fifteen minutes later, 'Still flying in cloud, estimated position near Sumburgh Head. Unable to see any hole in the cloud. Returning to Stromness.'

Eric Starling, in those days, was young at the game, but he always used good judgement and did not take silly risks as was the case with many young pilots who had recently obtained their 'flying ticket' and thought they knew it all. I got to know Starling very well in the years to come and, today, I often see him when passing through Renfrew on my way to London by air. Eric possesses the honour of holding the unique record of landing a Robinson Redwing biplane in 'easy virtue' street at one of the French seaports at night, namely, the Boulevard des Alliés, Calais. It was quite unintentional and came about in the following manner.

When he was learning to fly at a training school at one of the southern English airfields, he set out one pitch dark night to carry out his 'night flying test' and got himself hopelessly lost. After flying around for a considerable time, he saw lights in the distance on his port side. He headed towards them and found a town of considerable size beneath him and which boasted a well-lighted and broad street bereft of traffic. He had no idea where to look for an airfield and, with the risk of petrol running out, decided to land on that well lit street below him. He brought off a good landing and as he was extricating himself from his aircraft, he was suddenly accosted by a policeman who excitedly addressed him in French. It was then, to his amazement, that he learned he had crossed the Channel and had landed at the seaport of Calais in France. Furthermore, he was in a famous street, well known to visiting sailors. I didn't hear the rest of the story,[1] but it was rumoured that, upon his return to his home airfield the next day, his pals jocularly presented him with the 'Knight of the Garter' as a decoration for his resourcefulness. Be that as it may, on that night Eric Starling proved the makings of a good pilot who kept his head in the face of extreme danger.

On 30 January 1936, my wife presented me with a son, and it was decided he would be christened in Kirkwall by a friend of ours, Bishop Kessock, early in April. I arranged for a DH84 Dragon to take us up to Orkney and, as I was just recovering from an attack of flu, instead of piloting myself, I left it to one of our pilots, Adam Smith, to perform that duty. The party consisted of Mr Hamilton, our secretary; his fiancée, Connie Forbes; the godfather to be, David Tolmie of Stornoway; Mrs Nan MacKenzie of Inverness; Peter Angus of 1931 Avro days in Thurso; my wife with baby Richard in her lap; and lastly myself. I sat in the front on the right hand side of the plane, just behind the pilot. My wife and baby were immediately behind me and Miss Connie Forbes was in the seat behind my wife. (I mention these details in view of what was to come). It was a fine hot day with not a lot of wind and we flew a direct course to Kirkwall, by-passing Wick. On approaching Kirkwall, we were congratulating ourselves on a pleasant and smooth trip when the pilot shut off his motors to approach Wideford airfield. What wind there was blew from the north-east and the approach took us immediately over the Highland Park distillery. At that moment and without any warning, we hit the biggest air pocket I have ever experienced during my many thousand hours flying. I estimated we dropped 200 feet. Every loose article hit the roof. Those passengers not strapped in were thrown over the cabin and baby Richard shot from his mother's lap, hit the roof of the cabin, bounced off it and landed up in the lap of Connie Forbes sitting, as I have said, immediately behind my wife. Captain Smith kept his head and landed us safely while we were all trying to sort ourselves out and rubbing our bruises. Our poor little son was screaming his head off and it was found he had been badly bruised by the force with which he hit the roof. Sitting in the Kirkwall Hotel after dinner that night, we jocularly attributed the hectic air disturbance to the strong fumes arising from the Highland Park distillery. I said I would pass that one on to its owner, Walter Grant. He took it in good part and told me he had witnessed the tossing we had received as he was watching the aircraft approach from his front garden. He added, 'I'm very glad I wasn't in the plane.'

---

[1] The account of Starling's night landing in Calais is fully told in Starling's own words in: Iain Hutchison, *The Flight of the Starling*, (Erskine: Kea Publishing, 1992).

190

On 3 March, 1936, the Inverness radio station was ready for testing and Kirkwall was ready a few days after. I carried out the air to ground tests which were completed within the week, and the stations were ready to go into service by the second week of March. What an enormous difference that made to our flying technique. The whole character of our flying in bad visibility changed. We were now able to climb to a safe height which put us well above any mountains along the route and home straight on our destination. More often than not, we got above the clouds at 5,000 feet in winter and at other times we settled down to fly through them.

Sumburgh radio station opened in May. We advertised the commencement of our Shetland run for 3rd June. A few days before that date, an advertisement appeared in the Aberdeen and Shetland press announcing the opening of a similar service by our competitors the day before we were advertised to start. I immediately wrote a letter to Aberdeen Airways, Dyce, pointing out that our Sumburgh airfield was not open until 3rd June and refusing them permission to land until the airfield was officially opened. Foolishly, I did not send Jim Black, our Sumburgh agent, instructions to immobilise the airfield by placing obstacles over the landing area. I don't think, at that date, that we had fully appreciated the type of enforced competition we were up against. Our letter went unanswered and Aberdeen Airways' plane landed at Sumburgh with passengers the day before we were due to start, thus jumping our wicket and claiming to be the first company to operate the Aberdeen-Shetland service. The public reacted to that one with unconcealed disgust, but there were people in Shetland who appeared pleased, especially some of the councillors, who seemed to completely discount the work I had put in organising that route and the time and money spent on its development by Highland Airways.

However, we had the advantage of being able to place a Rapide aircraft on that run and which the offending company were apparently unable to match at the time. The speed of the Rapide and its extra safety over the stormy open sea leg, plus the more efficient heating system installed in the plane, appealed to the public, and we did not suffer very much from loss of traffic – at least to commence with. We were to be subjected to another jolt the following year and the spear shaft was an official one.

Our Shetland service from Kintore airfield commenced on 3rd June with myself as pilot. We had a full load of passengers and the weather was good. Climbing to six thousand feet, we reached Sumburgh by way of Kirkwall in one hour forty-five minutes. There was a representative gathering to welcome us at Sumburgh airfield, including some members of Shetland County Council, but not all. The Rapide proved itself splendidly on that run. Its rate of climb was very much faster than the DH Dragon, likewise its cruising speed, and the cabin was better upholstered, so much so, that the passengers made a point of expressing their appreciation. Captain Adam Smith piloted the return journey. I stayed over in Shetland with my very good friends, Mr and Mrs Bertie Ganson whose firm represented us in Lerwick and provided the road transport to and from Sumburgh airfield, some twenty-five miles to the south. It's a very twisty road, but the scenery is splendid.

We now possessed three very skilled pilots who maintained the services close on one hundred percent. I had less time for flying as the management was developing into a full-time job, so I discontinued regular service work. However, I acted as relief pilot along the routes when needed, and attended to all the charter flights, which were numerous, involving as far afield as London, Edinburgh, Glasgow and Stornoway. The latter town was becoming a very busy leg. Around this time, I stepped up the North Isles and trans-Pentland service by stationing an aircraft, plus a resident pilot and engineer, at Kirkwall. This aircraft became very busy and operated a late Kirkwall-Shetland flight in addition to the morning service. Commercial travellers found it convenient to fly up late in the day to Shetland from Orkney, which enabled them to commence their work early the following morning. Inversely, travellers from Shetland took advantage of the return flight to position themselves in Orkney ready for the following day. There were also a number of private ambulance flights cropping up from time to time and this arrangement also found favour with the Orkney County medical authorities and Surgeon Ian McClure who made full use of being able to rapidly transport dangerous cases to Aberdeen Hospital.

Thurso suddenly bobbed into the picture again. Aberdeen Airways were plugging that town hard and were taking away some of our traffic to Wick. There was only one temporary site that I knew about which would be reasonably safe to operate from, and that was the field from which I gave short flights from in 1931. It was situated on the Thurso-Scrabster road about a mile from the town. It was a better and safer field than the one at Claredon which the opposition were using, so I called on the owner, Jock Miller, to see if he would give me a lease of the ground on a permanent basis. He greeted me at his front door.

'It's a pleasure to see you again, Captain Fresson. We haven't met for a long time. What brings you this way today? I thought you had deserted us.'

That gave me my opportunity. 'That's easily answered. I am urgently in need of a landing field here and I have not been able to find a suitable site to operate from. I've come to ask you to let me use that park of yours on the Scrabster road that I hired in 1931 for the short flights.'

He invited me into his study, rang the bell, and told the maid to bring in some liquid refreshment.

'So you're wanting that park back?' he said. 'How long would you want it for?'

'Permanently,' I replied, 'or at least until the Council can be persuaded to build a municipal airfield.'

The whisky arrived and he poured out two heavy drams.

'I don't know,' he said. 'It's very difficult. I could let you have it for a few weeks, but permanently is a different matter. Here's fun,' he said, raising his glass. 'You see, Captain, I'm a sheep breeder as you know, and having that park used continuously would seriously interfere with my business. I want to help you, as we are old friends, but naturally, I must look after my interests first.'

I thought for a few minutes while I got rid of some of the Scotch.

'Would your difficulty be solved,' I enquired, 'if I confined the landings to one in the morning and one in the afternoon? I would arrange to have my groundsman herd the sheep off the actual landing run, and that would avoid taking them off the field and disturbing them. I do the same in the Orkney North Isles and it works out very well.'

'That might be the solution,' he said, 'I'll speak to my grieve.[2] Look back in a week's time and I'll give you the final answer.'

'I'll do that.' I bid him goodbye and went away thinking I had won my point.

Not so, however, because a week later, Jock Miller told me his grieve thought the continual landings might affect the sheep when they were breeding and they just couldn't take the risk. He was genuinely sorry he could not assist me. There was no other single field in the neighbourhood. I had tried them all. Accordingly, we had to drop the idea of operating from Thurso in 1936. So, for the time being, I left Thurso to the tender care of our competitors, knowing that they could only nibble at the fringe of the holiday traffic with such limited facilities.

I flew back to Inverness that afternoon in the DH Moth, and on arrival, found the Shell Mex manager, Mr Green looking for me. I contacted him and he came round to my office. He told me he had just received word from Glasgow that the head of their sales organisation in London wished to charter a plane to fly him and two departmental chiefs to Skye, Stornoway, Kirkwall, Sumburgh, and back to Inverness the same day, giving them an hour in each place.

'Can you do it in the time?'

I roughed out a programme on paper. Skye was the pivotal point. The only place I knew of on that mountainous island where I could land was a stretch of beach at Broadford Bay at low tide, which I had in mind for ambulance work. That meant an early landing at Broadford Bay in order to cope with such a big programme and get back to Inverness that night. I looked up from my notes.

'We can do it if I can catch the right tide at Broadford. I shall have to contact the harbour master. When do they want to start?' I enquired.

'As soon as possible,' Green replied.

I put through a call to the harbour master's office and we fixed a date when the tide would be low in the morning. Next morning, I was informed that the

---

[2] A 'grieve' is a farm manager.

Shell party confirmed the arrangements, so all I had to hope for was fine weather which was a 'must' on a tight flight of that sort.

Mr Green came to my office just after the arrival of the London train and asked if I would accompany him to the Station Hotel to meet Mr Wallace and his party. We were introduced and I took an immediate liking to Mr Wallace. He was a fairly tall, thick-set man and so friendly, considerate and affable, and his friends, Mr Lawson and another, also appeared good chaps. A friendship between Wallace and myself, and later between our respective wives, very soon developed and, ultimately, we became intimate friends. We sat down in the hotel and, over a cup of coffee, he explained the day's programme that they had in mind.

'Mr Green tells me you have everything laid on. When do we start?'

'Right away,' I answered, 'and the earlier we get to Skye the better, as we are dependant on low tide.'

Dragon aircraft G-ACIT was ready for us to take off and in a few minutes we were on our way to Skye. Climbing up to around 5,000 feet, we flew direct across mountainous country to Kyle of Lochalsh, where we had landed last year in the seaplane *Cloud of Iona*, and from there hopped across the water and put down on Broadford beach forty-five minutes after leaving Inverness. The beach ran north and south. Fortunately, the wind favoured us and we made an easy landing. A car was awaiting our arrival and the party were rushed into Portree, twenty-eight miles away. They were back by two o'clock, having lunched on sandwiches in the car on the return journey. We took off easily and headed for the north end of Skye, up the Sound of Raasay. It was a bright sunny day and my passengers were entranced with the beauty of the scenery and the colouring. Fifty minutes later, we were down on the tidal basin at Stornoway. Portree had phoned our agent, Lagley, who ran a car service, to meet us, and they were hurried into town. We departed from Stornoway at 4.30pm. Climbing again to 5,000 feet, we flew a direct course to Kirkwall, cutting across the north-west tip of Sutherlandshire and passing Cape Wrath on our left, then out over the sea to Orkney, fifty miles away. That trip by surface transport would have taken them two days, it took us exactly one hour and a quarter. We landed at Wideford at a quarter to six and I went down to town with my passengers. We partook of a hurried supper in the Kirkwall Hotel and after they had completed their business at the Shell installation, we hurried out to the airfield and left for Shetland at half past eight in the evening. The night was fine and at that latitude so far north, the light was good. In fact, in Shetland, it does not get really dark all night and one can see to read a newspaper at three in the morning. Soon we passed the North Ronaldsay lighthouse and commenced the sea crossing. Fair Isle loomed up ahead on our right and, in twenty minutes, we should be landing at Sumburgh. I had taken the precaution of phoning through to our Lerwick agent, Bertie Ganson, to send a car to meet the plane. Just north of Fair Isle, an ominous haze appeared ahead. Within a few minutes, the haze had turned to gloom and we found ourselves flying over the top of dense fog. I cursed my folly in not having asked the radio station to remain open for the flight. Although we had been flying in fine weather all day, I knew the Orkney and Shetland weather was unpredictable and should, therefore, have taken precautions. Mr Wallace asked me whether we would be able to land.

'Not unless we can find a hole in that murk,' I replied. 'It would most likely be possible to go down through it if the radio station was open, but it has been closed for five hours.'

'That's unfortunate,' he commented.

It was now getting on for ten o'clock at night. We flew around for a while looking for a hole, but without success. The white carpet extended north as far as the eye could see. I learned afterwards from the car driver who was sent to meet us, that the fog extended all the way from Lerwick to Sumburgh airfield and the visibility was down to a couple of hundred yards.

We returned to Orkney. I was a little afraid that, if we did not look sharp, the fog might settle down there. We ran into the clear abeam of Fair Isle and were back in the Kirkwall Hotel at 11.00pm, having been in the air for two hours. We sat in the lounge awhile over tea and biscuits, talking about the events of the day. My passengers were highly delighted with the speed and regularity attained during the major portion of the trip. We retired to bed after planning an early take-off for Shetland next morning. I was dog tired and slumber soon overtook me.

Next morning broke fine, but to my disappointment Mr Wallace told me at breakfast that they had now decided to give Shetland a miss.

'You see,' he said, 'we have to be in London for an important meeting tomorrow, but we will be back to complete the Shetland tour of inspection before long.'

We got into Inverness in time for lunch and they asked me to join them at the Station Hotel. I saw them off on the afternoon express.

At the end of the month, a call was made from Stornoway to carry six passengers to Edinburgh. I flew over in Dragon DH84 G-ADCT to pick them up. I was in some doubts, with so many passengers and constituting a full load, as to the take-off from the short run provided at the tidal basin. By getting the two rear passengers to come forward to the front of the machine, which would enable me to get the tail up quickly, I figured we could just do it, as there was a slight wind in our favour. The two passengers were instructed to watch for me raising my arm. Immediately I did so, they were to return to the rear seats. We got off with about fifty yards to spare. I raised my arm and back went the two passengers. Then commenced our climb to 7,000 feet, which was the altitude I had selected for the journey. Ahead lay one hundred miles of mountainous country topping nearly 4,000 feet in places. It was a run I had never before attempted and I estimated the elapsed time of the flight to take 1 hour 55 minutes for the 200 miles. It was a lovely day over Stornoway and the Minch, and likewise for the whole route except for several patches of cloud over the mountainous section. We crossed over Gairloch. Almost immediately, the high mountain tops came into view. The country over which we passed for the next hour was magnificent in its wildness and there was no sign of habitation for long stretches. We crossed Loch Mullardoch, Glen Cannich and Loch Affric and, shortly after, Loch Garry came into view with Invergarry nestling at the far end of it. Soon after, we picked up the end of Loch Laggan and, crossing over a 3,760 feet mountain range, there lay Loch Ericht nestling at the bottom of the mountains. Flying over the middle of Loch Rannoch and Loch Tay and another mountain range, we picked up Crieff on our left and it was then only a few miles to the Firth of Forth when the famous rail bridge came into view. Within a few minutes, we landed at Turnhouse, having covered the 200 miles in one hour and fifty minutes, five minutes faster than my estimate. The passengers were thrilled for they had seen country and mountain tops that no people in Stornoway had seen before, and that gave them something to talk about for a long time. By steamer and train, that journey would have taken over twenty-four hours.

During the middle of July, I gave local flights at Sumburgh for two days in an endeavour to ginger up the population to air travel and one hundred daring Shetlanders took to the air. It turned out to be good publicity. Our traffic figures showed some sign of improvement in consequence, and I expect our rivals also obtained some free advantage through our endeavours.

On 14 August, we added to our North Isles service by including Longhope on Hoy. Metal Industries had their local headquarters at Lyness and were engaged in raising the scuttled German fleet from Scapa Flow. Mr MacKenzie, their boss, was an old friend as I had met him at that miserable luncheon at Surgeon McClure's house on the morning in 1933 when I damaged the Monospar monoplane in the fog. We had subsequently met many times in Inverness and Kirkwall and, since that day, had become the best of friends. Some months earlier, he had suggested we extend the island service to his base as it would be of great advantage to his firm. He added that, together with their own workmen, they had many important visitors from the south who would make good use of such facilities. Ten minutes into Kirkwall, instead of an hour or two by surface, offered distinct advantages. I had surveyed Longhope in the Moth and found it very difficult to locate a suitable landing site owing to the rolling nature of the countryside and the extensive peat bogs which appeared to cover most of the island. In the end, I selected two fields at Snelsetter Farm, L-shaped with the east-west run going up a tidy slope. That slope would be of great help in landing and taking off downhill when loads were heavy and winds were light. Unfortunately, the surface was a bit rough and there was a ditch three feet wide separating the adjacent field to the south. I got Mr MacKenzie over with his foreman and he told me he would bridge the ditch and level the lumps without charge. That was a noble gesture and showed, I thought, how much people living in the more inaccessible districts appreciated air communications. To my mind, it is a great pity that, after the Second World War, the nationalisers overlooked this fact and withdrew the services I had commenced and operated with so much public appreciation.

World War One German fleet salvage operations in Scapa Flow (Orkney Library & Archive)

We flew our first service into Longhope the day after the field was serviceable, Mr MacKenzie being one of the first passengers. He was very pleased with the ease of the journey and the time saved and told me his principals in the south would be overjoyed. Longhope airfield became a very busy place and we ran many charters to and from the south for Metal Industries.

During August, I was flying duplicate services in the DH Dragon almost every day to Kirkwall and I was hard put to cope with the increase in traffic. There was little doubt that passengers, in the days before the radio stations were opened, were sometimes as scared as we were of skimming over the ground and sea, low down in bad visibility, and they now appreciated the ease, safety and comfort of high altitude flying. More people were also becoming interested in spending their holidays in beautiful and historic Orkney, which could now be reached with ease, speed and comfort.

That summer, I received an enquiry from the famous comedian, Harry Gordon, to fly sixteen members of his comedy troupe from Aberdeen to Inverness for a matinee show at the Empire Theatre. To do this would require two of our DH Dragons, but we hadn't two available at midday, only one. I asked them if they would mind flying in two shifts, which of course meant, the first shift would have to be prepared to depart from Aberdeen some two hours earlier than the second to ensure all arriving in time to open the show in Inverness after lunch. The next problem was whether we would be able to get both parties back to Aberdeen in time for the evening show at the Beach Pavilion? The answer to one aircraft for two return flights was in the negative, but happily, I remembered the Inverness-Orkney service plane would be available after its return to base, well before departure time for Aberdeen after the second show. So we were able to guarantee their return to Aberdeen by six o'clock. I made the two trips to bring the party over, and another trip for the return, which made three return journeys of over 600 miles for me for the day. The whole exercise went off without a hitch and Harry was very well pleased, so much so, that he gave us first class and valuable publicity during his show that night in Aberdeen. The three flights, which had enabled the famous comedian and his troupe to appear in Inverness and Aberdeen within a period of a few hours of each other, created a lot of local interest.

In September, the flights to Longhope were still on the increase, many charter flights being made from Inverness direct to Longhope. The weather was, however, capricious, for there was a lot of fog, low cloud and heavy rain during the first three weeks of that month. The radio homing stations were proving their worth and made our lives far less harassed.

In the third week in October, our baby son had to be taken to Edinburgh for a small nasal operation and I had to go into a nursing home also for nasal trouble which was the outcome of a broken nose received during a plane crash at the end of World War One. My wife, with the baby and myself, left Inverness by road for Edinburgh via Queensferry. The weather was bad; heavy rain and a gale blowing which appeared to increase with strength the further south we went. We pulled in to North Queensferry and there was a tremendous sea running in the Firth of Forth. There was some doubt as to whether the ferry boats would continue to operate. We were parked well down the quay alongside a concrete wall waiting for our ferry boat to come in. We could see it pitching and tossing in the firth as it laboriously ploughed its way over from the other side. Suddenly, without any warning, a tremendous wave broke over the sea wall and hit the roof of our car with a tremendous force. The noise was deafening and the car lurched with the shock of impact. Our poor little son was terrified. He let out a scream and nearly shot off his mother's lap. The ferry, with great difficulty, was tying up at that moment. The question was, would we get aboard before being struck by another well of water?

My wife said, 'I wish they would hurry up. This is a frightful place to be parked.'

I agreed. 'It's bad enough to break the roof in,' I replied.

I had hardly spoken when we were again hit, but by a smaller wave this time. At that moment, we were waved to go aboard. We were relieved to get away from the quay, but we were not out of the wood yet. The ferry pitched and plunged at alarming angles as she got out into the firth, and by the time we were

Firth of Forth ferry, *Robert the Bruce*, at South Queensferry. She was built at Dumbarton in 1934, and broken up in 1965 following completion of the Forth Road Bridge.

in mid-stream we began to get into difficulties. The gale came from the west and was slowly beating us downstream towards the Forth Bridge. The water got rougher and at times we were standing on our beam ends. Each time that happened, the steering appeared to fail and the nose of the ferry was flung round towards the Forth Bridge. Three quarters of the way across, one particularly vicious wave caught us and, before the skipper could do anything to correct the yaw, we were flung with a resounding crash against one of the bridge piers. The stern swung round and in the semi-darkness, we were caught amidships, bumping and scraping at an alarming angle against the pier we had struck. We thought the ferry was about to break up and sink. No boat could take that pasting for long. We were stunned and the position looked serious.

'We're all going to be drowned,' my wife shouted. 'We should have never attempted the crossing in this weather.'

I tried to remain calm, but I was not feeling it.

'I expect the Skipper knows what he is about. If he can only get clear of this bridge pier we should make it, providing the boat hasn't been holed,' I shouted.

After what appeared to be an endless time, but which was probably not much more than a few minutes, the ferry at last got clear and underway, heading straight into the gale and away from that killer pier. In another ten minutes, we were alongside the Hawes Inn slipway and we tied up.

'Thank God, for that,' my wife said, 'I never want to cross the Firth again in a storm like that.'

It was a near thing, there was no doubting that.

We were back in Inverness in the first week in November. All services were running with good loads and, on the day I arrived, I had to make a special trip to Kirkwall for the Post Office as 500 lbs of mail had turned up. Owing to a full load of passengers, the one aircraft could not cope with the excess mail. We flew north in formation, much to the interest of the passengers.

The surface of the Kintore airfield had turned out to be very rough and required levelling for next year's operation. Along with Mr Barrack at the farm, I marked out two strips at right angles to one another and he agreed to get the levelling ready early in the new year. Mr Barrack was a loyal and sincere friend to Highland Airways and to myself, and we owed him a lot. There was little doubt that without his help we would have been obliged to retire from the Aberdeen-Kirkwall-Shetland run.

The absence of a radio air station at Aberdeen worried me. As far as landing an aeroplane was concerned, Aberdeen had far worse weather over the year than Inverness and radio was vitally necessary in the performance of a safe and regular service to the north. Mr Gandar Dower obstinately refused to accept this safety measure at his airfield as he would then be compelled to allow us to use Dyce airfield should we so wish. While Dyce was a better airfield than Kintore by a long way, we did not need to use it as Kintore was quite satisfactory for our operations after surface levelling. No one could understand Mr Gandar Dower's mentality and his refusal made it very difficult to operate on many days. He had the use of our airfields at Kirkwall and Sumburgh and the benefit of the radio facilities installed there. As Mr Gandar Dower would not play ball with us, we charged him heavy landing rates at our airfields about which he complained bitterly to the Air Ministry and various MPs. The whole situation was so unfair that the Air Ministry would not take any notice of his complaint. This state of affairs continued until late 1939 when World War Two commenced. I well remember that there was a case around that time of one of Aberdeen Airways planes very nearly coming to grief under foggy conditions when groping along at low altitude trying to find Dyce airfield. Without warning, the pilot flew on to high ground and, before he knew what was happening, the plane had landed itself and was running up a grassy hill. The surprised pilot (not Eric Starling) fortunately acted quickly and cut his motors and pulled up without damage to the aircraft or himself and any passengers he might have had on board. He was stuck out in the blue with thick fog around him and it was a long time before he could obtain assistance. That was a chance of one in a million. I have never heard of such a miracle happening before or since. Surely, the devil looks after his own, so the saying goes.

During the summer, Mr Gandar Dower thought he would like to run a service to Inverness from Kirkwall in competition against us. He could not be stopped from using our airfield at Longman as, not only did it belong to the Inverness Town Council, but there was a radio station there, which, as I have said, gave him automatic rights to land. That was when I first met Pilot Starling, when he flew Mr Gandar Dower and another member of his firm into Longman airport one morning. The hero of the flight described at the opening of this chapter, Pilot Starling, remained on the airfield while the others went up to town. We had a chat and he told me his boss was looking into the possibility of opening a competitive service from Inverness to Orkney and Shetland. He also told me that he was anxious to build up flying hours so that he could go south and obtain a better job.

He appeared to be a very nice chap and I had come to look upon him as a very good pilot. However, instead of going south, he stayed on at Aberdeen to pioneer and pilot the four-engined DH86 sixteen-seater airliner on the Aberdeen-Stavanger air service which Mr Gandar Dower promoted, the following year. It should have been a good and useful service, if a connection could have been made between Aberdeen and London. I admired Mr Gandar Dower for having the courage to embark on a venture of such magnitude. He certainly did not obtain much encouragement from our civil aviation authorities of the day, although I believe the Norwegian authorities were most willing to give all the assistance they could to obtain such an air connection with Scotland and London. What I could not understand at the time was how Mr Gandar Dower expected Eric Starling to maintain such a service from Stavanger to Dyce in all weather without the aid of radio at the Aberdeen end. He was alright from Dyce to Stavanger because there was a radio station at that airport. Mr Gandar Dower's reticence on that very important matter may have had some bearing on subsequent official outlook. The press statement at the time is of interest in reference to this courageous pioneer venture, and one which I would have liked to have seen successful.[3]

Airways Chief attacks Air Ministry
Vital Norway Service Ignored
Norway grants extension to Oslo

An attack on the British Government and Air Ministry was made by Mr Eric Gandar Dower of Allied Airways (recently Aberdeen Airways) at a banquet at Stavanger on Tuesday, a fortnight ago. The Ministry, he said, refused not only to recognise his air service between Britain and Norway, but had completely ignored powerful pleas for aid to progress of the North Sea airline. A five year concession to carry air mail and passengers across the North Sea granted by the Norwegian Government to Allied Airways must cease unless the British Government aids financially this concern. More than £100,000 has already been spent by Mr Eric Gandar Dower, Managing Director of the concern, in providing an air link between Britain and Scandinavia. 'I speak deliberately in Norway,' Mr Gandar Dower said, 'because it is possible that my remarks may be more widely reported than if delivered in Scotland.' He accused the Air Ministry of apathy and of ignoring requests for interviews where the serious position arising out of even a temporary suspension of an important British air service, could be discussed with responsible

---

[3] Although a proving flight, with a DH89 Rapide, was undertaken from Aberdeen to Stavanger, the scheduled service that was subsequently launched with the DH86 operated to Stavanger from Newcastle, not Aberdeen.

officials. About this time, British commercial aviation history was made when Allied Airways brought Norway within two hours of Scotland for the first time. The four-engined Allied Airways airliner covered more than 700 miles of open sea between Aberdeen and Stavanger and back in a final bid to complete the vital link in a chain of air routes which may ultimately stretch from Leningrad to Canada, embracing Sweden, Norway, Scotland and Iceland on the way.

The importance of such an air route was stressed by high Norwegian officials and representatives of Scottish interests when the prospect of making Scotland the centre of vitally important international air traffic was discussed at the banquet which was given by the Mayor of Stavanger. With more than 200 air crossings of the North Sea to their credit, the Norwegian Government have granted permission to Allied Airways to extend their route to Oslo.'

This service ceased at the end of six months operations, as forecasted.[4]

To return to Mr Gandar Dower's visit to Inverness, he eventually advertised a service in and out of Inverness to the north. It ran for a few weeks, but very irregularly and died a natural death at the expiration of that time. The public did not take kindly to his invasion of our home base, knowing so well that we were frozen out of Dyce on a 'closed shop' policy. Consequently, support was entirely lacking and we were spared a cut throat war owing to public loyalty and goodwill towards the pioneer company.

Eric Starling today holds a senior position in the nationalised air service at Renfrew.[5]

Eric Starling, Roland Morris (flying instructor at Dyce) and Fresson's nemesis – Eric Gandar Dower. (Frances Vallance Collection)

---

[4] This report should be read with caution as some of the detail is inaccurate. The service between Newcastle and Stavanger ran for two summers, from 12 July 1937 and 19 September 1938, consisting of 166 round trips. It did not extend to Oslo.
[5] Eric Starling retired from BEA in 1971. He died in 1997, age 85.

Relaxing in Hankow in 1913, age 22.

(above right)
Resplendent in
Royal Flying Corps
uniform.

Fresson (centre) at Duxford,
January 1919. The aircraft is a
de Havilland DH9 'light bomber'.

Aircraft construction in China. The workshop (top). Wing sections (bottom).

En route to the first flight.

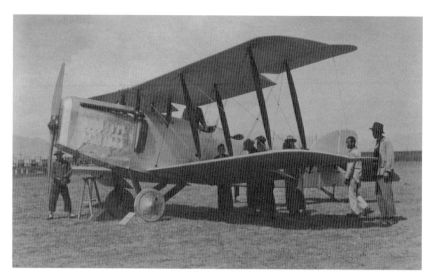

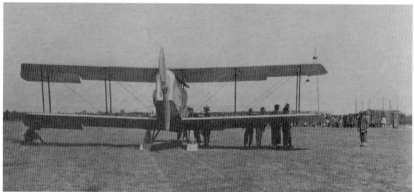

Assembled and ready to go (above and top).

The moment of truth.

Flying for Berkshire Aviation Tours Ltd

Flying Licence No. 310, 1919. Fresson's permit to fly the Avro 504K.

Cyril Pugh, Ted Fresson and Lance Rimmer pose before Avro 504K G-EBGZ on a souvenir postcard that they sold to joy-riders.

Engineer Jock Gillies, Christine Fresson, Bert Farminer, Lance Rimmer, publicity agent Frank Wolfson, and Ted Fresson, Kendal, 16 May 1929.

Two young North British Aviation passengers at Huddersfield, April 1929. Jock Gillies at the prop and Bert Farminer at the ladder which was strapped to the wings struts when the Avro 504K moved between joy-riding sites.

Real flying country. Gipsy Moth G-AAWO and Avro 504K G-EBGZ at Keswick, May 1929.

Keswick crowds gather for Sunday joy-riding undeterred by sultry clouds overhead (above and top).

Rainford Hall, near St Helens, one of many grand homes to which Fresson made informal aerial visits.

Avro 504K in Orkney. Fresson first took this aircraft across the Pentland Firth on 22 August 1931. (Orkney Library & Archive)

First landing in Orkney, G-AAWO at Corse field near Kirkwall, 19 April 1931.

Ted Fresson and Helen Pauer.

Wings folded and tail skid supported on a trolley, G-AAWO is escorted to Shearer's coal shed for overnight storage in Kirkwall. (Orkney Library & Archive)

Kirkwall and the Peerie Sea (centre left). (Orkney Library & Archive)

Passengers Gabriel (American Oil Co) and Smith (White Horse Distillers), Ted Fresson, and Sir Edmund Findlay (The Scotsman), first Highland Airways service Inverness to Kirkwall, 8 May 1933.

GA Monospar G-ACEW at Wick, intermediate stop on the Inverness-Kirkwall inaugural service, 8 May 1933.

G-ACEW in flight over the Moray Firth.

Dignitaries gather for the departure of the first flight on 8 May 1933.

Peter Angus with Fresson at Longman, about to depart for Shetland on 3 October 1933...

... and after a safe landing on the Isle of Bressay.

The first consignment of Scotsman newspapers being loaded for delivery to Orkney on the day of publication.

DH84 Dragon G-ADCT at Wideford, Orkney in August 1935, the first Highland Airways aircraft to be equipped with radio.

Pilot's 'office' – cockpit of the DH84 Dragon.

DH84 G-ACIT at Seaton airfield, Aberdeen, on 7 May 1934 for the first Aberdeen-Kirkwall service.

Football referee Peter Craigmyle disembarking from the Monospar at Longman after officiating at an Orkney v Shetland match in Kirkwall.

9

Getting the Measure of the Railways

A day or two after the New Year's Day 1937, we received two charters. The first was to take a business party to London and back, and the second was a return trip to Edinburgh for the same purpose. With the advent of our DH Rapide aircraft, and the better performance and comfort offered the passengers, the business community were beginning to take advantage of the immense saving in time that air charters offered. The London flight, for example, only took three and a half hours from Inverness and it was, therefore, possible for a business party to spend most of the day in London on their business and be back in their homes at night.

In addition, the New Year saw a big development on the Orkney Inter-Isles service, with Longhope in the forefront. Metal Industries found it of great assistance and the local inhabitants were also making full use of the facilities offered. Whereas the 'locals' would go into Kirkwall only when absolutely essential before the air connection came along, now that the journey only took ten minutes they appeared to be flitting in almost once a week to the cinema and to do their shopping. Our pilot stationed in Kirkwall was so hard put to it that I had to spend a few weeks in Kirkwall with another plane to help him out.

By this time, there were a number of companies in the airline business and in many instances they were cutting each other's throats. The Government had appointed the Maybury Committee to study the desirability of some measure of control in the licensing of air companies to certain routes. Accordingly, our Aberdeen rivals were in a hurry to stake their claim to the Aberdeen-Orkney-Shetland route and so force Highland Airways off that run irrespective of the years we put in preparing and educating the public to fly and having been first in the field. In addition, Highland Airways had spent a considerable amount of money on the development work and construction of an airfield at Sumburgh, of which our unwelcome competitor sought to take advantage. To assist in their plans, Aberdeen Airways persuaded the MP, Major Basil Neven Spence, to ask certain questions in the House of Commons. The debate was an interesting one in that the claim of Mr Gandar Dower's rights to the air route he was desirous of licensing was exposed in its true light. Mr C G Grey, founder and editor of the well known air periodical *The Aeroplane* expertly reviewed the issue and debate in an article dated 27 March 1937, which is reproduced ad verbatim. It is somewhat lengthy, but worth studying in order to assimilate the degree to which competition in air transport had developed at that date. The morality of the issue is also well dealt with in the debate and needs no further comment.

On the Air war in the North

War seems to be endemic in the North of Scotland.... Captain Fresson seems to have the advantage of having been there first and having founded Highland Airways Limited at Inverness several years before Mr Dower [sic] started to build an air transport network in the right hand top corner of Great Britain. Also, Captain Fresson has local backing in the persons of Col J J Robertson, DSO and Captain R Donald of Inverness, North of Scotland Shipping Company Limited, Aberdeen, and he has national backing from Major McCrindle, MC, Mr W L Thurgood and Mr J de C Ballardie, respectively of British Airways, Jersey Airways, Spartan Airways, all now in the British Airways fold.

What backing Mr Dower has, we do not know beyond his own combative spirit and considerable wealth. The 1937 campaign opened in the House of Commons on Wednesday, 3rd February, when Major Neven Spence, Unionist Member of Orkney and Shetland asked the Under Secretary of State for Air [Sir Philip Sassoon] whether the Air Minister had considered the application submitted by Aberdeen Airways Limited (Mr Dower's line) dated 13th December 1936, requesting that certain Airlines they were operating should be licensed in view of the recommendations made by the Maybury Committee that airlines should be licensed and would the Air Ministry license these airlines at an early date?

Sir Philip Sassoon said the application had been received but he would remind the Honourable Member that no licences yet exist, and that a good deal of parliamentary procedure will be necessary before further steps can be taken.

From this we judge that Mr Dower made an effort to jump in and stake his claim for licensed airlines at places, which for years have been well served by Highland Airways. But evidently, he jumped too soon and showed his hand to the perhaps slower witted, but very capable, directors of Highland Airways Limited.

Major Neven Spence then asked Sir Philip Sassoon why, in view of the growing importance of air transport to Orkney and Shetland, the Air Ministry had approved landing fees for Wideford Aerodrome, Orkney, and Sumburgh substantially higher than those of Croydon, for example, 25/-d for such craft as Dragons and 38/-d for Rapides, and whether, seeing that fares across the Pentland Firth to Orkney and Shetland were £1 and £2 10s 0d respectively, he would take steps to reduce the landing fees and so make possible the profitable use of a six seater aeroplane at fifty percent load.

Sir Philip Sassoon replied that the principle followed in fixing landing charges was to approve rates which appeared to be reasonable considering the cost to the aerodrome proprietors of providing and maintaining facilities according to traffic. So there appeared no justification for revising the aforementioned rates.

The point here is that those two aerodromes were laid out by Highland Airways Limited for their own use and Mr Dower wants to use them. Of this there is more to say later.

What the Maybury Committee did Recommend

Major Neven Spence's next question was whether the Under Secretary was aware of the recommendations of the Maybury Committee that there should be a standard scale of charges for all aerodromes throughout the country licensed for public use and the owners should conform to that scale. Sir Philip Sassoon said that the point was being considered. Here we may remark that there is a vast difference between considering a point of that sort and making regulations in the interest of one company to the detriment of the people who have done the spade work, and naturally do not wish to be cut out or undercut by rivals. Major Neven Spence then asked whether the Under Secretary was aware that no petrol or oil could be bought at Sumburgh, that there were no hangars there, that Aberdeen Airways had been refused permission to build sheds, and that as Sumburgh was the only practical landing ground in Shetland, the licensee, namely Highland Airways Limited, has a virtual monopoly of landing in Shetland. Would the Air Ministry, therefore, take over the aerodrome and operate it impartially in the public interest. Sir Philip Sassoon said that the licensing for an aerodrome for public use does not entail provision for fuel or housing. Permission to land was a matter for the owners of the aerodrome, and the acquisition of the aerodrome would be contrary to Government Policy.

That seems to settle those questions, but here again, there is more to be said later.

Major Neven Spence's parting shot was a question on whether the Maybury Committee recommended that main aerodromes should not be privately owned and whether, as Sumburgh was the only landing ground in Shetland, would the Under Secretary reconsider the question?

Sir Philip Sassoon, who always has a ready answer, pointed out that the Maybury Committee had also recommended that displacing or discharging existing owners of aerodromes would be unfair. Mr Garro-Jones, Labour member for Aberdeen North, who might not be expected to sympathise with such an evident capitalist as Mr Dower, threw in a question, asking whether this licence was subject to renewal and if so, would the Right Honourable Gentleman undertake not to renew it until the aerodrome has provided facilities which are in demand in the district, and are ready to be supplied by Aberdeen Airways? We presume he meant that Aberdeen Airways are ready to supply them and not that the facilities are ready to be supplied, but political language is apt to become journalese.

Sir Philip Sassoon squashed that by stating that the Government has no power to do that sort of thing. That being that, we can now discourse on some of the facts.

A few Basic Facts

In the first place, if and when the licensing of air routes in the north arises, Highland Airways have an obvious prior right to the lot. And if Mr Dower wants to run uneconomical parallel routes, then fairly obviously, his line would be without a licence. The landing charge argument is amusing. Mr Dower's machines have not been using Highland Airways aerodrome at Kirkwall, although Highland Airways were willing to share it on equitable terms. Mr Dower acquired a landing field of his own. Consequently, ever since the radio station was installed at Kirkwall, Mr Dower's machines have had the benefit of that station, which is run entirely at the expense of Highland Airways. Mr Dower has not contributed to the cost of the service, although Highland Airways have often been obliged to keep their Control Officer on duty several hours after their own services have been shut down for the day, so as to give free service to the competing company. That being so, one can hardly be surprised at Highland Airways extracting as big a landing fee from Mr Dower as they can when his machines land on their only available Shetland aerodrome.

We may say that, to get radio stations installed by the Air Ministry at Kirkwall and Sumburgh, Highland Airways had to guarantee to provide Control Officers at their own expense, because the local authorities would not help, although the local people are very keen on the accelerated mail and passenger service which has been provided for them for the past three or four years by Captain Fresson. Highland Airways had to choose between supplying the control themselves or doing without the radio, so they took on the responsibility. If they had not done so, they would not have had to throw their aerodrome open to public use.

Those Landing Charges – Moreover, we have information that Mr Dower's machines have only used Sumburgh aerodrome two or three times during the winter since the approved charges came into force. All through the summer, when Mr Dower's outfit was running more or less regularly, he was only charged 12/6d a landing. We think that even if they had been operating regularly during the winter, the higher approved charges would have been very low, considering it has to bear a reasonable share of the cost of the control for which Highland Airways have to keep two men permanently at Sumburgh.

We may add that Mr Dower has been informed, that if he likes to bear an equal cost of the control, Highland Airways will agree to modify the landing charges in spite of the fact that the existence of a radio station is the only reason why the aerodrome is public and although there is not enough traffic along the route for two services.

An Historical Incident – Here arises the interesting point that Highland Airways spent two years surveying, arranging for, and developing the Sumburgh route. The aerodrome was ready, the timetable was planned, and their machines were equipped with radio a whole year before the date the service began. As soon as the radio station was settled, Highland Airways advertised their starting date some weeks before. Three days or so before that date, Mr Dower published the statement that his company was about to start a Sumburgh Service, and gave the date one day before Highland Airways Official inauguration. Actually, Highland Airways are able and willing to supply all the machines that can be needed to carry passengers on the Shetland route, provided they are given the same consideration as they get from the Orkney people, namely, that passengers will notify their need for seats a reasonable time beforehand, and will give reasonable notice of cancellation, when they find they do not want them. This is worth mentioning, because a number of people, some of them who have been loudest in their demand for an air service, booked their passages south by steamer some time before, found at the last moment the steamer was not running, and then wanted to travel by air. The aeroplane on the regular service was full up and these people did not give enough notice to make a duplicate possible. Also we may mention that Highland Airways have run the Shetland service at least twice a week out of the three scheduled in the winter, until Sumburgh became flooded.

Shetland Accommodation – Then came the question of sheds and petrol. Highland Airways have been considering putting up a shed and they will do it as soon as they are sure that the indigenes and visitors to Shetland are going to use their air service enough to make it worthwhile. Also, they have to discover a non-floodable place for it. Petrol and oil are not wanted at Sumburgh because it is only a short hop from Kirkwall and aeroplanes can always carry enough petrol and oil to give them 100% for the return trip. This method is the better because petrol and oil cost more in Shetland than it does in Orkney. Furthermore, there is nothing to prevent Mr Dower storing his own petrol in cans, as do Highland Airways at Sumburgh, for emergencies.

Reciprocity – Another point is that although the aerodromes of Highland Airway at Orkney and Shetland are open to Mr Dower's outfit, reciprocal use of Mr Dower's aerodromes at Thurso and Dyce, Aberdeen, was refused until Highland Airways made their own arrangements at Aberdeen, whereupon Mr Dower offered the use of Dyce aerodrome after the permission had lost its value. We happen to know that in the presence of another director of Highland Airways Limited, Captain Fresson personally offered Mr Dower free landings at the Kirkwall aerodrome in exchange for free landings at Thurso, although Kirkwall has a radio station and Thurso has not. Similarly, Mr Dower was offered free landings at Kirkwall in exchange for free landings at Dyce. And that offer was also refused. Looking at the matter purely dispassionately, one cannot help thinking that Mr Dower expects Highland Airways to give everything while they get nothing in return.

We have watched this war from its very beginning, and so far as we have been able to learn, Mr Dower has never offered any concessions to Highland Airways. Highland Airways were there first. Captain Fresson has put up an amazingly courageous fight against weather, mechanical problems and finance. He has won the confidence and personal affection of the people of Inverness and the Orkneys. He has given them a passenger and mail service such as they had never imagined possible. Also he has the distinguished honour of being the first airline operator who has carried His Majesty's Mails under contract with the General Post Office, without surcharge. Consequently, he can claim in every way to be not merely a pioneer of air transport in the north of Scotland, but a pioneer of air mail transport in the British Empire. As we have explained frequently in this paper before now, Highland Airways had all their plans laid to extend their service from Inverness to Aberdeen, and when Mr Dower took a fancy to running direct from Aberdeen to Orkney and Shetland, Highland Airways showed no animosity. They were willing to co-operate on a fair for all basis. Mr Dower's policy seems evident in the questions asked in the House.

In early March, we received the first ambulance call from Stornoway. It was for a sick person arriving from hospital in the south who wished to avoid the long rail and steamer journey across the Minch. The patient was comfortably flown over from Inverness in fifty minutes. The chairs had been taken out of the cabin and a mattress placed on the floor and made into a comfortable bed. The hard beach at low tide and the tidal basin alongside the golf course had certainly proved their worth as emergency landing facilities over the past three years and they demonstrated conclusively the necessity of an airport to serve Stornoway..

I stayed the night and took the opportunity of calling on the Stornoway Trust Committee, who owned the ground of the Melbost golf course, accompanied by the Provost and Town Clerk. In all, I had made not less than fifty chartered flights between Inverness and Stornoway up to that time, and at last the value and the necessity of air travel had begun to penetrate the minds of those who had the control of the only land which was suitable for the construction of an airfield. Resulting from that discussion, we had at last got them to concede that they were prepared to release the golf course, or that portion of it, which would be required for the construction of an airfield. The remaining and equally important matter which had yet to be solved was over who would meet the cost of construction. I had at last got half the way over this thorny problem and I returned to the mainland to report to our Board.

I informed the chairman and members that the cost of putting the ground in order would probably, in my opinion, run to £10,000. That was a substantial sum and the question arose, who was to finance it? After considerable discussion as to ways and means of solving this problem, it was decided to send a delegation over to meet the Town Council and trustees of the Estate to try and hammer out a solution. It was left to me to make the arrangements. I forget how it all ended and who paid what, but after lengthy discussion the lease was settled later on in the year, and we sent a team of experts over to make the survey and estimate the cost.

At the end of March, we were booked to fly the Secretary of State for Scotland, Sir Walter Elliot, and his advisors to Wick, Kirkwall and Sumburgh, and return. Mrs Elliot and Dr Shearer of the Ministry of Health were among the party. It was the first time that a Scottish Secretary had ever used air transport to visit the outlying boundaries of Scotland and the flight therefore created history. I found Sir Walter and his wife charming people and after his trip with us he became a regular supporter of the future development of Scottish air travel. I later learned that the decision to fly was made after a rough trip in the Fisheries cruiser aboard which the party had set out from Edinburgh to Inverness. It was a fine day. We flew high and the air was calm, so Sir Walter and party had every reason to suppose that air transport was not only faster, but more comfortable than rolling about in a ship at sea.

Our traffic on the long distance sections was now increasing. Many more bookings were being made by residents in the south and it was evident to me that railway influence with travel agents all over the country was making it difficult for would-be southern passengers on our routes to book at their local travel agents. That state of affairs could mean loss of business. There appeared to be an agreement between the travel agencies and the railways prohibiting them from effecting bookings which were not approved by them and, so far, our company had not been approved. So, all southern bookings had to be made the hard way, that is, by letter, telegram or telephone to Inverness. We then either had to send the tickets on to the passenger or hold them for their arrival. It also meant that passengers had to remit the value of the reservations made direct to us. All this lengthy and irritating procedure could be avoided if the railways could be persuaded to authorise travel agencies to book for us.

I decided to tackle the matter and wrote to the Superintendent of Traffic at the L M S Railway Headquarters at Euston, enquiring whether they could see their way to accommodating us and expressing my willingness to call on them to discuss this matter should they desire to see me. In due course, a reply came back, intimating that one of their senior executives, Mr W P Bradbury, would be glad to discuss the matter I had raised if I would call on a certain date at his Euston office. At the appointed time I was ushered into Mr Bradbury's office and, after shaking hands, he introduced me to another person by the name of Wing Commander Arthur Measures. At that time, the British Railways group were about to float an air company to be known as Railway Air Services and the Wing Commander had been appointed as their Air Superintendent. Accordingly, he was there to take part in the discussion to protect the new rail air company's interests. Mr Bradbury was a tall man of lean stature and appeared extremely human and pleasant. We were later destined to become very close friends. The Wing Commander was of medium height and inclined to be on the stout side, and was slightly officious. As matters turned out, I was going to see a lot of him in the future.

Mr Bradbury opened the discussion saying they had considered the Highland Airways letter regarding the travel agency bookings, but they found some difficulty in granting permission in view of the fact that we were in direct competition with the Highland Railway which ran from Inverness to Wick and Thurso, and which carried all the Orkney traffic to those ports before the air service started.

'That is so, but,' I suggested, 'if the public wish to use the faster mode of transport, they will fly irrespective of your withholding booking facilities and that doesn't help you, in fact it only creates a public resentment towards the LMS.'

He appeared slightly taken aback at that interpretation of the position.

'What about the Inverness-Glasgow service the press report you are about to commence?' he enquired. 'Will you want the same facilities for that run?'

'Certainly,' I replied, 'if you are prepared to grant them, but for the moment I am chiefly concerned with the traffic north from Inverness.'

He went in to a huddle with the Wing Commander and finished up by telling me they would agree to my proposal for the northern routes, but not for the

Inverness-Glasgow run should we commence to operate. I took that proviso to mean that Railway Air Service would be casting their eyes on that one, which in the end turned out a correct prophecy.

They bade me goodbye and I left for home thinking I had not done too badly for a beginning. What I did not then realise were the far reaching changes that were about to occur following that meeting. From Mr Bradbury's conversation, one could read between the lines that they were very knowledgeable about our operations. I was perplexed as to where they had obtained so much information. Shortly after, we found out!

For many months, we had noticed a short stocky man wearing a bowler hat standing alongside our hangars at Longman airport, Inverness. George Griffiths, our chief engineer had also noticed him and had called my attention to his behaviour. Day in and day out, he was always there and never missed a day, fine weather or foul. The only difference in the latter case was that he always came armed with an umbrella. He carried a pencil and notebook and always appeared to be writing. We wondered what interested him so much. Eventually, we became suspicious. No one would surely waste so much time as he did without some purpose. I told Griffiths to put one of our boys on to following the man with bowler hat back to town to find out where he came from. To our astonishment, it turned out to be the railway headquarters in the Station Square. Next day, I was down at the airfield while the morning Orkney plane was being loaded and passengers going aboard. I stood a few yards away from the 'little man', where I was not too conspicuous. As soon as the mail bags were being loaded on to the plane from the trolley, he began to write. When the loading finished, he stopped writing. Then the passengers came out ready to embark. Out came the notebook and pencil again and more writing went on as the passengers stepped aboard.

'Good gracious,' I thought, 'he's noting the aircraft load. What's he up to?'

I walked up to him.

'You appear to be very interested in the mail and passengers going aboard that plane?'

He turned and gave me a blank look, but said nothing.

'Why do you take the trouble to make notes of our aircraft loading?'

'Because the boss told me to,' he replied.

'And who is the Boss?' I interrogated.

'The traffic manager,' he answered. 'I've been told to do it every day.'

'Are you working for the railway?'

'Yes,' he said, 'I'm in the Traffic Office.'

'You've been doing that for a long time?'

'Yes, over six months now, and it's jolly cold work sometimes.'

'Well, little man,' I said, 'you've been very honest. Go back to your boss and tell him we don't like the railways snooping around here. If it continues, we will have to call the police.'

He scuttled off and we never saw him or, to the best of our knowledge, any other body, taking loading notes again. So that explained it all. Those figures were being transmitted to London and Mr Bradbury was the recipient. No wonder he could tell me a thing or two.

A year or two later, I pulled Bradbury's leg about the incident. He laughed, and then told me another story, this time against myself, which occurred at Stornoway the previous summer. He and the Wing Commander had visited the Western Isles by surface transport, spying out the land on the islands which Northern & Scottish Airways were operating to, namely Barra, South Uist and North Uist. They had finally landed up at Stornoway where they were checking up on the air potential and a possible site for an airfield. They had been told I had spent years at that game and had decided on the Melbost golf course. Mr Bradbury went on to say that one sunny afternoon they were walking around the golf course when they espied a DH Rapide coming in from the east. They watched it circle the town, dropping off height.

'Do you think that plane is going to attempt a landing here, Measures?' Bradbury asked.

'No, Sir, I shouldn't think so. There's not enough level ground here for a seagull to land on.'

They were standing by the golf hut in good view of the tidal basin.

Mr Bradbury went on: 'To our astonishment the plane approached the northern end of the basin and Measures said, "Good God, that Rapide is going to try and land here, after all. Look out! There's going to be a crash".'

'Isn't there a sufficient run over there?' Bradbury asked the Wing Commander, pointing at the tidal basin.

'What, for a Rapide landing at 70 miles an hour? Not in your life, he'll never do it,' he answered.

'To our utter amazement,' Bradbury continued, 'that pilot made a beautiful landing and with quite a bit to spare. Wing Commander Measures couldn't believe his eyes. He said to me, "I've never seen a Rapide landed in such a small place before. Come on. Let's go and quiz the pilot."'

'We were both dressed as tourists,' Bradbury continued, 'and we went up to the pilot and had a chat with him, asking him what he thought about the golf course for an airfield. "Very good", he said. "I'm trying to get the rights, as we wish to run a service to Stornoway." We told that pilot we were tourists and were most interested, as the steamer and rail connections were so long and tedious. You made a wonderful landing with such a short runway. "Oh," the pilot said, "I'm used to that, I've done it many times before." On hearing the plane belonged to Highland Airways, we plied him with many more questions, couched of course, in tourist language. "Obliging sort of chap, that pilot," Bradbury said to me. "He told us all we wanted to know!" "You're returning to Inverness this evening?" we asked. "Yes, in about an hour's time." "Well, we'll wait and see how you get off." He bid us goodbye and left for the town with his passengers.'

Mr Bradbury was laughing by this time, having come to the end of his narration.

'What are you laughing at?' I enquired.

'You were the pilot,' he replied.

'Good Lord,' I said, as it all came back to me. 'Those two figures, one in a straw hat and the other with a cap, and both dressed in tweed jackets and flannel trousers. Who was your pal?' I asked.

'Wing Commander Measures,' he replied.

'Well you fooled me alright,' I had to admit. 'I had little idea when I met you in your office for the first time that I had actually been in conversation with you two before.'

'We know,' Bradbury said. 'We were laughing about it after you had left.'

A month or two later, we were surprised to receive a letter from United Airways, now changed to British Airways, informing us they had received overtures from Railway Air Services Limited, who were now operating a number of air routes throughout the country, proposing a merger of Northern & Scottish Airways, Renfrew, and ourselves, with the Railway octopus. They asked for me and our secretary, Willie Hamilton, to attend a meeting in London to discuss the proposal. They told us that the recent formation of British Airways involved operations to the Continent, and they, British Airways, thought a partial link-up of the internal routes to Railway Air Services would enable them to concentrate more on their new task.

As the meeting progressed, it was obvious that there would be advantages in being tied up with such a powerful group, and I had in mind Aberdeen Airways who were becoming a nuisance to us on the Aberdeen-Kirkwall-Shetland run. At the same time, I did not wish to lose my control of the northern routes to their Air Superintendent who, let alone being wholly unknowledgeable of the local requirements, had, as far as I could judge, no technical experience of operating aircraft. Wing Commander Measures had come from the RAF, it was true. But he was a Wing Commander in one of the non-flying departments on the administrative side. When asked for my views on such a merger, I said I was quite content to continue under the British Airways set up. As far as I remember, George Nicholson of Northern & Scottish Airways, who was also present, expressed the same views. The problem was left to Mr Roberts, the chairman of our board, and who also spoke for the new company, British Airways, to settle. Willie Hamilton and I returned home and became engrossed in other matters, not giving the subject any further thought.

Then to my surprise, two months later in early May, I received a chit from 'Old Man Roberts', as he was known to us, saying, he would be visiting us along with Wing Commander Measures to inspect our organisation at Inverness, Wick and Kirkwall and would like to return by way of Thurso. Would I have a plane ready and stand by to fly them up? I showed the letter to Donald and Willie Hamilton.

'Looks as if they are going in with the Railways after all,' they said.

'Funny thing that they didn't write to us and say what they were doing,' I replied. 'We can only wait and see. No doubt Mr Roberts will wish to discuss whatever they have up their sleeve.'

On their arrival, Roberts said they had been considering the Railway offer, but nothing would be completed until we had had an opportunity of finally discussing the matter again at boardroom level. I took our friends down to Longman in our car and they commenced to go through our sheds and stores. Measures was making criticism over our methods, why hadn't we this and that, and why didn't we do this or that, all of which would have meant the employment of many extra bodies at heavy expense. By the time we had got to the end of our tour, I had formed the opinion that Wing Commander Measures would have us run our organisation on RAF lines, but without the government purse to 'pay the piper'.

The weather was not very good at Orkney. There was heavy fog over the Pentland Firth. I flew above it and homed on Wideford radio station, dropping down over the sea on the north end of the airfield, and then in to land with a ceiling of around 300 feet. The same process of inspection and comment went on at Wideford and our town office before going to lunch at the Kirkwall Hotel. We left around three o'clock for Thurso. As there was no radio at Thurso, I decided to try and fly under the fog as I didn't like to chance breaking cloud at the other end without knowing exactly where I was. As it happened, the weather was clear over there and it was a pity I didn't find that out by telephone before we left as it would have made the flight much easier. The trouble was that I was worried and my mind was full of doubts about getting mixed up with the Railways. It was clear they had a very different outlook on operational methods to what I had. Moreover, I did not wish to lose my identity and authority to possible bureaucracy, restrictions and planning unsuitable to the requirements in our part of Britain. We had to remain flexible and British Airways had not disturbed our 'status quo' in that respect. As a result, our services were increasing and we were not losing money like most of the other independent air services in the south, with the exception of Mr Thurgood's excellent Jersey Airways Limited.

Mr Roberts said they wanted to see the Old Man of Hoy, that remarkable rock formation standing some 100 yards off the perpendicular cliffs of the island of Hoy. The pinnacle towers a hundred feet or more in the air and has the features of a man's head on the top, looking out over the Pentland Firth like a sentinel. It can be readily seen from the Thurso shore on a fine day. We flew out over the township of Stromness and rounded the north end of Hoy. Very soon the Old Man came into sight and, as we passed it, Mr Roberts and the Wing Commander obtained an excellent view. We were flying a few hundred feet above the area and within 200 feet of the Old Man's profile, and it presented a wonderful spectacle. Old Man Roberts was just saying what an extraordinary freak of nature it was that such a realistic profile could be carved out of the rock by the wind and rain, when we suddenly ran slap into the fog. I carried on 'on instruments', altering course a little to the right to make sure we would miss Dunnet Head on the cliffs east of Thurso. Occasionally, there was a glimpse of the water. I expected we should run out of it as we neared the other side. Suddenly, a voice sounded in my ear, 'Doesn't look too good, does it?'

'I expect it's only local,' I said.

After ten minutes we were still in it, when the same voice came up again.

'Don't you think we had better turn back?'

I then realised, he had the wind up.

'I'll keep on a bit longer,' I told him. 'We can always climb above it and continue on to Inverness if the worst comes to the worst.'

I took a quick look at him and his face betrayed his anxiety. My other passenger was quite demure. What a difference between those two, I thought. Shortly after, we flew out into the clear and we were about a mile offshore in Scrabster Bay making for Thurso dead on course. They spent an hour or so in Thurso, after which we left for Inverness and the south.

There were many meetings in London after that exploratory trip. Shortly afterwards, Wing Commander Measures visited us again with the intention of inspecting our arrangements at Sumburgh. By then, we had built our hangar, facing south east. Measures considered we should have sited it facing west.

'All the gales come from that quarter,' I told him. 'Anything from 80 to 100 miles per hour. The roofs would soon be off when the doors were opened to get the aircraft out.'

'One has to know the local conditions,' I added, just to show we were not so stupid.

No more was said. By then, I had definitely got the impression that everything we did had to be turned around in order, I supposed, to assert authority.

It was decided by British Airways that we would merge with the Railway Group the following August. We were to remain a separate company and were to operate under the name of Scottish Airways Limited. George Nicholson at Renfrew, and myself, would remain as directors and be in charge of the same

areas as hitherto, but the Wing Commander was to be the 'overlord'. British Airways would hold half the shares and the Railways the other half. I did not like the set up at all and I knew I was going to have trouble with Measures. His views and mine were clearly miles apart.

At that stage, I was beginning to wish I had tied up with Mr Gandar Dower for the opportunity had presented itself the year before. At least we had the same views on resisting bureaucracy and useless extravagance, which was looming on my horizon. Also, Mr Dower and I, out of business, were the best of friends. At least I thought so.

May 1937 was the month of the Coronation of King George VI, and on that day, the 13th, I looked up Sandy McLaren, the local representative of Star Photos, Perth, who kept the daily newspapers well supplied with photos of Highland Airways' developments.

'What about coming to Fair Isle with me today, Sandy? We'll take a good supply of the Coronation newspapers and there should be some good photographic material if we can make a landing.'

His eyes sparkled over such original possibilities. 'I would most certainly like to accompany you,' he said.

So, downing tools on whatever work he was doing, he rushed off to get his camera and slides filled and said he would meet me at the airfield in half an hour's time.

It was a brilliant day and, for some time, I had been meaning to try and effect a landing on top of the cliffs at the south end of that island. I had crossed over by boat in the summer last year and had found this possible landing place, the only one on the whole of Fair Isle. It was precariously situated some 200 feet above the sea, and the cliffs surrounded three quarters of the perimeter. So, if I overshot on landing, it meant disaster and a plunge into the sea 200 feet below. I had a little over 300 yards to play with. Sandy was down on time with his camera plates and a good supply of the various dailies. We bundled them into the Monospar, which I decided to use for the job, and off we flew. We landed at Kirkwall for lunch and set off for Fair Isle around two thirty. It was fine to North Ronaldsay, but after that, when we started crossing the sea, it turned hazy. We spotted the island some fifteen miles away, looking gaunt and rocky, like a lone sentinel stuck out in the middle of the North Sea. There was a slight wind from the north-east which was in our favour for the landing. Soon, we were circling the island. Sandy was sitting alongside me.

'There's the landing strip, Sandy, on the south end and to the east of the lighthouse,' I said as we came down lower to have good look.

'You've not got much room Captain,' said Sandy, 'and those cliffs they look forbidding.'

'Yes, I know, but don't worry. If I can't make it with certainty, we'll return to Kirkwall.' 'Strap yourself in,' I said, 'and keep quiet, I'm going in on a dummy run, to get the touchdown point in my mind. We've got to land within 20 yards over the cliff edge.'

Down and down we went, the engines ticking over slowly. I pulled the nose up so that the plane was nearly at stalling speed – the speed at which an aircraft ceases to remain airborne – and then opened the engines up a bit. The cliff loomed up ahead, sharp as a razor on the top edge.

'Must take care I don't touch the wheels on that edge,' I thought.

Suddenly the plane started to sink, and the cliffs rose up in front. I froze at the thought of smashing into them. Simultaneously opening the motors full out and slightly dropping the nose to pick up flying speed, I let the monoplane fall away to the right in a slight bank and as we came parallel to the cliffs. I commenced climbing again to safety.

'Whoof,' Sandy said, 'that was a near shave!'

'Yes,' I answered 'there's a bad air sinker along those cliffs. We were lucky to get out of that one.'

We started the run in again, higher up this time as the cliffs came near, and at the same spot the sinker started its evil work, but we were high enough and, with a little motor-running, we touched down within a few yards of the cliff edge. With full brake, we pulled up a little way past the centre of the run and, turning north towards the stone cottage, cut the engines. Within seconds there was a milling mob around us. The entire population had come to look at the very

first aeroplane to land on their island and, for most of them, the first aeroplane they had ever seen on the ground and at close quarters.

As we opened the canopy and stood up to get out, a loud cheer went up, and I saw old Mr Stout, the island's postmaster, whom I had met on my earlier sea trip and who manned the boat to take me ashore off the *St Magnus* steamer. He was pushing his way through the crowd to greet me. Sandy McLaren was thrilled at the prospect of a good all-time-first photographic scoop. As I got off the plane, Jerome Stout had reached us and gave us a warm welcome.

'You couldn't have chosen a better day to come,' he said. 'We are celebrating the Coronation with a big tea party and we all hope you and your friend will stop and share it with us.'

'We'll be very glad to, won't we Sandy, so long that you don't make it too late. I don't like the look of the sky. I think bad weather is not far away.'

Mr Stout agreed with my assessment and said they would commence tea at four o'clock.

'That will be fine. We will leave not later than five. We've brought you the Coronation newspapers as a souvenir, so perhaps you will distribute them in a manner fair to all as there are not sufficient to go round the whole population.'

'Right Captain, I'll see to that.'

I caught a glimpse of Sandy plying his trade in real style, with a number of the local beauties lined up for a front page news picture. It was soon four o'clock and we were ushered into a fairly big cottage. A sumptuous tea was provided, with crowds waiting outside to take the second and third shift. The King and Queen were toasted in good 'tea total' style and every one made merry, some playing musical instruments. I have never seen such a happy lot of people and there they were confined to an island of very small dimensions. The southern half only was habitable as the northern end was mountainous and was only good for grazing sheep, which they reared in quantity, using the wool that they processed for knitting the famous Fair Isle scarves and jumpers. After a lot of speech-making and reference to our arrival, I gave them a talk on my ideas for the construction of a better airstrip in the middle of the island. Time for departure drew nigh and we were both presented with a present for being the first aerial visitors. My present was one of the famous scarves and I believe Sandy McLaren received a pair of the locally knitted gloves. We were also each presented with one of the new threepenny bits.[1]

I was anxious to get off as, during our tea spell, the weather had deteriorated and we did not carry radio in the monoplane. I had plenty of room for take-off and was not worried. We shook hands with old Mr Stout, Mr Ingram, the lighthouse keeper, and some of the other inhabitants, and climbed into the plane to the accompaniment of cheers and calls of 'come back soon'. I had told Mr Stout that I would pay them another visit. Next time I wished to test a DH Dragon out on that small park so that if anyone was taken seriously ill, we could rescue them and take the patient into hospital at either Lerwick or Kirkwall. We were airborne long before we reached the cliff edge. The wind had increased and that helped the take-off considerably. We circled the island and dived at the crowd, scattering them in all directions before turning the aircraft on course for North Ronaldsay, thirty-five miles away. The visibility had dropped down to a couple of miles and the sea was getting up with white horses clipping the tops of the waves. There was absolutely no hope of rescue if our engines failed. We felt very much alone out there with the weather clamping down on us.

I now had a three quarter cross wind to contend with so I headed the aircraft more to the south in order to take up the drift and make sure we hit the Orkney North Isles. We plunged on through the murk in silence, flying low at around five hundred feet. In murky conditions one can see further at low altitude than higher up and I wanted to be sure I saw the islands as soon as they came into view. In twenty minutes, I discerned land. We had hit North Ronaldsay bang in the middle. That pleased Sandy McLaren for he said, 'Good navigating, Skipper.' We turned on to a more southerly course and very soon ran into better visibility and made Kirkwall fifteen minutes later.

As the years went by, I noticed that changes in weather and visibility frequently occurred over the sea between North Ronaldsay and Sumburgh. As

---

[1] This may be a reference to the twelve-sided brass threepenny coin that was introduced in 1937. A traditional silver threepenny coin was also minted.

soon as land was reached, the visibility invariable improved. I believe those phenomena are due to certain sea currents of different temperature and to winds when blowing from the eastern quarter.

We didn't land at Kirkwall, but flew direct to Inverness. Our trip had been an exciting one and Sandy obtained some first class pictures, which the national press swallowed up to our mutual benefit. That flight took place just about the time that the new threepenny piece was minted, and as I have said, we were given one each by Postmaster Stout before we left as a souvenir. Sandy McLaren had them suitably engraved with the date and in commemoration of the 'first landing on Fair Isle by an aeroplane.' I still have that threepenny piece and treasure it for there is little doubt 'they were the days' when flying was full of interest and fun, always with new fields to explore. Compare it with today. One gets into a plane at an airport that is second brother to a railroad station. The plane climbs to high altitude and one usually flies in cloud or above, the passenger seldom catching a glimpse of the ground, and when he does, the view, at very high altitude, is Lilliputian and hazy. It has become wholly detached from the picture and one is inclined to think, what has that to do with the comfortable surroundings one is sitting in? Then, at the end of the journey, the passenger is disembarked into another air station full of bustle. The whole set up is entirely detached from the romance and excitement of those adolescent days.

Early in June 1937, we opened up a new service between Inverness and Aberdeen. The air journey took forty minutes and, altogether, roughly an hour between town centres compared to the rail time of over four hours, and by road three hours. The fares were kept uneconomically low to commence with so as to compete with the first class rail fare and to attract passengers. We operated the service so that Invernessians could spend a day in Aberdeen shopping and as an encouragement to the business fraternity. It did not, however, catch on. I put it down to the good road communications. With petrol at one shilling and four pence a gallon, my 'would be' passengers could motor there and back in the day, allowing plenty of time for shopping at a quarter the cost of our cut price air fare. I suppose the same went for the business travellers. We withdrew that service at the end of the following year, 1938. It had the honour or dishonour, as the case may be, of being the only one we threw overboard.

One morning in the middle of the summer, we read in the daily papers that the Fleet was coming north and intended carrying out naval manoeuvres in the Moray Firth for a few weeks. The political situation in Europe was going from bad to worse and we wondered whether the announcement had any bearing on the European situation. Was this display of 'might' intended as a warning to Hitler who was raging through Europe? We had almost forgotten about it when one day a telegram arrived stamped 'On His Majesty's Service' at the top of the envelope. I opened it and the contents read somewhat as follows:

You are notified that from 'such a date,' naval exercises will be carried out in the Moray Firth until further notice. Your company is instructed not to fly over the Moray Firth route to Wick and Orkney. You should divert your aircraft inland behind Dornoch and fly overland to Wick and Orkney. Signed, "Tidewater", Invergordon.

I read, and re-read it, and wondered why we should be thrown off our direct route for a more difficult one. We only flew over the sea between Tarbatt Ness and Helmsdale, which represented the estuary of the Dornoch Firth. That surely could not be sufficient reason, to my mind, for asking us to fly a longer and more expensive course inland and which would add to the flying time of the out and return flights thus throwing our timetable out.

I took the telegram to Mr Donald and Mr Hamilton.

'What do you think of that?' I asked, 'and who is "Tidewater"?'

They studied it. Willie Hamilton said that it was the naval telegraphic code word for Invergordon Naval Command. I discussed the objections I had to this seemingly autocratic demand and our chairman, Mr Donald, agreed with me.

'But I'm afraid you can't do much about it,' he added.

I went back to my office and sat on it until next day when I sent a telegraphic reply stating:

Reference your telegram signed "Tidewater", regret we are unable to divert our aircraft from the direct course. Our route from Tarbatt Ness to Helmsdale only utilises a minute portion of the North Sea. Request you to arrange your western boundary two miles off the coast. You will then still have the whole of the North Sea to manoeuvre in. Signed, Highland Airways.

A week went by and we heard nothing further. Shortly after, I attended one of our monthly board meetings with British Airways in London. One of their directors, Major McCrindle, came over to speak with me after the meeting. I knew him very well and we were on good terms. He was a charming man and I believe he was a barrister by profession.

'What have you been doing to upset the Navy?' he enquired.

'I was out to dinner the other night and one of the senior officials of the Home Fleet, whom I know, was there. He asked me, "Who is that man Fresson you've got up in Inverness?" "Why do you ask?" I enquired. "He's got the whole of the Admiralty in an uproar." And he told the Major about my telegram.

I explained to Major McCrindle about the peremptory telegram ordering us to divert our services inland. To have complied would have caused us considerable upset and would have cost quite a bit in hard cash.

'And for what purpose?' I asked him. 'The Navy have got the whole expanse of the Moray Firth to carry out their exercises. Surely they don't want to run their ships ashore by manoeuvring right up to the cliffs along the coastline along which we fly. All I've done is to suggest they arrange a corridor, two miles off the coast, which they will probably observe anyway, in the interests of their own safety.'

'I see,' said the Major, 'well they seem very upset. You should have sent the telegram to us for attention. We could have put it through more diplomatically. However,' he smiled, 'don't worry yourself, I know one of the heads of the department concerned and will have a word with him.'

We left it at that.

Shortly after I was back in Inverness, a letter arrived from Invergordon, written on flagship notepaper and signed by the Admiral's Secretary, inviting me to lunch aboard his flagship at a certain time on a certain day. To say the least, I was somewhat startled and taken aback. I hurried down to Mr Donald's office (my office was in Macrae & Dick Limited's premises) and said, 'What do I do with that one?'

He read it and passed it across his big desk to Willie Hamilton on the other side to read.

'You've got yourself into the Lion's Den this time,' Donald said. 'You'll have to accept.'

So I wrote a polite answer, and told them I should be very pleased to present myself at the appointed time.

On the day, promptly at twelve thirty, I was being piped aboard the flagship as if I were an admiral, and an officer met me at the top of the gangplank asking me to follow him. He took me down to the ward room full of senior officers having their appetiser before going in to lunch. I was presented to the admiral's secretary who took me under his wing and introduced me to several officers. I soon found my feet. Suddenly the admiral appeared and one of the officers took me over and introduced me. Unfortunately, I cannot remember his name, but he was an extremely nice man. He enquired if they had looked after me and, on being assured, called several officers over and we got down to business before going to lunch. I told him I had seen Major McCrindle in London at our last board meeting and I was sorry to learn my telegram had been the cause of embarrassment, but I suggested that my request was a very reasonable one. Surely the Navy would not wish to exercise close inshore and therefore a two mile corridor might reasonably be conceded. I explained the upset and cost Highland Airways would be put to if forced so far off course. We should have to claim for any such losses. Would the Admiralty pay? The admiral asked one of his officers to produce a chart of the Helmsdale and Dornoch area and, when it arrived, they were able to assess the picture after I had laid out our route. It could then clearly be seen we would not interfere in any way with their exercises should they accede to my request. The admiral said they would discuss the matter further at lunch when other interested officers would be present. The lunch was a very nice one. The atmosphere, which was at first a bit chilly, warmed up and the other officers heard what their admiral had to say.

After some discussion, the admiral turned to me saying, 'I think Captain Fresson, we can fall in with your wishes, but please see that your pilots clearly understand that they are liable to be fired at if they wander off the corridor.'

I gave him and his other officers my assurance that their orders would be met. After lunch, having expressed my thanks for their consideration, I took my farewell from His Majesty's Navy and returned to Inverness feeling very well lunched and very well done by!

Mr Donald, and my good friend Willie Hamilton, were surprised to hear the successful results of my mission.

'It's not usual that the Navy can be budged,' he said laconically.

I wrote to Major McCrindle telling him how well they had treated me aboard the flagship and that the Navy had agreed to my suggested air corridor. So all was well that ended well and, although bureaucracy had been breached, no one had any hard feelings. I gave my pilots very strict instructions regarding adhering to that corridor. In fact, I instructed them to fly over the edge of the cliffs after reaching Helmsdale and to take special care on the Tarbatt Ness-Helmsdale leg.

'Steer for Dornoch after leaving Inverness and that should prevent any misunderstanding with the Navy,' I told them.

The month's naval exercises went by without any incident.

At the end of June, I flew one of our Dragons to London to be sold and I collected a new Rapide from De Havilland, Hatfield. We had decided to replace our whole fleet as quickly as possible with that type of aircraft, with the exception of G-ACIT which we retained. One of my passengers on the return flight was a Mr Tutt. He was flying north to inspect our Monospar monoplane as we had most reluctantly decided to sell it.

In the middle of July, I attended a medical board at Leuchars for the six monthly renewal of my pilot's licence. It was a fine day, so I flew a direct course there and back across the mountains in Moth, G-AAWO. On that trip, I passed over a wild stretch of the eastern Grampians which, unbeknown to anyone at that time, held a secret from World War One. Early in 1941, a naval Avro Anson aircraft went missing from the Lossiemouth air station and a search party was sent up into the Cairngorms to find the wrecked aircraft, which had been spotted from the air. The search party found themselves in a steep corrie, which they had to ascend. On nearing the top they unexpectedly came upon a strange looking aeroplane intact. The wings were tattered from exposure, but were still covered.

When they got alongside, they saw to their amazement the skeleton of the pilot sitting in the cockpit, clad in RFC leather flying kit. It turned out to be a Sopwith Camel and the Air Force number could still be deciphered at the tail end of the fuselage. The search party continued their search and found the Anson, with the crew all dead, not so very far away from the World War One Camel tragedy. On return to Lossiemouth camp, they reported their unexpected find and enquiries were immediately sent off to the Air Ministry in London. Within a few days some officers arrived from London and requested to be taken up the mountain to inspect the Camel. They said the number had been traced and the Sopwith Camel and its pilot had belonged to the RFC Fighter and Training Station at Montrose during World War One. It had been reported missing from a training flight during the winter months of 1917. It was assumed that the pilot must have landed in a snow drift, or otherwise it would have been impossible for the plane to have landed without severe damage. Also, had the ground been clear of snow, the pilot would not have remained in his aircraft to die, but would have attempted to foot it down the mountain to safety. It would have been impossible to do that in deep snow without the use of snow shoes or skis, and so the poor fellow was apparently committed to remaining in his cockpit hoping he would be rescued. Instead, he was probably frozen to death.

During the second half 1937, we received a shock, for it was announced that the Shetland airmail contract had been awarded to our unwelcome competitors at the cut rate of $1^3/_4$d per pound of mail. In as much as the Post Office were paying Highland Airways 4d per lb for the Inverness-Kirkwall section, a little over half the distance of that to Shetland, the absurdity of the tender from Allied Airways should have been obvious to the authorities. For at that price the air company were subsidising the carriage of His Majesty's mails. We were amazed at the Post Office policy for we had forfeited our exclusive rights to Sumburgh airfield in order to obtain a radio station, without which it was not possible to provide the regularity which would enable the mails to be carried by air. So, through our public-spirited action, not only had we lost the mail contract, but were faced with passenger competition – and the passengers were not all that plentiful.

Our directors and myself, rightly considered the Post Office had double crossed us. Another grievance was that the Postmaster General had called on us to provide a satisfactory operational record for twelve months before we were entrusted with the first internal airmail carriage in the British Isles. No such condition appeared to have been imposed or insisted upon with our competitors.

It was not so long before the Aberdeen-Shetland airmail regularity began to lag for, without a radio station at Dyce Airport, Aberdeen, it was not possible to operate a continuous schedule in all weathers. The reason there were no such facilities available may best be quoted in the very words of the managing director of Allied Airways Limited at a public address he gave at a luncheon in Lerwick. After accepting the privileges that Highland Airways had to give him, he naively stated that he had always had to treat Dyce Airport as if it were a closed garden because, if he made it public, he would have to admit competition to his own airlines. So, evidently, Mr Gandar Dower's interpretation of the old saying 'What's sauce for the goose is sauce for the Gander' was in negative terms, *viz* 'What's sauce for the Gandar, wasn't sauce for the Goose!'

The following extract from the *Shetland News* at the time indicated the difficulties of Allied Airways to deliver the mail regularly for there were many protests. I quote two letters to the press, which appeared at that time, to substantiate the position, and which poses the question as to why the Post Office took no action to right the complaints made.

Having read all there has been to read about the advent of the airmail and eulogies of the regularity of the air service to our isles, and being in possession of perhaps no more information than the average person, one is left wondering as to why the pioneer company, namely Highland Airways, has not been referred to or given any credit by our MP or in your "Leader" in connection with your statement that: 'The aeroplane service has been successful beyond expectation. In all weathers, the planes have arrived and departed with wonderful regularity.'

To the best of my knowledge, since the commencement of the air service at the beginning of June 1936, Highland Airways are the only company to have operated during last winter, and without a break this summer and up to the 23rd November this winter, excluding of course the few days when Sumburgh was flooded last January, which made landing impossible. I have recollections that Highland Airways operated to schedule throughout the gales of last January and February when our steamer service was delayed for days on end. Further, the fact should not be lost sight of that the carriage of mails by air of another company has only been made possible through the provision of Sumburgh Aerodrome which was constructed by Highland Airways at their own expense, after two years survey work and exploratory flights over the route from Orkney without radio assistance. It was this blazing of the trail which has made an air service possible from Orkney with safety and regularity. So let us not forget to give credit where credit is due and recognise the company who have alone created the unbroken schedule since the inception of the air service to our stormy Isles.

Later on, when the airmail consistently failed to arrive on time, another letter arrived at the *Shetland News* office in the following terms.

The Shetland Mail

I have looked in vain through your columns for a report of some action being taken by our city fathers to secure a much needed improvement in the mail service. My grievance is, I am sure, shared by numerous citizens who have to wait several days for the receipt of letters from friends in the south due to the delays in the arrival of the mail plane and, which delays of latter weeks, have made the present conditions quite intolerable. I had hoped that the local Chamber of Commerce would have tackled this matter through the proper official channels, but it would appear to the man in the street that this august body of estimable business men is suffering from some not yet diagnosed decline, and is following in the footsteps of our erstwhile Ratepayers Association, and rapidly lapsing into a state of coma, or moribund inactivity. It may be, however, that the Chamber of Commerce has dealt with this matter in committee and is presently taking some action to remedy this lamentable state of affairs, and to bring pressure on those in authority to take steps to alleviate this just grievance. Could not they help the long suffering Shetland public by tackling this matter in public?

In bygone days, the Lerwick Town Council had a Mails Committee which frequently proved very efficacious in keeping the mail carrying companies up to scratch, but the city fathers seem to be quite dumb in this important matter nowadays. I have made full and exhaustive enquiries into the reasons for the present disorganisation of the letter mail service, and find that the airline presently holding the mail contract is being run with no regularity whatever. Witness the state of affairs when no letter mails were received from the south from Tuesday the 14th to Monday the 20th January – six days. On the other hand, I find that the airline which does not hold the airmail contract has, up to this date, a practically unbroken record of regularity of operation in all weather conditions.

I am really surprised that our town councillors have not seen fit to bring this matter to the immediate notice of the Postmaster General with a request to have the carriage of our longed for letters put into the hands of those who have shown that they are competent to operate a regular service to and from the Northern Isles.

The foregoing quotations are only two of many which were received by the press in those days. It has always remained an intriguing mystery to those who were connected with Highland Airways why the Post Office should have required such searching evidence from our company that we were capable of operating the Orkney mail with a high degree of regularity. Yet they awarded the airmail contract of the Shetland route to a company who were not first asked to demonstrate, as we had done, their ability to operate to postal standards.

Later in the year, after many meetings between British Airways and Railway Air Services, it was agreed that the railway interests would acquire a half share in the Scottish air companies, which meant that on 12 August 1937 Highland Airways and Northern & Scottish Airways lost their identities and the two companies became welded together under the name of Scottish Airways Limited with registered offices at Renfrew. The amalgamation brought powerful backing, but we lost a lot of our independence.

Mr Roberts, our chairman, remained in office, as also did the other British Airways directors, including Major McCrindle. The railway directors were Mr W P Bradbury, W Yeaman, L M S Scottish Region Manager, and Mr J W Ratledge of David MacBrayne & Company Limited. George Nicholson and myself retained our directorships as before. On Thursday 12th August, we held our first board meeting at Renfrew and, after our chairman, Mr Roberts, introduced us all to the new members of the board, we got down to work. Wing Commander Measures was appointed managing director of the new company. I would have preferred that George Nicholson and myself should have become joint managing directors as I could not see how a newcomer could possibly cope with the complexities of the operations Nicholson and myself had grown up with. After all, the routes operated were organised by us. As it was not to be so, we had to make the best of a difficult job. The major issue discussed was the *modus operandi* of the new company. It was agreed that George would carry on as before with the southern section and I would remain boss of the northern section.

It was at this meeting that I first became aware of the difference in financial stability of the Western Isles services. Whereas Highland Airways had been making ends meet and were beginning to show a profit, Northern & Scottish had been in the red for a long time. Their traffic density did not appear as great as ours, but their operating mileage was much longer. Further, they were using an operationally more expensive type of aircraft than we were and all this added up to a not too rosy picture. It was at this juncture that I submitted to the new board that our accounts should be kept separately and shown separately at each board meeting. In due course, it was frequently murmured by one of the new directors that the more affluent 'brother' was helping to keep the poorer one.

Mr Bradbury, at the end of our first meeting, invited my wife and I to spend a long week end with Mrs Bradbury and himself at Rothesay where they were staying. It was a lovely sunny day and we gladly accepted. We drove down to the Greenock ferry in my one and a half litre Riley and we made the journey in record time. I don't think Bradbury was feeling too safe as he gently enquired whether I thought I was piloting a plane! However, we had a very pleasant crossing over to Rothesay and, on arrival at the hotel, we met Mrs Bradbury for the first time. During that weekend, Bradbury and I were able to get together on future procedure. I told him I thought the managing director arrangement had weaknesses but, as long as the Wing Commander would not interfere in technical matters, I for one would do my best to play ball. Bradbury appreciated my frankness and said that the appointment had been made because Measures had to co-ordinate the Railway Air Services with our operations and see that there was no overlapping or other divergences.

We left on Monday morning, the Bradburys returning to London and we to Inverness. On the whole, I now felt pleased with the way things had worked out and above all that we now had the railway goodwill with us instead of in opposition. That would smooth many a past headache out. Also, I had, I felt sure, a friend in Mr Bradbury and, as he was a senior official in the L M S Railway, I thought that, if I ever found myself in genuine difficulty, his help would be at hand.

Shortly after I had returned to Inverness, I flew Gipsy Moth, G-AAWO, up to Orkney and toured the North Isles to see how the new island timetable was working out. I discovered, to my astonishment, that the islanders were using the plane service to 'fly to market.' They were lining up at North Ronaldsay with produce, ducks, vegetables, chickens and eggs to be flown into the Kirkwall market. There was no question that the Island service was doing well and we were running to a high load factor and making it pay. Backing the boost given by the islanders were the commercial travellers and, in the summer, visitors took the opportunity of making a quick tour of the isles. The two daily services, early morning and late afternoon, enabled a return journey to be made in one day, giving passengers plenty of time for their visits. This arrangement was extremely popular with all and was the reason for the success of the exercise.

I stayed that night in Kirkwall at the St Ola Hotel and, as in the days when I was surveying the possibility of an air service in 1931/1932, I ran into the 'old school' in the private sitting room. The Deputy Town Clerk, who hadn't changed a great deal, was there, as were my good friends John Shearer and James Baikie, the contractor. I had their glasses filled up, included one for myself and we got to chatting over the amazing growth of Highland Airways. That name was to stick with us for quite a time, in spite of the takeover.

'Do you know what I saw today?' I enquired.

They waited in expectation.

'You won't believe it, but the North Isles folk are now going to market by air.' I told them what I had observed that morning, and they just smiled.

'We heard that some time ago,' said John Shearer. 'It's just too easy for them with the new timetable.'

'Funny no one thought of that one a long time ago,' said Deputy Town Clerk Smith.

The night drew on and Mrs Stevens, the owner of the St Ola, looked round the corner and, spotting me, came into the room.

'Well, bless me, if it isn't the Captain. How are you? We haven't seen you for quite a time.'

'I know, dear lady, but you see we have been busy changing our name and tying our fortunes up with the Railway Group, so I have been south a lot instead of north.'

'Well, my,' she said, 'you have gone a long way since you were giving those short flights out at Hatston six years back. With the news you bring, that calls for one on the house.'

She meant it, for she arrived back with double-doubles all round as a nightcap.

Next morning was a lovely day, just blue sky and sunshine. So, for old times sake and with the memory of Mrs Stevens reference to joy-riding days at Hatston six years back, I went up in the Moth and gave the town a quarter of an hour's aerobatic display just as they were going home for lunch. Everyone appeared to have seen, and enjoyed, the stunting, including myself.

I left around tea time for Inverness and, on the way, I made a new conquest by landing on another island whose inhabitants had never seen an aeroplane at close quarters before. It was the island of Stroma, just two miles across the Pentland Firth from that famous place, the John O' Groats Hotel. The hotel boasts of a pier and the island ferry boat starts from there on its numerous daily runs across to the island, the Sabbath, of course, being excepted. It was a tiny field I landed in; I paced it out, just 150 yards and a bit downhill but the Moth managed it easily. I told the islanders about the air ambulance service which the County Council had laid on and suggested they hack a landing strip out of the peat wastes on the west side of the island. Apart from the air ambulance, I explained the value of air communication to the island should any of them have need of rapid transportation south. I walked over the site I had seen from the air. It was reasonably flat and provided a run of at least 450 yards. The peat was not deep, but there would need to be some draining in the middle of the strip. One of the crofters departed and came back with some pegs and we soon had the strip marked off. I said I would return and inspect the work when they wrote and told me that the strip was ready.

I left the island late, having stayed far longer than I had intended. By the time I had passed Helmsdale, it was starting to get dark, but the night was clear and I decided to push on and effect a night landing at Inverness instead of landing at Golspie for the night where I had an emergency landing field. I had an arrangement with Macrae & Dick's garage that, if I circled over the garage at night time, they would send a couple of cars down to the Longman airfield and turn on their headlights into wind, and in the direction of south should there be little or no wind.

On 25th August, an SOS was received from Kirkwall. Could we carry the

Kirkwall football team to Thurso to honour a fixture made some time ago? Something had gone wrong with their surface travel arrangements and a plane was the only hope of them getting there. I set off in my trusty DH Dragon, G-ACIT, and found I should have to make two runs with eight passengers on each trip. Unfortunately, the wind was in the worst direction, which gave an uphill take-off. I got the lightest bodies on board and opened up. I only had 400 yards run and at the end was a stone dyke, four feet high, separating another field. We gathered speed very slowly, but by the time the middle of the run was reached, the tail was well up and I figured I could just do it. But I figured wrongly. The dyke loomed up and a quick glance at my air speed indicator showed I was wanting another ten miles per hour to become airborne. There was no time to shut off, so I did the only thing I could do. By pulling the control column right back very quickly, the plane lurched off the ground and cleared the dyke. I let her settle down, dropped on to the next field where I finished the take-off run with ease and we were airborne. I gasped with relief and the sweat was pouring off my face. As I mopped it up with my handkerchief, I thought of the second lot and the heavier ones waiting to be transported. Half the load in Thurso was useless, but how was I to lift a heavier load off. Half way across the Pentland Firth, an idea came to me. As the wind was not so strong, I decided to taxi to the top of the rise to the west of the Kirkwall airfield and take off downhill and cross wind. I landed the first lot at my old joy-riding site on the Scrabster road and hurried back for the remainder of the team. There was not much time as the match was due to start in an hour. With the remaining eight bodies aboard, I put my downhill take-off into effect. The plane came off the ground in half the run and we arrived in Thurso well on time.

I waited until the match was over to take one load back. The second lot had decided they would stay overnight and fly back by the air service from Wick next morning. That suited me fine, so I repaired to the Royal Hotel in Thurso.

Who should I run into there, but my old friend Peter Angus, the first passenger to fly the Pentland Firth from Thurso in 1931.

'Hello, Captain Fresson,' he said, 'I'm right glad to see you. We haven't met for a long time. You'll not be refusing a dram with me?'

I told him I was waiting to take eight members of the Orkney football team back to Kirkwall, but with a couple of hours to spare, figured just one would do no harm. We talked about old times and the first Shetland trip we had made in the Monospar away back in 1933. He then said he had seen the announcement in the press about our amalgamation with the Railway Group and wanted to know how it would affect me. The two hours soon flitted by and I was soon back at the field loading my return passengers aboard. It was turning to dusk and we circled the lit up town of Kirkwall to indicate I had brought a victorious team back from Thurso. I stayed the night and joined the 'old gang' in the St Ola. It had been a tiring afternoon and that near miss take-off had shaken me up. When I turned in, I slept like a log.

In the middle of September, my wife and I left for the south by car and we stopped off at the George Hotel, Perth, for afternoon tea. There was a point I wished to clear up about the Inverness-Glasgow service I was planning for next spring, so I took the opportunity of calling William Cumming, the secretary of the new company at Renfrew, on the phone before continuing our journey. During our conversation, I was told that it had been decided that the Inverness-Glasgow service would be operated from Renfrew.

'Who told you that?' I asked.

'The Wing Commander,' he replied.

'How did that happen? I've been working on that route for the past year and I want it integrated with the Kirkwall-Wick-Inverness run, timed to leave Kirkwall early in the morning so that the Kirkwall passengers can spend a day in Glasgow and return at night.'

'Sorry, old chap, but those are the orders,' he replied.

'Where can I get Measures?'

'He's in London as far as I know.'

'What's his phone number?'

He gave it to me and I got on the phone to the Wing commander. By then I was really ready to jump off the deep end. I was beginning to see how the Renfrew set up was working. Consultation was gong on without my being present. Eventually, Measures voice came through.

'That you, Wing Commander?'

'Yes, Measures speaking.'

'I've just been speaking to Cumming and he tells me you have instructed the Renfrew end to operate the Glasgow-Inverness service?'

'That's correct,' he answered.

'Why have you done that? Everyone knows that run has been in my mind for a long time. I want you to alter that decision. It's most unsatisfactory.'

'I can't do that,' he said, 'we want the service to tie up with the south.'

'But I want it to tie up with the north.'

By this time, the 'Wingco' was getting as heated as I was, and he said it was too late to alter the decision.

'Why wasn't I informed about it?' I howled.

'I never knew you were interested.'

'But I told you long ago.'

He said, 'It's no use continuing this conversation. We will have to talk about it later.'

I rang off.

'What's the matter?' my wife said when I joined her. 'You look pretty het up.'

'I should think so,' and I told her what had happened. I felt sure in my mind that the decision had been engineered by Renfrew and I was determined to get to the bottom of the matter.

I brought this matter up at our next board meeting and it was finally agreed that Renfrew would operate the service for the coming season and we would take over the following year. The traffic results would be compared and the final decision would rest on which way paid best. That appeared reasonable, so at that, I left it. What I liked the least was that such decisions could be reached without any consultation with myself. I decided to get this put straight at the first opportunity.

Early in the autumn, a new pilot arrived to take charge of the Kirkwall station. Captain Hankins was a senior pilot and had been recommended by George Nicholson to take on that onerous job. Talking with him one day, he brought the question of Fair Isle up and he asked if I would take him over and show him the landing drill so that he would be in a position to pick up any ambulance cases which might arise. I agreed because I knew he was an experienced joy riding pilot and was therefore proficient in short landings.

We set off on 11th November, a fine day, and I made the second landing within six months on the island, this time with Dragon, G-ACIT, as that aircraft would be used for the ambulance cases. This time there were no downward air eddies over the approaching cliff face, but also, there was no north-east wind to help shorten the landing. Nevertheless, we managed to pull up by the usual swing to the north during the middle of the landing run towards a wire fence, instead of towards the 200 foot cliff drop into the sea. We went up to the middle of the island with Mr Stout and a few of the islanders to settle on the site for a strip which the locals had undertaken to hue out of the hillside in their spare time. Mr Stout invited us to stay for lunch and we were served with some very tender Fair Isle mutton. The islanders were excited to see me back. We explained to Mr Stout the procedure to obtain an ambulance flight if needed. Also, I introduced Captain Hankins who told me he was prepared to undertake flights to Fair Isle now that he had seen me land. I explained that Captain Hankins was in charge of Kirkwall and to get in touch with him in the case of emergency. We left for Orkney after lunch and more presents were handed to us. The Dragon got off easily and therefore I had no fear about ambulance or emergency flights being undertaken with it.

On 19th November, I flew over to Stornoway for our final meeting with the Stornoway Trust Committee about commencing work on the Melbost airfield. I carried copies of the Agreement with me and I returned with the documents signed. I had been working to obtain that Agreement for nearly five years and now it was in my pocket. We had obtained a long lease on condition that we agreed to shoulder the cost of construction. There was, however, protection for

Scottish Airways should the long lease be broken and, with that safeguard, we were prepared to go ahead.

The LMS at Glasgow recommended a civil surveyor, a Mr Warren, to carry out the survey and, on 2nd December 1937, he and several members of his staff arrived in Inverness. I met them off the train and we lost no time in taking off for Stornoway. For good measure, there was a 50 mph wind blowing from the north and we ran into heavy snow storms across the mountains. We flew at 5,000 feet on an instrument course and ran into better weather over the Minch. I spent the day with Mr Warren, going over the golf course and marking the four landing strips we would require.

I returned in the evening as I had to fly to Kirkwall next morning to bring a party in from Metal Industries at Lyness to Inverness in time to catch the southbound express. The wind had abated quite a bit for the return journey and the flight was uneventful. The Lyness charter was carried out without incident, the fully loaded plane getting off easily on the downhill run. The Lyness landing strip had more than justified itself and Mr MacKenzie told me that the air connection was a great boon to their company.

We were near the end of the year and I finished it off by taking the scheduled morning service to Kirkwall, fully loaded with passengers and a big stack of His Majesty's mail. I looked forward to the New Year with some misgivings. I was still suspicious of the new set up, but I felt I had the sympathy of the chairman and British Airways directors to see I did not become engulfed in muddled thinking. I also had the support of Mr Bradbury, should any be needed. I had won my point at the board meeting, that I should be present at all meetings on policy held at Renfrew.

10

Last year of peace

The opening months of 1938 were exceedingly stormy, gales with high winds prevailing. These were not the only storms on the horizon for the situation was growing steadily worse in Europe.

As the Nazi war machine grew in might, so individual countries were beginning to be overrun. Life, however, went on as usual in Britain and it was not until Munich, later in the year, that our citizens began to realise that all was not as well as it should have been. However, with Mr Chamberlain's flight to Germany and his meetings with Hitler, the public appeared reassured with the message on his last return that 'We would have peace in our time.' As we all know, however, this promise was bust wide open a year later.

There was a similar militant movement on my own home front. Renfrew and the new operations director were still a constant source of worry to me in their ever increasing interference and arrival at policy decisions without consultation with myself in spite of the board ruling. I was placed well out of the way in Inverness and also heavily engaged in flying owing to the surging increase in traffic which necessitated many duplicated flights. Accordingly, I was unable to spend a great deal of time in the south. By the spring, matters had got to such a pitch that I requested the Glasgow operations manager to come up and see me. We sat on the edge of the airfield and talked. I insisted that orders should not be given without my consent, especially as they affected the Northern Section, and unless these practices were stopped, I would have to make a major issue of the matter. I told the operations manager that it appeared incongruous to me that the Southern Section management, who were making a heavy loss, should be dictating to me, who at least enjoyed a clean balance sheet. Matters improved after that set to and relations became less strained and more co-operative.

During the first week of January, the surveyors from Glasgow arrived for a second time and I flew them over to Stornoway to continue their survey of the Melbost golf links airfield. I remained with them for a few days and, as we had decided on a new technique, I assisted in laying out the runways we should require. Up until now, it had been customary to level off the whole of an airfield area, but from experience gained in the Orkney North Isles, where we had to be satisfied with narrow strips of ground pointing to different wind directions, it occurred to me that we could save a lot of money if the Stornoway links were laid off in four different strips, 150 feet wide, pointing north/south, north-east/south-west, east/west and south-east/north-west. We had also found from experience that we could land and take off in cross winds safely up to a forty-five degree angle and the four strips never at any time presented a greater wind angle than that. Accordingly, I requested the chief surveyor to survey and cost the two projects, namely for levelling the complete area and, alternatively, levelling the four runways one hundred and fifty feet wide. When the survey and costing was completed it was found that the saving in cost by employing strips amounted to many thousands of pounds. I now had to convince our board that flying would be safe using air strips instead of the conventional airfield. That I succeeded in doing.

The project was accepted and the airfield constructed on these unconventional lines. I believe it was the first airfield of its kind and set the pattern for future airfield construction. It was wholly taken up by the RAF and RNAS during the war and all modern airfields are constructed on the same principle today. The survey and costing took a long time and there were other delays which put back the commencement of constructing the airfield until the latter part of the year.

It was finished in August 1939, but never went into use. The outbreak of World War Two prevented us commencing the Inverness-Stornoway run, which we had advertised for 1st September 1939. Our new unused airfield was taken over by the RAF and completely reconstructed on a vast scale with tarmac runways. It played a major part in war-time operations for Coastal Command.

Our air service did not commence until towards the very end of the War, in 1944. Although all my hard work and patience had to wait so long before we obtained any benefit from that airfield, at least we had the satisfaction of knowing that our airfield had helped the war effort in no mean way.

As January progressed, so did the speed of the winds, and at the end of the month the island of Foula was reported to be running short of food. The supply steamer which provided a connection with the outside world through Walls, Shetland, had been unable to make the crossing for nearly a month. The Shetland authorities asked us if we could help and I sent Captain Wilson up to Sumburgh in a Rapide to organise a food drop, as there was no known place where we could land on Foula.

He took a number of home-made parachutes with him, which we roughly constructed from old flour bags. The parcels were in packages weighing five pounds and each parcel was attached to a 'chute. I told Captain Wilson to see the aeroplane door was removed before taking off from Sumburgh for Foula and to pick up Captain Johnstone, who was stationed at Kirkwall, to attend to the dropping of the food parcels. Captain Johnstone was to lie on the floor and have his legs strapped to one of the aircraft chairs as a safety precaution. There was a gale blowing itself out when the Rapide aircraft arrived over Foula and, on his return, Captain Wilson told me the air was exceedingly turbulent low down over the island and they had great difficulty in manoeuvring into position to effect the drops.

For the drop, he selected a portion of moorland near the cottages at the southern end of the island and the ten packages, each containing five pounds of food, were successfully dropped. All were observed to be collected. The press described this operation in the following terms:

Food Dropped to Starving Islanders
Foula Relieved by Plane after Thirty-four Days

After being isolated for thirty three days, Foula, one of the farthest flung islands off the north of Scotland, was relieved yesterday.

In the afternoon, ten packages of foodstuffs attached to parachutes were dropped on the island by a Highland Airways aeroplane, after a thrilling flight against a 50 miles per hour wind. The inhabitants of the island, which rises like a rock out of the storm-tossed seas, have had an unfortunate time this New Year. Following an epidemic of influenza, which affected every family, came the long-continued storms, until the inhabitants were almost at starving point. The plane piloted by Captain C B Wilson, which relieved the isle, left Kirkwall and flew over 200 miles of storm tossed seas against a fifty mile an hour gale. The intrepid pilot, who was accompanied by Captain J J Johnstone of Highland Airways

Limited, reached his objective and was able to drop much needed supplies to the marooned inhabitants of the little island before returning safely to Kirkwall.

Ten parcels were dropped by Pilot Johnstone by means of flour bag parachutes, fashioned for the occasion. Captain Johnstone lay on the plane floor, his legs tied to the seats in case he was humped out, and released his parcels through the door opening. The first parachute failed to open, but the groceries did not appear to suffer. The remaining parachutes all opened and floated gracefully to the heather where the islanders retrieved them and waved their hands to the plane which spent half an hour over the Island.

On reaching Foula, the plane circled round and made a complete survey of the island. The cliffs rise almost sheer out of the water and the island slopes up to a central peak. The only possible landing place was a small field, but the pilot decided it was too small to land in. The welcome spectacle of the aeroplane with its much needed supplies must have given heart to the islanders as at the hour it was still not possible to approach Foula by sea. Later, the steamer *Betty Bodie* reached the island.

Foula, wild and picturesque, was brought into prominence in a romantic fashion recently, when the film *Edge of the World* was shown.

In all, 400 miles were flown by the time Captain Wilson returned to Inverness that night. He deserved great praise for carrying out the 'food drop' successfully under such stormy conditions, as also did those who assisted him. Only recently, one read in the daily press that Foula was again cut off, this time for a much longer period, and they were completely out of supplies. And yet in this modern age and with state-run airlines, no steps were taken to bring air relief such as our commercial company successfully carried out twenty five-years previously. One is left wondering why, when equipment and techniques are so far advanced compared to that of the 'pioneering thirties'.

Captain Wilson joined us in January 1936. He was an extremely experienced pilot and, like myself, a product of World War One having learnt to fly with the Royal Flying Corps. He appeared fearless of bad weather and some of the trips he made into Kirkwall and Shetland, without modern aids, were a great example to us all. During World War Two, he flew as a Test Pilot for the Lockheed Aircraft Company at Speke airport, Liverpool. On one occasion, while testing a Thunderbolt single-seater fighter, the plane caught fire over the middle of Liverpool. Bernard Wilson gallantly stuck to his burning plane and manoeuvred it away from the city and over the River Mersey. He then turned the burning plane over on its back, dropping himself out, and then made a parachute descent into the middle of the river. He was fished out, without injury, by a boat. The burning plane crashed some distance away without doing any damage. The Lockheed Aeroplane Company rewarded Captain Wilson for his gallant action and soon he was back at his duties.

The gales persisted and continued into March, so much so that one day the mail steamer could not make the voyage from Mallaig to Stornoway. The Inverness postmaster rang up to enquire whether we could fly the stranded mails over. I was a bit sceptical, the wind was blowing at seventy mph and almost directly ahead on the flight over. That would mean two hours flying at altitude, and there was no radio station at Stornoway to home on. I hesitated taking the valley route in that gale. In the end, I decided to have a go. I thought the publicity would be good for the company so I told the postmaster to send the mails down to the airfield and we would get underway as quickly as possible. However, I warned him that I might have to turn back.

I took off with a very heavy load of mail, and I took Goulden, our radio mechanic, as my radio operator for the return journey above cloud. Wind usually increases in speed with altitude, so I decided to fly low on the outward journey. As soon as we got into the main Ullapool valley, we were trounced badly by most vicious bumps. I knew the journey was going to be a rough one, but I hadn't bargained for what we were getting. Ploughing through the bumps, which were likened to sledge hammer blows with the outer wing struts bending with the strain, we commenced rounding the bend at Braemore pass where the road bends sharply to the left and round up the valley to Dundonnell and Little Loch Broom. Then, without warning, a master gust hit us. The plane shuddered and I thought it was going to break up. It all but stood on its tail and I could do nothing with the controls. I thought we were lost. Never in my forty-one years as a commercial pilot had I ever encountered anything like that hammering in the air and I had been through some pretty bad ones in my time. My radio engineer poked his head through the cabin door and said, 'Are we going to crash, Captain?' Taking a mighty quick look at him as I was wrestling with the controls, I saw his face was as white as a sheet. There wasn't time to answer. I had to get that plane back on to an even keel while it was still in one piece. After what seemed an interminable time, the controls gradually started to function again, and the valley that drops down to Loch Broom came into sight. I immediately pushed the nose down and dived for the loch, clipping the tree tops down that valley. At last, we reached Loch Broom and flew low over the water and below those murderous blasts which were coming down the mountain sides.

Once past the Summer Isles, the going was much better over the Minch, and I heaved a sigh of relief when the cliffs of Chicken Head were sighted. The mail was handed over to the postie in the mail van, who was waiting at the Melbost Golf Club clubhouse nearby. We scrounged a lift into Stornoway for a rest before wrestling with the return journey.

As the gale would now be behind us, I decided to climb to 10,000 feet in order to get above the frightening turbulence experienced on the outward journey. With my radio operator, Goulden, as the only passenger, the aircraft was lightly loaded and so the plane climbed quickly and we were soon in the calm air. What a contrast to the outward trip. With the help of the gale on our tail, we reached Inverness, ninety-three miles away, in half an hour.

Before leaving for the town, I suggested to George Griffiths, our chief engineer, that the plane should have a thorough check in view of the buffeting it had received. No damage could be found, which spoke well of the de Havilland stressing. Nothing on earth would ever induce me to fly low through that valley again in the teeth of a gale of the magnitude we had experienced that day. The delivery of the stormbound Stornoway mail was a feather in our cap with the Post Office and it was the talk of Stornoway. It appeared the population were puzzled receiving their mail early after lunch, instead of the following morning, which was usual, as the mail steamer did not arrive in Stornoway until evening. All the same, I felt the GPO did not deserve that effort and risk which had been taken, having 'double crossed' us on the Shetland airmail contract the year before.

In the spring, we would be running to our summer timetable, and we completely reorganised our Shetland air communications. The Aberdeen run was altered to commence at Shetland in the early morning, arriving in Aberdeen just before midday, via Inverness. The return journey was scheduled to depart from Kintore at 12.40 pm reaching Sumburgh at 3.35 pm. To do this we built a hangar at Sumburgh and stationed an aircraft there, with pilot and engineer. In addition, on 3rd May, the Glasgow-Inverness service was inaugurated. The plane called at Perth on the way, and proceeded on to Kirkwall and Sumburgh, arriving at 12.35pm. A quick turn around was organised, and the southbound passengers departed at 12.45pm, arriving Glasgow at quarter to five, after calling at Kirkwall, Wick, Inverness and Perth. Thus Shetland was served by two services and, although they were operated to close on one hundred percent regularity, strangely enough neither carried the mail.

The month of May had not advanced far when a serious state of affairs came to my notice. One morning, the Renfrew plane arrived completely iced up and I was told that it practically fell into Inverness Airport. I did not see the pilot on that occasion. The aircraft could not proceed in that condition to Shetland, so we had to provide a substitute plane at short notice, which was not easy. A few days later, it happened again. This time I found and questioned the pilot. He told me he understood the managing director, who had no practical experience of flying, had issued instructions to the operations manager at Renfrew that the passengers were not to be subjected to the frightening experience of flying in cloud and pilots were accordingly instructed to climb above the clouds after leaving Perth to get over the mountains. At that time of year, 10,000 feet or considerably more had to be reached to get above the overcast. On many days it was impossible to climb sufficiently high to get above cloud, but in the process of trying, the aircraft got badly iced up with the results observed at Inverness. This dangerous practice had to stop. We could not afford a fatal accident on that or any run. I complained to Renfrew without any effect. They simply said they had their instructions and, if the pilots ran into icing, they were to return to Perth. The alternative would ruin the regularity of the service and was wholly unnecessary.

We in Inverness knew a safe and proper way to fly that sector with the aircraft we had available, which did not possess de-icing equipment. We called it the 'Dog's Leg Route' because we flew to Perth on two courses, which, drawn on paper, looked like a dog's leg. That way, we rarely encountered icing because we did not have to fly at an altitude higher than 5,000 feet, but it usually meant flying in cloud most of the way. It appeared that the only measure left in order to avoid the danger was to convert the pilots of the Southern Division to our way of thinking, and when they learned that we had experimented with the 'dog's leg' route via Drumochter pass at 5,000 feet altitude, without running into icing, they gave it a try and decided to ignore the instructions they had received. In future, and for the rest of the summer, that's the way the Perth-Inverness sector was operated – and without difficulty. Nothing was said, so we let sleeping dogs lie.

The opening of the Renfrew-Shetland service was celebrated by the town council at Scone airfield, Perth, and a luncheon was given in honour of the occasion. Many well-known people attended. Speeches flowed galore and after lunch an air trip over the city of Perth from Scone airport was given to prominent members of the council and community. To my surprise, I was asked to pilot the plane, which I did with pleasure. I stayed overnight and joined the northbound service next morning. Captain Barclay, who was piloting, invited me to fly the plane as far as Inverness. I well remember it was a beautiful day at Perth, blue sky and brilliant sunshine. Halfway over the mountains, we ran above cloud at 7,000 feet and it continued that way to Inverness, which was completely overcast.

In the middle of June, word was received that the Stroma island strip was completed and I flew up, with a Mr Muir as passenger, in the DH Moth to inspect the work. The islanders had made a good job and had levelled off some 400 yards of moorland. They had removed the top layer of peat and uncovered a firm clay and gravel surface along the entire strip. The wet part had been drained and the islanders must have put in a tremendous amount of work to prepare that strip, all by hand. It went to show how people living in the remote parts of our islands appreciated and yearned for air transport, as was the case a few years before when the people of North Ronaldsay hewed out their own airfield. We had a gathering in the islander's hall and I thanked them for the work they had so freely given, and I told them I would give them the utmost support for any air transport required.

My first job when I got back to Inverness, I told them, would be to write to the County Medical Officer and inform him that we could now care for any ambulance cases which might occur on the island of Stroma. I also promised that if any islanders wished to be uplifted, to travel south, I would give instructions for the Kirkwall-Wick plane to land en route and pick the passengers up. I had, however, to qualify the landings subject to wind direction, because if there was a strong crosswind it would be unsafe to attempt a landing. They undertook to light a smoke fire when the aircraft appeared overhead, which would indicate the wind direction and strength to the pilot. This they diligently attended to.

Before leaving, I promised to bring up a DH Dragon and give those who had worked on levelling the strip a free flight. They were to prepare slips of paper with the names of the prospective flyers and draw twelve names out of a hat. The lucky draws would be the ones chosen for a flight. Shortly after, when I knew I would be north, I wrote to the island postmaster and told him the day and hour I proposed landing, wind permitting. I dropped the letter by 'chute in front of a cottage on my next trip to Kirkwall. The flights were performed, carrying six passengers at a time. The lucky ones were thrilled and could not believe their island looked so small from a thousand feet up in the air. They gave me a tumultuous send off when I departed.

At the end of July, our Wick agent, Colonel Robertson, enquired if I could fly up in the Moth and give a fifteen-minute aerobatic display at that year's Wick gala. The Gala Committee had not forgotten the display I had given them during my joy riding visit, seven years before, in 1931, with the Avro 504K, and with Colonel Robertson as passenger. They wished me to repeat the performance and were prepared to pay a good fee. We made a deal. The plane was to arrive at around half past four in the afternoon and go straight into action.

I flew the Moth over the large crowd gathered in the sports field alongside the river and just behind the Station Hotel, dead on time. There was a large gathering. I put everything I could into that display and, after fifteen minutes, I decided I was getting too old for such high pressure flying and, by the time the stunts were over, my poor eyes were seeing things twice. After flying around a bit to regain my composure, I finished up with a good dive to within a few feet of the ground and pulled up almost vertically over the grandstand. I could see the spectators waving their pleasure as I left direct for Inverness without landing at our Hillhead airfield. Shortly after, a cheque, accompanied by a letter of great appreciation, was received from the Gala Committee for the display.

I have said very little about Colonel Robertson up to now, so it is appropriate that while I am writing about Wick, I should use this opportunity to say how much he helped the air service in those early days. He was, of course, a founder director of Highland Airways and, from our first day, his first thought was for the success of the company. He owned a garage and hardware business in the Main Street and had a very nice house on the Castletown Road on the outskirts of the town. Mrs Robertson was a charming lady and they had a very nice family. I, of course, met Colonel and Mrs Robertson on my first visit to Wick in 1931 and, from the commencement of the exploratory flights in 1931 onwards, I was always a very welcome guest in their home. He personally looked after our bookings and, for the first few years, always accompanied the passengers up to Hillhead landing ground daily and awaited the arrival and departure of the plane to make certain everything was functioning properly. He also provided the transport and took care of the local advertising. Nothing was too much trouble and so our business prospered under his vigilant eye. He used to board the service plane at Wick and fly to Inverness for our monthly board meetings and his counsel at those meetings was of great help to the other members of our board and myself.

During the early days of the service, he introduced me to a great friend of his, a Mr Georgeson who was a solicitor in Wick. Through that introduction, I got to know his son, Harold, very well. Mr Georgeson Senior was an original shareholder in Highland Airways and I am glad to think that his trust in us was well rewarded when we sold out to British Airways as was the case with the other original shareholders.

At the beginning of this chapter, I mentioned the growing threat of the Nazis in Europe and, arising out of that situation, we were given an Air Ministry contract to carry out Army Co-operation Flying at Inverness and Kirkwall for 297 Heavy Anti-Aircraft Battery. Mr Gilbert Ross was a captain in that battery and Colonel MacIntosh was the commanding officer. Their headquarters were in the drill hall alongside the old Inverness Academy school building behind our offices. Co-operation flights took place once a week. The aircraft had to fly on certain courses and at different altitudes up to 10,000 feet, while the Army practised training with ack-ack guns and working the radar equipment in readiness for any enemy aircraft, should they ever come their way. These exercises went on from one to two hours and became very boring. Bertie, as Captain Ross was known to his friends, sometimes used to accompany me and his company helped to pass the time. When the drill was over, we repaired to the officers' mess in the drill hall to discuss the evening's exercise, and spent a very pleasant hour or so with excellent refreshment always on tap. They were great days.

On one such occasion after one of the weekly exercises, the Isle of Skye cropped up in the conversation. I was talking about the beach at Broadford Bay, which I used for charter flying and ambulance flights. Bertie Ross said he knew Mr George Campbell, proprietor of the hotel there.

'What about making a trip in the Moth one evening when the tide permits and paying George Campbell a surprise visit?' he enquired.

A few days later, having checked the tide at Broadford, I gave Bertie Ross a ring on the phone and named the date.

'We'll leave around five in the afternoon, weather permitting.'

'That's on,' he said.

So at five in the afternoon, Thursday 21st July 1938, we set off in brilliant sunshine and blue sky in the Gipsy Moth for the beach at Broadford Bay. It was a beautiful summer's evening with very little wind but, being in a single-engined aircraft, I followed the valley past Achnasheen and along the railway through the pass, down to Loch Carron and over the water to Broadford. The tide was well and truly out and the beach looked dry and in good shape. After landing, we taxied up to the high water mark and soon a crowd gathered. I picked out a reliable looking man with good muscles and asked him if he would guard the plane while we were away. He agreed and was promised a reward. In particular, I asked him to see that the children did not clamber over the wings, which they always tended to do in order to get a glimpse of the cockpit.

We made our way up to the Broadford Hotel and mine host was at home. He greeted Bertie Ross like a lost brother and I was introduced. He appeared to know about me and gave me a real welcome.

'Well this, gentlemen, is a great honour. It's the first time we've had guests calling on us by air. The occasion deserves celebrating.'

It was really hot in Skye and I was thirsty after the flight. Bertie said he felt the same. The welcome grew steadily, until I was beginning to wonder how we would ever fly back that night. By this time, we had been there an hour or so and the party was going with such a swing that I could not get my passenger to leave and mine host was not giving any encouragement. In fact, he wanted us to stay the night. I couldn't as I had to fly a duplicate service next morning. By the time we got back to the plane, a large crowd had gathered. It was a strange sight for them to see an aircraft in Skye, and I am sure, for many, it was the first they had seen at close quarters in their lives. An examination of the plane confirmed our guard had done his duty and he received a very adequate tip for having done his job so dutifully.

With difficulty, we got the crowd back from the plane and I swung the airscrew. It started first go. I got my passenger aboard and swung myself into the rear cockpit and we were off. After climbing to a thousand feet or so, I circled the beach two or three times just to make sure I was in sufficiently good fettle to fly after such a welcome. I appeared alright so we swung off on a course of 090∫ magnetic, climbing to 7,000 feet, for, having absorbed sufficient 'Dutch courage' since the outward journey, I intended to fly the direct course across the mountains to save time as it was getting late. Around half way, we ran into cloud for a while and I did not feel too comfortable flying on instruments. But it was not for long and the sky was clear for the rest of the trip. We had a magnificent view of the razor-topped mountain peaks. Soon, we were gliding down into Inverness Airport having covered the seventy-five miles in fifty minutes.

My wife greeted us, saying, 'My, you're pretty late, what kept you so long? I've been waiting in the car for over an hour.'

I left Bertie to do the excuses while I attended to getting the Moth into the shed. Bertie Ross came up to our house and we finished the party off there.

In the third week in August, we had an interesting charter flight that was the first of its kind. A firm of fish curers in the island of Stronsay, north of Kirkwall, had a branch in Stornoway, and they required six of their senior fish girls to be flown to Stornoway for an important job. To travel by surface transport would have taken over two days. By air, it took exactly one hour and twenty minutes. The flight was mostly over sea and the only land we flew over was the Cape Wrath peninsula which was only fifteen miles wide. The girls had never flown before and were looking a bit nervous, but as soon as we were on our way, flying at 2,000 feet in smooth air, they had such a splendid view of the Orkney Isles that they soon forgot about any squeamishness. By the time I landed them at Melbost, they didn't want to get out. We left Kirkwall at 11.00 am and landed at Melbost at 12.20. Transport was ready and my passengers were in town at 12.30 pm, ready for work after lunch. No wonder the fish curer jumped at the price I offered him for the charter for he had saved two days wages for six employees, plus the surface transport to Inverness and across to Stornoway which would have come to about double the sum of the air charter. The girls were thrilled with their flight when they alighted. At the time, I thought they would be good publicity agents for the Stornoway-Inverness service when it commenced.

During September, terrific controversy started about an airport for Thurso and pressure to provide an airfield was brought to bear against the Thurso Town Council. The Air Ministry, at the request of the council, had sent up one of their surveyors to inspect several sites proffered and one had been chosen at Dixonfield Farm, which was owned by Sir Archibald Sinclair. Obviously Thurso was very much out of the 'air picture' at that time. Air traffic had increased enormously in the past three years and most of it, plus the mail, was going through Wick.

Thurso enjoyed a large summer tourist trade and the Royal Hotel had recently been enlarged and refurnished by Mr James Wilson, its owner, to provide seventy-five rooms. The small field operated by Allied Airways was unsuitable and dangerous for heavily-loaded aircraft and, in any event, was a closed shop to outsiders. So, besides having no regular air route, Thurso could not even receive charter flights from the south to accommodate its passengers. In spite of all this, the Thurso Town Council still jibbed at providing a municipal aerodrome. Once the Air Ministry had settled a location which would be acceptable, the battle really started. The town finance scrooges lined themselves against the business community and were locked in deadly combat. Mr James Wilson led the business community and they demanded action. They worked out the cost, including the purchase of the land and the construction. Having obtained Scottish Airways support, who agreed to rent the airfield and manage it, they submitted an extremely good business proposition to the Town Council and asked them to go ahead and get on with the job. Still the Finance Committee would not move. Today, Thurso has no airfield, and is not likely to have one, as Wick airfield was reconstructed by the Air Ministry during the War, and it now serves the whole of the north of Scotland. The matter is of historical interest, so I quote the letter submitted by Mr James Wilson to the Town Council Aerodrome Committee, written during September 1938, which places the matter in the right perspective. This letter, incidentally, was sent through the columns of the *Caithness Courier* so that the public might be aware of what was going on and the opportunity that was being missed.

Thurso Aerodrome

To the Editor, *Caithness Courier.*

As convenor of the Town Council Aerodrome Committee I think it is my duty to let the ratepayers know the truth of how this matter stands, as there has been fierce propaganda against the proposed aerodrome and a number of misleading statements made in public regarding the project.

The Town Council approached the Air Ministry to send one of their surveyors to advise them on a suitable site for a Municipal Aerodrome. The surveyor reported to the Town Council on six sites.

No. 1 site was on the farm of Dixonfield which he reported as most suitable. There was ample room for the required runways, no hills or obstructions and in close proximity to the town. Only the ground was wet owing to the main leader ditch being choked. No. 2 site at Weydale and No. 3 site at Claredon [Allied Airways' field], were both unsuitable, as was the case of Numbers 4, 5 and 6 sites.

The present aerodrome [Allied Airways'] holds a temporary licence from the Air Ministry who are at present urging the Town Council to forward the development of the Dixonfield site. The Aerodrome Committee forthwith approached Sir Archibald Sinclair, Bart, re the purchase of Dixonfield Farm and the price asked is £800 which the Committee think most reasonable. The interest on this outlay would be from £24 to £28 per annum.

Scottish Airways and Allied Airways, the two operating companies in Caithness, have been approached. The former sent their surveyor from

London who reported favourably on the site, had samples of the soil analysed, and found ample depth of soil for drainage. The proposal put forward by them was to make 600 yard runs in all the required directions at an estimated cost of £4,000. This scheme was submitted to the Air Ministry and approved. Allied Airways sent their surveyor from Aberdeen. He reported favourably on the site and estimated cost of full development of aerodrome was about £8,000. Both companies are willing to pay a total rental of £60 to the Town Council for the required ground and the Committee expect £40 for the rent of the farm.

Outlays

Interest on loan	£28
Rates on aerodrome	£18
Rates on farm	£ 4
Repairs to farm buildings	£10
Total outlay	£60
Income rental	£100
Profit	£40

The forty pounds yearly profit would go towards payment of the loan. At the end of about fifteen years, the farm of Dixonfield with aerodrome would belong to the ratepayers of Thurso which would not have cost them one penny piece. The generous offer of Sir Archibald Sinclair, Bart, to accept £800 for the farm makes this possible.

In March last year, I approached Captain Fresson, Scottish Airways, and Mr Gandar Dower, Allied Airways, regarding a landing arrangement at Kirkwall and Thurso (Claredon) aerodromes.[1] I suggested each company should give landing for landing, with the company having the greater number of landings to pay an agreed fee. Both companies accepted and the service was to commence on the 17th May 1937.

About 1st May, Allied Airways took an interdict in Court, preventing Scottish Airways from landing on the Thurso aerodrome, after that company had duly advertised this service in their timetables. Had Allied Airways honoured the arrangement of landing facilities to Scottish Airways at Thurso, which the latter company grant Allied Airways at Kirkwall and Shetland, it would be possible to have our airmail delivered in Thurso at about 11.30 am thus giving the community the opportunity of replying by airmail, leaving Thurso about 1.30 pm by the returning mail plane from Orkney. Passengers would also be able to travel direct to Inverness.

---

[1] Ted Fresson commented: "We did not like this airfield as it was too small and, in our opinion, dangerous except for the lightest loads. However, we agreed to deliver the mail from Inverness to Thurso in the hope that it would encourage the Thurso Town Council to provide a municipal airfield at Dixonfield Farm."

Letter No 2 from Mr Wilson, dated 22nd October 1938, reads:

I regret I have been unable to reply to Mr Gandar Dower's letter in your issue of the 7th inst having been away on business.

Mr Dower [sic] states he knows of no propaganda. Mr Dower invited the Thurso Town Council to a free aerial trip to Aberdeen knowing perfectly well there existed a difference of opinion in the Council regarding the aerodrome question. I call this practical propaganda. Six members of the Town Council took advantage of Mr Dower's generosity. No such bouquets were thrown to the Town Councils of Lerwick, Kirkwall and Stromness, all burghs served by Mr Dower's air service. Mr Gandar Dower gives his case away when he admits the NE-SW runway places Claredon Airfield under Class "E" of the Air Ministry's classification, the lowest by one. We want a Class "A" airfield for Thurso.

The difference of opinion existing between Mr Dower and myself is his refusal to open Claredon Airfield. Mr Dower has offered to purchase Dixonfield, develop it and make it public. Claredon is his own property; why does he refuse to make it public? Scottish Airways offers landing on all their airfields but Mr Dower wants to practise free trade on Scottish Airways and protection on his own. Mr Gandar Dower's service this summer was anything but satisfactory. Five daily services were advertised, but the timetable was constantly being changed and services cancelled. On the day of the Thurso Town Council's trip to Aberdeen, four passengers came off the midday train to travel by plane. No conveyance called at the hotel to take the passengers to the airfield. I telephoned Mr Dower's office and was informed that the service was cancelled as the plane was going to Aberdeen with the Thurso Town council. The four passengers had to stay until next day. Such incidents happen too frequently.

On 17th October 1938, I sent the following letter to Scottish and Allied Airways:

"Sirs,

In the event of the Thurso Town Council purchasing Dixonfield Farm for a Municipal Aerodrome, would you be prepared to take:

1. A lease of same for 21 years at a rental of £60?
2. Develop the aerodrome at your own expense?
3. Forego any claim for compensation from the Thurso Town Council at the expiry of the lease?

Yours faithfully

J Wilson"

Allied Airways acknowledged the letter, but informed me Mr Dower was away from home on business. Scottish Airways replied as follows:

"We acknowledge receipt of your letter of the 17th inst and in reply would state, that in the event of the Thurso Town Council purchasing Dixonfield Farm for a municipal aerodrome, Scottish Airways would be prepared to:

1. Take a lease of same for 21 years at a rental of £60 per annum
2. Develop the aerodrome at their own expense.
3. Forego any claims for compensation from Thurso Town Council at the expiry of the lease if an option to renew for a further 21 years is allowed.
4. Should the Town Council desire to take over the aerodrome after 21 years, Thurso Town Council would make a refund to Scottish Airways at valuation, of the costs they had been put to for putting the ground in order.

The last clause would be clearly understood to imply that, if Scottish Airways do not wish to renew the lease at the end of 21 years, they would not expect compensation at valuation. This would only be expected if the Thurso Town Council took over the aerodrome after 21 years at their own desire and wish.

We hope this clarifies the position and we would again reiterate that the Town Council can draw up the heads of the Agreement in their own words providing the principles laid down above are conformed to. The matter would then be submitted to the board of Scottish Airways for final ratification.

Scottish Airways Limited

E E Fresson"

Well, that's it in its entirety. Nothing further happened and Thurso probably lost for all time the chance of holding her position in air transport in the extreme north. Had Dixonfield been constructed, more than likely the Air Ministry would have developed it further during the War the same as they developed Scottish Airways' airfield at Wick and today they would have a modern airport.

The after effect of the Thurso controversy came when the Wick Town Council started to take fright as soon as it became known that we were prepared to take a lease of Dixonfield Farm at Thurso and construct an airfield there. They, for some unknown reason, got into their heads that we were going to cut Wick off with their airmail service and so commenced writing to Ministers, the Postmaster General and licensing authorities to bring pressure on Scottish Airways to continue the airmail service. In fact, all we wished to do was to route out the Inverness-Orkney-Shetland service through Thurso, and operate our Inverness-Wick-Kirkwall service as usual. I could not see what objections Wick

Town Council could have, nor what right to prevent us routing our aircraft to show the most beneficial operating results to the company and public. I was and always have been deeply conscious and appreciative of the great help given to me by the Wick authorities in my early struggle to launch the air service to the Orkneys. With the exception of Inverness Town Council, the Wick city fathers were the only public body to give us any help in those difficult days. However, to the best of my memory, I subsequently visited the Town Council and put their minds at rest.

One of the main reasons I wanted an airfield at Thurso was on account of weather. Frequently, it was extremely difficult and even risky trying to land at Wick. Situated bang on the north-east coast, the town was subject to sea mists and low cloud which frequently settled over the area, whereas Thurso did not suffer so acutely from that type of weather. In addition, as I have already said, Thurso was developing a very good tourist trade, more so than Wick, and, naturally, we wished to capture that business. Lastly, there was a demand for a service direct to and from Inverness and Orkney. However, it was not to be, and Wick retained all services for which no doubt, they were truly thankful.

For the second time, Mr Walter Elliot, Secretary of State for Scotland as he was then, used Scottish Airways for his northern tour. On 10th October, he flew with me to Wick and Orkney and we renewed our acquaintance. I gathered from what he said that it was the intention of the State Department to use air transport in future when and where practical. The flight was successful in as much that it enabled the Secretary to carry out his mission in one day and return to Edinburgh on the late afternoon train. That, of course, saved a lot of time compared to his old method of travel by fisheries cruiser or train. It was also an advantage to Scottish Airways as such publicity certainly encouraged air mindedness with the public.

Early in the autumn, I transferred Captain Hankins back from Shetland to Kirkwall to continue the management of the Orkney station. The traffic had now developed to such an extent that I needed someone in charge that could also manage the technical problems which were arising with the aircraft operations. Captain Hankins installed himself in Tankerness House in the main street just opposite St Magnus Cathedral, which was very old and full of historical charm. I spent many pleasant visits there.

In November, I was invited by the students at Edinburgh University Orkney and Shetland Association to lecture them on the "Operation of the northern Air Routes". The meeting was very well attended and my audience showed tremendous interest in the address, which was evidenced by the number of questions put at the end of the meeting. Without going into technicalities, I cannot describe the meeting better than quoting the *Scotsman* report:

Problems of Air Service
Technical Difficulties

The difficulties of promoting air travel between the Orkney and Shetland Islands and the mainland were discussed last night in an address given to the Edinburgh University Orkney and Shetland Association.

The history of the service was traced from the opening flight from Inverness to Kirkwall in 1933 and described as the forerunner of Great Britain's air line service. The section to Shetland was opened in 1936. Captain Fresson said that the development of passenger traffic to Shetland had been, to his mind, disappointing. In the first year, 852 passengers were carried and in the second year, 1,171. The total number of passengers carried from June 1936 to September 1938 was 2,599 of which 76% travelled by Scottish Airways' planes. As a comparison, the total number of passengers carried from Inverness and Aberdeen to Orkney over the same period numbered 5,002, not including those carried by another company, nor those who used the Wick-Kirkwall service. Even without that addition, the Shetland traffic had a lot of leeway to make up.

He attributed the disparity in traffic to the cost of air travel to and from Shetland. The position in relation to Orkney was a difficult one. Inverness or Aberdeen to Orkney was approximately half the distance as compared to Lerwick. The time saving factor which, after all, was what the air service had to sell, was not a great deal different to that of Orkney. It was difficult for them to reduce the fare because, per mile, they were actually receiving less from the Shetland run than they were from the Orkney run. Another economic difficulty lay in the fact that the traffic was largely a seasonal one. If the traffic could be more easily apportioned over the entire year, as was the case with Orkney, they should then be in a position to run a direct service from the mainland to Shetland with an attending reduction in fares. Yet, until the fares could be made cheaper, he did not see how the air service could be available to Mr Everyman.

Speaking of the technical difficulties of operating the service, it was pointed out that the airfield problem in the north of Scotland had always been a difficult one. They were forced to operate from very much smaller airfields than those more fortunate services operating in the south and to the Continent. Unfortunately, also, Orkney and Shetland were geographically placed in the direct path of depressions which brewed in the Atlantic and proceeded in a north-easterly direction. Low cloud accompanied by heavy rain was their worst enemy.

The meeting was concluded with a description of the machines used and the method of flying them under difficult conditions. After answering many questions, the meeting ended with a vote of thanks to Captain Fresson.

I returned to my Hotel for a late supper and went to bed hoping for an early start next morning. It was not to be as the weather was as bad as I had described it at the meeting the previous night with clouds right down on deck.

I used the morning to call round at the *Scotsman* to pay a visit to my old friend, Mr George Law. Since the amalgamation with Railway Air Services, we had drifted apart a bit as far as business was concerned, but I was very anxious that our personal friendship should not be neglected for I owed everything, and every success of the air service I had built up, to Mr Law. Without his valuable aid and sportsmanship in the early days, there would have been no air service as far as I was concerned. He was very pleased to see me and enquired what had brought me to Edinburgh. I told him about the lecture the night before at the university and he appeared most interested. I told him I had met a *Scotsman* reporter, so no doubt he would be reading about the address.

'I will look forward to that,' he said. 'I hear the Government are about to licence all air routes. How will that affect you?'

'It's difficult to say,' I answered. 'Being the pioneers, we have a good case, but there is so much politics tied up with flying today that anything could happen.'

'Let me know when you come down for the hearing and you and Mrs Fresson will come and stay with me.'

I was very pleased as that was the first time he had ever invited us to be his guests overnight. After some further talk, I said I must be getting out to Turnhouse as I had to get back to Inverness that afternoon, no matter what the weather was.

I took off after lunch with very little improvement in the meteorological conditions and flew most of the way in cloud. Fortunately, there was no icing as there was a warm front spread over Scotland.

The New Year was not far away and, had we but known it, 1938 was to be the last year we would be allowed to operate free from bureaucratic control. The year had been one of continued expansion and consolidation. Our traffic and freight had increased substantially since our tie-up with the Railway Group the previous year. By now, the name of Highland Airways had been completely superseded by that of Scottish Airways and most of the friction which had manifested itself during the first twelve months had mostly disappeared. We were working as a team, which was all to the good and as it should have been.

I had been hard put to it, with the management and with flying many duplicated services, to take care of the upsurge in reservations, but the results were worth the effort. The comparison of traffic figures are worthy of note. For the first year, 1933, we carried 1,400 passengers. For the eleven months ending,

November 1938, 7,500 passengers were transported on Scottish Airways northern routes. That figure did not include the passengers travelling on the Inverness-Perth-Glasgow route.

The mail figures were even more outstanding. In 1933 it was 10 tons, and the eleven months to 30 November 1938 was 80 tons. I have no records of the newspaper loads, but since the second year under contract to the *Scotsman* had been completed, we were carrying most of the daily national newspapers and the Aberdeen *Press & Journal*. The daily loads were always extremely heavy and, more often than not, we were obliged to put on a separate aircraft to take care of the mail and newspapers. From a trickle in 1933 climbing to 60 lbs a day, I should say 600 lbs daily would scarcely have covered the 1938 loading.

These remarkable results had been obtained in four and a half years and had only been attained by the extraordinary high percentage of regularity flown. Only in one year out of the four did the annual regularity fall to 97%, for two years it was 98% and one year 100%, which meant that not one single day was missed during a whole year's flying. I am afraid that standard is not maintained today, twenty-five years later, in spite of the great advance in technical equipment. Great credit was due to our pilots for such a record of regularity and safety. They flew through a high percentage of extreme weather. For posterity, I quote their names in order of joining the company: Cyril Coleman, J A Greenshields, Adam Smith, Bernard Wilson, Johnny Rae, George Holmes, John Veasey, Johnny Fielden, John Hankins and Johnnie Johnstone, with a little help from myself![2]

The pilots certainly could not have carried out their onerous task without the backing of a fine engineering and maintenance organisation behind them, led by George Griffiths and assisted by Bert Farminer, Arthur Dodds, Archie Macdonald, A MacLennan and our radio engineer, Theo Goulden, who maintained our radio sets to a very high standard of efficiency. The few failures we had with our radio, upon which the lives of the passengers and air crew often depended in bad weather, was remarkable. I must not forget the traffic and office staff, headed by Miss Jean MacDonald and Sandy Cumming. At any time, all of them, along with the engineering staff, would work overtime to further the efficiency of the company without increase in pay. The sense of *esprit de corps* and loyalty was intense. They were a great team of which I was proud.

And so we leave Stage One of the 'Birth of Highland Airways' and turn to 1939, with controls and a second World War to face up to, in which Scottish Airways played a very important part.

---

[2] Peter Clegg's research indicates that the correct order should read: Holmes, Greenshields, Coleman, Rae, Smith, Veasey, Fielden, Hankins, Johnstone and Wilson.

11

Final days of carefree flying

During the middle of January 1939, the Air Transport Licensing Authority under the Air Navigation (Licensing of Public Transport) Order 1932 sat in Edinburgh to deal with the applications by Scottish Airways, North Eastern Airways and Allied Airways (Gandar Dower) Ltd to operate air services. The proceedings opened up on Monday 16 January and were presided over by Mr A M Trustram Eve, KC.

My wife accompanied me and we set out by road from Inverness on the Sunday. Mr Law took a great interest in the proceedings and he had invited us, as I have already said, to stay with him at his house in Murrayfield Road. The house was named *Duncliffe* and it possessed huge iron gates which were kept continually locked. On ringing the bell, the twin gates would open silently and mysteriously, as if by some unseen hand as there was no one on the other side to greet the caller. One stood mystified as to what should be done. Would a footman arrive to show the way, or should one walk up the drive to the front door? As the former solution was not presented, one took the second and commenced walking, the iron gates then clanging shut by the same unseen hand.

I had got to know the procedure from several previous calls and that the gates were worked electrically by pressing a button in the front hall. It was, however, quite new to my wife and it was amusing for me to see her reactions.

'How ghost-like,' she commented, 'how does it work?'

I explained as we walked up to the front door, which was already open with a maid waiting to usher us indoors. After shedding our coats, we were shown into the drawing room to be greeted by our host. It was a lovely house and particularly large for a lone bachelor. We sat down to a five course dinner served in pre-war style with a good supply of wine and Scotch. After preliminary conversational skirmishes, the theme turned to tomorrow's proceedings.

'What time have you to be there?' Mr Law asked me.

'The Court commences sitting at ten o'clock.'

'Well, breakfast is served at eight. That should give you plenty of time. I'll give instructions for the maid to call you at seven. Who's your Counsel?' he asked me.

'Oh, Railway Air Services have briefed a Mr Gilbert Woodward from London', I replied. 'Our case is all prepared on the basis that we were the first company to commence operations along our routes and that there is insufficient traffic for two companies.'

We went into the smoke room after dinner and chatted about all that had happened since I first turned up at the Highland pipe practice in 1931. He wanted to know all the facts about our present passenger and freight figures and was very surprised to know we were carrying such high load factors. As the evening wore on, he pressed the bell and told the maid to bring in the whisky.

'We'll have a nightcap.'

Mr Law proposed a toast to the success of the licence applications.

At seven next morning, we were called and were down to breakfast on the dot of eight. Our host was already there waiting for us. 'How did you sleep?' he enquired of my wife, and 'help yourselves', pointing to the dishes on the hotplate, all in the same breath.

Promptly at quarter to ten, Mr Law's chauffeur arrived to take me to the Licensing Court proceedings. I left my wife to entertain herself as best she could until I returned at lunchtime. We stayed for three days, and by the morning of the third day, I was so exhausted by the long court sittings, that I was half an hour late for breakfast. Mr Law was sitting there stern of face. He made no bones about telling me I was late and he looked most displeased. I apologised and said I did not have to get to the Court until eleven that day, and that I was beginning to feel the strain of continual questioning and thinking up the right answers. Gradually, the atmosphere improved and I hoped he understood.

The Court commenced its enquiry on Monday 16th January by asking Scottish Airways to state their case for the applications submitted. These were for a number of services including Inverness-Shetland, Glasgow-Inverness and Aberdeen-Stornoway, with intermediate landings in each case. This application was opposed by Allied Airways and North Eastern Airways Limited. We claimed we should have a monopoly of civil aviation in that area to the exclusion of Allied Airways as we had pioneered the route and were four years ahead of Allied Airways who, in 1935, had stepped in with unwelcome competition on routes which were uneconomical for two companies to operate. Our Counsel emphasised that Highland Airways had:

Borne all the considerable development costs over a period of years.

Constructed and licensed all the northern airfields that held monopoly rights.

Accepted the Air Ministry demand that we should surrender their monopoly rights for the erection of radio air stations in the interest of public safety.

Such public spirited actions had not been matched by the applicants who wished to compete along the routes and who appear to have adopted a policy of 'all take and no give.' For that reason they had been refused a radio station at Dyce Airport by the authorities.

Many questions were asked by the President as to loads on the various sectors and we had to submit evidence that we were suitably capitalised to operate the service to the general benefit of the public. Our examination lasted all Monday and a part of Tuesday when the questioning was switched to Allied Airways Limited of Aberdeen which went through a similar cross examination. What was not interrogated in any sustained examination were the irregular operations which that company were in the habit of maintaining for a diversity of reasons. I could not understand our Counsel's apathy to this important bit of evidence and I felt the failure to drive this point home penalised us in the ultimate issue of the monopoly rights that we claimed.

On the Wednesday, North Eastern Airways were called to present their case, but they did not interfere with our application as they operated from London to York, Newcastle-on-Tyne, Perth and Aberdeen. Their managing director, Mr Jacques, had previously told me his company found it very difficult and risky operating in bad weather without radio facilities at Dyce. After the last applicant had been dealt with and given evidence, local witnesses representing local authorities from the north of Scotland were called. The chairman expressed the gratitude of the tribunal for their presence, remarking they had been of great assistance. The chairman went on to say that Scottish Airways Limited was applying for a number of services including Inverness-Shetland, Glasgow-Inverness, and Aberdeen-Stornoway, with intermediate landings in each case. The applications were opposed by Allied Airways Limited. The chairman indicated the tribunal's provisional views 'subject to all proper conditions being attached to the licences':

> Ideally, civil aviation north to Inverness and Aberdeen both inclusive, should be operated under single control, subject to the safeguards and interests of the public, which may be imposed. In this we agree with the contention of Scottish Airways. Scottish Airways claim they should have the monopoly of civil aviation in this area to the exclusion of Allied Airways. We think that a case has not been made out by Scottish Airways to exclude Allied Airways from this area.

This assertion appeared to us quite contrary to the facts already presented by our Counsel at the opening of the enquiry and contradictory to the President's opinion stated above. What more evidence could be available? We had educated the public to air travel, which was a costly process and we were in the field at least four years ahead of the competition complained of, with the services and air mail contracts already cut and dried and which had been in operation for two years at ninety-eight percent regularity. Finally, and most importantly, there was not sufficient potential for two services, which the chairman had admitted. What more evidence could we provide? We and nobody else could figure that one out, or ever did. The Chairman went on to say:

In default of single control, we are of the opinion that a case has been made out for the granting of licences to Scottish Airways and Allied Airways to operate services respectively from Inverness and from Aberdeen and that these licences should, subject to minor exceptions, be exclusive to each respective company.

All these however, may be affected by the Postmaster General to carry mails. We would invite suggestions from both applicants as to the best methods for the Authority to obtain the views of the Postmaster General upon this matter.

We appreciate also that conditions in aviation change rapidly. We have in mind the possibility on those and other routes of night flying, the utilisation of more rapid machines, the extension of ground organisation and of landing grounds and other factors which may affect these licences. Our views therefore, are to be taken as expressed upon the facts as existing today and on the evidence now before us. With this in view we invite suggestions as for the period for which licences should be granted. These are our present impressions on hearing again the directors concerned and the speeches from the three advocates. We have not yet finally decided any of the applications.

Later on in the month, we were informed that our applications as applied for were granted, but with the exclusion of operating in and out of Aberdeen. Thus 'the Cuckoo was left sitting in the pioneer nest.' One doubtful concession given to Scottish Airways was that we would carry the Aberdeen to Shetland mail from Kirkwall to Shetland every other day, and Allied Airways would be responsible for the carriage on the alternative days. This in effect was tantamount to the ruling of 'King Solomon', when two mothers claimed the same baby; the baby was said to have been cut in half and each mother took a cut. We did not like the idea of being a 'mother' at a cut rate paid by the Postmaster General under the uneconomical acceptance of Allied Airways bid to grasp the mail from Scottish Airways. We would have preferred a passenger taking up the weight utilised by the 'unwanted portion of the child.' To make matters more of an imposition, there were many days when Allied Airways could not or would not operate from Kirkwall to Shetland. We were then called upon to carry the mails on that sector and this caused us considerable embarrassment as we were frequently fully booked with passengers. I noticed that such occasions usually occurred on the days when the weather was extremely bad along the Aberdeen-Kirkwall route, which was of course, without radio assistance. In the end, I gave orders that passengers who we had contracted to carry were not to be unloaded for mail. In such cases, the mail had to remain in Orkney overnight and we carried it the next day. The new licensing arrangements carried on until 1st September 1939 when war was declared and both airlines were called upon to operate under Air Ministry direction.

Before leaving this subject, it may be of interest to note the letter I wrote to the *Shetland Times* on 12th January 1939, just before the Licensing Court sat. It dealt with the irregularity of the Aberdeen-Shetland mail service and corroborates what I have already written.

Sir,

On reading your recent story of the Shetland air mail, I was struck with the fact that possibly through lack of space, several important facts had been left out. We were told that on only two occasions had the air mail failed to leave Dyce, but somehow the number of times it had failed to reach Shetland was omitted. Seven times in July, August and September last, the Shetland air mail made no appearance at Shetland Airport according to the aircraft arrival record at that station, and yet on each of the seven days a Scottish Airways plane appeared in the log. We were also told that on one day all Scottish air lines were grounded by fog – not strictly accurate – as Scottish Airways air mail service has never in the past eighteen months failed to leave Inverness and what is more important, arrived in Orkney on schedule.

You quote an official as saying, "Wireless at Dyce should supply a service which would result in Shetland getting the mails with 100 percent regularity every summer and winter," but you do not say why there is no radio station at Dyce, or that the radio station at Sumburgh and at Orkney, which has helped the Shetland mail so much, was only provided through the unselfish attitude adopted by Scottish Airways when they made their aerodromes public on demand by the Air Ministry in order to provide radio stations for all services and the benefit of the public. I venture to suggest that radio could have been available at Dyce long ago had its owner been prepared to open his aerodrome to Scottish Airways as we had done to Allied Airways at Kirkwall and Sumburgh.

As you have given space for what you term a commendable effort on the part of Allied Airways to maintain an air mail service to Shetland, perhaps you will see the fairness of printing the aforementioned points and corrections.

Signed E E Fresson

There were further letters to the press on the irregular Aberdeen air mail service to Shetland which appeared later and will be referred to in its appropriate place.

I have said early in this narrative that the airfield site I originally chose at Kirkwall was situated at the farm of Hatston, but that I was unable to obtain the use of the land, although the tenant farmer was agreeable, owing to other interests which were likely to be affected by the opening of air communications. I had always hankered after getting that ground for an airfield as it was situated at sea level whereas Wideford was 200 feet above and often in fog when Hatston was in the clear. So, when a London representative from the Admiralty called on me at Inverness at the end of January asking if I could advise them of a suitable site in Orkney for the construction of a Naval Air Station, I immediately recommended the Hatston farm.

He told me they wished to construct four air strips and one had to be at least 1,500 yards long. By continuing the north-east/south-west air strip into another farm to the north-east, I figured all the requirements could be met at Hatston with the possible exception of the approach to the East/West strip which was downhill. My visitor, Commander Heath, said he would like to charter a plane to fly him up to inspect the site.

'That's easily arranged and I will fly you up myself,' I replied.

A telephone call to Whitehall soon confirmed permission and we set off in Dragon aircraft G-ACIT.

I was requested to make dummy runs from the eight points of the compass over the Hatston site with a view to testing the approaches. When that was completed, we landed at Wideford airfield and went into town for lunch. We returned to Hatston farm in the afternoon to walk over the ground and my Admiralty friend expressed the view that the site might be satisfactory. I warned Commander Heath about the boggy state of the ground in Orkney during winter months and recommended that hard tar macadam runways should be constructed. The commander looked at me in amazement.

'I have never heard of anything like that in airfield construction before,' he said.

'I am sure you haven't,' I replied. 'It is new thinking on my part after five difficult winters struggling to take off at Wideford airfield with heavy loads in a sea of mud. The Navy will never get away with the standard grass airfield in Orkney.'

They accepted my advice and, as far as I am aware, that was the first airfield constructed in the British Isles which was provided with hard strips for take-off and landing. When construction was completed, Hatston airfield obviously caused some hard thinking in the RAF because many senior officers arrived in Kirkwall to inspect the finished job. Within a couple of years, the 'hard strip' became standard practice for the wartime airfields constructed all over the country.

Commander Heath returned to London. Within a week he was back and accompanied by Admiralty surveyors. On this occasion we flew in a Rapide and repeated the dummy runs and approaches with the faster aircraft. We transferred the theodolites and surveying equipment into the waiting car at Wideford and I left for Hatston. On the way, I booked them in at the Kirkwall Hotel.

The result of that survey was entirely satisfactory. I was asked to advise on the directions the four runways should be sited. They agreed three, but queried the east-west strip as the approach towards the east was downhill. I was thinking that, if hostilities did not take place, we might be able to rent that airfield from the Navy, in which case our operations in and out of Orkney would be considerably eased and be far safer. Accordingly, I was all out to help the naval authorities construct such a splendid airfield. So I answered, quickly:

'If there is a strong wind from the east, then the strength of the wind will counter the slope downhill. On the other hand, should only light winds be encountered then there is nothing to prevent the pilot landing on the north-east/south-west strip.'

They accepted that viewpoint. After the airfield became operational and once the naval pilots got used to gliding down the approach hill low over the surface, the point was proved. They encountered no difficulty in using the downhill strip as the slope corresponded to the glide path of the average aircraft in use in those days. Shortly after the survey party had returned to London, I received word that the Admiralty were going ahead with the plan and construction commenced in the early spring.

The air strips were finished just in time for the early phase of World War Two. The hangars, maintenance shops and personnel quarters were still in course of construction for some time after 3rd September 1939. An arrangement was made between the Admiralty and Scottish Airways that they would use and manage Hatston in peace time, but that never came about as construction was finished coincidal to the commencement of hostilities. However, as we had given the Admiralty so much assistance with Hatston airfield, we hoped that we would be allowed the use of that airfield in the event of hostilities. That view was at first accepted, but we ran into trouble with the Commanding Officer, who succeeded Commander Howe RN, the first Commandant of the air station at the outbreak of war.

During the summer of 1939, the war atmosphere continued to develop as the weeks went by, but it appeared remote and daily life continued as before. In Orkney, our ambulance service was doing good work and was often called upon by the Orkney County Council. One evening on the last day of February, an urgent call was made at nightfall for medical assistance on the island of Sanday. The night was very dark and a young gale was blowing. To make matters more difficult, there were heavy rain squalls. Nevertheless, our station manager, Captain John Hankins decided to answer the call to fly a doctor out to the island. Apart from the difficulty of finding the island in the dark without radio or proper airfield lighting, the available run on the landing field at Sanday was no more than 300 yards and the only lighting would be car headlights. This flight I consider was the highlight of all our urgent ambulance flights and I have always admired the skill and courage of Captain Hankins in undertaking that call. I cannot do better than quote from the report appearing in the *Orcadian* newspaper of Thursday 2nd March 1939 respecting this mercy flight. I managed to get hold of a copy of this report through the good offices of Jack Watson, who was my traffic officer in those days and is now stationed at Kirkwall for British European Airways.

Kirkwall Pilot's Night Flight
Doctor Flown to and from Sanday

Scottish Airways Limited conveyed a doctor to and from Sanday in darkness on Tuesday evening. The flight was carried out in the face of several difficulties – rain-soaked and mud-treacherous airfield and periods of poor visibility, heavy rain showers and strong wind.

The flight began from and ended in flat calm at Kirkwall (Wideford Airfield). Strong gusts caused anxiety at Sanday. The flight was carried out without the aid of wireless, the Kirkwall radio civil aviation station having closed down with cessation of normal flying at dusk. Word came through by telegraph shortly after eight o'clock that the plane had landed safely at Sanday. There was no means of knowing later in the evening when the plane would leave for Kirkwall.

Pilot J Annesley Hankins, before coming to Kirkwall, carried out a considerable number of night flights with doctors on ambulance duty, between Glasgow and the Western Isles. The passenger to and from Sanday on Tuesday evening was Dr W A Sinclair who was called to a confinement in the north end of the Island. Mr Archibald MacDonald, Scottish Airways ground engineer at Kirkwall Airport, travelled in the plane also. On return of the plane, it was learned that mother and daughter were both well.

Captain Hankins, on taking off at Kirkwall set a course for Sanday with the aid of bearings he took on the lighthouses of Copinsay and Auskerry. The flight to Sanday occupied twenty minutes. Difficulty was experienced in landing. Several motor cars instead of one, had been set up with their headlights showing into wind, which however changed direction as the plane was heard approaching. Owing to the soft ground, the cars could not be shifted in time to indicate the new wind direction. Captain Hankins, when about to land, discovered from the feel of his plane and the speed he was approaching the car lights that they were pointing downwind. He immediately opened up and commenced to climb to a safe altitude, circled around and then landed across wind without mishap. [I would not have thought that possible if a young gale was blowing.]

Fresh anxiety was caused when another car, parked nearby, switched his lights on the plane as it was racing to a standstill. Fortunately, the pilot was able to avoid danger despite the dazzle. The doctor was conveyed by car to his case eight miles up the island. Two hours later, he returned and the home flight was then accomplished safely. Cars indicated the wind direction for the pilot at Kirkwall, which was reached shortly after 11 o'clock at night.

The plane used for the flight was a DH Dragon, G-ADCT. The plane was made ready and wheeled from the hangar, and warmed up ready for the flight, within twenty minutes of receipt of the telegram. Mr J S D Watson, the local traffic officer of Scottish Airways, carried out the ground arrangements and 'held the fort' until the plane returned. Among the people who had assembled at Kirkwall Airport to see the return of the plane, and who congratulated Captain Hankins on his achievement, was Mr Ian H McClure, Surgeon Superintendent at Balfour Hospital.

The flight created quite a stir in the Orkney Islands and it was not long before all the Islanders knew about the good work Captain Hankins did that night on Sanday. It was all in keeping with the Scottish Airways motto, 'The plane must get through'.

We were now getting near the summer season schedule. A new service, which would link London to Orkney in six hours, was underway. The service was planned to depart from Orkney at 6.25am, arriving in time to connect with the North Eastern Airways plane at Perth, departing 9.00am for Edinburgh, Newcastle-on-Tyne and arriving 12.30 midday at Croydon airport, London. The northbound flight by Railway Air Services would leave Croydon just before midday and reach Inverness, Wick and Orkney in time for dinner. Another feature of the service was that it would enable the public to spend half a day in Glasgow and return to their homes the same night. Fares were kept low to encourage people in the north to go to Glasgow or Perth for business, shopping or sightseeing. The plane reached Glasgow just after 9.00 am, departing on the return journey north just after 3.00 pm. It was subsequently decided that the previous year's Glasgow-Perth-Inverness-Wick-Orkney-Shetland service would also be maintained. Thus, the public travelling to and from Glasgow and Orkney had two service frequencies per day, which is outstanding compared to present day schedules. There is no doubt that service frequency has suffered with modern planning and that the north of Scotland was considerably better served in that respect in pre-war years. We carried all passengers who wished to travel and, more important, at the time they wanted. The modern claim that better service is offered today is incorrect insofar as frequency is concerned.

The *Caithness Courier*, reporting these new schedules, wound up with the statement:

...it is interesting to note that Highland Airways, now merged with Scottish Airways, reached their sixth birthday last week, as the first service from Inverness to Kirkwall was inaugurated and flown by Captain Fresson on Monday, 8th May 1933. On that first flight, the small monoplane *Inverness* was fully loaded with three passengers and a considerable load of newspapers. On Monday week, six years later to the day, two DH89 Rapide airliners left Longman airport fully loaded with passengers and mail and newspapers.

The traffic development over the first six years had been exceptional as a total of 1,500 passengers was carried for the first year and a total of ten thousand passengers were carried for the year ending 8th May 1939 over the northern routes. Inasmuch as our Rapide planes only carried seven passengers without mail or newspapers, that load involved a high number of flying hours. It was in 1939 that our maintenance organisation under George Griffiths proved its high degree of efficiency. We had only a comparatively small staff, and Goulden was our only radio maintenance engineer assisted at times by Griffiths, and yet they kept six aircraft in the air continuously. Our pilots also were flying an average of 120 hours a month, and I am sure Captain Hankins must have logged more than that, although it was against Air Ministry maximum.

The London service was not very well patronised at first. In any event, not so many people were travelling from the north to London, but we found the Inverness passengers interested. Unfortunately, owing to the outbreak of war, the service did not operate long enough to assess its true value.

On 1st June, I carried out a charter to Orkney, carrying four passengers to attend a meeting and dinner party, which took place in the Kirkwall Hotel. My wife and I were the guests of our good friend Mrs Mackay who owned the hotel. It did not really get dark in Kirkwall at that time of the year and our passengers appeared in no hurry to return. We did not take off until one o'clock in the morning for the return flight. The light was eerie and it was like taking off into another world, especially as we climbed, when wonderful pastel shades appeared on the horizon.

We flew at 3,000 feet and I was wondering what the landing was going to be like at Inverness as we had no landing lights out. After passing Wick, it started to get darker and by the time we were down to Tarbatt Ness we were flying in moonlight. There was no wind and the whole picture, I can well remember, was like a fairy land. We could see the airfield at Longman, and Inverness was quite distinct as we passed over. Most of the passengers behind me appeared asleep, excepting my wife who sat just behind me in the starboard front seat. She was apprehensive of the night landing. I turned, shutting off the motors, and commenced the descent and approach in from the sea. The lower we got the darker it appeared, and I switched on the aircraft landing searchlight which picked up the dyke alongside the Moray Firth. After that the going was easy and we made a good landing. My passengers had done so well at the party that they took quite a bit of waking. I think they would have been quite happy if I had left them in the cabin for the night.

Shortly after that trip, an urgent call came in from the Stornoway fish curers to ferry twelve lassies between Wick and Shetland. I had only one aircraft available so, having delivered the first six at Sumburgh, I had to turn around and return to Wick for the second lot. I was in the air for five hours and twenty minutes and all the girls arrived on time. I believe one or two of them had previously made the trip with me on the first 'fish girl' flight direct from Kirkwall to Stronsay a year or so before.

As the political situation worsened, we were given an Air Ministry contract to carry out Army Co-operation flying at Inverness, Kirkwall and Shetland for 297 Heavy Anti-Aircraft (HAA) Battery. The aircraft had to fly on certain courses and at different altitudes up to 10,000 feet while the ack-ack guns practised training. These exercises went on from one to two hours and became very boring.

As the war clouds gathered momentum and the Nazis swallowed up Austria in their rampage over Europe, so the army co-operation work increased. It was stepped up to three nights a week and I was kept very busy on the air co-operation flying. High altitude spotting and gun-siting was the order of the day. I can remember one evening was so clear that, flying at 10,000 feet over Inverness and towards Loch Ness, I could see the mountains alongside the Corran-Ardgour ferry, south west of Fort William some seventy miles away. It was a wonderful sight which never repeated itself. We would repair to the ack-ack mess after these flights and the details of the exercise discussed and analysed, and procedure for the following exercise would be mapped out. It was very necessary for the pilot to know the drill the gun crews were involved in as the flying had to be co-ordinated to give the gun crews the maximum value of training. I am happy to know that we did the job well and it was to be hoped the instruction was such that it accounted for a record bag on Huns at a later date.

On the 22nd July, Lord Malcolm Douglas-Hamilton joined our service to Orkney, returning to Inverness the same day. I believe he was on Air Force duty and he seemed very interested in the flight. It was the first time I had met him and I found him exceedingly interesting to talk to. He was the chief pilot on the Mount Everest flight in 1932. He took a great interest in our air service, I suppose because he was Chairman of Scottish Aviation Limited at Prestwick.[1]

A couple of days later, Willie Hamilton, our secretary, phoned me at my home in Ardersier, saying that the champagne magnate Monsieur Bollinger wanted a plane to fly over to Aberdeen to rescue a lady friend who was arriving on the North Eastern Airways plane from London. Could I do the trip? Curiously, M. Bollinger did not wish to fly to meet the lady himself, but detailed me to collect her off the London plane, transfer her along with her luggage to my plane and bring her back to Inverness as quickly as possible. The price did not matter so long as the job was carried out expeditiously and the good lady was not kept waiting on arrival.

I hurried in to Longman, picking up an engineer on the way to help me get Dragon, G-ACIT, out the hangar and start up the motors. We were off the ground in record time. I took my engineer along with me in case I required the motors restarting at Aberdeen and not because I was thinking of taking a chaperone. We reached Aberdeen just before the London plane got in, so I had time to arrange with the traffic people at Dyce to get the lady off the North Eastern service and transfer her direct to our plane without delay.

I met the lady, Mme Landers, in the traffic reception and was a bit non-plussed to find she could speak no English. My French had never been good. In

---

[1] Lord Malcolm Douglas-Hamilton (1909-1964) served in the RAF 1929-1932 and during World War Two. It was his brother, Douglas Douglas-Hamilton (1903-1973), Marquis of Douglas and Clydesdale, who flew over Everest in April 1933 and he was a founder of Scottish Aviation Ltd. Malcolm Douglas-Hamilton is now known to have flown a de Havilland aircraft to Spain for Franco's nationalists in 1936.

my younger days I had spent so much time trying to learn Chinese that I had never had much time to improve on my school French. It is true, I had a messmate in Hankow many years before, a Belgian engineer, who spoke French fluently and who spent many hours trying to improve my very English accent. I was accordingly able to explain I was sent by M. Bollinger to fly her to Inverness. Mme Landers was a very charming woman and extremely good looking and I had to agree that Monsieur's taste was of the best!

We arrived back in Inverness in record time. M. Bollinger was so pleased that he invited my wife and I to dine with them, at the same time handing me a substantial bundle of notes to pay for the charter. He spoke English pretty well, so the conversation was a triangular affair, he doing the translating. Most of it was about the possibility of war with Germany and in his opinion it was bound to come. Britain had let matters slide too long, he said, and refusal to support the French Government when they wanted to resist Hitler's walk into the Ruhr some year back had contributed, if not made war inevitable. We learned very much later that he lost his life in the debacle which was to so shortly overtake us.

Monday 31st July proved a red letter day for North Ronaldsay for the Post Office, who had been considering the question for the past two years (in tortoise fashion) at last decided to grant the island an air mail service. I chose our Dragon aircraft, G-ACIT, for the job as it was that plane which had an honourable mail record.

It was a bad day along the route from Inverness, with thunder, lightning and heavy rain. But the weather at North Ronaldsay was kinder and I arrived over the landing ground to find the whole island out in force to welcome the mail and myself for they knew the amount of effort I had made to improve their communications with the outside world. Before the advent of the air service, they used to be cut off for days and, even with fine weather, it took hours to reach Kirkwall whereas with the air service the journey only took a matter of fifteen minutes or so. Now their mail would arrive regularly and on time, so it was not difficult to understand their joy. How tragic, that after waiting so many years for the privilege they received that day, and after only one month's operation up to the end of August, it was suddenly taken away from them. For at the outbreak of war on the 3rd September, the island services were closed down by the Air Ministry and all North Isles landing fields were immobilised by building stone cairns over them. After the war, when Scottish Airways had spent several months with the Orkney County Council surveying the islands with a view to laying down permanent airfields, they were denied a resumption of the pre-war services owing to Nationalised Bureaucracy.

We in Scottish Airways, and the directors, considered we were providing an air service which was of life or death importance to those islands, and, in conjunction with other local routes, such as the trans-Pentland service and the

Orkney-Shetland service for the business community, which paid its way with the type of aircraft we used. The islanders accordingly lived to curse the day when socialism, which was supposed to exist for the people, sold them down the drain. Since then, I believe, depopulation of the Orkney Islands has become a very serious matter and all on account of reverting to outmoded transport. I reproduce an interesting article, which appeared in the *Orcadian* newspaper dated 3rd August, 1939, a propos the new mail service.

North Ronaldsay Air Mail
New Service started by Captain Fresson

North Ronaldsay, first of the Orkney Islands to enjoy a local air mail and first area in the British Isles to have an all round air mail, had the opening service on Monday, when Captain Fresson, Managing Director at Inverness for Scottish Airways Limited, piloted the inaugural plane. Every description of mail is now flown to and from North Ronaldsday – letters, postcards, printed matter and parcels. The air mail operating between Inverness and Kirkwall is for first class matter only, that is to say letters stamped at the full ordinary postal rate. The general mail flown to and from North Ronaldsay is carried at ordinary rates.

The North Ronaldsay mail plane operating three times weekly, sets out from Kirkwall at 11.30 am. The plane returns to Kirkwall immediately after landing at North Ronaldsay. Monday's inaugural mail weights were 57 lbs from Kirkwall and 82 lb from North Ronaldsay. Almost the entire population of the island greeted Captain Fresson when he landed. Rev A M Gordon, the Church of Scotland minister, on behalf of the islanders, gave welcome to Captain Fresson. Acknowledging the welcome, Captain Fresson said he looked forward to the day when he would be asked to fly to North Ronaldsay, all the goods required by the islanders, even their beer!! (laughter).

On the outgoing mail being loaded, Captain Fresson was carried shoulder high to the plane. The crowd gave a rousing cheer as the plane, G-ACIT, took off.

"One hundred years of Postal Service", our North Correspondent adds. Monday was one of the most important days in this little island's history. It saw the start of a direct connection to Kirkwall, three times a week, with a full parcel and letter mail by aeroplane.

The motor car and the railway train play little and no part respectively in the scheme of things out here, but the island has been quick to realise the great possibilities and advantages of the latest mode of travel, the aeroplane. Since the mail service was first established to the island nearly a hundred years ago, across the notorious strip of ocean, the North

Ronaldsay Firth, to the neighbouring island of Sanday, it has been plied by boat, first once a week by open sail boat, and eventually twice a week in winter and three times a week in summer by a powerful motor boat. These hazardous crossings to and from Sanday during past generations have indeed been a wonderful achievement, as during all the years, no mails, passengers or goods have been lost or damaged. No tribute is too high to pay to those heroes of the deep who, down the years, have maintained those precarious crossings with the utmost skill and daring, thereby carving for themselves an everlasting memorial and an undying gratitude from the island they have so faithfully served.

Now, as always, the old must give place to the new and the people to whom in the past the sea has been their very life's blood, have taken over a new departure and accepted this flying service with open arms. It is hoped the outer world will try to realise the great venture the island has made to forego their proven methods of communication for this new service. To quote His Majesty's words at a recent great event, ‚It is an act of faith'.

The island is resting in the belief that the possibilities and advantages of this step forward will be truly justified and that the powers that be will make it the success we feel sure it will be.

The last paragraph is touching, for I have already dealt on what 'the powers that be' were guilty of in the years to come. The reference to the stormy passage across the North Ronaldsay Firth is well mentioned, for from the air between the islands of Sanday and North Ronaldsay, I have seen raging seas comparable to the open ocean. How the motor boat made those crossings on stormy days is unbelievable. The crew were brave and very skilful men seeking no notoriety, but getting on with the job of serving their fellow beings. And they have been and are still at it since the end of the war, thanks to a system that falls far short of the high duty the boatmen display in their hazardous occupation and the course of duty.

We were glad to see the month of July terminate for it was a month of almost continued fog and we were all feeling the strain maintaining our service at one hundred percent under such conditions. We little knew it at the time but with the advent of August, it was the last month of 'peace in our time' which Prime Minister Chamberlain promised us on his return from his second abortive trip to Munich and Berchtesgaden after his talks with Hitler.

The North Isles service traffic was booming and on 12 August we carried no less than twenty-six passengers that day, which was a record for such sparsely inhabited isles. Several unimportant but pleasant incidents occurred within the next few days. Firstly, my brother Noel, who held a permanent commission in the RAF, turned up for a week's stay. He wished to visit the RAF Invergordon base and we set off in the Gipsy Moth, 'AWO', one afternoon soon after lunch and carried out a tour around the Tain peninsula, landing in fields and calling on various friends. We landed up at Tain for tea and, making a few more calls on the way back, we landed at the RAF airfield at Evanton around six o'clock. We both knew the commanding officer, Group Captain Busk, and we spent a very enjoyable evening in the officers' mess. Incidentally, I was on the RAF Reserve at the time and knew several of the officers stationed there. They wanted us to stay to dinner but we had to make our excuses as we were expected home to dine, but that did not get us off and to dinner we had to stay. It was near eleven o'clock before we got clear and it was a pitch black night.

The Group Captain said, 'It now seems you will have to stay the night. You can't fly back in the dark without any airfield lighting here or at Inverness.'

'I'll manage,' I replied. 'I have a pocket torch in the Moth and I will be able to see by that for actual touch down.'

One can always gauge the approach to Longman by the town lights. There was tense silence; such a thing had never been heard of before in service flying.

'Don't be silly, old boy, you will break your ruddy necks. Better stay the night and make an early start,' the Group Captain said.

I thanked him. 'We'll make it alright. I have landed like that on several occasions before. My brother can stay if he wishes.'

But brother Noel said he would accompany me.

'Well, have one for the road before you go.'

I thought we had had too many for the road already that evening, but agreed to a small one to placate him, as it was within his powers to prevent us leaving his airfield that night. We were about to leave the Mess quarters for the airfield, when several officers appeared and presented my brother with several rolls of toilet paper.

'What's that for?' Noel asked.

'For use on your journey,' they replied.

Brother's Noel's face was a study, but he took the rolls out of spite. We made a good landing at Longman and, after walking up to the town, we gave our RAF host a ring to let him know we were safely down.

'Jolly good show, old chap,' he said. 'Thanks for phoning.'

Two days later, a Saturday, we had a midday party in the Station Hotel and it was such a lovely day that I suggested a trip over to Stornoway for tea to several of our friends. I wanted to see how the construction of the airfield was getting on. We would leave around three thirty and meet at the airfield. On our way home by car to our house at Mid Kerrogair at Dalcross, a Handley Page Hampden bomber flew low over the fields. One engine was evidently not functioning properly as it was backfiring and throwing out a lot of smoke.

It disappeared and I said to my wife, 'That pilot will have a forced landing on his hands if he is not careful.'

We had barely finished lunch, when a farm labourer came up to the house and told me an aeroplane had crashed in the woods on the hill behind us and near Culloden Moor.

We jumped into the car and made our way towards the burning plane which was clearly visible by the columns of black smoke spiralling its way upwards in the calm air. On arrival at the scene of the crash, I found it was the Hampden we had seen and it was all but burned out. I cannot remember whether the crew got away with their lives, but I seem to remember the pilot was killed. The burning wreck had set light to the beech and silver birch trees and there was a good forest fire in the making. There was nothing we could do as the crew had been removed sometime before we arrived, so we left for Inverness and eventually caught up with our guests at the airfield.

We used Dragon, G-ACIT, and the passengers consisted of William Hamilton and Connie his wife, my wife, Robert Donald our ex Chairman, and a Mr Christie from Orkney who was the organiser of the Father Christmas aerial visits. We had a magnificent flight over the mountains at 7,000 feet and made an easy landing on the familiar tidal basin. My son's godfather, David Tolmie, met us and took my passengers into town. I said I would follow later if they would send the car back as I wanted to inspect the work on the airfield construction. I had not been over to Stornoway for some months and I noticed a big difference. The four runways were all completed and the foreman told me that they expected to be clear of the job in a few days as they were now only cleaning up. I must say, it looked fine. Four level and wide airstrips, six hundred yards long, constituted a large airfield in those days. I was just itching to land on it, but it was not to be. In less than two weeks, war had broken out and we were prohibited from commencing the Stornoway service. Shortly afterwards, our new and unused airfield was commandeered and completely cut up and rebuilt to four times its size for Coastal Command operations.

I hurried into town and joined the party at tea in the Caledonian Hotel. Afterwards, we went up to David Tolmie's office and spent a very pleasant hour before leaving for the airport. We waved 'goodbye – see you again soon,' and left him standing by the golf clubhouse around seven o'clock in the evening. That was the last time we ever saw David Tolmie, for the following October, when I was in London and laid up with an attack of 'flu, my wife phoned the Bradburys where I was staying to say that David was desperately ill with an attack of meningitis. The doctor in Stornoway was, for some reason, unable to treat him or maybe did not grasp what was ailing poor David. I knew from the description of the illness given by my wife when she said it was reported he was banging his head against the wall with the pain. After three days, he died. Had I been in Inverness, as soon as the news came through I would have flown over and brought him into hospital even though I had a temperature. The symptoms were exactly the same as other cases we had heard of in Inverness before I went south. His life might have been saved, but there might have been after effects. His death was a great loss to us and he had been liked by everyone. He had been a very good friend to me and had given unlimited assistance in my long endeavours to establish an airport at Stornoway.

The colouring over the mountains was beautiful in the evening light. Ullapool, set at the top end of Loch Broom mountains, looked so picturesque with the white painted houses lit up by the sun shining on the western horizon. The loch, without a ripple on the water, wound its way up into the mountain barrier in the east, over which we had to fly. Five minutes later we could see Ben Wyvis, 3,429 feet high, rearing up in the distance. The Glascarnoch valley stretched below with the mountain streams trickling down like silver threads into the valley river which is now a huge hydro electric reservoir. To complete the picture, the sky was blue with the sunset making striking contrast in light, and the air was so calm that one might just as well have been sitting in an armchair. My passengers and I were entranced. We landed at Inverness after a flight of fifty minutes and it was hard to believe that such a stormy route could have been so blissful and beautiful. All my passengers agreed and commented on a wonderful outing. I have always thought of that trip as the "calm before the storm" as, within two weeks, we were caught up in a blitz, the ferocity of which the world had never experienced before.

The following Wednesday afternoon, I was on my way to Kirkwall operating a duplicate service when, just off the coast at Helmsdale, I received a wireless telegraphy (WT) message over my radio asking if I could make an urgent government charter to London. I told them to wait while I figured the timing out. Within a few minutes, I radioed that I would be available at Longman at four o'clock. I then radioed Kirkwall asking our Traffic Officer to have my passengers ready to step into the plane on arrival. I didn't stop for petrol. I figured I had enough and we were off on the return journey within five minutes.

As soon as we reached Inverness, Dragon, G-ACIT, was refuelled while I was introduced to Captain Sawyer who had come over by road from Poolewe on the west coast. My wife had brought me a small bag for the night and we were off for the south within twenty minutes. I took aboard our radio engineer, Goulden, who could work the WT channel, as I wanted range on the London trip owing to the radio stations being so far apart.

We set course straight for Hatfield, de Havilland's private airfield which housed their factory and excellent club. It was a fine afternoon and the going was easy. We droned on and on for several hours. As we were coming up on Doncaster, it was evident our petrol was not going to carry us through non-stop.

So a hasty landing had to be made and fuel taken aboard. We arrived at Hatfield at nine o'clock at night, five hours after leaving Inverness, as dusk was beginning to fall. We said goodbye to Captain Sawyer who thanked us for a very smart job, and he hurried on to the War Office in London. From the remarks he made on the way down, I gathered the war news was not good and that emergency measures were about to be organised.

I was anxious to make a night flight back to Newcastle-on-Tyne as the weather report for next day was fog, but we had had nothing to eat since breakfast. So I hurried Goulden into the club where we had a good drink to buck us up and then we made a meal out of sausages and biscuits which were placed on the bar as appetisers. I saw the barman looking at me a bit curiously, so I called him over and offered to pay for the food, at the same time explaining my haste and that we had no time to dine. The barman was very nice about it and a good tip left him in good humour.

I hurried Goulden out to G-ACIT, which had been refuelled. He swung the airscrews and we took off as night was gathering, following a compass course for Doncaster. There was a radio station there which we could work and we picked it up as we were approaching Stamford. By that time it was quite dark, but the visibility was good insofar as the lights of the towns were concerned. As we pulled up on Newark-on-Trent, we suddenly began to run over broken fog banks and a radio message from Doncaster confirmed that fog was commencing to form there. We still had thirty-five miles to go, or twenty minutes more flying.

There was no means of knowing how quickly the fog might clamp down, and to be caught up in the sky at night with thick fog at Doncaster could only end in disaster. I told Goulden to obtain weather reports every five minutes and to alert Doncaster for a string of bearings. That meant the sending of bearings every minute or so without calling the station. They brought us in almost dead overhead and I could see the airfield lights through broken fog. We dropped down quickly through a fairly large hole and picked up the landing lights. We hadn't been on the ground an hour when the fog closed down on us like a wet blanket. We went up to the control tower and had a chat with the officer in charge, asking him if he had a late report or forecast for tomorrow's weather. He had, and it was far from encouraging. Somebody with a car kindly took us into Doncaster to the Danum Hotel where we managed to book in.

Next morning, we were down for an eight o'clock breakfast. The forecaster of the night before was quite correct; one could not see thirty yards down the road. We hung around a bit and Goulden found a tobacconist to replenish his tobacco pouch. There was nothing to do, so we hied ourselves out to the airfield. It was situated almost opposite the Doncaster Race Course, which was the scene of an early aviation rally in 1909, when such famous names as Latham, Henry Farman, Blériot, Valentine, Pixton, Cody, Védrines, Hucks, and Weyman took part in the early Blériot, Deperdussin, Antoinette, and Morane monoplanes and Henry Farman and Cody biplanes.

We went up to the control room and had a look at the latest weather reports along our route. It appeared that fog extended all the way up to and beyond Perth and it was not expected to clear that day. We thought we would hang around in case the fog lifted at Doncaster sufficiently for us to take off. All the conversation was channelled into speculation as to whether there would be war.

Hitler was about to attack Poland and we were bound by treaty to go to her defence. But how we were going to do that, nobody, among those who were discussing the situation in that control tower at Doncaster, on Friday 25th August 1939, appeared to know. By eleven o'clock, the fog lifted a bit and one could see a couple of hundred yards. I had no maps, so I obtained the magnetic course from control on Newcastle Airport at Woolsington.

The Inverness weather report came through and it indicated blue sky and visibility fifteen miles, light north-east wind. That was good enough for me. The Met Office gave the fog and upper cloud height as 4,000 feet so I asked Goulden if he was game for a flight above the overcast. He said he was. I obtained clearance and we took off with full tanks. We were scarcely off the ground when we were completely enveloped in fog, so dense that I could scarcely see the wing tips. I trimmed the plane to a medium climb and settled down to concentrate on instrument flying. Up and up we went, two thousand – three – four thousand feet and we were still in the murk. 'Hmm,' I thought, 'the Met Office are a bit out here.' I wondered whether I was committed to cloud flying all the way. We had no auto-pilots, which could take over from the concentrated manual control, in those days. As we approached 5,000 feet, the cloud got lighter and at 5,500 feet we flew out into the clear and into strong sunshine. I flattened out at 7,000 feet so that I could pick up the Newcastle radio station quickly, as the higher one flew, the greater the radio range.

It was a beautiful sight below, just like flying over an enchanted snow field. After some twenty minutes, Goulden managed to contact Woolsington air control and we got a bearing, which showed us a bit to the west of our course. That meant an easterly wind was affecting us at seven thousand feet. I made an allowance for the drift and we carried on until, at the end of an hour's flying, we began to get near Woolsington. The bearings were changing rapidly, which indicated we were approaching from west of the airport. The drift had been more than I had anticipated from the east. After one hour and five minutes flying, we were reported over the station. Perth was the next radio station we had to home on and Goulden obtained the magnetic course to steer from Newcastle control. Near the end of our estimated time of arrival over Perth Airport, I caught a glimpse of the Firth of Forth and the coast, the first sight of land we had so far obtained. It was gone in a moment, but I saw enough to enable me to check our position, which was dead on course. Fifteen minutes later we were over Perth station and we reset course for Inverness. As soon as we had crossed the Grampian Mountains, the whole countryside opened up and visibility was as far as the eye could see. We landed at Longman at one forty-five, having taken two hours and forty-five minutes for the trip.

That was my last long flight during peacetime. We were home for a late lunch and I was glad to be back. It turned out that the fog persisted south for another day or two, so if we had waited for the weather to clear, it would have been a long wait.

Next day an ambulance call was required for Stornoway to take Doctor Leys over to an urgent case. I landed on the new airport for the first time. It was a great thrill in view of the length of my labour in obtaining an airport for Stornoway.

On 29th August, I received another urgent call from a government official at Stornoway who had to catch the afternoon express from Inverness for consultations at the War Office in London. As luck would have it, the Doncaster fog had caught up with us and there was only fifty yards visibility at Longman airport. We had no white line to take off from and the direction was towards the town. I had to use the boundary fence to keep straight as the cloud flying instruments were not engine driven and would not work until we were airborne.

It was difficult trying to keep a straight course looking sideways and I had three goes before I managed to get airborne. I had to climb quickly to clear the town chimneys and I prayed the motors would keep turning. To add to my mixed feelings, I struck a sinker air pocket over the town and we started to lose height. Down and down we went and I got hotter and hotter waiting for the crash. Then, suddenly, I flew into an upward current and we were well on our way. I came out at a thousand feet. Ten miles away, the countryside was clear all the way over to Stornoway. It was not possible to land at Longman on the return journey. I had ascertained that the top of Culloden Moor was clear, so I directed a car to be there to await our arrival on the return flight. I picked up my passenger, Mr Sutherland, on the new airport, my second and last landing on the airport as we constructed it, and I landed at the Culloden field without difficulty.

I only made two more flights that week, on the Thursday and Friday, and they were the last of peacetime flying for six years to come for, on Sunday 3rd September 1939, Mr Chamberlain, the Prime Minister, announced over the radio that we were at war with Germany. So the blow had fallen.

We sat in our drawing room at Mid Kerrogair listening to the radio and the Prime Minister's scathing attack on Germany's bad faith. It was a lovely summer's day, completely swamped by the gravity of the situation. Knowing the antipathy of the Socialists over the past three years to manufacture arms with which to protect ourselves, I considered that we were in great danger for we were wholly unready to fight a war against fully armed Germany.

12

Rapides at war

On Monday 4 September 1939 the Air Ministry ordered the cessation of our air services and withdrew the radio facilities along our routes. Thus, the naval base at Scapa was cut off from rapid communication with the south.

For Scottish Airways, war meant considerable changes including our freedom of action. The closure of our air communications affected the Admiralty badly and we were soon faced with the problem of service personnel turning up for transport to their units, and technicians on their way north for urgent duties in Orkney and Shetland. Urgent signals were despatched to the Air Ministry. In the meantime, I assumed the responsibility of retaining one Rapide aircraft, G-ADAJ, for Admiralty and Scapa communications.

A spate of charter flights occurred, which was tantamount to a regular daily service. It took exactly ten days to solve that 'Gilbertian' situation. It subsequently transpired that the Air Ministry had notified our Renfrew operations office three days after the outbreak of war that the Orkney service should be resumed as early as possible, but without radio facilities. For some reason, which I was unable to discover, that message was not passed on to Inverness, and it was some ten days later that I received direct instructions from Mr Collins, Ministry of Civil Aviation, to resume the Orkney service as soon as possible.

As Scapa Flow was to the Navy, so the airfield we had built at our own expense in Shetland was to the RAF, who immediately requisitioned it, together with our fifty-foot span hangar. A squadron of Gloster Gladiator fighters was sent to Sumburgh to give air cover and to patrol the northern sea approaches from Europe to the Atlantic. For the past three years, we had been exhorting the government to give financial assistance for constructing airfields at Wick and Shetland which would be of urgent and strategic value should war break out and which had rapidly been becoming a distinct possibility.

The air magazine *The Aeroplane*, backed by its well-known editor, C G Grey, joined forces with us in urging the Chamberlain government to act, but no notice was taken of those exhortations. Accordingly, Scottish Airways was forced to proceed on its own in order to provide an air link with Shetland. At considerable expense, it had an airfield constructed, which provided an 800 yard run in a north-south direction and 600 yards east to west.

That airfield was of sufficient dimensions for the operation of Gloster Gladiator fighters. So, owing to commercial enterprise, the Royal Air Force was able to provide immediate air cover to the Northern defence group immediately war broke out. In addition, we had a fifty-foot span hangar built, which was invaluable to the maintenance of the RAF fighters. To my knowledge, no official appreciation was ever extended to the company or myself who located, surveyed, established and financed such facilities that were so valuable to defence in the early and critical stages of the war.

Shortly, more confusion followed for, on 27 May 1940, I received a 'call-up' notice from the RAF to report to Gillingham, Kent, in ten days time under my reserve commitments. I immediately notified the Air Ministry department who were responsible for our operations that I would be leaving Inverness to take up my Reserve RAF duties in ten days. There was a lot to be done in a little time. My house had to be let and a thousand and one things to be sorted out. Over and above all the worry, there was the daily flying to be done owing to a great shortage in flying staff. Also, someone had to be found to take my place and there was none with the first-hand experience and knowledge which I possessed.

On the day before my departure, with luggage packed, sleeper ticket booked and issued and within a few hours of boarding the express train for London, an urgent departmental signal was received, instructing me to remain where I was. In due course, I was informed that I was to remain in Inverness and take charge of the air communications for the north of Scotland on behalf of the Air Ministry. That meant everything had to be unscrambled, including the persuasion of the prospective tenant of our house to cancel his lease, which he was naturally reluctant to do.

Passengers, mail and newspapers for the forces in Orkney and Shetland increased to embarrassing proportions, and we were at our wits end as to how we would carry the loads with the few small aircraft and limited staff that we had at our disposal. In 1940, as I approached my fiftieth birthday, I had perforce to rejoin the regular pilots' roster, which duties I continued to carry out for the duration of the war in addition to the responsibilities for the management and operations of the air routes.

With the advent of winter and deteriorating weather conditions, the absence of radio facilities were bearing hard on our pilots and myself in maintaining the regularity which was called for under war conditions. If the Admiralty did not receive its air mail at Scapa Flow, or couriers were delayed, such a position could have serious results in the conduct of the war effort. Against this apparent stupidity of those responsible for this situation, I was told by a high ranking RAF officer that the Germans flying up the European coastline could be heard using their radio for local operations in plain language. So I wondered why deny such urgent facilities to us? Without radio stations to home on, we were forced to fly at low altitude. I have described in earlier chapters the risks involved in that sort of flying and the danger of collision involved in being forced up into the overcast without the pilot being able to determine his exact position for the descent. A further obstacle was also placed in our way. We were denied the coastline route which we had always followed in the early days before radio stations were provided. That forced us into flying over high ground inland, which made it virtually impossible for us to operate when the cloud base was down to 500 feet, an altitude which was ample for the coastline route. Unless we could get these crippling conditions altered, it was clear to us that we would not be of much use to the war effort as we would be grounded many days of each month. If that happened, the Admiral-in-Charge at Scapa would be mostly affected, so I finally decided, why not present the problem to him?

An appointment was made for the afternoon of 13 October 1939 through his secretary, Lieutenant Commander Laybourne, and I was duly presented to Admiral French on board the *Iron Duke*, Scapa Flow. I found him very sympathetic and helpful. He listened to the problems which I placed before him.

'If we withdraw the restrictions we have placed on your company operating along the coast route when the weather and cloud conditions are down to 500 feet, would that be on any assistance?' he enquired.

'It would indeed, Sir', I answered, 'but we would still be back to 1933 methods of crawling along at low altitude in bad visibility, and it is not an easy or particularly safe approach to Orkney at low altitude. The regularity would still be affected, though in a lesser degree.'

He could not hold out any hope for the resumption of radio navigation, which led me to wonder if the Admiralty were responsible for the impasse, but he did say that he would authorise the coastal route being made available to us under low cloud conditions without further delay. That at least was something gained. Our conversation had been prolonged and it would be dark long before I could get back to Inverness. Night flying was prohibited, besides being very restricted without radio. I was, therefore, obliged to remain the night at Scapa Flow and Lieutenant Commander Laybourne made arrangements for me to stay on the *SS Voltaire* which was used as a guest ship for Admiralty personnel and visitors.

There were a number of interesting naval officers at dinner, and later in the ward room we chatted about the war and other matters well on to midnight. Retiring around midnight, it was not long before I was in a sound sleep. It had been a long day. I was awakened in the very early morning by the sound of numerous feet clanging about on the steel decks and orders being shouted around. This went on for an interminable time and I wondered what the Navy were up to at that unearthly hour. Gradually, the noise subsided and I fell asleep again.

An orderly brought me a cup of tea at eight o'clock.

'Whatever was going on in the early hours?' I enquired. 'The noise was enough to wake the dead!'

He appeared reluctant to answer me.

'Didn't you hear, Orderly?'

'Yes, Sir, I was up helping.'

'Helping? Whatever were you helping, at that unearthly hour?'

He hesitated. 'A terrible thing happened, Sir. The *Royal Oak* was blown up last night in the Flow and there's a heavy death roll. The wounded were brought here and to the hospital ship. It was terrible to see them, Sir', he said. 'Men covered in oil and choking, and others badly hurt by the explosion. I'm not supposed to tell you all this, Sir,' he went on, 'so please don't mention it to anyone here.'

I gave him my word and immediately got up to shave. It was not until after breakfast and when being ferried over to Scapa Pier in a naval launch that I fully realised the horror of what had happened. The sea was covered by a film of black fuel oil. Countless bodies soaked in black oil floated around with the debris and it was clear the death roll had been heavy. What on earth could have been the cause? Nobody appeared to have a clue. It was not until sometime after that we learned that a German U-boat had managed to breach the defences and had plugged at least five torpedoes into the *Royal Oak*, around one thirty in the morning of 14 October 1939, at a cost of 786 officers and men.

Apparently, there was a gap between two 'block ships' at Kirk Sound, which I have referred to earlier in this book, and with great skill the U-boat commander, Kapitänleutnant Günther Prien, steered between the block ships and swirling waters through the narrow gap presented in the dark. It was reported shortly afterwards over German radio by Lord Haw Haw that the crew could see a man on a bicycle going home, they were so close to the shore. For quite a while, no one could guess how the U-boat could have got in and, what was more incredulous, got out and away again. There were rumours that the commander must have followed on the stern of a warship through the boom of one of the larger channels, but that did not explain how the U-boat got out.

Arriving at Scapa Pier, I was soon in the air on my way back to Inverness, stunned by what I had witnessed. Three days later, Scapa had an air raid and the *Iron Duke* on which I had met Admiral French four days previously, was damaged by near misses, causing her to settle on the bottom in shallow water. However, she continued to do her work in that condition throughout the war. A few bombs also fell on South Ronaldsay, blasting holes in farmland.

By the middle of November 1939, the lack of radio navigation assumed an urgency not hitherto appreciated by officialdom in London for, on the 16th, I was detailed to fly a Group Captain Croke to Shetland on an urgent RAF mission. I assumed at the time it was something to do with the limited airfield facilities at Sumburgh Head, for it was obvious that, if the northern approaches were to be fully covered and patrolled, a far larger airfield would be needed than that provided by Scottish Airways.

We landed at Hatston Naval Air Station in Orkney for lunch and continued the journey to Shetland afterwards. A few miles north of North Ronaldsay lighthouse, with fifty-six miles of open sea in front of us and a very narrow landfall at the other end, we ran into a wall of cloud which stretched right down to the sea surface. I had no means of knowing, or finding out, whether these conditions continued all the way to Shetland. It was quite obvious that, if they did, we stood a pretty hopeless chance of finding Sumburgh Head and landing, and perhaps a very good chance of running slap into the vertical cliff face of Fitful Head, which reared up to over 900 feet to the west of our airfield. Accordingly, I returned to the island of North Ronaldsay and landed. My passenger was not at all pleased over the interrupted journey and enquired the reason. I explained the position to him and he was amazed to hear we had been deprived of radio navigation since the outbreak of hostilities.

'I mean to find out who is responsible for this chaotic state of affairs when I return to London', he said. 'Here we have air communications engaged on a most important job in the defence of the north and yet we are denied the means of operating in bad weather.'

And look into it, he apparently did, for within a short time we had the radio stations restored, enabling us to reopen the Shetland route which had remained closed since the commencement of hostilities. We, however, had to use coded messages which slowed us up a bit at first, but we soon got accustomed to it. It was a reasonable price to pay to regain the directional bearings.

Our landing field at North Ronaldsay was situated on the south end of the island and adjacent to the post office and the local store, both of which were operated by Mr James Swanney, who was also our agent. The service to North Ronaldsay had not been restored after the outbreak of war and so they did not see us very often. Mr Swanney soon arrived, enquiring if he could be of assistance. I explained the circumstances and he invited us into his house. We were met by Mrs Swanney who soon produced tea and cookies. While we settled down to this pleasant interlude, Group Captain Croke became interested in what Mr Swanney had to say about the changed life the air service and air mail had brought to the island.

'Just to think, Group Captain', he said, 'we waited over four years for our air mail, which commenced at the beginning of August 1939, only to lose it as soon as the war started a month later. Without our air service to Kirkwall, which we had grown accustomed to for the past four years, and which enabled us to get into Kirkwall in the morning and return at night, we feel completely cut off.'

I sympathised with him deeply, having been so closely associated with the islanders and I knew how much they had lost in amenity by the withdrawal of air communication.

After an hour or so, the weather appeared to improve so we bade farewell to the Swanney family and took off on another attempt to reach Sumburgh. Out to sea, we soon picked the low cloud up again, but in patches this time. After five minutes or so, we flew out into the clear and were able to see Fair Isle looming ahead on the starboard side, looking dark and foreboding in the misty conditions.

I sighed with relief at having run clear of that low cloud, but my relief was short lived for suddenly, to the south of Fair Isle, I spotted a big monoplane a bit higher than we were. I called to the Group Captain and he came forward and took a look. We both agreed it looked like a German Dornier pencil light bomber[1] and we were just mincemeat for him for we carried no armament. Suddenly, the dark looking monoplane turned towards us. Had he spotted us, we wondered? Hoping that he hadn't, I dived quickly for sea level with the intention of flying low for Fair Isle. Our plane was camouflaged and at sea level we stood a chance of reaching the island without being spotted and effecting a landing on the south end until the Dornier had passed on. But that was not to be, for as I commenced to go down, so did the other plane which by now was much nearer and heading towards us. We held our breath for there was little doubt that we had now been observed. The DH Dragon biplane's flying speed was far too slow to even try and keep on the unarmed tail of a Dornier. We had to reach Fair Isle. It was our only chance. I opened the engines flat out, skimming a few feet above the waves. There was just a possibility of reaching the shore before the enemy caught up with us. We had all but reached the rocky coastline when the intruder came within shooting range. 'The bullets will soon start tearing us to pieces now,' I thought, with the perspiration streaming down my cheeks, when suddenly we both exclaimed, 'It's an RAF Anson.' What a relief that was.

The incident showed how extremely moist air could magnify the size of an aircraft flying some miles away, for neither of us had any doubt, when we first saw the Anson, that it was a far larger aircraft. The incident had certainly put the wind up us. Had it been an armed enemy plane, I very much doubt we should have escaped with our lives. The Anson apparently recognised us as a friendly aircraft for it veered off and resumed its southerly course, no doubt to continue his patrol for U-boats.

On arrival at Sumburgh airfield, our manager, Jim Black, met us. I thought he was looking at us curiously.

I said, 'What's wrong?'

'You look a bit shaken, Captain. Was the weather very bad in the south? It has been a shocking day here.'

'Yes, we did run into bad weather north of North Ronaldsay, but after an hour's wait there, it cleared up.'

---

[1] Possibly an aircraft of the Dornier Do 17 series, which were nicknamed 'The Flying Pencil'.

I introduced him to the Group Captain and then told him about our experience with the Anson.

'Come along to the house', he said.

It was a stone cottage situated by the Pool of Virkie and was, I believe, like our agent's house at North Ronaldsay, the local post office which Mrs Black operated. There was a wharf nearby which the local fishing boats used. Apart from that, there did not appear to be much happening that would distinguish one day from another, except maybe a howling storm, which would whip the sea in to a boiling cauldron.

We stayed overnight twenty-five miles away in Lerwick. Our Lerwick agent, Bertie Ganson of Ganson Brothers Limited, sent a car to fetch us and my passenger enjoyed the marvellous view which presented itself along the coastline to Lerwick as the road winds up and down hill and often along sections of road cut out from the hillside.

Next day, we left Sumburgh in time to catch the night express from Inverness for London. Group Captain Croke had heard of the inland route that we had been transferred to west of Hoy, Thurso, Kinbrace, Dornoch and Invergordon. We had flown up the coast route owing to low cloud conditions, so, as the following day was clear, I flew low over the back country behind the Caithness and Sutherland mountains which stretched along the coast from just above Latheron to Dornoch. That run involved the journey around Hoy in Orkney and an excellent view of the Old Man of Hoy was obtained. We flew low across the moors south of Thurso, and the 500 foot plateau beyond Kinbrace could be seen as we were passing Achintoul Lodge which Mr George Law occupied in the early days of the war, and which I have referred to in an earlier chapter.

That route was an excellent one for safety as the war hotted up and Hun aircraft became more numerous. Our aeroplanes were camouflaged peat and green colour and the top wings merged with the peat and heather surroundings. Looking down from a height, it was very difficult for enemy aircraft to spot us. On many occasions shortly after having left for Inverness, I received a radio message from Orkney to return there as enemy aircraft were in the vicinity. If I was over half way across the Pentland Firth, I pretended I hadn't received the message as I knew I was safer over those moors than risking the return Pentland Firth crossing which would show up my plane clearly to the enemy.

There was a small cottage at the bottom of the escarpment some miles south of Kinbrace. It was miles from anywhere and I always used to fly low over that cottage on the northbound run and give the good lady who lived there a wave. She would come rushing out of the back door to respond. Sometimes I used to drop a morning newspaper to her. I felt sorry for her living in such uninhabited and lonely surroundings and hoped my morning aerial salutations brought her a little relief from boredom.

We were nearly into December and the so-called phoney war dragged on while the Nazis finished off Poland. We brought the New Year in with misgiving. Poland could not hold out much longer and, it was said, we were not strong enough or properly equipped to make a diversion in Poland's favour along the Maginot Line. So we waited for the Nazis to make the first move.

In the meantime, Hatston airfield had been mostly completed and a fine air station it was. It was commanded by a very nice officer named Commander Howe. He was aware that I had a hand in the siting and construction of the Hatston Naval Air Station and he was also aware of how inadequate our landing field at Wideford had become with the enormous loads we were having to cope with under wartime conditions. He accordingly kindly gave us permission to use Hatston airfield providing we conformed to Naval movements taking priority. I gladly gave that assurance and what a difference a full-sized airfield made to our operations and to the peace of mind of our pilots.

After seven years' use of the Wideford airfield, we were obliged to face up to the fact that its usefulness had become inadequate for modern needs. We, and the public, owed Wideford and its generous owner, Mr Anderson, a great debt of gratitude for it had served its purpose in establishing the passenger and airmail service to the Orkneys. It had also served in developing the aircraft loads from a trickle in the beginning to the 'rushing stream' which was now on the point of flooding its banks. So, it was with many pangs of regret that I advised Scottish Airways to discontinue the lease of that airfield as soon as the new RAF aerodrome at Grimsetter nearby was constructed the following year.

On landing with the mail plane at Hatston towards the end of the first week in January, a Naval Petty Officer was there to meet me as I descended from the aeroplane. He informed me that Commander Howe wished to se me in his office. He greeted me with 'Hello, Captain Fresson, I've got a job for you to do.' He had with him a high ranking Naval Officer to whom I was introduced. His name was Admiral Somerville. He was of medium height with a typical sea-faring look and he possessed a charming personality.

'The Admiral wishes you to fly him up to Fair Isle. We hear you have made several landings there and, as Admiral Somerville's visit is urgent and of great importance to the war effort, will you take the job on? Our pilots have flown up to Fair Isle and say there is no place they could land, so we are depending on you!'

'I'll be very pleased to take the flight on, but it will be necessary to wait until the wind conditions are right.'

The small landing area available on Fair Isle was exceedingly tricky and dangerous unless conditions were exactly right.

'I will contact you the first moment weather conditions are satisfactory', I said to him.

It was left at that and, a few days later, on Tuesday 10th January, I phoned Hatston from Inverness to say that the Inverness Meteorological Office had informed me that we might expect slight easterly winds in the Fair Isle region and, as that was satisfactory, would they let me know when I arrived at Hatston on the normal service if Admiral Somerville would be available.

On my arrival at Hatston airfield, there was the Admiral with Commander Howe waiting for me. Having ascertained how long the visit on the island would take, I arranged with my traffic officer to have the southbound passengers delayed until three thirty in the afternoon. Arriving over the Fair Isle, I circled the landing place at 1,000 feet. Admiral Somerville was sitting just behind me and, when I pointed out the landing ground, he exclaimed like others had done, 'Surely it's not possible to land there?' He had observed that the ground was encircled for three parts of the perimeter by cliffs and that there was a nasty drop into the sea if we overshot. I assured him I would not take unnecessary risks and, if the approach looked risky, we would return to base. I was flying the trusted Dragon aircraft, G-ACIT, and I could land that plane on a pocket handkerchief.

As we dropped lower, I observed to my dismay that the wind was fairly strong and not in the right direction, coming too much from the north. Fortunately, the neck of ground connecting the landing area to the rest of the island was in the north. I therefore decided to land on one wheel and turn in a slight circle as we touched down, so that, when the second wheel was on the ground, we would be heading for the narrow neck into wind. This way we made a good landing. However, I confess that the strong cross-wind take-off worried me, also the backing wind, as that meant the approach of a depression and probably bad visibility for the return journey. I kept all that to myself and accompanied Admiral Somerville on his search of the island. An introduction was made to Mr Stout, the island's chieftain, and to the lighthouse keeper whose name I believe was Ingram and whom I met on my first survey of the island by steamer some years back. It appeared that the admiral was looking for a suitable site for the navy to construct a radar scanner and we were all sworn to secrecy. We were taken to the top of a hill in the centre of the island and, on the way up, I discovered a site that had good possibilities of being constructed into a landing strip. It headed north-east by south-west and was just right for prevalent winds. We hadn't been out an hour when it began to rain. My foreboding about the depression appeared correct. We had landed at 11.30 am and it was nigh on one o'clock before we got back to the village on the south end of the island. The admiral had found a suitable site for his radar scanner.

We were invited to one of the houses for lunch, and a wonderful lunch it was. Soup, chicken, canned peaches and local cream. Our hostess had gleaming ginger hair and Admiral Somerville teased that poor woman until she was blushing furiously. At the end of lunch, we were presented with Fair Isle hosiery gifts and, by the time we were ready to take off at 3.00 pm, I felt like having a good afternoon siesta.

During lunch, the weather had deteriorated badly. We said goodbye to our very hospitable friends and clambered aboard. There was no doubt in my mind that the admiral had thoroughly enjoyed his impromptu outing when he was able to drop the mask of officialdom and rank. We made a cross-wind take-off and rose in half the distance available. Passing over the sheer cliff edge, the air was very turbulent as we commenced a climbing turn on a south westerly course.

It was raining heavily and the visibility was down to a mile or so. I hated that stretch of lonely water to North Ronaldsay without radio bearings to help me. It was so easy to fly past the north end and miss the Orkney Isles, and we had not too much petrol to go looking for them. The tanks had been kept purposely low so as to facilitate a quick take-off under such restricted conditions. As usual, when the visibility was back over the sea, I borrowed Francis Chichester's technique, which he employed on his famous island hopping from New Zealand to Australia, by steering a deliberate error to one side of the target and, after a calculated elapsed time, I steered at right angles to the course.[2]

In this particular case, it meant steering ten degrees south of the true course which, if continued, would take me to the left of my target of the Orkney Isles.

---

[2] In 1929 Francis Chichester flew from Croydon to Sydney in a Gypsy Moth, becoming the second aviator to make such a journey solo. In 1931 he made the first east-west solo crossing of the Tasman Sea. He gained later fame as a long-distance and round-the-world yachtsman. He was knighted in 1967.

I calculated the point of turn-off so that, after half an hours flying, it would be roughly abreast the island of Stronsay and to the east of it. By such means, one would avoid missing the northern tip of North Ronaldsay and getting lost over the ocean.

It was an eerie and lonely feeling groping one's way across the sea, low down and hemmed in by mist with no shipping around. Every way seemed the same way and one had to stick rigidly to the planned flight and to the compass course set. At the end of the half hour after being airborne, we turned west and within five minutes picked up the island of Stronsay. Within fifteen minutes, we had landed at Hatston airfield. Admiral Somerville thanked me for carrying out a difficult job for him and bade me farewell. I was never to meet him again as shortly afterwards he was transferred to the Mediterranean. I was sorry as he had been such good fun. I then picked up my waiting south bound passengers and delivered them to Inverness in good time for the afternoon express.

During breakfast at our house at Dalcross, near Ardersier, shortly before hostilities commenced, there came a knock at the front door. I answered the door and found two individuals who, after greeting me, said they were from the Air Ministry and wished to know if I could advise them where to find a likely site for an Air Ministry RAF airfield near Inverness. They said they had been advised to call on me. It had so happened that, for some months, we had come to the conclusion that our airfield at Longman had become obsolete with the heavy increase in traffic and aircraft loads and a thorough search of the district had been made for a new site. Longman would have cost too much to extend as it involved buying up and closing down two farms. I had chosen ground which my present house occupied, but the land belonged to the Earl of Moray and was heavily invested in farming. The question was, should I disclose the Dalcross site? The farmer wanted to get me out of my house as the lease was up, so it occurred to me that it might be possible to make a deal with these people so that, if they took over the land, we might retain our house.

So I said to them, 'We have the very place for you, capable of indefinite expansion. If I disclose it, would the Ministry consider my interests in the matter?'

They said they were unable to answer that question, but would make enquiries and call back and see me.

They returned within a few days and said the Ministry were prepared to do all they could to preserve any reasonable interests if it was within their jurisdiction. My mistake was that I did not get it in writing. Accepting their word, as we were also keen on getting a full size airfield for Inverness, I said to them, 'Gentlemen, you are standing on the very place.'

'What, here!' they exclaimed in surprise.

'Yes, come and look.' I took them into the fields in front of the house and pointed as far as they could see to the east and west and certainly a mile to the south.

'The ground is undulating in places and there are woods here and there, but that is no difficulty for modern machinery. One thing, however,' I warned as a parting shot, 'you will require tarmac runways because the ground will become very boggy in winter. The drainage fall is very slight.'

Off they went and we saw them marching over the fields for several days before they returned and said, 'Thank you, Captain. This is the place and you have saved us many weary days of search.'

'Good. Now tell the Air Ministry, my interests are twofold. I wish to retain the lease of this house and we would like the rights for Scottish Airways to use the airfield on terms to be arranged suitable to both sides.'

They promised to hand this information on and, later, other and more senior officials came to see me and said, as far as they could see, there would be no objection to my retaining the house on lease and, as for using the airfield, they felt sure that in peace-time an arrangement could be made with the Ministry.

Towards the end of 1939, we heard the land had been requisitioned and that work would commence on construction shortly. It was after my arrival back from Admiral Somerville's Fair Isle trip that we woke up one morning to the sound of tractors and terrific thumps on the ground. Looking out of the window to see what was going on, there was a tractor with chains pulling all our beautiful sycamore trees down and tearing up our hundred years-old lawn. I rushed down in my dressing gown and got hold of the foreman and asked him to stop such senseless destruction, until I could get a message through to Air Ministry in London.

'The garden', I told him, 'does not come within the area required for airfield purposes and, at any rate, this house is for my use.'

'Sorry, Captain', he said, 'I am only carrying out my instructions.'

However, he gave me until lunch time to try and get an official ruling form the Air Ministry.

The phone wires buzzed that morning, but to no purpose. The area of my house, I was told, was to be used for the erection of hangars.

'But', I answered, 'the arrangement with your representatives who called to see me six months ago was that my interests would be covered.'

'Sorry', they said, 'we have a war on our hands, and Dalcross is a first priority airfield.'

So that was that. Not only did I lose the trees, but I lost the house and had to be out by the end of April. Every morning, for the next few days, we awoke to the crunch of falling trees and, by the end of the week, our beautiful garden was no more. I had then to get busy to find another house and that came about in a most fortuitous manner.

Early in 1940, an official request came through for a charter from Stornoway to Inverness. It was a blind take-off in fog from Longman with no hope of landing there on the return. I made sure that our emergency field at Culloden Moor was fog-free and took off using the boundary fence to keep the plane in a straight line. There were no white lines on Longman airfield to assist fog take-offs. On the return journey, we landed high up on the moors not far from the old battlefield. Alongside the Culloden Moor landing field there was a house and petrol pumps belonging to one of the most worthy citizens of Inverness, Willie Michie.

He was a first rate humorist and, in his job as chief auctioneer for Fraser's Auction Rooms, he would keep the bargain hunters in stitches of laughter by his witty remarks during the sales. Along with his charming wit, he was an excellent connoisseur of a good dram. On descending from the plane, one of my distinguished passengers confided he had a bottle of a 'first class Scotch Blend' and, as we had a wait before our road transport would arrive, he suggested breaking the bottle.

'We haven't any water or glasses', he said. 'Can you take it neat?'

'Oh, that's easily remedied. Come along to the house by the petrol pumps and I am sure Willie will fix us up and enjoy a dram himself.'

On knocking at the door, Mrs Michie answered, and said her husband was out. Could she be of help? I told her we had just arrived from Stornoway and, as our car had not arrived, might we use the phone. Also, could we have a few glasses and some water? She acquiesced and showed us into her sitting room and, while I was phoning, Mrs Michie went to see about the water and glasses. On rejoining my three passengers, the chappie with the bottle was looking glum.

'She's brought each of us a tumbler of water', he complained, 'and there is no room for the whisky.'

'Oh dear, that's sad. I must get that sorted out.'

Ringing the bell, Mrs Michie returned looking quizzical. Explaining our difficulty, she blushed with embarrassment.

'I'm so sorry', she said. 'I didn't know you had a bottle with you. I will get a jug immediately.'

She came back with a half full jug and we were able to pour the water in the tumblers, back in to the jug.

That whisky really tasted good. It was an excellent brand, but coupled with the tricky flight and the cold dank air outside, it was a great booster. Shortly after, Willie returned. On introducing him to my companions, the owner of the bottle invited him to join us in a 'hootie'. As the warm liquid disappeared down Willie's throat, he confided to us that his wife had told him of the embarrassment she had caused us and he added, 'Just to think that such a thing could happen in 'ma hoose'.'

We talked on for a bit while waiting for the car when Willie asked me if I was still living at Dalcross.

'Yes, but not for long now. The Air Ministry are turning us out and I've got to find another in double quick time.'

'Would you wish to buy one?' he enquired.

'Yes, at the right price.'

'Well, you go and see Mrs Gordon Cumming at 12 Mayfield Road. I hear she is thinking of selling her bungalow. It is a very nice one with a good garden and garage.'

Just then, our car arrived and we bade the Michies farewell. I promised to get in touch with Mrs Cumming at once.

The next day we went around to see her. Yes, she was willing to sell if she could get her figure. I asked what she wanted and she told me. My solicitor friend, Harold Georgeson of Wick, got busy with the negotiations and within a month the house was ours. We moved in early April. It was with great regret we left our very nice residence in the country. However, it was really for the best, as the war soon started to hot up and it was far more convenient for me to be in town than nine miles away, especially in times of emergency or when VIPs were coming and going, and also with emergency charter flights cropping up at any odd moment.

My next important passenger was Mr Clement Attlee. He flew north with me to Orkney on 30th March 1940. I well remember the trip. He sat in the front seat of the cabin just behind me and, on one or two occasions, I tried to engage him in conversation on the way to the Pentland Firth. The windows of all passenger aircraft, under war time regulations, were blinded by camouflage and only the cockpit windows were clear. The passenger in the front seat could look out by bending well forward and I thought Mr Attlee might be interested to see the mountains we were passing over. He appeared to look very white and tired.

Passing over the southern shoreline of the Pentland Firth, on our way to the west end of Hoy, a large battle cruiser appeared ahead, dead on our track. Standing naval orders said 'Aircraft were not to fly directly over warships' so I commenced to veer off course to the east. Suddenly, signal lights commenced blinking away frantically on the cruiser. I had no signalling light installed on my aircraft to reply with, even if I had understood the flashes, which I didn't. We had nearly got abreast of the cruiser when she suddenly started shooting us up with her anti-aircraft guns. Suddenly, we were surrounded with white bursts which rocked the Rapide aircraft severely. I called to Mr Attlee and told him we were being fired on and to hold on tight as I was about to put the plane into a steep dive. He quickly leaned forward quickly and took a look as I pushed the nose of our aircraft down. We were flying, my logbook tells me, at 2,000 feet. We came out of the dive at a few hundred feet over the sea. By that time the firing had ceased and we scuttled low down around the Old Man of Hoy and into safety. Mr Attlee looked whiter than ever and became a little unbending, engaging me in conversation about the shooting.

On landing, I reported the incident to the commander at Hatston, who promptly got busy to find out the ship responsible. There was quite a flap on in view of the importance of our VIP. I learned later it was an Australian cruiser which had opened up on us because we had not answered their signals. All the same, their aircraft recognition should have been better than it apparently was because a DH Rapide biplane was unlike any of either our, or our enemy's, war aircraft of that period. However, they didn't hit us, which showed up their aerial gunnery and there the matter ended as far as we were concerned. I accepted it along with the many other risks our pilots and myself took operating in war-time air communications.

The weather in April was particularly bad. In fact, the weather had been continuously bad all the winter. Snowstorms were prolonged with heavy gales. That winter without radio was particularly hard on all pilots and, as I look back on the effort made through all the continuous nervous strain imposed on the air crews, the highest praise is due to the pilots concerned, John Hankins, Henry Vallance and Bernard Wilson.

30 April was another eventful day for myself. The Orkney Isles and the Pentland Firth were covered in low cloud and drizzle. I was returning from Orkney with a full load of passengers, flying low over the water around Hoy with visibility of around a mile. Suddenly, we ran into a clear patch and found ourselves bang in front of two warships carrying out target practice and, to make matters more alarming, we were between the warships and the target. No notice had been given to our operations room of this hazard. I took quick action. The only chance of dodging those shells was to drop down to sea level which we did pretty quickly. We flew along almost touching the wave tops with the shells passing overhead until we were well clear of the warships.

The war took an important change early in April for the Germans attacked Norway and sent a landing force to Narvik in the far north to protect it, that port being of supreme importance to the Germans as it controlled the shipment of iron ore supplies which came from the hinterland mines near the Swedish border. Trondheim was also overrun. The attack was very sudden and at the time was described as the 'Rape of Norway', a country which had for many years been on the best of terms with Germany.

At that time, I flew to Shetland a party of important Norwegians who would make their way across to Norway by sea and effect a secret landing. I surmised those VIPs were charged with the formation of the Norwegian patriots and underground. As time went on, we were to play an important part in flying members of the 'underground' to and from Shetland RAF base which would attend to their transportation to and from secret landing and embarkation spots along the rocky Norwegian coastline. We used to get quite familiar with the couriers' faces and then one day we would not see a particular face any more. It was not hard to guess what had happened. They were extremely brave people whom we all learnt to admire and respect in their dangerous work.

On 10th May 1940 sparks really began to fly. The war was now rapidly shifting westwards for Holland and Belgium were attacked by the German armed forces. There was a terrific stir in this country and all our aircraft, except Dragon, G-ACIT, were mobilised and despatched to France to assist at the evacuation of Dunkirk. Later, the operation was considered too dangerous for unarmed and slow types of aircraft such as our Rapides and on 2nd June they were returned to base.

We had a fortnight's respite when our aircraft were again commandeered, this time to assist in the evacuation of France. I was left with Dragon G-ACIT in Inverness to carry the Scapa Flow passengers, mail and documents, not forgetting the couriers.

On 16 June, 1940, G-AFOI left Heston for Bordeaux with a Ministry of Supply party who would endeavour to obtain a large quantity of industrial diamonds before France was overrun. On arrival at Bordeaux, our pilot, Captain Prentice, in view of the imminent approach of German forces, arranged a deadline for their departure the following day. The following morning, the defeatism prevalent in the French Officers' Mess, caused mainly by conflicting radio broadcasts in French and German, did not contribute to their ease of mind. Incidentally, the Rapide crew of three slept in the aircraft cabin overnight – with the radio operator's socks drying on the fixed aerial! At noon, the Ministry of Supply party arrived and they took off for the open sea following the River Gironde. Their fuel margin to reach England was very small. Pilots of varying nationalities, with aircraft of varying degrees of age and air worthiness, had 'nobbled' all available fuel and some had pranged on the runway.

Approaching Biscay, Captain Prentice concerned himself with petrol and decided that they must refuel at Nantes or face the possibility of ditching in the Channel. Approaching Nantes, the pilot did a few circuits, but no German movements were observed. The aerodrome was deserted. They helped themselves to fuel and took off over the sea to England. Engine trouble developed and eventually, flying on one engine, Captain Prentice diverted to Jersey. A Jersey Airways DH86 was discovered in a hangar where it had been in for Certificate of Airworthiness. No Jersey Airways staff were available, so the crew 'borrowed' one of the engines. John Rawse, the engineer, did a marvellous piece of work. The following morning, there was great enjoyment when the 'borrowed' engine was run up. By this time, the Ministry of Supply team had deserted the sinking ship. The Rapide crew then got involved in the evacuation

of Jersey and, loading a party of varying nationalities, set off for Exeter where they arrived safely. It was a great piece of work by the pilot, engineer and radio officer, as an engine change was a major operation, more especially as the DH86 engine installation was different to that of the Rapide.

As I have already said, between 1935 and 1939 we had constantly advocated airfield-building in the north of Scotland as a necessary defence project. We pressed the Government unsuccessfully to show their interest through giving financial support, which now became a mad rush in wartime and at double the cost. Wick airfield had just been completed with a turf surface, as was the normal practice of construction in pre-war days. As soon as winter set in, it rapidly became a quagmire and became unserviceable. We had been accustomed to such conditions for years while using smaller types of aircraft, but for the RAF, with larger and heavily loaded aircraft, they just could not leave the ground in the winter when the turf was waterlogged. A hurried scramble ensued to construct hard tarmac strips. We, however, were constantly taking off and landing in a sea of mud alongside the hundreds of Irish labourers and machinery engaged in the construction of the air strips. One would have thought that even officialdom would have learnt its lesson from Wick and proceed to construct hard tarmac strips at Dalcross, especially after my warning. With ostrich-like habits, the Air Ministry failed to apply the lesson or pay any heed to my earlier advice, and Dalcross was opened with the customary grass surface. The RAF moved in and, within two months or so, history repeated itself. Most of their aircraft stuck in the mud, just the same as happened at Wick, for it rained and rained during that winter of 1940. We continued to operate from Longman, which fortunately had a hard gravel subsoil.

During these troubled times for the RAF, the Hatston airfield, with its hard tarmac air strips, was functioning daily without the slightest difficulty. I believe a deputation from the RAF again visited the Naval Station of Hatston and left duly impressed, for shortly after, tarmac strips became standard in RAF airfield construction. With the advent of the multi-engined bombers, which would carry extremely heavy loads of bombs, aircraft were becoming larger. A hard and smooth surface for take-off and landing was therefore essential. It was then that the old fashioned grass aerodrome ceased to exist.

After Dalcross airfield was modified to hard runways, Sumburgh airfield, situated at the southernmost tip of Shetland, remained the only grass airfield in the north of Scotland. Once its role in the war effort was decided upon by the early part of 1941, reconstruction commenced. It was a difficult airfield to reconstruct as its level area was very limited. Consequently, it amounted to a major engineering job and costly alterations had to be made to the surrounding countryside. On the north side, the Pool of Virkie, which was a tidal basin, had to be filled in to a great extent and a large number of high dunes had to be levelled. To the south lay the beach alongside the North Sea, and to the east was Sumburgh Head, rising to some 300 feet with a lighthouse on the top of it. To the west some four miles away lay Fitful Head, towering to over 900 feet with the ground sloping up gently from the airfield. So to construct the north-east/south-west strip, a cutting of 200 feet in width and some forty feet deep had to be made through the sloping ground to the sea coast at the southern end of the site.

The construction, if I remember correctly, took over a year to complete, but when finished it was a fine airfield for post-war Shetland. It could never have come into existence had it not been for the war, for the cost of construction was enormous. Had it been carried out before the war, when I was urging the Government to build airfields, it would have cost a third of what it did under wartime conditions with highly paid Irish labour. With the completion of Sumburgh airfield, we were assured a chain of modern post-war airfields to operate from.

During the recent invasion of Holland, Belgium and France, the Germans used aircraft extensively for dropping saboteurs in the rear of the Allies and they landed Junkers aircraft in fields with troops aboard. To make sure this did not happen in the north of Scotland and the Western Isles, so they thought, the authorities erected poles along the roads, on the beaches and in fields near the towns so as to prevent such landings. Actually, if the enemy had wished to carry out landing operations, they could have crashed landed their aircraft without injury to the air crew or troops aboard, or for that matter, they could have dropped the troops by parachute. I suspect, therefore, that the immense amount of work employed on this stunt was more for psychological reasons vis-à-vis the local population. Even the road across Rannoch Moor, which was too narrow for aircraft to land on, received its share of many miles of poles at extravagant cost. However, be that as it may, I received a call to fly a party of surveyors over to the Western Isles with a view to organising the immobilisation of the beaches along the western sides of Barra, South and North Uist.

We set off on 27th July 1940 to carry out this work. The sun was shining, which made the trip not only pleasant, but enabled us to make quick progress with the survey. A local architect, Mr Hamish Paterson, who was a member of the Royal Engineers, was in charge of the survey party and I, of course, knew him quite well. Commencing at the island of Barra, we spent the day flying up miles of hard sandy beaches. The area was vast and it was soon obvious that the project was absolutely impractical. It would have taken a small army many years, and half the forest trees in Scotland, to complete the job. We landed at our rough landing field at Sollas that evening and went into Lochmaddy to stay the night at the local hotel. We planned to finish the survey of Harris and Lewis next day and fly straight back from Stornoway to Inverness.

It was not to be, however, for next morning, when we awakened, the island was covered with thick fog. We had no radio officer with us, which would have enabled us to climb above the fog and make the direct flight back to Inverness. Radio communication had been restored a week or two before, but all messages had to be sent in code. Otherwise, I could have operated the radio myself and obtained my own bearings. Therefore, we were stranded in Lochmaddy with nothing to do but play billiards and walk around the village. That night we had a real big party with the locals, the fog swirling around outside. We retired to bed, hoping the morning would break clear. Not so, however. If anything, it was even thicker than the day before. We could not see twenty yards ahead. To make matters worse, our host informed us that the whisky stocks were running low. With the war on, he said to me, he didn't expect such a big demand on his resources without notice.

'Hasn't the local store got a case left?' we enquired.

'No', he said. 'I had that off him yesterday.'

Our hearts sank. What was there to do in fog-ridden Lochmaddy, without a dram to keep one going in the evening, my passenger bemoaned.

'Let's go out to the landing strip', I suggested, 'and ask the radio superintendent to despatch a message to Renfrew to send a radio officer up on the Renfrew to Sollas scheduled service. Around midday the fog will likely lift a hundred feet or so, thus allowing the service plane to get in on radio bearings.'

Out we went in the local taxi. Sure enough, on the west side of the island the fog was up quite a bit and one could see possible breaks with the sun trying to get through. Our message went off and a reply soon came through that Jimmy Mitchell, our chief radio officer who had been on the Jersey forced landing, was coming up to assist us. The plane got down quite well with about a mile of visibility and we greeted Jimmy Mitchell as a long lost brother.

We got our plane started and took off. Climbing on an easterly course, we were swallowed up in fog within a few seconds. One thousand feet and we were still in it. At fifteen hundred feet, the sky got lighter and at 2,000 feet, we broke out into blue sky and sunshine. It was a beautiful sight with the white cloud carpet below us and deep blue sky above. After twenty minutes or so, we caught a glimpse of the island of Raasay through a hole in the fog. That meant we were just east of Skye and ahead, covered in cloud, were the Easter Ross mountains which rose to three or four thousand feet. We were flying at six thousand feet which was high enough for safety, so I carried on through cloud. The radio officer at Sollas had obtained a weather report for us giving an overcast sky at Inverness but good visibility. At an estimated position half way across the mountains, I asked Jimmy Mitchell to get me a bearing on Inverness airfield.

He started to tap away on his key. I waited and still the tapping went on. After five minutes or so, I called back, 'What about the bearing, Jimmy?'

'I can't get one', he replied.

'Why not?'

'Inverness have asked me for the code word for the day, and they say the one I have is incorrect so they won't give a bearing.'

'What in the hell has happened?' I queried. 'Didn't you get the code word when you left Renfrew?'

'Yes, but they must have given me the wrong one.'

'Have another go,' I said. 'Tell them the name of the pilot and say we are caught up in cloud over the mountains and must have a bearing.'

After a while he called to me. 'Inverness say they cannot break regulations. No proper code word, no bearing.'

'Damn', I said to myself. What a muddle. Here I was, caught up in cloud and doing the very thing that I refused to do yesterday without the help of radio. While this conversation was going on, we were being thrown about quite a bit and it took me all my time to keep the plane under proper control by instruments. It was therefore difficult to consider our position calmly.

After a couple of minutes intermittent thinking while trying to concentrate on the instruments, I figured the sensible thing to do would be to alter course to the north-east to make sure of descending over the Moray Firth at the end of the calculated elapsed time of the flight. By this time, at least a quarter of an hour had passed since Jimmy told me he couldn't get a bearing on Inverness when, without warning, we suddenly flew out of cloud and there, in front of us, was the Beauly Firth. We were dead on course. That was a lucky break. In another quarter of an hour we landed at Longman airport, home safely, and none the worse for an extremely bad error that had been made by the officer in charge at Renfrew. He had apparently given us the code word for the following day. The beaches on the west coast were never immobilised.

Two weeks later, the air battle of Britain was at its peak. In the midst of it we had a distinguished visitor, Sir Alan Brooke. In July, the Secretary of State for War recommended that General Brooke should replace General William Ironside in command of Home Forces. He was now on a tour of inspection. He had with him several members of his staff and I was instructed to fly him to Wick, and to Castletown where there was only a small field to effect a landing. On completion of his inspection, we returned to Evanton RAF airfield on the Cromarty Firth, and eventually to Inverness where they caught the express train back to London. Sir Alan thanked me for the speedy manner in which I had enabled him to carry out his northern survey in one day, which would have taken three days by surface transport. My memory of the occasion is taken up with the interest Sir Alan Brooke took in our operation, for he had heard that we flew the communications on days when the Fleet Air Arm and RAF were grounded. He had great charm and I took an instant liking to him.

With the fall of France, the air battle for Britain was stepped up and by 13th September the decisive battle in the air was fought. London was being savagely attacked, but in the north of Scotland we were more or less free from enemy intrusion. One night during that period, we were awakened by air raid sirens, but nothing appeared to happen and we went to sleep again. Next day, we were told that the aluminium works at Foyers had received a visit from the Luftwaffe and had been hit. But according to reports, not much damage was done.

After September, we began to get the occasional raider sneaking along our routes and Wick airfield was attacked. I remember landing there in the autumn of 1940 and seeing a Heinkel bomber, apparently intact, on the Wick airfield. I was invited to see the Heinkel and it was in a fearful mess. The gunner was riddled with our fighter bullets and slumped in the cockpit dead, and the rest of the crew were wounded. The plane was covered in blood. There had been several of them, but they were intercepted by our fighters out at sea.

An alarming incident occurred shortly afterwards. Captain Vallance had left Inverness in a Rapide with a full passenger load for Orkney. The weather was bad with low cloud lying over the firth, north of Cromarty, and which extended up to roughly one thousand feet. Above, the visibility was clear. Henry Vallance, flying above the cloud, had reached the vicinity of Tarbatt Ness, some thirty miles north of Inverness, on course for Kirkwall by the coastal 'bad weather' route. He happened to glance down to his left at the swirling mist below him when, suddenly, he stiffened in his seat. Without warning, a Heinkel bomber suddenly appeared, climbing out of the cloud below. What was he to do? The

Rapide was unarmed and, even had it been otherwise, the speed and climb of our aircraft could in no way match the German raider. It was not long before the Heinkel pilot spotted the Rapide and commenced a climbing turn to give Henry the 'once over' and, probably, a burst of machine gun fire, which would soon have finished of him, his seven passengers and his radio officer. Fortunately, as Henry told me afterwards, he remembered that the Heinkel had no rear machine gunner and so, if he could keep on the Heinkel's tail and send radio SOS signals, a fighter might arrive in time to chase the enemy off.

The enemy was still five hundred feet below the Rapide and Henry acted at once. He dived at the enemy's tail and positioned himself well to the rear and slightly below the Heinkel which was still climbing. As he commenced to dive, Henry shouted to his radio operator (I have forgotten his name) to send out an SOS call to Inverness advising he was being attacked by an enemy plane and to send word to Dalcross airfield for help. During the ensuing five minutes, Henry was having all his time cut out keeping on the Heinkel's tail owing to the higher speed and climb of the enemy. All this time, SOS messages were flowing like a stream from the Rapide's transmitter when, suddenly, for no apparent reason, the Heinkel veered out to sea and made off.[3]

Henry promptly returned to Inverness. Poor chap, his face was as white as a sheet and he was in no fit state to continue the service at that moment. The passengers were unloaded and, as they had been unable to see what was going on owing to the blackened out windows in the aircraft, were inquisitive to know why they had returned to Inverness. When told of their narrow escape, their faces were a study. After a rest of half an hour, Henry set off again for Orkney and duly reached Kirkwall safely with his passengers. By that time, several of our fighters had been alerted and were flying around the area.

On Sunday 13th October 1940, we were requested by the Air Ministry to send a plane over to Lossiemouth Naval Air Station to transport the Duke of Gloucester and four of his staff to Wick, and then return to Lossiemouth with a stop at Evanton. Departure time from Lossiemouth was fixed at 10.00 am and, although I had been flying on the regular services every day of the preceding week, as a director of the company I volunteered to give up my Sunday and take the flight.

On arrival at the naval station, I was taken to the commanding officer who presented me to the Duke and his staff of officers. The route we were about to follow was much the same as General Brooke had taken two months earlier, except that the point of departure and return was different, and I was not expected to fly on to Castletown as that journey was to be made by road. We took off at precisely ten o'clock in brilliant sunshine on a direct course for Wick

---

[3] In *A Flying Start to the Day*, (Godalming, 1986) and *Wings over the Glens*, (Peterborough, 1995) Peter Clegg notes that the German aircraft was not a Heinkel He111, but a Junkers Ju88.

over the Moray Firth. It was very hazy, but we got above the haze at 3,000 feet. After a while, the coast of Sutherland and Caithness came into view and I well remember it presented a beautiful sight with the sparkling sunshine lighting up the mountains and the deep blue sea leading to their threshold. I called His Royal Highness's attention to this scenic splendour and he got a good view by looking out of the cockpit window on the port side.

Wick was reached at 10.35 am and the military were out to receive my distinguished visitors. I was requested to wait through the day while the party

went off in staff cars to carry out their inspection. The time of departure for the south was said to be at 1600 hours, so I went off to Colonel Robertson's house, which was within an easy walk of the airfield, and spent the day with them. Colonel Robertson, having been in the army during World War One, was most interested to learn who my passengers were. Mrs Robertson and her two daughters were likewise interested in the flight and we sat and talked until lunchtime. The fare in Colonel and Mrs Robertson's house was always of the best and that luncheon was no exception. Suffice to say, I enjoyed a short rest afterwards, preparatory to continuing my journey.

Sharp on four, the plane was all ready for take-off, but my passengers had not arrived. It was close on 1700 hours before we were ready to leave for Evanton. We flew down the Caithness coastline and, when we picked up the Helmsdale valley running up to Kinbrace, the Duke of Gloucester showed interest as he told me he had frequently stayed at a lodge which we could just observe, during the pre-war shooting seasons. He wistfully said to me that it would be a long time before he would be able to visit that lodge again.

We spent an hour at Evanton. I was entertained in the mess while HRH and his staff were closeted with the senior station officers. We left late in the evening. Dusk was falling and, by the time we reached Lossiemouth, it was nearly dark and the ground flares were out to assist me with the landing.

I had to return to Inverness and, after being thanked by HRH for giving up my Sunday for him, I went along to the control room to phone Macrae & Dick's garage to request that they should send a couple of cars down to Longman so as to give me a flare path to land by. I was not prepared to emulate a 'Moth landing by hand torch' in a Rapide which touched down at near 70 mph against the Moth's 38 mph. There was also the difficulty of the approach as Inverness town lights, which used to be of great assistance, were now blacked out.

By the time I was in the air, it was pitch dark. There was no sign of the moon, but the coastline was dimly visible in places. On arrival over Inverness, which I could barely make out, there was not a car or light to be seen on the airfield. I flew around waiting for the cars to arrive. Fifteen minutes went by, but still there were no cars and I flew as low as I dared over the garage to wake them up, but to no purpose. What was I to do? I was in a real jam. It would be no use returning to Lossiemouth, even if I could find it in the dark without radio, as the ground flares would have been retrieved long ago. There was nothing for it but to try a landing with the sole aid of my nose headlight. Flying over the airfield, I could just discern the edge of the sea which lapped alongside. I flew out on a time course and shut off the motors after making the turn for the run in. Having switched on the landing light, the sea was clearly visible, but when the shore was reached, I was too high to see distinctly. There was nothing for it but to repeat the whole procedure. This time I got down as low as I dared over the water and approached entirely on a compass bearing to pick up the correct direction of the airfield for landing. It was very difficult to keep my eye on the compass, the Sperry Directional Gyro, and the water which was not more than twenty-five feet below me. This time I picked up land, namely the town rubbish dump, which extended for a couple of hundred yards before the airfield perimeter was reached. I could not be too sure whether the aircraft was heading in the right direction or was too much east or west of the full length of the aerodrome, which was not very large in those early days of the war. There was nothing left but to take a chance. The flaps were down and I eased the plane on to the ground. She touched down and settled on the tail wheel. I jammed the brakes on and the plane quickly came to a halt in one piece. I was sweating profusely and at the same time cursing the attendant at Macrae & Dick's garage.

Turning the plane east and taxiing along until the fence on the eastern boundary could be seen, it did not take long to locate the hangar which was adjacent to that fence. Walking up to town and going straight to the garage, I found the attendant and asked him why there was no car to meet me? All he said was that he was alone and had no one to send.

'Why didn't you ring up Mr Hamilton? He would have answered my call for help.'

The attendant hadn't thought of that.

'How did you think I was to land on such a dark night as this, without lights?' I shouted at him, for I was seething with rage at his seeming indifference.

He looked blankly at me. 'I don't know,' he replied.

And he couldn't have cared less, and that was all the satisfaction that one could get from him. My neck and the aircraft could have been broken for all he cared. I was lucky to get away with that one.

I had a nasty experience before the close of the first year of the war on a trip to Kirkwall. I have mentioned earlier that it was our custom to reposition the venturi tubes driving the Sperry Cloud flying instruments alongside the hot exhaust pipes to prevent them freezing up and putting the Sperries out of action. The aircraft I happened to be flying had been newly allocated to us and our engineering staff had not got round to that modification. However, I had the Reid & Sigrist instrument, which was driven from the engine, for emergencies.

I set off with a full load of passengers and mail along the inland route described earlier. Turning on course to pass over Invergordon, I commenced to climb to 5,000 feet. We entered the clouds around 500 feet and after ten minutes we had gained our altitude and turned on the new course to Thurso over high ground behind Invergordon. The coastal mountains on our right were completely enveloped in cloud. We had barely got set on the new course when, without warning, the windscreen became completely iced up. It was clear ice, the most dangerous form of icing, and guaranteed to bring any aircraft down if exposed to such conditions for more than ten minutes. At the same time, the Venturi tubes outside the aircraft froze up and the Sperry cloud flying instruments ceased to function. With the amount of ice which was rapidly building up over the wings and aircraft, I could not climb higher to get out of the icing layer. In fact, the plane was beginning to lose height. To make matters worse, the air screws and the engine carburettors were also becoming affected and so the aircraft was losing power when it was most needed.

In a short time, we were down to 3,000 feet and that was danger height with hills over 2,000 feet below us. Immediate action was necessary. If we carried on as we were doing, we would all be killed. Cromarty Firth lay on our right about ten miles away and with high ground in between. Our only hope was to reach Cromarty while there was sufficient altitude to get over the high ground. Altering course, we struggled along for five minutes, losing height quickly. We were then down to 2,000 feet by which time I estimated we should be past the high ground. I pushed the nose down, with power on, in a shallow glide. I could not make it too prolonged as there was high ground on the far side of the Cromarty Firth.

Inverness Town Clerk Smith-Laing, Provost Mackenzie, Director of Postal Services Sir Frederick Williamson, Postal Superintendent Measham, and Ted Fresson at Longman inaugurating the Orkney Air May, 29 May 1934.

Air Mail being delivered to Longman by Royal Mail motor cyclist, 1934.

Dignitaries assembled at Kirkwall for the arrival of the first Air Mail. Provost Slater, wearing his chain of office, officiates.

A hearty welcome from the people of North Ronaldsay upon the arrival of the first Air Mail on 1 August 1939.

The first Air Mail from Inverness to Stornoway being delivered by Assistant Postmaster Brown to Captain Eric Starling while Ted Fresson looks on, 16 February 1948.

Ted Fresson valued Royal Air Mail appointment as acknowledgment of the professional integrity of his air services in the north of Scotland.

Inauguration of air services to Sumburgh, Shetland, 3 June 1936. These were to be under the care of Captain Adam Smith, fourth from the left.

The hangar at Sumburgh. Its position was to be questioned by BEA, but Fresson knew Shetland's prevailing winds.

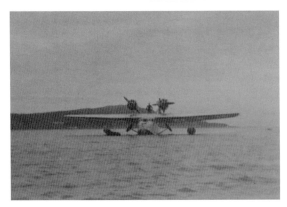

Cloud of Iona *at Renfrew (top) and moored on west of Scotland waters at the outset of the 1935 survey flight.*

A little technical trouble in Sinclair Bay, Caithness.

Wick harbour. The narrow entrance used by Cloud of Iona *for its departure is evident.*

At Dyce Airport, Aberdeen, probably during Cloud of Iona*'s return to the Isle of Wight following abandonment of the survey at Kirkwall. (Eric Starling)*

Ted Fresson meets Postmaster Jerome Stout while lighthouse keeper Ingram looks on following the first landing on Fair Isle on 13 May 1937.

Celebrations on Fair Isle during Fresson's Coronation Day visit.

This informal group with a Dragon at Wideford includes Ted Fresson (left), Gwen Fresson, and, on the far right, Captain John Hankins.

Sir Basil Neven Spence gesticulates his confidence of victory during his aerial electioneering tour in June 1945

Inverness-shire councillors, led by Cameron of Lochiel, on the Isle of Barra, August 1945.

*DH84 Dragon, G-ACIT,
seen here in Scottish
Airways wartime
camouflage at Renfrew,
24 July 1945.
(John Stroud)*

*Similarly camouflaged is
DH89 Rapide, G-AGIC,
at Inverness, 27 July
1945. (John Stroud)*

*Rapide line-up at Longman, Inverness: G-ADJG, G-AEWL, G-ADAG, and
G-AGIC. Note the masked passenger windows.*

A rare glimpse of Ted Fresson in his Scottish Airways uniform. Accompanied by his wife, Gwen, and his mother, the occasion was the award of his OBE in August 1943.

Taken in 1940, Ted Fresson has inscribed this photograph 'Bernard Wilson crash while sober!' While the hazards of ice accumulation in flight were well known, at this time the role of icing in preventing a successful take-off were not.

Inauguration of the service between Inverness and Stornoway on 24 May 1944. This gathering at Stornoway includes Provost Hugh Mackenzie of Inverness on Fresson's left, and Provost Alistair Mackenzie of Stornoway on his right. Chief Engineer George Griffiths stands behind.

Inverness railway station and marshalling yards with Longman airfield behind, 1947.

George Griffiths and his engineers (above) and Ted Fresson and his pilots (below). Henry Vallance is sitting to the right of Fresson. Notice that it's the pilots who get the ladies!

A busy scene around Rapide G-ADAJ at Kirkwall in BEA livery (above), and with Ted Fresson (below).

Ted with a Canadian
charter passenger at
Stornoway with his
Proctor, G-AMGE
(above), and with his
DH60 Gipsy Moth,
G-AAWO (right).

Gwen Fresson with G-AAWO at Inverness in July 1984 (above), and Richard with his sister Betty at the unveiling of Edmund Miller's painting, A Flying start to the Day, *at Inverness Museum in May 1985. (Peter V Clegg)*

After seven minutes, I cut the power and pushed the nose down steeper. By now ice was beginning to break away from the aircraft in big lumps. Down and down the altimeter wound. One thousand, seven hundred, six hundred, five hundred feet. I suddenly caught a glimpse of water. In another few seconds we were clear of the cloud at 400 feet and dead in the middle of the Cromarty Firth. The quick mental arithmetic, while struggling to keep the aircraft right way up with my remaining Reid & Sigrist instrument, had proven accurate.

I was pleased with myself. We altered course and flew up to Tain and along the bad weather coastal route. On disembarking at Kirkwall, the passengers had no idea what had been going on. I didn't tell them. As the saying goes, 'Ignorance is Bliss' and I left them in it. That was one of the days the Met slipped up for we had no warning that cloud icing of the clear and worst type might be prevalent that day.

I had my first taste of an air raid in early December 1940 when I was in London attending an Air Ministry medical board examination for the six monthly renewal of my pilot's licence. I had taken the opportunity of spending a couple of nights with my mother at her Northwood home for I had not seen her for over a year. She surprised me with her fortitude which she displayed along with the rest of the London inhabitants vis-à-vis the Hun bombing raids. She was alone as my daughter, Betty, had joined the WRAF and was stationed near us at Lossiemouth. I said goodbye to her with some hesitation and begged her to come up and stay a while with us and get clear of the air raids. But she would not leave her home.

There was a booking for me on the sleeper leaving Euston for Inverness at 7.25 pm that night. Arriving early, I sauntered into the Euston Hotel for tea and to while away the time. I had not been waiting long when the air raid sirens commenced their cacophony. Suddenly, without warning, there was a high whistling sound followed by an explosion which veritably rocked the Euston Hotel. A 'heavy weight' had landed just outside in the courtyard. Many females sitting in the lounge let out a scream while more explosions followed. I wondered whether the station and track had been damaged and went out to enquire. The head porter got on the phone to traffic control and it was established that no damage had been done. The departure had been put back to eight that night to give the raiders time to get clear of the district. That was my first initiation into what the poor Londoners had been putting up with for several months and I figured how lucky we were to be living in Inverness, clear of such frightful happenings.

It was a relief when we pulled out from Euston and arrived safely back in Inverness. My work, although hard at times, was, I thought, a picnic compared to what the poor citizens of the south had to put up with.

We saw the New Year, 1941, in without further incident,

13

Wartime Tribulations, Tragedies and Triumphs

Inverness Ack Ack Battery No 297 with whom, it will be remembered, we carried out pre-war anti-aircraft exercises, was transferred to Sumburgh towards the end of 1939. Its camp was situated some two miles west of Sumburgh airfield on rising ground and at the base of Fitful Head. The buildings comprised the usual Nissen huts and were located on a track leading off the main Sumburgh to Lerwick highway. It was a wild and windswept place with no protection from the 70-80 miles per hour gales which swept in from the west during the winter months.

The Officers' Mess was situated near the camp entrance and I was always a welcome guest if I was stormbound in Shetland. On a fine summer's day, a magnificent view was obtainable on the southern rocky coastline, Fitful Head, 928 feet high, towering over the camp immediately to the west. All from Inverness, the camp commandant was Colonel J MacIntosh, his deputy was a great friend of ours, Captain Gilbert Ross, and their lieutenants were Donald Walker of Leys Castle, Willie Melville, Macleay and Hogg. They ran a most hospitable mess and were always delighted to receive visitors as they were few and infrequent. They were completely cut off from their fellow men and, to make life more congenial, I was in the habit of bringing their mail and daily newspapers with me on the early morning air service. The delivery was effected on the approach to the airfield when I would make a run directly over the battery site and my radio officer would pitch the parcel out of the plane door as soon as he saw my hand go up in the cockpit. We seldom, if ever, missed the target so the camp received letters from wives and sweethearts and others, before eleven in the morning. The battery always said they could set their clocks by the time of our arrival, a claim also made by the Royal Observer Corps look-out at Fortrose, situated opposite Fort George some ten miles up the Moray Firth from Inverness.

I well remember one occasion when I was held up overnight by an eighty mile an hour south westerly gale, which had assisted me in making the journey from Kirkwall to Sumburgh that morning, a distance of some eighty-four miles, in twenty-three minutes compared with the usual time for that leg of forty-three minutes. As the return journey to Kirkwall against that gale would have taken near on three hours, plus the risk of taxiing and taking off in such turbulence, I decided to bed in at the battery mess that night. The landing had been spectacular, to say the least. There were twenty RAF ground staff ready to assist me land, as the wind was fifteen miles an hour in excess of my minimum flying speed. Their duty was to grab the plane as soon as I reached ground level. As I flew overhead, I could see them clustered at the intersection of the two runways. Before landing, I gave them a demonstration of a plane flying backwards by closing down my motors until my airspeed was seventy miles an hour, five miles an hour over the stalling speed of the aircraft, the minimum speed at which the plane would remain airborne. I was thus flying at ten miles an hour less than the wind so it accordingly blew me backwards. No one there had ever seen that trick before.

The approach was extremely bumpy and difficult. It had to be very accurately judged because if I missed floating down, so to speak, on top of the landing crowd, the plane would in all likelihood have been blown over on its back. With seven passengers and mail aboard, such an occurrence would have been serious to say nothing of the entire loss of the aircraft. I still remember that landing as if it were yesterday. Throttling down to an airspeed of just over eighty miles per hour, the plane came down practically perpendicularly. I was undershooting a little, so I increased the airspeed and, as I got above the landing party at around twenty feet, I shut the motors, dropping down right on top of them. They made a quick grab of the lower planes with several men straddling the tail. We did not risk unloading the passengers as that would have lightened the plane too much. Inch by inch, the taxiing to the nearest hangar progressed, with the men holding on to the main planes and being half dragged along. After what seemed an interminable time, we reached the lee of the hangar where the plane was strongly picketed to the ground and it safely rode out the night there.

The scene on Sumburgh airfield that day was incredible. Everything which was not securely tethered appeared to be flying through the air. In the early days of the war and before the RAF had installed petrol pumps for refuelling their aircraft they used five gallon petrol tins. The empties were stacked in their hundreds alongside the hangars. A number of these had broken loose in the gale and were cavorting through the air when we landed. A number of corrugated iron roofing sheets were also flying around and I was told that one airman was actually decapitated by one of those iron sheets through failing to observe one in full flight in his direction. It was a mystery to me how my aircraft and handling crew were not hit by those dangerous missiles and how we managed to taxi that plane into the lee of the hangar without it being blown over. Even walking was extremely difficult and it was a job to keep one's feet.

Colonel MacIntosh and Captain Ross invited me to stay the night in their camp. A first class dinner was served, preceded by plenty of Scotch whisky at fourteen shillings and sixpence a bottle to liven and cheer the night as the gale thundered against the corrugated iron mess hall and anteroom. By the time dinner was over, everyone was in excellent 'spirits' and we proceeded to play a darts match. During the middle of the game, Donald Walker was throwing his dart when Willie Melville stepped in front of the scoreboard to pick up a dart which had failed to penetrate the target. Donald's next shot was even worse, or may be it was intentional, for it hit Willie Melville right on the 'rear end of the season'. A banshee howl went up as he leapt at least three feet into the air. Everyone was reduced to howls of laughter while the wretched Willie went through the painful process of trying to extricate the dart from his anatomy. We played on well into the night without further incident.

Next morning, the gale had abated to a mere fifty miles per hour and I took off early on the long trip back to Inverness, my ground speed being reduced to sixty miles an hour against the tail end of the gale.

Sumburgh airfield, 28 July 1945.

Entertainments National Service Association (ENSA) parties were using the air communication services in increasing numbers and we carried many celebrated artistes during the war. Will Fyffe and his party travelled north with us over the New Year, and later George Formby and his wife flew with me to Orkney. A film had recently been shown in Inverness of George with his famous ukulele and my small son, Richard, aged five, had much enjoyed the performance. He happened to be with me on the bus which was taking the passengers and air crew to the airfield. I was talking to George Formby and his wife when suddenly I felt a tug on my sleeve.

'Who's that?' asked Richard in a whisper.

I told him and added, 'You saw him on the cinema a few nights ago.'

He appeared a bit stunned and then asked in a low whisper, 'How did he get out of the picture?'

That was such a good one that I passed it on to George and his wife. They were greatly amused and tried to get Richard into conversation, but he retired into his shell like a tortoise and even I couldn't get a word out of him.

In the spring, Sir Alan Cobham arrived in Inverness. I was requested by the Air Ministry to lay on a plane for him as he was on a mission for the Air Ministry to find suitable sites for the parking of aircraft as they came off the production line. It was not a very pleasant day for weather and the cloud and visibility was low when we crossed the Pentland Firth. I remember being rather taken aback when Sir Alan appeared somewhat perturbed that I continued the flight over sea to Orkney in such visibility, for he had taken on many celebrated and difficult long distance flights in the pre-war days when aircraft were not as reliable as the DH Dragon, G-ACIT, in which we were flying. I assured him that the weather was good for that part of the British Isles and there was no need for worry. He evidently trusted me for he said no more.

He found two sites on that trip, Dounreay, which is now converted to an atomic power station, and Dornoch golf links, which lost much of its original layout in the levelling work which subsequently took place in preparing two lengthy landing strips. Both sites housed many planes during the war prior to allocation and delivery to the respective squadrons, therefore our trip was far from wasted.

A few weeks later, towards the end of May, Captain Harry Reed of Allied Airways encountered motor trouble crossing the Moray Firth on his way to Orkney from Aberdeen. He managed to reach the Caithness coastline at Latheron on one engine. He crash-landed on an extremely small field situated at the edge of the cliffs and not far from the local cemetery. He received injuries from which he died within a day or so. This was a shock to us as we did not think it possible for anyone to get killed in a forced landing with a DH Dragon, an aircraft which landed at such low speed.

Pilot Reed was a very nice chap and we all liked him. It was the first fatal accident which had occurred on the north of Scotland air routes since the inception of the air services in 1933. I was charged with the duty of taking a wreath from our company, staff and myself up to Wick for the funeral, which took place on 2nd June 1941. He was buried in the little Latheron cemetery, near the scene of his crash.

During late summer, Commander Howe, the officer commanding Hatston airfield, was transferred south and was succeeded by a Captain Henry Fancourt. While the former had shown himself only too willing to co-operate with us in allowing the use of Hatston airfield, the latter instantly disapproved of such facilities being accorded civilian operators. We could not use our old grass airfield at Wideford as the war loads we were carrying daily were exceptionally heavy, and occasionally the aircraft had to carry a small overload to cope with all passengers and mails from the south, which, incidentally, benefited the Navy. It was not long before Captain Fancourt commenced to put the screw on us.

He issued an order that no more than one of our aircraft should be on his airfield at one time. This restriction worked satisfactorily for a time, but one day in the early winter, when the ground at Hatston in between the hard strips was liquid mud owing to days of heavy rain, I landed from Shetland to find two more of our Rapide planes on the deck, having got off schedule owing to the bad weather. It was an incident quite beyond our control. We were lined up awaiting Control to signal taxi-out for take-off on the duty strip. My attention was suddenly attracted to a figure, with a walking stick waving around the top of his head like a helicopter rotor, floundering through the mud. Eventually, the figure dragged himself from the quagmire on to the tarmac and, as my plane was the nearest to him, he commenced shouting at me, 'What the hell do you mean, allowing my orders to be disobeyed?' He was white in the face with maniacal fury.

'What's wrong?' I asked.

'Wrong!' he exploded. 'You have orders that only one Scottish Airways plane is to be on this airfield at any one time. There are now three.'

I endeavoured to explain that the situation was beyond our control. The services were not running on schedule owing to the very bad weather along the route and we were not deliberately flouting his orders. That explanation did not appease him, for he shouted at me, 'I'll see you off this Station,'' turned on his heel and floundered back through the mud. Within a few days we received a request from the Admiral at Scapa asking us to make arrangements to use another airfield in view of urgent representations made to him by the new commanding officer at Hatston.

What were we to do? I immediately flew north and arranged an interview with the Admiral. He asked me to lunch aboard his flagship, situated in Melsetter House at Longhope on Hoy, where I found him extremely courteous and sympathetic to the dilemma we were placed in. He appreciated the use the Navy obtained through our communication flights, but said he had to support his Hatston commander as he carried the responsibility for the safe and effective operation of Hatston.

An RAF airfield had just been completed on the Orkney mainland at Skeabrae, about fifteen miles away to the west, and another RAF airfield was in the process of being built at Grimsetter, a mile down the road from our Wideford mud-bound airfield. In fact, it was the Orkney terminal for our competitors, Allied Airways just before the outbreak of war. Return to Wideford was out of the question. The Air Ministry were unable, or unwilling, to bring pressure to bear on the Admiralty and eventually arranged for us to use Skeabrae.

With the long road journey, and the intensive comings and goings of RAF aircraft which were greatly in excess of the Hatston traffic, our services for a time were severely impeded and retarded. We were working long hours to get through the day's operations. This went on for nearly two months, until I was told that four hundred yards of tarmac had been laid on the first runway at Grimsetter. I immediately asked Air Ministry permission to use this short strip as it was just sufficient for our needs providing the wind was not too strong from the port or starboard side. In that case, we would temporarily revert to Skeabrae. Permission was granted on condition we could come to a suitable working arrangement with the contractors. This I was able to do as I knew Andy Sharpe, the local manager of Balfour Beatty, the engineering firm constructing Grimsetter.

Our aircraft landed many times a day and, for safety reasons, the workers had to be off the strip. Every time our aircraft landed meant considerable inconvenience to him as this slowed down the work. However, the strip grew longer every week and it was not long before the second strip was underway and our crosswind difficulties vanished. I could never understand Captain Fancourt's mentality in chasing us out of Hatston. After all, we were serving the three Services and, as far as I know, we did not interrupt the Hatston naval operations in any way as any naval aircraft taking off on operations would naturally be given priority by the controller in the tower. Finally, Hatston in all probability would not have existed had it not been for my co-operation with the Naval air services just prior to the outbreak of war.

1942 began with a month of atrocious weather. My logbook notes daily entries of rainstorms, hail and sleet, low cloud, flying above cloud all the way, very bumpy, heavy snowstorms, etc, culminating on 27th January in the complete isolation of the islands of Sanday and North Ronaldsay. The steamer had not been able to make its calls at those islands and we were called in by the GPO to come to the rescue and fly the mails in. There were several days of undelivered mail stacked up which were quickly disposed of by DH Dragon, G-ACIT, in spite of heavy snowstorms. Needless to say, the islanders turned out to welcome and thank us for coming to the rescue. We frequently carried out ambulance flights to the North Isles even although the Air Ministry would not allow a resumption of the air services during hostilities. I made several efforts to get the authorities to consent to reopening even a reduced service of three times a week, but without success. It was a great hardship on the population, cut off from the mainland in time of war, to be denied air transport which they had become so accustomed to.

Early in 1942, one of our planes was struck severely by lightning while passing over the Thurso area in snow cloud. The aircraft was very badly damaged. Captain Vallance, reporting on the incident upon his arrival in Inverness, said there was a terrific explosion accompanied by a violet flame and heavy fumes. His compass was put out of action, but fortunately the Sperry direction gyro was still functioning on the course he had set and he used that instrument to direct him towards the coast so that he could drop down to sea level where the risk of any further electrical damage could be avoided. Ultimately, he flew out of the snowstorm and reached Helmsdale without further incident and from then on the weather to Inverness improved.

On landing, it was found that the nose of the aircraft was perforated as if it had been shot up by machine gun fire. The radio trailing aerial fairlead had exploded and pieces had punctured the top plane. The aerial had been fused off and the radio set damaged. The port side of the aircraft body had been struck and the three ply skin split. Captain Vallance and the passengers had been badly shaken to say the least. It took our engineering staff two weeks to put that plane in order. All the ferrous metal parts, including the pilot's canopy, had to be demagnetised which involved a lengthy process and special equipment which we did not possess. Fortunately, the RAF at Evanton was able to help us out and we flew all the magnetised parts of the stricken Rapide there for demagnetisation.

The trailing aerial of our aircraft measured some sixty feet and, when in the trailing position, offered a first class conductor for lightning. Usually, the Meteorological Office would warn us, along with the weather report for the day, should there be any likelihood of cumulo nimbus cloud, which harboured electrical storms. With that warning, we would fly with the trailing aerial wound in on the winch positioned on the left side of the aircraft and within the pilot's reach. However, despite this precaution, our aircraft were not immune to lightning strikes. The lightning penetrated the nose of the aircraft and, contacting the winch full of copper wire, completely fused the wire into a solid block. To reach the winch, the lightning would pass between the pilot's legs. Not a happy thought. The only way one could avoid getting mixed up with lightning was to fly low over the sea, but that was not always possible.

I remember a bad case before the War, when one of Jersey Airways' four-engined DH86s was struck while flying over the English Channel. The lightning stripped one of the lower wings of all its fabric and tore a hole in the floor so that the unhappy passengers could see the sea beneath them. With the lift of one wing gone, the pilot had a difficult job keeping the plane on an even keel. Nevertheless, with great skill, he managed to effect a safe landing at Southampton airport. Later on, we had two other incidents of aircraft being struck, but not to the same degree as Henry Vallance's plane as the pilots had received the Met warning and were flying with their aerial wound in.

On 24th August 1942, my sister-in-law, Mrs Pobjoy, and her daughter, Shirley Ann, left their home at Cheltenham to holiday with us. They travelled to Crewe and caught the London-Inverness express connection that night. Their sleepers had been commandeered, which meant sitting up all night, a very uncomfortable experience as in wartime the trains were always crowded with troops. They were told the Duke of Kent and his staff were aboard. Later on that Tuesday morning, it was reported that the Duke of Kent was on his way to Iceland. He would be flown up from Alness seaplane base near Invergordon, that afternoon, Tuesday 25th August, in a Short Sunderland flying boat of Coastal Command.

I happened to be on the Inverness-Kirkwall run that day and the Met Office reported bad weather along the route as far as the Pentland Firth where conditions improved. I mention these weather details as they are directly connected with the tragic sequence of events which followed.

We flew north, above the cloud, at 4,000 feet and found the Pentland Firth bathed in sunshine with the sea looking a deep emerald green. We departed from Kirkwall around one o'clock in the afternoon on the return trip and, as usual, flew around the west side of Hoy, across to Thurso, in sunny weather. We caught up with the low cloud again at Thurso where I turned off on the south-easterly course to bring the plane over Dunbeath on the Caithness coastline, and which we passed over, above cloud, at 1.30 pm. On picking up our radio bearing from Inverness, I altered course, landing at Inverness twenty minutes later.

At approximately the same time as we departed from Kirkwall, the Sunderland flying boat took off from the Cromarty Firth. There had been, I was told, a last minute change in captains on board the flying boat, which had delayed its departure. The Duke of Kent and his staff were aboard. The Sunderland carried a rear gunner in the tail of the aircraft and his only communication with the rest of the crew was by inter-com phone. Apparently, the Sunderland climbed above the clouds and headed for the west side of Hoy before changing course for the over-sea flight to Reykjavik. Fifteen minutes of flight on course would have taken the flying boat into clear weather over the Pentland Firth, but for some unknown reason, after being airborne for a little over five minutes, the captain was heard by the rear gunner to say over the intercom, 'Let's go down and have a look.' Knowing as he must have done that there was a very low ceiling on the first part of the trip, I never understood what possessed that captain to take such unnecessary risks. The aircraft was fitted with the latest radio navigating instruments and there appeared absolutely no reason for what transpired. He had only to fly on course for another ten minutes and he would have had the whole of the Pentland Firth in view. However, down they went and at about 200 feet they broke cloud to find themselves in a narrow valley running parallel to the coastline north of the small village of Berriedale. That valley extends roughly three miles northwards and, at the end, the ground rises sharply up from near sea level to a thousand feet. With the poor visibility, the pilot evidently failed to see the sharply rising ground in time and, although he must have pulled the flying boat up into a sharp climb at the last moment, he failed to clear the top and the Sunderland crashed into the crest of the escarpment. The aircraft clock found in the wreckage had stopped at half past one, the time I was actually flying overhead and changing course for Inverness. The Duke of Kent and the crew must have all been killed instantly, but the rear gunner in the tail was miraculously thrown clear. He was, however, injured and rendered unconscious. According to later reports, he regained consciousness before darkness set in and, in great pain, set off on foot to obtain help. He picked up a small river and followed it downstream. Darkness soon enveloped him and he stumbled along through the night. In the early hours of the morning, the stream led him to a crofter's cottage near Dunbeath. In a semi-conscious condition, he woke the family by knocking on the door. They tended him and later gained the rear gunner's story of what had happened. The crofter immediately set off to the nearest village to report the tragedy to the police.

Later in the morning of 26th August, I was informed about the incident through RAF Fighter Control at Drumossie. As the whereabouts of the wreckage was not accurately known, we were asked to keep a look out on our flights north. After lunch, I set out on a charter flight to North Ronaldsay via Kirkwall and I made for the Dunbeath area. I flew inland a few miles up the coast from Berriedale and over the same small valley into which the Sunderland had evidently descended.

Suddenly, we came upon the wreckage strewn over a large area at the top of the escarpment. The aircraft had evidently caught fire for the wreckage was still smoking. The fragmentation had been severe. I descended to one hundred feet and circled the crash site. The four engines were scattered around the wreckage, which looked like a large dump of sardine cans and soup tins. The only recognisable part of the seaplane was the rear gun turret, rudder and tail fin, which had broken away from the main structure at the point of impact. My radio officer and I could distinguish three or four bodies lying amongst the debris. It was obvious that the considerable amount of fuel aboard had caught fire and had melted much of the light alloy wreckage. The position of the crash was some eight miles south-west of the village of Dunbeath situated on the coast, and the altitude was around eight to nine hundred feet above sea level. The seaplane must, therefore, have crashed in cloud.

After climbing the plane to 2,000 feet to obtain strong radio signals with Inverness, my radio officer, on instructions from myself, tapped out a message to Inverness Control informing them that we had located the crashed Sunderland and that, as far as we could tell, there were no survivors. We asked them to inform Fighter Control at RAF Command headquarters at Drumossie Hotel, high up on the southbound road out of Inverness.

During the period I was searching for the missing Sunderland, I had noticed what appeared to be the tail plane of an aeroplane lying alongside a stream in a valley running due west of Dunbeath. After my radio officer had despatched the message, I went back to take another look at it. I was puzzled how it could have got there as there was no further aircraft wreckage to be seen nearby. The ground to the south rose steeply to the base of Scaraben rising to 2,034 feet. I came to the conclusion that further wreckage must be around somewhere for that tail plane to get in that peculiar position.

'Let's make a search from the top of that mountain,' I said to my radio officer, Stewart, who was as intrigued as I was over that tail. 'There's surely been another crash around these parts.'

Round and round we climbed in circles and, as we came to the top of Scaraben, we found what we were searching for roughly 200 feet below the north summit. The crash lay spread out on a plateau. It appeared to be the wreckage of an Avro Anson that had hit the top of the mountain and crashed down the slope to the plateau beneath. There were several bodies lying around, but I could not see the tail plane although the outline of the wings was visible. That explained it; the tail plane had broken adrift on the point of impact, which undoubtedly occurred in cloud, and had floated down to the stream below. With that mystery solved, we continued our trip to North Ronaldsay.

On the return journey, we deviated and took another look at the remains of the Anson. It lay approximately five miles west of the Sunderland remains. I went up to RAF HQ immediately after landing at Inverness. There, I met Group Captain Somerville and made my report to him. He took me down to the mess bar, which was fairly full of officers as the time was getting on for six o'clock in the evening, and made notes of my description and report of the wreckage. Next day, he phoned to say they had traced the aircraft. It was an Avro Anson and had been missing from Kinloss airfield for the past three weeks. He said the aircraft had been on a training flight and, when it failed to return, an air search lasting several days had been put into operation without success. The group captain said they were grateful to me for finding the missing Anson and reporting it to them. Next day, they were to send out a party to climb the mountain and bring the dead down.

At the time, it appeared somewhat ironic that the Duke of Kent had to lose his life to enable that missing Anson to be found. Had it not been for the disaster which overtook the Sunderland, the Anson wreckage might have remained undiscovered for years in that wild and mountainous country.

At the beginning of hostilities, Scottish Airways was made responsible for the carriage of the naval mail, couriers, personnel, etc, to Scapa Flow base and Kirkwall Naval HQ situated in the Kirkwall Hotel. Later, this arrangement was superseded as the naval authorities set up their own air communications flight at our airfield at Longman, Inverness. They built themselves a huge hangar alongside ours at a cost of well over £100,000 and stationed a number of aircraft and pilots in Inverness. Their Headquarters were at Donibristle on the Firth of Forth. Not only was this move duplicating what was already available, but also it was of immense cost to the country.

At first, the pilots were drawn from Jersey Airways and from Scottish Airways' headquarters at Renfrew and all went well for a time. Later, those experienced pilots were transferred to more senior duties and replaced by junior personnel resulting in loss of regularity when the bad winter weather set in. On such occasions, not only were we expected to take care of their cancellations by carrying the passengers and mail, which of course we were unable to do, but at times we were subjected to severe delays at terminal airports owing to the inability of the new pilots to let down at the first attempt. Sometimes our aircraft were stood off for forty minutes until the naval plane either managed to land or decided to break off the run in. Our timetables became chaotic under such conditions and I was ultimately obliged to complain and ask for radio priority for our aircraft. That involved standing off the naval aircraft for five minutes or so.

In this connection, I recollect an incident which occurred at Sumburgh airport early in 1944. I was waiting at our traffic office to carry out the return flight to Inverness when I had a real set to with a high ranking naval officer who turned up at Sumburgh at the last moment and demanded a seat to Kirkwall. Low cloud persisted over the northern part of the route that day, and Naval Air Communications were cancelled. The senior naval officer therefore demanded a priority seat to Kirkwall on our service. He was told very politely by our traffic manager, Jim Black, that there was no accommodation for him as our aircraft was fully booked up with Air Ministry and civil passengers, plus a heavy load of service mail bags. The latter amounted to a considerable load on its own as all mail and light parcels at that period of the war were being despatched by air owing to restricted sea communications. Our friend with the large number of stripes wouldn't accept that explanation.

'My presence is required in Scapa urgently,' he insisted. 'You must take me.'

'Perhaps, Sir,' our manager replied, 'you had better talk to the pilot of the aircraft who, incidentally, is the northern director of our company.'

I thought at the time that this was a very adroit move by Jim Black. He got rid of the burden in a manner worthy of a King Solomon. I could only repeat what had already been said.

'I have no authority to offload any passengers or mail,' I told him.

'I must get to Scapa today,' he insisted. 'You've got to take me.'

Patiently, I explained, 'We are constantly up against this difficulty and there is nothing we can do about it. At the outbreak of war, we operated the Naval Air Communications until the Admiralty chose to terminate our services and commence their own communication flight. If they can't carry you, that is their responsibility and not my company's. Better make your complaint to the Admiral.'

I turned to make my way to the aircraft and he shouted after me, 'I'll report you for this when I reach Scapa Flow.'

I didn't hear anything further about that skirmish so I presumed the Air Ministry had suitably dealt with the complaint if one was made, which I doubt.

It was around that time, if not the actual day, when I taxied into position for take-off from Sumburgh at the western end of the long strip and was warming the motors up, that suddenly I became aware of a terrific roar overhead and tracer bullets commenced tearing up the tarmac immediately in front of the nose of my aircraft. Suddenly, a Hun Heinkel aircraft swept into view, flying low right along the strip shooting up RAF aircraft parked each side.

'Phew!,' I said to myself. 'Lucky thing for us that gunner didn't pull the trigger a few seconds earlier. We would have all been dead meat.'

I watched the Heinkel make a climbing turn to the south towards Sumburgh Head and disappear into low cloud. I didn't wait to be shot at again. In case that pilot decided to make another circuit, I opened up both engines and the Rapide was soon airborne. Into cloud we scampered, just as fast as I could make it, where I remained in an invisible state all the way to Kirkwall. That was a miraculous escape for the passengers and myself. I evidently wasn't meant to die just then.

As in 1941, the weather at the end of 1942 was atrocious and this carried on into the new year. On the morning of 15th February 1943, a terrific cold frontal storm broke over Inverness and along the Wick-Orkney route. The visibility was moderate, but a gale of eighty miles per hour, and probably gusting higher, was bending the trees almost double. To make matters worse, there were frequent snow storms and the turbulence inside them was worse than anything we had known. The aircraft, which had left just after nine in the morning for Kirkwall and piloted by Captain Cash, got as far as Helmsdale when the turbulence got completely out of hand and threatened to break the aircraft up. Very wisely, Captain Cash decided to return to Inverness. I was on the airfield to meet him, the radio station having informed me of what was happening. Captain Cash was a very experienced pilot and had been flying a long while in the Far East between Singapore and Hong Kong where some of the most turbulent weather in the world is encountered.

As Captain Cash had only recently joined us, I decided to make an attempt myself. I asked the four passengers if they were willing to try again to reach Kirkwall, and they said they were. As usual, we carried a very heavy load of mail. I got as far as Fort George, seven miles north-east from Inverness, and decided this gale consisted of everything I had ever experienced on the route. I was completely beaten. The bumps were appalling and the outer wing struts were bowing dangerously. That signalled extreme danger because, if the inter wing struts failed, the aircraft would break up in mid air. I was amazed that the plane had held together as far as Helmsdale and back, and I credited Captain Cash with more courage than I possessed for not turning back long before he did. With difficulty, I turned the aircraft through the heavy bumps and landed back at Longman airfield ten minutes after taking off. Fortunately, the landing party had not left the airfield and we radioed for them to catch us in. Captain Cash had waited to see how I fared. I told him I'd flown in gales equal to this one, but never had I experienced such vicious turbulence. It beat that memorable trip from Inverness to Stornoway a few years back with the delayed mails. I complimented Cash for getting as far as he did, but added that I thought, for the safety of the aircraft and passengers, he should have turned back earlier. We drove back to the office and I cancelled all flying for the day.

During the war, all passengers had to be screened by military control, and at Inverness, the army, which was responsible for this work, had an office next to ours in Macrae & Dick's premises. The Naval Air Communications passengers also had to go through the control. That morning, we learned that the Navy was operating a Handley Page Harrow, seating around twenty-four passengers, up from their headquarters at Donibristle. It was piloted by a senior pilot who decided to ignore our decision not to operate that day. Having a much larger aircraft than ours, perhaps he thought that this might be a good occasion for the Navy to get one across us for a change. He decided to continue the flight to Kirkwall.

One of their passengers, a military officer, refused to travel on hearing that Scottish Airways were not operating. Captain Adby, the control officer, later told me that the officer had remarked, 'If it is not good enough for Scottish Airways, it is not good enough for me.' So he stayed in Inverness.

The naval Handley Page Harrow took off and, to my surprise, safely reached Kirkwall. It departed from Kirkwall after lunch with twenty-one passengers aboard, including one Wren. The plane was observed to pass over Wick. Fifteen miles south, and some way out to sea of Lybster, the Harrow broke up in the gale and fell into the sea, killing all passengers and crew. I believe a brief radio message was intercepted by Kirkwall radio station in the form of an SOS. It was a salutary lesson in the art of knowing just when to draw the narrow line of safety limits and, fortunately, we knew it. Otherwise there would have been another tragedy that day. I thought again – Captain Cash was lucky to have got away with that Helmsdale trip.

Early in 1943, I received an official letter from Orkney. It contained an autographed excerpt from the "Minutes for the Meeting of the Business Committee of Orkney County Council", dated 15th January 1943. It is an historical document and I reproduce it in full.

Orkney County Council
Excerpt from Minutes of the Business Committee of Orkney County Council
15th January 1943.
Air Services – Captain E E Fresson

The Chairman drew the attention of the Committee to the fact that Captain E E Fresson, Inverness Director and Senior Pilot of Scottish Airways Limited, had recently completed twenty-five years of active flying in China, Canada and throughout Britain. In giving a brief summary of his outstanding career as a pilot and pioneer of Civil Aviation, the Chairman reminded the members that Orkney owed its air mail to Captain Fresson who had also founded the Daily Air Service between Orkney, the Shetlands and the South in 1933, while prior to that in 1931 he had linked the Islands with the Scottish mainland and had also been responsible for the pre-war network of local airlines between Kirkwall and the outlying Isles. Captain Fresson had also inaugurated a service between Kirkwall and Aberdeen on 7th May 1934 and had co-operated most helpfully with the County Council in bringing sick persons from the Islands to Kirkwall for hospital treatment.

The Chairman stated, that Captain Fresson's achievements had commanded the respect and admiration of all Orcadians, and that his energy and work in promoting Civil Aviation had conferred a great boon on the County.

Several other Members also paid tribute to Captain Fresson's personal record as a pilot and to the punctual and reliable service which he had provided and upheld in spite of war conditions which have rendered the maintenance of such a service increasingly difficult.

The Chairman moved: "That this Committee offer to Captain Fresson on behalf of the County Council of the County of Orkney, their hearty and sincere congratulations on his completion of twenty-five years active flying and their deep appreciation of the work which he has performed in establishing various air services which have proved so beneficial to the County."

This motion was seconded by Provost Flett and unanimously agreed to by the Committee which instructed the Clerk to transmit an excerpt from the Minutes to Captain Fresson.

Signatures: Alex Calder, Convener,
             Sutherland Graeme, Vice Convener,
             P C Flett, Provost of Kirkwall,
             James G Marwick, Provost of Stromness,
             J Harcus, Member
             R Slater, Member
             Douglas M Wood, County Clerk

I was deeply appreciative when I received this token of recognition for it was the only one I received from any of the councils in the territories which the advent of the air services benefited during the fifteen years I was connected with them. Shetland probably benefited mostly, but that island appeared more interested in the competition which appeared as soon as I had provided the facilities after several years of expense and labour. Stornoway was in a similar category. For years they made matters difficult and evaded the responsibility of the need for an airfield, but once the air service had eventually become established, twelve years after I commenced my long search for landing facilities in that difficult terrain, they were the most vociferous against any interference in *their* air communications.

Later on, the Western Isles, Stornoway and Lewis proved to be my loyal friends. I do not know whether the Orkney County Council's discussion and minutes of their meeting on the 15th January could have spread further south. If not, it was a coincidence that I was to be the recipient of a further honour a few months later.

On Thursday 6th May 1943, my wife, my son Richard and myself left on the night train for London. I was taking my first holiday since the war commenced, three and a half years before. We were bound for Cheltenham to stay with the Pobjoys who had a house at a delightful little village, named Bishops Cleeve, in Gloucestershire. Mr Pobjoy held a senior design appointment with Rotol Airscrews and had his office in Cheltenham. I was recovering from a recent attack of influenza, so it was a relief for me to get away from the hard daily grind of air communications in wartime. Bishops Cleeve is situated about seven miles to the north of Cheltenham and settles at the bottom of the Cotswolds on the road to Winchcombe.

The weather was sunny and warm and all the fruit trees were in full blossom. Under these delectable surroundings I was soon myself again. I used to go with Mr Pobjoy, or Pobby as he was known to the family, to the local village pub in the evenings and there was always a fair attendance of RAF officers from the nearby airfield, which specialised in towed glider pilot training. Those pilots were destined to crew the large towed gliders which were subsequently to be employed for the attack on the coast of France that became known as D-Day.

One evening, I got talking to one of the officers whom Pobby knew, and when he became aware that I was engaged in wartime air communications and was a member of the RAF Reserve seconded to Scottish Airways, he invited Pobby and myself to visit his airfield one evening to watch the night training in progress. He also suggested that I could have a flight in one of the training gliders if I wished.

We fixed a date in the middle of the following week, a Wednesday I believe, and Pobby and I duly arrived at around nine at night, darkness having nearly set in. We were entertained in the mess and then went out to see the aircraft. The gliders were two seaters and were towed off the ground by Miles Magister aircraft. By now it was dark and we proceeded to the end of the strip from which the flying was taking place.

Our squadron leader friend, whose name now eludes me, explained the instructional procedure. The instructor and pupil sat in tandem and were towed up to a height of 2,000 feet where the release handle would be pulled and the pilot of the glider was then left to find his own way back to the airfield and effect a landing. The landing area was lit up by marker lights and the gliders carried wingtip lights so as to avoid collision in the dark.

After watching a number of pupils, with and without instructor, being towed off into the darkness, our RAF host asked Pobby if he would like a flight. Pobby didn't think he would – he was all for having an engine in front of him and not being let loose in the dark without one.

'I'm sure Captain Fresson would like a go,' he added.

Having passed the buck to me, I said I would go up for a flight providing the instructor came along with me. So I climbed into a very narrow seat in the front cockpit and the RAF instructor got into the rear seat. We did a bit of cockpit drill through the intercommunication system and then got hooked up to a Miles Magister towing aircraft. The technique for holding station with the towing plane on the climb was explained to me on the ground and I spent a few minutes getting used to the layout of the instrument panel. When I was ready, the instructor gave the signal and we commenced to gather speed down the runway. Very quickly, the towing aircraft ahead with its red port wing, green starboard wing and white tail lights shining brightly, left the ground and I pulled the glider off.

'Keep the nose level with the tail light,' the instructor told me. The glider's controls were coarser than our Rapide aircraft and it was some time before I managed to keep proper station with the plane towing us. We wobbled up and down and from side to side in the inky blackness with those three lights in front, climbing higher and higher into the sky. There was no moon but the stars were out in full array. The altimeter crept up to 1,000 feet. By then I was in good control, or at least I assumed so as no further corrections came from my companion behind. At 2,000 feet, he said 'Cast off now.' I pulled the lever he had previously pointed out to me and we were suddenly adrift in the dark night with no power to assist us should I boggle the approach.

The towing plane's lights quickly disappeared into the black night and I settled down to obeying the orders of my instructor.

'Glide at forty miles per hour,' he said. 'And put the nose down to increase speed for turns.'

Having got me settled into the instrument flying, he said, 'Can you see the airfield?'

I hadn't a clue where to look as I had been so preoccupied with flying that strange aircraft. I could not take my eyes off the instruments for long, but I eventually managed to pick up the lights of the airfield far below to the port side. I was told to make wide circles around the field, gradually dropping off height. When we got below 1,000 feet, I made sure to keep to the windward side of the landing strip so as to be certain we touched down into wind. At first I was at a loss to know which the windward side was. It was south westerly when we took off, so it was not difficult to sort that one out with the compass. The fantasy of that flight was the utter silence except for the swishing of the air passing over the wings. When we got down to 500 feet, my friend behind began taking control of the situation and, following his instructions, we came in nicely over the boundary lights and he took over for the landing. We touched down and came to a halt. We then waited for transport to tow us back to the airfield apron. That was a wonderful experience, but I was a bit scared at first.

'Well done,' my RAF friend said. 'For a first launch, you did very well. We will have to enrol you as a glider pilot.'

'No thanks,' I replied, 'I think I will stick to powered aircraft.'

We found Pobby in the mess being well entertained by other officers.

'How did you get on?' he asked.

I told him all about the flight in the glider and said to him, 'Why don't you have a go?' Pobby was a private aircraft owner before the war, and had done quite a lot of flying.

'It's a bit queer at first, but you soon get used to it.'

'No,' said Pobby. 'I haven't the experience you have. We'd better be getting back home. It's nearly midnight.'

My wife was very surprised to hear I had actually been up in a glider and, thinking over the flight, I would not have minded having another go! Eventually, after the war, I organised a gliding school at Dalcross, Inverness, for the Air Training Corps (ATC) and remained commanding officer of the unit for a couple of years. We towed the gliders off the ground by winch, and were able to reach 600 feet and take advantage of ascending air currents, thus making sustained flights after a good deal of practice.

Next morning, my hostess, Elaine, gave me a letter. 'It must be an important one. It's from the Prime Minister,' she said.

'You're pulling my leg?'

I took it and, sure enough, the words 'Prime Minister' were printed in the left hand bottom corner. I opened the letter, wondering whatever Mr Churchill was writing to *me* about. It was headed '10 Downing Street' and dated 11th May 1943. It had been to Inverness and forwarded on to me at Bishops Cleeve. It read:

I am desired by the Prime Minister to inform you that it is his intention, on the occasion of the forthcoming list of Birthday Honours, to submit your name to the King with a recommendation that he may be graciously pleased to approve that you be appointed an Officer of the Order of the British Empire.

Before doing so, the Prime Minister would be glad to be assured that this mark of His Majesty's favour would be agreeable to you, and I am to ask that you will be so good as to communicate with me accordingly at your earliest convenience.

Naturally I was pleased to get this letter, but as no mention was made as to why I was to receive this decoration, I was left wondering what it was all about. I could only assume it was connected with my aviation work in the north of Scotland. However, at the investiture at the end of July, my conjectures were confirmed.

After my return home, the Under Secretary of State for Scotland, Mr Allan Chapman, and his party, arrived in Inverness on 17th June 1943, on their way to Shetland. He had a number of important meetings and speeches organised in connection with the war effort on that day, and it was most essential that he arrive on time. We were faced with a poser. Orkney was enveloped in fog, but there was a low ceiling at Grimsetter airport which enabled us to reach Orkney on time, though with difficulty.

However, Shetland, including Sumburgh airport, was covered in fog. I was on the roster of two pilots for the Shetland run that day, and the Chapman party were allocated to my aircraft. We arrived at Orkney on time, landing just after Captain Vallance who had left Inverness just ahead of us. A second weather message from Sumburgh was awaiting me at Orkney. The conditions remained the same with the exception that there was now around two hundred yards visibility on the airfield. Normally, we would cancel the flight under such conditions owing to the dangerous approaches to the airfield. When I told the Under Secretary this, he was sympathetic, but very worried.

'What am I to do about those meetings which are organised?' he queried. 'This is a serious matter. What bad luck the weather is so contrary today.'

We stood around awhile. I asked Captain Vallance what he thought. He, like Captain Hankins, could land under the most impossible conditions.

'I don't know what to say,' he replied. 'There is that devilish Pool of Virkie entrance to get through. If the radio bearings are only a little out, you've had it!'

However, this was wartime and risks had to be taken, so I said to Mr Chapman, 'I will have a go at it if you like to accept the risk.'

He agreed without any apparent hesitation. His assistants didn't have any say in the matter.

At fifteen hundred feet, we were flying in sunshine and in forty minutes were given an overhead signal by Sumburgh radio station. The drill was to make the original approach so that the plane was at an altitude of 1,500 feet above the radio station when given the signal 'motors overhead'. The pilot would then turn off on a magnetic course of 135 degrees and descend on a flat glide at ninety miles per hour. That brought the aircraft down to sea level off Sumburgh Head and to the east. During the last 500 feet, a turn to the north would be made and radio bearings would be taken off the Sumburgh station until a magnetic bearing of 285 degrees was obtained. The plane would then be on a true westerly course, which would normally bring it in through the Pool of Virkie gap. Once in, and by following the shore, the north-east/south-west landing strip could be picked up. One, however, had to be certain about the correctness of the westerly bearing received. It was possible to check it as there was a fisherman's stone hut built on the coastline rocks that was directly on the course. It was very difficult to find in foggy weather.

The first descent was commenced and the sun was left behind as we entered the murk. Down we went, one thousand feet, seven hundred feet, five hundred feet... Turn to the north commenced. Bearings began coming in from the radio station at the request of my radio officer: 315 degrees magnetic, three hundred and ten, three hundred... We were now flying on a northerly course and getting near our turning point to the west at 285 degrees. Being so near the station, bearings changed very quickly. Now we were down to 290. The course was altered to north-west so as to make the final turn less sharp. By this time, we were flying at approximately fifty feet over the sea, which could just be discerned below.

'Two eighty-five,' my radio officer called out.

We turned in towards the gap and held tight to the bearings, which continued to come through to hold the plane on the correct course. Suddenly, I espied the rocks and took a quick look around for the fisherman's hut. Visibility was only a hundred feet or so. I couldn't see it. I daren't risk continuing the run in, so opened up my motors, at the same time turning north, and climbed up above the fog again. We flew south and then came in over the radio station for the second time and the same procedure started all over again. Again, we approached the rocks, but again, no fisherman's hut could be discerned. So up again we roared into the sunny weather and we tried for the third time. By now I was beginning to feel the strain and so it was with great relief that I saw the hut right ahead of me on the third run in. Once through the gap, the visibility went up to a good three hundred yards, having improved in the last hour since we left Orkney. There was, accordingly, no difficulty in picking up the strip and we landed safe and sound.

The radio superintendent came over and told me I had received ninety bearings.

'It seemed like 190,' I replied. 'However, thank you for such good co-operation, for I have important passengers.'

I introduced the superintendent to Mr Chapman. The Under Secretary thanked us very sincerely for having got him to Sumburgh in one piece. He had no idea how bad the conditions were until he had the opportunity of observing at first hand.

Today, nearly twenty years later, I am told the Shetland plane does not land unless the cloud height is seven hundred feet with the wind from the western quarter, and 1,000 feet with the wind from the east. The smaller and more highly manoeuvrable plane is, of course, far more suited for that kind of flying than the large 45-seater planes in use today. Unfortunately, the smaller plane is wholly uneconomic to operate, largely brought about by trade union regulations and restricted working conditions.

On 27th July 1943, the Investiture took place at Buckingham Palace. It was a fine sunny day and my mother accompanied my wife and myself to the palace. I am very glad that my mother was able to attend as she died suddenly of coronary thrombosis the following January. Besides being very happy that I had been honoured by King George VI, it was the first time she had been inside Buckingham Palace and she was most interested in the Court procedure.

We were first shown into a large ante-room and the recipients, according to their degree of honour, were segregated into separate rooms. Meanwhile, the guests were shown into the throne room, which was heavily guarded by the Home Guard. It was a long room with a dais situated in the middle. An aisle leading to the dais was partitioned off and the honoured recipients filed slowly along in order of seniority. I could see my mother and wife sitting on my right as I moved along the aisle very slowly.

Well ahead of me was Naval Commander Ben Bryant, the famous submarine commander. The recipients bowed and curtsied and were presented by the king with their gong after their name had been read out by a chamberlain standing next to him. Occasionally, the king would converse with the more important individuals and I noticed that Commander Bryant was in conversation quite a long time. I was certain he had many exciting experiences to interest His Majesty. After Commander Bryant, there was a clear run of some ten minutes when my turn came to be presented. To my surprise, the king detained me and asked me many questions about our operations. He was extremely interested to know that I had found the wreckage of the Sunderland flying boat on which his brother was killed, and to hear about our experiences with enemy aircraft in our unarmed planes and how we managed to avoid being shot down. He kept me talking for at least five minutes and I found him delightful and so unassuming to talk to. With so much royal attention, I began to think I had got into the wrong Honours group and should have been ahead with the CBE class!

We had a job getting away from the palace as all taxis were taken up and my mother was unable to walk far owing to a weak heart. Also, we were besieged by photographers from the press anxious to take our photo. I could not help but think that was organised by the press in Scotland as other recipients did not appear to be getting so much attention. It was getting on for one in the afternoon when we managed to hail a taxi and we adjourned to the Piccadilly Hotel in time for a well earned lunch.

To add to the excitement, it was a hot sunny day and we were glad to sit down in the lounge and relax over a well earned appetiser. Halfway through lunch, we discovered we had Orcadian company for, sitting a few tables away from us, we espied Billy Scarth who, in the early formative days of the air service, used to be with the firm of Macrae & Robertson, solicitors in Kirkwall, who were the factors for the Hatston Farm, which I so desperately needed for an airfield in 1933.

H W Scarth held an important post in the conduct of the war, and we frequently had him as a passenger on our aircraft. We got to talking after lunch about old days in Kirkwall when suddenly he asked, 'What brings you to London in these hectic days?' My wife replied for me and described our visit to Buckingham Palace that morning. That was the first he had heard about my decoration. He was very pleased that I had at last received recognition for my work.

He departed and we sat and watched the multitude of London dwellers going their various ways. I found myself speculating what part they were all taking in the war. One thing stood out clearly in mind, they were a lesson to the world in the part they had played a year or two back in withstanding the vicious aerial onslaught the Hun had made on the capital of Britain.

We returned to my mother's house in Northwood for the night, and next day were on our way back to Inverness via Renfrew where I collected a new aircraft to augment our fleet. That brought our total to six de Havilland Rapides, representing thirty-six seats per day, or seventy-two if we duplicated the flights. From that figure it can be deduced, we had considerable mail and freight capacity.

In December 1943, Fighter Command at Raigmore, Inverness, gave me a magnificent Christmas party. We had never seen such a spread at dinner since pre-war days and the festivities went on well into the night. To most of us, I think, it was apparent that the end of hostilities could not be so very far away. Our bombing raids over Germany had reached such a crescendo that production in Germany must have been severely curtailed and, against that, the enemy had the Russian onslaught to cope with – plus the Russian winter, which defeated Napoléon.

14

Preparation for Peace

We brought in the New Year of 1944 with a party for our pilots and friends at our house at 12 Mayfield Road. It went on until the early hours. We also celebrated New Year's Day with a restricted service to the north when only loads affecting the war effort were carried. Among the pilots attending, I remember Captain Vallance, Captain Riley and Captain Cash, plus Red Haynes and Tony Raven of the Radio Control at Longman airport. We had all had a very heavy year's work and every pilot was flying his full 120 hours allowed by the Air Ministry per month, myself included. That represented 1,400 hours in the air annually, mostly under high pressure. The engineers, under George Griffiths, must not be forgotten, for it was they who kept our aircraft running. Complete engine failure, with aircraft always fully loaded, under cloud-flying or sea-crossing conditions, would have meant disaster. Looking back, I don't think I ever worked with such a fine bunch of fellows. In those days, they did not have trade union doctrines and restrictions to bother them. I was indeed proud to lead them.

On 4 January 1944, I left Inverness with Rapide, G-AERN, to ferry it back to Liverpool. It had been borrowed from the Associated Airways Joint Committee during the early part of the war and we had now been allocated a new plane. I attended a board meeting in Renfrew that day and planned to continue the flight to Liverpool on the morrow.

Dawn broke with shocking weather being reported almost all the way to Preston. I could not fly at altitude as heavy icing was forecast. The only way I could get through was to try and crawl underneath the low overcast. According to my logbook, I had 500 feet to play with, plus heavy rainstorms that cut visibility down to half a mile while flying through them. To be caught in the overcast with icing around could easily have meant my 'last flight.' I took off from Renfrew and headed down the Clyde and around Gourock Point, following the coast past Ayr and down to Stranraer. There the weather improved a bit insofar as the rainstorms with their bad visibility ceased. I managed to cut across land to Luce Bay and then over the Solway Firth, picking up the Cumberland coastline at St Bees Head which I followed to Morecambe Bay on the other side of that bit of water. Blackpool hove in sight and with it, better weather.

Arriving at Liverpool, I flew across the Mersey to have a look at Hooton Park airfield, my old joyriding base from 1929 to 1933. The only change I could discern was that the Pobjoy's house had been reduced to rubble. After landing at Speke Airport and handing the aircraft over to Wing Commander Measures and

Captain Gordon Olley, who were operating the Associated Airways Joint Committee, I took the opportunity of paying my old joyriding partner of days gone by, Captain Lance Rimmer, a visit. He had a wartime job working for a company who were manufacturing Avro Lancaster bombers under licence at Speke airport. He hadn't changed much. He was surprised and glad to see me again. He and his wife lived at Hoylake, south of the Mersey and, I believe, are still there today.

Returning to Glasgow by train that afternoon, I went to Renfrew to stay with Captain Barclay. John Hankins was also there. I hadn't seen him since he left the Northern Section at the beginning of the war, and so my visit was doubly pleasant. We three visited the cinema in Paisley after supper. Halfway through the performance, a message was flashed on the screen for Captain Barclay. He looked agitated and uncomfortable upon his return.

'What's the matter?' I asked.

'It's a telephone message for you,' he said, 'from your wife in Inverness.'

Some sixth sense of foreboding flashed through me. 'Is it bad news?' I asked.

David nodded his head in affirmation.

'Then keep it until the picture is finished,' I asked him. I don't now remember what was being shown, but it was an extremely good picture and I wanted to see the end of it.

When we got outside the picture house, I said, 'Now David, what's it all about?' The reply staggered me.

'Your wife phoned to say she had received a phone call from your brother, Kenneth, in London. Your mother died suddenly from thrombosis at five o'clock this afternoon.'

I was stunned. I had no idea my mother suffered seriously from her heart. When David told me in the cinema there was bad news, I thought maybe one of my relatives, or perhaps my son Richard, had been taken ill.

My brother had added that my presence, as the eldest member of the family, was required urgently in London. Before I could leave for the south I had the new aircraft to deliver from Renfrew to Inverness in replacement of the plane I had just delivered to Liverpool. I phoned brother Kenneth from David's house and said I would leave on the night train from Inverness the following day as I had to get that plane to Inverness next morning. The war effort had to go on. He agreed.

I caught the London express on the Friday night of 7 January, and went straight to my mother's home at Northwood. The funeral was to take place the following week at Golders Green crematorium. My father had died in May 1939, so now both my parents had gone.

The first matter requiring attention upon my return to Inverness was to sort out a complaint from the admiral in command at Scapa Flow. In the defence of Scapa Flow against attacking aircraft, the Admiralty had erected a balloon barrage which flew at varying heights above the Flow. It was a formidable defence as each balloon was anchored to the surface by a heavy wire cable. We all took jolly good care to avoid that barrage when flying in cloud and we allowed a wide safety margin to the west of our route around Hoy. Apparently, during my absence, Captain Vallance had completed a trip in cloud from Inverness to Kirkwall with a strong westerly gale blowing and had not allowed sufficiently for drift. Consequently, he had unknowingly flown slap through the balloons and, more amazingly, he had got away with it – a chance of one in a thousand. There was not much I could do about it after the event, but I thought it wise to call on the admiral in person and explain how the error had occurred.

I found the admiral in poor humour.

'You know, Captain Fresson,' the admiral said, 'if it had been a pilot without much experience, some allowance might be made, but for one of your very experienced captains to err like that, there is no excuse. It's a miracle the plane was not wrecked and all the occupants killed.'

I agreed with him, but expressed the opinion that no one in his right senses would deliberately fly through a maze of cables attached to that balloon barrage. I also told the admiral that it was not easy to maintain an accurate course on the inland route in cloud with a strong cross wind blowing as there were no radio aids with which to check.

Having told Henry in future to steer a westerly error under cross wind conditions to make sure he did not wander to the east, that was the end of the matter as far as I was concerned. No one more than Henry realised how lucky he had been and he took jolly good care not to repeat the performance.

Two months later, I had an alarming experience in Dragon, G-ACIT, not far away from those cables. I left Inverness for Kirkwall with a 1,000 lb mail load and one passenger. There was a seventy mile an hour gale blowing in the Pentland Firth. To make maters worse, there was low snow cloud down to 150 feet and extremely turbulent blizzards floating around from time to time. I caught up with the gale near Helmsdale. The trip in poor visibility across the Pentland Firth was rough and the fear always present that the high cliffs of Hoy would not be picked up in time for, in the blizzards, visibility was virtually nil and the plane was being roughly thrown about. Safely reaching the south-west corner of the Hoy cliffs, we entered another blizzard. The mail was piled to the roof and the lone passenger sat just behind me. I carried no radio officer and was flying at a hundred feet or so above the sea when a terrific squall all but turned G-ACIT on its back. The mail tumbled over the cabin and the left wing dropped vertically, pointing at the foam-flecked rollers only a few feet below like some monster waiting to clutch us in its grasp. The shifting mail bags made the plane sluggish on the controls. For a few seconds it was touch and go as we slithered down towards the white wave caps lashed in fury by the gale. At the last moment, when we had little further to drop and I thought my end had come, the left wing gradually came up with plenty of top rudder to help it. We settled right way up, kissing the gigantic wave tops. After a terrible tussle, we rounded Hoy and flew into calmer weather.

I stayed that night in Kirkwall. Nothing would induce me to risk the Hoy corner low down again under such conditions. Dragon, G-ACIT, still lives and is working for Mr Peter Masefield, former managing director of British European Airways. For the past fourteen years it has been used as a joyriding plane at Blackpool. Mr Masefield recently bought it and has had it rebuilt for the second time. He uses it as a personal communication plane and has invited me to fly it again whenever I am near Oxford airfield where I believe it is housed. In all, I flew over 1,000 hours in that aircraft.[1]

May was upon us and on the 24th of that month we were requested by the Air Ministry to provide a regular air service between Inverness and Stornoway, almost five years after the original date we had planned to open that service before the outbreak of war in 1939. With the type of aircraft we were using, the route was a difficult one during the winter months as icing was prevalent at the altitude we had to fly to cross the Easter Ross mountains, which in many places topped near the 4,000 feet level. We had no de-icing equipment on the Rapide

---

[1] G-ACIT now resides at the Science Museum, Wroughton, Wiltshire. Sir Peter Masefield died in 2006, age 91.

aircraft or airscrews, and the carburettor intakes were not wholly cared for under such conditions. We had, therefore, to carefully watch the meteorological icing warnings and, when the red flag was out, we kept to the valley route, low down whenever possible.

I flew the inaugural service and had as passengers the Provost of Stornoway, Mr Alistair Mackenzie, and several councillors. Our chief engineer, George Griffiths, came along with us and our senior radio officer joined the flight. We had a pleasant trip across the mountains in fine weather and went into town for lunch which the town council was giving to celebrate the air service they had been waiting so long for. Before we left Inverness, the Met Office reported that there was a weather front steaming up from the south-west and it was expected to reach the Hebrides during the afternoon. However, my appetite was not adversely affected by that report as, if necessary, I had radio to help me home at altitude.

The lunch was long and excellent and by the time we had got through all the speech-making it was getting on for half past three in the afternoon. Provost Mackenzie made an excellent address, working up through the years I had been looking for an aerodrome for Stornoway and the success that eventually came my way, only to be thwarted by the outbreak of hostilities in September 1939.

By the time we were ready to depart to the airfield for the return journey with a full load of return passengers, the weather front predicted by the Met Office had duly arrived The cloud ceiling was not much more than fifty feet. I planned the return flight at 5,000 feet across the mountains. At 3,500 feet we got above the first layer and I turned to my radio officer to obtain a tail bearing on Stornoway so that I could calculate the drift, if any. To my amazement, he was slumped in his seat. George Griffiths was sitting in the rear of the cabin so I asked the passenger nearest me to tell him to come forward.

'Sparks appears to be ill. Will you take a look at him?'

I was worried, finding myself in the position encountered in 1931 over the Pennines and which I made up my mind not to get into again.

George Griffiths bent down to have a good look at the radio operator and in a few moments he leant into my cockpit and said, 'The only thing that is wrong with him is that he's dead drunk.'

'Dead drunk?' I gasped. 'What in the devil are we going to do?'

It was not known how far the front penetrated to the east and whether Inverness was in it. There was seven people's safety in my care and to try and grope one's way down into Inverness airport without accurately knowing one's position was fraught with considerable risk as was demonstrated years ago with the Moth.

There was no alternative, but to brace myself for some very accurate dead reckoning flying, so I told George Griffiths 'Try and shake some life into him, you've got to get him awake somehow.'

We continued climbing and were now at over 4,000 feet. George slapped the radio officer's face and shook him to no avail. Suddenly we flew over a clear chasm in the clouds, about a mile wide. I could se the sea and white horses which were whipped up by the wind quite distinctly. I made up my mind at once to duck down under it and try and get back into Stornoway airfield underneath the low cloud ceiling. At least we knew we were above water for the descent. 'Warn the passengers I am diving down quickly and returning to Stornoway,' I yelled to Griffiths. 'OK,' he replied and then came back to attend to the radio officer.

As we reached sea level, George Griffiths said, 'I've got him awake at last.'

'Try and make him understand that unless he can get a radio bearing on Stornoway, he's likely to lose his ruddy life along with us all,' I shouted.

After a few minutes and to my relief, 'Sparks' started to tap on his key. He came back with a mumbled bearing that I could not understand. We were now on the return course and the cliffs on Chicken Head were ahead and sticking into the murk.

'What did you say?' I yelled. 'What's the bearing?'

I could just catch 320. That showed us a bit south of the course which was all to the good. He got me another bearing which was 315 and showed we were drifting north. I altered course 10 degrees to the south. The visibility was only about half a mile and the gloom made our position look desperate. Five anxious minutes after, the cliffs were seen as we were almost upon them. I could only see a little way up those cliffs before they merged with the mist. Following them to the outskirts of Stornoway town we managed to pick up the road leading to the airfield. The cloud was so low that the plane was not more than 50 feet above the road. We had to be careful we did not hit any cottage roofs along the roadside, as the plane roared over them. I was thankful when suddenly a tarmac strip appeared just in front of me. We landed across wind. I had no inclination at that moment to go looking for the right strip into wind. The passengers had, of course, witnessed the disgraceful position and they were most sympathetic and thankful they had been extricated from a difficult position and so said all of us – not least myself. We repaired to the town after phoning for transport, and we stayed the night.

Next morning, the front had passed through and the weather was good enough to fly without radio assistance. I said nothing to my operator until we got back to Inverness, when I called him to my office and told him he was fired.

'You placed us all, including yourself, in considerable danger through becoming intoxicated during lunch and the only redeeming feature lay in the fact that you managed to get the vital bearings to locate Chicken Head.'

I sent a report of the incident to Head Office at Renfrew and my reasons for the dismissal. Consequently, I was staggered to hear about two weeks later that the same radio officer had been re-employed by the Renfrew boys. No notice was taken of my protest. It was an unbelievable state of affairs that the Renfrew management had condoned drunkenness when the individual was on duty and had imperilled the safety of aircraft, passengers and crew.

Two weeks later, Britain invaded the Normandy coast of France. D-Day had arrived. We had just finished breakfast and the radio was on. We were waiting for the nine o'clock morning news when the announcer came on the air to say that, during the preceding night, a great armada of convoys and their escorts crossed the Channel to the Normandy coast and that the task of landing was in progress. Further announcements would be made during the morning.

How thrilled we were. We were conscious of the bravery of those of our countrymen who were committed to the bloody task of driving the Hun back from the coast so that the final offensive could begin. The big gliders, for which the pilots were being trained at that airfield near Bishops Cleeve the year before, were now in full action and being towed across by Douglas Dakota aircraft.

At our next board meeting, which I attended a week or two later at LMS railway headquarters at Euston, I complained about the radio officer episode. An enquiry was ordered and that was the last I heard of it. I went out to Harrow to see Air Commodore Herbert Brackley who was in charge of the newly formed RAF Transport Command. The idea had been growing in my mind that I might be of better service to my country as a pilot for the Dakotas, which were now operating a new technique in invasion tactics. No doubt, before France could be recaptured, many more such airborne drops would be required.

Air Commodore Brackley received me courteously and opened up the interview, 'Well, Captain Fresson, what can we do for you?'

I explained my visit to the glider school near Bishops Cleeve the year before and the interest I now had in glider towing technique being used in the invasion of France. With this new phase in the war effort, I enquired whether my qualifications could not be better used by offering my services as a Dakota towing pilot, instead of plodding along the Inverness-Orkney-Shetland route, which now appeared to be well out of the centre of operations.

'How many hours flying have you logged to date?' he enquired.

'A little over eight thousand,' I answered.

'Hmm,' he said, 'that's a good figure. I will see what can be done. I shall of course have to get in touch with the Air Ministry to ascertain that you can be released from your present war duties and also find out about our own requirements for air crews.'

We talked a bit about pre-war flying and he then took me down to their club room which provided a good bar.

Over a drink, I recalled to mind our first meeting in 1927 at Croydon Airport when he was air superintendent for Imperial Airways.

'I was looking for a job as pilot, but you turned me down as I had not then logged the number of flying hours which met the company's requirements.'

'Ah, yes, you had just returned from the Far East!'

'You have a very good memory in remembering that interview,' I said. Eighteen years have passed under the bridge since then.'

In bidding me goodbye, he said he would write me as soon as he had made the necessary enquiries.

I returned to Inverness and told my wife what I had done. She was not enthusiastic. She need not have worried, however, for a week later I received the following communication from Major Brackley, turning my application down. I quote the letter:

Air Commodore H G Brackley, CBE, DSO, DSC,
Headquarters, Transport Command, Royal Air Force,
Harrow, Middlesex.

16th June 1944

Dear Fresson,

Thank you for your letter of the 13th June. We have got the Dakotas and completed our training and are doing our stuff. There is no shortage whatever of pilots, in fact, everyone is very flush here and they are complaining they get no flying. As you can imagine, the ambulance role is one of the many we are doing at the moment. This is all worked in the glider towing, paratroop dropping, supply dropping, etc, all with the same type of aircraft. If I can see any opportunity of fitting you in, I will do so. Frankly, I cannot at the moment.

Yours ever,
H G Brackley

I replied to that letter on the 20th June 1944.

Dear Brackley,

Thank you for your letter of the 16th June. If you have a sufficiency of pilots, then of course I recognise my proposition is of no interest. I feel I am doing so little for the war effort stuck away up here that I was hoping I might be able to assist in releasing younger men for more onerous duties. Of course, if the ambulance role is connected with glider towing, etc, I should have been glad to have taken this on also. Apart from pilotage, however, I was also hoping my long experience in aviation matters might have been of some value to the ambulance and supply organisation. I am naturally sorry you can do nothing for me as I gained the impression when I saw you that opportunities to use my experience might occur.

Yours sincerely,
E E Fresson

That was the end of the matter. I heard nothing further, so continued my duties in the north of Scotland. Apart from the hope of doing something more constructive for the war effort, I was also hoping to obtain experience on larger aircraft. With the tremendous impetus given to air communications in Scotland by the war on the Glasgow-Hebrides and Inverness and Aberdeen-Orkney-Shetland route, I felt certain the six-seater de Havilland Rapide would be unable to cope with the post-war traffic.

Practically everyone was now using the air service and very few the sea route owing to restricted sea services and the danger incurred by enemy action. Having become accustomed, over a period of years, to reaching Edinburgh, Aberdeen and Glasgow in minutes as compared to days by the alternative surface routes, I was confident that the greater percentage of the islanders would continue to use air travel. In that conclusion, I was ultimately proved to be correct for the post-war traffic quickly developed to five times the pre-war traffic and it was the Dakota that superseded the Rapides.

I have recorded earlier in this narrative that we were called upon to transport members of ENSA. During the war years, we flew many important members of the theatrical and musical professions to entertain the Navy, Air Force and Army contingents stationed in Stornoway, Shetland and Orkney. In 1944, the celebrated pianist Leff Pouishnoff became a familiar figure and I used to make a point of piloting him myself. I introduced him to friends of mine in Orkney who possessed a grand piano. We were asked to dinner the next day and it was a very good dinner too for war time rationing. We sat talking after the repast when suddenly our hostess exclaimed, 'Oh, Mr Pouishnoff, wouldn't you like to try our piano?' There was an awkward silence.

Leff Pouishnoff did not reply immediately, then he suddenly said, 'You know, Madame, your request reminds me of a story told in New York City about a famous hostess who, some years ago, invited the celebrated violinist M. Vivaldi to dinner. He was late and the hostess began to worry that he had forgotten the date. When her guest eventually arrived, she hurried to the front door to greet him.

'Oh, Mr Vivaldi, I had begun to think you had forgotten our invitation,' and then noticing he was without his violin, exclaimed, 'Why, you haven't brought your violin.'

'Dear Lady,' Vivaldi exclaimed, 'for the simple reason my violin doesn't eat dinner!'

'You see' said Leff Pouishnoff, 'if you had asked me to play for you instead of asking if I would like to try your piano, I would have been delighted.'

There was a prolonged silence. It was only broken when Leff looked at me and said, 'I will play for you the *Glazounoff Sonata*.'

It was the first time I had ever heard that composition and it was a masterpiece. I can never understand why it has not been recorded.

I flew south with Pouishnoff next day after showing him around the beautiful St Magnus Cathedral, which dates from the tenth century, and taking him over the ruined Earl's Palace. Being a great lover of historical buildings, he was charmed. He stayed with us that night in Inverness and we were treated to a private recital. Leff Pouishnoff was a very witty person and was born, I believed, in or around Odessa. He was in Moscow when the Bolshevik Revolution broke out in 1917 and, after the fall of the Kerensky Government, he decided to get out of Russia if possible. He had friends in Odessa, to whom he fled from Moscow, and he managed somehow or other to reach Persia where he told me he became a Persian citizen and remained so for some years. Eventually, he was able to make his way to Britain and, after a while, changed his nationality to British. Since then, he had made Britain his home and became renowned as one of our top pianists.

My wife and I first heard him play at the Usher Hall, Edinburgh, where he was booked to give a Chopin recital. I remember well that he was dressed in a velvet smoking jacket for we both had commented that it did not look very professional, arriving on the concert platform in such garb. However, he gave a superb concert for which he received a great ovation. At the end of the concert and after many encores, he made a little speech and apologised for his unusual clothes.

'The fact is,' he added, 'I have just come from Aberdeen and I've lost my clothes.'

That announcement tickled the audience so much that he was greeted with a roar of laughter. Obviously, he had never heard about the classic stories told of the Aberdonians. A year or two later, I mentioned this episode to him. He said, he did not understand at the time why such a simple remark should have convulsed his audience with so much mirth and laughter, but he had been made wise since.

By October, our armies were in Holland and the end of the war was in sight. Accordingly, the railway companies were thinking about peacetime operations to replace the rigidly controlled wartime services. On 4th October, I received a visit from a Mr Dennis Handover who had joined Railway Air Services the year before as air adviser. He had previously held many important posts in aviation and came to the railway group from BOAC. He was accompanied by his wife and they were booked to fly to Orkney that day. The weather was bad and they did not see much of the route as we were in cloud most of the way there and back. Handover, however, managed to get an idea of our organisation in Orkney and, on his return to Inverness, decided to stay a few days for a post-war discussion. My wife and I found them to be exceedingly nice people.

Right away he recognised that there were special problems in running air services in the north of Scotland, which did not exist in the south. We had long discussions and my views on post-war operations were noted with interest. We took them by car over to Loch Maree so that they might see the type of country we flew over on the Hebrides routes. Unfortunately, it was pouring with rain and he couldn't see much. We had tea at the Loch Maree Hotel and returned to Garve Hotel where they were to stay the night. The road was flooded for most of the way as it was raining so hard. Miss Mackenzie, the proprietrix, greeted us. She was an old friend of mine and had flown on many trips to Stornoway with me. We stayed to dinner and Mr Handover plied me with questions regarding our five years of war operation, which he appeared most interested in.

He expressed surprise when he learned of our high record of regularity.

'Never less than 97% in any one year, and often more,' I told him.

To attain that, I explained, meant a first class team of flying crews, and as much credit was due to the engineering staff who worked under George Griffiths, and his second in command Bert Farminer, whom it will be recalled was my chief engineer in my old joyriding days. We were completely self-contained and were in a position to rebuild any aircraft, however badly it was damaged. Our stores contained a most comprehensive list of spares, sufficient for several years. I showed him our drying sheds, which gave our overhauled aircraft another 100 lbs or so of payload by extracting all moisture from the woodwork. In addition we carried out all complete engine overhauls and had our own engine testing bench. He had a long talk with our chief engineer, George Griffiths, who had so ably welded the team into such an efficient unit. In A MacLennan, we had an expert wood worker and in Theo Goulden, a first class radio engineer, he was told.

He said afterwards that he was agreeably impressed with what he had seen and had little doubt we were in a first class position to change over rapidly to peacetime operations on a profitable basis. I saw a lot more of Handover during the next two years in his London headquarters in Grosvenor Street where new offices for post-war operations had been acquired by the Railway Group.

January 1945 was a month of continual snow blizzards of exceptional intensity. The Kirkwall newspaper, *The Orcadian*, of Thursday 1 February narrated the events of that month in the following descriptive article.

Air Line Beat the Snow
How Scottish Airways Kept us Linked

Foresight, vigilance and hard work maintained the 'Orkney lifeline' – our daily air service – through the recent weeks of Arctic weather. Mails and newspapers came through with almost 100 percent regularity, a further triumph for Scottish Airways Limited.

Proof that the public take a good deal for granted lies in the fact that the very regularity of the Inverness-Kirkwall air service caused many people to think that the mainland of Scotland was having easier weather than Orkney. The reverse was the truth.

The Scottish Airways routes to Scotland, as well as Orkney, would have closed early in the snowy spell but for the steps taken to beat the exceptional heavy falls experienced in the Inverness area. The ground staffs of Scottish Airways everywhere, and the pilots and radio operators, must be congratulated in having pulled off a magnificent job of work. When the local airliners were grounded overnight, in blizzard weather, they had to be watched every moment until dawn, and often till well on in the day. Then, runways having been cleared, they took off and overtook schedule.

Bad at Inverness: The Arctic weather conditions have showed up many weaknesses in our daily habits. Houses built for Orkney's reputed clime, suffered burst water pipes. Roads were blocked with whole areas isolated. On the Scottish mainland, surface railroads were running hours late, all contributing to the dislocation of our daily lives. Boats and buses were very late, or entirely cut off. In view of that upheaval, it is especially worthy of note that Scottish Airways delivered the Orkney mails and newspapers regularly and with very little upset in their timetable.

Because of this phenomenal regularity in such appalling weather conditions, one wonders whether people are not disposed to take the comings and goings of Scottish Airways as a foregone conclusion, and possibly the thoughts that Scottish Airways are not meeting with the difficulties we have ourselves.

There was even an impression that Scottish Airways were able to keep on running because their airfield at Inverness was not suffering from the effects of snowfall, as did other airfields on the Scottish mainland. How wide of the mark this was, shown by the fact that Inverness had to contend with twelve inches of snow over most of its airport landing area. When the snow commenced, the aircraft had to roll their own runways before taking off was possible. After that, a system of rolling was put into action so as to pack the snow hard. After every fall of snow, the rolling process was continued. Inverness, therefore, had a runway of frozen snow as hard as concrete and it was only by that resourcefulness [which was my idea incidentally] and the assistance of the RAF authorities at Inverness which enabled Scottish Airways to maintain the only air connections operated continuously between the mainland, Orkney and Shetland during the two Arctic weeks. [The RAF authorities at Longman were at first reluctant to roll the snow. It was quite contrary to their usual practice of using snow ploughs. I had to explain that we reduced the pressure of our aircraft tyres, which prevented the aircraft skidding on the rolled snow, before they would act.] Actually, landing and taking off were the least difficult part of maintaining operations.

The severe snow storms, Scottish Airways pilots were called upon to fly through day after day, and the skill which was employed to avoid dangerous icing conditions, speaks well for its pilots – Captains Vallance, O'Reilly, MacFarlane, Hayes and Fresson, and the radio operators who flew with them.

Orkney gained one over Shetland inasmuch as Scottish Airways efforts brought our mails and newspapers regularly. Scottish Airways do not hold a mail contract for Shetland. [Nevertheless, we delivered a lot as the Aberdeen mail was diverted through Inverness on many occasions during that shocking fortnight.] Thanks are due to the Naval authorities and RAF at Sumburgh and Grimsetter, and Longman, Inverness, who kept the airfields open for civil air communications.

Personally planning and conducting the Scottish Airways efforts at Inverness and elsewhere was Captain E E Fresson OBE, the Inverness managing director of the firm, its senior pilot and founder of Highland Airways Limited, the pioneer concern responsible between 1931 and 1933 for launching Orkney's daily airline and its associated routes.

I can now divulge an incident which occurred during that fortnight's blizzard, and which was withheld from the press at the time. Captain William Baillie left Orkney ahead of me late one afternoon, with a full load for Inverness, in a heavy blizzard extending far south. I left shortly after with a heavily loaded aircraft. We both took the east coast route. It was agreed that I would fly 500 feet lower than he so as to avoid the risk of collision in snow cloud.

Roughly half an hour after take-off, my port engine petered out without warning. My position was roughly fifteen miles out to sea off the Helmsdale coast and I was flying on radio bearings given every five minutes by the Inverness radio station. We were flying at 1,500 feet to avoid engine icing and, as I have said, we were heavily loaded. That heavy load was nearly our undoing as I was unable to maintain height on one motor and we gradually began to lose height.

I called Radio Officer Stewart to come forward.

'Radio Inverness and tell them our port motor is out of action and that we are losing height. Also give them our approximate position, ten to fifteen miles off the coast north of Helmsdale. Say I intend edging into the coastline, but cannot go too near as visibility is nil.'

He started working his Morse key as hard as he could go. He appreciated the danger, caught up as we were in heavy snow, visibility nil, and insufficient power to maintain height, with a rocky coast abeam.

I edged in nearer to the coast, but was afraid of running into the cliffs, which were several hundred feet high, or the mountains behind them. Gradually, we sunk lower. We were down to 1,000 feet when R O Stewart told me Inverness had acknowledged our message and had reported it to the RAF. Not that they were able to help us. While struggling to keep the plane on a straight course on instruments, my eye suddenly caught sight of the port motor oil gauge. It was still registering oil pressure which meant the dud motor was still turning over. That could only mean one thing – the slow running jet was functioning and I deduced from that, that the main jet was choked with some foreign matter. If I could suck the foreign matter through the main jet, I would recover power. I therefore opened the throttle lever suddenly and the motor picked up for a moment. I repeated the throttle movements nearly a dozen times, moving it backwards and forwards, thus causing a heavy suction on the suspected choked jet. Suddenly the motor burst into life and kept on functioning. The trick had succeeded and saved us.

Inverness reported clear weather and I prayed for that motor to keep turning until we were out of that white hell. The minutes went by and the motor was still functioning when the blizzard began to get lighter. Up until then, it had been a semi-dark grey colour. Within a few moments we were in the clear and Tarbat Ness was visible about five miles ahead and slightly to starboard. We landed safely at Longman airfield. None of the passengers were any the wiser of the near miss they had had to a watery grave.

George Griffiths and I immediately had a post mortem.

I said to him, 'Better change the carburettor before letting that plane in the air again if you cannot find the cause of the stopped main jet.'

He agreed.

Next morning I was flying the same plane. As soon as I got down to the airfield, I asked Griffiths 'have you found the cause?'

'No,' he answered. 'I've had the carburettor to pieces and checked all the petrol pipes from the filter to the carburettor and cannot find a trace of dirt. It must have got sucked through the jet. I have also run the motor for a good fifteen minutes on the ground without loss of power.'

I accepted the position without question.

The traffic officer loaded up the plane, again an overload. It was that way nearly every day. It didn't appear to affect the take-off or flying as long as the two motors kept turning over. I quickly forgot yesterday with the thought that 'that sort of thing can't happen to me again so soon.' I took off towards the west side of the town.

I had reached about eighty feet and was just over the River Ness when the same motor cut dead on me again. I had not attained proper flying speed and I only had around eighty miles per hour on the clock, just ten miles over the speed necessary to keep the plane airborne. I had to turn to get back to the airfield, but turning took more power and I just hadn't got it. Quickly taking the only chance possible, I put the nose down slightly to keep what airspeed I had, thereby losing valuable height, and gingerly made a flat half-turn until I was heading across the airfield, cross wind. Dropping the aircraft down slowly, we touched down on one wheel and came to a stop. Griffiths had to send a car out to tow us in as it was impossible to taxi on one motor. To say I was shaken by this second event was to put it mildly. That was twice in twenty-four hours I had nearly been killed. Nothing like it had ever happened on the Orkney run during the past twelve years.

The passengers were transferred to another plane and I again left for the north, having told Griffiths, 'Change the motor if you can't find what is causing the trouble.' He agreed, being equally disturbed as I was, having witnessed the whole affair.

On my return from Orkney I found that Griffiths had located the trouble. The supply petrol pipe from the petrol filter was made of gut reinforced with a steel wire core. The gut had flaked and a small piece had got into the jet chamber of the carburettor. The flake was transparent and was almost invisible. Hence the reason it was missed on the previous day's examination. To prevent a repetition of that trouble, we submitted the details to de Havilland's at Hatfield and they supplied a special 'banjo' filter to attach to the float chamber of the carburettor. It was an alarming thought that one little piece of disintegrated gut might have cause the loss of an aircraft, plus seven passengers, radio officer and pilot.

We were now ready to go into action as soon as we had been demobilised from wartime and ministerial control. Our great headache was the lack of suitable aircraft. The civil conversion of the Douglas Dakota was of assistance to the longer routes, but we considered that type of aircraft would be too expensive to operate on the shorter haul stages such as we were faced with. What we required was a monoplane reproduction of the pre-war DH86 four-engined bi-plane, seating 14-16 passengers, with variable pitch air screws and de-icing equipment.

The intensive planning for post-war operations that I have mentioned was connected with the White Paper issued by the Government in the early Spring, which stated that those companies controlled by the railway companies would be responsible for the operation of all internal air lines in the country. The *Scotsman* editorial in their publication dated Friday 6th April 1945 said:

Civil Airlines Development Plans

Day and night flying in fast passenger planes with the latest safety and all weather devices are envisaged in the ambitious plans being prepared by the railway and shipping companies for the post-war development of internal air-routes in Britain and linked up with the Continent.

Scotland's share in the scheme of things to come foreshadows a marked expansion in the network operated by Scottish Airways and its associated companies, the pioneers of civil aviation in Scotland, who have a notable record of achievement throughout their history of the past ten years. At the moment, their plans are contingent on the ultimate decision of the government policy as outlined in the recent White Paper on rail, sea and air travel coordination.

A few weeks later, the *Shetland News* commented on the Shetland/Aberdeen services in relation to the White Paper. It stated:

Mr Douglas M Wood, County Clerk at Orkney, wrote stating that when the Government White Paper containing proposals for Civil Aviation was issued, it stated that those services controlled by the railway companies would be responsible for the operation of all internal airlines in the country. Mr Wood had been told that this decision had been modified and that the present monopoly of the Aberdeen-Orkney-Shetland route held by Allied Airways (Gander Dower) Limited was to be continued. The matter, he said, was to be raised at Orkney County Council, the Clerk of which said he had no hesitation in saying that Scottish Airways Limited, one of the Railway Group, should be permitted to resume their service on this route, with communications to Edinburgh and London. Scottish Airways were actually the pioneers of this route, but were excluded from it by the Licensing Tribunal in January, 1939. Later Mr Wood wrote that Orkney County Council had instructed him to communicate with the Minister of Civil Aviation, regarding the question of Scottish Airways being allowed to resume their service from Aberdeen to Orkney and Shetland.

Major Adie of Shetland, said he heartily agreed with the object of that letter. He had no interest whatever in either air company, but he did think there was the danger of a monopoly being started here. They suffered already from a monopoly on the sea, and he thought the Shetland Council should write to the Air Ministry and ask for the reinstatement of the service between Shetland, Inverness and Aberdeen by the pioneer company.

Major Adie added that he had found out that, owing to the irregularity of the carriage of mails by the Aberdeen company, the Admiralty instructed the GPO to send all their mails via Inverness. Now, the Aberdeen company had the mail contract, but they had never been able to carry all the mails and, through delays and one thing or another, Scottish Airways had carried the mails from Inverness. These had been routed from Aberdeen by rail or car to Inverness and were carried by the company that did not have the mail contract.

Since January 1943, over 250 tons of first class mail had been carried from Inverness. It was also very difficult to leave Shetland and get to

Aberdeen. One could only do so via Inverness and by surface transport to Aberdeen. In these days of poor railway services, it was much better to travel by air. Mr Robertson agreed, but thought it would be a grave disadvantage if, willy nilly, one had always to go to Inverness if one wanted to reach Aberdeen. What he would like to see was the company running the mails from Aberdeen up to Shetland up to date. Scottish Airways had always run up to time, and he took his hat off to that company.

Those two articles accurately recorded the position as it was by the end of June 1945. In an earlier chapter, I have already described the support Shetland gave the company who had muscled in on all our years of preparation, and of the injustice done to us at the Licensing Court presided over by Mr Trustram Eve in 1939. The present praise now given to us by Shetland would have been of better assistance to us, and them, if it had come in January 1939 instead of 1945.

The Armistice was signed at Rheims on 7th May 1945 and the war in Europe was over. Japanese hostilities continued in the Far East, but that did not affect our change over to peacetime duties.

We had maintained an air communication service second to none during six years of war under bad weather conditions and enemy action. Throughout that time our continuity did not fall below ninety-seven percent and often went to one hundred percent. Together with Railway Air Services' routes between Glasgow and Belfast, and our Southern Section, we had flown 4,000,000 miles, carried 1,000,000 passengers, and 4,000,500 lbs of mail and freight. The press, in reporting these figures, went on to state:

These impressive totals, says a statement by the LMS Railway, encourage the operators in plans now being made for peace, which will bring new and greater opportunities for swift transport throughout Scotland.

That was what was thought then, but the LMS Railway administration, although they did not know it or even guess it at the time, had a second guess coming. They little knew that, within a year or two, the deadly poison of bureaucracy would descend all over the country and destroy Scottish Airways and them overnight. What, however, it could not destroy was the record of pre-war and wartime service commercial aviation gave to the country.

15

'Dead Hand on Aviation'

Parliament was dissolved on 15th June 1945 and polling day was fixed for 5th July. The wartime National Government had ceased to exist and a caretaker government ruled until the polls.

On or about the third week in June, I received a phone call from Major Neven Spence, MP for Orkney and Shetland. Could we provide a plane to take him around the Orkney North Isles and to Fair Isle on an electioneering campaign? He wished to leave Kirkwall on Wednesday 27th June. I arranged to meet him in the Kirkwall Hotel on the evening of Tuesday 26th June, and I left Inverness in Dragon G-ACIT with my wife and son, Richard, at noon on the Tuesday. We landed at Wick and had lunch with our good friend Harold Georgeson at his home. We set off in the afternoon for Kirkwall. In the evening, Major Neven Spence and I got down to mapping out the tour. He would require about three hours at each island. The islands to be visited were Stronsay, Sanday, Eday – where there was no known landing field, Westray, Papa Westray – also with no known landing field, and North Ronaldsay. We finished that round on the afternoon of Friday 29th.

We found a good field to land on at Papa Westray without difficulty, but Eday was a poser. We flew round and round for quite awhile and were unable to locate a field which appeared anything like suitable for the Dragon to land upon. There was only one site which had the necessary length, but it was situated on quite a sharp slope. It was that or nothing. The wind blew up the slope and was too strong for us to land downwind and up the gradient. We therefore approached the downhill run gingerly. The plane touched down and effected a landing with the tail still up. The wind assisted in a quick pull-up. I had a long wait there. The electorate had many questions to put and have answered.

Next morning, Saturday, Mrs Neven Spence accompanied her husband on the Fair Isle trip. I decided to try landing on the partially constructed airstrip which, at my suggestion during the early part of the war, the naval authorities had commenced to build on the side of a hill and situated in the middle of the island. It was about 250 yards long and very narrow. However, it looked better than the site on the south end of the island with its drop of 200 feet into the sea around most of its perimeter. After a couple of dummy runs, I managed the landing with only a few yards to go. The islanders were delighted to see me back after nearly five years and gave me a great welcome. I went to the meeting with the major and his wife and he had a full attendance. The islanders were a strong

'Liberal Camp' and my Tory candidate had a tough meeting. He was, however, received well. His visit by air created a first class impression. I heard afterwards, that while they did not feel inclined to betray their Liberal loyalties, they agreed with a lot that Major Neven Spence had to say to them. So, in their novel way, they thought they would assist him by remaining neutral – so they did not vote at all.

We spent three hours on the island and, with regret, took our departure from such a genuine welcome. The take-off with our light load was easy and we landed in Kirkwall in the late afternoon and celebrated Orkney's first aerial election with a first class dinner at the Kirkwall Hotel. My wife and I were the guests of the major and his good lady.

A little over a week later, the results came in from the polls. Major Neven Spence had retained his seat in Orkney and Shetland by an increased majority.

Within a week or two, the Socialists were returned to power with a very high majority. The country was stunned. To think the electorate had thrown Winston Churchill overboard – the man who had saved them from Nazi tyranny. It was said that the Forces were responsible, but that is a matter for conjecture. Whatever the reason, the country was on the verge of disastrous legislation and many were going to be hurt in the process, myself included.

Immediately after the new government had taken its place in the House of Commons, it was announced that Lord Winster would be the new Minister for Air. I went to see him in the House of Lords and he seemed to be a friendly and reasonable minister. He assured me that my position was secure and that, in the new organisation, Scottish Airways would be valued for operating air services in Scotland. Unfortunately, Lord Winster did not last long as Air Minister. For some unknown reason, he was replaced by a far less amenable minister.

Soon after the election, Sir Steven Bilsland was appointed Chairman of Scottish Airways. George Nicholson, who was Director of the Southern Section, and myself were introduced to him prior to a board meeting which was held in the Glasgow offices of coastal shipping company David MacBrayne Limited, which operated the Western Isles shipping routes as far north as Stornoway, and were shareholders in Scottish Airways. We were told at that board meeting that our post-war plans were to continue as intended before the election.

In August, I took the annual Inverness County Council flight, with councillors led by Cameron of Lochiel, their chairman, to Barra. Barra had no airfield and all aircraft landings and take-offs were made on the beach at low tide. On arrival, the County Clerk enquired the latest time they would have to report at the beach for the return journey before the tide came in.

'Seven o'clock in the evening is the absolute deadline,' I replied.

'If you arrive any later, we may be held up for the night, so don't be late,' I warned Mr McKillop the County Clerk.

It was a lovely day and, after lunch, my radio officer and I hired a small rowing boat and rowed over to a sandy island opposite the Castlebay Hotel where we spent the afternoon swimming. Our plane was parked by Sir Compton Mackenzie's bungalow at North Bay. Time had gone quickly and it had soon turned five in the afternoon.

'We had better be getting back,' I said to my companion, 'if we are to catch the tide for take-off.'

We dressed quickly and rowed back to the hotel, had a quick tea, then hied out to North Bay and were ready for take off at 1830 hours, just half an hour before the deadline.

The motors were warmed up ready for a quick get away as soon as Lochiel and the councillors arrived. The weather was beginning to deteriorate. I could see a bank of low cloud coming up from the south. By seven o'clock, our departure time, the sun had been replaced by cloud and the visibility reduced to a few miles. There was still no sign of our passengers and the tide rolled in relentlessly. At 1930 hours, the tide was too high for take-off when we espied a car coming along the coast road some way off.

'That must be them,' we both remarked in disgust.

Sure enough it was, and the time 1945 hours. When told they were three quarters of an hour too late for the tide, the County Clerk McKillop said he had been pressing the party to hurry to no effect. Lochiel seemed peeved and asked when they could get away.

'Nine thirty at the earliest and it will be nearly dark by then. Besides, look at the weather. It has changed a lot during the past hour.'

I was annoyed with them for making it so difficult for me.

'Why can't you leave now?' he persisted.

Lochiel was evidently thinking about a half-moon strip of soft high water sand for take-off. I got exasperated with him. The others were all standing around.

I thought a moment and then said, 'There is only one way we can get off now, Sir, as far as I can see.'

'What's that?' Lochiel enquired eagerly.

'Just this. If we can obtain and place a chair on the beach and you will sit in it, it might be possible for you to do a 'Canute act.' And when the tide recedes, we can take off immediately.'

His fellow county councillors let out a roar of mirth.

'That's it,' they said, 'who'll fetch the chair?'

Cameron of Lochiel went red in the face, took the hint and subsided. I could see he was not feeling too gracious about having his leg pulled so effectively.

We eventually managed to leave at 2045 hours, but to do so we had to take off in a semi-circle on a narrow strip of hard sand left by the now outgoing tide and which was adjacent to the high water mark of soft beach. It was a tricky take-off with a full load. If the plane had touched the soft sand on the continuous turn I was obliged to make, we would most likely have turned turtle. I left word with our agent to phone Inverness and get the radio boys out to help us home as there was very little daylight left. Flying low over the sea, we reached the north end of Skye where we caught up with the weather front and ran into clear weather. Climbing to cross the mountains, we passed over Gairloch. Ahead, the mountains were covered in cloud. We managed to contact Inverness radio station and they gave me a bearing which they could not guarantee. They said it was subject to night error. Just after that, the Achnasheen valley opened up before us and looking very black below. In half an hour we landed at Inverness in the dark with the aid of car lights.

On 29th August, Captain Balfour, former wartime Under Secretary for Air, arrived in Inverness. In pre-war days, he used to be a director on the board of Whitehall Securities, owners of United Airways whom we joined in 1935. I had seen him on several occasions since then. The last time occurred in 1944 when I visited him at his office in Whitehall in an effort to persuade him to assist us in obtaining a tarmac airstrip for the Longman airfield at Inverness.

The purpose of his visit was to inspect the recently constructed airfield at Dounreay, which had never been used by the RAF for whom it had been constructed at great cost. It had three magnificent tarmac airstrips and was situated away in the wilds, west of Thurso. It is now the home of the Dounreay atomic station. I flew him up in Dragon, G-ACIT, and, after landing and inspecting the airfield, a caretaker came running out and asked us what we meant by landing there. The airfield was closed, he told us, at the same time asking our names. I told him my name, which he appeared to be acquainted with, and introduced my passenger as Captain Harold Balfour, recent Under Secretary for Air. His face changed to an apologetic look. 'Oh!' he exclaimed, 'I am sorry, gentlemen, for bothering you, but my orders are to see that no one uses this airfield and I had no word of your coming.'

Captain Balfour, now Lord Balfour of Inchrye, put him at his ease and we left shortly after for Orkney.

Two weeks later, our chief pilot, Captain Henry Vallance, was honoured by the king for his remarkable service during six years of wartime flying with Scottish Airways. The award was celebrated by the company at an evening banquet given in Henry's honour at the Caledonian Hotel, Inverness, and was presided over by our new chairman, Sir Steven Bilsland.

In his speech, Sir Steven said, 'We meet tonight in honour of Captain Vallance, chief pilot of the Northern Section, in appreciation of the distinction recently conferred on him by His Majesty the King, whose commendation he received in appreciation of his work in maintaining air lines in Great Britain.'

After referring to the foundation work of Mr Robert Wotherspoon and Mr R Donald, Sir Steven went on to say, 'But we have met particularly to honour a gallant and distinguished pilot of Scottish Airways Limited, Captain Vallance.' [Applause] Sir Steven said that he wished also to take the opportunity to pay sincere tribute to the pilots, ground staff and also the administrative staff under the splendid leadership of Captain Fresson, who had maintained that vital service of airways during the six years of war. [Applause] He had before him a letter from the Ministry of Civil Aviation conveying to all of them the appreciation of His Majesty's Government and a copy of which would be given to each member of the staff. Captain Vallance was one of a splendid team.

Sir Steven continued. 'I want to say a word about that team which had done so well under the inspiring and able leader ship of Captain Fresson all through the war.' [Applause] 'Scottish Airways, in this area, have supplied a key service and very much has depended on the regularity of that service, carrying passengers of first importance and also dealing with matters which had had an extremely important bearing on the war effort. We are all very proud of the reputation which has been built up by all of you. Their war job was ending and their peace time job beginning. Very considerable plans were being developed by Scottish Airways, which must await various decisions on the part of the government before they could be put into operation.' Ending his speech, Sir Steven Bilsland then asked the Company to drink to the health of Captain Vallance. After a deal more speech-making, the dinner ended.

Seventeen years after that award to my friend Henry Vallance, he now has the great responsibility of flying 150-seater Douglas jet aircraft, operated by KLM, from Amsterdam across the Atlantic, a position of very great trust indeed. I have presented Sir Steven Bilsland's address at Henry Vallance's dinner fairly thoroughly. Although I have not by any means quoted it in full, I consider it helpful to put events which were to follow in their right perspective.

During the middle of October, Allied Airways Limited received some publicity in their efforts to persuade the Aberdeen Town Council to support them in overthrowing the Air Ministry's intention of allowing us to resume the Aberdeen-Orkney-Shetland service which, it will be remembered, we pioneered in 1934. The *Press & Journal* reported the Town Council discussion as follows:

North Air Plea Supported
Allied Airways request for sharing declined

Aberdeen Town Council yesterday adopted a recommendation of the Lord Provost's Committee, supporting the move to restore the Orkney and Shetland Air Service formerly carried on by Scottish Airways Limited. At the same time, the Council turned down a request from Allied Airways, to hear a deputation from that firm and, meantime, to withhold support for the move.

By the KING'S Order the name of
Henry Vallance,
Pilot, Scottish Airways Ltd.,
was published in the London Gazette on
14 June, 1945,
as commended for valuable service in the air.
I am charged to record
His Majesty's high appreciation.

Winston S. Churchill

Prime Minister and First Lord
of the Treasury

Henry Vallance – and the
parchment conferring his
King's Commendation for
Valuable Service in the Air.
(Frances Vallance Collection.)

343

Orkney and Shetland County Councils and Orkney Town Council had asked the Minister of Civil Aviation for augmented services between these areas and the south, particularly Aberdeen.

It was in these representations that the suggestion was made that Scottish Airways, who originally operated the route, but who were excluded from it by the Licensing Tribunal in 1939, should be permitted to resume their service. The request from Allied Airways was conveyed to the Aberdeen Town Council in the following telegram: "Regret Council's support of Orkney and Shetland representations regarding Aberdeen air service. Our new service on peacetime basis adequate for all needs. Orkney and Shetland councillors interviewed and express complete satisfaction with our new programme. Proposed action now unnecessary. Request Council receive deputation from directors and meantime withhold representations to Minister."

The Council were unanimous, on the motion of Treasurer Morrison, in deciding to take no further action on the telegram. The treasurer said they had not heard representations from one side, and he did not see why they should see representatives of the other side.

Thus, in our effort to right the injustice inflicted upon us by Mr Trustram Eve in the 1939 Licensing Court hearing at Edinburgh, the post war fight was on.

It however, did not last long for we and Allied Airways were soon to become involved in a bitter fight with the dead hand of bureaucracy, for on the 1st November 1945, the new Socialist Government declared its attitude to civil aviation in a speech made by the new Air Minister, Lord Winster. Also involved was Group Captain David F McIntyre of Prestwick Airport who had designs of running in competition to our Southern Section on the Renfrew-Belfast service. They were about to launch a Prestwick-Belfast run with a converted 25-seater Dakota at a fare of thirty shillings single. That was roughly half of the fare we were charging. We were very much pre-occupied with this threatened invasion and cut throat competition of our territory when Lord Winster made his announcement of nationalisation in the House of Lords.

The press announcement on 2nd November quoted the details in the following report:

State to Own All Civil Air Transport
Three Corporations to run Services under Ministry

The Government's policy to bring civil aviation under state control was outlined in the House of Lords today by Lord Winster. It was described by Viscount Swindon, former Minister of Civil Aviation, as 'a most disappointing and damning statement for the prospects of civil aviation.'

"The practical working plan on which we were all agreed to mobilise all our assets ready to fly at any time is sabotaged 'for political theory'," he declared. "It is a sorry day for aviation." Lord Winster went on to say that, "The State will operate all British air transport services, own all airports used for scheduled services, and provide all radio, meteorological and air traffic services. The Brabazon Committee will be retained and the existing flying companies will be free to continue only until the new organisation is established." Prestwick was to be made an International Airport.

So the rumours which had persisted for the past two months had now become reality.

Following Lord Winster's statement, he assured me that insofar as Scottish Airways were concerned they would remain as a Scottish Division under the state corporation to be formed for the operation of the British and European air routes, and he again told me my position would be secure in view of the valuable services Scottish Airways had provided throughout the war. He requested me to do all I could to bring about successful transition from wartime to peacetime operations. I left him, thinking that perhaps after all, state control could be made to work, but I failed to take into account the scheming and jockeying for power which eventually reared its ugly head and the type of individual who would hold control against which there would be no appeal. In other words, civil aviation was to be operated under a Dictatorship.

Not so long after my interview with Lord Winster, he resigned his appointment as Air Minister and he was replaced by an individual whose ideas were not so honourable or appreciative of the work performed by our company over the past fourteen years. Ten days later, I received a letter from our Chairman, Sir Steven Bilsland, which indicated the policy under which Scottish Airways Limited would function until the great takeover by Socialism-cum-Bureaucracy occurred. The letter is worthy of reproduction.

I had a meeting in London last week with Sir Harold Hartley to discuss the situation created by the Minister's speech on 1st November.

The position is that we will continue to operate our services until the new organisation has been formed. Furthermore, it is important that we should not relax our efforts in any ways to develop and advertise our services and to ask for any additional aircraft that are needed to meet public demand. The Director General of Civil aviation told Sir Harold that he would welcome any suggestions from us as to new routes.

With regard to capital expenditure, it has been arranged that any new aircraft for which we have not already paid be hired, and the terms of hire are to be negotiated.

With regard to other schemes of urgent development involving capital expenditure, Sir Harold has asked me to put them up to him without delay, so that they may be discussed at the Ministry.

We will be discussing the whole position at our meeting on 30th November.

We met in Glasgow on 30th November for a Scottish Airways board meeting and most of the time was taken up in discussing the events of the month. Our directors appeared to be under no misapprehension what it would mean by being swallowed up by the Socialist octopus which had so suddenly descended upon us. We had all been under the assumption that the civil aviation plans agreed by the Coalition Government for post-war operations and to which we had already contributed a lot of hard work and planning, would be maintained by a Socialist Government. Under nationalisation, there would be no individuality or incentive or pride in the job as we had become accustomed to under commercial enterprise.

One newspaper ably described the situation as the 'Dead Hand on Aviation', and went on to say

> In some respects the civil flying scheme under proposed nationalisation repeats the broad lines of the Swinton scheme approved by the late Coalition. There will be three "chosen instruments" with assigned routes of operation. But whereas the Swinton scheme did seek to make use of the experience and knowledge of pre-war and present day operators and held out to them an inducement of financial rewards for enterprise, the Socialist Government proposals jettisons such experience and kills the incentive to development.
>
> The north of Scotland and the islands which are appreciative of the enterprise and the operators who serve them and who are looking for still further advantages, will note that their familiar services are to disappear. They will have to take what some large organisation, whose interests will be many, thinks is good enough for them.
>
> In passing, it may be remarked that the terms to be offered to dispossessed operators are 'infamous'. They are to be given only the value of their physical assets and nothing for goodwill. They have run financial risks in building up that goodwill but the Socialist Government proposes to step into their businesses and 'rob them of the fruits of their enterprise'.

We were not to feel the force and effect of those statements for another fifteen months. How true that forecast was, will be apparent later.

We gave a big party at our house for the New Year's festivities. Invited were all those who had taken part in the wartime air operations. Pilots, engineers, air control, Fred Haines and Tony Raven, plus wives attended and the party went on well into the early hours. New Year's Day was a holiday and we only ran the mail plane to Orkney and return. It was to be the last of a series of New Year parties we had held for the past few years for those who did so much for the war effort. Our son was sent out to sleep so that he would not be disturbed by the revelry.

The New Year brought serious thinking. If we could obtain a Scottish Division operated by Scottish Airways personnel as part of the new set-up and on the lines I understood Lord Winster to be sympathetic to, then nationalisation would only mean a change in financial ownership and that should not affect us. I could not see, at that period, any difference to the Treasury holding the purse strings to that of the LMS Railway Company. I certainly learned when it was too late that there was a whale of a difference.

First I had to get public opinion behind me. Again, I learned later that, in a Socialist Dictatorship, that also meant precisely nothing. I had been invited some weeks before to speak at the Rotarian lunch in Aberdeen on the 8th January 1946, and I decided to make the "Scottish Air Division" the main theme of my address. The Aberdeen *Press & Journal* fully reported my speech which is quoted from their issue dated 9th January 1946:

Claim of Scotland to run own Airways
Separate Division wanted for Pioneer Companies

Captain E E Fresson, pioneer of civil aviation in Scotland, wants a petition asking the Scottish Secretary to intercede for a separate division to operate air ways in Scotland within the framework of the corporation proposed for European and internal routes. Now is the time for such a move by municipalities, Chambers of Commerce and other business organisations, he told the Aberdeen Rotary Club yesterday. Suggesting the present companies should be the basis of such an organisation, he remarked that other claims in this direction savoured of "You've grown the plums and we are now going to eat them." Others who claimed the right for themselves had never, to his knowledge, run an air service in Scotland. They had had the same opportunities as the pioneers of 1933-39, but had not seized them.

Captain Fresson got a resounding "Hear, hear," from his Rotarian audience when he declared that government policy should develop along the lines of a Scottish Division within the greater corporation rather than absorb the present organisations into a corporation with its headquarters in London, and with no special interest in, or knowledge of Scottish needs.

Advocating that Scottish Airways and Allied Airways should be the backbone of such an organisation, he pointed out that they had pioneered, maintained and developed a large network of routes over the past thirteen years. They had plans and facilities for considerably enlarging their post-war operations. They held mail contracts. They had an experienced and specialised staff who knew every rock in Scotland. What had been achieved, he emphasised, had been done successfully by individual effort which gave a man drive to work twenty-four hours a day if necessary. It gave him a pull over any organisation swamped in some big undertaking.

Those views were given wide publicity throughout Scotland by the national press. A leading article commented:

Captain Fresson, as the pioneer of civil aviation, is entitled to a respectful and cordial hearing on the subject. His knowledge is gathered from day to day experience of founding and developing successful air services over a period of thirteen years. It is, in fact, the useful knowledge in which the Minister of Civil Aviation and his bureaucrats are lacking.

In parenthesis, it should be said here, that the pioneers of civil flying in the north of Scotland and elsewhere are being meanly treated under the scheme of nationalisation. They are to be flung out of business and probably out of employment with no compensation for their pioneering labours and risks, but with nothing but the price of their physical assets. The Socialists are treating the mine owners more liberally.

The Press obviously had a better slant on the "crystal ball" than I had at that time, and were able to foresee what was to happen two years ahead. I, on the other hand, believed we were to be allowed to continue operating the Scottish routes as a division within the framework of the corporation that was in the process of formation. In the meantime, our operations continued as usual and without any interference.

In the spring we were informed that the corporation, which was to operate the European and internal air routes, would be known as British European Airways and under the chairmanship of Sir Harold Hartley, with banker Gerard D'Erlanger as managing director. Sir Harold was the former chairman of Railway Air Services, which had also been taken over under the new set up, and Gerard D'Erlanger was ex-Air Transport Auxiliary (ATA), which was engaged in ferrying aircraft from the factory to the squadrons of the RAF during the war.

The first hint I got that British European Airways had become a reality came to me by telephone on Monday 2nd April 1946 when our secretary, William Cumming at Renfrew, phoned through to say that my presence was required on Wednesday 4th to meet British European Airways officials who were flying up from Northolt. They arrived just before lunch, in good style, by a Dakota aircraft which had been converted to peacetime requirements. George Nicholson, Wing Commander Measures, and several others along with myself, were awaiting their arrival in the Scottish Flying Club when they were ushered in by Secretary Cumming. We were introduced individually and, when it came to my turn to meet Gerard D'Erlanger, I felt he was hostile. During the speech-making after lunch, it became evident to me that the position of our company in future was to be on an "Overlord vis-à-vis Peasant" basis. When everyone had talked themselves to a standstill, the party left to be shown around our headquarters.

Later, they flew back to Northolt, and George Nicholson, Cumming and I discussed the future with foreboding. We sensed we were in for difficult times ahead. And we were not far wrong. I stayed over in Ayr that night with the Nicholsons and, on my return north, I was engaged in an interesting survey of the North Isles with a Dr Williamson, who was anxious to discover the location of seaweed beds. The plastic age was nearly upon us and it appeared that seaweed was sought after in connection with its manufacture.

We set off for Inverness in Dragon, G-ACIT, and flew at 400 feet around all the islands and coastlines. That appeared the best altitude to detect the seaweed beds. The doctor sat just behind me with a map and noted with pencil where the deposits could clearly be seen from our plane at the altitude we were flying. We spent three days on this work and the results, Dr Williamson told me, were most satisfactory.

He returned to Edinburgh on the regular service to Inverness and I stayed over in Orkney as I had some work to do on the reorganisation of the Orkney North Isles airfields. They were too small for modern needs and required extending. Arrangements had already been made with the Orkney County roads surveyor, Mr John Robertson, to make a survey of the airfields at North Ronaldsay, Sanday, Stronsay, and Westray, and we left next morning by air to commence the work, with two of his staff equipped with theodolite and measuring equipment.

I stayed in Orkney a week, running the survey team backwards and forwards to Kirkwall each day. By the end of that time, we had four airfields mapped out, which would give us three strips of 500-700 yards on each field. Our present fields only had a maximum of 400 yards, and some less than that. Also the surface was in its original rough state. We intended levelling the surface on the new strips. Within a month, we received an estimate of somewhere around £7,500 to carry out the work and I laid the matter before our board at our next meeting at the end of the month. They approved the expenditure, but our chairman considered it better to submit the tender to the Minister before officially accepting. It took some months to get a reply, but in the end the proposal was shelved. The new corporation did not appear interested with small shuttle services, no matter how much air communications meant to the islanders. Here was our first taste of nationalised service and we wondered what would be the fate of our other routes. Fourteen years later, the Orkney North Isles are still without the air connections they had grown to depend on for a number of years before hostilities.[1]

Shortly afterwards, when I was in Renfrew discussing the 1946 summer timetable with our traffic manager, I was introduced to an individual I had not seen at Renfrew before. It subsequently transpired that he was from the British European camp at Northolt, Middlesex. I had the Northern Section timetable worked out and we wished to integrate the Inverness-Glasgow section with services of the Southern Section to Ireland, Isle of Man and London. We assumed we were to carry on with the de Havilland Rapide in the absence of any other, and more suitable, aircraft.

It turned out that the stranger was attached to the new BEA traffic office in Northolt, and he opened up on me by saying that the intention was to provide three different types of aircraft for the Scottish runs. They all had different cruising speeds, which would make the aircraft non-interchangeable on a given route without hopelessly upsetting the timetable. On enquiry, he admitted they had little or no spares with which to service the aircraft, and more important, no engineers qualified for maintenance and no maintenance equipment. Without any of the aforementioned prerequisites, the airline would be a shambles within a week. I told him I wouldn't look at it. He looked at me with a pained expression on his face and replied in an aggrieved voice, 'Well, Captain, it's at least a plan.' I was thunderstruck. If that was an example of the new nationalised outlook and planning, we were going to have passengers stranded all over the country.

'A plan?' I said to him. 'You can take it back to Northolt. We're responsible for operations this year and Rapides we stick to.'

He turned on his heel and disappeared, and unbelievable as it may seem, that was the type of mentality encountered during the first year's operations of the new corporation.

I also learned during that visit to Renfrew that British European Airways, which was dealing with the question of post-war aircraft for Scottish operations, were negotiating with the Ministry for the allocation of a number of German Junker Ju-52 monoplanes. They were to be converted to fourteen-seater aircraft and were powered by three 450 hp radial motors. The aircraft were wholly uneconomical to operate and the motors were extremely unreliable as the Germans had mass produced those engines on the basis of one hundred hours operating life.

I suggested to Wing Commander Measures, who was acting for the purchase of these planes, that the whole proposal should be dropped and warned him about

---

[1] Loganair revived air services to the North Isles of Orkney from 1967.

the unsuitability of the German wartime engines and their maximum life of one hundred hours. But if they were set on purchasing these aircraft they should at least arrange to have American Pratt & Whitney Wasp radials installed and the German engines scrapped. Failure to do this, I warned him, would have disastrous results. It will be seen later how my warning came true. Apart form the technical disadvantages to using Ju-52s, I tried to impress on him the cost in fuel alone would be prohibitive for a suggested seating capacity of fourteen persons.

My advice was disregarded and a number of Ju-52s were made available the following year at a conversion cost of approximately £12,000 a piece. Not only were the BMW engines fitted, but most of them had exceeded their maximum permissible hours with the disastrous unreliable results I anticipated after the aircraft became operational.

Soon after the war ended it came to my notice that a new pilots union was in the process of formation. By the middle of 1946, the union had a branch at Renfrew and it appeared I had two militant 'Brothers' on my staff at Inverness. One day I received a letter from Wing Commander Measures stating he had received representations from the British Air Line Pilots Association (BALPA), Pilots' Executive Council, Glasgow, to the effect that they had received a letter from a member based in Scotland. Quoting from that letter, it went on to say, 'The writer of the said letter refers to certain features, which he considers to be most undesirable, of the operations to and from Inverness of Scottish Airways Limited.' There were four points raised. The first three were beyond the company's control and were the concern of the Air Ministry. The last complained that pilots were expected to fly in high winds, and cancellations because of high winds were regarded with disapproval by the resident director at Inverness – which was me. My reply to that complaint was termed in the following phraseology:

No pilot is forced by me to fly any route which he does not feel capable of doing. The question of flying in very strong winds is a necessity in this part of the world, if a high degree of regularity is to be maintained, and which of course, is so essential for the success of the service. We have flown in these high winds for the past thirteen years and no pilot has ever grumbled before. If there is any pilot on this station who feels he is incapable of carrying out the high standard of flying we have maintained for so long, then he has only to say so, and his services can be dispensed with. Incidentally, Allied Airways (Gandar Dower) Limited match our services in such boisterous days.

My reaction to all four complaints was that they were pettiness and an endeavour to stir up trouble. I went on to say in my letter that, 'I think the name of the complainant should be asked for and he should be questioned by the company as to his motives in making these complaints. I should add that, whoever he is, he has not been honest enough to first come to me and present his case. Instead he went behind my back and made representations to the British Air Line Pilots Association.'

I eventually found out who they were. One came from another air company and was a notorious 'Bolshie' and the second had very recently joined our company from abroad. He had been engaged on administration in the RAF and no doubt the kind of flying he was suddenly precipitated into, from an office desk, came as a shock to him. I blamed the first individual for the incident. The second got himself involved as he had not the right mentality to cope with some of the situations he was faced with. About that time, I also had some trouble with a newly formed Radio Officers Association.

I have mentioned the occurrence as it was an early pointer to change that was maturing under the demoralising effect of nationalisation. Our engineers were the next victims. Hitherto, we had a loyal and hard-working team of the highest standard. My chief, George Griffiths, and myself took a personal interest in them all and we had worked for the past ten years in perfect harmony. It was therefore with concern and sorrow that I observed the deadly poison of soulless bureaucracy permeating into one or two individuals. These happenings were additional indication of things to come.

Years after, many of my old staff have remarked to me that there was nothing like the old days. They would dearly like to have them back. 'One is just a number in a big Corporation, and of course, under the thumb of union decisions,' one individual said to me, which, whether they like it or not, they have to follow. However, the full force of this changed outlook did not have its full impact until that fateful changeover had become effective, when further happenings crept into my daily life.

Towards the end of 1946, I noticed an ever-increasing trend to overlordship on the part of my Renfrew colleagues. I found decisions were again being arrived at without reference to me. That had not been the case throughout the war. I did not pay a lot of attention to this trend in its early stages, but as the practices persisted, I began to protest without avail. It appeared that orders, unknown to me, were being sent from our new bosses-to-be in London, and that the Renfrew management were accepting and putting them into effect. Later, I found to my detriment, the answer to this subservience. The ground was being prepared for the new management of the nationalised Scottish air routes.

On the 27th September, the Southern Section had their first fatal accident. One of the Inverness aircraft, Rapide G-ADAJ piloted by Captain Hayes, was indirectly involved. Captain Hayes was making a scheduled flight from Inverness to Renfrew and, as he arrived over the airport in cloud, another

Rapide, G-AFFF, was approaching from Port Ellen, Islay, on the west coast. That aircraft, Captain Hayes told me afterwards, was making heavy going of homing on Renfrew airport and the pilot appeared to be inexperienced in the technique we employed for letting down in cloud. After a quarter of an hour or more of hanging around in cloud waiting for the other aircraft to get down, our pilot got fed up and asked for a priority landing, which was granted. Captain Hayes landed within five minutes of being given permission, but the other aircraft in the meantime flew into high ground some miles to the north of the airport, killing five passengers, plus the pilot and radio officer.

There was an enquiry held at Renfrew by the Air Ministry, which I attended, a month or two later. The conclusion arrived at was that the pilot of G-AFFF, Captain Stephens, may have mistaken the bearings given to our aircraft, G-ADAJ, which made its final approach on Renfrew airport from the south. Such a misconception would have headed Captain Stephens north in cloud towards the 1,500 feet Craigton Hill, at the east end of the Kilpatrick Hills, which he flew slap into. The finding appears incorrect to me inasmuch as the registration letters of the aircraft receiving the bearings are always prefixed by the radio station, prior to transmitting the original or subsequent bearings, excepting the final phase of approach when bearings are given in a string, that is, one bearing quickly after another. Our pilot, Captain Hayes, was blamed for crashing in on G-AFFF by asking for priority. It appeared to me at the time, that if Captain Stephens was unfamiliar with the procedure and was holding up the let-down of another aircraft, he should have been given a bearing and altitude to fly on by the radio station and told to stand off for five minutes. Whoever was to blame, it was an unnecessary accident which destroyed a twelve-year-old clean bill of flight. That incident proved how essential it was for pilots to receive specialised route training and I found out later that Captain Stephens was a pilot lent to Renfrew by the Pilots Pool and he had not received specialised training on the Western Isles routes, which we considered so important for safety.

I visited Renfrew Airport the day following the accident and saw the first German Ju-52 aircraft, which the Air Ministry had converted for civil use, parked on the tarmac. I was asked by the Renfrew chief pilot, Captain Barclay, if I would like to fly it. 'Certainly,' I said. I was interested to see how the aircraft performed and I flew it around for half an hour, making several landings and take-offs in order to appraise the performance of the aircraft on our small airfields in the north.

The Junkers Ju-52 had a tremendous amount of power for the carriage of fourteen passengers and, as I have said, was an extremely expensive and uneconomical aeroplane to operate. Furthermore, it required a small mobile power plant to start up the motors. There were very few aircraft and engine spares available and not enough starting units to go round any of our airfields. I was not impressed and I foresaw trouble with that machine if and when it was used on the Western Isles and northern air routes. I advised the Renfrew management they should insist on sticking to the Rapides until a suitable replacement was made available. That advice went unheeded in London and, early in 1947, the Junkers Ju-52 was operating the services from Glasgow to Stornoway, Aberdeen, Orkney and Shetland. Later, we shall see the chaos which ensued.

During November, Captain Hayes was again in trouble, but this time through a different cause and which was completely out of his control. For the third time since the commencement of hostilities in 1939, one of our aircraft was struck by lightning. It happened while Captain Hayes was flying the return Stornoway-Inverness service at 11,000 feet in clear air above cloud. He was passing through two pinnacles of cloud, which extended up from the cumulus nimbus cloud below, when the aircraft suddenly bridged the gap between the pinnacles. That allowed the stored up electrical energy in one of the cloud pinnacles to discharge through his plane to the other pinnacle. He was approximately half way across the Easter Ross mountains when it happened. As usual, there was a loud report and the cabin was filled with acrid fumes. The radio was put out of action, as was the compass. Fortunately, 'Smokey' Hayes, as he was known to his fellow pilots, kept his head, and as in the case of Captain Vallance some years earlier, he used his Sperry Directional Gyro to steer an easterly course which would take him out over the Moray Firth for a let-down without radio through the cloud. Captain Hayes successfully broke cloud off the coast by Fort George and soon landed at Longman airfield. On examination, the usual holes in the nose were observed and the radio aerial had been burned off. Again, it took our chief engineer, George Griffiths, a week or two to demagnetise all the ferrous metal parts in the nose of that Rapide.

With the arrival of November, the first public criticism of the nationalised airways began. An article appearing in the *Glasgow Herald*, dated Monday 4th November read:

Disappointment at Government's Failure to Meet Obligations
In particular there is disappointment and hard feeling over the failure of the Government Airways Corporations to meet their obligations. None of the Scottish services listed in June, in a somewhat modest programme of development, has materialised although the target date in almost every instance was October. Doubts about the capacity of British European Airways have seemed to be confirmed by suspension of services on their own main routes, caused by shortage and unserviceability of aircraft, etc.

On the 16th November, an Avro Anson arrived in Inverness with the Parliamentary Secretary to the Minister of Civil Aviation, Mr George Lindgren, aboard. He and his party stayed at the Caledonian Hotel. A reception was laid on to meet the civil authorities and I was invited to meet him.

During our conversation, he told me they were planning to put 100-seater aircraft on the north of Scotland run when they could get them built. These aircraft, he told me with glee, were to carry one hundred passengers at the third class railway fare. I remember looking at him in amazement. I commented that such rates would cost the taxpayer a lot of money.

'And,' I enquired, 'where are the airfields in the north of Scotland to accommodate such large aircraft?'

He hadn't thought about such contingencies. I let the matter drop. The whole nationalised situation was developing into a fantastic set-up.

Our last free year of commercial operations, 1946, had gone well with us. For the most part, free from political interference, we carried 28,000 passengers up to the end of September compared to 13,200 in the corresponding period of 1945. Over two million miles per year were then being flown by Scottish internal services. Finally, to end our year's commercial operation, we made a profit of approximately £8,000 for the year. We would have hoped to double that figure in 1947 had we been able to continue free from State interference. There was no profit the following year, or ever after on the Scottish air routes. As the losses mounted, the Scottish routes were conveniently named 'social services'.

What an easy and convenient way to brush off crude inefficiency. The London set-up had been warned that the Scottish routes could not be operated at a profit on the grandiose scheme they envisaged, but no heed was given and hence the resultant losses, which were enormous – £500,000 for the first year on Scottish routes, and considerably more in the years to follow.

16

State 'control'

During the first week of the New Year of 1947, George Nicholson, William Cumming and myself were summoned to attend a meeting in London with the Nationalised Administrative Heads of the newly formed British European Airways who, under Government charter, were to operate all European routes formerly administered by British Airways and all the internal British airlines operated by various commercial interests. The railway companies had considerable representation in most of the British air companies for which Wing Commander Measures acted as the co-ordinating director under the LMS chairman, Sir Harold Hartley.

Sir Harold was the first chairman of British European Airways and the managing director was Gerald D'Erlanger whom I had met at Renfrew the year before. We were interviewed by these two executives. Nicholson and Cumming went in first and I was the last. I was greeted by Sir Harold Hartley with a smile and hand shake. I, of course, knew him well. I received a scowl from his companion.

'Sit down, Captain Fresson,' said Sir Harold Hartley. 'We have brought you three down to London to acquaint you with the new set-up of Scottish Airways, which will be dissolved on the 1st February and taken over by British European Airways. Mr D'Erlanger, as you no doubt know, will be the managing director of British European Airways and he will explain the new appointments for the Scottish Division of the new corporation.'

Gerald D'Erlanger stared at me. I was under no misapprehension of the distaste with which he viewed my presence. In a cold and pitiless voice, he told me that George Nicholson had been appointed the Scottish Division director and would represent that Division at the BEA board meetings. William Cumming was appointed senior executive officer. 'You will be the area manager for north of Scotland and come under the jurisdiction of the aforementioned gentlemen who will function from Renfrew headquarters. You will be given a contract for six months.'

I sat there stunned. I just could not believe my ears.

D'Erlanger evidently read my thoughts and remarked, 'Take it or leave it.'

Sir Harold Hartley looked at me, I thought with sympathy, and made some remark to try and ease the tension. I recovered my equanimity and informed D'Erlanger that I was amazed to hear that I had been placed in a junior position to George Nicholson when I was senior to him in age and operational experience.

I added, 'Since the amalgamation of Highland Airways with Scottish Airways, my section has been the only one that showed a profit through the years and that surely indicated better management.'

He replied, 'I am not here to argue with you.' He repeated, 'Take it or leave it.'

I had to think this serious event out in calmer water.

'How long before you require an answer?' I asked.

He stated a time. I cannot remember exactly, but it was within a few days. I undertook to let him know in writing. The meeting terminated. Sir Harold shook hands with me and wished me good luck and D'Erlanger said, 'Good Morning', upon which I turned on my heel and left the room.

I met George and William Cumming outside and they said they hoped that we would still work together as in the days of the recently defunct Scottish Airways. They then walked ahead of me, arm-in-arm, talking seriously and looking very excited. There could be little doubt that they were delighted with the situation. For myself, I was placed in a humiliating and very insecure position.

When British Airways sold out their share in Scottish Airways to the railway company interests in 1939, Major McCrindle, one of the new directors of the reorganised British Airways, that subsequently became British Overseas Airways, had said to me that if I was not treated properly in the new set up of Scottish Airways, I could always rely on him to see that I obtained a suitable appointment with British Airways. So, after my interview with Sir Harold Hartley and D'Erlanger, I at once went to see Major McCrindle and reminded him of his offer. I explained what had been said to me and he appeared very surprised. Apparently he knew D'Erlanger well and said he would speak to him. I asked him not to do that. I would prefer it if he could arrange a transfer for me to British Overseas Airways. He undertook to investigate the matter. However, he was not successful, so, against my better judgement, I agreed to stay on with British European Airways on a six month contract. Subsequent events proved that decision to be disastrous. The changeover would take place on 1st February 1947.

I returned to Inverness and, as the days went on, the press became critical of the new set-up of Scottish affairs. It appeared that, along with the Renfrew appointments, there was to be an additional body to overlord our operations under the august title of the Scottish Advisory Council on Aviation. Its Chairman was to be Sir Patrick Dollan who was a Lord Provost of Glasgow from 1938 to 1941. I was unaware that Sir Patrick had any past connection with, or knowledge of, the complexities of aviation. I was told he had functioned on different social boards, but that was not going to assist us much in the stormy months ahead.

The first shot came from *The Bulletin* dated 11 January 1947, which quoted the views of the Lord Provost Perth, John Ure Primrose, who had been appointed as a member of the Scottish Advisory Council on Aviation and who held constructive and knowledgeable views. His brother had held a high rank in the RAF and I met him before the war when he was Air Adviser to the Post Master General for airmail operations. I quote the report *The Bulletin* as it appeared:

'Dictation from London on the future running of Scotland's already efficient airways should be resisted', declared Lord Provost J Ure Primrose, Perth, a member of the Scottish Advisory Council on Aviation, in a charter in the operation of nationalised Scottish air routes to be submitted to the Civil Aviation Authorities.

The Lord Provost states that the Scottish Division proposed under nationalisation should have charge of the operation of both internal and European services operating out of Scottish airports and should enjoy powers of operational management. The Advisory Council should resist the forcing of technical matters on them by London over the heads of the Scottish technicians. Scottish airfields, says the charter, sometimes call for different standards than those made for English and Continental airfields. The Scottish Division should not be bound in all instances to the rigid requirements laid down in the south.

'Scottish Airways, who are to be nationalised to form the base of the Scottish Division, have operated internal air services in Scotland for thirteen years with almost a clean bill so far as accidents are concerned,' the Lord Provost declared. 'At all costs, the Scottish Division should avoid having a host of unwanted personnel from the south foisted upon it. Excessive centralisation should be avoided at all costs, the charter stated. The efficient management of air services requires an extreme degree of flexibility and instantaneous decisions. This cannot be attained under excessive centralisation, especially if it is situated in London.' The Lord Provost says that the introduction of the 'pilot's pool' system in Scotland should be resisted. The system of employing and training pilots to be specialised on their routes should be continued for safety and regularity. Scottish Airways' only fatal accident occurred last September with a pilot borrowed from the south who had not been specifically trained over Scottish routes.

Looking back on events, I must say, Lord Provost Ure Primrose spoke with great wisdom and he confirmed my views which were identical and which I voiced at several public speeches early in 1946 for the safe operation of the Scottish routes at high regularity percentage. Further, a Scottish Division operated by the personnel who had learnt the special technique required through the years would have saved the public several million pounds which were squandered on an unwieldy set-up and run by men with a war operation mentality and to whom cost meant nothing. As this story draws to its conclusion, we shall see the sorry state our well esteemed airlines were reduced to by the central colossus of socialist politics and inefficiency.

After my London visit, I had not been back in Inverness more than a few days when I was called upon to fly the Shetland service owing to the indisposition of one of our pilots. The weather had been appalling with heavy rain, and many of the fields, I well remember, were flooded. In fact, Sumburgh airfield, between the strips, looked pretty wet. After landing at Kirkwall on my return, I was asked by the Post Office if I would delay the southbound service and fly the mails out to North Ronaldsay and bring in accumulated mails from the island, which had been cut off for over two weeks by storms and high seas. There was a strong wind blowing, which would be of assistance as I was told the landing ground was badly flooded and the ground very soft. I agreed to carry out the charter provided my southbound passengers consented.

We took off from the Hatston airfield around two o'clock in the afternoon on the first of three round trips as there were many passengers who had also been marooned at Kirkwall and on North Ronaldsay. The press reported the relief of the marooned island in the following terms:

Orkney's Epic Flight

The finest feat in the civil flying Orkney career of Captain E E Fresson OBE, the pioneer of Britain's internal airlines, was performed on Tuesday 14th January when he relieved the weather beleaguered island of North Ronaldsay using a land machine for a job that almost demanded the services of an amphibian aircraft. The island had been cut off from transport for seventeen days. The pre-war green field aerodrome made for Captain Fresson by the men, women and children of the island, and now seldom used, was the scene of the pioneer's latest exploit.

An island correspondent describes three landings made there on Tuesday by Captain Fresson as 'the most sensational spectacle in Orkney's sixteen years of civil aviation.' The aerodrome was flooded by rain water. The surrounds were covered by native sheep that normally live outside the short dykes encircling the island. As Captain Fresson, flying de Havilland Rapide, G-AGDG, circled overhead, the islanders cleared the sheep off the landing ground and on to the shore. The aircraft, a faster plane than the last remaining de Havilland Dragon, G-ACIT, so well known in Orkney, then sped down to 'land'. The landing had to be made in a semi-circle run around the rain lake. As the machine touched down, its wheels showered so much water out of the ground that the inhabitants feared disaster. An eye-witness said, 'You would have thought he had landed in the flood water after all. It was for all the world like a flying boat landing on the sea.' The plane skidded and slithered alarmingly, but came safely to a standstill.

The islanders crowded around to congratulate Captain Fresson and to sympathise with him for having marooned himself with them. He replied, 'No fear, we shall take off alright.' The prophecy proved correct. The plane made in all three double trips that day between Kirkwall and North Ronaldsay. The three take-off performances, less spectacular but definitely more hazardous than three landings, were accomplished with a fair margin of clearance despite the loads carried. Each flight from Kirkwall occupied fifteen minutes, the return journeys requiring twenty minutes each owing to the strong head winds.

The enterprise of the Post Office was responsible for the day's flying. The Post Office chartered the plane and the first flight from Kirkwall to North Ronaldsay and back again was a Post Office affair. Outward, the plane carried 948 lbs of mail and no passengers. Captain Fresson flew without a wireless operator to keep down the weight, operating the radio himself. 363 lbs of mail and two young women students were carried on the return journey. Four passengers were carried on the second outward flight and seven schoolchildren on the return journey. There were no passengers on the third outward flight. On the return trip seven adult passengers were carried.

The North Ronaldsay flying involved some smart staff work on the part of the Post Office and Scottish Airways. The Head Postmaster in Kirkwall, Mr David Scrimgeour, by chartering the plane for the mail flights, made the aeroplane available to the North Ronaldsay members of the general public. The Scottish Airways Kirkwall staff, who put in a great deal of extra work on Monday night and Tuesday, were R McKerrell, Orkney branch manager; John Watson and H Fisher, traffic officers; Robert Bain, driver; Kenneth Wards, airport assistant and Miss Ivy Cooper, clerkess. Orkney ex-members of the RAF, and certain serving members, stated to the *Orcadian* that only a pilot who had had joy-flying experience in all sorts of odd corners of the country could have effected the feat achieved by Captain Fresson in his North Ronaldsay landings and take-offs on Tuesday.

I have quoted the newspaper story of this flight in full detail as it demonstrates the value of flying to people living in the outlying parts of Scotland – a service which, I am sorry to say, they have not enjoyed since the Rapides were taken away by nationalisation.

The day of our handover to British European Airways dawned on 1st February 1947. It was a Saturday and I was recovering from an infection which had laid me up for the past three days. I did not feel fit to fly myself down to Renfrew, more especially as there was a south westerly gale blowing and the clouds were down to 500 feet with rain at times. I phoned my office and asked them to get hold of the off-duty pilot, Captain Hayes, and tell him I wished him to fly Rapide, G-ADAJ, to Renfrew with me as passenger.

We set off at ten in the morning in bad weather. Icing conditions were reported at 2,000 feet and above, and the cloud base at Renfrew around 100 feet. Accordingly, we decided to try and fly under the murk and we set off down the Caledonian Canal. After passing Fort William, the wind speed increased from the south-west and, halfway down Loch Linnhe, we were hit by a blast akin to the one I experienced before the war when flying the mails on a Post Office charter to Stornoway in a 70 mph gale. Pilot Hayes turned round and looked at me.

'Go on a bit further,' I said. 'We must get to Renfrew if at all possible.'

On arrival at the Crinan Canal, which we intended following, all the hills were in cloud and so the air became a bit calmer and we were able to reach Renfrew by circling around the coast off Ardlamont Point and cutting across the spit of land over Rothesay to the Clyde, nearly clipping off the chimney pots in the process, we were down so low. I was glad to get out of that plane. I had had a taste of the passenger's feelings in turbulent weather and it was quite different to being in charge of the controls.

I spent the afternoon at Renfrew at a meeting anent the winding up of Scottish Airways with Nicholson and Cumming. In the evening, George Nicholson drove us up to the Central Hotel where the 'handing over ceremony' was to be held. We had hired a room where we could all change. At seven o'clock in the evening, Sir Steven Bilsland, our chairman, opened the proceedings. He said that Scottish Airways Limited had passed into history, but would be reborn as a virile division of British European Airways and would contribute a wealth of flying experience and technical skill to the new company. Sir Steven went on to say that, from May 1933 until January 1947, aircraft of the company had flown nearly 10,000,000 miles and had conveyed 339,812 passengers. That was a record which would compare favourably with any other airline in the world.

Among the guests were Sir Harold Hartley, chairman of British European Airways, who welcomed the pilots and technical staff to the new Division; Sir Patrick Dollan, chairman of the Scottish Advisory Council on Civil Aviation, and the Earl of Selkirk, a member of the Scottish Advisory Council. Several pioneers of Scottish Airways – Captain E E Fresson OBE, George Nicholson, William Cumming and David Barclay were present and they recalled many of the early adventures of the original companies. Also present was Mr George Lindgren, Parliamentary Air Secretary to the Socialist Government; senior members of some of the trade unions and some of the senior staff of Scottish Airways.

In ending his speech, Sir Steven Bilsland made his first point to Mr Lindgren. He said, 'I hope that security of the gentlemen who have spent many years in making such a profitable success of Scottish Airways will be taken over by British European Airways. I would like to know that the Government intend honouring that wish Mr Lindgren. I refer particularly to Captain Fresson, Mr Nicholson and Mr Cumming.'

'Most certainly, Sir Steven,' he replied. 'What football club would, of its own free will, get rid of their star players? There will most certainly be a most welcome place for those gentlemen.'

I have quoted those proceedings, as later it will be seen that such assurances were merely a figment of the mind, if not actually double-talk.

I hadn't been back in Inverness more than a day or two when I learned the Inverness Town Council had received a letter from Mr George Lindgren, Parliamentary secretary to the Socialist Ministry of Civil Aviation who were responsible for operating the post war airfields, enumerating the advantages of Dalcross airport to Longman airport adjacent to the town. He pointed out that, whereas Longman airfield had served Inverness and the Highlands well in the past, it had many grave disadvantages in comparison to Dalcross, which outweighed anything that can be said in its favour.

The writing was on the wall. We were about to be uprooted from Longman which we had operated out of for the past fourteen years without accident. Dalcross was a first class airfield and, as I have said earlier, it was I who had recommended the site to the RAF just before war broke out. It was then my intention to move out of Longman owing to its limited size, but during the war Longman airfield was greatly extended by the RAF who used it alongside us throughout hostilities. With a little alteration, it was as large as Renfrew, Dyce or Edinburgh Turnhouse. The cost of operating Longman did not exceed a few hundred pounds a year whereas Dalcross would run into many thousands of pounds. I was therefore of the opinion that we should wait and see how aviation developed in the north before vacating Longman. Dalcross would not run away overnight whereas Longman could easily disappear for building purposes at a moments notice if we vacated it. I replied in a letter to the *Inverness Courier* urging a policy of wait and see, and pointing out the heavy increased costs of operating out of Dalcross, to the heavy increase in road transport costs and to the loss of time which would be incurred.

Within a week or so, I got my knuckles rapped sharply from the British European Airways chairman who sent a message through Mr Cumming, Renfrew, instructing me not to interfere and saying that I was cutting directly across 'London Policy'. That was the first intimation I received that the Scottish Division was to be a 'Division' in name only, and that our experience gained over the years was to be bypassed. In other words, we were expected to assume the role of 'yes men'.

The next jolt received was the advent, in the early spring of 1947, of the German Junkers Ju-52 which I have referred to earlier. Without warning, our DH89 Rapide aircraft were partially withdrawn to be superseded by the Junkers aircraft. Instead of leaving us with the Rapides with high payloads of around 1,200 lbs, which we had gone to a lot of trouble and expense in effecting by building a drying-out room to extract the moisture from the wooden components during annual overhaul, we were ordered from London to dispose of those aircraft and retain a bunch of Rapides of later registration which only had a payload of around 800 lbs. On enquiring into the reason for this extraordinary uneconomical action, it appeared that the decision was arrived at by an individual in the London hierarchy who considered that the aircraft with old registration letters should be the first Rapides to be disposed of.

After that order had been carried out, much against our better judgement, we were told that the Rapide was wholly uneconomical, as it only carried a limited and unprofitable load. The whole incident was completely irrational, and no doubt had been dealt with by an individual of the mentality I had met at Renfrew the year before, who dealt in 'plans'.

Having got rid of the aircraft, which helped us to make a reasonable profit the year before, at Renfrew, the Junkers Ju-52 went into action. In less than a month, our Renfrew-Stornoway and Aberdeen-Orkney-Sumburgh air routes were in complete confusion and dislocation. These German aircraft were breaking down all over the outlying airfields and, if and when the motors stopped, they could not be restarted without a special power-driven starting truck, which the northern stations were not supplied with. That meant the pilot had to keep his motors running while the passengers were disembarking and embarking. In the event of a motor having stopped, a starting truck had to be ferried by air from Renfrew. That took a lot of time and was extremely costly. We had no spares at outlying stations and headquarters at Renfrew were not much better off. As most of the motors were found to have exceeded their one hundred hours, they were extremely unreliable and spares were a vital necessity.

Passengers were kept waiting out at airfields from early morning to late evening, and were lucky if they got carried at all that day. There were no catering facilities when our base was transferred to Dalcross and no heated waiting rooms. In Aberdeen, passengers bound for London often had to await the arrival of an aircraft coming up from London, and that plane could be anything from an hour to several hours late even though the weather was good all along the route. I made it a point to find out what caused such delays and it appeared that departure of the London-Aberdeen plane was dependant on its arrival from Madrid or some other far away continental city. Some bright individual in the London set-up had the idea of integration and utilisation of aircraft worked out on paper without any thought being given to the possibility of the aircraft being able to operate to a strict schedule. Motor trouble, which, I have said, was frequent in those days immediately after the war, together with adverse continental weather had not been taken into account.

By the time July was reached, the public were screaming their heads off. MPs were asking questions in the House of Commons, not only about the frightful inefficiency of the newly nationalised airways, but the operating losses which were mounting into millions of pounds.

In the early days of 1947, I used to attend the monthly meeting of the newly formed Scottish Advisory Council of Aviation, but after a couple of months I gave it up as a waste of time. It involved travelling from Inverness to Glasgow and it had become clear to me that the Council was functioning in name only. Its chairman, who knew nothing about aeroplanes, used to arrive off the night train from London, completely briefed with instructions from Northolt. Whatever we suggested from our end was rarely taken any notice of. Those who held high office in London Headquarters mostly came from the Air Transport Auxiliary ferry service which had been responsible for delivering planes from factory to dispersal fields strewn around the British Isles, or to RAF squadrons, during the war. They may have known about ferrying work, but they had about as much idea of operating our Scottish air services as 'an ape had with a bad headache'.

No sooner had we been taken over, than our staff was increased from 75 bodies all told at Renfrew and Inverness plus outstations to something in the region of 400. Trade union rules were creeping in and demarcation of jobs being imposed making the labour charge very costly and wholly uneconomical.

BRITISH EUROPEAN AIRWAYS (Scottish Division).

Telegrams BEALINE Inverness

Telephone Inverness 720/1.

Struthers Lane,

Academy Street,

INVERNESS.

10th February, 1947.

H. Vallance, Esq.,
17, Affleck Street,
ABERDEEN.

My dear *Henry*, *Cheque*

    Very many thanks for the 20 cigars safely received. As I asked you to get them, I must insist on making due retribution. I therefore enclose P.O. for 5/-, and thank you very much for the trouble you went to in getting them for me. If you can manage some oysters on the next trip, I shall be delighted to get them. I had my first dozen for three or four years down in London last week, and they cost 1/- each.

    I am most interested to hear you had a good trip to the Far East. I think you are well out of this country and that you did the right think in joining K.L.M. The new set-up is not at all pleasing to anybody who is a free thinker or has any initiative whatsoever. You are indeed lucky being able to visit all these other countries, especially New York City.

My wife joins me in kindest regards to Mrs V. & yourself. Hope the Son in law is making good progress.

Yrs. [signature]

P.O.

Large aircraft were being used for administration flights on a large scale and the whole set-up was soon entangled in red tape and masses of printed orders, which were hardly issued before they were countermanded by a host of amendments true to civil service style. The organisation was also engulfed with decoration schemes comprising a red line and a 'key' which had to be 'exactly so' around walls of offices and waiting rooms, plus a BEA crest, and other oddities of a like nature which occupied a host of wasted man hours for all concerned.

The London headquarters of British European Airways rapidly became a nest of departments with the heads of each department vying with one another as to who should have the maximum of staff. They no doubt figured the bigger their department, the higher and more profitable status they acquired in our organisation which was already top-heavy. In Scotland, we were hamstrung. We had no independence and our efforts to reorganise

under the so-called Scottish Division on business-like lines was not countenanced. In fact, as events subsequently proved, we only earned black marks in our endeavour to get our services back to normal, and to make them pay.

By May 1947, it had become evident that our operations were to be conducted on a grandiose style comparable to long distance continental air routes. No thought was apparently given to the difference in earning power or traffic density of the two totally different operations.

Early in the spring, I wrote to the managing director of BEAC in London, Gerard D'Erlanger, regarding the extravagant changes that were taking place on the Scottish routes. I referred to the inadvisability of moving to Dalcross and to the operation of large aircraft on the northern Scottish routes. I warned him that if we vacated Longman airfield and moved to Dalcross, the cost of our operations would increase considerably. Our present transport costs at Longman airfield during winter was £25 per month. If we moved to Dalcross, the charges would be in the region of £250 in the winter and probably £350 in the summer. These increased costs only applied to passenger transport. Over and above, we would be faced with additional transport expenditure for engineers and operating personnel. I went on to say:

There are no proper waiting room facilities at Dalcross, whereas the Air Ministry have only just completed a very nice block of traffic offices at Longman airfield. Ultimately, new buildings will have to be built at Dalcross at extra expense. At present, there are three airfields on the Inverness-Kirkwall route, within five minutes or so of the centre of the towns, namely, Inverness, Wick and Kirkwall. I doubt whether there are three towns on any one route throughout the country which can boast such timesaving airfields right up against the town they serve. It would be a retrograde step to upset this happy trinity.

Lastly, the close proximity of the Longman airfield to Inverness is of great interest to visitors and, as soon as the restaurant and tea rooms are functioning on that airfield, the local traffic potential, coupled with the tourist trade, could be greatly extended. Additionally, the publicity value must not be overlooked. Finally, the maintenance cost of Dalcross as compared to Longman, will be extremely heavy.

Regarding the larger aircraft, it is my opinion, and I have fourteen years experience to go by, that the heavy flow of traffic which would call for aircraft of the Dakota class will be from London to Edinburgh and Aberdeen via the east coast.

The type of aircraft required on the Glasgow-Inverness-Orkney-Shetland run is a de Havilland DH86 sixteen-seater aeroplane, redesigned as a monoplane which would cost a fifth of the sum required for a large aircraft providing barely twice the number of seats. Also, maintenance would be considerably more economical for the smaller aircraft, and that type of plane could be run to a high utilisation figure per annum through frequency of services, thus reducing the operational costs considerably and giving better service to the public.

To settle any doubts about the safety of Longman airfield, a Dakota aeroplane should be sent up with one of our pilots to make practical tests of take-off and landing on the available airstrips. Should the tests be satisfactory, then Longman airport should be retained. After all, Dakotas were operating out of Longman throughout the war without difficulty or danger.

May I again emphasise the mistake must not be made of trying to run the Scottish services on a par with the continental routes. The two conditions are as different as chalk is to cheese. Failure to recognise this dictum will result in huge losses and poor regularity. Lastly, you will remember at the lunch at Northolt at the beginning of the month, Sir Harold Hartley, our chairman, said he looked to Scotland to make its own airways pay. That being the case, our advice should be accepted.

I did not receive a reply to that letter. We were hustled out to Dalcross the following August. At the same time, all our maintenance was shifted to Renfrew along with our staff and substantial stock of spares. Our Renfrew friends were surprised to note how George Griffiths had catered for any eventuality. In wartime it took a long time to obtain spares. The want of a spare part could ground an aircraft indefinitely. We were never caught out.

I have gone into the outcome of nationalisation at this stage in some detail as it will clarify and explain later events and the appalling losses which were to occur before the year was through. When these losses ultimately became known, the 'ATA Boys' had the temerity to term our once profitable air routes as a 'social service' and that in plain language meant, the taxpayer was expected to make good the huge and totally unnecessary deficit. We still had a number of Rapides at Inverness for our local operations, and they came in extremely handy in assisting to transport the passengers held up by Junker breakdowns.

In the spring of 1947, I took steps to improve the landing strip on the island of Stroma, situated in the middle of the Pentland Firth. Immediately after the war, the island was sold to private interests in the south. When I could obtain permission to recommence the North Isles service, I planned to incorporate Stroma. Under the Scottish Division set up, I had not the authority to get on with the job at my own discretion, as was the case in the past. I first wrote to the new owner, whose name I have forgotten, explaining my proposals and asking if he would he bear the cost of providing a small bulldozer if he was in agreement. I added that air transport from Inverness to the Stroma should be of assistance to him when he visited the island. He agreed to my plans and, on the 6th June, I flew Mr Phillips of William Tawse Limited, well-known contractors at Aberdeen, to the island to advise on the drainage and surfacing. At that time, I was unaware that the nationalisers had no intention of recommencing the much wanted local isles services, which Kirkwall Roads Surveyor, Mr Robertson and myself had spent so much time surveying the previous year. We were just on the point of ordering the small bulldozer when I got word that the island of Stroma would not be included, if and when the North Isles services were recommenced.

In the third week in April, I received instructions to proceed to Aberdeen to take over Allied Airways' affairs and weld them into the nationalised corporation. On arrival, I found that Mr Gandar Gower was away at his favourite holiday resort in Switzerland so, in his absence, the takeover was effected through his representative in charge. It was an unpleasant chore and I would have preferred someone else to have carried out the job – but there it was. I have always felt that, at that moment, 'GD', as he was commonly known to us all, and myself became friends in adversity. We had both been blatantly robbed of many years' hard work and effort. The press were humming around looking for a good story. The first question they asked me when I arrived at Dyce airport administrative block was:

'How do you feel, Captain, in taking over your Rival's business?'

I disliked that question and answered, 'No comment.'

They pumped other questions at me, which I refused to answer. On completion of the necessary documentary work, I left our station officer in charge to carry on the daily working of the air services, such as they were. The Aberdeen *Press & Journal* next day reported my visit in the following terms:

Captain Fresson, British European Airways' Scottish Director, commendably declined publicity – pictorial or otherwise – when he went to Dyce Airport for the preliminaries of taking over Allied Airways (Gandar Dower) Limited on behalf of the Government. Somebody less decent might have revelled in it.

For MP Gandar Dower,[1] in whose absence in Switzerland the northern airline has been taken into state hands, was Fresson's one and only keen rival in the pioneering days of the north of Scotland and outer islands air routes. Competition at times, was intense.

I sometimes see GD when I am in London, either at the Royal Aero Club or for an appetiser at his home in the West End. He hasn't changed a lot in looks, but is more mellowed, along with myself, in outlook I think.

On 5th July, I flew Sir Harold Hartley down from Shetland to Inverness. It was raining hard most of the way, but we landed at Longman airfield in time for his rail connection to London. He had a talk with me on the airfield apron. He thanked me for an excellent flight and said he was glad to have flown with me for the first time. I gathered, from what he said, that he would shortly be relinquishing the chairmanship of British European Airways for that of British Overseas Airways. (This actually came about at the end of the month.) He said he realised how difficult things must be for me, but told me to keep a cheery outlook on the problems which faced me. I have often since thought that he knew that his successor to the chairmanship was gunning for me, although he did not put it in so many words. I was sorry to see him go. He was the only friend I had amongst the Philistines.

Around the middle of the month, a phone call for me came through from Dalcross, from a pilot who had just landed in a Miles Hawk monoplane from

---

[1] Eric Gandar Dower stood for election as a Unionist candidate in the 1945 General Election, winning the constituency of Caithness & Sutherland by a mere six votes. The previous MP of 22 years was the Liberal, Sir Archibald Sinclair. Following a dispute with his local Conservative Association over his decision to renege on one of his election promises, he served the remainder of his term to 1950 as an Independent.

London. I picked up the phone and asked what I could do for him.

He said, 'I have an introduction to you, Captain Fresson, from a mutual friend in London. He told me to get in contact with you as you might arrange for my transport into town.'

I did not place 'the friend' who gave the introduction. He went to say that he was touring the British Isles by air under his own steam and that he came from Australia. I went out in my car to meet him. He was of medium height and there was nothing about his appearance much different from the average person one came up against in those days.

On the way into town, I became suspicious. This visitor had steered the conversation into my relationship with the new corporation. He asked a number of pertinent questions about the British European Airways set-up and asked my reactions to the changes which were being made. I was puzzled. If he came from Australia, why should he be interested in British European Airways or my opinions? It suddenly occurred to me that he might have been sent up from Northolt. I egged him on a bit and in the end I was certain I was correct. He was no actor and quite the wrong type to send on such a mission. I told him just what I wanted London to know in case they had sent him.

Shortly after, another incident of a similar nature occurred and I then became certain that I was being quizzed by order of higher authority. It happened at lunch after one of our Glasgow meetings. I was placed next to the female secretary of the British European Airways Scottish Advisory Council chairman. I had sat next to her on previous occasions. She was anxious to know my opinion on many controversial matters and what I thought about the set-up in BEA. Did I like or believe in nationalisation and so on? I was then certain that the Australian flyer's questioning was tied up with one and the same source.

I talked it over with George Nicholson afterwards and he agreed it was more than likely there were 'informers' adrift in the corporation. There appeared to be an atmosphere of being watched.

Early in July, I relieved a pilot on the Inverness-Orkney-Shetland run. Arriving back at my home for afternoon tea, the phone rang. On picking up the receiver, a voice said, 'Hello Fresson, is that you?'

'Yes. Who's that speaking?'

'George Nicholson,' came the reply.

'I've rung up to tell you I have been fired. I'm to carry on until the end of September, when the Scottish Division is to be dissolved.'

'You're pulling my leg', I said.

'No, it's the truth. I was sent for yesterday to go down to Northolt and the managing director told me I was out.'

I distinctly remember saying, 'I expect it will be my turn next.'

'It looks like it,' he said. 'They seem determined to smash the Scottish Division.'

'I'll be down to Renfrew soon and we will have a chat about this situation.'

'Fine,' he said. 'Let me know when you are arriving and come and stay with us.'

He rang off. I turned to my wife. 'Nicholson has been sacked,' I said.

She looked incredulous. I told her the rest of the story.

'I'm afraid that's the beginning of the end of our so called Scottish Division.'

I went on with my job as best I could while waiting to be called to London at any moment. But no word came.

At the beginning of August, we moved from our Longman airfield to Dalcross. The Junkers were still breaking down and hanging passengers up for sometimes hours. At Longman, passengers could wait comfortably in the Inverness Station Hotel and partake of meals when necessary. At Dalcross, there was no proper waiting room, let alone a coffee bar or dining room. There also was no heating. During August it did not matter so much, but when the winter came around, our passengers were in for a grim cold wait should the Junker aircraft fail to appear.

Just about that time, rumblings in Parliament commenced. In *The Scotsman* of 3 July 1947, Socialist member for Tradeston, Mr John Rankin, is reported as having asked the Parliamentary Secretary for Aviation, Mr Lindgren, how many Ju-52s had been converted, the total cost of their conversion and on which routes these machines were operating. Mr Lindgren replied that ten Ju-52s had been converted at a cost of £125,000. These aircraft were operated by British European Airways on five of their Scottish services, but were to be replaced in the autumn of that year.

February to October represented eight months' use of these aircraft for £125,000!!! How could the Scottish routes earn enough to pay that price? And we had been asked to do our best to operate the routes at a profit. That was just the first rumble of the financial volcano. An eruption was about to take place before the end of the year. Actually, we managed to get shot of the Ju-52s at the end of August. That arose through an incident which occurred around the first week of that month.

One of the Junkers arrived at Aberdeen from Orkney with the aircrew almost on the point of asphyxiation by carbon monoxide gas. Passengers sitting in the front seats nearest the cockpit were also affected. Half way across the Moray Firth, exhaust gasses from one of the motors broke free, penetrated the cockpit, and invaded the cabin, the door leading to the cockpit being open. The crew shut off the cabin and opened all the cockpit windows, but that was not enough. Slowly and surely, the crew were gradually getting torpid. They radioed Dyce airport reporting what was happening. They then tried shutting down one motor at a time to find out which was the offending engine out of the three installed. By the time they had located and shut down the responsible motor, they were over Banffshire with still forty miles to go. They only just made it.

On hearing about this grave incident, I strenuously urged Northolt to withdraw the Ju-52s at once, even though it might cut our passenger capacity, and replace them with DH 89 Rapides. The Junker aircraft had been nothing but a nightmare ever since they were put on the run after the takeover on 1 February.

For the first time, London responded to a request made by me. They went further and replaced the Junkers by sending up one or two Dakota twenty-five seater aircraft which operated at never more than half load.

At that stage I should have thought their correct and proper plan would have been to place an order with the de Havilland Aircraft Company for a dozen DH86s with the new Mark II Gipsy Six motors fitted with constant pitch airscrew. The DH86 had a capacity of fourteen to sixteen seats, and would have tided them over until the de Havilland Company had produced their new DH Heron monoplane to replace them. Had they had the common sense to adopt that plan, and to retain the Rapides to carry on the service until the DH86s were available, a very different financial picture would have resulted.

At the end of August, I was staying overnight at the Kirkwall Hotel. During the early part of the evening, I was looking out of the lounge windows watching the harbour movements, when I heard a voice addressing me. I turned around. It was one of our old passengers.

'What's gone wrong with Scottish Airways?' he enquired. 'In the old days, we could set our watches by your timekeeping. Now we never know when or at what time we are going travel!'

The question was put in a loud voice. There were a number of other visitors in the lounge who looked at me as soon as they heard the question. I had to think quickly if I was to produce an answer that could not be pinned on me as an act of disloyalty.

After a short pause, I answered. 'You are not travelling by Scottish Airways any longer, Sir. You made your last flight with that company on 31st January.'

I have forgotten the passenger's name, but he looked uncomfortable.

'I am sorry, Captain', he said. 'The travelling public would give a lot to get Scottish Airways back again.'

I excused myself as I did not wish to get caught up in any controversy. One never knew who was listening.

With the advent of the Dakotas, we gradually began to regain some semblance of a timetable, but we soon found they could not operate in the low cloud conditions, which the Rapides were able to do. Neither, during the previous seven months, had the corporation taken any action to train the pilots for that specialised type of operation on our routes which I have referred to as so essential. My impression remains that we figured the percentage of regularity that winter at around 60-70 percent as against Scottish Airways 97-100. However, after eight months of never knowing when the Ju-52 planes would arrive, it was like coming out into the sunshine to see the aircraft running to a reasonable schedule again.

George Nicholson phoned me in the middle of September to say there would be a helicopter arriving at Renfrew on the 16th. Would I like to go down? If so, he would try and arrange a flight for me. 'I certainly would,' I replied. I mentioned the matter to Brigadier Murray who resided in Caithness and who sat on the board of the Scottish Advisory Air Committee.

'Why don't you come with us?' I asked, having met him casually in the lounge of the Station Hotel, Inverness, that day. 'You would enjoy a helicopter flight.'

He said he would like to. Accompanied by my wife, we motored down together and arrived in time for lunch at the airport of Renfrew.

It was a nasty, gloomy day. The cloud base was around 500 feet and a fairly strong wind was blowing from the west. I wondered whether a helicopter could fly under such conditions. Apparently it could, as the Brigadier and myself were ushered aboard the helicopter for the first flight after lunch. I don't mind admitting it, I was a bit scared. The machine only had one engine and if that failed over heavily built-up Glasgow we were in for serious trouble. However, we set off by rising vertically from the hangar apron and flew over John Brown's shipyards on the other side of the river. The helicopter had a curious sideways movement and, when struck by a gust, it would shudder in a most disconcerting manner. I took a quick look at Murray. He must have sensed I was looking at him for he looked round at me and pulled a wry face. From that, I gathered he, like myself, was not exactly at his ease. After circling the shipyards several times, we made off in the gloom over central Glasgow. It was like entering nightfall. With the Central Hotel as the pivotal point, we circled around the city and ended up about a hundred and fifty feet over the main entrance of the hotel where we hovered for at least two or three minutes. We could see all the pedestrians below gazing up at us. By that time, I was tremendously interested, for it was an out-of-this-world experience.

We arrived back at Renfrew airport exactly forty minutes after take off. The pilot made one circuit of the airfield, dropping off height and arriving in front of the hangars at around 100 feet. Then, for me, the most amazing thing happened. The helicopter suddenly ceased to move forward. We were hovering over the hangar apron from where we had started. Our pilot moved the throttle of the motor back slowly and we began descending vertically. As we were about to touch down, he gave a slight movement forward of the throttle and we settled on the ground without a tremor. It was an amazing experience and I was grateful for having had the chance of that flight.

Seven months after nationalisation, I now did very little routine flying. Two new pilots had joined us, ex-RAF, by the names of Captains Forbes and Thacker. Once he had familiarised himself with our specialised requirements, I posted Captain Forbes to Aberdeen. He was a first class pilot and, by September, he was flying the night service out from Northolt to Edinburgh and Aberdeen. I made several trips with him and became intensely interested in the RAF Gee-H navigational aid which I had not come into contact with before.

It was all very interesting after the crude methods we had been using throughout the war, although I must say that, when we had got used to calculating drift and course in our heads from bearings on the station one was making for, it was extremely accurate and we never failed to reach our destination directly overhead the radio station, even under blind conditions over the whole route. The bombers' Gee-H system, however, went into reverse, so to speak, because they homed the aircraft on their target from the point of departure whereas we were homed by the point of arrival. Furthermore, we had to obtain our homing bearings by wireless telegraphy calls. On Gee-H the positions of the aircraft were constantly fed from the guiding station. Captain Thacker did well for us on the Orkney and Shetland service, very often flying overtime to rescue stranded Ju-52 passengers.

Towards the end of 1947, my work had become mostly administrative and I now seldom flew a scheduled service, excepting as relief pilot. The work involved frequent visits to Aberdeen, Sumburgh, Kirkwall and Renfrew. I continued to carry out all ambulance flights that cropped up in the Northern Isles. I was the only pilot left who was experienced in landing in those small and rough island landing grounds. Mostly, my old friend Dragon, G-ACIT, was used for those flights, although I had often made use of the DH89 Rapide which landed faster and, of course, this was more difficult. My last ambulance flight of the year was made on 13th September, to bring a sick case from the island of Sanday to the Balfour Hospital, Kirkwall.

We had not stationed any aircraft in Kirkwall since we were forced by the government to close down the North Isles service at the beginning of the war, so the plane had to depart from the nearest base, Inverness. The Kirkwall newspaper, *The Orcadian*, describing the flight in their issue of 18th September 1947, said,

Orkney's old aerial friend was seen and heard lumbering over the sky again last Saturday. Pilot at the joy stick of this veteran de Havilland Dragon, G-ACIT, was airways pioneer Captain E E Fresson OBE.

This aircraft was bought new in July 1933 by Highland Airways and was rebuilt by George Griffiths and his team in Inverness two years ago, with spares obtained from Australia owing to them being unobtainable in this country. Her job last Saturday was to convey a lad from Sanday to hospital in Kirkwall. Two hours, Inverness-Sanday and Sanday-Kirkwall. That was the Dragon's excellent time on this mercy mission.

The patient was seventeen year old David Cromarty Leith. The family were on holiday in Sanday. Young David, tall for his age, had been under medical treatment in Edinburgh before coming north, was reported to be doing well in Kirkwall's Balfour Hospital. The lad's father is a nephew of Mr James Irvine, West Brough, Sanday.

During the fourteen years I had been flying in the north of Scotland I cannot remember our company ever failing an ambulance call, be it at night or in the foulest weather, and many calls came from Shetland. Even with that record, we were criticised by some Shetland councillors who complained that we carried patients who were stretcher cases on a mattress placed on the floor of the aircraft after the seats had been removed. The councillors, I gathered, considered we should have provided an aircraft fitted up on the lines of a road ambulance, but they did not say who was to meet the prohibitive cost. We never received a complaint from any patient who, no doubt, were only too happy to enjoy the privilege of being transported from Sumburgh to a modern hospital in Aberdeen within two hours, in reasonable comfort. There were, and I suppose always will be, some folk whom one can never please.

A few weeks earlier to that island ambulance charter, an article had appeared in the journal *Modern Transport* on the subject of 'Airfields in the Orkney Islands'. I have already recorded that, since the middle of August 1946, I had been busy in improving the landing strips for the Orkney Isles. I had always deemed it urgent that the North Isles should have their air service restored to them. I quote the article, presenting the uncalled for delay and indecision on the part of the bureaucrats in re-establishing those communications.

It is to be hoped that with the human weakness credited to civil servants in their leisure hours, some responsible myrmidons of the Ministry of Civil Aviation, listened to the edition of *Country Magazine* broadcast by the BBC recently. It deals with life in the Orkney Islands and included impassioned pleas for the restoration of the air service between the mainland and its outer islands.

This valuable service was provided until 1940 by Scottish Airways Limited, but there is at present no indication of its restoration, despite the presence in the British European Airways fleet of one de Havilland Dragon, admirably suited for the purpose and, indeed, specially reconditioned by Scottish Airways in 1945 with that in mind.

As it was, some of the participants in the broadcast programme were compelled to spend three or more days away from home. Inter-island boat services do not work daily, whereas the air service, operating two return trips every other day, involved less than fifteen minutes flying, against three to six hours by sea.

The recent statement by the Ministry of Civil Aviation on the subject of aerodromes referred to the need of detailed surveys as some of the landing grounds used before the war are considered too small for the medium-sized aircraft which would provide a faster and more efficient service. The survey carried out by Scottish Airways after the war showed that all the fields would enjoy one strip not less than 700 yards long, and other strips were from 500 to 600 yards in length. There is no knowing what medium-size aircraft may be officially in mind, but the Dragon or Dragon Rapide would be perfectly adequate for the traffic likely to be derived from communities of up to 300 people, and it would be far better to commence operations with this well-tried type, rather than wait for further surveys.

That article ably described the gist of the matter. The surveys which I have previously mentioned, carried out by the Orkney County Council surveyor, Mr Robertson and his team, more than catered for the DH Rapide which could carry seven passengers and luggage and, working a two-trip a day timetable, could transport fourteen passengers each way. For an average population of 300 souls per island, that was more than sufficient. Furthermore, an aircraft stationed at Kirkwall would have been able to care of all the air ambulance services in Orkney and Shetland, thus avoiding the present long and unprofitable positioning of aircraft from Renfrew to Kirkwall and Shetland, and return to Renfrew base after the mercy flight had been completed.

There was another case to be made for stationing a Rapide with pilot and engineer at Kirkwall, for the aircraft could have been profitably used to restore the Kirkwall-Shetland evening service which we used to operate for the commercial travellers. In addition, the local trans-Pentland run which in pre-war days we and Allied Airways found very popular, could have been revived.

The North Isles service was never recommenced, although at the end of 1947 it was generally believed from statements issued by the minister concerned, that they would be restored. In fact, I was told by the minister that they would be restored, and as late as September 1947 I was called on by the Ministry of Civil Aviation to make a special flight to North Ronaldsay and Stronsay with an Air Ministry surveyor to inspect the airfield sites we had in mind for reconstruction. The ultimate failure on the part of the Socialist government's chosen instruments to restore air connections to those remote islands, and the hardship imposed, has to my mind, been largely responsible for the depopulation of the islands which has occurred since the end of the last war. I visited North Ronaldsay in my Percival Proctor aircraft during 1955, landing on the same field the inhabitants carved out with their hands and rough tools before the war. They were delighted to see me and there were many expressions of regret that the dead hand of nationalisation had cast its curse on that and the other islands.

By November, it was apparent that all was not well for BEAC from what Air Minister Lord Nathan described as 'the first socialised industry in this country' in a speech made at the beginning of the month. Following that, the *Glasgow Herald* published a leading article which stated:

State aviation has had a bad year. The twelve months which have elapsed since the Scottish Advisory Council was appointed have been notable for more broken promises than for extension of air services. In fact, not much more flying is being done now than at the end of the war. The Scottish Division of British European Airways set up at Renfrew in February, in fulfilment of frequent Parliamentary promises, has lost both its independent status and its original commander.

The *Sunday Express* published an article by Squadron Leader William Simpson DFC, one of our famous fighter pilots, in which he headed his article 'Show Down on the Air Road to the Isles'.

'It was not like this in the early days of Scottish Airways, friend. I am sorry, but that is the truth.' The speaker was a priest from Benbecula in the Hebrides. The place: the beach airport on Barra. The seat he had booked was already occupied by a VIP. This priest expressed to me the common feeling throughout Scotland. Commenting on VIPs, the priest went on to say, 'It is crofters and other ordinary folk who fly, and British European Airways is giving an inferior service to the most air minded people of Britain'

During a comprehensive air tour of the islands and Highlands, I had ample experience to justify this view. Since fifteen years ago, when pioneer Captain E E Fresson opened the first scheduled air service between the mainland and Orkney, the ordinary folk of many remote islands have learned to accept air travel as a matter of course. And as the airlines grew, sold largely on the results of air ambulance flights that saved countless lives, Scottish Airways began to make a profit.

Things have changed for the worse since British European Airways took over the assets and operations of Scottish Airways. Pilots and radio officers have yet to learn by experience the intricacies of flying to remote small islands, often in fog.

He then goes on to comment on the unserviceability of aircraft. That flying and engineering personnel plus management in Scotland, are working on the end of remote control from London. He tells passengers' tales of woe. Of hours spent in tea-less wooden huts, waiting for planes that never arrive. Of the heavy burden in ill-will that British European Airways has earned and suffered, and a spate of odious comparisons with Scottish Airways. Naturally, he states, the political issue of nationalisation versus private enterprise is raised, and with it, a growing resentment that control of Scottish air travel should have passed into English hands. He finished off his article with:

Scots say that under either private enterprise or nationalisation, the personnel of Scottish Airways alone knew how to operate the peculiarities of air services to remote islands with complete efficiency.

The *Investors Chronicle* also published an article under the heading:

Parasite Drag on Air Transport

Commercial Aviation is undergoing a change which, if continued to its logical conclusion, must destroy it. It is being turned away from its real purpose, the conveyance of people and goods at high speed, to other less simple, less open, and as the writer believes, less desirable purposes.

The article then goes on to deal with the three corporations which have been formed and says that the corporation handling the South American traffic is the only company which remains in touch with reality.[2] 'Otherwise, the corporations BOAC and BEA look to Government funds for their continued existence.'

All of the above quotations coincide exactly with what Mr Nicholson and myself had continually preached until our throats were hoarse. Not only were we not listened to, but we became marked men, ready for the public executioner for the advice we gave.

By the time December arrived, the press commenced to expose the financial losses and again the *Sunday Express* came out with an article, this time from Group Captain Dudley Saward OBE, headed 'Why our Air Lines lose Money'. This article was dated 7 December 1947. I quote the most pertinent extracts, which also coincide with the fears I felt within a month of being taken over. The Group Captain said:

> I left British European Airways because I do not like to see good money wasted, and because I want to see British aviation organised on sound, paying lines, free from the dead hand of the civil service,' (That remark gets right down to one of the main causes of the troubles of nationalisation.) 'First of all, why do we have three corporations to run one state enterprise? Why have triplication of fabulously-paid higher grades?

How right the Group Captain is, for the rate of pay per annum of the chief executives of the three corporations referred to at that time was:

BOAC Chairman	£7,000 plus £1,000 expense allowance
BEA Gerald D'Erlanger	£6,500 plus £1,000 expense allowance
British South American Airways	£6,000 plus £ 500 expense allowance.

In each of the above cases, the expense allowance is exclusive of overseas visits, special large scale entertainments, and car and chauffeur. I should add, that to the above figures, must of course be added the three managing directors' fees, probably within £2,000 of each of the above payments, and for three managerial staffs. Divided by three would have effected a big saving. Group Captain Saward goes on to ask:

> Why have triplication of research, training, maintenance, buying, equipment and stores departments, ticket selling, commercial and general

---

[2] British South American Airways Corporation was initially run by Air Vice Marshal Donald Bennett. He placed a high priority on efficiency and running to schedule, but the airline experienced several aircraft losses and was eventually absorbed into BOAC in 1949.

administration, advertising and traffic handling? How much economy is needed, can be judged from the monthly losses:

January 1947	£260,200
February 1947	£342,300
March 1947	£353,500
April 1947	£305,100
May 1947	£267,400

And those figures are operating expenses only. One has to bear in mind, that BEA had a number of their aircraft virtually given to them, that most of their ground facilities were provided, and that they got their equipment at a ridiculously cheap price.

In addition to the aforementioned triplication, must be added, as far as BEA were concerned, the unnecessary repetition of organisation within English, Continental and, until recently, Scottish divisions.

Here I venture to add that, if the Scottish Division had been given complete home rule, the profit that company made the previous year could easily have been doubled in 1947. When I say 'complete', I also mean complete divorce from Ministry of Civil Aviation handling of airfields which helped to put BEA expenses sky high.

To the above quoted mismanagement, must be added, says Group Captain Saward, the Control muddle, which was considerable. One particular item was the failure to equip the aircraft belonging to BEA with the 'Gee' equipment, which was the minimum radar which was considered safe by 'Bomber' Harris for RAF aircraft when not over enemy territory. Eventually, the proposal was approved and the target date of fitting that equipment to the Dakota aircraft was the end of December 1947. It was said there would be no difficulty in obtaining a contractor to fit the equipment. Quoting the Group Captain's words:

In January, air crews were complaining about the failure to fit the radar equipment to their aircraft. I again raised the matter, pointing out that a Scottish firm [meaning Scottish Aviation, Prestwick] was putting similar equipment in certain foreign operators' aircraft at considerable speed. These contractors had efficiently and speedily fitted radio and radar equipment to Dakota aircraft of the Allied Air Forces during the war years. I was rebuked. I was told there were political difficulties about placing an order with a Scottish firm. I suggested that we were not interested in politics, but in seeing that our aircraft were safe. So it went on. In April I warned, that if something was not done quickly, our Dakotas would have to face another winter without radar equipment. By June, one prototype had been fitted and when I left in September, only three had been finished. During the war, all the twenty-three Dakotas would have been completed within a month.'

One can deduce from the above indictment that, rather than give the work to a firm who were not in the political swim, safety of aircrew and passengers were a secondary consideration to the then vicious set up in BEA. The article continues with a citation of minor abuses of privilege, all adding to costs, but the most damning statement is contained in the last few lines:

Finally, I would like to mention an ominous aspect of a state corporation. I refer to the code of disciplinary procedures set out in Northolt Station Route Orders in September 1947 providing for a system of punishments up to dismissal without notice with entries in the 'accused's personal file'. I was horrified and frightened to find such a thing in civilian commercial organisation.

That ends the article and I have presented the main facts in order that the reader may obtain a mental picture of the set up which we in Scottish Airways were precipitated into and for which Cumming and myself were about to suffer ignominy and ruination.

Two weeks later, and just to see the old year out, on 21 December there was another contribution to the *Sunday Express* by Squadron Leader William Simpson DFC. The title this time was 'What a Way to Run an Airway'.

A statement of account for the first year's operation of one of our three nationalised airlines, the British European Airways Corporation, will be laid before the House of Commons tomorrow. That is to say, the printed balance sheet will be available to MPs. But there is not likely to be an opportunity for debate on it until the next session of Parliament, and perhaps not even then.

This is a pity, for the figures, the first to be made public, of a British nationalised air transport undertaking will be startling.

Taxpayer Pays. Behind this Christmas shock for the taxpayer, lies a story of a mushroom organisation built up to operate the British air routes, to the capitals of Europe and between main towns of Britain and the remote islands around our coasts. Interested observers, including myself, have watched BEA grow up and lose money, with alarm. It is an organisation which bears a close resemblance to a military air force where expense is no object, and it has the same faults and qualities. [It was, of course, being run by wartime ATA heads and senior personnel.] The Government told BEA to go ahead and show the British flag to advantage in a 'big way'. This has been done and how!

The business organisation is appalling, top heavy and cumbersome which shocks the pioneers of the many airlines that were amalgamated and nationalised into BEA. Those pioneers who are with BEA have lost the power and opportunity for initiative which they once used to profitable advantage. They know how to make money out of aviation, but are now powerless to put their business experience into practice.

The *Scotsman* leader of the 23 September, ended up the commentary of the disaster of nationalised air transport in the following words:

It has been known for a long time that the State system of civil aviation has been run at a heavy loss. The accounts of BEAC, published yesterday, show that for the first eight months, the Corporation had lost £2,000,000. The State air line was operating on a seller's market for many people travelled by air owing to a shortage in shipping.

Evidence that State aviation is proving a very costly experiment for the tax payer is apparently now inducing the Cabinet to review their air policy. The heavy looses piled up by the state corporation justify the views of those who maintained that a new and expanding industry would have been more successfully operated by private enterprise on a public utility basis.

BEAC's policy now is to economise by eliminating services which are not self-supporting. Their restrictive attitude augurs ill for the development of aviation in Scotland. Its expansion here has not been limited by shortage of aircraft which could have been made available by private operators. Unfortunately, the dead hand of state control had deprived Scotland of an opportunity which is not likely to recur, of creating an aviation industry of comparable importance to its shipping trade.

It is quite understandable that the Ministry would welcome a cessation of criticism, but the record of state aviation is so uninspiring that it badly needs the stimulus of criticism if there is to be any hope of greater efficiency.

That, I think, represented a fair assessment of the position ending my last year with Scottish aviation, with the exception maybe that the Ministry of Aviation also bears considerable responsibility for the grandiose way at which it set up its own department for the operation of the Scottish airfields. Fire tenders big enough to put several houses on fire out, manned by many bodies who sat on their 'chairs' most of the day doing nothing – some stations even had putting greens to help pass the time. There was a State manager for each airfield which could have been managed by the BEA manager on the spot with a junior assistant, and so on. All the heavy costs involved were reflected in high landing charges for BEA aircraft, out of all proportion to the number of passengers carried and the fares charged.

The pre-war system worked very well for the small number of aircraft movements in Scotland. The operator managed the airfield and the Air Ministry provided and operated the radio stations. That cut out Air Ministry operating charges being reflected in the landing fees and made landing rates reasonable. It would be interesting to know what the Air Ministry Civil Department cost the taxpayer over and above. Whatever it was, one can be sure that BEA's Trojan losses created a very steep bill.

17

The BEAst strikes

The New Year 1948 was spent quietly among our local friends. 'Gone with the Wind' best described the celebrations among our staff, which over the years had been a unique and happy feature in our home at Mayfield Road for all flying and engineering staff had been transferred to Renfrew, along with our aircraft, during the last half of 1947. They left me Dragon, G-ACIT, and one engineer, Archie MacDonald, to maintain it. I now had no prescribed flying duties, but in the absence of any instructions to the contrary, I presumed I was still expected to carry out charter flights or air ambulance calls as they arose. Otherwise, why station an aircraft at Inverness? DH Dragon, G-ACIT, had been returned to Renfrew early in December for its annual overhaul and I ferried it up on 5th February via Dyce airport where I was due to carry out my monthly check on operations at Aberdeen.

My first charter of the year came from the Ministry of Civil Aviation to transport three of their airfield inspectors to the island of Westray on 11th February. The North Isles air service still appeared to be under consideration at that late date. The Westray charter was to be the last operational flight I made for the Northern Section of British European Airways as it subsequently created a storm of inhuman criticism. The flying field at Westray was some three miles away from the village. While the inspection was underway with Mr Johnson and his party from the Ministry, a taxi arrived from the village. The driver brought a message from the hotel asking me to return and phone Surgeon McClure at the Balfour Hospital, Kirkwall, as my services were urgently needed for a 'serious case' ambulance flight.

On arriving at the Westray Hotel, I was connected to the Balfour Hospital without loss of time. Surgeon McClure came to the phone.

'Is that you Captain Fresson?' he asked.

I replied in the affirmative.

'We have just received an urgent call, old chap, from the island of Stronsay, asking for an immediate air ambulance. A small boy has been crushed by a farm tractor and the island doctor says that, unless he can be flown into Kirkwall Hospital for urgent attention, he is likely to die. I understand an immediate operation is necessary.'

I told Surgeon McClure that I was in Westray on an Air Ministry charter, but would return to the airfield and explain the urgency to my passengers and would leave for Stronsay within a quarter of an hour. 'You can tell the Stronsay doctor to have his patient on the flying field within twenty-five minutes.'

I hurried back to the Westray landing ground and explained to the Civil Aviation representative, Mr Johnson, what had happened. He agreed I should make the trip immediately.

'In fact,' he said, 'we have completed our work here during your absence, so we will come along with you, if that is alright, and it will save you the trouble of flying back from Kirkwall to get us.'

Within the twenty-five minutes, the patient, a small boy, was being put aboard the plane at Stronsay and inside ten minutes I landed him at Hatston airfield, Kirkwall. An ambulance was awaiting our arrival and the poor little chap, who appeared to be under the influence of a sedative, was in hospital within a few minutes. He was operated on at once and I learned next morning before leaving with my Air Ministry friends for Inverness that he was out of danger. They had caught him just in time.

Details have been given at some length in view of the aftermath that occurred. The press gave the flight some publicity and within a few days I received a short terse letter from the manager of British European Airways at Renfrew saying it was understood I had carried out an ambulance flight to Stronsay on the 11th inst, and I was requested to inform them who had given me the authority to make the flight, and that in future, I was not to carry out any further flights of a like nature. I replied, saying I had not received any instructions forbidding me to carry out mercy flights. In fact, I understood the reason for stationing Dragon, G-ACIT, at Inverness was for that very purpose, plus the carrying out of any charter flights which might occur. I concluded by adding that, if I had not been near at hand to carry out that mercy flight call, the surgeon at Balfour Hospital told me the boy would most certainly have died for he was sorely injured. I forget how the matter ended, but the instructions for me to desist in answering any ambulance calls in future were not withdrawn. Subsequently, there were press criticisms over this incident, which were tied up with other matters and will be related in sequence.

On 22nd February, the *Sunday Express* displayed in large type on the front page an announcement:

70 BEA pilots face sacking

HQ officials and Scottish pioneers to get notices. Men who made the Air Roads to the Isles – Cuts caused by travel ban and £2,000,000 loss. At the same time, three pioneers of the two independent Scottish companies, which were absorbed by BEA upon nationalisation, are to be dismissed.

The *Press & Journal*, Aberdeen, on the 23rd February, confirmed the previous day's report, but added:

"There will be no drastic changes in reorganisation or serious staff reductions in Scotland, Sir Patrick Dollan, Chairman of the Scottish Advisory Council on Civil Aviation," assured a reporter of the *Press & Journal* yesterday. "Many of our services have to be stepped up by 100% this summer and we need all the pilots and radio officers we have," he said. Rumours of dismissal of three Scottish pioneers in aviation – Captain Fresson, Captain Barclay and Mr Cumming, was denied by Sir Patrick. "The reorganisation is bound to bring about changes and these may be in executive posts, but," Sir Patrick said, "should any of these three be affected, then an alternative job will be offered."

Sir Patrick was either pulling the wool over the eyes of the public or he was grievously misinformed, as events will confirm.

The Glasgow *Bulletin* commented very ably in its leader on 23rd February about the mess that one year of nationalisation had created in the country:

If anything can shock the reluctant into a true appreciation of the Scottish position of civil aviation, surely we have it now in the news that three of our pioneers in civil flying are likely to be 'axed' by British European Airways.

Not only have the Labour Government killed Scottish flying enterprise, but their 'chosen instrument' now seems to be in process of dealing as unceremoniously with the pioneers they took over as they did with the other pioneers who would have nothing whatever to do with a nationalised set up, which was plainly foredoomed to disaster.

In fact, the only Scot who seems incapable of being shocked into facing the facts is Sir Patrick Dollan, Chairman of the Scottish Advisory Council, who was yesterday still handing out the usual stuff about Scotland having a better deal than ever, in spite of all the official forecasts from the south about the absolute necessity for cuts in services and everything connected with them.

These pre-war services were laid down and built up by native Scottish enterprise, by people like Fresson and Cumming, for whom we are told, there is likely to be no future under British European Airways. If those people had been given any sort of freedom after the war, they could and would have developed services far beyond anything that had been possible before, but instead Scotland was saddled with the incubus of a 'chosen instrument' which has all too plainly been finding it a struggle to maintain anything like the pre-war standard.

Under protest by people who saw what was happening, the Government eventually gave Scotland an 'Advisory Council', one of the most obvious pieces of 'political eyewash' in the Labour Cabinet's short career. The council has no doubt given London its advice, but how much of it has been taken? According to Sir Patrick Dollan, at various times, quite a lot, but all the public can judge from is tangible results, and these results have brought neither new services nor an improvement in old ones. The reverse, in fact, for complaints by users in the north in particular is that the services are worse than ever they were.

And what can Scotland do in the face of this shocking display of nationalised ineptitude? Precisely nothing it seems.

The press had accurately summed up the situation. I can't say I was surprised at the turn of events in view of the lavish and stupid manner under which our well-organised business had been turned upside down. Ever since George Nicholson was fired in the previous July, I knew I was on insecure ground and that it was only a matter of time. It was with grief that I gazed on the sad and chaotic state our efficient airlines had been reduced to, and which had taken us over fifteen years to build up. We had served the country faithfully during five years of difficult wartime flying, in unarmed aircraft, which were always open to attack at any moment without the power to defend or retaliate against the enemy who roamed the skies along our routes.

The continual parrot cry of the politicians, that Scotland enjoyed a far better service under the chosen Government instrument was too much for the Scottish public to swallow. For it was they who came to know the hard way, exactly what had been going on since the airlines were pitched under the hands of bureaucracy in its worst form.

It would be a great loss for me to leave the air routes which had become my one ambition in life, but under the circumstances, I was prepared to relinquish office, provided suitable arrangements could be determined. I, at that time, had reached the middle fifties, and could not hope to pick up a compensating post equal to what I had built up over the years. I, accordingly, decided to leave for London as soon as possible and seek an interview with Gerard D'Erlanger at his home in Kensington, when I could talk to him uninterrupted, about my future, for he held the final word.

I flew to Aberdeen in Dragon, G-ACIT, on Wednesday 18th February and caught the night plane down to London. I put up at my London club, the Royal Aero Club in Piccadilly, and got in touch with banker D'Erlanger on the phone at his house. He said he would see me on Saturday 21st February at 10.00 am.

I kept the appointment punctually and was ushered into the drawing room. The minutes ticked by, then an hour, and still no sign of my quarry. I could hear him talking to his children who appeared to be playing in the garden. I sat waiting until after midday. I had been there two hours or more when he suddenly appeared without any apology. His look was no more pleasant than when I had met him in January 1947 with Sir Harold Hartley. After looking through me, and still standing, he said, 'You wanted to meet me?' I briefly referred to the newspaper articles reporting my impending dismissal and asked him if it were true that I was about to be dismissed from the Corporation. He said a final decision had not been taken. I suggested to him, that if he wished to get rid of me, I would resign from the Corporation inasmuch as I no longer had any authority in the operation of the Scottish air routes, and provided the Corporation would adequately compensate me for the loss of my livelihood. He replied that he would see what could be done, or words to that effect. The interview was short and at an end. He opened the door of the drawing room. I picked up my hat and coat and was ushered out of the front door.

The following Friday in the House of Commons, Sir Basil Neven Spence, MP for Orkney and Shetland, accused British European Airways of waging a 'cold war' on Scots and the pioneers of Scotland's internal airways and declared that the services would have been better under private enterprise. The *Daily Record*, in its report, said:

> Sir Basil referred to the reported dismissal (since denied) of the three well-known Scottish airmen on grounds of redundancy. Angrily demanding, 'Who created the redundancy?' he went on to say, 'There was no redundancy before the war. The services were organised with the correct number of people. I think it is a monstrous thing for these Corporations to create redundancy and then proceed to kick out men who have spent their lives building up these airlines. The Scottish Advisory Council on Aviation,' he said, 'did everything but give advice. The day after the report of the dismissals in certain papers, Sir Patrick Dollan had stated that the notices of these men were not being sent out.' Sir Basil, who uses a plane more than any other member of the House, told the Government why the Scottish internal air lines were not paying. 'I came down the other day from Aberdeen to London in a 21-seater aircraft as a sole passenger. Does it not occur to British European Airways that, in running these internal airlines, it would be far better to have twenty passengers at £10 a piece, than four at £25?'

Earlier, Mr Alan Lennox-Boyd, Conservative MP for Mid-Bedfordshire, had reiterated the Opposition's determination to denationalise the Corporation as soon as they returned to power. In 1951, when the Tories were again in office, Mr Lennox-Boyd failed to carry out that promise when he became Minister for Civil Aviation.

On Thursday of the following week, Mr Cumming, Captain Barclay and myself reported to Mr J V Wood, managing director at Northolt. We were shown into his office, one at a time. He appeared a kindly man, and it was apparent he had been delegated to carry out the 'dirty work'. Having asked me to take a seat, he said, 'I am sorry having to tell you, Captain Fresson, that there is no place for you in the future set up of British European Airways.'

'I had gathered that already from the press,' I replied, and I asked on what ground I was being dismissed. I was informed that there were no complaints. I then said that there must surely be some reason for depriving me of the business I had created and knew more about than anyone in the Corporation. He made no reply to this observation, other than it was the Board's decision.

'Will the Corporation adequately compensate me?' I enquired.

'We have agreed to pay you £2,000,' he answered.

I could hardly believe my ears. 'That amounts to the public theft of my business!'

'Those are strong words,' he answered.

'Well, doesn't it?' I retorted. 'How am I going to live on the interest of such a wholly inadequate sum as that. You must surely realise that, at my age, I shall be unable to obtain a commensurate job. And as for aviation, there is practically nothing left which this Socialist government hasn't seized.'

He gazed at me, I thought with sympathy. 'I am only informing you of the decision of the Board.'

'In that case, there is nothing more to be said.' I bid him good morning and left.

As I walked along the passage, I was thinking that D'Erlanger, after my interview last week at his house, had done nothing to obtain a just and honourable settlement, and this confirmed the suspicion in my mind that he was responsible for the situation. As I turned a corner in the passage leading to the front entrance, I ran slap into him. Before I could say a word, he glared at me, and disappeared quickly into an office on his right. I met Cumming at the Orchard Hotel, Ruislip for lunch. He had been told exactly the same thing. David Barclay, he said, had received a last minute reprieve. Sir Basil Neven Spence's reference in the House of Commons to his valuable air ambulance work, which, incidentally, I had spoken to Sir Basil about previously, had caused a change in attitude. I was told that David had been interviewed and told that he would be given the chance of organising an air ambulance division.

We flew back to Renfrew that night. One of our pilots, whom I had always counted as one of my friends and who had been attached to the northern routes during the war, was on the same trip. He saw us seated, but passed by although there was a spare seat at hand, and he chose a place in the extreme front of the Vickers Viking aircraft. He appeared frightened to talk to Cumming and myself, which indicated the fear of persecution.

There was a battery of cameras and reporters to meet our plane on arrival at Renfrew. The news of our meeting, and its result, had reached the Glasgow press and we were showered with questions. The date of my departure from the Scottish airlines had been fixed for the 31st March 1948 and, as William Cumming and myself had not come to any decision on our future action in relation to our dismissals, we agreed to make no public statement at that moment. We merely confirmed the report that we had been sacked.

I went down to Ayr to stay with George Nicholson that night and we sat up late discussing the political theft of our business. It seemed to me, like a nightmare. I had been to see Mr Lindgren, the Socialist Parliamentary Secretary for Air, whom I had previously met on his visit to Inverness in the autumn of 1946. He appeared pleased to see me and called a colleague in to the discussion. I asked him if the Air Minister would take action to prevent British European Airways ruining me. After some consultation, they both eventually agreed that it would embarrass the Attlee Government, should my case be brought to the House of Commons. They could not, or would not, give any just reason for the British European Airways policy. I left, thinking that perhaps Mr Lindgren was sympathetic, but in that I was subsequently to be proved wrong when the debate ultimately took place in the House of Commons for he did his best to justify the British European case. Lord Winster, whom I think would have befriended us, had been replaced by another Minister who did not appear to have the same degree of discrimination between right and wrong.

I returned to Inverness to work out my last month, but there was nothing for me to do. I flew up to Kirkwall in Dragon, G-ACIT, on the 23rd of the month to say goodbye to my staff, and on the 30th March I flew over to Dyce to bid my adieu there. They all appeared too frightened to say much, but I could sense their sympathy for me.

I flew back in the afternoon, crawling along low down over the hills and moorland south of the Banffshire coastline. I landed at Inverness Dalcross airport at four thirty in the afternoon. It was my last flight in that aeroplane, which had become a trusted steed. Next day, unbeknown to me for I was not advised of the situation, a plane was sent up from Renfrew with an engineer and pilot, and G-ACIT was then flown to Renfrew. I did not know it had gone until two days later. I had asked to be allowed to purchase that DH Dragon. I was proposing to use it for air ambulance work in the Northern Isles if British European Airways did not restore the facility, and also for air charters. I was brusquely refused, and, to make sure I did not keep that plane, it was removed in a stealthy manner out of my reach.

Following the reprimand that I received in the middle of February in connection with the Stronsay ambulance flight already described, and following the removal of the DH Dragon from Inverness at the end of March, there occurred two calls from the Orkney County Council for ambulance flights to take an urgent surgical case from the island of Westray to Kirkwall Hospital. Quoting Dr Bannerman, Chief Medical Officer of Health for Orkney, 'British European Airways said they could not carry out the mercy flight because they had no suitable plane available.' And yet they had my Dragon, G-ACIT, in Renfrew, which we specially retained and rebuilt for that work. It can only be concluded that it was not the aircraft they were short of, but a pilot who knew those landing fields in the North Isles. Having got rid of me, they at the same time got rid of the one person who could have met the ambulance contract BEAC had with the Orkney County Council.

With Renfrew's inability to do the job, a steamer had to be sent to Westray to bring the small patient, Inga Brown, seven years old, into the Balfour Hospital. The sea journey took six hours against the flying time of fifteen minutes. The press reported that the girl was seriously ill with acute appendicitis, and the sea was very rough. The press also quoted that it was understood that the BEAC pilots at Aberdeen refused to make the trip because the landing ground at Westray was not licensed. I suspect, in that case, it was also because none of the pilots could land a Rapide, which was the only type they had available for the job, on the small field at Westray. It was possible to do so safely, if one had the 'know how' because I had frequently landed there in that type of aircraft. In any event, the law did not require a field to be licensed for a charter flight or for ambulance flights.

Meantime, a storm of protest was raised about the dismissals. The Inverness Chamber of Commerce, supported by the Aberdeen Chamber and others, organised a protest meeting on 9th April in the Inverness Town Hall, which seated 400 persons. The place was packed. The MP for Inverness, Sir Murdoch Macdonald, and Lord Malcolm Douglas-Hamilton together with Mr Eric Linklater, the famous novelist, spoke, as also did Provost Ross and certain councillors.

In its leading article, the *Highland News* of 27th April 1948 described the situation created in the following terms:

Indignation of the summary dismissal of Captain E E Fresson and the other senior Scottish executives of British European Airways Corporation is growing throughout the country. It is certain that the question will be aired in the House of Commons after the Easter recess, probably by Sir Murdoch MacDonald MP for Inverness-shire who is well aware of the distressed surprise that the announcement caused. Sir Murdoch has already raised the matter privately with the Under Secretary for Civil Aviation.

This is a matter above party politics and it is more than possible that, when the question reaches the floor of the House, criticism will come not only from the opposition side. In the country at large, protests of the harsh and altogether stupid action of BEAC high command are being crystallised through such democratic channels as the newspapers, chambers of commerce, local authorities and public societies, whose only interest is to see fair play for both these pioneers and for the air travelling public.

It seems possible, that the 'Fresson case' will become something akin to the historic case of 'Jenkins' ear',[1] but instead of forcing the Government to take action against a tyrant foreigner, it will force an investigation into the despotic and thoroughly inefficient rule of one of the Government's most disastrous ventures.

The word that sticks in everyone's gizzard in connection with the dismissals is that used by BEAC in its very self-conscious announcement 'Redundant'. The only thoroughly experienced, top men in the Scottish Division, the only men to reach the top the hard way, the only men with an intimate knowledge of the routes, and the public they serve, in fact, the men who planned and pioneered it all, 'Superfluous?' Scottish people just won't believe it. The people of the Highlands and the Islands who 'bless' the name of Fresson, who brought the world to their door, would have a stronger word for it, a short sharp word of three letters.'

The Editorial writer in the *Stornoway Gazette* has struck the nail right on the head when he says:

One does not look to Government Corporations for gratitude, but one would like to know who have taken the place of these pioneers, how they were chosen and what their qualifications are. The weeding out process that has taken place in BEAC since the Government took over, savours rather of a 'bloodless purge'.

All the men who built up the services are gradually being dropped, not because they are redundant – many more officials have been taken on than have been displaced – but because room is being made for other people. But will we get an answer to this charge? No, certainly not, if it is left to the Corporation. Certainly not if it is left to the mealy mouthed Ministers who refuse to give answers in the House to questions about their economically disastrous ventures in the air, on the ground, and under the earth. Will details be revealed of the shifts and manoeuvres that provided plenty of jobs for the 'boys'. Or about timetables slashed and

---

[1] A reference to the War of Jenkins' Ear (1739-1742). British declaration of war on Spain was legitimised by the alleged severing of Captain Robert Jenkins' ear by Spanish coast guards when they boarded his brig off Havana eight years earlier. The ear incident was used as an excuse by Britain to pursue conquest of Spanish territories in the West Indies.

altered to fit the whims of the planners and which put the convenience of the passengers a poor second? Of vastly increased fares and of planes running with only a third of their complement of passengers?

The only satisfactory answer is for the affairs of BEAC to be investigated by an impartial Enquiry. Public opinion demands this, and the people's voice will not be stilled until such a step is taken.

So ends the leader.

Earlier in my story, I said I would again refer to Stornoway which, during the pre-war years, was so reluctant to give any help in establishing an airfield. Once the air service had really got under way, the population became my staunch supporters. Its town council and councillors were as demanding as any other part of the north of Scotland in their protests against my dismissal. One newspaper even reported they were considering offering me the Freedom of Stornoway, but I never heard anything about that officially. Anyway, such an honour did not mature either there, or anywhere else.

I am afraid the demands in the last paragraph of the *Stornoway Gazette* editorial went unheeded, for the Socialist Civil Aviation Parliamentary Minister, Mr George Lindgren, gave no sympathy or help to public opinion. With every effort made by MPs to get the fantastic mess sorted out that British European Airways had got themselves into, plus their frantic desire to get rid of me, Mr Lindgren's answer was always to the effect that the 'question' was a matter for the Corporation and outwith government interference. So, having given birth to the monster, the Socialists washed their hands of any responsibility for their deeds. A very convenient, but perhaps dishonest way of evasion.

On the 31st March, I said goodbye to my Inverness staff, packed my belongings, and left the office I had occupied for the past seven years. I was allowed to retain the Gipsy Moth, G-AAWO, and Mr Donald of Macrae & Dick, who had taken over our old hangars at Longman airport, allowed me to house it there. Within a week or so, the Aberdeen *Press & Journal* newspaper hired me to carry out a photographic survey of the north of Scotland towns along with their photographer. We also included the Cairngorm Mountains and the small lochs to be found on the slopes of those mountains. Some excellent results were obtained in twenty-odd hours of flying time.

At the beginning of May, I was informed that the Conservative Party intended to raise the question of my dismissal and compensation in the House of Commons. The date was 31st May 1948 and it is recorded in Hansard Vol. 451, No. 126. I was later invited along with my wife to stay with Colonel and Mrs J R H Hutchison (Glasgow Central) (now Colonel Sir James Hutchison) at Forgandenny, south of Perth, to spend the night and to provide information for the forthcoming House of Commons debate. I was told by my host that Mr J S

C Reid, MP for Hillhead, Glasgow, and an eminent barrister, would present the case on behalf of the Conservative and Unionist Party.

That same evening, there was a big assembly, under the chairmanship of Lord Dunglass DL,[2] in the Central Scotland Ice Rink, Perth, to hear Mr Winston Churchill speak. I was invited to accompany my hosts. We were late in getting back to Forgandenny and so the notes on the debate to come were completed next morning.

I arrived at the House of Commons at two o'clock in the afternoon on Monday 31st May 1948. I was shown into a box at floor level. Beside me sat a British European representative who had been sent to take notes of the debate. I knew him slightly. He told me he did not like the job he had been assigned, but it was a question of 'do as you are told or be fired'.

Mr Hutchison had evidently been told of my arrival, for he came along and went over several points which Mr J S C Reid required to be checked. The attack on the Minister of Civil Aviation, through his Parliamentary Secretary Mr George Lindgren, then commenced.

Mr Reid (now Lord Reid) was a very well-known barrister and a very skilful one, for he presented the case in masterly form. For the purpose of my story, I will content myself with referring to the more pertinent passages in his address to the House.

The case, which Mr Reid built up step by step, was to prove that British European Airways had no legitimate reason for dismissing me. Scotland was, he said, disturbed and alarmed by developments in the Scottish air services. Then, suddenly, came the announcement that the man who had created aviation in Scotland had been dismissed. Then Scotland got really angry and, the Minister may know, there were protest meetings – large protest meetings – held in many places; there were resolutions passed by all manner of local authorities, chambers of commerce, and the like. Indeed, in one local authority in Stornoway, two Socialist members of the Council went so far to propose that Captain Fresson should receive the Freedom of the Burgh, and one said that the way Captain Fresson had been treated was no great credit to the present government. That was a Socialist bailie in Stornoway. Perhaps they were far enough away so that the whip may not have reached up there. Not only that, but we had speeches and pronouncements by prominent men of all parties. We had the whole press, local and national, up in arms and nobody had a good word to say for the Ministry. He went on to quote the final paragraph of the *Scotsman* editorial of 10 April 1948:

> The pioneers of Scottish aviation have been dismissed by BEAC on the ironical pretext that the services of men of unrivalled experience and knowledge are redundant. A protest meeting at Inverness last night

---

[2] Lord Dunglass was later better known as Sir Alec Douglas-Home.

voiced the indignation in the Highland area at the harsh treatment by BEAC of Captain Fresson, the founder of air services in the Highlands. The people in the north of Scotland, where Captain Fresson has worked for fifteen years, are surely in a better position to estimate the value of his services than the heads of a bureaucratic concern in London. No explanation of the arbitrary dismissal of this pioneer has been offered by BEAC despite the widespread protests by local authorities and other bodies in the Highlands.

A public meeting in Kirkwall on Monday emphasised the duty of BEAC to pay adequate compensation to Captain Fresson. This is a moral and not a political issue. It is intolerable that a public corporation should be above accounting for its decision in a matter which provokes so much popular feeling and which raised important issues about the efficiency and control of Scottish Aviation.

'In their first report,' Mr Reid said, 'British European Airways drew attention to the fact, that it had been necessary for them to speedily start from scratch. That may well have been so in other departments of their work. It was emphatically not so in Scotland, but they chose to make it so, because they chose to turn things upside down when there was absolutely no need for them to do so. They chose to turn services, which were practically self-supporting, into services which incurred crippling losses with the result, of course, that the Minister had to interfere. He could interfere then. Why cannot he interfere now?'

By this, he meant to direct British European Airways to either utilise my knowledge of the Scottish routes, or pay me adequate compensation for my undeserved dismissal. The Socialist argument was that the minister was incompetent to interfere in a matter that was purely an administrative one.

Then Mr Reid went on to say, 'If the Minister would accept responsibility, I should of course, confine my criticism to him. The old and good rule should hold that, where a Minister is responsible, his subordinates and others ought not to be criticised, but as the Minister disclaims responsibility, it is necessary for me to direct my criticism to the actual wrong-doer. The chairman and most powerful influence in British European Airways is Mr D'Erlanger. Whereas Sir Harold Hartley appears to have reasonable views, whereas the Minister when he saw fit to make pronouncements had more or less reasonable views, this gentleman had anything but reasonable views. I will not expatiate upon the facts of Captain Fresson's case. He had given fifteen years of devoted service to the Highlands with universal satisfaction. He had received resolutions long before this matter cropped up. He was decorated during the war for his services and what has happened since shows the prestige which he has acquired in the Highland area.'

Mr Reid's masterly presentation of the case, plus the widespread public indignation aroused over it, failed to move that Minister of Air or his colleagues. If the full Hansard report is read, it is not difficult to see the Party resentment which I feel was behind the stark refusal of Mr Attlee's Government to protect me from savage persecution.

Three years later, the Conservatives returned to power. I went along to see the Minister for Air, Mr John S Maclay, regarding reopening the matter of adequate compensation which the Tory Party said in 1948 should be paid to me. To my utter surprise, Mr Maclay told me that the new Conservative Government were not prepared to reopen my case. So what was honest and right for the Conservatives in 1948, appeared no longer to apply in the spring of 1952. It's a topsy turvy world, which makes politics a doubtful profession!

On the 1st July, I left Inverness to receive training for a three-year executive post that had been offered to me in Kenya. My wife came down to Alloa with me and stayed for the first week before returning to our home in Inverness. On the Monday morning, I had just left my wife reading the morning paper in our room, to go down to breakfast, when I heard her cry out in anguish. I hurried back to find her in tears. She handed me the *Daily Express* saying, 'Pobby has been killed.'

'What?' I exclaimed and hurriedly read the report.

The day before, Mr Pobjoy, the designer of the engines in my first plane in 1933, was returning by air from Finland after discussions with the Finnish Government, which was interested in a very advanced tractor he had designed. His plane had reached the London Control Zone. The weather was extremely bad with low cloud down to a few hundred feet and poor visibility. A number of planes were 'stacked' in the air in the 'hold off' area, and his wife Elaine was awaiting his arrival on the tarmac. Suddenly, she heard a sound like a clap of thunder in the air a few miles north-east of the airfield and near my parents old home in Northwood.

Sometime later, an announcement came through that an RAF Avro Lancaster plane, bringing Sir Edward Gent back from Singapore, had collided in cloud with the Scandinavian plane which Mr Pobjoy, my brother-in-law, was on and had cut it clean in half. Both aircraft fell into a wood two miles away from Northwood and burned out. Everyone was killed.

It was a great shock to us and a terrible tragedy for Pobby was a brilliant engineer and he was on the point of a great success with that tractor. Unfortunately, the detailed drawings of his tractor were still in his head, and so his wife, Elaine, and daughter, Shirley, now Lady de Freyne, were unable to benefit from the contract which had been signed in Finland.

Sometimes one is said to have fateful premonition and that appeared to have been the case with Pobby. Before he departed from Finland, and upon being told there was a complex weather front with attending low cloud over the south of the country, he proceeded to send a telegram from the Finnish airport to his insurance company in London requesting them to insure his life for that flight, for a considerable sum.

I went off to my first day's training in no mood to absorb very much information. I spent the rest of the summer at Alloa and passed an examination towards the middle of October. I was due to leave for East Africa by flying boat from Southampton on 23 November 1948.

As I still had my Moth aeroplane, the *Press & Journal* again contracted me, this time to fly their photographer over the Braemar Games at Ballater, which were in progress on Tuesday 9th September. We obtained some first rate pictures of that famous gathering. The weather was kind to us, and we were able to get low down in the valley to get the shots. Over the following week-ends I used to motor up from Alloa and return on the Monday. The *Press & Journal* photographer and I carried out a number of week-end air photo excursions. One of importance was in the Loch Cannich area which was due for post-war hydro electric development.

In August, my wife's sister, Elaine Pobjoy, came to stay with us in Inverness and, on the 3rd of November, I flew her up to Orkney in my Moth, G-AAWO, to say goodbye to my friends, the Reids, at Braebuster Farm, ten miles east of Kirkwall. We landed in a tiny field alongside the farm house. I overstayed our time and got caught up with darkness and bad weather at Helmsdale on the return journey. I was forced to land while there was a little light left and touched down on the same field three miles north of Helmsdale that I first used for the Avro landing in 1931. After picketing the moth down, we returned to Inverness by the night train. Because of unfavourable winds, it was several days before I could rescue the Moth.

I eventually flew it back solo on the Saturday 6 November. The wind was still unfavourable, blowing from the west but at greatly reduced speed, which meant a downwind take-off. The local physician, Dr Gray, and Sandy Grigor, an old friend who owned the Belgrave Arms Hotel in Helmsdale, came along to witness the take-off. They were scared I would not make it in the restricted downwind run. They did not understand the acceleration the downhill run would give and I had no doubts that the Moth would make it. In fact it came off the ground half way down the slope. It was my last cross-country flight in that machine, which had been in my possession for seventeen years since 1931. That little plane had been rebuilt two years before by George Griffiths, just after Dragon, G-ACIT, was similarly dealt with. The motor had also received a complete overhaul and so 'A-WO' had many flying years ahead of it, but not with me. I made a farewell flight around Inverness on Saturday 13 November and, next day, Sunday, a pilot friend of mine flew 'A-WO' to Balado airfield near

Kinross, south of Perth. The owner of that airfield, Mr MacDonald, said he would store it and find a buyer for me.

That last flight was like parting with an old friend and I well remember I had tears in my eyes. 'A-WO' had flown many thousand miles with me and was responsible for the original survey of the Inverness-Orkney route in 1931 and 1932. I just hated parting with it and had considered shipping it out to Kenya. I came to the conclusion, however, that it might be unsuitable for that type of flying, owing to the long uninhabited distances one had to fly over.

I put 'A-WO' back into its Longman airfield hangar that night for the last time and locked the door with a heavy heart.

18

Inverness to *Salcombe*

The ninth of November 1948 dawned. At breakfast, I read in the *Daily Express* a small reminder of the function, which was to take place in the Caledonian Hotel in my honour the following day. I always think newspaper leader writers are so very skilled in putting so much meaning into so few words, and the small leader article in question that day was no exception to the rule. It ran:

> The men of the north take farewell of a pioneer tomorrow. With tiny resources and immense faith, Captain Fresson taught Scotland to fly. His mail passenger planes reduced distances, once measured in days, to hours. His air ambulance, on moor or beach, saved many an island life. And he made it all pay. He was taken over by the Government air monopoly, employed for a while, then ruthlessly discarded. Now he leaves for part of the Empire where there is still outlet and reward for men with the right spirit.
>
> He goes with the blessing and good wishes of all who admire a bonny fighter.

My eyes became misty as I put the newspaper down. It was a marvellous little tribute and I kept the cutting for my scrap book, which I am now quoting from and have been quoting for most of this life story of mine.

All day and the next day, 10th November, the day of my farewell party, I was busy supervising the packing up at 12 Mayfield Road in readiness for my departure a week hence. The house had been sold and that also had a tone of finality in what had descended upon my wife and myself. We had been so happy in that home and had hoped that we would have had many more years spared to us, along with our young son Richard, to enjoy it.

However, it was not to be and I kept on thinking as I got ready that night for the farewell dinner, to which some ninety guests were to attend, including a few notables in the north of Scotland and maybe one or two from the south, what a fickle thing fate is. For, had the electorate not let our famous Prime Minister Mr Churchill down, after having saved the country from a terrible fate, I and my family would not at that moment be making our exit from a home and town we had grown to love so well.

On arrival at the Caledonian Hotel at 7.15 pm before the dinner was due to start, we went into the ballroom where the banquet was staged to take place. A wonderful sight met our eyes. There was a big rectangle of tables seating thirty guests each side, with twelve seats each end. In addition there were an additional eight seats provided behind the two sides. In the middle of the rectangle formed by the tables, a striking tableau met the eye, arranged by Mr J S Nairn. A scale model of the town of Inverness made by the students of the Edinburgh College of Art made up the centre piece, and it was surmounted by an illuminated arc of fluorescent lighting, representing the sky. Model aeroplanes were suspended over the model of the town, making their way to Orkney, Lewis, Aberdeen, and the south, along the air routes which I developed. A model of the monoplane *Inverness*, which commenced the service from Inverness to Orkney on 8th May 1933, topped the tableau, and the flowers which were grouped around in great profusion, made the scene most striking and beautiful. Mr Nairn had put a lot of hard work into a lovely tableau which enchanted the guests, my wife and myself.

During the dinner, Stewart Kay and members of the Caledonian Hotel Orchestra played Highland airs. After the speeches and presentation of a beautiful antique silver tray to my wife and I, films were shown of the inauguration of the Inverness-Orkney air service at Longman airfield in 1933 and the mail plane taking off for Orkney on the first internal air mail service in Britain at the same airport in May 1934. Mr Wotherspoon, one of the founder directors, intimated that the original air mail pennant flown by my plane was to be presented to the Burgh of Inverness for safe custody and would be placed in the museum.

I sat in the middle of the left side array of thirty chairs, on my left Sir John Gilmour, who was a director in the firm on whose behalf I was going to Kenya, on my right Provost Hugh Ross. Three seats away from Sir John Gilmour sat Sir Murdoch MacDonald, our MP; next to him my wife's sister, Mrs E Pobjoy, and on her left Mr A Trotter, editor of the *Scottish Daily Express*. Then Miss J Ross, Mr R Donald, Highland Airways' chairman, Mr N MacArthur, and Mr and Mrs Scott Swanson. On the right of Provost Hugh Ross sat the famous author Mr Eric Linklater, next to him my wife, Mr and Mrs Wotherspoon, and Mr and Mrs James Grigor. Mr and Mrs William Hamilton, Highland Airways' secretary in the early days, and Colonel and Mrs J Robertson, Highland Airways' Wick director, Mr J South and Mrs Lowe. There were, in all, ninety guests. An excellent dinner was served under the direction of Mr B V Marler. There were many speeches, but it would take too long to quote them all. It will suffice if I mention Mr Linklater's historic address, which I reproduce from the *Inverness Courier* dated Friday 12 November 1948.

Mr Linklater, proposing the health of Captain Fresson, said that when he had heard the sound of Captain Fresson's private plane in the sky the other day, he felt uncommonly sad, because he realised that the plane circling around his house [Moth, G-AAWO] marked the end of a chapter, a chapter in their history which Captain Fresson had composed and written. Captain Fresson's plane in the sky had been as familiar a sight as the doctor's car on the country roads. Today the sight of a plane in the sky was common enough, but if they cast their minds back fifteen years ago, they would remember their skies were relatively quiet.

Then came Captain Fresson, blazing the skywards trail through the Highlands to the islands of the north and the islands of the west. (Applause) Nowadays they were inclined to take aeroplanes in the sky as something to be taken for granted, but he was reminded that it had been said that the history of civilisation was the history of communications. They in the Highlands were in a position to substantiate that statement, because they did know what an immense advantage to their comfort and convenience and to their whole way of life, the coming of the aeroplane had been. (Applause)

Describing Captain Fresson's achievement as comparable with those of General Wade, Mr Linklater said, that there was this difference – that General Wade's intentions of opening up the Highlands with roads was rather repressive, whereas Captain Fresson's intention of opening up the airways had been expressive, for it had enabled the people of the north to give expression to their desire to travel.

The effect of the air services which Captain Fresson had introduced had therefore been radical. He [Mr Linklater] could speak of their effect in Orkney, because he had watched the services from their beginning. After the aeroplanes had come, they had seen something like a benign revolution. An inter-island service had been established, and three times a week people came into Kirkwall. Patients in dire need of medical attention were brought in, and lives were saved in many cases. 'And so,' commented Mr Linklater, 'when I saw Captain Fresson's plane flying down the Cromarty Firth to Inverness for the last time, I realised what a melancholy closure it was to a pioneer's achievement, that Captain Fresson should be leaving us.'

Referring to the series of protests made in the summer against the enforced severance of Captain Fresson's connection with BEAC, Mr Linklater said that those protests were unhappily unavailing. 'It is a new and, I think, a very serious thing in our national life,' declared Mr Linklater, amid applause, 'that protests made by responsible bodies, whose charge is the welfare of the community, should receive no reply from an organisation, whose authority has been given to it by the government.'

All of them were aware of the difficulties created in Europe by the descent of an Iron Curtain, but in the summer this year, something like a tin curtain descended across Scotland, and responsible people in Scotland stood on one side demanding an explanation, and the powerful people charged with the conduct of air services, stood on the other side, saying nothing. Captain Fresson was no ordinary employee of that corporation, and that he should be forced to leave that corporation which had taken over the property he had created, and no explanation should be forthcoming in response to authoritative responsible demands, was something new in this country and something very 'sinister'. We shall remember what Captain Fresson has done for our good, and we shall also remember the manner in which he has been forced to leave the country.

It was a repetition in miniature of something that happened in 1620, when the Pilgrim Fathers left Britain to seek a new home, continued Mr Linklater, for there was this point of resemblance that Captain Fresson, like the Pilgrim Fathers, left because he had a conscience. He had no doubt, that if Captain Fresson had chosen to become a 'yes man' and to 'kow-tow' and do as he was told, he could have had a 'cushy' job with the Corporation, but his conscience would not have permitted him to behave in that manner. (Applause) For that, Captain Fresson deserved their respect. 'His departure is a protest against bureaucratic 'tyranny',' Mr Linklater declared, 'and the time may come when many more of us may have to protest against bureaucratic tyranny. He has been a pioneer. He may also be an example. Our protests were ineffective, but perhaps Captain Fresson's protest may be more effectual than ours.'

Mr Linklater concluded by declaring that Captain Fresson deserved success in East Africa. His pioneering the Highlands was done in the public interest, and they owed it to him – and those who succeeded owed much to him, which he doubted they would acknowledge – to wish him good health, good fortune, and all possible happiness in his new surroundings in East Africa. (Applause)

The toast was enthusiastically pledged, and the company sang 'For he's a Jolly Good Fellow'.

Provost Ross presented the silver tray in a happy speech to Captain Fresson. As Provost of the Royal and Ancient Burgh, he felt proud, he said, to present him with a memento in recognition of his services to the Highlands. Captain Fresson was leaving them and going to a part of the Empire. They all regretted his departure and they wished him well in Kenya. 'With this handsome silver tray,' said the Provost, 'go our best wishes for your health and happiness in the land where you are going, and when you return to Inverness, you can depend on a real Highland welcome.' (Applause)

A bouquet was presented to Mrs Fresson.

I replied at some length to thank the people of Scotland for their loyalty and the very great friendship they had bestowed upon me. Perhaps the reader will bear with me for making reference to one or two of the most pertinent paragraphs. Again quoting the *Inverness Courier*:

Acknowledging the toast, Captain Fresson, who was greeted with prolonged applause, recalled that [as mentioned in Chapter 1] in October 1911 he left London for Shanghai, a young man of twenty with the spirit of adventure, and he walked right into the Chinese Revolution of 1911 which overthrew the Manchu dynasty and made China a republic. Now, thirty-seven years later, he was leaving the country, not because he was seeking adventure, but because he had been condemned by the government of the day for making a success of the business he had come to Inverness fifteen years ago to create, and sentenced without trial or appeal by the cynics the government had placed in power to operate nationalised aviation in this country. 'Such action appears to be a warning against rule by dictatorship and confiscation, which is totally foreign to the British character and ways of living.' He went on to recall the difficulties of the early days in operation, and the obtainment of the mail contract. He was delighted that the friends who had backed him in those early days were present this night, namely Mr Robert Donald, the Highland Airways chairman, Mr Wotherspoon an original director, and his good friend Willie Hamilton, secretary to Highland Airways. He said he was also lucky to have acquired such loyal and efficient staff in George Griffiths, his chief engineer who had built up a wonderful maintenance station at Inverness, and his assistant Bert Farminer, who had grown up in the early days as apprentice with the Tom Sopwith aviation company at Brooklands during 1912 and onwards. And then a local man, Alexander MacLennan from Fochabers, a wizard in woodworking and carpentry, who carried out most of the rebuilding of our wooden aeroplane components and which called for great skill.

Then there were the pilots, Captains Bill Holmes, Bernard Wilson, John Hankins, Henry Vallance, B T O'Reilly, Bill Baillie, Cash, J A Greenshields – to name a few, who did so much to encourage air travel by their supreme skill and unremitting care for the passengers' safety, comfort and peace of mind. (Applause) He was also extremely grateful to the press – *The Scotsman*, *The Daily Express*, *The Aberdeen Press & Journal*, *The Bulletin* and lastly, a deep sense of gratitude to *The Orcadian* and Mr James Mackintosh, its owner, who gave us free booking and agent's facilities in Kirkwall for a number of years and until we could get on our feet.

I also mentioned at some length the grievous mistake of British European Airways in turning our organisation upside down, which had been 'cut to suit our figure,' from experience gained over a number of years. I cited their policy in subsequently raising fares on the Aberdeen-Edinburgh-London run just as they were getting the passengers in numbers to travel. My words, quoting the *Inverness Courier* were:

'The fares were bounced up in 1947 against my advice. The traffic at Aberdeen and Edinburgh just withered, but since the fares were reduced to their original figure, the traffic had returned.'

Ending the occasion, Colonel Neil MacArthur moved the vote of thanks to all who had contributed to organising the dinner.

The beautiful solid silver tray presented to me weighed 9 lbs and was inscribed with the following words:

Presented to
Captain E E Fresson, OBE
Founder of Highland Airways
At a Farewell Dinner given in the Caledonian Hotel, Inverness
On 10th November 1948.
By his many friends in Inverness and throughout Scotland
In appreciation of the great services rendered by him
To Aviation in Scotland.

Three nights later, Saturday, my wife and I were entertained to another dinner given by our more intimate friends, in the Station Hotel, scene of the inauguration of Highland Airways and the opening of the Longman airport by the Duke of Sutherland in May and June 1933. We enjoyed a novel menu inasmuch as the first letter of each item of seven lines was so worded as to spell our name 'Fresson'. I believe Dudley Carlin, the manager of the Station Hotel, was responsible for the clever make up of that menu.

My last week-end was spent in helping to complete the packing at home. My wife went south with me and saw me off from Southampton, returning to Inverness, to hand the house over to the new owner. On Wednesday 17 November we left by the LMS night express for London. There was a large crowd to see us off and bid me god-speed on my long air journey to Nairobi, East Africa. The flying boat was due to depart from Southampton on Tuesday 23 November and we went to stay with our friend, Cecil Horne, for a few days at his lovely home situated on the bank of the Thames at Mapledurham, near Reading.

I had first met Cecil Horne in 1935 when he landed at our airfield in Inverness in his private plane. He had just arrived from a shooting holiday in the Orkney North Isles and a fault had developed in the motor of his American Stinson monoplane on the way down. He stayed overnight while George Griffiths repaired the motor. We were glad to be of help to a private owner and he let me fly his plane before he left for the south. We became very good friends and I would accompany him in seeing London West End life, during frequent visits to town, before the war.

He went out of his way to make our stay an enjoyable one. On the Friday, he kindly lent us his car to run over to West Downs Preparatory School, Winchester, to fetch our son Richard, who had been given special leave by Mr Tindall, his headmaster, to spend the week-end at Mapledurham and accompany us to Southampton to see me off on the Short Solent flying boat.

Over the weekend I took ill with fever and had to send for a doctor. There was some doubt on the Saturday evening as to whether I would be fit to leave on Monday afternoon. However, I made sufficient recovery by the time the doctor came on Monday morning and was allowed to leave the house to catch the three o'clock train for Southampton.

It was a very foggy day and it took that train $2^3/_4$ hours to cover the 47 miles. As we neared Southampton, the fog cleared. The taxi driver who took us to the hotel told us it had been sunny there all day. We were booked in at the Hotel Polygon which appeared to be the official hotel for BOAC passengers. My friend, Mr Whitney Straight, who held high office in BOAC, had given me an introduction to the company's station superintendents all along my long route to Africa, and I took advantage of that to call on Mr Bingham who was in charge of the flying boat service in Southampton. He told me to ask for him as soon as we arrived at the flying boat landing stage next morning. 'Be along about half an hour before the departure time and we will get you through the formalities ahead of the other passengers.' I thanked him for it gave me a chance to pick the seat in the flying boat which I wanted. Mr Bingham was extremely helpful and, while flying between stages, I wrote and thanked him for his courteous help.

Dinner in the hotel that night was not a very cheerful affair. First there was the parting from my family. Next, I didn't know what was ahead of me. I was aware from experience that to clear up a mess in a business when the old management and directors held a powerful minority shareholding was to court making enemies, however tactfully the transition was put into effect. Shortly after dinner, my wife took our schoolboy son up to bed and I sat in the lounge reading my last evening newspaper in Britain. My mind would not concentrate, and I began to study the other occupants of the lounge, wondering what the morrow meant to them. Some of them might be my fellow passengers on the Solent flying boat *Salcombe*, registration G-AHIV.

I was aroused from thoughts by my wife's voice. 'Let's have a drink to cheer things up,' she said. I called the waiter and I gave him my order. He hurried away and, on his return and while pouring the soda water into the glasses, he remarked, 'Going on the flying boat tomorrow, Sir?' I wondered how he guessed that. Perhaps my face expressed my feelings too clearly, for one who had acquired the habit of keen observation in his daily contact with human nature. 'Yes,' I answered. I tipped him and he departed to another table. My wife and I retired early. We were to be called at 6.30 am for breakfast at 7.30 am. I did not sleep well that night.

Going back on what Mr J S C Reid had said in his address to the House of Commons, and Mr Linklater's address at my farewell dinner a week before, I just could not think how it had come about that I should be in my present position. Britain and its way of life, its conception of fair play and just reward where it was due, just did not match up with the fact that I had been driven out by a system that was entirely foreign to my concept of British justice. The whole of Scotland had told me only too plainly that my work had been of public benefit and yet I had been treated like a criminal. In the end I gave up and started the old trick of trying to count sheep going through a gate and eventually fell into an uneasy sleep. I was glad to get up when the bedside phone rang to tell us that the hour of 6.30 am had arrived.

The morning was again free of fog. It had dawned a fine day, but with high overcast. We breakfasted, and made our way by taxi to Pier No 50. Mr Bingham was there to meet us and, after I was through the formalities, he introduced Captain E Rotheram who was the skipper of our flying boat *Salcombe*, at the same time mentioning I was a friend of Mr Whitney Straight. The captain was a genial chap and invited me up to the cockpit after we had got on course. I spent three to four most interesting hours, right across France to the Mediterranean and on to Sardinia, observing the technique of navigating and flying a modern aircraft. I was grateful to him as it took my mind off my recent departure.

I bade my family goodbye. 'I'll see you in three months, I said to my wife, for she would follow me out to Kenya by ship, leaving in January 1949. Our son would return to West Downs Preparatory School and would fly out for his summer holidays with us in Nairobi. I chose my seat amidships on the bottom deck and shortly after was greeted by a fellow passenger whose name was Hargreaves. He later told me he was connected with the Calico Printers Company of Manchester. He was a most companionable passenger throughout the journey and I was truly glad of his company.

The cabin door was closed, I gave Richard and my wife, who had a handkerchief to her eyes, a final wave through the cabin porthole and we commenced our long taxi out into the Solent for take off. The time was 9.00 am prompt to the second of the advertised time of departure, and I recollect thinking what an efficient company BOAC were.

We taxied a long way down Southampton Water and commenced the take off opposite Woolston where I used to cycle down from Putney, London, in 1906 and 1907 to stay with my Uncle Noel who was in charge of the famous racing boat *Flying Fish* and which took part in the Monaco races of that day. It was owned by the Duke of Westminster and was powered by Wolseley Motors, in which firm my uncle was a member.[1] The boat was built by Saunders Roe of Cowes. My mind flew back to the many exhilarating trips I had the good fortune to make in those far off days down the Solent at forty miles per hour, which was a high water speed for the 1900s.

My mind came back to Mother Earth as the motors of the flying boat were suddenly opened up. We were off the water in forty-five seconds, which was very good as the ship carried a heavy load of petrol for the 1,300 mile non-stop flight to Augusta in Sicily where we would spend the night before flying on to Alexandria next day for lunch, and then on to fabulous Luxor on the Nile, for the second night stop.

We caught up with the clouds at 4,000 feet and were through and on top in brilliant sunshine at 5,000 feet. The country which had exiled me lay hidden beneath the clouds behind us.

[1] Noel M Robins was Fresson's uncle on his mother's side. He was marine manager to the Duke of Westminster who had a great interest in yachting and powerboat racing. Robins crewed for the Duke in powerboat racing at Monaco and Cannes and is credited with saving the Duke's life at Cannes.

Epilogue

by Richard A Fresson

The unique aspect of my father, which set him apart from all other aviation pioneers, was that he was both a qualified engineer and an aeronautical engineer by practise, an excellent pilot in all aspects of flying and navigation, and he was a very astute businessman. It was this last aspect which was to give him employment after he was dismissed by the politically orientated BEA.

Sir John Gilmour of Calders Brewery, which was then part of the Inde Coope and Allsopp brewery group at Burton upon Trent, asked him to go out to Kenya and take over Taylor's Brewery, which Inde Coope had just taken over, in order to restructure it and start expanding the operation. He felt that the sensitivities of the family would be understood by my father after what he had been through, and he had no doubt that he would proceed sympathetically with the task of keeping the late owners on side as it were. Thus it was that, on 23 November 1948, he found himself on the BOAC Solent flying boat, developed from the Short Sunderland with small cabins each accommodating four people in absolute luxury. He spent much of the time on the flight deck as guest of the captain. He kept a detailed log and there were stops at Augusta in Sicily, Alexandria in Egypt, then on to Luxor where they stayed overnight. At 0615 hrs they departed for Khartoum for the leg to Kampala. This entailed crossing the 400-mile Sudd area which is a massive swamp infested with crocodiles. At Kampala he disembarked and took the East African Airways flight to Nairobi.

The next five years were frantic with a new brewery being built at Ruaraka on the Thika road from Nairobi, and a new scheme of retail agents with a modern distribution service being created. This was accompanied by the introduction of new brewers and financial staff. During this period, he flew in his spare time for an old RFC pilot whom he knew from the 1914-18 war and who had an air charter firm and was short of pilots. In this capacity, he flew all over Kenya and was lent an aircraft for our family holidays when we flew down to Malindi.

At the completion of his contract with Taylor's Brewery, he went to Kitale to do consultancy work and he flew spraying flights for the agency tasked with the control of locusts which were wreaking havoc on the various estates in northern Kenya. This was to have a profound effect on his life later as the liquid used to spray the locusts contained a very toxic material which was later used by the United States Air Force in Vietnam as a defoliant to expose the Vietcong. It was highly carcinogenic as was discovered some years later when many of the aircrew on those operations developed cancer. It was exposure to these chemicals that caused his death in 1963.

In 1953, a chance meeting at the Kitale Hotel with a guest whom he had known when stationed at Hatston as a pilot in the Fleet Air Arm resulted in the suggestion that my father join him as his co-pilot in taking a Miles Messenger to its new owner in England. This venture started from Kisumu airport in July 1953. The flight took some ten days and was action packed in a way that would do any adventure story proud. The log that he wrote of the flight included very difficult weather conditions, maps that gave very little detail to allow accurate map reading, frustrating bureaucracy at various airports, a faulty compass due to a spare magneto being placed by an engineer too close to the compass, and the odd incident of engine trouble. Nevertheless, some 5,500 miles later they arrived safely at Gatwick.

In 1955, just before he returned to the UK for good, he undertook to arrange the delivery of three ex-RAF Chipmunks from the Empire Flying Training Scheme based at Bulawayo, which was closing down, to a flying club based at Nairobi West airport, with two club members to help. This entailed a trip of some 1,200 miles. The Chipmunks' safe flying endurance was little more than two hours at an average of 90 knots so this required at least ten refuelling stops without the convenience of airfields at the required intervals. This meant landing on roads, and arranging for fuel in Jerry cans to be driven to the appropriate location. Refuelling was done by hand and all the fuel was strained through cloth filters to ensure that no fuel blockages occurred in flight since the source and cleanliness of fuel could not be taken for granted. On this trip, he did all the navigation which again was difficult due to the featureless nature of much of the bush country. Regrettably, one aircraft was lost during take-off from one of the improvised refuelling stops, but the pilot was not injured.

On his return to Scotland in 1955, he purchased the Dalmore Filling Station at Inverness. He also bought a Proctor aircraft and set up a company called Charter Flights. This was based at Longman in the Bellman hanger used by the Naval Air Service during the war and now belonging to Macrae & Dick Ltd, his old partner in Highland Airways. He had many charters for newspapers, various corporate charters, and a contract for Army Co-operation work. This continued until 1960 when he decided that, as his 70th birthday was approaching, he should hang up his flying helmet. He died at Inverness Royal Infirmary on 25 September 1963, some five days after his 72nd birthday. The effect of the locust spray had taken another victim.

Just as James Swanney, North Ronaldsay's postmaster, had predicted, the work of my father in bringing aviation to the north of Scotland was recognised and valued in the years after his death. Various events marked the anniversaries of the air services that he introduced and monuments were unveiled in his honour at Inverness and Kirkwall airports. My mother was able to witness many of these before her own passing in 1984 at the age of 76. In 1973, by which time

BEA had been combined with BOAC to create British Airways, the fortieth anniversary of the first Highland Airways service was marked. Following this event, Patrick Gillibrand , the airline's head in Scotland, persuaded the airline's pension trustees to award my mother a widow's pension, which was very much appreciated and to a certain extent made amends for the past treatment of my father.

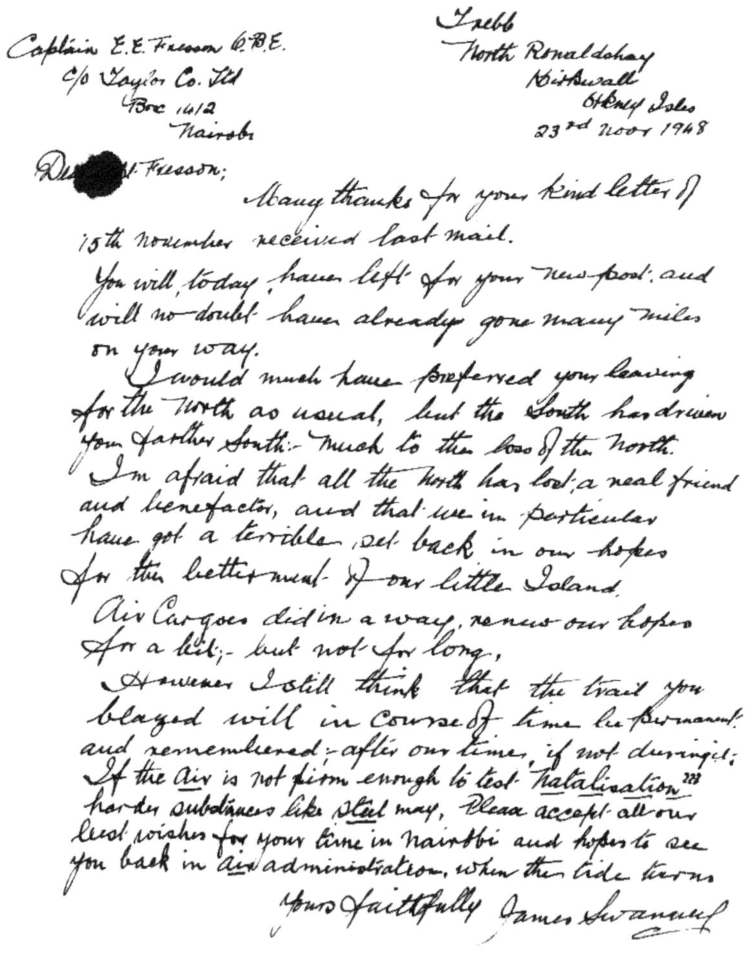

Captain E.E. Fresson C.B.E.
C/o Taylor Co. Ltd
Box 1412
Nairobi

Trebb
North Ronaldshay
Kirkwall
Orkney Isles
23rd Noor 1948

Dear ~~████~~ Fresson;

Many thanks for your kind letter of 15th November received last mail.

You will, today, have left for your new post; and will no doubt have already gone many miles on your way.

I would much have preferred your leaving for the North as usual, but the South has drawn you farther South:- much to the loss of the North. I'm afraid that all the North has lost a real friend and benefactor, and that we in particular have got a terrible set back in our hopes for the better meal of our little Island,

Air Cargoes did in a way, renew our hopes for a bit;- but not for long,

However I still think that the trail you blazed will in course of time be permanent and remembered:- after our time, if not during it; If the Air is not firm enough to test "Natalisation" harder substances like steel may, Please accept all our best wishes for your time in Nairobi and hopes to see you back in air administration, when the tide turns

Yours faithfully James Swanney

Letter from James Swanney, North Ronaldsay, to Edmund Fresson, 23 November 1948.

Artistic licence has been employed in this painting of Highland Airways' Monospar crossing the Pentland Firth. It is painted in a style sometimes found adopted by the railway companies of the period and displayed in the compartments of railway carriages.

Commemorative first day cover posted in Inverness on 29 May 1934 to mark Highland Airways' introduction of the Orkney air mail.

This cover, franked in Wick on 1 December 1934, marks the incorporation of Caithness into the air mail service.

First day cover to mark the 60th anniversary of the first air mail.
(Iain Hutchison)

This special cover marked the 65th anniversary of the North Ronaldsay air mail service. (Iain Hutchison)

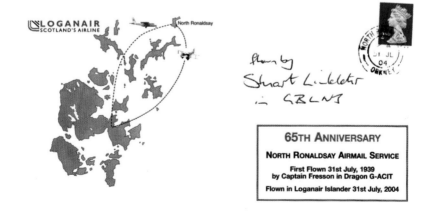

De Havilland Dragon, G-ACIT, is an iconic aircraft for Highland Airways. It was initially preserved at the Science Museum, Wroughton, in this colour scheme.

LICENCE for
PILOTS
Of AIRCRAFT.

ROYAL
AIR MA

Fresson's cherished air mail pennant on display at Kirkwall Airport. (Iain Hutchison)

G-ACIT is now displayed at Wroughton in Highland Airways markings.

G-BJOP is one of several Loganair Britten-Norman Islanders to be named after Ted Fresson. (David Dyer Collection)

In 1935, Highland Airways merged with Northern & Scottish Airways to form Scottish Airways.

Veronica, Richard, Mark and Simon Fresson at Inverness Airport following the unveiling of Ted Fresson's statue airside.

The statue is now located at the main entrance to Inverness Airport. (Iain Hutchison)

Aviation historians R E G Davies, John Stroud and Iain Hutchison at Inverness at the 60th air mail anniversary in 1994. Davies wrote about Fresson in his book, Rebels and Reformers of the Airways, *while Stroud saw the first edition of* Air Road to the Isles *to press in 1966. (Iain Hutchison)*

Memorial to Fresson's first air service to Orkney at Kirkwall Airport. Both dates in the inscription are incorrect by one year. (Iain Hutchison)

Erected
To the Memory of
Capt. E.E. Fresson
O.B.E.
Who pioneered the
Air services to and
Within these islands in
1932 and operated the
First airmail service
In the United Kingdom
In 1933

Final resting place of Ted and Gwen Fresson in Tomnahurich cemetery, Inverness. (Richard Fresson)

IN
LOVING MEMORY OF
A DEAR HUSBAND
AND FATHER
CAPT ERNEST EDMUND
FRESSON, O.B.E.
OAKLANDS, INVERNESS,
PIONEER OF HIGHLAND AIRWAYS
WHO DIED ON THE 25TH SEPT 1963.
AND HIS BELOVED WIFE
GWENDOLINE HOLLOWAY
WHO DIED ON THE 24TH JULY 1984.

THE FRESSON TRUST

The Fresson Trust is an aviation charity set up in 1991. Its objectives are:

1. To offer bursaries or similar contributions to residents of the North-East and Highlands & Islands area of Scotland who are appropriately talented and wish to begin or pursue a career in aviation in the area, as pilots, engineers or other associated employment, but do not have sufficient financial resources to do so.
2. To support the establishment of suitable local museums and archives to house memorabilia and aircraft (civil and military) with a Highlands and Islands connection, thus preserving our Aviation Heritage.
3. To arrange and promote events to commemorate the anniversaries of Captain E E Fresson's aviation activities throughout the area, and more recent aviation achievements, in order to create and retain public awareness of aviation history in the north of Scotland.
4. To engage in fundraising activities in a variety of ways to help provide the Trust's bursaries, and to assist in its other objectives.

Contributions to the Trust: Anyone wishing to contribute to the Trust and its aims should contact the Treasurer by email at:

Memorabilia: The Fresson Trust has a range of memorabilia available for sale. This includes prints of the aviation paintings of Edmund Miller and aviations histories by Peter V Clegg.

Miller is a founder member and former chairman of the Guild of Aviation Artists and his paintings are displayed at several Scottish airports and museums. Clegg is a former journalist and was public relations manager of Dan-Air. He has written several books on aviation pioneers. Copies of these paintings and aviation histories may be obtained through the Trust web site.

www.fressontrust.org.uk

A charity registered in Scotland No. SCO20054

Acknowledgements

The publisher would like to thank the following for helping bring about this Second Edition of *Air Road to the Isles*. First and foremost is Ashlene Pickthal. Ashlene is Richard Fresson's sister-in-law and it was she who undertook the mammoth task of re-typing Edmund Fresson's original manuscript. Without her work, I seriously doubt if you would now be perusing this volume. Next is Richard Fresson, who consented to the republication of his father's memoir and has been a continuing support and propagator in bringing the Second Edition to press. Right at the beginning of our discussions, Richard indicated that any proceeds from the book should go to The Fresson Trust, and the Trust's subsequent support, not least in securing some National Lottery funding to help launch this new edition, has been invaluable. One of the founders of The Fresson Trust is Peter V Clegg. Peter has written extensively on Fresson and on the other pioneers of aviation in Scotland and beyond, and I am grateful to Peter for his enthusiastic backing. Tahnks are extended to Magnus Linklater for following in the footsteps of his father, Eric Linklater, by providing a Foreword to this new unabridged volume of *Air Road to the Isles*.

Edmund Miller's paintings have illustrated Peter Clegg's books over many years and the originals of many of these paintings are now to be found in Scottish airports and museums. Ed is a Full Member of the Guild of Aviation Artists and it is one of his paintings that graces the cover of this book - his willing help with this is greatly appreciated. The original manuscript required some considerable editing, and I thank Douglas Nicolson for casting his eagle eye over the final proofs with the same dedication that he has applied to previous Kea publications. Dougie Martindale's fine maps help the reader to follow Fresson's travels, and I express thanks to Dougie for turning these around so quickly. A portfolio of line drawings appeared in the original edition and, with kind permission of the artist, John Blake, this is given a new airing in this volume. Most of the photographs have been provided by Richard Fresson and are from the Richard Fresson Collection unless otherwise indicated. Efforts to establish copyright of some photographs have not always been successful and apologies are offered to anyone whose images are reproduced without their express permission. Photographic assistance from Peter Clegg, David Dyer, Robert Foden, David Mackie at Orkney Library & Archive, and Frances Vallance is acknowledged with thanks.

Iain Hutchison

Index

Captain Fresson had his own unique writing style. He frequently recorded his contacts as the likes of 'Mr Mackintosh' without reference to forenames or initials. Some of these have been identified, but many have not. Spellings have not been confirmed in many cases, e.g. MacIntosh, Mackintosh, etc. For the purposes of adding some clarity, occupations have been added in the Index where possible. Place names have been presented as they were known during Fresson's time, but may have subsequently changed, notably in China.

440

Serious fun

is the theme of these two books

Former TriStar training captain *John Morton* explains all you need to know about what happens during a passenger flight
while *Graham Perry* takes a wry look at the last fifty years of flying, and at the determination of the people who have made it a safe every day event.
Illustrated by *figment*

Flying People – *bringing you safe flying, every day*
Graham Perry
"Well written, explanations which my young son understands and which I find fine as a pilot." Amazon reviewer.   £12.95

Whatever were you thinking of, Captain?
A Handbook for Airline Passengers
Captain John L Morton
"...puts over the material in such an easily-assimilated form, spiced with recollections and humour." *Aircraft Illustrated* magazine.   £8.95

Kea Publishing, 14 Flures Crescent, Erskine, Renfrewshire PA8 7DJ, Scotland.
Please add 10% for UK postage and packing; 25% for other destinations.
www.keapublishing.com